ArtScroll Series®

Rabbi Nosson Scherman / Rabbi Meir Zlotowitz
General Editors

Let My Nation

*Based on Talmudic
and Midrashic Sources*

Published by
Mesorah Publications, ltd

Serve Me

*Marching to Sinai
to Receive the Torah*

YOSEF DEUTSCH

FIRST EDITION
First Impression … May 2004
Second Impression … April 2006
Third Impression … May 2009

Published and Distributed by
MESORAH PUBLICATIONS, LTD.
4401 Second Avenue / Brooklyn, N.Y 11232

Distributed in Europe by
LEHMANNS
Unit E, Viking Business Park
Rolling Mill Road
Jarow, Tyne & Wear, NE32 3DP
England

Distributed in Australia and New Zealand
by **GOLDS WORLDS OF JUDAICA**
3-13 William Street
Balaclava, Melbourne 3183
Victoria, Australia

Distributed in Israel by
SIFRIATI / A. GITLER — BOOKS
6 Hayarkon Street
Bnei Brak 51127

Distributed in South Africa by
KOLLEL BOOKSHOP
Ivy Common
105 William Road
Norwood 2192, Johannesburg, South Africa

ARTSCROLL SERIES®
LET MY NATION SERVE ME
© Copyright 2004, by MESORAH PUBLICATIONS, Ltd.
4401 Second Avenue / Brooklyn, N.Y. 11232 / (718) 921-9000 / www.artscroll.com

---

ALL RIGHTS RESERVED
The text, prefatory and associated textual contents and introductions
— including the typographic layout, cover artwork and ornamental graphics —
have been designed, edited and revised as to content, form and style.

No part of this book may be reproduced
IN ANY FORM, PHOTOCOPYING, OR COMPUTER RETRIEVAL SYSTEMS
— even for personal use without written permission from
the copyright holder, Mesorah Publications Ltd.
except by a reviewer who wishes to quote brief passages
in connection with a review written for inclusion in magazines or newspapers.

THE RIGHTS OF THE COPYRIGHT HOLDER WILL BE STRICTLY ENFORCED.

ISBN 10: 1-57819-364-8 / ISBN 13: 978-1-57819-364-6 (hard cover)

The layout of this book is based on that of Let My Nation Go, designed by Deenee Cohen, DC Design.

Typography by CompuScribe at ArtScroll Studios, Ltd.
Printed in the United States of America by Noble Book Press Corp.
Bound by Sefercraft, Quality Bookbinders, Ltd., Brooklyn N.Y. 11232

לעילוי נשמת

ר' אברהם ב"ר עזריאל יהודה הי"ד
שרה Maca ב"ר זאב הי"ד

עזריאל יהודה ב"ר אברהם הי"ד
מינדל ב"ר אברהם הי"ד
שמואל ב"ר אברהם הי"ד
ישראל ב"ר אברהם הי"ד
עקיבא יהודה ב"ר אברהם הי"ד

My grandfather's sister's family of seven who died *al kiddush Hashem*.

Although their lives were taken by Hitler, ימח שמו, their memory lives on in eternity.

תנצב"ה

לעילוי נשמת
ר' יונה דב ב"ר אהרן ע"ה

Throughout the war,
my grandmother's brother was *moser nefesh*
to keep intact the traditions of his family.

While in forced labor camp in the Ukraine,
he was a tailor who sewed uniforms,
a position that afforded him the opportunity
to observe the Torah and the *mitzvos*.

After the war, all he wanted was to go to Eretz Yisrael
and continue his life as the dedicated Jew he was.

Tragically, the British shot him near the shores of Haifa.

He died at the age of 33,
leaving his expectant wife a widow
and his unborn son an orphan from birth.

תנצב"ה

Haskamah by Harav Shmuel Kamenetzky, שליט״א

בס״ד

שמואל קמנצקי
Rabbi S. Kamenetsky

2018 Upland Way
Philadelphia, Pa 19131

Home: 215-473-2798
Study: 215-473-1212

בס״ד ג׳ אייר נעננו ונשמח לנק׳

לכ׳ הרב הגאון מו״ה לוי יצחן קפלוא

ר׳ נלאה ושלום הסת״ן ברוב״ט שליט״א

קבלתי הספר חמדת א בל, וראיתי דוגמא וחלק
ניכר יעסוק בהרחב בהלכות ד״ו ואולי הרחה יהנו הפוסקים
הפולדי. הקונו׳ יושקפן בעיון דיני דמעי וכל דבר ועניני
גדר ה׳.

דינינו מלוק, הנה נעננו להאריך הקונו׳ קדוש
אמיו הספר נדרו ולהאירמה.

דורש הפנלה
שמואל קמנצקי

Introduction

Shlomo HaMelech, the wisest of all men, taught: *"V'chut hameshulash lo bimheirah yinasek* — The three-stranded cord is not quickly severed." Therefore, I owe an especially great debt of gratitude to the *Ribbono Shel Olam* for allowing me the opportunity to publish this, my third book. Having been granted the privilege of publishing my first book, *Let My Nation Go*, that tells the story of the Exodus from Egypt, and my second, *Let My Nation Live*, that tells the story of the salvation of the Jews in the time of Mordechai and Esther, Hashem has once again blessed me by enabling me to publish this third book, *Let My Nation Serve Me*, the story of the Giving of the Torah at Sinai. As in my previous books, I am humbled by His generosity and can only hope that I bring honor to His Holy Name.

The basic premise of this book is similar to that of the previous two books. It is a collection of Talmudic and Midrashic sources that have been woven into a tapestry that describes the period after the

Exodus from Egypt, picking up the story where the first book, *Let My Nation Go*, left off — after the Parting of the Sea. It proceeds through the encampments from Marah through Mount Sinai, telling the story of the manna, the war with Amalek and the Giving of the Torah, among others. The book concludes with the terrible sin of the Golden Calf and Hashem's forgiving the Jews, on Yom Kippur, some three months after they had sinned.

As in my previous books, I make no claims that the story presented here is the definitive account of what happened during this period. It is merely one version drawn from the vast body of information available on the subject. I am confident that I have formulated a story that is in accord with many Torah-true opinions. At the same time, I am fully cognizant that, considering the many Midrashim and seemingly conflicting views, I am unable to present a version that is absolutely definitive.

Understanding Midrashim requires a great deal of discernment, since some are meant to be taken literally and others metaphorically. I have presented a subjective view as to the events that have taken place and understand that a different view of the events would be equally acceptable. I have therefore endeavored to provide meticulous footnotes so that the readers may go back to the sources and draw their own conclusions as to the intent of the Midrashim.

I would like to thank Rabbi Yaakov Yosef Reinman, the masterful writer who edited the entire manuscript. As he has done with my previous books, he deftly wielded his phenomenal skill and professionalism to produce exceptional results once again.

Special thanks to my beloved Rebbi, Rav Yirmiyah Gugenheimer, who continues to offer me encouragement and *chizuk* throughout my work. His insights and guidance are invaluable.

R' Kalman, you are the oxygen that brought life into my writing. Without your direction, there would not have been a first book, let alone a third.

I would also like to take the opportunity to express my deepest gratitude to my dear parents, who have played a direct role in this book's coming to fruition. They have been a constant source of support, and they continue to guide me in the right direction day after day. My dear grandmother has always been a great source of strength, constantly encouraging me to be productive and to value each and every day of my life.

Introduction

I would like to express my appreciation to my older brothers, each of whom is there in his own unique way, to offer me positive feedback and encouragement on my manuscripts.

My children are a great *chizuk* to me. They are also great motivators, always turning up the pressure by asking, "When's the next book coming already?"

And of course, without my wife's constant support, there are no books. Thank you.

I would like to express my deep thanks to Deb Hoefnner, the talented artist who has painted the beautiful illustrations for the covers of my books, and to Eli Kroen, Hershy Feuerwerker and Leah Weiner of Mesorah/Artscroll, who turned the artwork into a striking cover.

I would like to convey my gratitude to the others at Mesorah/ArtScroll who invested their time and talents, some beyond the call of duty, to make this book a work of quality and beauty. Mrs. Esther Hoberman and Mrs. Mindy Stern reviewed and commented on the manuscript and reworked the footnotes. Ovadyah Stavsky typeset the book, and he and Devorah Scheiner entered the myriad revisions and corrections. Mrs. Faigie Weinbaum did the final proofreading. Avrohom Biderman has been immensely helpful in the production of the book.

A special thanks to Efraim Perlowitz, a true friend, who has been a pillar of support and assistance in the development of the book.

Last but certainly not least, I want to thank all readers who have taken the time to read the previous books and have continued to encourage me to write. I appreciate all your comments and especially your criticism, which I accept as a challenge to maintain the quality of my work and always seek to take it to next level.

Yosef Deutsch

Rosh Chodesh Nissan, 5764

Table of Contents

Prologue: The Memory of Sinai 9
1 ﺱ *Journey Through the Desert* 15
2 ﺱ *Bread From Heaven* 35
3 ﺱ *Double for Shabbos* 61
4 ﺱ *Miriam's Well* 83
5 ﺱ *Amalek Attacks*. 97
6 ﺱ *Arrival at Sinai* 135
7 ﺱ *A State of Preparation* 157
8 ﺱ *We Will Do and We Will Listen* 175
9 ﺱ *The Great Day Arrives* 191
10 ﺱ *The Giving of the Torah* 213
11 ﺱ *The Ten Commandments* 237
12 ﺱ *Forty Days in Heaven* 277
13 ﺱ *The Golden Calf* 297
14 ﺱ *Uproar in Heaven* 331
15 ﺱ *Moshe Returns* 351
16 ﺱ *Remorse and Retribution* 367
17 ﺱ *Forgiveness* 381
Appendix: Dating Matan Torah 401

Prologue:
The Memory of Sinai

Deals can sometimes be struck overnight. The offer is made and accepted, the contract is signed, and it is done. But when Hashem gave the Torah to the Jewish people, it was anything but an overnight deal. The preparations for the momentous event were already being laid years and even centuries earlier. The Jewish people went through the crucible of bondage in Egypt and a number of ordeals in the desert before they could enter into the Divine covenant of the Torah. Sometimes they were successful, and sometimes they were not so successful. But they kept moving forward tenaciously, and in the end they reached their goal.

The history of the Jewish people leading up to the Giving of the Torah can be explained with the following parable.

A world-famous king had a daughter, an only child, and he doted on her. When she reached marriageable age, the king was very worried about finding her the perfect mate. He wanted a man of strong character, someone smart and resourceful, but how was he to find such a man?

The king locked his daughter away in a castle fortress surrounded by a deep moat. The walls were high, thick and unbroken by any doors or windows.

"I am looking for a fine son-in-law," the king announced, "and I am running a test. The princess is inside the impregnable castle fortress with a retinue of servants. I am prepared to give her hand in marriage to anyone who can get to her. All who are interested may come and make the attempt. Do not bother to bring me your pedigrees to show me the quality of your families. I am not interested. Do not bother to bring sacks of money to show me how wealthy you are. I am not interested. I need no nobles, no aristocrats, no princes, no business magnates or industrialists. Blue blood and green money mean nothing to me. I just want a man of strong character, good values, resourcefulness and robust intelligence. If you succeed in reaching the princess, you are indeed qualified, and I will be happy to have you as a son-in-law."

For weeks and months, great and handsome suitors came from all over the world, eager to win the princess' hand in marriage. But try as they might, they could not breach the doorless and windowless walls of the castle. The walls were made of solid stone, too thick and solid to be pierced, too tall and slippery to be scaled. The men circled the castle and attacked its walls, but to no avail. They suffered the heat of the day and the cold of the night as they struggled to find a way to reach the princess, but eventually, they all threw up their hands in frustration and left.

One day, a young man with intelligent eyes arrived at the castle with the hope in his heart that he would marry the princess. He surveyed the castle and quickly realized that any attempt to break through the walls or scale them would be a futile endeavor. But still, he thought, there must be a way into the castle, something everyone has missed. It is a puzzle and I will figure it out.

Patiently and methodically, he walked around the castle again and again, seeking the slightest sign of an opening, but he saw nothing. Then he carried out an inch by inch examination of the walls, and he suddenly noticed that in one place the thin mortar between the stones was ever so slightly thinner. He looked more closely still and noticed that the thinner mortar formed the faint outline of a small window.

Encouraged, he scraped away the mortar, and indeed, the stones in that spot were small and shallow. He removed the stones, and lo and behold — a window! The only problem was that the window opening was too small for a person of normal size to enter.

Undaunted, he poked his head through the window and called out, "Your highness! Honored princess! I cannot get in through this window, but since I have found an opening, the least you can do is talk to me."

There was the sound of footsteps, and then the princess appeared. "You are right, good sir," she said. "You have done better than all the rest. I am impressed. But you have not yet won my hand in marriage. This is not called reaching me. But do not be discouraged. If you have gotten this far, you will also find the door and gain entry to the castle."

Invigorated by the princess' assurance, the young man returned to the walls for an even more minute inspection. For days, he examined every stone, every crevice, every speck of mortar, until he finally saw a line of mortar so thin that it was barely visible to the eye. He traced the hairline mortar and discovered the almost invisible outline of a door. He could barely control his excitement as he scraped away the mortar and removed the stone. There before him was the door he had been seeking for so long.

He opened the door and walked into the castle, but to his dismay, all the doors to the chambers and apartments were locked. Without the keys to the doors, all his effort would be for naught.

"Your highness! Honored princess!" the young man called out in anguish. "I have striven so hard to reach you. I found the window and the door, and I have gained entry to the castle, but what is the use if I have no keys to the doors?"

"You are right, good sir," the princess called back. "I will tell you where to find the keys."

She gave him exact instructions, and he found the keys. It took a great amount of effort to match the keys to the locks, but he did it, opening one door after the other. Finally, he reached the last door. He found the right key, inserted it into the lock and turned it. The door opened, and he found himself in the princess' apartment. She was sitting on a thronelike chair surrounded by her attendants.

The princess gave the young man a smile of congratulations. Then she sent a message to the king that one of her suitors had been successful. The king welcomed the young man with great honor. Eventually, the young man became one of the richest and most powerful people in the kingdom.

In the same way did the Jewish people come to receive the Torah and enter the covenant with Hashem. They had to go through much hardship and adversity before they found the opening to Hashem, and even then, they needed Hashem's kind assistance to complete the last part of their journey to Him and become His chosen people.

Furthermore, the Torah itself is not an open book, easily understood by anyone who opens to one of its pages. It is full of depth, meaning, secrets and mysteries that can only be discerned after long and hard toil. The Torah is like the daughter of the king sealed in an impregnable castle. Intelligence, unflagging effort and sincere prayer are the keys to unlock the secret delights and mysteries of the Torah.[1]

The Torah writes with great urgency about the importance of remembering the stand at Mount Sinai (*Devarim* 4:9-10), "Only take heed and watch yourself very carefully so that you do not forget the things that your eyes saw all the days of your life, lest this memory leave your heart. Teach your children and grandchildren about the day you stood before Hashem your L-rd at Chorev [Sinai]."

There is a difference of opinion among the *Rishonim* regarding the inclusion of this exhortation in the formal counting of the 613 (*taryag*) mitzvos. The *Ramban*, among others, considers the prohibition to forget the stand at Mount Sinai one of the *Taryag*. The *Ramban* sees special importance in remembering that Hashem gave us the Torah Himself rather than through Moshe. In the future, an alleged prophet might arise and produce signs and omens to gain the confidence of the people. Should he then rescind all or part of the Torah, the people might believe him or at least consider it a possibility. But if we remember that Hashem revealed Himself to us and gave us the Torah, we will know that any prophet who claims otherwise is not to be believed. That powerful memory will dispel any trace of doubt from our hearts.[2]

The *Ramban* further explains that this is the reason the revelation was accompanied by so many fearsome spectacles — the thunder, lightning and ear-shattering sounds. Hashem wanted the experience

---

1. See *Meam Loez* p. 514.
2. *Ramban, Lo Saaseh* 2 on *Rambam, Sefer HaMitzvos*.

of Sinai to be etched in the memories of the Jewish people so deeply that it would be carried forward for all future generations.³

The *Rambam*, among others, disagrees with the *Ramban* and does not consider the exhortation never to forget Sinai among the 613 mitzvos. He sees this commandment as a repetition and extension of the eleventh mitzvah, which commands us to learn the Torah and obey its commandments.⁴ Nonetheless, the *Rambam* agrees with the critical centrality of remembering the revelation at Sinai. He just does not consider it one of the 613 mitzvos.⁵

The *Tur* writes that when a person makes the blessing over the Torah he should have in mind the revelation at Sinai and the fact that Hashem chose the Jewish people from among all the other nations and brought us to Sinai. He also writes that in remembering the stand at Sinai we should visualize the image of the fire that reached "into the heart of the heavens" and all the other spectacular manifestations. These are the events that are embedded into the Jewish consciousness, and therefore, these are the images that we must refresh in our own minds.⁶

The events and episodes described in the following pages are based on the descriptions in the Torah, amplified by the Talmud, the Midrash and the commentators. They form the core of the national Jewish memory, the hallowed memories of the experiences that led to the Giving of the Torah and the formation of an eternal covenant that binds us to the Almighty, the experiences that formed us as His firstborn nation, His own chosen people about whom He had declared (*Shemos* 4:22-23), "Send forth My nation and let them serve Me!"⁷

---

3. *Ramban* to *Devarim* 4:9.
4. *Peirush Megillas Esther* to *Ramban*. See *Rambam, Hil. Talmud Torah* 1:8.
5. *Rambam, Iggeres Teiman.*
    See *Smag* 13. See *Smak* 15, *Yere'im* 359. See *Menachos* 99b; *Kesubos* 5b; *Yoma* 19b, 38b; *Avos* 3:8; *Yoreh Deah* 246. See *Yalkut* 271; *Zayis Raanan*.
6. See *Tur* 47 and *Bach*.
7. See *Rashi* to *Shabbos* 89b; *Shemos* 4:22.

1 Journey Through the Desert

It had been a night of the most spectacular miracles. The sea split open to allow the great multitudes of the Jewish people to cross to safety, and then the waters closed over the heads of their Egyptian pursuers and destroyed them. At long last, the Jewish people were free. Hashem had smashed the chains of their bondage in order to bring them to Mount Sinai and give them the Torah. Now nothing stood in their way. It was full speed ahead to Sinai.

As dawn broke over the Yam Suf and its surroundings, there was an excited stirring among the Jewish people. The intense spirituality of their unforgettable encounter with the Master of the Universe still electrified the air. The cloud pillars that had protected them from the Egyptian fusillades, those glowing ramparts which represented the Divine Presence, returned to take up their positions at the opposite ends of the multitude. The sea was calm. The shoreline glittered with mounds of golden ornaments and jewels, remnants of the opulent Egyptian army, which the sea had washed up on the shore for the Jewish people.

Moshe moved among the people, exhorting them to begin the journey to Sinai. "Hurry! We must move quickly. Hashem awaits us at Mount Sinai. There is no time to waste."[1]

But the people did not respond so readily to his call; they were not eager to leave the shores of the Yam Suf and head into the desert. Some were simply bedazzled by the spiritual aura of the place and wanted to linger there as long as possible.[2] Others were intent on collecting the vast piles of Egyptian booty that lined the shores of the sea in a panorama of ownerless wealth beyond their wildest dreams.[3] Yet others had not yet severed their emotional ties to Egypt, the ancestral home of the Jewish people for over two centuries; they could not bring themselves to take the irrevocable step of turning their backs on Egypt and striking out into the desert.[4]

As the day wore on, however, the cloud pillars, beacon and protective shield of the Jewish people, detached themselves from the encampment and slowly moved away from the sea and out into the desert. The message was clear. Hashem wanted the Jewish people to leave all other considerations behind and embark on the great journey to Mount Sinai.[5]

"Come, my people," Moshe exhorted those who still hesitated. "The signs are clear. It is time to begin the journey."[6]

The people nodded and turned their hopeful faces toward the desert.

For the next three days, they traveled through a desolate wasteland known to us as the Shur Desert, the word *shur* meaning wall; by turning their backs on Egypt and venturing into the desert, they entered a wall of protection from the outside world. The word *shur*

---

1. *Ibn Ezra; Ralbag*. See *Abarbanel* to *Shemos* 15:22.
2. *Zohar* 60a; *Tur Al HaTorah; Ralbag* to *Shemos* 15:22.
3. See *Mechilta, Rashi; Tur, Rabbeinu Bachya* to *Shemos* 15:22; *Tanchuma Yashan Beshalach.*
   This behavior would not go unnoticed. The Jews would soon lack drinking water in Marah as punishment for tarrying at the Yam Suf and not hastening toward Sinai to accept the Torah (*Kli Yakar*).
4. *Akeidah* to *Shemos* 15:22.
   Some suggest that there were still among them idol worshipers who could not forego their habitual practice of worshiping idols and wanted to return to Egypt (*Mechilta*).
5. *Zohar* 60a.
6. *Mechilta; Tur Al HaTorah* to *Shemos* 15:22.

can also mean vision, indicating that Hashem always kept the Jewish people in His sight, so to speak.⁷

Unfortunately, the Jewish people were not alone in the desert. Danger lurked just beyond the outskirts of the enormous multitude. The neighboring nations, many of them allies and satellites of the Egyptian monarchy, were fully informed about the latest development in the Egyptian crisis. They knew about the catastrophic plagues that had devastated Egyptian society. They knew about the mass exodus of millions of former slaves, the dramatic pursuit by the cream of the Egyptian military and the shattering climax in the heart of the sea. They knew about all of this, and they burned with a desire for retribution. The Jewish people could not be allowed to escape to safety without so much as a scratch.

Thirsting for Jewish blood, these nations sent commandos and irregulars to stalk the encampment and harass the Jewish people at every opportunity, to wait in ambush and attack anyone who ventured beyond the protective shield of the cloud pillars.⁸

These marauders posed a real danger to the Jewish people, especially to those who carried with them "the idol of Michah" and were not worthy of miraculous protection.⁹ Nonetheless, Hashem sent massive snakes and scorpions into the desert around the perimeter of the encampment to seek out and destroy any marauders who

---

7. *Shemos Rabbah* 24:4; *Radal*; *Rashash*; *Maharzav*; *Yefei To'ar*.

Although named "Kuv," it was called "Shur" because Shur is an acronym for the dangers found in the desert: *Saraf, V'akrav, Raav* — serpents, scorpions and hunger (*Yefei To'ar*).

See *Zohar* 60a for another interpretation.

Some suggest that within this desert there were two cities. One was called Aisom, the other Shur (*Ibn Ezra*).

Some suggest it was a total of four days with Shabbos included, but they did not travel on that day. Others disagree, stating that since they had not received the laws of Shabbos and *techumin* (the limits on the distance one may travel on Shabbos) till the following week, they did travel on Shabbos.

Some suggest that it took them only one day, but it was indeed a three-day journey that lasted only one day. It was inconceivable that the Jews would be able to survive for three days without water, as we will see shortly (*Saadiah Gaon; Rabbeinu Bachya; Midrash Ohr Afeilah*).

Some suggest that the reference to "three days" in the Torah refers to three camp stops they made on their journey (*Chizkuni*). Perhaps this view can resolve the differences of opinion regarding how many days it took to reach Marah. This would indeed explain the Torah's term of three days and why they were able to survive without water (see *Lekach Tov*).

8. There are various opinions as to when this took place. Some are of the opinion that this generalized set of events took place over the forty-year period in which the Jewish people were in the desert. Others are of the opinion that it in fact took place at this very time.

9. *Mechilta; Shemos Rabbah* 24:1; *Avos D'Rav Nassan* 34.

lurked there. Not a single member of the Jewish people, not even the most undeserving, was harmed.[10]

The Place of Bitter Waters

As they trudged through the desert for three days, the Jewish people were preoccupied with their journey.[11] Hashem expected them to take this opportunity to reinforce the faith that had blossomed in their hearts at the Yam Suf. As they walked through the desolation of the wilderness, suffering thirst and weariness, they would come to the realization that their fate and their destiny lay solely in His hands and they would appreciate all the more the wondrous miracles He would perform for them. Hashem wanted them to prove themselves deserving of further miracles and worthy of receiving the Torah.[12]

But the Jewish people were too preoccupied. They talked about the past and the future. They busied themselves with this and with that, but they did not devote any time to the study of those parts of the Torah that were already in their possession. They starved themselves of the spiritual nourishment of Torah, and so their faith in Hashem melted under the desert sun. Their morale dwindled along with their water supply and soon they were complaining of thirst.[13]

Some go so far as to suggest that despite the great miracles they witnessed, many Jews wanted to return to Egypt to worship idols now that they were free and no longer slaves (*Mechilta*).

Some suggest that the Jews were being judged as a group and not as individuals; thus they were deserving of these miracles even though the idol of Michah was with them (*Avos D'Rav Nassan*).

10. See *Mechilta; Meam Loez; Shemos Rabbah* 24:1; *Radal*.

11. On Rosh Chodesh Iyar they left Marah and arrived at Eilim. From there they traveled to Alush, arriving there on the 15th of Iyar. See *Ibn Ezra* to *Shemos* 15:27 who indicates that they were in Marah for just one day.

12. *Rabbeinu Bachya; Akeidah; Malbim* to *Shemos* 15:22.

13. *Mechilta; Targum Yonasan* to *Shemos* 15:22; *Bava Kamma* 82a. See *Midrash Ohr Afeilah* and *Kli Yakar* to *Shemos* 15:22; *R' Efraim Al HaTorah*. See *Maaseh Hashem*.

Some suggest that this "test" was all part of Hashem's master plan for training the Jews in how to deal with suffering in order to bring them even closer to Him (*Abarbanel*).

Based on this, an ordinance was made by Ezra to read from the Torah on Monday, Thursday and Shabbos. This would prevent any neglect in Torah learning over a three-day period. This view suggests that the Jews did travel for three days since they left the Yam Suf.

Some question the ordinance based on this incident alone, since the Jews did not go through three consecutive days on the road without Shabbos intervening. In Egypt the Jews surely learned Torah, and thus there is no reason to assume they did not learn — at the very least — on Shabbos. This is assuming that the Jews did not travel on Shabbos, as some suggest.

On 25 Nissan they arrived in Marah and pitched camp. There was no drinkable water in Marah, at least none that anyone could discover. They searched high and low and even dug fresh wells, but there was no water to be found.[14] Actually, there was a spring of brackish water, but it was bitter to the taste. The constant blowing of the north wind had sapped the water of its natural sweetness and left it undrinkable.[15]

The encampment was in an uproar. Children wailed, and mothers wrung their hands. Men wandered desperately from cluster to cluster, hoping to hear about any solutions that might have been found. A mob began to form.

Three men stood together in the shade of a tent. One of them, an older man named Kumiel, was slightly stooped, and he kept stroking his gray beard. The other two, who were named Peliav and Achiash, were in their early 20's, and they hung on every word Kumiel was saying.

"We have to be patient, my young friends," said Kumiel. "Moshe has brought us this far. He will intercede with Hashem for us and take care of this problem as well."

"So what are you saying, that we shouldn't worry?" said Peliav.

"What am I supposed to do about my babies?" asked Achiash. "Babies are so fragile. They can die of thirst so easily. We must get water!"

"You should definitely be worried," said Kumiel. "I'm worried. My children aren't babies anymore, but they also need water. And so do I. And so does my wife. A person cannot live without water. But at the same time, we cannot lose our heads. We have to keep looking for water. And we have to pray. Everything will work out. You'll see."

A shadow fell across the tent as another man joined them.

---

14. *Peirushim U'Pesakim, R' Avigdor Tzarfani*, to *Shemos* 15:22.
15. *Mechilta (Netziv); Seder Olam; Rabbeinu Bachya; Alshich; Yalkut Reuveni.*

This was to the detriment of the Jews in that there would be reason to give them the benefit of the doubt for their complaints if they did not have any water, but according to this view, they had water to keep themselves alive; it just wasn't satisfying. (See *Mechilta; Tanchuma Yashan; Rabbeinu Bachya; R' Avraham Ben HaRambam.*)

Moshe himself speculated about the purpose of the bitter water. He rationalized that it would have been more understandable if there were no water at all than to have water that was undrinkable (*Shemos Rabbah, Ki Sisa*).

At the time it was not yet called Marah. It was given the name Marah, which means bitter, because of this episode.

"What's this I hear?" said the newcomer. "We have to be patient? We have to pray? The problem is with Moshe, I tell you."

"There you go again, Nagdor," said Kumiel. "Why do you have to be so negative?"

"Negative? My throat is so parched I can barely talk, and it's all Moshe's fault. You call that being negative? I call that being realistic."

"Listen here, Nagdor, how can you blame Moshe?" said Peliav. "Does he know where to dig the wells? Does he have water hidden away that he hasn't told us about?"

"That's right, Nagdor," Achiash added. "How about showing a little respect. Moshe really took the Egyptians apart, didn't he? And he split the sea for us, didn't he? Or have you forgotten?"

"No, I haven't forgotten," said Nagdor.

"So how can you blame Moshe for what's happening now?" said Achiash. "What is he supposed to do about it?"

Nagdor leaned forward and spoke from between clenched teeth. "He has no idea where he's going, I tell you. Look, if Hashem brought us through the sea and led us into the desert, He must have had water and food prepared for us. So why haven't we found it? Because we're lost, I tell you! Moshe has taken a wrong turn somewhere, and we're lost in the desert!"[16]

Kumiel put his hand on Nagdor's arm. "Calm down, young fellow," he said with the wisdom of age. "Just be patient for a little while longer. Everything will work out."

As the men were talking, they could hear a rumbling sound drawing nearer. The rumbling grew louder by the minute until they could make out the sound of angry voices and the sound of sandals tramping on sand and pebbles. From a distance, the mob came into view in a cloud of dust. A mass of men shouting and brandishing their staffs filled to overflowing the walkways between the rows of tents.

Peliav gasped. "It's a mob. And they're headed to Moshe's tent."

"Quick, let's get behind the tent," said Kumiel.

"What for?" said Nagdor. "Let's follow and see what happens."

"We don't want to associate with them. I can see Erev Rav among them. They're only going to get everyone into trouble."

"What's wrong with the Erev Rav?" said Nagdor. "They're not Jewish? So what if they were once Egyptians? They converted, and

---

16. See *Rashi; Abarbanel.*

now they're Jewish. Why are you discriminating? They're as thirsty as the rest of us, and they're not afraid to speak out and do something about it. They've got spirit and courage, I tell you. We could borrow a page from their book."

"Well, you can stay here and watch," said Peliav. "Kumiel, Achiash and I are not interested. Behave yourself, Nagdor."

The mob drew closer, and the angry shouts pounded against Nagdor like a wave. Suddenly, he felt a hand grab him. It was a tall man with the dark skin and the colorful garb of an Egyptian. His name was Toltep. Two other Egyptian-looking men stood behind him.

"Nagdor, my good friend, how are you?" said Toltep. He pointed to his friends. "You know Dernak and Bubmose, don't you? We're on the way to Moshe's tent. Come join us. We can use all the support we can get."

"You think it's such a good idea?" asked Nagdor, suddenly having second thoughts.

"I think it's a great idea," said Toltep. "Aren't you thirsty? Don't you want to do something about it? Come with us. You're not going to accomplish anything standing here."[17]

And so the mob continued on to Moshe's tent, growing in size and anger as it swept through the encampment. This was the third time they tested Hashem in the desert. Altogether, they would do so ten times, each time triggering a crisis.[18]

The mob, seething with anger, gathered around Moshe's tent. "Give us water, Moshe!" they shouted. "Water! Water! Water!"

Moshe raised his hands for silence. He thought about the water that was too bitter to drink and considered the possibility of throwing honey and sweet figs into it to make it drinkable. But he didn't know if that was what he should really do.[19] As he stood there, he lifted his eyes to Heaven and prayed to Hashem for an answer. How could he provide water for the thirsty people?

Hashem did not immediately answer his plea. Instead, He first castigated the people for their impetuous behavior and their lack of fortitude and faith.[20] Moshe conveyed this rebuke to the people, and

---

17. *Mechilta (Netziv); Zayis Raanan; Rokeach; Ohr HaChaim; Lekach Tov; R' Avraham Ben HaRambam; Malbim*. See *Abarbanel; HaKesav VeHaKabbalah*.
18. See *Arachin* 15a.
19. *Tanchuma Beshalach* 24.
20. *Shemos Rabbah* 43:2.

the effect was immediately evident. The air seemed to go out of the mob as they shrank back in confusion. Nagdor pulled away from Toltep and his friends Dernak and Bubmose and moved to the side. He closed his eyes and concentrated his thoughts on the remorse he was feeling, and he prayed for a speedy resolution to the problem.[21]

Once again, Moshe cried out to Hashem on behalf of the Jewish people, and this time, Hashem immediately directed him to get a branch from a bitter tree.[22] The type of tree this was has not been identified with any certainty. It may have been a willow, an olive tree, a pomegranate tree, a fig tree, a cedar, ivy or perhaps even oleander. But whatever it may have been, it was truly amazing that a tree of any kind would be growing in the barren wastes of the desert.[23]

Moshe engraved the holy Name of Hashem on the branch, and then he tossed it into a large well whose waters had been found to be bitter.

"Draw water from this well," Moshe declared to the people. "It is drinkable now. Give gratitude to Hashem for the miracle He has performed for you, and slake your thirst."[24]

The crowd that had been a volatile mob just a short while before now fidgeted nervously. The branch had not changed the appearance of the water; it still retained that brackish look.

Toltep, the former Egyptian, stepped forward. He peered doubtfully at the water. Then he took a deep breath and scooped up a handful, but he did not bring it to his mouth. He wrinkled his nose and poured it back.

"On second thought," he said, "I'm not going to take that stuff into my mouth. It looks just as bitter as it was before. And what's more, that magic branch Moshe tossed into it may have made it even

---

21. *Mechilta.*
22. *Mechilta; Yalkut* 256.
23. *Mechilta; Shemos Rabbah* 23:3; *Yalkut Reuveni.*
   According to the opinions that suggest the Jews did not have any water whatsoever, Hashem first revealed a water source and then a tree that would sweeten it.
   Those who suggest it was a willow point out that it is common for the willow to grow near a source of water (*Tosafos Al HaTorah*).
   The species *hirduf* or oleander that grows on the seashore has the appearance of a rose-like flower. It is a bitter tree or shrub that is poisonous for animals, when eaten. (See *Etz Yosef* to *Tanchuma* based on the *Aruch's* interpretation. See *Toras Moshe* of R' Aryeh Kaplan.)
24. *Mechilta; Targum Yonasan* to *Shemos* 15:25; see *Chovos HaLevavos, Bitachon* Ch. 4; see *Zohar* 60b.
   Some suggest that Moshe used his staff and placed it in the water. Others suggest that Hashem revealed the Tree of Life that was hidden by the Satan and it was

more dangerous. It might cause illness. How are we supposed to drink this?"

"In the Name of Hashem," said Moshe, "I assure you that you needn't worry. The water is safe to drink. Hashem is your Healer. The water He has provided for you will not make you ill."

Nagdor stepped forward. "I will be the first to taste it."

He filled a cup and took a long drink. The people watched his face anxiously and were rewarded by an expression of pleasure.

"Delicious!" he exclaimed when his cup was empty. "I've never tasted sweeter water. Here, I want to fill my jug and take it to my family."

The thirsty crowd surged forward, and Nagdor just managed to fill his jug before the crowd forced him away from the well.

The sweet waters flowed and flowed until all the people had drunk their fill and a peaceful calm returned to the Jewish encampment. Gone were the anxious eyes and the worry lines. Gone was the angry grumbling, replaced by the happy sounds of children at play and the murmur of pleasant conversation.[25]

The miracle of the sweet water of Marah, the people realized, had opened new frontiers in the annals of the Jewish march to nationhood. They had found a bitter tree growing where no vegetation could possibly survive. One of its bitter branches had sweetened the bitter waters.[26]

There was a profound lesson of faith to be learned from this, a lesson far greater than many they had learned in the past. A bitter ingredient can transform a bitter product and make it sweet. Similarly, the ways of Hashem that may sometimes appear incomprehensible and bitter tasting can sweeten the bitter circumstances of life in the most miraculous ways.[27] As long as we have faith in Him, learn His Torah and place our trust in His all-powerful

---

its natural sweetness from Gan Eden that sweetened the water. Anyone drinking from this water was healed from all possible illnesses (*Tikkunei Zohar* 21a; see *Rabbeinu Bachya*; *R' Efraim Al HaTorah*; *Yalkut Reuveni*; see *Torah Shleimah* 15:261). Others suggest that this branch was from the *Etz HaDaas*. The very tree that brought death into the world would now sustain the Jewish people (*Chemdas Yamim*).

25. See *Meam Loez*; *Torah Shleimah*.

Some suggest that the Jews were examined like a *sotah*. The very fact that the water turned sweet suggested that Hashem had pardoned them. (See *Zohar Nasso* 124b.)

26. *Shemos Rabbah* 23; *Yefei To'ar*; *Tur*; *Ramban*.

This would be similar to someone being poisoned by a snakebite where the very remedy to heal it would be the venom itself (*Meam Loez*).

27. *Targum Yonasan*; *Mechilta*; *Maaseh Hashem*.

Hashem could have made a miracle and sweetened it without the aid of a tree or

hands, nothing will stand in the way of our success. Thus began the conditioning of the Jewish people to prepare them for the acceptance of the Torah. The future held many hardships and ordeals in store for them, and only by strengthening their faith would they survive as a people.[28]

There was also an even greater lesson in the events at Marah. The people had been concerned about their health, worried that the waters might be harmful to them. Now they understood that neither food, water, pure air or medicine are the true causes of healing. Sickness and health are in the hands of the Almighty. Obey the word of Hashem, said Moshe to the people, and He will shield you from all maladies and evil decrees and cure those who are already ill. In the merit of faith and Torah study, you will be protected against eighty-three illnesses common to Egypt. Otherwise, if you are lacking in faith and deficient in your observance, if you are guilty of a near rebellion as had occurred at Marah, He will expose you, Heaven forbid, to illness and injury. For, at the root of all things, He is the Doctor of All Doctors.[29]

Furthermore, if the people would be conscientious in their faith, study and observance, they would also be guaranteed a high level of spiritual health and well-being and entry into the next world. They would avoid spiritual illness in this world and the necessity to be spiritually cleansed before being allowed into the next world.[30]

---

anything else (*Chizkuni; Bechor Shor*).

There were a number of miracles here: the fact that water isn't readily available in a desert; that they found a tree in the first place; that this tree provided sweet water. This was a lesson in faith meant to teach the Jewish people that prayer, Torah and believing in Hashem are the ingredients to overcome any and all obstacles. (See *Ramban*.)

Others compare the miracle of Marah with the concept of "*tzaddik v'rah lo* — the suffering of the righteous" and expound on how a bitter life can make one's life in Gan Eden sweet (*Alshich*).

See *Moshav Zekeinim* and *Alshich* on the connection between the *parah adumah* (red heifer) and this concept.

28. *Abarbanel*; see *Tanchuma Yashan* 18 in *Beshalach*.

There is a question as to why the Jews did not receive the "Well of Miriam," which provided water in the desert, at this point. It seems to have been an opportune time to benefit from the Well which came through her merit. One view suggests that the Well came through the merit of Miriam while the manna would come through the merit of Moshe. It would have been disrespectful for Miriam's merit to precede Moshe's merit (*Tosafos*).

29. See *Rashi; Rabbeinu Bachya; Targum Yonasan; Tur.* See *Malbim's* interpretation. See *Akeidah* for his interpretation of the symbolism of Hashem acting as a doctor.

30. *Mahari Kra* 15:26. See *Netziv* to *Mechilta*.

A Time to Study

As peace and calm returned to the Jewish encampment at Marah, the thoughts of the people turned to the great events that awaited them at Mount Sinai. But first they would need preparation. There would have to be safeguards against a recurrence of the lack of faith, indeed the near mutiny, that had resulted from the bitter waters, and what could be more effective than a solid dose of Torah and mitzvos? Furthermore, they needed to be given certain mitzvos to ensure that their financial dealings with each other would remain amiable and harmonious.[31]

In order to accomplish these purposes, Hashem gave them a preview of the Torah at Marah. They had already been given the "*Sheva Mitzvos Bnei Noach*," the seven universal mitzvos that even gentiles are commanded to observe. Hashem also gave them at least three more mitzvos — Shabbos observance, honoring parents (*kibbud av va'em*) and basic civil and business law (*dinim*). According to some opinions, He also gave them circumcision (*milah*), the forbidden thigh vein (*gid hanasheh*) and the red heifer (*parah adumah*).[32]

Hashem wanted the Jewish people to become familiar with his positive commandments (*mitzvos asei*), to be ethical and moral in their conduct of business and commerce, to have high standards of personal integrity, and to go beyond the letter of the law (*lifnim mishuras hadin*). The time they would spend learning and studying these laws would raise their spiritual level and improve their relationships with each other.[33]

---

31. *Mechilta; Rashi; Midrash HaGadol; Targum Yonasan* to *Shemos* 15:25. It was in the merit of accepting these laws that the Jews would be worthy of eating the manna and drinking from the Well in the desert for forty years (*Shemos Rabbah* 25:7). See *Ramban* who explains that these laws included proper ethics and moral behavior for people to abide by so that peace and serenity would remain within the camp.

The letter of the words the Torah uses — "שָׁם לוֹ" — can be rearranged to spell שָׁלוֹם, a reference to the Jews learning about living in peace with one another (*Tosafos Al HaTorah*).

32. See *Sanhedrin* 56b; *Yalkut* in *Beshalach* 256 and 257. There were eleven mitzvos in total (*Yalkut Shimoni*). See *Seder Olam* and *Sanhedrin* 56b who maintain that they received ten mitzvos. See *Tosafos* there who questions the count.

Some commentaries question whether the count included the various laws of Pesach and *tefillin* which have already been mentioned in the Torah.

See the *Gra*, who writes that Moshe did not tell them about Shabbos till they reached Alush. Thus, the first Shabbos they observed wasn't until the following week.

See *Yerushalmi Beitzah* 2:1 and *Tosafos* to *Shabbos* 87b s.v. *Atchumin*.

33. *Mechilta; Ibn Ezra; Lekach Tov.*

Some suggest that although they were taught many laws here at Marah, these laws were not established until *Kabbalas HaTorah* (the Giving of the Torah) or later when the Mishkan was raised (*Tosafos*).

In addition, Hashem imparted to them very valuable information about the natural environment. He taught them the intricacies of horticulture so that they would know which plants were edible and which were not. He pointed out to them the various trees, flowers, herbs and seeds that had medicinal value and those that were poisonous.[34]

In essence, Hashem was teaching them that they should seek guidance in all matters from the Torah, its mitzvos and ideals, and from the knowledge it contained regarding all matters. Regardless of the appearance of a natural world that runs under its own steam, a person's progress through the world is determined by the faith in his heart, the Torah and *tefillah* on his lips, and the mitzvos with which he fills his hands.[35]

Twelve Springs, Seventy Palm Trees

Six days after the Jewish people arrived at Marah they were once again on the move. On Rosh Chodesh Iyar, they journeyed to Eilim and encamped in the oasis they found there.[36]

After the tribulations at Marah, the sight of the lush oasis was a feast for the eyes. Groves of tall and stately date palm trees swayed in the gentle breeze, and bounteous sweet water cascaded from the gurgling springs.

The oasis at Eilim was a miracle but not a mirage. From the time of creation, Eilim had been no more than a parched and barren stretch of sand awaiting the day it would bloom in the desert and provide healthful food and drink for the millions of people in the Jewish encampment. And indeed, just before the Jewish people arrived, Eilim was miraculously transformed.[37]

How many springs were there in Eilim and how many palm trees? We know there were twelve springs representing the twelve tribes and seventy date palm trees, each of a different species, representing the seventy elders, but what exactly does this mean?[38]

---

34. *Rabbeinu Bachya.*
35. *Abarbanel; Alshich.*
36. *Yemos Olam* to *Seder Olam* Ch. 5; *Abarbanel.* This was a Sunday; they would remain there for eleven days. Others suggest they would remain there for twenty days (*Ibn Ezra*). See *Mechilta.*
37. *Mechilta* to *Shemos* 15:27; see *Netziv; Sifsei Chachamim; Ibn Ezra; Ramban; Sifsei Kohen.*
38. Each spring was specifically designed to accord with the specific nature of each tribe (*Sifsei Kohen*).

According to some opinions, this is the precise number, twelve and seventy. If so, this was a remarkable miracle within a miracle. Not only did the barren wasteland suddenly produce trees and springs, but also, only twelve springs and seventy date palms sustained the entire people.[39]

According to others, however, twelve springs and seventy date palms were too few to provide ample water and food for several million people. Instead, they suggest that there were twelve springs for each of the twelve tribes, for a total of 144, and seventy palm trees for each of the seventy elders, for a total of 4,900 date palms. This higher number could certainly have provided ample food and drink for all the people.[40]

In Eilim, the people continued to study the laws and precepts they had learned and reviewed at Marah. They lacked nothing. In fact, Hashem was teaching them an important lesson. As long as they would devote themselves to learning the Torah and fulfilling its commands, the yoke of daily cares would be removed from them. Hashem would provide for all their needs and leave them free to study and learn.[41]

Crisis at Alush

Eleven days after they encamped at Eilim, the Jewish people set out into the desert once again, ever aware of the great events that awaited them at Mount Sinai. The excitement and anticipation were great. The sojourn at Eilim had been exceedingly pleasant and comfortable, with food and water in such plentiful supply. Nonetheless, to their credit, they were eager to be on their way.

---

39. *Zayis Raanan* to *Mechilta*.

Imagine what the Jews must have felt like, in retrospect, seeing that a little patience and eventual travel from Marah would have brought them this great abundance of food and drink. It is a lesson in faith and trust in Hashem that just because one suffers in the present, it does not mean that the following day Hashem cannot produce great sustenance in the blink of an eye (*Chofetz Chaim*). This concept can be understood with the verse mentioned in *Shacharis*, "U'vetuvo mechadesh bechol yom tamid maaseh Bereishis — And in his goodness renews daily, perpetually, the work of creation."

40. Some suggest that the seventy palm trees represented the Jewish nation at the time Yaakov went down to Egypt. The family total at that time was seventy (*Zohar Chadash*). See *Rabbeinu Bachya* and *Toldos Yitzchok* for other opinions suggesting that there were seventy different palm trees for each tribe. These trees were seventy different species of date palms. They were each different in appearance and taste (*Sefer HaBahir* 53).

41. *Chizkuni*; *Sifsei Kohen*; *Netziv* ibid.

This would be the only time throughout the next forty years that the Jewish people would find fruit in the desert (*Abarbanel*).

Although they knew that as they traveled through the desolation of the desert their supplies of food and water would inevitably dwindle, they were not concerned. They had learned their lesson, and they were confident that Hashem would provide for them, regardless of where their encampment was located.[42] After they left, Eilim returned to its original state. The trees and springs disappeared, and it was once again nothing more than a barren wasteland.

On 15 Adar they arrived at Alush.[43] The encampment at Alush would witness one of the most eventful and significant episodes in Jewish history. It would begin with a temporary deterioration of the fragile character of the young nation, the fourth time they tested Hashem in the desert. It would culminate with one of the most

---

42. See *Seder Olam* 5; *Sifsei Kohen*.

43. See *Shabbos* 87b as to whether this was on Shabbos or Sunday, and if they received the manna on Sunday or Monday.

See *Mechilta, Ibn Ezra* and *Rabbeinu Bachya* who say that it was on Shabbos that they arrived in Alush. But *Seder Olam* and *Lekach Tov* say that it was on Sunday. The events were as follows: According to the *Mechilta*, Rosh Chodesh Nissan was on Thursday and Rosh Chodesh Iyar was on Shabbos, making their arrival in Alush on Shabbos as well. According to *Seder Olam* everything was pushed up a day, with Rosh Chodesh Nissan on Friday, Rosh Chodesh Iyar and the 15th on Sunday. Incidentally, *Rashi's* view is that the 16th of Iyar was on a Sunday.

One premise of the disagreement concerns when the laws of Shabbos were given and what laws regarding Shabbos the Jews were required to practice. How could they have arrived in Alush on Shabbos? Some suggest that they were not given the laws of Shabbos until the 16th of Iyar, a Sunday or Monday. Thus, in Marah they had not yet received them and the first Shabbos they observed was either the 21st or 22nd of Iyar. Others suggest that they were given the laws of Shabbos in Marah but were not required to keep the laws of *techumin*. Others suggest that Moshe had already been given the laws, but did not relay them to the Jews yet. See *Tosafos Al HaTorah*; *Tosafos* to *Shabbos* 87b; see *Gra* and *Yavetz* to *Seder Olam*; *Yerushalmi Beitzah* 2:1; *Pirkei D'Rav Eliezer* 18; *Tosafos* to *Pesachim* 117b; *Bereishis Rabbasi* 13; *Devarim Rabbah* 3:1; *Radal*; *Rashash*; *Midrash Tehillim* 92; *Mechilta* to *Shemos* 16:28; *HaKesav VeHaKabbalah*. All these sources deal with the question of when the Jews received the mitzvah of Shabbos, what part of the laws they received and how long after Moshe received the instructions from Hashem did he relay them to the Jews. Some suggest that they kept Shabbos as soon as they left Egypt. Others posit that the Jews kept two Shabbasos before *Matan Torah* — the 21st of Iyar and the 28th. On the 15th of Iyar they were in Marah, on the 16th they received the manna, and the 21st was when they collected the manna on Shabbos.

The Torah writes that they arrived at a destination in the Sin Desert between Eilim and Sinai. Although the Torah does not state here that they arrived in Alush, they nevertheless did. From Eilim they traveled to the Sin Desert, and from there they traveled to Dafka and then to Alush. See *Ramban* to *Shemos* 16:1; *Seder Olam* 5; *Rokeach*; *Bamidbar* 33:11-14.

For the purposes of this book both approaches will be used; however, *Lekach Tov* makes it clear that we follow the view of *Seder Olam* and not the *Mechilta*.

The word "Alush" comes from the word *"lushi,"* which means knead. In the merit of Avraham preparing bread for the three angels the Jews received the manna (*Bereishis Rabbah* 48:12).

miraculous occurrences ever, an event that would forever define the loving relationship between Hashem and His chosen people.[44]

In Alush, the food supplies of the Jewish people finally ran out. They had left Egypt, thirty-one days earlier, with sacks of plain bread wafers (*matzos*) and livestock on the hoof, enough for sixty-one meals per person. The food had miraculously remained fresh until the very end. At two meals per day, there was food for thirty days. On the thirty-first day, there was food for only one more meal. By midday, all the food was gone. There were no emergency reserves of bread. The livestock were depleted. What would the millions of people eat that evening? Where would they find food in the depths of the barren desert? No one had the answers to these questions.[45]

Immediately, the level of their faith plummeted once again. Dissension spread through the encampment like wildfire. An angry mob formed around the tents of Moshe and Aharon. The mob was a cross-section of the people, the old and the young, the leaders and the common people, the righteous and the not so righteous. The Erev Rav especially was heavily represented.[46] At Marah, the mob had directed its wrath at Moshe alone. This time, Aharon was a target also.[47]

"Moshe! Aharon!" they shouted. "Come out and stand before the people. Don't hide in your tents. Face up to your responsibilities."

Inside their tents, Moshe and Aharon could hear the angry rumbling of the crowd, and they stepped out to confront them.

Shouts of protest were coming from all sides, one after the other. Moshe and Aharon waited silently for the people to vent their anger and frustration.

Achiash and Peliav pushed their way to the front of the crowd. Achiash clambered onto a rock so that he was elevated above the

---

44. *Arachin* 15b.
45. *Shemos Rabbah* 25:4; *Maharzav*; *Yefei To'ar*; *Targum Yonasan*; *Mechilta*; *Lekach Tov*; *Rashi*; *Sifsei Chachamim* to *Shemos* 16:1-2. See *Maaseh Hashem*; *Sifsei Kohen*; *Ibn Ezra*; *Abarbanel* to *Shemos* 16:2. Some commentaries note the calculation as 30 days. Others note the total meals as 62. See *Riva* and *Maharal* for their tally as to how we get the number 61.

See *Maharal* who states that the Jews had what to eat for the coming night but not for the next morning.

See *Abarbanel* who suggests that they ran out of food because it began to spoil.

46. *Ibn Ezra*; *Rokeach*; *Ohr HaChaim*; *Malbim* to *Shemos* 16:2; *Rashi*; *Sifsei Kohen* to *Shemos* 16:7.

See *Zohar Bereishis* 28b that the Erev Rav were descendants of Amalek. See *Meshech Chochmah*.

47. *Mechilta*; *Ibn Ezra* to *Shemos* 16:2.

rest. "The people are on the verge of starvation," he shouted. "How long will you, Moshe and Aharon, wait before you do something about it? What are my babies supposed to eat tonight? We have no more food left."

Peliav climbed up to stand beside his friend. "And don't you accuse us of complaining against Hashem. No, we are faithful Jews. We are complaining against you, against the two of you, Moshe and Aharon. You have cooked up some kind of secret scheme between you.[48] You brought us here to this place knowing full well that there is nothing here for us to eat and that our food supplies are exhausted. What is your scheme? Why are you doing this to us? Why are you bringing starvation on innocent people?"[49]

A short distance away, the three friends from the Erev Rav had found a rock of their own from which to harangue the crowd.

"My friends, look at me," shouted Dernak. "From my skin and my clothing you can readily tell that I used to be an Egyptian, but I decided to join the Jewish people. I gave up my fatherland, my people and my birthright to join the community of Hashem. But what are our rewards, yours as emancipated Jewish slaves and ours as converts to your faith? Starvation! That is our reward! Now, I ask you, wouldn't it have been better to remain in Egypt? At least, you would have had full stomachs. And if the Egyptian taskmasters would have threatened your lives, who wouldn't prefer a quick and merciful death by the sword over a slow and agonizing death by starvation?[50] Do you know what it means to die of hunger, to feel the pain of your innards being hollowed out and your belly swelling? Moshe and Aharon, what have you done to your people? You have taken them out of the frying pan into the fire!"

"It's true," shouted Nagdor, who had joined his friends on the rock. "I would rather have died a well-fed slave than starve as a free man."[51]

The shouts rang out from all over the crowd.

"Hear! Hear!"

"No starvation without representation!"

"We want food!"

"Bread before freedom!"

---

48. See *Minchah Belulah*.
49. See *Ramban; Abarbanel; Ohr HaChaim; Netziv*.
50. See *Mechilta; Rashi; Bechor Shor* to *Shemos* 16:3.
51. See *Mechilta; Rashi; Bechor Shor* to *Shemos* 16:3.

Toltep joined his friend Dernak on the rock. He held his hands up for attention. "Think back to the good old days in Egypt, my friends. We had plenty of meat, fish and fruit. True, the work was hard, and the hours were long, but those who were enterprising could always find some scraps of quality food. And look where we are now, stuck in the middle of this ridiculous desert, millions of us, and not a morsel of bread among us. What's going on, Moshe and Aharon? Is this some cruel joke? We were so much better off in Egypt."[52]

Peliav called for attention. "Now wait a minute, Toltep, my friend. You have a rosy view of what life was like in Egypt. Let's not forget that you were on the other side most of the time, if you know what I mean. You only joined our people near the end. So how would you know what it was like for us? Speaking for myself and for most of us here, we didn't have the opportunity to eat the meat, fish and fruit you mentioned. I never got anything more than dry bread, but I'll tell you something, a piece of dry bread sounds very good to me right now."

"Hear, hear!" came the shouts from all around.

Peliav held up his hands. "I'm not finished. Listen to me. In Egypt, I worked as a cook, would you believe it? My masters ordered me to prepare roast meat, usually ram or venison, and they never allowed me to put a morsel into my mouth. I had to stand there and smell the mouth-watering aromas of the roasting meat, knowing that I would never have the pleasure of tasting it. Believe me, it was painful. But still! Still! I would rather be back there in Egypt, standing in front of that untouchable roasting pot and eating my piece of dry bread, than die of hunger and starvation here in the desert.[53] I, for one, am ready to turn around and go back."[54]

Among the Erev Rav, Bubmose now sought his turn to speak. "You are all talking about food. And I agree that food, or rather the lack of it, is a critical issue." He looked around with a lewd leer on his face. "But let's face it. There are other issues, if you

---

52. See *Bamidbar Rabbah* 7:4; *Tur Al HaTorah*; *Ralbag*; *Abarbanel*.
53. *Shemos Rabbah* 16:4; *Zeh Yenachmeni*; see *Abarbanel*.
  Some suggest that the Jewish people consciously did not eat what the Egyptians were eating because the Jewish people were stringent about not mingling and uniting with them in any way. This was similar to keeping their traditional names and dress codes. The Jewish complaint here was that in Egypt they would be rewarded for abstaining from eating meat and so it was tolerable. Here there was no meat to be found and no reward as a consequence (*Chasam Sofer*).
54. *Yalkut Reuveni*.

know what I mean. In Egypt, we could enjoy all sorts of other pleasures, if you know what I mean. But here in the desert, the rules are so strict. No parties. No revelry. How is a person supposed to enjoy himself?"[55]

Nagdor gave Bubmose an odd look. "I don't think this is the time to bring up those issues, Bubmose, my friend. We have to remain focused. We're talking about food here. We're talking about starving babies. We're talking about survival. We're talking about life and death, I tell you! You all remember the plague of darkness. During those three terrible days, many of our Jewish people perished, in particular those who wanted to remain in Egypt. I admit it. I was one of them. I would not have been surprised if I had died during the great darkness, but I was spared. Standing here now, in this terrible predicament, I see that I was right to want to remain in Egypt. It would have been better to die in the darkness than to starve to death here in the desert."[56]

Peliav was nodding vigorously. "Nagdor is a little extreme in his views, I think. But I have to agree with him that a quick death would have been preferable to starvation in the desert. You know, I am a firstborn. I think I would have preferred to die in the plague of the firstborn than to die of starvation here in the desert."[57]

Kumiel tugged at Peliav's sleeve. "Help me get up there," he said.

Peliav grabbed him by one arm and Achiash by the other, and together they lifted him onto the rock.

"My friends, I feel there are some points that have to be made," said Kumiel. He stroked his gray beard as he collected his thoughts. "With all due respect, Moshe and Aharon, our quarrel is not with Hashem but with the two of you. We have complete faith in Hashem. We haven't forgotten all the miracles He performed for us to break us free from Pharaoh and the Egyptians. And don't think we've forgotten so quickly the miracles at Marah. No, our problem is with the two of you.[58] We feel that somewhere you've made a wrong turn when you negotiated with Pharaoh. You've gone off the

---

55. *Riva* 16:3.
56. See *Mechilta; Lekach Tov; Ohr HaChaim*. Had we stayed in Egypt, only the wicked would have died and that would have been the end of it. Now in the desert everyone will die, including the sages and righteous (*Netziv*).
57. *Maaseh Hashem*.
58. *Abarbanel*.

track of your mission. Hashem sent you to free us, but why did you have to take us into the desert? You could have worked out to have us remain as free people in Egypt. Or else, you could have led us toward Canaan through habitable places where life can survive. It doesn't make sense that we should have to spend a month in the desolation of a desert, with no wells, no rainfall and no food.[59] If Hashem had wanted us to die, He could have killed us in Egypt."[60]

"I agree!" shouted Toltep. "Why take us through the desert? Why couldn't you have taken us through Philistia? That's the quickest way to Canaan, and there is plenty to eat and drink there. We blame you, Moshe and Aharon, for our predicament. You chose to take us into the desert, and because of you, we are all going to die right here in — "[61]

Shouts of anger and frustration drowned out the rest of Toltep's harangue. People began to push and shove, more to vent their anger than because they had anywhere to go.

Achiash jumped off the rock and ran to the back of the crowd where he had glimpsed his wife Beruchah holding their young children and anxiously watching the proceedings. He grabbed his young sons and daughters and pushed through the crowd until he stood in front of Moshe and Aharon.

"Take my children!" he screamed. "You feed them. You give them water. Their lives are in your hands. I cannot help them. You brought us here. You find the solution."[62]

Yet underneath all the angry complaints there was also a strain of helpless pleading. Many people were not intent on assailing Moshe and Aharon. They just stretched out their hands to them, like hungry children beckoning to their parents, pleading for a morsel of food. These people were not a threat about to turn to violence. But others were.[63]

The complaints and the accusations were morphing into ominous mumbled threats. Here and there, demonstrators reached down and

---

59. *Ramban*; see *R' Avraham Ben HaRambam*; *Abarbanel*; *Alshich*; *Maaseh Hashem*.
60. *Sforno*.
61. *Ramban*; see *R' Avraham Ben HaRambam*; *Abarbanel*; *Alshich*; *Maaseh Hashem*.
62. See *Sifri, Devarim* 2.
63. *Tosafos Al HaTorah*. Some suggest that the reason the Jewish people were not punished for their attack against Moshe and Aharon was because in some ways they were right. Although they were guilty of their lack of faith in Hashem Who had proven time and time again that He answers their prayers, nevertheless "on paper" their arguments were valid in that they were a congregation of 600 myriads of people in the middle of a desert with no food in sight (*Abarbanel*).

picked up rocks and sharp stones. Crazed by the prospect of imminent starvation in the desert, the mob turned ugly and menacing. Moshe and Aharon stood before them bravely, listening to their complaints without responding, letting the crowd vent its anger. But the situation was rapidly deteriorating. At any moment, the first stone was likely to be hurled through the air, and if that should happen, pandemonium would break loose.[64]

Something had to happen. And right away.

---

64. *Mechilta* to *Shemos* 16:10.

Bread from Heaven

2

Even as the angry demonstrators milled about with stones in their hands, Hashem was already informing Moshe about the solutions that would immediately become apparent. First, however, Hashem rebuked the Jewish people for their rebelliousness and lack of faith. Nonetheless, Hashem still regarded them as His beloved people, and He set in motion for their benefit a miracle such as the world had never seen.[1]

"Behold," Hashem replied to Moshe, "I am about to rain down bread from the heavens, and then people shall go out and gather it daily. This will be a test for them to determine whether or not they will follow My Torah. On the sixth day, they shall prepare what they bring; it will be twice as much as they gather daily."

The food would not be actual bread but rather a spiritual breadlike substance that would one day be called manna. No longer would families have to worry about where they would find food for their

---

1. *Lekach Tov* to *Shemos* 16:12.

next meal. All the food they needed would rain down from the heavens in ample measure, to provide sustenance and satisfaction to every single member of the Jewish people.

Having received his prophetic message for the Jewish people, Moshe stepped forward to deliver it; since the protest had been made in public, the response would be in public as well.[2] Aharon stood at his side, ready to interpret and clarify Moshe's words for the benefit of the people. Being extremely tall, Moshe towered above everyone else, and when he extended his staff into the air, the entire crowd saw it and fell silent.

"My people, please calm yourselves," he began. "It is understandable that you were upset when your food supplies ran out and you had nothing lined up to replace them. After all, you're only human beings with human feelings and human failings. But what's this about wanting to go back to Egypt when things get a little difficult? That is foolish and immature. And what's this about accusing my brother Aharon and me of leading you into the desert by our own designs? What a ridiculous thought! Do you think we have any say in what happens? Do you think that we are the ones who set you free, who broke your chains and took you out of Egypt? What are we — Moshe and Aharon? We are nothing. Believe me, this is not humility. We know what we are, but I tell you — we are nothing. We are incapable of taking anyone out of Egypt. We are incapable of deciding on a travel itinerary for a people numbering in the millions. We are incapable of performing miracles and providing food for the people through our own powers. We are nothing — helpless and directionless, simple receptacles for the voice of Hashem and instruments of His intent."[3]

Moshe paused for a moment, and then he continued in a loud voice.

"Shame on you," he declared, "that you thought, for even a moment, that we have the capability to perform miracles on our own. It is disgraceful."

---

2. *Sechel Tov* to *Shemos* 16:6; see *Abarbanel*.

3. *Mechilta; Netziv; Rashi; Sechel Tov; Rashbam; Ramban; Ibn Ezra* to *Shemos* 16:6,7.

It was because of this modesty that Moshe was the only individual to whom Hashem referred as "My servant." In addition, Moshe also merited the subjugation of the Jews toward him, exclusively. (See *Chullin* 89a; *Midrash Ohr Afeilah* to *Beshalach*; *Rambam, Hil. Melachim* 2:6.)

The people bowed their heads in humiliation.[4]

"If you find yourselves here in the desert in such trying conditions," continued Moshe, "it is because Hashem wants you to be here. He is the One Who took you out of Egypt. He is the One Who brought you here. He is the One Who will feed you and sustain you now and in the future.[5] But know that you are being tested. Instead of talking nonsense about returning to Egypt, show Him that you have faith in Him. Rely solely on Him, and He will show you that He has heard your cries of anguish and He will send you what you need right away."[6]

Moshe raised his staff high, and the people shrank back before the force of Moshe's words.

"During the next twenty-four hours," he continued, "you will see wonders such as you have never seen before in your life. One will take place this evening, and the other tomorrow morning. This evening a great flock of plump quail will fly in from the desert, and you will be able to eat your fill of succulent meat.[7] You will not have to go back to Egypt to get a portion of meat.[8] Hashem is being kind to you. You hungered for meat, and He will give it to you. But you do not fully deserve such a miracle. You are still full from today's morning meal, so why were you complaining so vehemently about your lack of meat? Your livestock is not yet depleted completely, so why are you saying you have no meat? You could still make a meal from the animals you have left, but of course, you want to keep them rather than eat them. Furthermore, unlike bread, meat is a luxury; you don't really need it for your sustenance."[9]

"So are we getting the quail," asked Toltep, "or aren't we?"

---

4. *Sanhedrin* 110; *Lekach Tov, Malbim* to *Shemos* 16:7.

5. See *Rashi; Sifsei Kohen.*

6. *Midrash HaChefetz; Sechel Tov* to *Shemos* 16:9.

7. *Mechilta; Rashi; Ibn Ezra; Abarbanel; Ralbag* to *Shemos* 16:6,13.

   There are differing opinions as to when the quail actually fell. Some understand "*bein haarbayim*" as meaning in the latter part of the afternoon; others suggest that they fell in the period of twilight. See *Rabbeinu Bachya.*

   There are those who suggest that the whole idea of having the quail come at night to be eaten by the Jews was by Moshe's own volition, and not commanded to him by Hashem (*Alshich; Abarbanel; Malbim*).

8. *Alshich.*

9. See *Yoma* 75; *Mechilta; Rashi* to *Shemos* 16:8; see *Meiri* to *Chullin* 84; *Rambam, Hil. Dei'os* 5:10.

"Oh, yes, you will get them," Moshe replied. "You will get more than you can possibly eat in one night."

"Then we will eat some more tomorrow," said Nagdor.

"No, you will not," said Moshe. "They will last only the one night."

"So will we get more tomorrow night?" asked another man respectfully.

"No, you will get them only this one time," said Moshe. "Hashem will not give you the quail with the glowing radiance of His countenance, as a gift that comes from the heart. Instead, you will have to prepare hurriedly. You will not have time to prepare them as you might like. Hashem is giving you the quail as a sign that He has the power to feed you in any manner He chooses, but at the same time, He wants to show you His displeasure with your behavior on this day. It was really inappropriate."[10]

"And what will happen in the morning?" asked another man.

"Tomorrow morning," said Moshe, "you will wake up and see the ground covered with bread from heaven. Bread is the most basic food a person needs to survive. It is not a luxury food like meat. Therefore, you were justified in being concerned about the depletion of your bread supply, and Hashem will replenish your stores in a loving, affectionate and most miraculous manner.[11] You will get the bread early and have as much time as you need to prepare it to your liking, even all day if you wish. You will have enough to eat until your hunger is fully satisfied. Go home to your tents. Soon you will have plenty to eat."[12]

Just a short time earlier these very people had formed an unruly mob, but now they turned away, meek and shamefaced. The reassurances they had heard from Moshe and Aharon had alleviated their fears and concerns, and now they were filled with remorse at their

---

10. *Mechilta; Rashi; Abarbanel* to *Shemos* 16:8; *Iyun Yaakov* to *Shemos* 16:12 ; *Rif* to *Yoma* 75.

Night is a time of judgment, hence the meat descended at a time that lacks affection. The manna, on the other hand, came down in the morning, a time of mercy and compassion (*Zohar* 63a).

See *Abarbanel* and his explanation as to how the meat was a sign of Hashem's love, like a father to a son. See *Chasam Sofer* as to why the Torah uses a different expression of faith when talking about the quail and about the manna.

11. See *Yoma* 75; *Mechilta; Rashi; Chasam Sofer* to *Beshalach.*

The *Chasam Sofer* notes that it is interesting that despite the abundance of quail the Jews ate, they never became satisfied or full. Yet, with the more modest portion of manna, the Jewish people became full despite the fact that they never saw an abundance. It is well known that one who cannot see the food he is eating is less likely to become full, yet the manna satisfied the Jews.

12. *Ramban; Sechel Tov* to *Shemos* 16:6,7; *Yoma* 75 with *Rashi* and *Maharsha.*

disgraceful behavior. They opened their hands surreptitiously and let the stones they were holding slip out and fall to the ground. They turned back and looked at the desert, and fear gripped their hearts. They knew that they had earned a punishment for what they had done, and they repented in their hearts and begged Hashem's forgiveness.

Suddenly, the cloud pillars of glory appeared before them in the merit of Aharon. The cloud pillars were the symbol of the Divine Presence among the Jewish people, and their appearance at this moment signaled Divine forgiveness. The people breathed a collective sigh of relief. Their repentance had been accepted. All was well again.[13]

A Blizzard of Quail

Toward evening, the sky to the southeast, in the direction of the Red Sea, was suddenly darkened by a colossal flock of birds.[14] The birds seemed oblivious to any need to find their nests for the night. Instead, they flew straight across the desert and landed right on the outskirts of the Jewish encampment.[15] Miraculously, they

---

13. See *Ibn Ezra HaKatzar* to *Shemos* 16:7; *Mechilta; Ibn Ezra; Ohr HaChaim; Zayis Raanan; Abarbanel; Baal HaTurim; Netziv* (to *Mechilta*); *Rokeach* to *Shemos* 16:10.

14. *Ramban* to *Shemos* 16:6; *Bamidbar* 11:31; *Sforno; Abarbanel; Radak* to *Tehillim* 78. See *Targum Yonasan* who writes that the quail blew in from the Mediterranean.

It is the accepted opinion that the birds in question were a species of pheasant or quail. See *R' Avraham Ben HaRambam* who specifically offers the Arabic word for *slav*; he translates *slav* with the Arabic words *alsoman* and *alseluee* which are in fact a quail. See *R' Samson Rafael Hirsch*.

There are varied opinions as to how many episodes of the *slav* there were. Some are of the opinion that the *slav* began now and lasted for the next forty years just as the manna. The manna was given greater attention in the Torah because of its greater miracle and lessons for the Bnei Yisrael to learn.

Others are of the opinion that the *slav* lasted for one night and returned in response to their complaints a year later on the 23rd day of Iyar. Based on the opinion that there were two episodes of the *slav*, there is a question as to whether the present *slav* carried with it the same factors and miracles as the one mentioned in *Bamidbar*, about which the Torah offers more detail. See *Tur's* explanation of why they complained in the second episode when they already had *slav* available.

According to the view that suggests that there were two *slav*s — other than the retribution that took place in the *slav* episode mentioned in *Bamidbar* — the facts remain basically the same in both occurrences, with just minor and subtle differences. (See *Mechilta D'Rashbi Beshalach*.)

For further detail as to the opinions of how many *slav*s there were and what the implications of the differences are, see the following: *Arachin* 15b, *Rashi* and *Tosafos* there. See *Ramban; Akeidah; Riva; Rabbeinu Bachya; Tur; Bechor Shor* to *Shemos* 16:6; *Chizkuni* to *Beha'aloscha; Pane'ach Raza; Sechel Tov* to *Shemos* 16:35.

15. *Tosafos* to *Shemos* 16:7; *Ibn Ezra* to *Beha'aloscha*.

did not disperse upon landing but stayed crowded together so that it was easy to collect them.[16]

The birds flew straight at the encampment with the force and ferocity of a blizzard. Soon the ground was completely covered and piled high with birds, but the impact of their hard landing did not kill them. They were very much alive and fresh for the eating.[17] The piles of quail reached three feet in height,[18] and they were so vast that they could be seen from thirty-four miles away, a full day's travel across the desert.[19]

The more vigorous among the men quickly gathered piles of quail and hurried home to share them with their families. Those who were weaker or somewhat handicapped also did not have to worry. The weakest among them was able to gather, with hardly any expenditure of effort, ten full *chomer* measures of quail, the equivalent of about 1,000 pounds or half a ton.[20] All they had to do was reach out their hands and take the quail. They did not have to bend over or reach up to get them. The piles were on the level of the person's heart, the least stressful position from which to take something. It was not even necessary to turn around. Wherever they looked, in any direction, they were surrounded by piles of quail. [21]

In actuality, among the choice poultry meats, quail ranks with the lowest in quality. It is a fatty, pretentious food that is harmful to a person's health.[22] The quail that flew in from the desert were so fatty

---

16. *Sifri* to *Beha'aloscha*; *Netziv*.

17. *Lekach Tov* to *Beha'aloscha*.
   See *Targum Yonasan* to *Beha'aloscha* that this wind was destined to blow away the world if not for the merit of Moshe and Aharon.

18. *Mechilta*; *Mechilta D'Rashbi* to *Shemos* 16:13. This was two cubits high.

19. *Mechilta*; *Mechilta D'Rashbi* to *Shemos* 16:13; *Bechor Shor* to *Bamidbar* 11:32; see *Toras Chaim* of R' Aryeh Kaplan.
   It was a day's travel in all four directions.

20. See *Rashi* to *Bamidbar* 11:32; *Lekach Tov*. See *Mechilta* to *Shemos* 16:15. It was a measure of 675 gallons or over 400 egg volumes of food. See *Toras Chaim* of R' Aryeh Kaplan. See *Sifri* who offers even a greater amount of potential meat consumption.
   The majority of the quail landed outside the camp. The person in the middle of the camp had to walk the furthest to retrieve the quail. It was that person who collected 10 *chomer* measures. Someone on the outskirts of the camp like the tribe of Dan could have easily collected much much more (*Gra* to *Beha'aloscha*).

21. *Mechilta*; *Mechilta D'Rashbi* to *Shemos* 16:13, *Bamidbar* 11:32 with *Rashi*.

22. *Yoma* 75b with *Rashi*; *Kli Yakar* to *Shemos* 16:7; *Abarbanel*.

that even a small bird would balloon during roasting until it filled the entire oven.[23]

In general, quail have a taste similar to meat and fish.[24] These quail, however, differed in their taste, depending on who was eating them. The righteous found the quail quite a mild food and pleasant to the taste, while the wicked, who had bombarded Moshe with their thorny complaints, found the quail meat thorny in texture and difficult to eat.[25]

The questionable pleasures of the quail meat lasted only during that one night. By morning, all the quail and quail meat had disintegrated and disappeared without a trace. The lesson was clear. Despite all the worries and doubts of the fainthearted, Hashem could provide food in the most miraculous ways whenever and wherever He chose to do so. Once was enough to teach the lesson.[26] In addition, it was imperative for the quail to vanish, because the place the quail occupied was needed for the manna that would fall in the morning. It would cover the entire ground, and the quail needed to be cleared away.[27]

The Bread of Angels

During the night of 16 Iyar, in the third watch of the night, thirty-one days after the Jewish people had left Egypt, the manna fell for the first time.[28] It would continue to fall every day except Shabbos for the next forty years, providing full sustenance for millions of people in the barren wastelands of the desert.

---

23. *Yoma* 75b. This was retribution for a request that was improper and thus the people got an inferior choice of meat (*Maharsha*).
24. *Chizkuni* to *Beha'aloscha*.
25. See *Yoma* 75b with *Maharasha*; *Hadar Zekeinim* to *Shemos* 16:13.
26. *Eliyahu Rabbah* 12; *Abarbanel*; *Chasam Sofer* to *Beshalach*.
27. *Abarbanel* to *Beshalach*.
   See *Rabbeinu Bachya* who suggests that, based on the view that the quail fell nightly, by the time the quail fell, the manna had liquefied itself into a stream. By early evening there was no manna to be found, which allowed for the presence of the quail without difficulty. See *Chizkuni* and *Ibn Ezra* who write that the manna fell outside the camp. See *Malbim* to *Shemos* 16:13 who says that the manna did not fall inside the camp because the *slav* were there at the time.
28. *Zohar* 66b; *Rabbeinu Bachya*; *Meam Loez*. (A night is divided into three watches. The third watch is usually understood to be from 2 a.m. to 6 a.m. in a 12-hour night that begins at 6 p.m. and concludes at 6 a.m.)
   Some suggest that the manna actually fell two days later, on the 18th day of Iyar. This, interestingly enough, happens to be the same day as Lag BaOmer. See *Chasam Sofer* to *Shemos* 16:3.

The manna was one of the things that was created at twilight on the sixth day of creation right before Shabbos, but it did not materialize in the world until the Jewish people appeared in the desert.[29] The essence of the manna was spiritual, and it resided in the heavens where it sustained the ministering angels in a spiritual sense. Accordingly, it was called *lechem abirim*, the bread of angels.[30]

Never before had the world witnessed the miraculous phenomenon of the manna. There was no hint in any of the news bulletins or the legends that circulated in the world, of a food that fell from heaven and sustained an entire people in the desert.[31]

Before dawn, a frigid north wind passed through Gan Eden on its way to the desert. It swept the floor of the desert clean, while a gentle rain washed away any debris so that the ground was left clean, level and smooth. At the break of dawn, a glittering golden dew, thick as a light rain, fell from the sky and coated the desert floor with a gilded sheen. The ground was now ready to receive the manna from the heavens.[32]

The manna, being spiritual in its essence, underwent a transformation, like wheat being milled, as it passed through a bank of clouds called *shechakim*, where it took on a more physical form, although it retained the heavenly flavor of Gan Eden. The final nature of that physical form was tailored to the specific person who

---

29. *Pirkei D'Rav Eliezer; Tanchuma Yashan; Lekach Tov* to *Shemos* 16:15; *Avos* 5:8.
  See *Radal* to *Pirkei D'Rav Eliezer* 3 who comments about an apparent contradiction as to when the manna was created.

30. *Zohar; Rabbeinu Bachya; Yoma* 75a; *Tanna D'Vei Eliyahu* 14. See *Ibn Ezra* to *Shemos* 16:13 regarding his description of manna that is found today.
  The manna, upon entering the worldly hemisphere, changed into a different physical form in both shape and taste. Others suggest that the Jews did not eat from what the angels eat, but rather from what they prepared.
  See *Ramban* to *Shemos* 16:6; *Zohar* 61b; *Zohar Balak* 384 about the spirituality of the manna and how it is similar to what the angels eat.
  Some suggest that one's soul also benefits from the manna. The *neshamah* also ate from the manna (*Tosafos Al HaTorah*).
  Some suggest that in Gan Eden also the manna would be eaten. The final letters of the words כְּזֶרַע גַּד לָבָן spell out "Eden" (*R' Efraim Al Hatorah, Shemos* 16:31).

31. *Ramban* to *Shemos* 16:4,6. See *Zohar* 61b.

32. *Mechilta; Yalkut; Ibn Ezra; Rabbeinu Bachya.*
  See *Ramban* 16:4 who suggests that rain may have fallen along with the manna.
  In fact the manna for the righteous was edible and ready just as rain is drinkable as it falls. This was the complete opposite of grain from the ground that needs preparation to become edible bread (*Abarbanel*).

collected it. The manna was warm and moist, ready to eat, as if it had just come out of the oven.[33]

The manna passed through the clouds and fell to the ground in complete silence, coming to rest on the bed of gilded dew, which protected it from any dirt that may have remained on the ground. After the manna fell, a second coating of dew fell from the skies and covered the manna, protecting it from any dirt and insects that might alight on it.[34]

In the end, each piece of manna took on the form of a thin round disc with a hard frosted glaze above and below it that kept it warm and fresh all day.[35] It resembled a biscuit, with a hard crust on the outside and a soft, moist filling within.[36] The appearance of the filling, which was actually the manna itself at the time of its descent, was truly singular and distinct. It was white and round like a coriander seed with a golden-yellow tinge like a mustard seed, and it had a gleaming radiance like a pearl or a piece of well-cut crystal.[37]

---

33. *Rabbeinu Bachya; Yalkut Reuveni;* see *Tanchuma Yashan* to *Shemos* 16:21; *Chagigah* 12b and *Maharsha; Tehillim* 78:23. See *Malbim* to *Bamidbar* 11:5; *Alshich* to *Tehillim* 78.

This would obviously be only for the righteous, for the wicked had to prepare it themselves.

The spiritual nature of this food was necessary as a preparation to accepting the Torah. As *Chazal* teach us, the Torah was only given to those that were eaters of the manna. See *Tanchuma Beshalach* 20; *Kometz HaMinchah, Shavuos.*

34. *Mechilta* to *Shemos* 16:14; *Rokeach* 16:23; (*Netziv*) *Sifri* to *Beha'aloscha* 11:9; *Lekach Tov* to *Shemos* 16:14.

The falling of the manna was unlike rain which descends in a noisy and cool fashion. Like the *Lechem HaPanim* (Show Bread) of the Temple which was sanctified food and which remained hot and fresh for eight days, the manna remained fresh and warm throughout the day (*Shaarei Aryeh* p. 158).

35. *Rashi; Onkelos* to *Shemos* 16:14. It was as paper thin as the thickness of dust or ashes (*Sechel Tov*).

Some suggest that they were like round balled hailstones in appearance (see *Rashbam; Bechor Shor*).

Others suggest it was a sticky doughlike substance created by the combination of the manna and dew when they united (see *Ramban*).

36. See *Sifri* to *Bamidbar* 11:9; *Lekach Tov; Sechel Tov* to *Shemos* 16:14; *Rokeach* to *Shemos* 16:23.

It is in memory of the manna that on Shabbos the *challah* is covered both on top and bottom (*Shibbolei HaLeket, Siman* 68). Some question this, since on Shabbos the manna did not fall.

Others suggest that there was no dew on top of the manna. When the dew rose in the morning, the fresh manna lay on the moist and clean ground (see *Ibn Ezra; Ralbag*).

The *Gemara* suggests that the manna looked as though it were in a chest, similar to a jewelry box where women keep their jewelry.

37. See *Bamidbar* 11:7; *Rabbeinu Bachya* to *Shemos* 16:4; *Yoma* 75a; *Mechilta* to *Shemos* 16:5; *Rashi; Ibn Ezra; Sechel Tov* to *Shemos* 16:31.

Some suggest that the manna came in the form of *kitniyos,* as a bean or pea in appearance. In Poland the word for pea or bean is related to the word manna (*Maaseh Hashem*).

Afterward, when the people collected the manna, it became drier and crustier in varying degrees, depending on the person who had collected it.[38]

After sunrise, the upper layer of dew evaporated into the air, leaving the manna and its bed of gilded dew visible to the people who would come out to collect it.[39]

The people got up in the morning and said the *Shema*. Then they went outside, and to their utter amazement, there it was. The ground was covered with a substance they had never seen before.[40]

The people wandered back and forth, looking at the manna with puzzlement and wonder. They asked each other questions, but no one had adequate answers. It was a mystery.[41]

Toltep stared at the manna and scratched his ear. "*Man hu?*" he said, reverting to his native Egyptian tongue. "What is this thing? Where did it come from?"[42]

Peliav shook his head. "I've never seen anything like it. Perhaps it is some kind of food that grows only in the desert. Moshe told us we would have food this morning. This is what he meant."[43]

"But how did it get here?" asked Nagdor.

Peliav shrugged. "Maybe it is a gift from Heaven."

"I wonder what it is," said Kumiel. "Perhaps you are right, Peliav. There is a popular food in these parts called manna that is quite unfamiliar to most other people.[44] I've seen it, and there is a vague similarity. But this is something completely different.[45] This looks like food that has come out of an oven; it looks fully prepared. It

---

38. *Rokeach* 16:23. This involved the wicked, who had to grind and prepare the manna in its entirety.

39. *Rashi* to *Shemos* 16:14. This prevented the Jewish people from having to break the layer of ice that was atop the manna initially (*Rokeach*).

Some offer a view that the evaporation of the dew and exposure of the manna was similar to removing a peel and exposing the seed inside (*Rishonim*).

40. *Sifri* to *Bamidbar* 11:9; *Lekach Tov* to *Shemos* 16:14.

Others suggest that the Jews collected the manna before the sun would rise in the morning (*Midrash Shocher Tov*).

This was also dependent on a person's level of righteousness. The righteous had little to do to collect the manna, while the wicked had to go long distances to retrieve their manna portions.

41. *Mechilta; Chizkuni; Bechor Shor* to *Shemos* 16:15.

42. *Rabbeinu Chananel* to *Shemos* 16:15.

43. *Akeidah* to *Shemos* 16:15.

44. *Sefer HaShorashim* p. 259; *Rabbeinu Bachya* to *Shemos* 16:15.

45. See *Rashi; Malbim* to *Shemos* 16:15; *Succah* 39b; *Daniel* 1:5.

gives the appearance of a high-quality food, and it is obviously warm, freshly baked and ready to eat."[46]

Just then Achiash and his wife Beruchah came by. They were carrying their children, who were rubbing the sleep from their eyes.

Beruchah turned to one of her friends standing nearby. "I don't know what this is either, but I love it already. You can imagine what this is going to do for our lives. No more cooking and baking in a hot kitchen. No more peeling and cutting and scraping until your hands become red and chapped. This is my idea of Heaven. Now all I have to do is take care of my crying babies. Do you think a taste of this stuff would make them stop crying?"

"I don't," her friend replied. "I'll settle for the no cooking, no baking. Ask for too much and you get nothing."[47]

Achiash took a piece and was about to put it into his mouth, but Nagdor grabbed his wrist.

"Careful, my friend," he said. "How do you know that it's safe to eat this thing? Who knows, it may make you violently ill."

"You are quite right, my young friend," said Kumiel. "There is no sense in taking chances. Let's go ask Moshe what to do. First, we need to know if we can eat it and, if so, if it needs any special preparation."[48]

The sun had barely risen above the horizon when Kumiel and his friends arrived at Moshe's tent. But they were not the first. A large crowd of the curious and baffled had come to ask Moshe similar questions.

"My dear people," Moshe told them, "this food is a gift to you from Hashem. It is safe to eat, and it needs no preparation to make it edible. Hashem has already prepared it for you."[49]

As the people walked away from Moshe's tent, eager to begin collecting the manna, Beruchah said to her friends, "Did you hear Toltep refer to this as *'man hu'* in Egyptian? Well, I think I'll call it manna, because when all is said and done, we still don't really know what it is."

"That is a good idea," said her friend. "It needs a name, and manna is as good as any other. In fact, it's better."[50]

---

46. See *Rashi* and *Gur Aryeh*; *HaKesav VeHaKabbalah* to *Shemos* 16:15.
47. *Tzeidah LeDerech*.
48. See *Alshich*; *Malbim* to *Shemos* 16:15.
49. See *Rashi*; *Alshich*; *Malbim* to *Shemos* 16:15.
50. See *Chizkuni*; *Bechor Shor* to *Shemos* 16:15; *Pesikta Zutra*; *Tzeidah LaDerech*; *Tosafos Al HaTorah* to *Shemos* 16:31.

And so the name spread among the women, and eventually, the food that had once been called *lechem abirim*, the bread of angels, came to be called manna.[51]

As the day progressed, the manna continued to fall. By the end of the morning, the piles of manna were sixty cubits high. Every single day, the windows of Heaven opened wide, and enough manna fell to last the Jewish people for 2,000 years. Relatively speaking, more manna fell in the desert than water during the Great Flood. Kingdoms even in the distant east were able to see the mountainous piles of manna that fell from the heavens to feed the Jewish people, and the Name of Heaven was abundantly sanctified.[52]

After the dazzling miraculous display for the benefit of the surrounding kingdoms, the manna dissolved until there was only enough left to provide a full *omer* measure for every man, woman and child in the encampment.[53]

Different Modes of Gathering

The relationship of the people to the manna differed from group to group. The righteous Jews rose early and went out to gather the manna during the first two hours of the day. The less righteous Jews were not so zealous about gathering the manna. They rose a little late and went out to do their gathering during the third and fourth hours of the day when the sun was already quite high in the sky.[54] The lazy Jews did not go out to gather their portions of the manna until after the fourth hour of the day, but by then the hot morning sun had melted all the manna.[55] It was too late for that day, and these lazy people had to go hungry until the next day or subsist on small donations from those who had the foresight to come earlier.[56]

The manna that melted in the midday sun did not go to waste. It ran off in streams that joined into a mighty river and flowed into the

---

51. *Tehillim* 78:25; *Lekach Tov* to *Shemos* 16:31; *Pesikta Zutra*.
52. See *Shemos Rabbah* 25:7; *Maharzu*; *Yalkut Shimoni* 258; *Yoma* 76a; *Radak* to *Tehillim* 78. See *Rashi, Tosafos* and commentaries in *Ein Yaakov* for further explanation.
53. See *Ben Yehoyada* to *Yoma* 76a.
54. See *Rashi* to *Shabbos* 117b; *Rashi*; *Sechel Tov*; *Ralbag* to *Shemos* 16:21.
   Some suggest that the Jews began to collect the manna before sunrise (*Ibn Ezra HaKatzar* to *Shemos* 16:21).
55. *Toldos Yitzchok* to *Shemos* 16:13; *Targum Yonasan* to *Shemos* 16:21.
56. *Rabbeinu Bachya* to *Shemos* 16:21; *Akeidah* to *Shemos* 16:20.

Mediterranean Sea. The dew that fell with the manna irrigated the land, providing vegetation for the animals.[57] In addition, the animals had the singular benefit of drinking from the liquid manna as it flowed to the sea.[58]

There were also other differences among the groups besides the time of day they would go out to do their gathering. The dynamics of the gathering itself were also different, but we are not sure exactly how they differed.

According to some opinions, the righteous, who spent their time learning Torah, found the manna waiting for them on their doorsteps, warm, fresh and ready to eat without any preparation; they didn't have to interrupt their studies to provide food for their families. The manna came to them on its own. All they had to do was reach out and take it. Moreover, their portions of the manna never lost their full freshness and never needed reheating, always remaining exactly as when first delivered.[59]

The less righteous Jews received their portions of the manna in the form of raw dough that still needed baking. It also did not come to their doorsteps. Instead, they had to go out beyond the encampment for a short distance, and there they would find the manna waiting for them. All in all, the effort they had to expend to retrieve and prepare their portions of the manna was fairly minimal.

The Jews on the lowest spiritual level, the mean-spirited chronic complainers lacking in faith and gratitude, had a much harder time with the manna. They had to go deep into the desert to retrieve their portions. The manna they found there had fallen in the form of hard

---

57. See *Targum Yonasan; Lekach Tov* to *Shemos* 16:21; *Mechilta; Rashi*. Later we wll see that the nations of the world would benefit from the taste of this manna when eating these animals. *Targum Yonasan* suggests that it was the Jews who ate these animals and enjoyed the taste of the manna as well.

Some suggest that this prevented anyone from leaving over any manna in their homes. Most however suggest that the collected manna left over became wormy but the manna left untaken outside is what melted and liquefied into a stream of water. (See *Abarbanel*.)

For this reason some suggest that the manna was not found in the courtyard areas of their tents. At the very least they would have to leave the camp, going into the desert to retrieve the manna. Would the manna have been placed across the courtyard areas of the tents, the stream of melted manna would have soaked the camp, dampening and wetting the ground and causing much difficulty of movement throughout. It was because of this that manna did not fall and rest in that area. See *Mechilta; Malbim* to *Shemos* 16:13; *Zeh Yenachmeni*. See *Rokeach* to *Shemos* 16:13.

58. *Rokeach; Yalkut Reuveni*.

59. See *Maharsha* to *Yoma* 76a; *Rokeach; Panim Yafos*.

kernels that had to be milled and pounded in a mortar and taken through the entire bread-making process. Most of these people's time was consumed by the preparation of the manna, leaving them little time for mischief.[60]

Others suggest that the relationships were exactly the opposite. The manna fell in a manner that accommodated the patterns of the individual. The righteous Jews, who were active and zealous in all their actions, received their portions far afield. The laziest Jews, who were slow to move from their positions, received their portions simply by stretching out their hands; they did not have to exert any more effort than they ordinarily would. The average Jews, who would customarily make some effort, found their portions outside but close to the encampment.[61]

Yet others suggest that the mode of delivery depended on the physical condition of the individual. People in excellent health would have to go far afield, people of moderate health would go just outside the encampment, and ailing people had it delivered to their doorsteps.[62]

The Rules of the Gathering

Hashem sent the manna to provide sustenance for the people, but He also used it to test their faith in Him and observance of His commandments. The first law of the manna that Moshe gave the Jewish people was to collect only for that day's needs.[63] The amount of manna allotted to

---

60. See *Yoma* 75a and *Maharsha* there. *Mechilta; Tanchuma Yashan* to *Beshalach* 22; *Shemos Rabbah* 24:3.

Those not righteous had to travel a *mil*, a distance of 2,000 *amah*, which is the *techum Shabbos*, the distance one may travel on Shabbos.

A major motivation in proper adherence to Hashem's commandments was that on one day a person would find manna at his doorstep due to his righteousness. If, however, on a particular day he sinned and did not repent, he would be considered wicked and would have to travel to get his manna. It would be public knowledge and evident to all that this person had sinned, and the embarrassment would be overwhelming (R' Yaakov Galinsky). Others argue with this premise based on a *Sifri* in *Beha'aloscha* which states that the clouds traveled with a person outside the camp. Therefore, one was obscured by the *amud anan* (pillar of cloud) and could not be recognized when going out to collect the manna. Others respond with the notion that sinners were not protected by the *anan*, as noted by the war with Amalek (*Shaarei Aryeh* p. 148).

See *Malbim* to *Shemos* 16:14 where he explains that the manna itself had many variations in its physical being.

61. *Tanchuma Yashan* to *Beshalach.*
62. *Hadar Zekeinim.*
63. *Zohar* 62a; *Mechilta, Rabbeinu Bachya* to *Shemos* 16:4; *Ibn Ezra* to *Shemos* 16:19. *Chovos*

each person was an *omer* measure (equivalent to 43.2 eggs, somewhere between 2.66 and 4.66 quarts by volume, or 2 kilos), enough for the two meals of the day. They were not to be concerned with the food they would need the next day. Just as Hashem had provided for them this day, they should have faith that He would keep His promise and provide for them the next day as well.[64]

Should anyone gather more than his share, the manna itself would call out, "The stomach of the wicked is always empty." In other words, the unauthorized food he had taken would do him no good.[65]

At first, the people protested that this law gave unfair advantage to rich people such as Nachshon ben Aminadav, whose large household staff could gather a disproportionate amount of manna, thereby leaving the common people with only meager meals.

Moshe quickly reassured the people that their concerns were baseless. Rich or poor, fat or thin, large family or small family, it made absolutely no difference.[66] The allotment of the manna was by the individual, and the portion of an *omer* measure was universal to all Jews. Anyone who ate less than an *omer* measure would suffer from malnutrition. Anyone who ate more than his allotted *omer* measure would be considered a glutton,[67] and his gluttony would cause the portions of other family members to be reduced proportionately, causing them to suffer malnutrition.[68]

HaLevavos, Bitachon Ch. 4.
 Hashem wanted the Jews to know that anyone who follows His commandments and honors Him properly will never have to worry about sustenance for himself and his family.
 It is this manna that would bring the Jews to a very high level of faith and belief in Hashem. The Sages mention a custom that whoever says the verses in the Torah concerning the manna each day, will never experience a shortage of food or lack of support (*Sefer HaManhig, Hilchos Shabbos* 44; *Rabbeinu Bachya*).
64. See *Rashi; Lekach Tov* to *Shemos* 16:16 . See *Rashi* to *Shemos* 16:39; *Eruvin* 83b. See *Toras Chaim,* who explains that an *eifah* is 5 gallons or 22 liters. This meant that the *omer* was a half gallon or 2.2 liters. See *Tosafos* who writes that it was a *kezayis* (olive-size measure).
65. *Zohar* 62a.
66. See *Lekach Tov; Mechilta; Netziv; Rabbeinu Bachya* to *Shemos* 16:16.
 Some suggest that the reference to rich and poor was one that dealt with children and not fortune. The concern here was that a larger family would receive more manna on average than a smaller family. Moshe replied that the manna was the same regardless of family size; it would still be one *omer* per person (*Chemdas Yamim*).
67. *Lekach Tov; Mechilta.*
68. *Abarbanel* to *Shemos* 16:17.

Another law required that the head of each household go out to gather the manna for the entire family.[69] It would be immodest for the women to go out and mingle with the gatherers. As for the children, they had to stay with their teachers and learn the holy Torah. Each head of household was required to collect an *omer* measure for each individual in his family. A family of five, for example, received five *omer* measures.[70] He was prohibited, however, from collecting for another family.[71]

Some suggest that each family member, older or younger, larger or smaller, ate an *omer* measure of the manna, and miraculously, all were satisfied by the exact same amount.[72] Others suggest that the bigger people ate more, while the younger and slimmer people ate less. The "one *omer* measure per person" rule applied to the family as a whole; the number of *omer* measures the family gathered was equal to the number of people in the family, but the exact apportionment within the family itself depended on the respective individual's need for food.[73]

It was the responsibility of the head of the household to take a basket or a large sheet with him when he went to gather the manna. He would take the amount of manna that appeared to be an *omer* measure for each member of his family. The exact measurement would be taken when he came home. He had to try to be as accurate as possible, because an error would cost him dearly. If he took too much he would have to trek back out to the desert to replace the manna he had taken without authorization. If he had taken too little, he would have to return to the desert to gather more for the hungry mouths in his family.[74]

---

69. See *Zohar* 63a; *Lekach Tov*; *Rabbeinu Chananel*.

70. *Abarbanel*; *Malbim* to *Shemos* 16:16. See *Rabbeinu Bachya* to *Shemos* 16:16.

The righteous person did not have to go out to collect the manna. With the manna falling right at his doorstep, he was able to utilize this valuable saved time to learn Torah (*Tosafos*).

Some add that the Torah's use of the word "*ish*" (man) in 16:16 suggests that this a child was excluded from having the right to collect the manna (*Shaarei Aryeh* p. 143).

71. *Shaarei Aryeh* p. 144. The *Shaarei Aryeh* suggests, however, that one was allowed to eat from another family member's portion. This was unlike the laws in place for the *korban pesach*.

72. R' *Avraham Ben HaRambam*; *Ohr HaChaim* to *Beshalach*; *Devarim* 8:3. See *Chasam Sofer*, *Choshen Mishpat* 12; *Orach Chaim* 181; *Yoreh Deah* 294.

Since the manna was a spiritual food, it was not related to one's appetite or size. Spiritually, all souls are equal in size and matter and since the manna was a spiritual food, it sufficed regardless of a person's age or size (*Alshich*).

73. *Sifsei Kohen*; see *Zohar*.

74. *Rashbam*; *Akeidah*; *Reav*; *Bechor Shor*; *Chizkuni*; *Sforno*; *Maaseh Hashem*. See *Lekach Tov*; *Abarbanel*.

Considering the consequences, most heads of households made a conscientious effort to gather the correct amount designated for their families. And when they returned home they found that, miraculously, they had gathered precisely the right amount. There would be no need to return to the desert after all.[75]

Once the manna was distributed to the family members, the entire manna had to be consumed before the next day. In addition, the manna was only allowed to be used for eating. Selling the manna or using it for any other purpose was strictly forbidden.[76] The entire portion had to be eaten, with nothing left over for the next day. Hashem had promised to deliver manna every day.[77] Therefore, to set aside food for the next day would show a profound lack of faith in Him.[78]

But what if someone did not want to eat so much? After all, an *omer* measure was a sizeable amount of food. What if a child could not eat the entire amount? What if a person was more spiritually inclined and was not accustomed to filling his belly with food? Did he have to force himself to eat the full amount?[79]

No, he did not. He could eat as much as he wanted and leave the rest to other family members or give it away to the lazy people who came out too late to gather their own portions of manna.[80] If there was still leftover manna, he could throw it into the stream of melted manna flowing to the sea, as long as he did not hold it in store for the following day.[81]

---

75. R' Saadiah Gaon; Rashi; Chizkuni.
76. *Minchah Belulah; Abarbanel* to *Shemos* 16:15.
   Some question how it was possible to save the manna for anything, considering that it melted and liquefied itself by day's end. (See *Abarbanel*.)
77. *Ibn Ezra* to *Shemos* 16:19
   Some suggest the manna was symbolic of mitzvos. One should never leave mitzvos for another time. They should be done immediately (*Tosafos; Abarbanel* to *Shemos* 16:20).
   Some suggest that the evening meal was the deadline to rid oneself of the manna. After that it was considered *nossar* (left over), and at that point it would spoil. See *Panim Yafos* and *Sforno* who write that this was the case after Shabbos as well.
78. *Mechilta; Lekach Tov; Ibn Ezra* to *Shemos* 16:19-20.
79. See *Netziv* to *Shemos* 16:19.
80. *Tanchuma Yashan; Ibn Ezra* to *Shemos* 16:19.
   This, however, raises the question regarding what was mentioned earlier. It was considered unhealthy for anyone to eat less than an *omer*. Some suggest that this only applied if they ate less as a means of savings the manna for the following day (see *Ralbag; Rabbeinu Bachya* to *Shemos* 16:21).
81. See *Pane'ach Raza*.

Most of the Jewish people obeyed the law and did not leave over any manna until the next day, but a small group of people flaunted the law and stowed away their leftover manna in their tents. The Jewish women, however, obeyed the law without a single exception.[82]

Not surprisingly, among the lawbreakers were the notorious Dassan and Aviram, who had cast themselves as the nemeses of Moshe and Aharon from the moment they had come to Egypt to liberate the Jewish people. Now again, they chose to ignore Moshe's laws, perhaps because they lacked faith in Hashem, perhaps because they wanted to test Moshe's leadership and his reaction to their insubordination.[83] Moshe had summoned the people for an announcement of major importance the next day. When the people assembled, it would become known that some had disobeyed him. Dassan and Aviram wanted to see what he would do about it.

On the first day the manna fell, Dassan and Aviram ate only part of it. In the evening, they made a great display before their friends of stowing the manna away in their pantries.

But Hashem would not allow their perfidy to go undetected. Toward morning, maggots and fruit flies began to circle over the leftover manna. But this was only the first and smallest of the miracles that were about to take place.[84] Huge red and white worms infested the manna in such vast numbers that they filled the entire tents.

The people were already assembling for Moshe's important announcement when a great commotion disturbed the tranquility of the encampment. The huge red and white worms burst forth from the tents of Dassan and Aviram in two long orderly rows, the worms piling on top of each other in their urgency to march. They snaked their

---

82. *Lekach Tov* to *Shemos* 16:20.

83. See *Sforno; Akeidah; Abarbanel; R' Efraim Al HaTorah* to *Shemos* 16:20.
    The commentaries will always presume that any lawlessness that took place among the Jews would first and foremost include Dassan and Aviram. These individuals were wicked from their childhood and had always been involved in any lawlessness, chaos and disorder (*Etz Yosef* to *Shemos Rabbah; Tanna D'Vei Eliyahu* 18).

84. See *Sechel Tov; Rokeach; Sifsei Kohen; R' Efraim Al HaTorah* to *Shemos* 16:24 and commentaries to *Yeshayah* 14:11 as to the difference between *tolaim* and *rimah* (types of worms).
    The issue at hand is the word *tolaim* mentioned regarding the leftover manna and the word *rimah* mentioned in reference to the lack of *rimah* when the Friday manna was left over. Most suggest that *rimah* precedes *tolaim*. They are creatures that do not eat food, but either begin the rotting process or are the first parasites when spoiling begins. Others posit that at first white worms began to crawl, followed by red worms that were the main parasites of the manna.

way among the tents, the thunderous vibration of their movement fairly shaking the ground. Almost instantly, the news of what Dassan and Aviram had done spread through the encampment like wildfire.[85]

But that was not the end of it. Once the existence of the leftover manna became common knowledge, it immediately began to rot, giving off a horrendously putrid stench, like a decomposing carcass that had been left for a long time in the sun.[86]

Moshe had been prepared to speak to the people about the rules governing the gathering of manna for Shabbos, but this outrageous distraction aroused his furious anger.

"How could you do such a thing?" he cried out. "How could you so wantonly disobey Hashem's instructions.[87] The manna was a test of your faith, and those of you who broke the law have failed miserably. After seeing all these great and wondrous miracles Hashem has performed for you, how can you remain untouched and unaffected? How can you not have faith in Him? How can you not believe Him when He tells you He will give you more manna tomorrow? How can you not obey Him when He tells you not to leave anything over at the end of the day?"

Moshe paused and let his angry words sink into the hearts of all the assembled people.

"And there is something else," he continued. "The manna is food from Heaven, the bread of the angels, a precious gift from Hashem. The manna has a spiritual essence even though it takes on a material form. It is holy! It is pure! And look what you lawbreakers have done. You've caused it to become infested with maggots and worms.

---

85. *Mechilta; Shemos Rabbah* 25:10; *Yefei To'ar; Tanchuma Tetzaveh* 11; *Tanchuma Yashan* to *Beshalach; Midrash Ohr Afeilah; Rashi; Gra* to *Shemos* 16:20; *Aruch* to the word *klan; Rokeach* to *Shemos* 16:24.

This would be another of the ten times the Jews tested Hashem in the desert (*Arachin* 15b).

86. See *Rashi; Mechilta; Rokeach; Abarbanel.*

Many commentaries reverse the order of the Torah as it deals with this leftover manna. Under normal circumstances, decay and spoilage in food precede the infestation of worms. Other, however, posit that in dry matter such as wood and fruit, it is common for worms to form without a previous stage of rotting. It is only something hot, sweet and moist that tends to spoil before the arrival of worms. (It is interesting to note that the manna was in fact warm and extremely sweet, and according to some, moist as well.) They believe it to be unnecessary to reverse the order and change the wording of the Torah without absolute necessity. In fact, others suggest that it was crucial that the decay did not take place first, for if it did, they could never have been exposed. Once they saw the manna rotting, it would have been thrown away and the *Kiddush Hashem* would never have materialized. (See *Aruch* to the word *tola; Ramban; R' Saadiah Gaon; Akeidah; Abarbanel; Ohr HaChaim; Malbim.*)

87. *Mechilta* to *Beshalach; Rokeach* to *Shemos* 16:20.

You've caused it to become so degraded that it smells like a rotten carcass. What an outrage!"[88]

Moshe was so overcome by pain and anger that he could not go on with the announcements he had prepared. He was so upset that he overlooked his responsibility as a leader to forewarn the people not to gather the manna on Shabbos. As a result, some Jews would desecrate the next Shabbos by going out to gather the manna.[89]

The Manna Solves Mysteries

An interesting benefit of the "one *omer* per person" rule was that it helped solve mysteries and resolve disputes.

For instance, there was a dispute between a professed slave owner and the man he claimed as his slave.

"It is well known that this man belongs to me," he told the court. "I can prove I bought him a long time ago. I want him returned to me right away."

"Not so fast," said the alleged slave. "It's true that I once belonged to you, but you set me free a long time ago. I am a free man, and you have no claims on me."

"You can't just claim that I freed you," the angry owner retorted. "Where is your proof that I set you free? I can prove that I bought you, but you cannot prove that you were freed. That makes you my property."

The judge listened to both sides and nodded his head. "Very well, we will issue a ruling tomorrow. Please come here right after you gather your manna, and make sure you bring your manna with you."

The next day, the man who claimed that he owned the slave came to court with his manna in a basket. The judge ordered the manna measured. There were exactly eight *omer* measures.

---

88. *Sifsei Kohen* to *Shemos* 16:21.
   One reason for this was that the manna and the desert offered the greatest conveniences for the Jews. They never had to go to the bathroom, they never sweated and there never were bugs. Now this spiritual food was not only made non-spiritual but was brought down to the lowest depth of a food's makeup. See *Devarim Rabbah* 7:11.
89. See *Vayikra Rabbah* 13; *Tosafos* to *Shabbos* 87b; *Shemos Rabbah* 25:10; *Rashi* to *Shemos* 16:22; *Mattos* 21:31.
   Some suggest that Moshe reasoned that with the manna falling on Monday, he would wait till the end of the week to remind them about the Shabbos laws as they pertain to the manna. When Moshe became angered at the Jews who were leaving over the manna, it caused forgetfulness and therefore the Jewish people were not reminded not to go out on Shabbos. (See *Yefei To'ar* to *Shemos Rabbah* 25:10.)

"How many people are there in your family?" asked the judge.

"Well, let's see," said the man, counting on his fingers. "Me. My wife. One son and five daughters. Eight!"

"And you have exactly eight *omer* measures of manna," the judge pointed out.

"So it matches," said the man. He smiled smugly.

"Yes, it does," said the judge. "But where is the *omer* measure for this slave you supposedly own?"

The man realized he had been caught red-handed, and his face grew red to match the color of his hands.

"Case dismissed," said the judge.

The manna was also used to determine the paternity of children in cases where the identity of the father was uncertain. For instance, a married woman divorced and remarried within three months, and then she had a child seven months later. Who was the father? Was the baby a full-term child fathered by the first husband or a premature seven-month child fathered by the second husband? Once again, the manna held the answer, because the household of the real father received the portion of the disputed child.[90]

This was another reason for the law that the manna must be consumed or discarded on the day it was gathered and nothing was to be left over for the following day. If people had been allowed to stow away manna for another day, they could add to their daily basket from their reserves and claim more members in the household, and the manna would no longer be such a positive proof.[91]

A Food of Many Tastes

Because of its spiritual essence, the manna was unlike any other food. The sustenance it provided depended very much on the righteousness and spiritual level of the person eating it. The holier and purer the person, the more satisfaction and pleasure he derived from the manna. Yehoshua, Moshe's closest disciple, derived as much pleasure from the manna as the rest of the Jewish people combined.[92] The manna, being the bread of the angels,

---

90. *Lekach Tov; Mechilta*. See *Yoma* 75a; *Zohar* 63a.
    See *Shaarei Aryeh* who writes that were someone allowed to collect for another family, this proof used to adjudicate disputes would not have been available.
91. *Chasam Sofer*.
92. See *Yoma* 76a; *Kometz HaMinchah* to *Beshalach*; *Malbim* to *Bamidbar* 11:4.
    In fact the numerical value of "*lechem abirim ochal*" ("the bread of angels [men] ate"; *Psalms* 78:25) is the same numerical value as the word Yehoshua [391] (*Steipler*).

also elevated the spiritual level of the people who ate it and guarded them against the evil thoughts that eating could sometimes trigger.[93]

Before any modification, the taste of the manna was like that of a honey-glazed wafer or doughnut. Some say it was like a pancake drenched with honey. Others say it was like a paste or batter made from fine flour mixed with honey.[94] Yet others say that the manna was sweet as a honeycomb.[95]

The manna also held deep reservoirs of many different tastes. People on a high spiritual level were able to connect intimately with the spiritual essence of the manna and derive its full potential of 546 different tastes, from fatted calf to casseroles.[96] They could configure the taste of the manna to their personal preference, no matter what they wanted or fancied. It also assumed the smell of that food, but it always retained its original shape and form; according to some opinions, it even assumed the texture of that food.[97] Its spiritual essence allowed it to transcend its physical form and provide the tastes and smells the people desired.[98] And to accomplish this, the people did not have to state their preference. They only had to think that they were in the mood for a particular food, and the manna would instantly resemble that food.

The *omer* measure of manna which came down from the heavens for each individual Jew was more filling than any other food they had ever eaten. In fact, the manna increased their appetites and made them want to eat even more.[99] But no matter how much they

---

93. *Sifsei Kohen.*
94. See *Mechilta; Rashi; Yonasan Ben Uziel; Abarbanel; Ibn Ezra; Tosafos Al HaTorah* to *Shemos* 16:31; *Yoma* 75a; *Challah* 1:4. See *Rashi* in *Pesachim* 37a. See *R' Avraham Ben HaRambam* and his Arabic translation.
Others suggest that it was like dough fried or baked in a pan. Others suggest that it tasted very sweet, as though it came from a jug filled with honey.
See *Berachos* 57b where it says that the manna was sixty times the sweetness of honey. *Midrash HaChefetz* to *Shemos* 16:31 writes that the manna was not connected to honey in any way. The Torah only compares manna to honey because that is the closest thing to which to compare it. See *Meam Loez.*
95. *Rokeach* to *Shemos* 16:31.
96. *Shemos Rabbah* 25:3; *Maharzu; Yefei To'ar; Yalkut Shir HaShirim* 986; *Mechilta; Rokeach* to *Shemos* 16:31; *Maharsha* to *Yoma* 75b; *Ben Yehoyada; Midrash Tehillim* 23. The 546 is significant because it is the numerical value of the Hebrew word "*matuk,*" which means sweet.
97. See *Yoma* 75a for the difference of opinion on this subject. See *Kli Yakar* to *Shemos* 16:15.
98. *Zohar; Kometz HaMinchah* to *Beshalach; Malbim* to *Bamidbar* 11:5. See *Alshich* for a similar view.
99. *Maharsha* to *Yoma* 75a.
Similar to the *neshamah yeseirah* that allows one to eat more on Shabbos, the spiritual nature of the manna allowed one's appetite to expand accordingly.

ate, even if they consumed it all day, they never suffered the consequences of overeating or digestive disorders. At the end of their deeply satisfying meals, they would eat the final morsel and think about the most delicious, mouth-watering dessert, and they would have it. And they didn't even get fat![100]

All this great variety of taste was available to people who were at least on a minimal level of spirituality. Those basically devoid of spirituality or those who simply ate without thinking of any preference in taste did not have access to the vast array of tastes in the manna. Nonetheless, the manna by itself adjusted to the particular situation of these people.[101]

The very young and the elderly usually prefer foods with a sweet honey taste or the smooth flavors of oil.[102] Adolescents, on the other hand, have a strong preference for the taste and texture of breads and breadlike foods. These foods appeal to their palates and also provide them with the nutrients they need at these junctures in their lives. The manna on its own provided them, according to their age, with the tastes and the nutrients they needed.

For the nursing infant, the manna provided the mother with the healthful foods that enriched her milk and made it tasty for the child.[103] For the ailing, the manna took on the tastes and textures of bread made from fine flour, honey and oil, foods that are restorative for sick people.[104]

---

100. *Tosefta Sotah* Ch. 4. Once again this only applied to righteous people (*Malbim*).
This was not the case regarding the *slav*. Overeating of the poultry meat would have serious health effects in the future.

101. *Tosefta Sotah* Ch. 4; *Zohar*; *Minchas Bikkurim*; *Panim Yafos*; *Kometz HaMinchah* to *Shemos* 16:16; *Malbim* to *Bamidbar* 11:5.

102. Some suggest that the manna tasted like sweet honey before it was processed through the mortar, and like oil after it was processed. See *R' Saadiah Gaon; Rashbam* to *Shemos* 16:31. The *Zohar* says that this applied to those who were not righteous, who could have only this taste.

103. See *Shemos Rabbah* 25:3; 5:9; *Yoma* 75b and *Ben Yehoyada*. See *Tanchuma Yashan* to *Beshalach*.
This was one of the reasons the manna came from the sky. The spiritual nature of the manna was likened to the purity of bread before the sin of Adam. After Adam sinned, all ground produce brought with it refuse and waste in one's harvest (*Malbim* to *Shemos* 16:4). Some are of the opinion that the manna was the same spiritual food that Adam himself ate while he was in Gan Eden (*Akeidah*).
See *Ibn Ezra HaKatzar* to *Shemos* 16:5 for his commentary on the interchangeable taste of honey and oil.

104. *Tanchuma Yashan* to *Beshalach*; *Otzar Midrashim* p. 288.
Hashem purposely did not use meat as a foundation of the manna, but instead used bread. The consumption of any food has an immediate effect on the body. One of the reasons we do not eat meat from a non-domestic animal is because the

For pregnant and nursing mothers, the manna could not be made to resemble the five foods harmful to their digestive systems — cucumbers, melons, leeks, onions and garlic. Although according to some opinions it always retained the form and texture of the wafer, it took on all the other properties it was made to resemble, including taste and smell. If it had been able to resemble these five restricted foods, it would also have taken on those properties that made them harmful to pregnant and nursing women.[105]

The marvelous qualities of the manna were available to righteous Jews. For the wicked, unworthy Jews, the manna was singularly uncooperative. It would not assume any of its multitudinous tastes. Furthermore, no matter how hard these people worked at preparing and baking the manna, it always tasted like plain dough kneaded in oil.[106] Others, however, suggest that the differences between the righteous and the wicked only affected the process of gathering the manna, but in the enjoyment of its varied tastes, all Jews were alike.

It was another story altogether for the Erev Rav and the other nations of the world. Hard as they tried, they were never able to gather any of the manna, despite its vast abundance. Somehow, the places to which they went were always bare when they got there.[107] The Erev Rav did manage to get nourishment by drinking from the streams of liquefied manna that ran off toward the sea.[108]

The gentile nations did not even have that opportunity to experience the manna directly. When they drank from the streams of melted manna, the taste was bitter in their mouths.[109] Some suggest that they did find some manna but that it tasted like bitter coriander seed.[110]

---

predatory and cruel nature of these animals will transfer to the person who consumes them. Animals that do not eat meat, but instead consume grass or pasture, bring tame and calming influences to the person who eats their meat. Thus, eating lion meat, for example, will bring forth lion behavior. Eating veal or meat from a sheep or cow will cause the calm and tranquil nature of these animals to be mirrored in the person. With this in mind, Hashem wanted the manna to be reflective of bread, because of its simple and pleasant makeup as a food source, so that the Jewish people would benefit from these qualities (*Abarbanel* to *Beshalach*). See *Ramban* to *Vayikra* 11:13.

105. *Yoma* 75a with *Rashi* and *Maharsha*. See *Iyun Yaakov*.
106. *Zohar*; *Rabbeinu Bachya* to *Beha'aloscha*.
107. *Zohar* 191; *Yalkut* 258; *Sifri* to *Haazinu*; *Midrash Avchir*.
108. *Zohar* 191. The Erev Rav always found themselves outside the camp and did not have their residence within the camp. They weren't worthy enough to merit the protection of the pillar of cloud. This would have great consequences in the war with Amalek.
109. *Tanchuma Yashan* to *Beshalach*.
110. *Shemos Rabbah* 5:9; *Tanchuma Yashan* to *Beshalach*; *Yalkut Shimoni* 258.

Others say that they never even got that far; the manna never entered their mouths. The gentile nations did, however, have one opportunity to experience the manna indirectly when they ate the animals that had drunk from the streams of the manna; the taste of the manna lingered in the meat. The virtuous gentiles acknowledged and praised the good fortune of the Jewish people to share the bread of the angels, while the evil gentiles, jealous of the Jewish good fortune, would grind their teeth in frustration.[111]

Other Benefits of the Manna

One of the most amazing aspects of the manna was that, when consumed by righteous people, it produced no waste products. It was absorbed completely into the 248 limbs with perfect wholesomeness and efficiency, as if these people were heavenly angels.[112] And with a righteous person, the spirituality of the manna he had eaten in his lifetime would protect his body against decomposition, worms and the foul odors of death.[113]

Furthermore, the manna brought blessings to the Jewish homes even before it was consumed. It filled the tents with the fragrant scent of spices, flowers and perfumes. A sweet aroma also lingered over the women long after they had eaten the manna.[114]

The manna also brought other gifts along with it. Spices and fragrances, precious stones, pearls and gems, fine garments, pomegranates and exotic fruits, all of these fell from the heavens along with the manna, leaving the Jewish people satisfied, prosperous and content.[115]

---

111. See *Tur; Lekach Tov; Sechel Tov; Mechilta* to *Shemos* 16:21; *Yalkut Shimoni* 258.
    Many consider the animal of note to be the deer.
    Others suggest that the gentiles weren't even that fortunate. They would have no knowledge of the manna's taste. It would be the Jews who would taste the manna when eating these animals (*Targum Yonasan*).

112. *Yoma* 75a; *Mechilta*; Rashi to *Shemos* 16:14; *Midrash Shocher Tov* 78; *Malbim* to *Bamidbar* 11:4.
    When a Jew consumed a food that wasn't manna, it was absorbed by the manna and thus produced no waste matter as well. This however would only last for a year. After they complained at the time of the *slav*, the Jews were lowered in their level of holiness and at that point non-manna food reacted normally. Hence the need for laws of "*Veyaseid tiyeh al oznecha*," which refer to the proper behavior when relieving oneself (*Maharam Ben Chaviv*). See *Devarim Rabbah* 7:11.

113. *Meam Loez*.

114. *Yoma* 75a and *Ben Yehoyada*. See *Zohar*. The manna also gave rise to a naturally pleasant complexion and skin tone, so it was unnecessary for them to use makeup or cosmetics.

115. *Yoma* 75a and *Ben Yehoyada*; *Tosafos* to *Shemos* 16:5,17.
    Some suggest that the Jewish people could not make use of this jewelry. Only the *nesiim*

How They Earned the Manna

When the angels visited Avraham's home, he showed them great hospitality and served them bread, meat, butter and milk. In his merit, his descendants, the Jewish people, were given the spiritual manna, the bread of angels, this magnificent substance that could deliver the tastes of meat, butter and milk.

The manna fell for the first time in Alush, which is reminiscent of Avraham's instructions to Sarah when the angels came. "*Lushi*," he said. "Knead bread for them." That hospitality was rewarded with manna.[116]

Moshe's merit was another important factor in the financial security and the manna that the Jewish people enjoyed.[117]

Finally, the Jewish people themselves earned the manna that fell for them from the heavens by learning and studying the portions of the Torah they had recently received at Marah. The lesson was clear. With proper dedication to the study of the Torah and the observance of its mitzvos, Hashem would provide them with all their needs without any effort or struggle on their part.[118]

(tribal princes) could collect these items and safeguard them for the use of the Mishkan (*Meam Loez*).

Some question the significance of the falling pomegranates since one was able to have the taste of a pomegranate if he chose to.

There is one opinion that babies who were born were clothed from the excess clothing their mothers had after delivery. As it is known, the clothing grew with each person throughout the years in the desert. With the completion of the pregnancy, this excess clothing (no longer needed) would be used to clothe them. See *Devarim Rabbah* 7:11; *Devarim* 29:4; *Tanchuma Bamidbar* 2.

116. *Shemos Rabbah* 25:5; *Maharzu*; *Eliyahu Rabbah* 12; *Tanchuma Yashan*.

Although Avraham served the angels "*basar v'chalav*" (meat and milk), it is evident that after the Torah was given to the Bnei Yisrael the manna didn't include tastes that combined these ingredients at one time. See *Chomas Anach*. *Panim Yafos* in *Beha'aloscha* explains that the manna tasted like something forbidden if that is what a person had in mind, because the food they were actually eating was permissible. *Chidushei HaRim* disagrees.

117. See *Taanis* 9a; see *Iyun Yaakov*; *Tanchuma Bamidbar* 2.

118. *Shemos Rabbah* 25:7.

See *Yedei Moshe* for his interpretation of why the Jewish people did not sing *shirah* (songs of praise) upon receiving the manna.

3 Double for Shabbos

What would happen on Shabbos? Would the manna fall? Actually, Hashem had already given the answer to Moshe in the original prophecy about the manna. He had said, "On the sixth day, they shall prepare what they bring; it will be twice as much as they gather daily."[1]

Although there was little to do in the preparation of the manna, especially for the righteous, Hashem wanted the people to rise early and with great diligence on Friday morning and invest time and effort into the preparation for bringing the joy of Shabbos into their homes.[2] They were to pay loving attention to the choice of special foods for Shabbos.[3] In effect, He was telling them that the food for Shabbos would arrive on Friday.

---

1. *Shemos* 16:5.
2. See *Shabbos* 117b with *Rashi*; *Sforno*; see *Lekach Tov* to *Shemos* 16:5; *Orach Chaim* 250, *Beis Yosef*.
   Some suggest that this information was given to Moshe without the specific intention that it be told over to the Jewish people (*Ohr HaChaim* to *Shemos* 16:22).
3. *Rashi* to *Beitzah* 2b.
   As will be seen later, one was allowed to leave over the manna only on Friday, with the specific designation that it was in honor of Shabbos (*Netziv*).

As of Friday morning, however, Moshe had not yet relayed this information. The people had not yet been told how and when they would be supplied with food for Shabbos. The answer came indirectly on Friday morning. When the people gathered their daily portions of manna, they discovered that additional manna had fallen on that day. They had received a double portion.

What form did that double portion take? Some say that they gathered two *omer* measures per person.[4] Others say that the *omer* measures they gathered on Friday contained the special blessings of Shabbos and therefore lasted for two full days.[5] Others suggest that they gathered one *omer* measure but later discovered that they actually had two. What's more, they found that the double *omer* measure miraculously fit into their single *omer* containers.[6] Some suggest that the double measure that fell on Friday came in the form of two attached loaves of bread.[7] Others suggest that in addition to the *omer* measure that fell on Friday, there also fell two attached loaves of bread for Shabbos.[8]

In any case, the people were dumbfounded. Why had they received a double portion on that day? The princes of the tribes immediately went to Moshe for guidance.

"Why is today different from every other day?" one of them asked. "Why has so much manna fallen today?"[9]

"What can we do with so much manna?" asked another. "We can't eat it all up in one day."[10]

---

4. See *Mechilta; Rashbam* to *Shemos* 16:5; *Midrash Shocher Tov* 92; *Ibn Ezra* to *Shemos* 16:22.

Some add that the Bnei Yisrael collected one *omer* in the morning and when they saw that the *omer* didn't dissipate after the fourth hour they knew that Friday was different from other days and collected a second portion after that (*Shaarei Aryeh* p. 152).

5. See *Maharal* to *Beshalach*.

6. See *Rashi; Be'er Yitzchok* to *Shemos* 16:5; *Zeh Yenachmeni; Chasam Sofer; Akeidah; Alshich* to *Shemos* 16:22.

7. *Sechel Tov*; see *Mechilta*.

8. *Zeh Yenachmeni; Bereishis Rabbah* 11:2; *Yefei To'ar*.

According to this, three *omers* in total fell on Friday. Perhaps a connection can be made between the six days of creation and the manna. While Hashem fashioned three creations for each day of the week, on Friday he made double, fashioning six creations. Beasts, animals, creatures, Adam, Chavah and the souls of the world were all created on Friday (*Mishnas R' Eliezer* 20).

9. *Mechilta*; see *Ibn Ezra*.

Some suggest that all along the belief of the *nesiim* was that they would collect only one *omer* and that, through preparation and the Shabbos blessing, it would suffice as two. When they saw that upon collection two *omers* emerged, it was then that the *nesiim* questioned Moshe about the double portion of manna (*Malbim* to *Shemos* 16:22).

10. *Sifsei Kohen*.

"That's right," said a third. "And if we can't finish it, we can't leave it over until tomorrow either. We haven't forgotten those horrible worms that materialized from the leftover manna. Nor have we forgotten how angry you were when Dassan and Aviram left over some of the manna."[11]

"You needn't worry," Moshe replied. "I've known about this all along. Actually, I should have told you about it before, but my anger at Dassan and Aviram caused me to have a lapse of memory regarding the laws and my responsibility to tell you about them."[12]

Some say that Hashem gave Moshe instructions about the Friday double measure because, even though they had not yet received the Torah, they were required to observe Shabbos once they learned about it at Marah. Others suggest that it was only for practical purposes; since the manna would not fall on Shabbos, it was important that they prepare on Friday.[13]

"I will explain everything to you," said Moshe. "You received a double portion today because no manna will fall tomorrow. One portion you received is for your regular needs today. The other is to be put aside for tomorrow. As you know from what we learned in Marah, Shabbos is meant to be a day of rest; labor is forbidden. You

---

11. *Chizkuni; Bechor Shor; Maaseh Hashem* to *Shemos* 16:22.

12. *Mechilta; Rashi* to *Shemos* 16:22; *Rokeach; Rabbeinu Meyuchas; Shemos Rabbah* 25:10; *Yefei To'ar; Yedei Moshe.*

Others suggest that Moshe did tell the Jews about collecting a double portion on Shabbos. The *nesiim* were never told what to do with the extra manna, and that was what they asked Moshe — what should they do with the additional portion? (See *Ibn Ezra; Abarbanel.*)

Other suggest that Moshe never referred to Hashem's address of earlier in the week. Moshe responded to Hashem's address to him at Marah where Hashem guided him in the laws of Shabbos (*Midrash HaChefetz*).

There is a question as to the sequence of events that took place during the week. The chain of events was as follows: On Sunday night/Monday morning the manna came down. On Monday, Moshe commanded the Jews not to "save" any manna for the following day. On Tuesday, Moshe was angered because there were Jews who did leave manna over for fear it would not return the next day. Moshe had in mind to tell the Jews about the laws of Shabbos and the double portion of manna that would come later in the week, but forgot. On Wednesday and Thursday, the Jews gathered the manna properly. On Friday, the Jews gathered a double portion. On Shabbos, no manna fell but there were Jews who went out anyway, looking for it. See *Seder Olam* 5; *Meam Loez; Sefer HaParshios; Rashbam.*

13. *Netziv* to *Mechilta.*

This is consistent with the view that, although the laws of Shabbos were taught at Marah, they were not as yet implemented. Moshe believed that this applied to this Shabbos as well. In fact, all opinions agree that — unlike the previous Shabbos at Marah — the Jews were required to observe this Shabbos in Alush.

will not be allowed to cook or bake on Shabbos. All your preparations have to be done today."[14]

"But what will happen," asked one of the princes, "if we leave it over? Will it become rotten and worm-infested?"

"There is no cause for concern," Moshe assured them. "Since Hashem wants you to leave the second portion for tomorrow, nothing will happen to it. And besides, the blessing of the holy Shabbos will preserve it from spoilage.[15] In fact, if you leave over part of your Friday portions they won't spoil either. The blessings of Shabbos will preserve them."[16]

---

14. *Rashi; Sforno; Ralbag* to *Shemos* 16:23.

Others suggest that this preparation applied only to the first *omer*. The second *omer* would be eaten raw.

Others suggest that the food in question was that which was bought, for the manna itself was readily edible without a need for preparation (*Pnei David*). This view presents difficulties in that — as mentioned earlier — no exchanges or sales were allowed to be made with the manna.

15. *Rashi; Alshich* to *Shemos* 16:24; *Mechilta; Chizkuni; Ralbag* to *Shemos* 16:24.

In fact, the blessing of Shabbos would enhance and enrich the manna to even a greater level than during the week.

Others suggest that this only applied to those who saved it because they were commanded to, in recognition of Shabbos. Those that left over the manna as a lack of faith would find the manna wormy and spoiled (*Netziv; Shaarei Aryeh* p. 263).

On this premise, some ask that if one wanted to prepare manna for Shabbos on Wednesday for example, would it dissipate and melt before that time. Some suggest that, since it was for Shabbos, it would remain fresh and edible, while others suggest that this blessing was only provided for Friday, since the mitzvah of preparation for Shabbos specifically designates Friday as opposed to any other day of the week (*Shaarei Aryeh* p. 156).

Others suggest that they could eat as much as they wanted. They didn't need to measure the consumption of exactly one *omer*. If they ate 1.5 *omer* on Friday, that would be fine. The blessing of Shabbos would allow the remaining half-*omer* to last and sustain someone for the rest of Shabbos (*Ramban; Tur; Tosafos Al HaTorah* to *Shemos* 16:25).

Each *omer* provided two meals a day. With that being the case, the Jewish people had four loaves ready on Friday. By Friday night there were three loaves and Shabbos morning there were two loaves. It is a known fact that the double portion of Friday is memorialized by *lechem mishneh* (two loaves) on Shabbos. Based on the number of loaves that lasted through Shabbos, some suggest that this is one reason why there are those who are lenient about *lechem mishneh* for *shalosh seudos*, because by the evening meal on Shabbos all that was left was one loaf.

Others suggest that each half-*omer* provided two loaves of bread, totaling eight loaves. This left six loaves for Shabbos, allowing for two loaves for the three meals of Shabbos, with complete *lechem mishneh* at every meal.

Mechilta says that from the *pasuk* of 16:25, which repeats the word *hayom* three times, we learn it is a mitzvah to eat three *seudos* on Shabbos (see *Shabbos* 117b; *Orach Chaim* 274,354; *Yere'im* 92; *Tosafos Al HaTorah* to *Shemos* 16:5; *Daas Zekeinim* to *Shemos* 16:22; *Moshav Zekeinim* to *Shemos* 16:25).

[Note: There are a number of customs based on these issues, and we are in no way suggesting that any one is more correct or proper.]

16. *Maaseh Hashem* to *Shemos* 16:24.

As marvelous as the manna was in the eyes of the people, the manna that fell on Friday was a marvel of marvels. In many ways, it was the same as the daily manna, yet it was also different and distinctive in many ways.[17] The spiritual nature of the manna combined with the special spiritual blessings of Shabbos to produce a food of such high spiritual level as the world had never seen nor would ever see again.[18] The aroma was extraordinarily heavenly, the taste was extraordinarily sublime, and it glittered with an extraordinarily golden color.[19]

The Shabbos manna never shrank in size no matter how long it was cooked or baked, nor did its taste and texture ever deteriorate during the process of preparation.[20]

The concept of "double for Shabbos" is a recurrent theme. The manna's taste and aroma were twice as good on Shabbos.[21] The sacrifices, candles, songs and praise were doubled on Shabbos, and the punishment for its desecration was twice as severe.[22]

Reassured by Moshe, the princes of the tribes returned to their people and brought them up to date. The people were calmed, and they set aside the additional manna they had gathered for the following day.[23]

The First Shabbos

Not all the Jews accepted Moshe's instructions with equanimity. A small group of wicked men, whose faith in Hashem and respect for Shabbos were weak, saw this as an opportunity to undermine Moshe's authority and credibility with

---

17. See *Mechilta* to *Shemos* 16:5 and 16:22; *Rashi*.
18. *Sifsei Kohen*.
    See *Bereishis Rabbah* 11:2,4; *Shabbos* 119a; *Etz Yosef* about the blessing that Shabbos offers to food and the flavor that Shabbos adds, which food eaten on the weekday does not have.
19. See *Mechilta*; *Tanchuma Yashan*. It had a special perfume scent for women on Shabbos as well (*Chemdas Yamim*).
    See *Malbim* to *Shemos* 16:31 for his explanations of the various differences between the manna of Shabbos and that of the rest of the week.
    See *Shaarei Aryeh* p. 204 who writes that, during the preparation of the manna on Friday for Shabbos, one had to have in mind what taste he wanted for the manna for Shabbos. One was, however, forbidden to do so on Shabbos since it would change that food into what he wanted, and this would be similar to a *melachah* of food preparation on Shabbos.
20. *Sforno* to *Shemos* 16:5; *Mechilta* to *Shemos* 16:23.
21. *Midrash* in *Torah Shleimah* 16:22 § 119.
22. *Rabbeinu Bachya* to *Shemos* 16:23,28. See *Tur* and other *Rishonim* to *Shemos* 16:5. *Midrash Shocher Tov* 92 writes that this included the commandments to "Remember" and "Safeguard" the Sabbath.
23. *Lekach Tov* to *Shemos* 16:24.

the people.[24] Most prominent among these were the infamous Dassan and Aviram.[25]

Late Friday night, Dassan and Aviram went out for a stroll so that they could speak in full privacy.

"Moshe says there will be no manna tomorrow," said Dassan. "What do you think we should do about it?"

"There's much to do," said Aviram. "We should have no problem. We have food left over from today."

"Do you believe him?"

Aviram shrugged. "I suppose. Do you?"

"Maybe," said Dassan. "But I have an idea. Moshe is going to have to do some hard explaining tomorrow morning. Are you with me?"

"Of course I'm with you. Now, tell me the plan."

"This is how it goes. I have a little manna left over from today. You probably do, too. We have to go to our friends in the opposition, the ones that would love to see Moshe embarrassed, and ask for their cooperation. Some of them must have some manna left over. Now, if we collect all this manna, we should have quite a bit."

Aviram looked puzzled. "All right, but what do we do with it? How does it embarrass Moshe?"

"Here's the move," said Dassan. "We stay up very late, until everyone is asleep, and then we go out into the fields and scatter the manna in different places. In the morning, it will appear as if some manna did fall during the night, although not as much as on a regular day. But Moshe said nothing would fall. People will laugh at him."[26]

"Brilliant!" said Aviram. "Simple but absolutely brilliant."

---

24. *Targum Yonasan; Abarbanel* to *Shemos* 16:27.
25. See *Shemos Rabbah* 25:10; *Mechilta; Rashi* to *Shemos* 16:27.
26. Some question the physical possibility of this deception. At best, Dassan and Aviram had four *omers* between them, hardly enough to convince anyone that this was a legitimate fall of the manna. Some offer that Dassan and Aviram's intention was only to show the possibility that manna would fall on Shabbos. Others suggest that there were additional wicked Jews who joined Dassan and Aviram in this deception, raising the manna amount. This, however, does not come close to the miles of manna that fell daily.

It is interesting to note that originally the Jews, like Dassan and Aviram — lacking proper faith — had saved their manna, having worried that there would be no manna on the next day. When Shabbos came, the very same wicked Jews who had earlier worried that no manna would fall, now went out on Shabbos expecting to see the manna — contrary to the words of Moshe!

The next day, the people rose early and were relieved to see that the manna left over from the night before had not spoiled nor become worm-infested.²⁷ They said their morning prayers and prepared to go home for the morning meal. But something did not seem right. They were still full of questions, which they discussed among themselves, but nothing alleviated their confusion.

"What exactly did Moshe mean," asked one fellow, "when he said all preparations should be done on Friday? Is there anything we are allowed to do today?"

"And what did he mean," asked another, "when he told us not to gather the manna on Shabbos? Did he mean for cooking and baking only, but we can gather manna if we want to eat it raw?"²⁸

"I think he said," said another, "that manna won't fall on Shabbos, period. But now that you mention it, maybe he meant that even if manna did fall it would be forbidden to gather it."

"It's not clear to me either," said the first fellow. "Maybe he meant that manna won't fall in the morning, so we have to save some manna from yesterday. But maybe the manna will fall later in the day or tonight, so we should go out and check."²⁹

The people decided to approach Moshe for clarification.

"What should we do?" they asked. "Should we go now and gather manna in the fields?"

"Absolutely not," said Moshe. "Today is Shabbos, and no manna falls on Shabbos. There is no manna out there. But you have plenty of manna for today, since you all got a double portion yesterday. Use it for the morning meal and for the evening meal before Shabbos ends."

"But are we allowed to eat leftover manna?" asked one fellow. "I know that it isn't spoiled, but it's still *nossar*, left over. We weren't allowed to eat the *nossar* of the *korban pesach* in Egypt. Is there a problem with the *nossar* of the manna?"

"There is no problem," said Moshe. "As I told you before, you gather manna for six days, but on Shabbos you rest. Hashem gave you a double portion yesterday just for this purpose. So you don't

---

27. *Sechel Tov, Gra* to *Shemos* 16:24.
28. *Gur Aryeh; Chasam Sofer; Pnei David; Tzeidah LeDerech.*
29. *Ibn Ezra; Chasam Sofer; Be'er Yitzchok; Gur Aryeh* to *Rashi* on *Shemos* 16:25.

It was Moshe's original forgetfulness that prevented him from detailing the laws slowly and methodically to the Jews, and that led to their having a number of unanswered questions.

have any problems with *nossar*. Go home and enjoy your Shabbos."[30]

Moshe had answered the people's questions to their satisfaction, and they began to stream to their tents in a festive mood. A short distance from Moshe's tent, Dassan and Aviram, accompanied by a small group of men, had planted themselves in their path.

Dassan held up his hand. "Stop! Where is everyone going?"

"We're going home," said one man. "Our families are waiting for us to start the morning meal."

"Well, haven't you forgotten something?" said Dassan.

"That's right," said Aviram. "Haven't you forgotten that you should be going out to the fields to gather the manna?"

"There's no manna today," said the man. "It's Shabbos."

"So how do you know there's no manna on Shabbos?" said Dassan.

"Because we've just come from Moshe, and he told us so."

"Really?" said Aviram. "Did he say nothing would fall? Or maybe not a lot? You know, maybe today is a slow day, and only a little fell."

"No, he was very clear," said the man. "No manna falls on Shabbos."

Dassan and Aviram exchanged knowing glances.

"Ahem, I don't mean to disillusion you," Dassan said to the people, "but I have different information."

The people were confused.

"What do you mean?" they shouted. "Tell us."

"We have it from reliable sources," said Aviram, "that some manna did in fact fall this morning. I think we should check it out."

"It can't be," the people protested. "We heard it from Moshe."

"Well, Moshe isn't perfect," said Dassan. "We've been saying this all along. You can't rely on him completely. He's just another human being like the rest of us. He can be wrong sometimes. He can make mistakes. Who knows, maybe even deliberately. Look, let's check out this report. If it turns out that there is some manna in the fields, we'll know that whatever Moshe tells should be taken with a grain of salt. Let's go."

---

30. See *Ohr HaChaim* to *Shemos* 16:25; *Tzeidah LeDerech*.
Some consider "your Shabbos" to be a reference to life. Six days refers to the 6,000 years of this world and Shabbos refers to *Olam Haba*, "A day that is completely Shabbos." A person should try to collect as many mitzvos and good deeds in this world as he can, because once he passes away and enters the World to Come, there will no longer be any opportunities to collect mitzvos (*Abarbanel* to *Shemos* 16:25).

Dassan and Aviram turned and headed for the desert beyond the encampment, with their small group of followers right on their heels. After a moment of hesitation, a number of other people, overcome by curiosity, also joined them, until there was quite a crowd.[31]

Out in the desert, their eyes searched eagerly for any sign of manna that had fallen that morning, but there was not a single scrap to be found. There was only sand and rocks as far as the eye could see. The people gave Dassan and Aviram disdainful looks and headed back to the encampment, their faith in Hashem and in Moshe restored.

Presently, Dassan and Aviram were left in the desert by themselves. They looked at each other in wonderment. Where had all the manna gone? Suddenly, they heard the loud caw of a bird, and they looked up simultaneously. High above them circled a black bird holding a little scrap of manna in its beak. There was the cause of the failure of their plan. The birds had scooped up every last bit of manna that they had scattered in the desert the night before.[32]

This unfortunate incident was the sixth of the ten times they tested Hashem in the desert.[33] They had failed to undermine Moshe's authority. Moshe had escaped embarrassment, and it was they, Dassan and Aviram, who had suffered embarrassment instead. To make matters worse, they had desecrated the Shabbos and caused a number of other Jews to do so as well.

This was an especially great tragedy, because the damage it caused was incalculable. Had the Jewish people kept this one Shabbos flawlessly, they would have been immune to the persecution of the gentile nations. No nation or kingdom would have been able to dominate or control them. They had missed a golden opportunity.[34]

---

31. Ibn Ezra; Sforno; Bechor Shor to Shemos 16:27.

32. Sefer HaMatamim; Taamei HaMinhagim, Likutim 98. See *Magen Avraham, Orach Chaim* 322:7.
It was very befitting that these wicked people had to travel to the furthest point that is allowed on Shabbos on the assumption they would find manna. Had they been righteous, it would not have been necessary for them to go out to find the manna, since it would have been at their doorstep.

33. *Arachin* 15b.

34. *Shabbos* 118b. This is a reference to Amalek's ability to fight with the Bnei Yisrael. If the Jewish people would honor two Shabbasos, they would immediately be redeemed from their exile. See *Shemos Rabbah* 22:12 and commentaries as to whether it is one or two Shabbasos and the differences of opinion.
Some suggest that this, in fact, was the only Shabbos the Jews observed properly in the forty years in the desert. See *Devarim Rabbah* 3:1; *Sifri Zuta* 9:4; *Yerushalmi Taanis* 1:1.

By the late afternoon of that first Shabbos, worries and questions once again beset the people.[35] What would they do if they ate the evening meal after Shabbos? Would the manna last into the night? What would they eat tomorrow? Would the manna resume falling in the morning? Would manna fall that afternoon to be gathered after Shabbos was over, so that there would be food for that evening and the next day? Would manna fall in the night for the next day's food?[36]

Once again, they brought their concerns to Moshe.

"Let me make it very clear," said Moshe. "Today is Shabbos, and there will be absolutely no fall of manna on Shabbos. Hashem Himself honors Shabbos and will not break His own laws. Nor will any manna fall tonight. But you can rest assured that everything will resume tomorrow morning, as it was earlier this week.[37] When you wake up tomorrow morning, you will already find that the manna has fallen.[38]

"And one more thing, just because the manna you had left over from yesterday did not spoil, do not assume that you can leave it over tonight as well. The blessing of Shabbos kept it fresh. Whatever you leave over tonight will not be protected. It will become spoiled and worm-infested.[39] Do not be stingy. You will have plenty of food tomorrow. Eat your Shabbos meals without any concerns. Enjoy the rest of your Shabbos."[40]

---

35. *Hadar Zekeinim* to *Shemos* 16:25.

36. *Tzeidah LeDerech.*

37. *Chasam Sofer; Netziv* to *Mechilta.*

38. See *Mechilta; Rashi; Sifsei Chachamim; Lekach Tov; Reav; Tosafos Al HaTorah* to *Shemos* 16:25.
From this *pasuk* we learn that the laws forbidding the collection of manna applied to the festivals as well as Yom Kippur. See *Mechilta; Rashi; Tosafos* to *Beitzah* 2b; *Pesachim* 116a.

Some question what the Jews did eat following Yom Kippur. Although on Shabbos the manna didn't fall, on Friday they received double and ate it on Shabbos. Following Shabbos, the manna would spoil if not eaten. Since eating on Yom Kippur day was obviously forbidden, what did they eat on Motza'ei Yom Kippur? The *Sfas Emes* suggests that they ate meat that one time. Accordingly, it is quite likely that even on that day the Jews did not miss out, since it was these animals that drank from the liquefied manna and carried with them the taste of the manna. See *Targum Yonasan* 16:21.

Others suggest that since the children had to eat, the manna fell on Yom Kippur as it would on any weekday, to feed them. And just as the blessing of Shabbos kept the manna fresh from the previous day, so too was the case on Erev Yom Kippur. (See *Shaarei Aryeh* p. 199.)

39. See *Sforno; Maaseh Hashem; Sifsei Kohen* to *Shemos* 16:25; *Divrei David* (*Taz*). See *Chizkuni,* who disagrees with this view.

40. *Mechilta; Tosafos; Malbim* to *Shemos* 16:25.

Hashem's Rebuke

After the Jewish people desecrated the Shabbos, Hashem rebuked Moshe sharply. The rebuke was directed at the Jewish people in general and also at Moshe individually.

Although Moshe had not desecrated the Shabbos himself, he had to bear some of the responsibility. He had failed to transmit the Shabbos law properly and in time, to prevent the Jewish people from desecrating the Shabbos; he had only made them aware that there were prohibitions involved in the manna not falling on Shabbos.[41] He also should have posted sentries around the encampment to warn people not to go out to look for manna.[42] Furthermore, by neglecting to teach the people the laws in a timely fashion, but only at the last minute, some of them may have gotten the impression that Moshe had improvised the laws rather than received them from Hashem.[43] Finally, he was taken to task because all Jews are responsible for each other.[44]

Others suggest that Moshe really did not deserve a rebuke on his own. But as the saying goes, "The cabbage suffers along with the thorns." When the farmer pulls the thorns from the cabbage patch, some of the cabbage is inevitably uprooted as well. Although Moshe was like the cabbage among the thorns, he suffered along with them.[45] Still others suggest that the rebuke was not directed at Moshe at all, but at the Jewish people. Hashem said it to Moshe solely for repetition to the Jewish people later and in private, in order to spare them embarrassment.[46]

"I gave you and the Jewish people," Hashem said to Moshe, "two prohibitions — not to leave over the manna during the week and not to go out to gather the manna on Shabbos — and you have transgressed them both. How long will you continue to disobey My

---

41. *Midrash Aggadah;* see *Sforno; Rokeach; Bechor Shor; Maaseh Hashem* to *Shemos* 16:28.
    They thought that all that was required in honoring Shabbos was not to collect the manna, and that the laws of carrying in a public domain and the restriction against traveling did not apply.
42. *Rokeach* to *Shemos* 16:28.
43. *Sifsei Kohen* to *Shemos* 16:29.
44. *Sefer Chassidim.*
45. *Rashi; Ohr HaChaim* to *Shemos* 16:28; *Bava Kamma* 92a. The *Maharal* explains that Moshe, who is the *prat*, must be joined together with the *klal*, and thus was guilty along with the Bnei Yisrael.
46. *Sechel Tov; Ibn Ezra* to *Shemos* 16:28. This follows the law that one should rebuke in private so as not to hurt the feelings of a sinner.

laws and commandments?[47] Don't you appreciate the importance of Shabbos, that it is comparable to the entire Torah? Shabbos represents the very essence of creation, the essence of faith and belief in Me. And now that you have desecrated the Shabbos, it is as if you have violated the entire Torah.[48]

"Since before the creation of the world, I have kept Shabbos locked away in My treasure house, and I have presented it as a gift to the Jewish people and not the gentile nations.[49] In the merit of Shabbos, I have given the Jewish people the three festivals, the land of Israel and the World to Come. Don't you realize what a treasure I have given you?[50]

"All the miracles I have performed for you were in the merit of Shabbos. I brought you forth from Egypt. I split the sea for you. I gave you the quail and the manna.[51] And these are only a prelude to many more miracles I have in store for you. And yet, you cannot keep even the few mitzvos I have given you."[52]

Moshe accepted Hashem's rebuke with humility. He then assembled the Jewish people and spoke to them. "You all saw that, miracle upon miracles, a double portion of manna fell from the heavens on Friday so that no manna would have to fall on Shabbos.[53] Why? Because Hashem honors Shabbos and rests on that day, so to speak, just as He did after the six days of creation. He also wants you to rest on Shabbos, just as He did.[54]

"On Shabbos, you may not carry, but even if you are walking with empty hands and empty pockets, you may not go more than 2,000 cubits (*amos*) beyond the boundaries of the encampment. If you should go walking and find yourself more than 2,000 cubits beyond the encampment, you must remain in that place until Shabbos is over, moving no more than four cubits in any direction. You must also know that it is forbidden to carry an item four cubits in the public domains of the encampment.[55]

"Remember always, Shabbos is comparable to the entire Torah."

---

47. *Midrash Chadash Al HaTorah; Midrash Ohr Afeilah; Ibn Ezra* to *Shemos* 16:28; *Shemos Rabbah* 16:17.
48. *Mishnas R' Eliezer; Shemos Rabbah* 25:12; *Yerushalmi Nedarim* 3:9; *Akeidah* to *Shemos* 16:29.
49. *Sechel Tov* to *Shemos* 16:29; see *Shabbos* 10b; *Shemos Rabbah* 25:12.
50. *Mechilta; Sechel Tov; Yalkut.*
51. *Mechilta; Sechel Tov* to *Shemos* 16:28; *Yalkut* 261.
52. See *Tanchuma Yashan* to *Beshalach.*
53. See *Rashi* to *Shemos* 16:29; *Sechel Tov; Maharal.*
54. *Shibbolei HaLeket* 27; *Midrash Shocher Tov* 92; *Ibn Ezra* to *Shemos* 16:29.
55. See *Rashi; Ralbag; R' Saadiah Gaon; Abarbanel; Maharal; Rokeach* to *Shemos* 16:29.

How exactly did the people desecrate the Shabbos on that fateful day? What exactly was their transgression? Some say they transgressed the prohibition of *techum Shabbos*, going too far beyond the boundaries of the encampment.[56] Some say they transgressed the prohibition of *haavarah*, carrying the receptacles for gathering the manna through the public domains (*reshus harabim*) of the encampment.[57] Others suggest they transgressed the prohibitions of *muktzeh* and *nolad*, the use of items that did not exist in their current form before Shabbos.[58] Yet others suggest that they transgressed the specific prohibition against gathering manna on Shabbos.[59] Although this prohibition was applicable only for that particular generation, it was nonetheless a full-fledged part of the Shabbos laws.

The Jewish people accepted Hashem's rebuke, and thereafter, they were scrupulous in their Shabbos observance.[60]

A Symbol for the Ages

During this time, Hashem instructed Moshe to tell Aharon to take a full *omer* measure of the manna and put it into

---

56. As seen earlier, much of this discussion is tied to the travels of the Jews and the question of whether they had arrived in Alush on Shabbos or Sunday. Some suggest that they were given the laws of Shabbos in Marah but were not required to keep the laws of *techumin*. Others suggest that although they were given all the laws, they were not required to observe the Shabbos just yet. See *Tosafos Al HaTorah* to *Shemos* 15:25; *Tosafos* to *Shabbos* 87b. See *Gra* to *Seder Olam*; *Yerushalmi Beitzah* 2-1; *Eruvin* 48a, 51a; *Sotah* 27b; *Pirkei D'Rav Eliezer* 18; *Sefer HaMitzvos* of the *Ramban* 321. See *Devarim Rabbah* 3:1; *Radal*; *Rashash*; *Midrash Tehillim* 92; *Netziv* to *Mechilta* on *Shemos* 16:29; *Rashi* to *Shemos* 16:29; *HaKesav VeHaKabbalah*; *Moshav Zekeinim*; *Alshich* to *Shemos* 16:25.

All these sources deal with the dispute as to when the Jews received the mitzvah of Shabbos, what part of the laws they received and how long after Moshe received the instructions from Hashem did he relay them to the Jews.

Tosafos in *Pesachim* 116 writes that the laws of Shabbos were instituted already while in Egypt. The words *"ki Hashem nasan lohem"* written in *Shemos* 16:29 regarding Hashem having given the Jewish people the Shabbos have the numerical value of 646, the same as the words *b'eretz Goshen* (in the land of Goshen) (*Tosafos* to *Shemos* 16:29).

57. *Chizkuni*; *Ralbag* to *Shemos* 16:25,29.

58. See *Panim Yafos*.

59. *Midrash Chadash Al HaTorah* to *Shemos* 16:27; *Pirkei D'Rav Kahana* 14; *Sforno*; *Meshech Chochmah* to *Shemos* 16:27.

This gathering would be prohibited as *me'amer* according to most authorities.

Others suggest that the prohibition was because of the *melachah* of *tolesh*, disconnecting something from its source of nutrition (*Sforno*). Many of the opinions debate if the prohibition applies to something not connected to the ground. See *Shaarei Aryeh* p. 177.

60. *Ibn Ezra*; *Rashbam* to *Shemos* 16:30. See *Midrash HaChefetz*.

The commentaries agree that this excludes *mekoshesh* (gathering). See *Bamidbar* 15:32-36. There are varied opinions as to how many times the Jewish people did not keep Shabbos. Did they keep only one Shabbos, or did they keep every Shabbos other than this one and the one that the *mekoshesh* desecrated?

safekeeping for future generations.⁶¹ It would serve as an eternal witness to the Jewish people that their ancestors had placed their faith in Hashem and that He had fed them in the desolate wilderness with food from the heavens.

Moshe transmitted these instructions to Aharon the following year when the Mishkan was built. At that time, he told Aharon to take an *omer* measure of manna, seal it into an earthenware jar⁶² and place it near the Holy Ark, the *Aron Kodesh*.⁶³ Aharon promptly took an *omer* measure from his own portion of the manna and placed it in the jar near the *Aron Kodesh*.⁶⁴

Nearly 900 years later, there was a famine in the land of Israel. The prophet Yirmiyahu informed the Jewish people that they lacked merit because they did not devote enough time to Torah study.

"But we have no time to study Torah," they protested. "We have to earn a livelihood."

Yirmiyahu held up the ancient earthenware jar for everyone to see. "Do you know what this is?" he said. "This is the jar of the manna that Aharon preserved for future generations. The manna fell from the heavens, and it sustained our ancestors in the barren desert for forty years. If you want, you have the time to learn Torah. As for your livelihood, Hashem will find a way to sustain you."⁶⁵

---

61. *Ohr Same'ach* on the Torah; *Sechel Tov* to *Shemos* 16:34.

Many suggest that this took place a year later. See *Ibn Ezra* to *Shemos* 16:32; see *Malbim*; see *Alshich* to *Shemos* 16:33 as to why Aharon was the one to do it. (See also footnote 78.)

62. *Mechilta*; *Rashi*; *Lekach Tov* to *Shemos* 16:33.

There are varied opinions as to what kind of jar it was. Most believe that the jar of choice was earthenware, which would best preserve the manna for a long period of time. Others suggest its type was determined by the meaning of the word *"tzintzenes."* Some suggest that it was glass (*Minchah Belulah*; *Abarbanel*; *Zeh Yenachmeni*; *Gra* to *Mechilta*). Others suggest that it was made of copper (*Ibn Ezra* to *Shemos* 16:33). R' *Samson Rafael Hirsch* says it was made of stone.

This jar was bought from sanctified money; thus the manna placed inside it became *hekdesh* (consecrated) and was therefore allowed to be kept in the *Kodesh HaKodashim* (Holy of Holies) (*Shaarei Aryeh* p. 165).

63. Many suggest that this took place the following year. It was mentioned here only because the Torah relates all aspects pertaining to the manna. Since the Mishkan was not yet built, Aharon could not have possibly placed the manna beside the *Aron* (Ark).

Others suggest that this took place after forty years in the desert, when the manna stopped falling (*Tosafos Al HaTorah*). See *Panim Yafos*.

See *Alshich* for a different view.

64. *Shaarei Aryeh* p. 202.

65. See *Mechilta*; *Zayis Raanan*; *Rashi*; *Malbim* to *Shemos* 16:32; *Rashi* to *Yirmiyahu* 2:31.

The manna showed that just as its two *omers* could satisfy someone, a righteous Jew who lived a life of holiness could survive with little food. Hashem would also arrange that one's livelihood could be maintained by the least amount of effort, so that the rest of his time could be spent learning (*Chasam Sofer*).

For all future generations, the preserved manna would be a symbol of Hashem's patience with the Jewish people and His readiness to sustain an entire nation in the most difficult situations. Moreover, the everlasting freshness of the manna was a reminder that only Hashem holds the key to a person's continued livelihood and success.[66]

Some suggest that the jar of manna, the *tzintzenes ha'man*, will be preserved until the appearance of Eliyahu the prophet and Mashiach, speedily and in our days.[67] Others say it will be preserved until the Patriarchs are resurrected during the time of the Resurrection of the Dead.[68]

The Manna's Spiritual Impact

The manna did far more than sustain the Jewish people physically in the desert. It also had a profound impact on their spiritual condition. It provided food for their bodies so that they would not die of starvation, but it also provided food for their souls, so that they would grow in stature and come closer to Hashem.

The manna established the singular relationship between Hashem and His chosen people. Ordinarily, one would expect the servant to procure food and prepare it for his master. Yet Hashem said, "I took the Jewish people out of Egypt so that they should serve Me. Nevertheless, even though I am the Master and they are My servants, I will tend to them. I will prepare the food and serve it to them."[69]

Hashem also showed His love for the Jewish people by reversing for them the manner in which food is produced. Ordinarily, food grows from the ground, and the dew that falls from the sky covers it. With the manna, Hashem brought forth food from the sky and placed dew on the ground underneath it.[70]

The manna also provided the first opportunity for the first blessings related to food, the *Bircas HaMazon*, the Grace After Meals.[71]

---

66. See *Sifsei Kohen; Lekach Tov; Malbim* to *Shemos* 16:32-34.
67. *Tanchuma Beshalach* 21; *Yalkut HaEzuvi; Pane'ach Raza; Tur* to *Shemos* 16:33. This is hinted at in the words "*lemaan yiru es halechem*" (so that they will see the bread), where the first letters of each word spell Elyah, a reference to Eliyahu.
68. *Zeh Yenachmeni*. See *Lekach Tov; Rabbeinu Bachya*.
69. *Tanchuma Yashan Shelach*.
70. See *Mechilta; Lekach Tov*. See *Rashi* to *Iyov* 36:31.
    This bread would be pure of dust and refuse, which are normally found in products from the ground. Coming from the sky, it would be as pure and pristine as rain (see *Malbim*).
71. *Berachos* 48b. See *Rabbeinu Bachya; Abarbanel* to *Shemos* 16:12.
    Since the *slav* (quail) was requested in an unreasonable manner, no blessing or laws

It would have been just as easy for Hashem to send down a larger measure of manna weekly, monthly or even yearly. In fact, He could have sent them at one time the entire amount they would need during all the years of their stay in the desert. But Hashem chose instead to send it down daily. Why? Because He wanted the relationship of the people with their Creator to be warm, close and immediate.

Had they received enough manna for longer periods of time, they would not have worked so hard to maintain a strong connection with Him. There would be nothing motivating them daily to have trust and faith in Him. But with an empty pantry at the end of every day, and with no means to fill it on their own, the Jewish people were conditioned to engender a deep and abiding faith in their hearts, to repent for their shortcomings and to pray to Him every day. Parents who worried about feeding the hungry mouths of their children understood that their survival and prosperity depended on their faith, observance and meticulous attention to their obligations. [72]

Our Sages have taught us that someone who has food for today and worries about tomorrow is a person of little faith.[73] The generation that ate the manna knew the meaning of real faith. They had literally nothing at the end of each day, yet they had faith that they would not go hungry the next day. They knew that Hashem would take care of them and provide them with the livelihood they needed. There was no need to worry about tomorrow.[74]

---

were instituted because of it.

The *Tzlach* in *Berachos* 20a writes that Moshe himself instituted the blessing of *HaZan* ("Who nourishes" — part of Grace After Meals).

There is great discussion as to the blessing that was made upon the consumption of the manna. Some suggest that they made the blessing "*Hamotzi lechem min hashamayim*" (Who brings forth bread from heaven) (*Rama MiPano*; *Sefer Chassidim* 1640; *Bnei Yissaschar*). The *Bnei Yissaschar* also writes that during the week they didn't make a blessing, but on Shabbos they said "... *vetzivanu leechol seudos Shabbos* (... and commanded us to eat the meals of Shabbos), because although during the week a blessing was not necessary, on Shabbos, because of its natural holiness, the manna took the role of a *korban* (*Bnei Yissaschar* 3:3). See *Rashba* to *Berachos* 48b. Others suggest that there was no blessing on the manna since it was not designated with a specific taste (*Bamidbar Rabbah* 7:4; *Yedei Moshe*; see *Pardes Yosef* to *Beshalach*). Others suggest that a blessing was made simply based on the food one thought about. If one had in mind meat, it would be *Shehakol*; if one had in mind a fruit it would be *Ha'etz*. (But the oil, milk and honey would have all been *Shehakol*; see *Hashmatos* and *Miluim* to *Torah Shleimah*).

72. See *Mechilta D'Rashbi*; *Yoma* 76a; *Rashbam*; *Chizkuni*; *Rivash* to *Shemos* 16:4. *Rabbeinu Bachya*; *Sforno* to *Devarim* 18:16. See *Maharsha* who writes that smaller families would have survived by buying food from merchants who circulated in the desert.

73. *Mechilta*.

74. *Rabbeinu Bachya*; *Alshich*.

Even if one is secure about his food for the future, one must continue to pray so that the food he already has should become full of blessing (*Zohar* 62a).

Indeed, all the laws regarding the manna were designed to further this attitude and this relationship. It was forbidden to gather more manna than was needed for that day, and it was also forbidden to leave over any manna for the next day. Doing either of these would have shown a lack of faith in Hashem. Similarly, it was forbidden to go out to gather manna on Shabbos. Having received a double portion on Friday, a faithful Jew would be secure in the knowledge that Hashem had given him what he needs.[75]

It is no wonder then that the manna was considered a vehicle for the blanching of the sins of the Jewish people. By encouraging them to focus on prayer and repentance, the manna kept them pure, holy and free of sin.[76]

The daily fall of the manna also taught the Jewish people that their livelihood depended on their devotion to Torah study. Hashem was prepared to feed them daily so as to free them from worldly concerns and responsibilities. On the other hand, those who did not devote themselves to Torah study would have to invest much time and effort in order to put bread on their tables.[77]

For this reason, Hashem would later command that the *terumah* tithe be given to the Kohen. The Kohanim were dedicated to Torah study and to their obligation in the service of the *Beis HaMikdash*. Therefore, Hashem commanded that they have their food provided for them.

For this reason as well, it is customary to support and sustain sages and scholars who devote themselves to Torah study. Although there is no manna for these people today, we are obligated to free them from the obligations of earning a livelihood and other responsibilities that might interfere with their studies.[78]

The phenomena of the manna were also a metaphor for life itself. Regardless of how much a person gathered, be it a lot or a little, in the

---

75. See *Rashi; Sforno* to *Shemos* 16:4.
76. See *Yoma* 75a with *Rashi* and commentaries.
77. *Shemos Rabbah* 25:9; *Yefei To'ar; Sforno, Ohr HaChaim.* See commentaries to *Avos* 13:17 — "If there is no food, there can be no Torah."
  This explains why the righteous did not have to go out and collect, while the wicked did have to strain themselves.
78. *Rabbeinu Bachya* to *Shemos* 16:4.
  Some suggest that this is hinted at in the Torah when Moshe tells Aharon to place the *omer* of manna away for safekeeping as a lesson that food will always be ready and available for those committed to a life of Torah and service to Hashem (*Rabbeinu Bachya; Alshich; Malbim* to *Shemos* 16:4) (see fn. 61).

end everyone was left with the same amount, an *omer* measure per person; no matter if he was rich or poor, he was left with the same *omer* measure. In life as well, people may exert huge efforts to accumulate much wealth, but in the end, all die and leave the world with the same amount. Only the accumulation of spiritual wealth is lasting.[79]

The Many Miracles of the Manna

All in all, the manna was the result of, and attended by, numerous miracles. These included:

- The very fact that the manna fell.
- The manna fell from the sky even though food normally is derived from the ground.
- The manna's two major tastes of oil and honey depended on the individual.
- The manna had numerous interchangeable tastes.
- The manna was completely absorbed into a person's body, producing no waste products.
- The spiritual essence of the manna prepared the Jewish people to receive the Torah.
- The spiritual nature of the manna shielded Jewish people from evil thoughts.
- A vast amount of manna fell daily.
- The manna only fell near the Jewish encampment, nowhere else.
- The manna accompanied the Jewish encampment on all its travels.
- After the morning gathering, the remainder melted into a stream of liquid from the heat of the sun.
- The manna never spoiled before it liquefied.[80]
- Regardless of how much or how little one gathered, the final amount was always one *omer* measure per person.
- A double portion fell on Friday, one for that day, the other for Shabbos; it was as though the manna itself kept Shabbos.
- Unlike the rest of the week, no manna fell on Shabbos.
- Leftover manna became rotten and worm-infested overnight.

---

79. See *Akeidah*; *Malbim*; *Kli Yakar*; see *Rabbeinu Bachya*; *Ibn Ezra*; *Alshich* to *Devarim* 8:3. Others add that regardless of one's amassed spirituality and mitzvos in this world, whether a lot or a little, all Jews have a portion in the World to Come.

80. As mentioned earlier, this was only the case with uncollected manna. Manna left over with the intention of saving it became wormy.

- Manna left over from Friday to Shabbos did not rot.
- The manna of Shabbos had a distinct taste.
- The manna was able to adjudicate disputes.
- For 900 years, the manna remained fresh in the Ark.[81]

Forty Years of Manna

The Jewish people, according to the Torah, would continue to eat the manna for forty years, until they stood on the threshold of Eretz Yisrael.[82] The cessation of the manna was as painful and traumatic to the Jewish people as the feeling of an infant separated from its mother's bosom.[83]

To be precise, the manna started to fall on 16 Iyar, just over a month after they came out of Egypt, and it stopped on 7 Adar, the day Moshe passed away, just before they entered Eretz Yisrael. If we calculate the time, we find that the manna fell somewhat less than forty years.[84] According to some opinions, the statement that "the manna fell for forty years" is only an approximation and does not imply that it fell for forty complete years.[85] Others suggest that the *omer* measure of manna gathered on the final day that it fell miraculously lasted until 16 Nissan, when they no longer needed it.[86] The Jewish people crossed the Jordan River on 10 Nissan. They made the *korban pesach* in Gilgal on 14 Nissan. On 16 Nissan they brought the *omer* offering, and thereafter, they were permitted to eat *chadash*, the grain of the new harvest.[87] In addition, the cakes they took with them from Egypt on 15 Nissan had a taste similar to that of the manna. Therefore, in a sense, the Jewish people enjoyed the manna, or a food that resembled the manna, for a full forty years.[88]

---

81. *Ibn Ezra HaKatzar* to *Shemos* 16:5; *Abarbanel*, end of *Shemos* Ch. 16.
82. *Shemos* 16:35.
83. *Sifri Beha'aloscha* 11.
84. See *Emunos V'Dei'os* of R' Saadiah Gaon.
85. *Lekach Tov*; *Maeseh Hashem* to *Shemos* 16:35.
86. *Sifsei Kohen* to *Shemos* 16:35.
87. All commentaries agree that it was only due to the absence of manna that they ate from the *chadash* grain. See *Tosefta Sotah* 11:2.
88. See *Mechilta*; *Rashi*; *Ibn Ezra* to *Shemos* 16:35; *Seder Olam* 10; *Tosefta Sotah*; *Kiddushin* 38a; *Yehoshua* 5:11 and commentaries there. See *Pane'ach Raza* to *Devarim*.

The varied opinions are all based on the Torah's ambiguous statements about the Jews

A question arises regarding the view that the one-*omer* measure of manna that fell on the day of Moshe's passing lasted until 16 Nissan. Since this manna would have to be "left over" every night for fully five weeks, would it have become rotten and worm-infested as it did when Dassan and Aviram left manna over until the next morning?

There was a difference, however. Dassan and Aviram left over manna when it was falling every day. Hashem wanted the Jewish people to show their faith in Him by not leaving over the manna for the next day. But after Moshe's passing, the manna ceased to fall; there was no longer a Divine promise of manna every day. Therefore, leaving the manna over was no longer a faithless act, and there was no need for the leftover manna to become rotten and worm-infested. As a case in point, we see that manna left over on Friday night did not spoil, because there was no expectation of manna falling on the next day, which was Shabbos.[89] We also find that the manna sealed in the jar for posterity didn't become rotten for 900 years, because its being left overnight was not a faithless act.[90]

Others suggest that the manna continued to fall for thirty-eight days after Moshe's passing.[91] Still others find a hint in the language of the Torah that implies that the manna continued to fall for an additional fourteen years, the seven years of conquest and the seven years of apportionment, for a total of fifty-four years. Only afterwards, when the Jewish people actually settled in the land, did the manna cease to fall.[92]

According to those who say that the manna continued to fall after Moshe's passing, it is generally agreed that it came in a diminished form. It no longer had interchangeable tastes based on the preference

---

eating the manna until they came to an inhabited land, and coming to the edge of the land of Canaan.
Some suggest that the manna lasted till the 15th.

89. *Pane'ach Raza* to *Shemos* 16:19. See *Lekach Tov; Griz* to *Shemos* 16:35.
See *Tur Orach Chaim* 292, *Bach*. Some suggest that according to the opinion that Moshe died on Friday but was laid to rest on Shabbos, it was common for the manna to stay fresh Friday night into Shabbos. An extension to this would seem rational since, like Friday night, no manna fell after Shabbos either.

90. *Alshich; Lekach Tov* to *Shemos* 16:35.

91. *Rabbeinu Bachya;* see *Sechel Tov* to *Shemos* 16:32; according to others it was thirty-nine days.
According to some the manna lasted 70 days longer; 24 days from his passing in Adar Rishon, 30 additional days of Adar Sheni and 16 days of Nissan.

92. See *Mechilta; Mirkeves HaMishneh; Yalkut Shimoni* to *Yehoshua* 5.

of the one eating it. Rather, it had a uniform sweet taste like that of honey cake.[93]

Regardless of whether or not the manna fell for the full forty years, the persistence of this incredible phenomenon for such an extended period of time was the greatest of all the miracles Moshe performed.[94]

---

93. *Sifsei Kohen* to *Shemos* 16:35.
94. *Ibn Ezra* to *Shemos* 16:35. Unlike other miracles which lasted a short time, this miracle lasted for forty years.

4 Miriam's Well

After spending a turbulent week in Alush, the Jewish people traveled on and encamped in Refidim on 23 Iyar.[1] The name Refidim is reminiscent of *rifyon yadayim*, which literally means a weakening of the hands; in other words, a deterioration. In this case, it reminded the people of the deterioration of their connection to the Torah.[2] They were neglectful of the study of Torah, and by their desecration of the Shabbos, they showed laxity in their observance of the mitzvos they had received at Marah.[3]

---

1. *Seder Olam* 5.
  Others suggest it was Sunday, the 22nd day of Iyar (*Gra* to *Seder Olam*). These disputes once again are all dependent on the dates and times of their previous travels. As seen earlier, there is a question if the manna fell on Sunday or Monday of the previous week, which depended on their travels on Shabbos.
2. See *Mechilta* to *Shemos* 17:1; *Sanhedrin* 106a; *Pirkei D'Rav Kahana* 3; *Shabbos* 118a with *Maharsha*.
  Although Amalek did not threaten the Jewish people until later, it was in Refidim that the Jewish people would suffer.
3. *Sanhedrin* 106a with *Maharsha*; *Rif* to *Shabbos* 118a; *Targum Yonasan* and *Sechel Tov* to *Shemos* 17:1.

As a result of this deterioration, two tests awaited them at Refidim — a lack of drinking water and a treacherous attack by their archenemy Amalek.[4] There had always been water in Refidim, but in anticipation of the arrival of the Jewish people, all the wellsprings dried up. Water is the symbol for Torah, and the lack of water told them allegorically that they were parched for Torah. It would also be a test of their faith. How would they react this time in the face of adversity?[5]

Anger and Frustration

By the time the Jewish people left Alush, they were already seasoned desert travelers. They knew from their bitter experiences in Marah that water was scarce in the desert. They were fully aware that they could not expect every successive encampment to have reliable sources of water, and so they made sure to take on adequate stores of water in Alush before they set out into the barren desert.[6] If they needed more motivation, Moshe had also urged them to bring along extra supplies of water because of the uncertainties of the desert.[7]

When they arrived in Refidim, therefore, they had sufficient stores of water to last for a while. Nonetheless, they immediately set out to assess the water situation. Would there be enough water when the supplies ran out?

---

4. *Rashi* to *Sanhedrin* 106a; *Bechoros* 5a; *Targum Yonasan*.
5. *Rokeach*; *Targum Yonasan* to *Shemos* 17:1,3.
6. See *Ramban* to *Shemos* 17:1; *Be'er Yitzchok* to *Shemos* 17:2.
   Some suggest that they had dirty water or bitter water available in a worst case scenario. At the very least it would provide the animals with sustenance (*Yefei To'ar*).
   Some question why the liquefied manna could not be a source of water. They respond that the manna dissipated each day, and a fresh batch fell the following day. In addition, as seen earlier, Hashem did not want any leftover of the previous day's manna so that they would constantly have to show faith and pray for the following day's sustenance. This, however, does not explain why they could not drink from this liquified manna day to day and thus sustain themselves for the next forty years. Some suggest that in fact this was possible. The Jews, however, were looking to complain despite the fact that they had with what to sustain themselves. Others suggest that since they did not have water visually, they felt the lack of it. This was seen a year later in their complaints that brought upon them the tragedy of the *slav* (see *Derush Shmuel*). Others suggest that the water of the manna also became wormy, making it undrinkable. See *Shaarei Aryeh* pp. 166-167 for varied opinions on this subject.
7. *Tosafos Al HaTorah* to *Shemos* 17:5.

It did not take them long to discover that there was no water at all in Refidim, not even bitter water as they had first found in Marah.[8] Hashem expected the people to respond with a show of trust and faith, to recognize that their fate lay in the hands of the Almighty and to cry out in prayer to Him. Unfortunately, the mean-spirited, wicked and rebellious among the people once again sought to sow dissension among the people.[9]

A group of nervous and apprehensive men gathered in the shade of a large tent.

"Has anyone seen any wells in this place?" Nagdor raised the question that was on everyone's mind.

"No, we haven't," replied a man with darting eyes.

"Has anyone found any water?" Nagdor called out. "A well? A stream? A pond? Anything?"

All the men shook their heads.

"This place is completely dry," said the man with the darting eyes. "You can take it from me. I've looked everywhere."

"I tell you, I can't believe it," Nagdor cried out. "How could we fall into the same trap again and again?"

"What are you talking about?" asked his friend Peliav. "What trap?"

Nagdor took a deep breath to calm his nerves. "It's that Moshe again. He's done it to us again.[10] We never learn our lesson. He just leads us around the desert by our noses to any place he chooses. He doesn't feel he has to answer to anyone, not to us, not to Hashem. He's like the king. He does anything he pleases and goes wherever he pleases. And we go along."

"Now wait a minute, Nagdor," Kumiel interjected. "There you go again, jumping to conclusions. The young are so rash and impetuous. Why don't you stop and think for a minute? Does Moshe steer the cloud pillars in the direction he chooses? Eh?"

He paused to give Nagdor a chance to respond, but the question was clearly rhetorical; it did not call for a reply.

---

8. *Zeh Yenachmeni; Sechel Tov; R' Avaraham Ben HaRambam; Tosafos* to *Shemos* 17:2.
9. *Targum Yonasan* to *Shemos* 17:2.
   Some suggest that these were the same people who would eventually join Korach's rebellion against Moshe (*Tur*).
10. Some suggest that Aharon too was included in their complaints (*Ibn Ezra; Ramban*). Others suggest that Aharon was excluded as he was the master mediator of peace and was beloved by all (*Mechilta; Yalkut* 262).

"Of course not," Kumiel continued. "No one is fool enough to believe that Moshe controls the cloud pillars. Hashem does. Well, didn't you notice that we are following the cloud pillars? Moshe is leading us in the direction indicated by the movement of the cloud pillars. So how can you accuse Moshe of our current troubles?"[11]

"I don't know, Kumiel," said Nagdor. "You're too smart for me. Maybe I agree with you, maybe I don't. Someone has to answer for this fiasco. If it isn't Moshe, then we have to direct our complaints to Hashem.[12] Some of us here have enough water to last for a while, but what about those of us who do not? What will Hashem do for us? Can He devise a source of water right here in the desert that will serve us in the long run?[13] Is He even aware of our needs and wishes? The situation as it stands now is unacceptable. Every time we travel to a new encampment we risk a new crisis of water. How can we live like this, never knowing where we will be getting our next drink?"

Achiash raised his hand. "I'm with you, Nagdor. I don't know if I would phrase it in such provocative terms, but I agree that we have to do something and do it fast. I, for one, do not have any water. For me the crisis is right now! I say we go directly to Moshe and throw the problem in his lap. I don't think he has the ability to do anything, but let him struggle with it. Let him look for a solution. He is the one who brought us here. It is his responsibility to see that we all do not die of thirst."[14]

As the discussion continued, more and more anxious men joined in and offered their comments and opinions. Among them were Toltep and his two friends from the Erev Rav.

"Nagdor, my friend," said Toltep. "I am inclined to agree with you. I have some water in my tent, but I don't fool myself into thinking that we don't face a very grave problem. I have no argument with Moshe. After all, what is he supposed to do? No, my argument is with Hashem. He is endangering our future, our very survival, by putting us into these situations."[15]

"I also have some water," said Peliav. "While I'm not prepared to speak out against Moshe or Hashem, as others seem to be, I don't

---

11. *Abarbanel.*
12. *Ralbag* to *Shemos* 17:2.
13. *Pesikta Rabbah* 13; *Etz Yosef; Ralbag;* see *Be'er Yitzchok.*
14. *Rokeach; Ibn Ezra; Tur* to *Shemos* 17:2.
15. *Ibn Ezra; Tur; Tosafos* to *Shemos* 17:2.

delude myself about our situation. We may have just enough for now, but my family is going to have to ration this water. Who knows what conditions we will find in future encampments? This is the desert, you know, and your chances of not finding water are better than your chances of finding it. I agree that we have to do something. I just don't know what it is."[16]

As the discussion progressed, it grew more and more heated. Tempers ran high. Men shouted in anger and frustration.[17]

"Friends, we are in trouble," shouted Toltep's friend Dernak. "The stores of water we have put away are meaningless. They'll be gone before you know it. The present is like the blink of an eye. We are facing the future right now with absolutely no water, and what are we going to do?[18] What will happen to our beloved children? What will happen to our ever-thirsty livestock? How will we survive?"[19]

"We want water!"[20]

A storm was brewing. Fire flashed in many eyes. The angry grumbling grew louder and louder.

Nagdor held up his hands for silence.

"My friends, we must act now, I tell you," he said. "The leader of this journey must be held accountable. If Moshe is at fault, then we must demand that he come up with a solution. If he is helpless, we will stone him as a false prophet. Then we will challenge the Master of the Universe to provide us with drinking water. If He is capable of giving us what we need then we will gladly serve and worship Him. Otherwise, we will rebel against Him and seek other places in which to worship. Let's go!"[21]

The people shuffled their feet nervously when they heard these seditious words, but they were too distraught to object. They fell in

---

16. *Maaseh Hashem* to *Shemos* 17:5.
17. *Lekach Tov; Ramban; Malbim; Netziv* to *Shemos* 17:3.
18. *Abarbanel; HaKesav VeHaKabbalah.*
19. *Shemos Rabbah, Yedei Moshe* 26:2; *Sechel Tov; R' Yehudah HaChassid; Abarbanel* to *Shemos* 17:1.
   The Jewish people went out of their way to lengthen and stretch and extend their arguments as much as possible by including their children and animals when the premise of their arguments was simply a lack of water (*Ramban*).
20. *Alshich.*
21. See *Mechilta; Sechel Tov* to *Shemos* 17:2 and 17:7; *Shemos Rabbah* 26:2; *Maharzu; Tanchuma Yisro* 3; *Pesikta Rabbah* 13; *Midrash Petiras Aharon* p. 12 in *Otzar HaMidrashim*; p. 91 in *Beis Midrash* 1.
   Some suggest that Moshe ran to his tent at this point for fear he would in fact be stoned.

behind Nagdor and the other leaders, and soon a roiling mob surged through the encampment toward Moshe's tent.

Moshe listened to their grievances, then it was his turn to speak.

"Didn't I urge you to bring along extra stores of water?" he said. "Didn't you understand that there would be a water shortage for a while? At the time, you just nodded and did as I suggested. You had no arguments and complaints. Now, all of a sudden you are all up in arms as if this is my fault.[22] Be logical. If you think it was I who took you out of Egypt, why are you testing Hashem? And if you acknowledge that Hashem took you out of Egypt, why are you berating me? You know perfectly well that I cannot produce water in the desert on my own. You know perfectly well that everything I do and say is at Hashem's command. I am no more than His messenger.[23] We've been through this at Marah. So if you attack me, you are really attacking Hashem, Heaven forbid. How dare you risk such a thing? Repent immediately if you don't want to be punished.[24]

"Take heed, my people, because you are traveling down the wrong road. Why do you insist on testing Hashem's patience and forbearance? Please, I beg you, enough already! If you want results, you should pray rather than complain. Hashem will listen to your prayer and send you water."[25]

The people hung their heads in embarrassment, and they returned silently to their tents. But they still did not have any water other than the water they had brought with them from Alush.

The place where they had encamped was called Refidim, but after the contentious behavior of the Jewish people, it was renamed Masah U'Merivah. Masah, meaning testing, recalled that they tested Hashem. U'Merivah, meaning contention, recalls that they argued contentiously with Moshe. The testing was obviously a graver offense.[26]

---

22. *Tosafos* to *Shemos* 17:5.
23. *Abarbanel.*
24. *Malbim; Sforno* to *Shemos* 17:2.
25. See *Malbim* to *Shemos* 17:3.
26. *Mechilta; Targum Yonasan; Ibn Ezra* to *Shemos* 17:7; *Sifri Beha'aloscha.* There is a question as to who gave it the name — Moshe or Hashem?
   Some suggest that the Jews were never in doubt about Hashem's presence among them. They were just unsure if they were worthy of miracles or if their sins prevented them from experiencing further miracles (*Alshich*).

This unfortunate incident was the seventh of the ten times they tested Hashem in the desert.[27]

Moshe's Prayer

Within a few days, the water reserves were completely exhausted. The children cried out for water. The livestock bleated their distress. The people grew impatient and frustrated, but they did not respond in a faithful manner. They did not cry out in prayer to Hashem. They did not plead with Moshe to intercede for them.[28] Some people knew that the Jewish people were destined to receive water in Miriam's merit, but they were reluctant to approach a woman with their problems.[29] Instead, they grumbled and complained, and as the crisis deepened, their cries and demands grew more belligerent and strident.[30]

Hashem was testing the Jewish people once again, and they were failing miserably. After the fiascoes at Marah and Alush, Hashem was giving them another opportunity to reach a higher spiritual level, to strengthen their trust and faith in preparation for the Giving of the Torah, but they did not rise to the occasion. Rebellion was brewing. Moshe was running out of time.[31]

Although the people had made personal attacks on Moshe, disparaging his character and his motivations, he did not hold it against them. He never even considered turning his back on them in their hour of dire need.[32] The plight of his beloved people struck a deep chord in his heart, and he immersed himself in prayer before Hashem on their behalf.[33]

"Please help me, Hashem," he pleaded. "Help me show them the folly of their ways. Help me show them the futility of their chronic complaints. In the meantime, look upon them with compassion. Their reactions are understandable in a way, because You have placed them in a painful situation. Be patient with them, Hashem, and in time, they will indeed pass the tests You give them. But now they are enraged. They are so angry that they are ready to stone me,

---

27. *Arachin* 15b.
28. *Mechilta* to *Shemos* 17:3; *Shemos Rabbah*; *Maharzu*. See *Be'er Yitzchok* to *Shemos* 17:2.
29. *Sifsei Kohen.*
30. *Lekach Tov*; *Ramban*; *Malbim*; *Netziv* to *Shemos* 17:3.
31. *Malbim* 17:1; *Ralbag* to *Shemos* 17:7; *Abarbanel.*
32. *Lekach Tov* to *Shemos* 17:4.
33. See *Targum*; *R' Saadiah Gaon* to *Shemos* 17:4.

so angry that I fear for my life.[34] I heard them speaking among themselves that I am a false prophet and should be stoned, and I was ready to run and hide in my tent. Hashem, I am in an impossible situation. As Your messenger, I bear the burdens of leadership patiently, but I must also protect myself. Hashem, is my life in danger?"[35] It would have been easy for Moshe to distance himself from the people who were reviling him and rebelling against his leadership. But he remained steadfast in his devotion and loyalty to his people. He prayed for them with all his heart.

"Do not let their words upset you," Hashem told him. "They are exhausted, distracted and distraught, because they have no water. Forgive them, just as I forgive them even though they are impudent toward Me.[36] Guide them as a shepherd leads his flock. These are My people, and I have raised you up so that you will be their leader." [37]

Hashem went on to reprimanded Moshe for having slandered the Jewish people.[38] "And do not accuse the people of murderous intent against you.[39] It is a long way from verbal abuse to physical assault. And anyway, do you think they can hurt you if I do not approve it?[40] Go walk among the people and see if there are any arrogant people who will denounce you in public.[41] Walk among them and see if they will stone you or even lay a finger on your coat.[42] Walk among them with an escort of the weak and the elderly, who offer no protection from attack, and see if anyone so much as looks at you."[43]

Moshe did as Hashem had instructed him. He walked through the encampment, through the midst of the worried crowds, and saw

---

34. See *Ohr HaChaim* to *Shemos* 17:4.
35. See *Mechilta; Shemos Rabbah* 26:2; *Sifsei Kohen* to *Shemos* 17:5; *Abarbanel; Ibn Ezra; Rashi; Sechel Tov; Tosafos* to *Shemos* 17:4; *Tanchuma Beshalach* 22; *Etz Yosef; Midrash Petiras Aharon* p. 12 in *Otzar HaMidrashim*.
36. See *Shemos Rabbah* 26:2; *Matnos Kehunah; Rashash; Mechilta; Sechel Tov* to *Shemos* 17:5.
37. *Tanchuma Beshalach* 22.
  This statement will have great importance after the Jewish people would worship the Golden Calf. See beginning of Ch. 14.
38. *Rashi* to *Shemos* 17:5.
39. *Rashash* to *Shemos Rabbah*.
40. See *Zohar* p. 64a; *Abarbanel*.
41. *Yedei Moshe*.
42. *Mechilta; Rashi* to *Shemos* 17:5; *Yalkut* 764.
43. *Abarbanel*.

that he had nothing to fear from the people. They had heard Moshe validate their pain and distress, and now they greeted him in their midst with awe and accorded him the highest honor and respect.[44]

A Stone From Chorev

The time had finally come to provide water for the people.

"Leave the encampment here in Refidim and journey to Chorev,"[45] Hashem told Moshe. "I have designated one of its stones as the source of water for the Jewish people. The water will come from the stone itself, not from a wellspring, and it will flow all the way to the encampment at Refidim.[46] I want the people to know that the water is coming out of a stone. Some may think that it is really coming from a well you discovered when you tended sheep for your father-in-law Yisro.[47] We must avoid that, so bring with you the elders of Israel. Let them witness this great miracle I am about to perform for you. Let them assure the people that the water is coming from a simple stone and nothing else.[48]

"Take along your staff that you have used to perform miracles in the past. With that staff you will bring forth water from the stone.[49] The people will have plenty to drink, and their complaints will come to an end. They see the staff as a force for destruction. They saw it bring plagues and ruin on Egypt. But now they will see that this very same staff can be a force for the good.[50] They will enjoy a miracle within a miracle, for the staff that transformed water into blood will draw fresh water from a stone."[51]

---

44. *Tanchuma Beshalach* 22; *Sforno*.
45. *Ramban; R' Avraham Ben HaRambam* to *Shemos* 17:5.
    See *Pirkei D'Rav Eliezer* 44. This was 2 *parsangs* (about 4½ miles) away from Refidim.
46. *Ramban* to *Shemos* 17:5. *Ramban* also suggests the possibility that either strong youth or animals carried the water back for the Jewish people.
47. *Alshich*.
48. *Mechilta; Rashi* to *Shemos* 17:5.
49. *Targum Yonasan* to *Shemos* 17:5.
50. See *Rashi; Mechilta; Tanchuma Beshalach* 21.
    Many question the meaning of this because what was tragic for the Egyptian people was in effect good for the Jews. Some suggest that even if that may be the case, there was still an indirect tragedy as a result. In this case, however, there was only a positive result from the staff. This was something new, never witnessed by the Jewish people.
51. *Ramban; Chizkuni; Sforno* to *Shemos* 17:5.

Moshe did as Hashem had instructed him. He set out for Chorev escorted by the elders of Israel, who walked behind him, and a large retinue.

Chorev was actually another name for Mount Sinai, the place where the Jewish people would receive the Torah in the very near future. It is the permanent abode of the *Shechinah*, the Divine Presence. This is the place where Moshe saw the *sneh*, the burning bush that was not consumed.

Hashem wanted the water to come from Chorev specifically, because life-giving water is the symbol for life-giving Torah.[52] Furthermore, just as the manna was spiritual in its essence, so was the water from Chorev, and as such, it would help prepare the people to receive the Torah.[53]

When Moshe arrived in Chorev, he saw before him numerous stones, and he could not determine which was the one he was to strike with his staff. But Moshe was on such a high spiritual level that he could sense when he was near the *Shechinah*, and as he approached a particular stone, he became convinced that it was the designated one.[54]

"Do not choose the stone yourself," Hashem told Moshe. "I do not want people to be able to accuse you of trickery and question the integrity of this miracle. I do not want them to say that the water is really not coming from the stone but from some secret subterranean well you found a long time ago. Instead, I want you to have the elders choose the stone you are to strike with your staff. I assure you that whichever stone they choose will gush forth water when you strike it."[55]

The History of the Well

The miraculous well that would provide water for the Jewish people for nearly forty years in the desert was one of the ten things created at twilight at the end of the sixth day of creation. From that time, it had already been designated as the miraculous source of water for the newly emancipated

---

52. *Tosafos* to *Shemos* 17:6.
53. *Kometz HaMinchah, Shavuos*.
54. *Midrash Aggadah Chukas; Midrash Petiras Aharon; Ramban* to *Shemos* 17:6. See R' *Saadiah Gaon*.
    Some suggest that this was the only rock in Chorev and that it was apparent to Moshe to which rock Hashem was referring (*Abarbanel*).
55. See *Shemos Rabbah* 26:2 and commentaries.

Jewish people in the desert.[56] Two thousand years later, the miraculous well figured prominently in the dispute between the shepherds of Avimelech and the shepherds of Avraham over the ownership of the wells of Gerar. The wells rightfully belonged to Avraham, but Avimelech's shepherds stole them and claimed they had belonged to Avimelech all along. The miraculous well provided Avraham with proof of ownership. The waters rose up to meet Avraham's sheep when they appeared at the well; they did not rise up for Avimelech's sheep.

At that time, Hashem promised that one day these same waters would rise up to come toward the Jewish people in their time of need. Now, seven generations later, this promise was being fulfilled.[57] The merit of Avraham's giving the angels water to drink and standing near them in readiness to serve their needs had a part in alleviating the plight of his descendants. The Jewish people were rewarded that the *Shechinah* would stand by the stone waiting for Moshe and that the waters of the miraculous well would flow to them in the desert.[58]

This was also the well to which Rivkah went to draw water for Eliezer's camels. While all the other shepherds had to draw water from the well, the water rose up to Rivkah and filled her jugs with water. This too foretold that the waters would one day rise for her descendants, the Jewish people.[59]

Nonetheless, despite this long and glorious history, this miraculous well would always be known exclusively as Miriam's Well. Her acts of kindness when she saved the Jewish infants in Egypt from Pharaoh's decree of drowning and sustained them would now stand in good stead for the fledgling Jewish nation and sustain them in the desert for the forty years of their national infancy.[60] Her kindness toward her infant brother Moshe when she stood beside the water and kept watch over him also helped sustain the Jewish people in the desert. Finally, Miriam led the women in singing *Shirah* at the Yam Suf. Now she was rewarded

---

56. *Pirkei D'Rav Eliezer* 19. See *Pirkei D'Rav Eliezer* 3 and *Radal* there who write that it was created on Monday.
57. See *Bereishis Rabbah* 54:5; *Yalkut Shimoni* 764.
58. See *Shemos Rabbah*; *Tosafos Al HaTorah* to *Shemos* 17:1; *Bava Metzia* 86b.
59. *Bereishis Rabbah* 60.
60. See *Anaf Yosef*.

that the people would sing *Shirah* in her merit for the miraculous well that would sustain them in the desert.[61]

An Engineering Marvel

The well was contained in a large round stone. Its opening lay sealed inside the stone so that no water ran from it.[62] Moshe struck the stone a fierce blow with his staff, which was made of sapphire, and the stone split open in two equal parts, exposing the opening of the well.[63] At first, the opening oozed blood, and a few of the mockers in attendance snickered. But in an instant, a great fountain of water burst forth from the stone.[64] At that moment, all the stones on the mountainside also split open and gushed forth water, just as all the waters of the world split when Moshe split the Yam Suf.[65]

The opening of the well inside the stone was like a spout with a sieve at its end. Other pores in the stone also opened simultaneously and gushed forth water from similar spouts.[66] The well drew water from the deepest chasms of the earth and sent it skyward in a jet thick as a pillar, reaching higher than any water had ever reached since the days of the Great Flood.[67] The water then cascaded downward and flowed like a river to Refidim, where the Jewish encampment was located, and came to an end at the resting place of the *Shechinah*, which was at Moshe's tent before the Mishkan was built.[68]

In all the encampments during the forty years in the desert, the central point of the miraculous well would be near the *Shechinah*. The princes of the tribes would come and call out, "Arise, O well!"[69]

---

61. See *Bamidbar Rabbah* 1:2.
62. See *Tanchuma Bamidbar* 2; Rashi to *Avos* 5:6.
63. *Mechilta*; Rashi; *Zayis Raanan*; *Rokeach* to *Shemos* 17:6; Rashi to *Avos* 5:6. See *Tosafos* to *Kiddushin* 30b.

See *Yalkut Chukas* 763 which states that later after Miriam's death, Moshe was required to talk to the rock. This may be understood by an example: One hits the young to teach a point but speaks to the adult with reason and respect to bring out a point. The same applied with the rock. After forty years, Moshe would have to show respect to the rock and speak to it to give out water.

64. *Midrash Shocher Tov Tehillim* 105.
65. See *Yalkut Tehillim* 819. See *Let My Nation Go* p. 352 fn. 70.
66. See *Tosefta Succah* 3:3.
67. See *Radak* to *Tehillim* 78:16; *Eileh HaDevarim Zuta*; *Tosefta Succah* 3:3; *Minchas Bikkurim*.
68. *Tosefta Succah* 3:3; *Minchas Bikkurim*; Ramban to *Shemos* 17:5.
69. See *Bamidbar Rabbah* 1:2; *Bereishis Rabbah* 70:5; *Maharzu*.

As the water began to gurgle, the princes took their staffs and drew ditches in the sand in the direction of their respective tribal encampments, twelve paths in all. The water burst forth and flowed through these twelve ditches, forming twelve surging rivers that ran through the twelve tribal encampments. Each of these rivers then split into numerous tributary rivulets that ran to the tents of the individual families, providing them with water with the least effort possible. The result was an engineering marvel, a complex of waterways, irrigation ditches and streams flowing in many different directions.[70]

The soil of the encampments also benefited from these miraculous rivers and streams. The water made the soil so fertile and lush that it produced the finest fruit trees and vegetation. The figs, pomegranates and other fruits were as succulent as those that existed in the Garden of Eden before Adam sinned and was expelled, as delicious as those that would exist in the World to Come.[71]

The central rivers that ran alongside the tribal encampments were so wide that it was impossible to ford them without either wading through the water or crossing by boat to the other side.[72] The entire Jewish encampment, although in the middle of the stark and barren desert, now resembled a seaport in a river delta, its waters dotted with boats and sailors.[73]

---

70. *Bamidbar Rabbah* 19:26; *Maharzu*; *Bereishis Rabbah* 70:5; *Tosefta Succah* 3:3; *Yalkut Pekudei* 426; *Tanchuma Kedoshim* 7; Rashi to *Tehillim* 78:16.

71. *Bamidbar Rabbah* 19:26; *Yalkut Pekudei* 426; *Shir HaShirim Rabbah* 4:3; *Tanchuma Kedoshim* 7.

It goes without saying that this Midrash, as well as others, should not necessarily be taken at face value. As has always been the premise of this book, I bring down the Midrashim, opinions and views as I see them and leave it up to the reader to come to their own conclusions as to which Midrashim are to be taken literally and which are to be taken homiletically or symbolically. No one is to suggest that the specific events described above did not take place exactly as I have presented them, but they do raise some interesting observations: What was the necessity of these delectable fruits when the Jewish people had the manna? Where exactly was the manna through all this and to where did the liquefied manna stream amidst all this water? Also, according to the opinion that the *slav* fell daily, the desert must have been an amazing sight to behold with tons of *slav* scattered through the camp at night, manna scattered across the campsite in the morning, all in the midst of waterways flowing across the encampments of the Jewish people.

72. See *Bamidbar Rabbah* 19:26; *Maharzu*; *Yedei Moshe*; *Tosefta Succah* 3:3.

Some suggest that they would be able to boat themselves to the Mediterranean Sea and discover large treasures there.

73. Commentaries to *Tehillim* 105:41.

The rivers also served the Jewish people as guides through the desert during their travels. The twelve rivers indicated the exact spots where the respective tribes were to set up their camps, and the tributaries helped individuals find their way if they ever got lost.[74]

The Jews realized what an awesome gift Hashem had given them, and they sang *Shirah* to show their appreciation.[75] But once again, as was the case with the manna, the extent of the gift depended on the righteousness of the individual using it. The righteous enjoyed all the benefits of the water coming directly to their tents in abundance, while the wicked often had to walk hours to retrieve their rations of water, and then they had to lug it back to their tents.[76]

As for the gentile nations, they marveled at the good fortune of the Jewish people. They too wanted to sample this miraculous water, but as was the case with the manna, they found it nearly impossible to get a taste of it. If they took a ladle of the water and brought it to their lips they would find the ladle empty. Those who went to extraordinary efforts and managed to get a few drops into their mouths were not rewarded either. They would find the water brackish and bitter.[77]

The well inside the stone would travel with the Jewish people through the desert for nearly forty years. It came to an end when Miriam passed away, but it returned shortly thereafter in the merit of Moshe and Aharon.[78]

---

74. See *Bereishis Rabbah* 70:5; *Bamidbar Rabbah* 19:26; *Yalkut Pekudei* 426; *Shir HaShirim Rabbah* 4:3.
75. See *Targum Yonasan* to *Bamidbar* 21:17.
76. *Tanna D'Vei Eliyahu* 12; see *Rabbeinu Bachya* to *Shemos* 17:6.
77. See *Yalkut Shimoni* 258.
78. See *Seder Olam* 10; *Taanis* 9a with *Rashi*; *Maharsha*; *Shabbos* 35a with *Rashi*; *Yalkut Shimoni* 764.

5 Amalek Attacks

The Jewish people remained in Refidim for one week, after which they traveled directly to Sinai. They were barely two weeks away from receiving the Torah, but they were far from ready for the occasion.[1] Instead of purifying themselves through Torah study, prayer, the observance of the mitzvos and implanting an abiding faith in their hearts, they seethed with discord, dissension and conflict.[2]

Seven times had they tested Hashem in the desert, repaying kindness with ingratitude.[3] Hashem had brought them forth from slavery in Egypt and split the sea for them. He had fed them meat and manna in the desert although they had not prayed to Him with

---

1. *Seder Olam* 5. According to the *Gra*, they arrived in Refidim on Sunday, the 22nd of Iyar, since it had already been established that the 15th of Iyar was a Sunday and the manna began falling on Monday the 16th.
2. *Abarbanel.*
3. *Tanchuma Beshalach* 25; *Pirkei D'Rav Eliezer* 44.

humble supplication. He had sustained them with miracles although they had voiced their discontent slanderously and contentiously to Hashem and Moshe.[4]

But now, in Refidim, they had gone too far. They had dared to question the presence of the Almighty by saying, "Is Hashem indeed among us?"[5] They had neglected the study of the Torah, desecrated the Shabbos,[6] sneered at the laws and mitzvos of the Torah and even threatened to turn to idol worship. Such disgraceful behavior would not go unpunished and ignored. An appropriate retribution awaited the Jewish people, a calamity that would bring them quickly to higher levels of trust and faith in Hashem.[7]

The retribution could have been a further deprivation of food and water, as they had suffered at Marah, Alush and when they first arrived at Refidim. But that would have been counterproductive. The Jewish people had already shown that they were inclined to respond to deprivation with contention and rebellion. Their spiritual level would thus have fallen even lower than it already was. Instead, Hashem sent them an implacable enemy that would terrify them and inspire them to repent quickly and seek Hashem's protection. Once and for all, they would learn that their only hope for the future was to serve Hashem faithfully and pray for His mercy.[8]

Amalek, descended from Eisav, would pounce on the Jewish people in their moment of great weakness. Yitzchak had blessed Eisav that should the Jewish people ever decline spiritually, the descendants of Eisav would gain the upper hand and rule the world with their swords. In their present condition, the Jewish people, having neglected Torah and prayer, had left the door open for vengeful predators of Amalek.[9]

---

4. *Tanchuma Yashan Yisro; Pirkei D'Rav Eliezer* 44; *Matnos Kehunah; Bereishis Rabbah* 65:20.

5. *Pirkei D'Rav Eliezer* 44; *Mechilta*.

Some suggest that they believed Hashem was present in principle, but not with them while they were traveling in the desert (*Radal*).

6. *Zohar*.

7. *Tur; Lekach Tov* to *Shemos* 17:7; *Mechilta* to *Shemos* 17:8; *Pesikta Rabbasi* 13; *Shir HaShirim Rabbah* 2:15.

Others suggest that they were corrupt in the laws of weights and scales, showing unethical behavior in their business practices (see *Tosafos to Kiddushin* 32b; *Sifri Ki Seitzei*).

It is interesting to note that the numerical value of Amalek and of the word *safek* (doubt) is 140. This would suggest that because the Jews were in "doubt" of Hashem, Amalek arrived (*Iturei Torah*).

8. *Malbim* to *Shemos* 17:8.

9. See *Bereishis Rabbah* 65:20, *Maharzu; Ralbag* to *Shemos* 17:16.

The impending catastrophe could be explained by a parable.

A father was walking along a path, carrying his child on his shoulders. They passed a beautiful fruit tree, and the child said, "I want a fruit."

The father plucked the fruit from the tree and gave it to his child. The passed a sparkling fountain, and the child said, "I want a drink of water."

The father filled a cup and gave it to the child. Then they met a man coming toward them, and the child said, "Excuse me, sir, have you seen my father anywhere?"

"After all I have been doing for you all along," the father said angrily, "you ask if I am even here? How ungrateful can you be?"

The father threw the child from his shoulders, whereupon a dog sprang forward and bit the child.

Hashem had been carrying the Jewish people on His shoulders, so to speak. He had brought them forth from Egypt and spread the protective shield of the cloud pillars over them. They cried out in panic at the Yam Suf, and He split the sea for them. They wanted meat, and He gave it to them. They wanted bread, and He gave them the manna. And after all that, they declared, "Is Hashem indeed among us?"

If such is their ingratitude, then Hashem set upon them the Amalekite dogs to attack them and sink their teeth into their flesh.[10]

Ancient Foes

The roots of Amalek's hatred for the Jewish people ran very deep. Hundreds of years earlier, Yaakov and Eisav, Yitzchak's twin sons, had been engaged in intense rivalry from the moment they were born. Yaakov was faultless and scholarly, while Eisav was a savage man of the sword. Eisav was the older of the two, but Yaakov was convinced that the birthright of the firstborn rightfully belonged to him.

At the age of 15, Eisav returned famished from a hard day of hunting and sold his birthright to Yaakov for a bowl of red soup.[11]

---

10. *Shemos Rabbah* 26:3; *Rashi* to *Shemos* 17:8; *Pesikta Rabbasi* 13.

There are some who question the word "Amalek" mentioned in *Shemos* 17:8. Some are of the opinion that it refers to the nation of Amalek in general. Others are of the opinion that it refers to the generic name of the king and leader of Amalek, similar to the term Pharaoh used for the king of Egypt. It is unlikely that it refers to Amalek the son of Elifaz since he would have been over 300 years old at this time. See *Ibn Ezra* and *Shaarei Aharon*.

11. See *Targum Yonasan* to *Shemos* 17:8; *Shir HaShirim Rabbah* 2:15. See *Let My Nation Live* p. 169.

Many years later, when Yitzchak was old and blind, Yaakov prevailed on Yitzchak to give the blessings to him instead of to Eisav as he had intended. When Eisav discovered Yaakov's deception, he was infuriated and swore in his heart to kill his younger brother as soon as the opportunity arose.[12]

Yaakov fled his father's home to escape Eisav's murderous wrath. But Eisav was not so easily deterred. He plotted and schemed and refused to rest until he exacted his revenge and recovered the birthright and blessings that, in his opinion, were swindled from him.

Shortly after Yaakov fled, Eisav summoned his son Elifaz and said, "Go off in pursuit of my brother Yaakov. You know what that scoundrel has done to me. I want you to defend my honor and the honor of our family. When you overtake that thief, I want you to kill him. Then the birthright and the blessings will revert to me. Do this for me, and also for yourself, because if I retrieve what is rightfully mine, someday it will be yours. Do you hear me?"

"Yes, Father," said Elifaz.

"Swear you will do it! Take a solemn oath that you will avenge my honor and recover my loss."

Elifaz bowed his head and swore.

But he was ill at ease with what he had undertaken, and he sought the advice of his concubine Timnah.

"Are you out of your mind?" she said to him. "Do you think it is so easy to overcome Yaakov? If it were such a simple matter, your father would have gone to do it himself. He is no wilting lily when it comes to fighting and killing. He doesn't want to take a chance, so he sends you to do it."[13]

"So what do you think I should do?" he asked.

"Exactly the opposite of what your father wants. Make yourself useful to them. Dig wells for them and build roads. Befriend them. Believe me, you don't need them for enemies. They can destroy you."

Elifaz pondered his concubine's sage advice, but he was still in a quandary. He had sworn to his father that he would kill Yaakov, and he was bound by his word. Furthermore, Elifaz had been taught

---

12. *Lekach Tov* to *Shemos* 17:8; *Ki Seitzei*; see *Sefer HaYashar* to *Parshiyos Vayechi* and *Shemos* for details of some of the battles the Jews had with Eisav and his children.
13. *Hadar Zekeinim* to *Beshalach*.

since he was a little child that honoring one's father was a paramount value. Eisav had honored his father in an exemplary fashion, and no less was expected from Elifaz.

Elifaz had a conflict. Although no paragon of virtue, he had enjoyed a close relationship with his great-grandfather Avraham and his grandfather Yitzchak. He had an appreciation for the pure and righteous life that Yaakov had chosen to follow. He respected his uncle and did not want to harm him, but what was he to do? He had sworn to his father.

In the end, he decided to accept his father's mission, but he did so with a heavy heart, hoping that somehow he would be spared this evil deed.

Mounting a speedy camel, he set off in pursuit of his uncle Yaakov, and before long, he overtook him. Yaakov took one look at him and understood what was happening.

"So you have come to kill me, Nephew," he said.

"I've come on a mission from my father," said Elifaz stiffly.

"And the mission is to kill me, right?" asked Yaakov.

Elifaz remained silent.

"I've known you all your life, Elifaz. You don't want to do this thing."

Elifaz nodded even as he drew his sword. "You are right, Uncle, but I have no choice."

"But you do have a choice," said Yaakov. "There is a way that you can avoid shedding the blood of your own family, yet you will have fulfilled your father's mission."

Elifaz slipped the sword back into its scabbard and looked hopefully at Yaakov. "I am listening," he said.

"You see all these precious stones and gold?" asked Yaakov. "If you take them all away from me, I will be destitute. Alone on the road and penniless. According to the Torah, a destitute person is considered like a dead person. You can make me dead without killing me."

"I love it," said Elifaz. He drew his sword again. "Prepare to be robbed, Uncle. Your life or your money."

"You can have my money," said Yaakov.[14]

Elifaz returned home with the sacks of Yaakov's treasures, relieved that he had been spared the stain of innocent blood on his

---

14. *Hadar Zekeinim* to *Beshalach*; Rashi to *Bereishis* 29:11.

hands. He would eventually merit *ruach hakodesh*, Divine inspiration, because of his righteous act in letting Yaakov live.

But Eisav was not happy when he heard Elifaz's report. "You what? You took his money? I told you to kill him, and you took his money? Is this some kind of joke?"

"It's not a joke, Father," said Elifaz. "According to the Torah, a destitute person is considered like a dead person."

"You're joking, aren't you? A son of mine should talk like this? I thought I brought you up properly, but this! This! It's too much. You're giving me chest pains."

"You wanted him dead, Father, and he is as good as dead. The Torah says — "

"Enough! I don't want to hear what the Torah says. Did I ask you to give me a sermon or to kill that thief brother of mine? I wanted him dead. Dead! You know, no-heartbeat dead, no-breathing dead. Dead like a dead camel, not a pauper. What would you do if I told you to kill a camel, would you take away his saddle? Bah! Go away. You're useless. I'll find someone who speaks my language, someone ruthless who knows what dead is."[15]

That someone was Elifaz's son Amalek. Here, Eisav found a kindred spirit. Eisav and Amalek were very close, practically soul mates. Eisav's rage and bloodlust burned in the heart of his grandson.

"Send me, Grandfather," shouted Amalek as he leaped to his feet. "I am ready to go do your bidding. You've taught me all the skills of combat. I know exactly what to do. It will be an honor and a pleasure. I give you my solemn oath."[16]

Amalek went off to tell his father Elifaz what he was planning.

"Not a good idea," said Elifaz. "Because of your great-grandfather Yitzchak's blessings, Yaakov and his future descendants have inherited both this world and the next. If we can reach an accommodation with them, we will gain a share in the World to Come. If we antagonize them, we will lose that as well."[17]

---

15. See *Sechel Tov* to *Beshalach*; *Devarim Rabbah* 2:20; *Matnos Kehunah*; *Maharzav*; *Yalkut Mishlei* 947.
16. See *Sechel Tov* to *Beshalach*; *Devarim Rabbah* 2:20; *Maharzav*.
  The very essence of the word "Amalek" is bad. The numerical value of Amalek is 240, the same as that of the word *mar*, which means bitter (*Pane'ach Raza*).
17. *Tanna D'Vei Eliyahu* 24; *Yeshuos Yaakov*; *Rimzei Eish*.

Amalek heard his father's words with disdain in his evil heart. He was determined to do his grandfather's bidding. But he still had to contend with his mother, who was determined to stop him.

"Amalek, my precious, don't be a fool," said Timnah. "You think the fancy footwork and swashbuckling swordplay you learned from your grandfather are going to help you against Yaakov? Ha! Don't make me laugh. Yaakov has a higher power working for him. You don't stand a chance with your little tin sword."

Amalek rolled his eyes. "Mother, please don't start. And for your information, my sword is made from the finest tempered steel. If you ever saw me in battle, you would know the full meaning of a higher power."

"Spare me, my dear. Look, I only mean your own good. And mine, too, of course. I don't want to put on clothes of mourning for my precious son. But you don't think you are taking a risk. I see that. Fine." She paused and continued in a lowered voice. "But did you consider the other risk?"

"The other risk? What other risk?"

"You know, the 400-year thing."

"What are you talking about, Mother? Please don't be so mysterious."

"All right. If you're asking me, I'll tell you. Remember the prophecy your great-great-grandfather Avraham received? The Almighty told him that his descendants would be enslaved by a foreign nation for 400 years. Prophecies are serious business, my precious."

"I know, Mother, but what does that have to do with me?"

"Why, everything. If you kill Yaakov, then who will fulfill that prophecy? Whose descendants will be enslaved? It won't be Yaakov's. He hasn't even married yet. So that leaves our family. So, my precious, are you prepared to be a slave?"[18]

There was no way around Timnah's argument. Reluctantly, Amalek abandoned his plans to pursue Yaakov. Instead, he would wait for the prophecy to reach its fulfillment. Then he would honor the oath he had made to his grandfather Eisav. He would

---

18. *Hadar Zekeinim* and *Chizkuni* to *Beshalach*.

attack and wipe the memory of Yaakov and his family from the face of the earth.[19]

The nation Amalek established waited impatiently for many years. When the Amalekite king heard the news of the enslavement of the Jewish people in Egypt, he congratulated himself on his prudence. The prophecy had indeed come true, as he suspected it would. Fortunately, his grandfather had refrained from killing Yaakov; if he had, he and his family might have been the ones down there in Egypt lugging stones for the pyramids. Years later, the Amalekite king heard the news about the miraculous events that led to the release of the Jewish people from bondage, but he was not impressed. He would find their weak points, their vulnerabilities, and then he would strike like a serpent in the night.

Amalek's first attempt against the Jewish people involved a coalition of nations in the region. As soon as the Jewish people emerged from Egypt, the Amalekite king was already engaged in shuttle diplomacy in his attempt to organize a coalition. The surrounding nations agreed that the Jewish people were a common threat and that a coalition force should intercept and destroy them. The armies were mobilized and placed under the command of a joint general staff.

Then the news of the splitting of the Yam Suf struck like a bombshell. Moreover, they heard about the protective shield of the cloud pillars that protected the Jewish people from missiles and projectiles. The foe was apparently too formidable. All the nations recalled their officers for consultations, which was a euphemism for withdrawal from the coalition. The only nation that maintained a state of belligerency was Amalek.

Not to be deterred, the Amalekite king mustered his army and traveled hundreds of miles across the desert to attack the Jewish people by the sea. Moshe saw them coming and uttered one of the Divine Names of the Almighty, and the Amalekites were instantly thrown into a confused retreat. They slunk back to their homeland to lick their wounds as they prepared for the inevitable next round of the conflict.[20]

---

19. *Hadar Zekeinim* and *Chizkuni* to *Beshalach*.
20. *Tanchuma* to *Ki Seitzei*.

Presently, the Amalekite king heard that the Jewish people were traveling through the desert and was overjoyed. He practically salivated like a hungry dog. "At last!" he declared. "I've waited all these years, and now at last, I will honor my grandfather's oath. No more delays, no more prophecies, no more excuses. There's no more time to waste. Let's go!"[21]

That very day, the Amalekite king sent out his agents and spies to gather intelligence for an impending assault. It did not take them long to return.

"Great news, your majesty," they said. "We have seen the enemy, and they are ours."

"All right," said the Amalekite king. "Enough with the poetry. Give me facts."

"Certainly. The Jews are weak, both physically and spiritually. Our wise men tell us that when the 'voice of Yaakov,' the spiritual condition of the Jews, is in decline, then the 'hands of Eisav,' the military might of our people, will be in the ascendancy.[22] Well, believe me, their voice is not even a whisper these days. As for their physical condition, they are a basket case. According to our reports, they are having serious supply problems. Their logistics are awful. We hear they've been stuck in the desert without food and water for some time. It seems their G-d has abandoned them."[23]

The Amalekite king rubbed his hands together with relish. "Great news! Excellent! All right, we have to have a major strategy session. All systems are go. Water the camels and get ready to ride!"[24]

---

21. *Tanna D'Vei Eliyahu* 24.
   Amalek was the one who told Pharaoh that the Jews were escaping Egypt with no intention of returning after the agreed-upon three-day journey. See *Let My Nation Go* p. 328.
22. *Tanna D'Vei Eliyahu* 24; *Akeidah*; *Abarbanel* to *Beshalach*.
23. See *Sforno* to *Shemos* 17:8; *Pirkei D'Rav Eliezer* 44.
   Amalek would use his knowledge of magic and sorcery to overwhelm the Jews. Water has the ability to wipe out any spells or charms brought about by magic, and with the Jews lacking water, Amalek felt secure that he would succeed in his fight against the Jewish people (*Beis HaLevi*; *Sanhedrin* 67).
24. Some suggest that Amalek had a Kabbalistic interpretation of his expected success against the Jewish people. The letters of Amalek include *ayin, mem, lamed* and *kuf*. They stand for the words Amram (*ayin*), Moshe (*mem*), Levi (*lamed*), Kehas (*kuf*). Amalek believed that his name was an omen in an abbreviated sense that he could overtake the Jewish people. What he was not aware of was that the end letters of the names of those Jewish people — Amram (*mem*), Levi (*yud*), Kehas (*tuf*), Moshe (*hei*) — spell the word *misah*, meaning death. This meant that if anyone challenged them, they would die (*Moshav Zekeinim*; *R' Chaim Paltiel*; *Imrei Shefer*). See *Let My Nation Live* p. 172 for a similar error made by Haman, a descendant of Amalek, who felt that his name alluded to being victorious over the Jews.

A Different Version

According to other opinions, the Amalekite enmity for the Jewish people had different roots. A young woman named Timnah, a princess from the mountainous kingdom of Seir, came to Avraham and asked to be converted. He rejected her. Later, she approached Yitzchak with the same request. He also rejected her. Finally, she offered to become Yaakov's concubine. Once again, she was rejected.

Filled with the fury of a Seirian princess scorned, she offered to become Elifaz's concubine so that she could have at least some connection to Avraham's family. Elifaz accepted her, and she bore him Amalek. This angry former princess indoctrinated her son with a deep hatred for Avraham, Yitzchak and their descendants, and he grew up to become the nemesis of the Jewish people.[25]

Why did Avraham reject her bid for conversion when he actively sought converts? Some suggest that she was of illegitimate birth and therefore could not be accepted into a Jewish family.[26] Others say she was rejected because she was not sincere. Her intention was really to marry into the Jewish people. In this case, her conversion would have been invalid.[27] Some suggest that Yaakov would have accepted her as his concubine, but his mother Rivkah rejected her.[28]

Amalek Seeks Advice

The Jewish people represented a new belief in one G-d, Who demanded that mankind live up to His moral standards. The Amalekites wanted to undermine the faith of the newly emancipated Jews and thereby destroy

---

25. *Tzeror HaMor* to *Beshalach*; see *Ramban* to *Bereishis* 36:12; see *Sanhedrin* 99b with *Maharsha* and *Rif*. See *Let My Nation Live* p. 41.

According to *Rashi*, Timnah was actually the daughter of Elifaz and then became his concubine.

There are those who question how the Bnei Yisrael would be allowed to battle with Amalek when they were specifically commanded not to fight with the family of Eisav, as in the case with Edom. The answer to that is that Amalek was excluded from that commandment because he was the son of a concubine (Timnah) and not legitimately honored as a member of the Eisav legacy.

26. See *Ein Yaakov* and commentaries to *Sanhedrin* 99b.

27. *Beis Yisrael* to *Parashas Ki Seitzei*.

28. See *Yaaros Devash*, *Derush* 2, 7*Adar*; *Derush* 3, 7*Adar*; *Derush* 12, *Hesped*.

Many suggest that the Patriarchs were wrong for not accepting Timnah, and for her efforts she merited a son like Amalek.

their religion.²⁹ They also wanted to destroy the Jewish nation because of the deep hatred that was part of their malevolent legacy.

Besides the desire for vengeance against the Jewish people, the Amalekite king also believed that it was politically critical for him to destroy them. He believed that he was the rightful heir to the land of Canaan, because Yitzchak should have given the blessings to Eisav, his firstborn son. He did not recognize Eisav's sale of his birthright as valid, claiming, as his grandfather had, that it was executed under false pretenses. Yaakov, he claimed, had swindled Eisav twice.³⁰

The reports of the vulnerabilities of the Jewish people in Refidim had given him great encouragement, but he was also a realist. He needed a coalition in order to be successful. He wanted the cooperation of the other nations in the region, who were also threatened by the advancing Jewish multitude, if he hoped to be successful. But he needed a plan.³¹

The Amalekite king turned to a celebrated soothsayer and wizard named Bilam for advice. Bilam had been a palace wizard and adviser to Pharaoh and a sworn enemy of the Jews. His advice had been instrumental in the enslavement of the Jewish people in Egypt. Now, the Amalekite king needed him to devise a plan of attack that would annihilate the Jewish people once and for all.³²

"Bilam, you come highly recommended," said the Amalekite king. "I have heard that your advice is virtually guaranteed to be effective. I want to annihilate the Jewish people, but it is apparently a highly risky venture. Look what happened to Egypt. How ungrateful those Jews are! After the Egyptians were so good to them and took them in during a deep famine, that is how they repay them? Can you imagine what they would do to us? Their G-d has

---

29. See *Malbim*.
30. *Malbim to Devarim* 25:18. See *Malbim* to *Beshalach* for a completely different view of Amalek's motivation to attack the Jewish people.
31. See *Sechel Tov* to *Beshalach*.
32. If the names "Bilam" and "Amalek" are added together, they equal 282, the same numerical value as "*b'mitzrayim*" (*Yalkut Reuveni*).

The name Bilam can be an acronym for the following words: *basar* (meat), *lechem* (bread), *etz* (tree), *mayim* (water). These were the very things the Jews complained about. This was one of the reasons the Jews were now being attacked. They complained about "meat," the "manna (bread)," the bitter water into which Moshe threw the "tree," and "water" when Moshe hit the rock at Masah U'Merivah (*Chasam Sofer*).

extraordinary powers. That is a great concern of ours. So we need your advice, Bilam. Can you help us?"³³

"Your majesty, if I may be so bold," said Bilam, "you have a serious problem on your hands, but you've come to the right place. I have experience dealing with them, and I know what makes them tick. The first step you have to take is to gather intelligence. Find out if their children are assembling in their classrooms to study Torah. That is the most powerful weapon in their arsenal, and I'm afraid you do not have any weapons that can neutralize it. But if they have become lax in Torah study, then you have a chance. After all, you are also a descendant of Avraham, and you can call on his merit to work on your behalf."

"We're one step ahead of you, Bilam," said the Amalekite king. "We already have the reports you suggested, and I'm happy to tell you that the Jews have become very lax in Torah study and their observance of the mitzvos also leaves a lot to be desired. As for their prayer, not much to talk about."³⁴

"Excellent, excellent," said Bilam. "You are a man after my own heart. We will do great things together."

"Thank you. So what's the next step?"

"The next step, if I may be so bold, is to put together a lethal offense. Inform your neighboring nations about our discussions and persuade them to join the coalition once again. They have nothing to fear. Mobilize your armies, and make sure you have a large representation of sorcerers, wizards and magicians. Place people celebrating their birthdays in the front lines, because people don't usually die on their birthdays. You may look at this as an astrological superstition, but trust me, it is well tested and widely accepted. Oh yes, and one more thing. Have your stargazers identify people who are fated to live through the rest of the year. Send those people to the front lines as well, so that even if the fighting gets fast and furious, with no clear victory, your soldiers will not be killed."

---

33. *Mechilta* to *Beshalach*; *Esther Rabbah* 7:13.

Some suggest that all Amalek wanted to do was to weaken them physically so they would not be a threat to the other nations, but not necessarily to wipe them out (see *Yefei Anaf*).

34. See *Bereishis Rabbah* 65:20; *Esther Rabbah* 7:13; *Ruth Rabbah Pesikta* 3:4.

There would be a sense of irony in that it would be Bilam himself who would end up blessing the Jews and cursing Amalek, stating they were destined to fall mightily for being the first nation to attack the Jewish people after they left Egypt. See *Shemos Rabbah* 27:3; *Bamidbar* 24:20.

"Consider it done," said the Amalekite king. "Anything else?"

"Yes. Attack the Jewish camp at the point where you will find the least faithful Jews. That is where you can make a breakthrough."[35]

"Go fight the Jews," said Bilam. "You will succeed. The Jewish people are protected by the merit of their ancestor Avraham, but you are also a descendant of Avraham. So your merit cancels out theirs. They apparently do not have the merit of Torah and mitzvos now either. Furthermore, as a descendant of Eisav, in my opinion, you have a distinct advantage over the descendants of Yaakov. Don't forget that Yaakov's sons sold their brother Yosef into slavery. That was not such a nice thing to do. So the advantage is yours. The time is ripe. You will attack and destroy them."[36]

Following Bilam's advice, the Amalekite king once again called a conference of the neighboring nations for the purpose of forming a coalition, but they were still reluctant to join. They were terrified of the G-d of the Jews and feared that they would suffer the same fate as the Egyptians.

"I will make you a proposal," said the Amalekite king. "Here is what I suggest. We will form a coalition and attack the Jews. If the battle seems to be going against us, then you can all retire from the field and leave my army to suffer defeat by itself. And if the battle goes well, then stay with us and share in the spoils. You are not exposing yourselves to risk. We're the ones who will be taking the risk."[37]

Five of the neighboring nations were swayed by his proposition and joined the coalition. It was agreed that Amalek's army would man the southern flank of the coalition forces, because Amalek's lands were located in the southernmost part of the region. Assured of and emboldened by the assurances of support from their neighbors, the Amalekites set off for the front without waiting for them to bring their armies forward.

---

35. *Meam Loez* to *Beshalach*; *Esther Rabbah* 7; see *Yalkut Reuveni*; *Rabbeinu Bachya* to *Shemos* 17:9; *Yerushalmi Rosh Hashanah* 3:8; *Yotzer* to *Parashas Zachor*; see *Tanchuma Tetzaveh* 9; *Beshalach* 28; *Mechilta*; *Yalkut* 2:364; *Midrash HaChefetz* to *Shemos* 17:9.

36. *Esther Rabbah* 7; *Yalkut Beshalach* 262.

As noted, Amalek is also an acronym of the names: Amram, Moshe, Levi, Kehas. Amalek thought that this indicated that he had the ability to overcome the Jewish people whose leaders descended from the tribe of Levi (*Yalkut HaEzuvi*).

37. See *Esther Rabbah* 7; *Mechilta*; *Tanchuma Beshalach* 25; *Tanchuma Ki Seitzei*.

See *Zayis Raanan* and *Netziv* for the logic behind it.

They gathered an army of one million soldiers, many of them sorcerers, wizards, magicians and other practitioners of the occult. Most of the soldiers also had their birthdays on the day the fighting was to take place. The Amalekite army stormed across the desert in a northerly direction, covering 400 *parsahs* and reaching the Jewish encampment in the space of a single day, a most miraculous achievement.[38]

The Assault Begins

On 29 Iyar, Amalek began its assault on the Jewish people.[39] The Amalekite armies did not attempt to probe the Jewish defenses and set up ambushes and deceptive maneuvers. Nor did they send the Jewish people a declaration of war, as was the custom among nations. Consumed by hatred and an arrogant confidence in their own abilities, the Amalekites launched a surprise, unprovoked frontal assault. The Amalekites were a terrifying sight, charging across the desert as they brandished their swords and spears in the air. They flashed toward the Jewish encampment like a relentless tidal wave of carnage.[40]

---

38. *Mechilta; Targum Yonasan* to *Shemos* 17:8; *Tanchuma Beshalach* 25; *Etz Yosef; Sefer HaYashar; Divrei HaYamim LeMoshe* in *Otzar Midrashim* 261; *Ibn Ezra* to *Shemos* 17:8; *Yotzer* to *Parashas Zachor*.

According to some, it was over 900 miles that they traveled overnight, a miraculous feat. According to others, it was 1,200 miles.

According to some interpretations, Amalek amassed an army of 18 million people; according to others it was an army that totaled 400,000. See *Midrash Abba Gurion* 3 to *Megillas Esther*.

According to R' Aryeh Kaplan, Amalek could have been coming from the Arabian Peninsula, perhaps from Yemen or Medina.

39. *Panim Yafos Beshalach.*

See *Sefer Yetzirah* 1:43 who writes in the name of the *Ravad* that the war took place on the 10th of Av. Some suggest the discrepancy to be nothing more than mistaken print.

Amalek knew that the Jewish calendar follows the moon rather than the sun. Knowing that their astrological strength stems from that, he picked Erev Rosh Chodesh, a day when the moon cannot be seen, an omen he felt would help him in his fight against the Jews. In the end, the Jewish resistance uncharacteristically lasted until the following night, which was the month of Sivan when the new moon is present, and this gave the Jews the strength to prevail.

It is interesting to note that the 29th day of Iyar according to some opinions fell on Shabbos rather than Sunday. (This has major ramifications as to the date of *Matan Torah* the following week.) See *Bnei Yissaschar, Iyar Maamar* 1, who writes that the war took place in Iyar, but does not specify a date.

40. See *Mechilta; Abarbanel; HaKesav VeHaKabbalah* to *Beshalach; Sifri* to *Devarim* 25:17-19; *Midrash HaChefetz* to *Devarim* 25:18.

See *Imrei Noam* who writes that Amalek tried three times to slay the Jews. The first time was when he let Pharaoh know that the Jews were escaping Egypt. The second time was at the Yam Suf and the third time was now.

But how would they penetrate the protective shield of the cloud pillars that turned the Jewish encampment into an impregnable fortress?[41] And if they should somehow manage to get inside the cloud pillars, who knows if they would be able to escape in one piece.

Amalek had a plan. Amalekite agents had earlier obtained clay tablets from the Egyptian archives that documented the ancestry and lineage of every Jew.[42] Having familiarized themselves with this information, they went ahead, well in advance of the Amalekite army, and struck up friendships with various Jews. They engaged them in casual conversations and even offered them business opportunities and secure investments. Many Jews were impressed with the charm and wit of these alleged local merchants, and they accepted invitations to conduct further meetings at rendezvous points outside the cloud pillars.

The Jews who took this bait were, of course, those of little faith. The righteous, faithful Jews were not concerned with business opportunities. Why would they want to start businesses when Hashem was shielding them with cloud pillars and feeding them bread from the heavens and water from a rolling stone? Did He need their help in providing for their sustenance? So they spent their time studying the Torah and doing mitzvos, ignoring the blandishments of the unctuous Amalekites.

Those greedy Jews of little faith, however, ventured out of the cloud pillars in their quest for business opportunities, and the Amalekite army pounced on them like a swarm of locusts and slaughtered them.[43]

In addition to these greedy would-be entrepreneurs, there was no shortage of victims for the Amalekite attackers. Men who had not been circumcised, usually because of medical complications, were required to stay outside the cloud pillars, as were those who were ritually

---

This is a reference to the Torah's use of the word *zanav* (tail), for Amalek attacked the Jews from the tail end of their camp.

41. *Midrash HaChefetz* to *Devarim* 25:18.
42. See *Pesikta D'Rav Kahana* 3; *Pesikta Rabbasi* 12; *Tanchuma Ki Seitzei* 9.

The *Ohr HaChaim* says that just to find the Jews while they were hidden by the clouds was a difficult task by itself. It was only because of the Jews who were outside of the cloud's protection that Amalek knew where the Jews were camped at this time.

43. See *Lekach Tov*; *Sifsei Kohen Ki Seitzei*; *Tanchuma Ki Seitzei* 9.

impure.⁴⁴ The Erev Rav, who were spiritually weak, and other sinful Jews were also denied the privilege of living under the cloud pillars. These people were also physically debilitated, some of them bearing the lingering effects of their slave labor and all of them deprived of the full benefits of the manna and well water because of their sinful ways.⁴⁵

These unfortunate defenseless Jews had to pitch their tents on the outskirts of the encampment. Like a rock badger stalking its prey, the Amalekite army pounced on them without warning and slaughtered many and took many others hostage.⁴⁶

The tribe of Dan, although they lived inside the encampment, were not accorded the protection of the cloud pillars because a number of them were followers of "the idol of Michah." The Amalekites wreaked havoc on the people of Dan, killing and abducting many of them.⁴⁷

The wanton slaughter of defenseless Jews drove the Amalekites into blood frenzy. Many of the Amalekite soldiers were so intoxicated with bloodlust that they got down on their hands and knees like dogs and lapped up the blood of their victims.⁴⁸ In doing so, they proved true to their name Amalek, which can be read as *am lek*, a nation that licks, expressing their depravity by licking up Jewish blood with gruesome relish. Like blood-sucking flies and mosquitoes, they hovered over their slaughtered victims, their thirst for Jewish blood unsatisfied.⁴⁹

---

44. *Pesikta D'Rav Kahana; Abarbanel; Pirkei D'Rav Eliezer* 44; *Yedei Moshe* to *Bamidbar Rabbah* 13:3. See *Yevamos* 72a. See *She'elos U'Teshuvos Imrei Tzedek* 93.

45. *Sifri; Targum Yonasan* to *Devarim* 25:18; *Pirkei D'Rav Eliezer* 44.
   Many of them were still weak and unable to fight due to the residual effect of the harsh labor in Egypt and the travels in the desert (see *Targum Yonasan and Rabbeinu Bachya* to *Devarim* 25:18).
   The manna contained nutrients and vitamins only when it was joined with the learning of Torah. These sinners who rejected Hashem were thus weakened physically because there was nothing in their bodies to give them strength. See *Rabbeinu Bachya; Sifsei Kohen* to *Devarim* 25:18.

46. *Tosafos* to *Shemos* 17:9; *Pesikta Rabbah* 12; *Pesikta D'Rav Kahana* 3; *Chemdas Yamim*.

47. *Mechilta; Sechel Tov; Targum Yonasan* to *Shemos* 17:8; *Pesikta D'Rav Kahana* 3; *Lekach Tov; Targum Yonasan* to *Devarim* 25:18; *Targum* to *Shir HaShirim Rabbah* 2:15.
   The Torah uses the word *nechshalim* to describe the weakened condition of the Jewish people. Dan, weakened by the sin of idol worship, was compared to a snake (*nachash*) in the blessings of Yaakov. The Torah alluded that the Jews weakened by sin were *nechshalim*, those of the *nachash*, a reference to Dan (*Nachal Kadmonim*).

48. See *Tanchuma Yashan Yisro* 4; *Mechilta; Zohar; Tanchuma Ki Seitzei* 9; *Pesikta D'Rav Kahana* 3.

49. See *Pesikta D'Rav Kahana* 3 p. 26; *Tanchuma Ki Seitzei* 9; *Chemdas Yamim; Kli Yakar* to *Beshalach*.
   Also *am yelek*, a nation swift like the locust called *yelek*. Others make reference to Amalek as a bear (*R' Efraim Al HaTorah*). Others, as a sneaky snake (*Zohar Bereishis*).

Then they mutilated and castrated the bodies, hurling the signs of circumcision into the air and shouting with cruel mockery, "Take back what belongs to you!" Their hatred of the Jews was so deep that they wanted to eradicate them physically and spiritually; they could not bear the sight of the signs of Jewish identity.[50] They also taunted and molested the dazed male survivors, thereby polluting the Jewish people.[51]

Most nations go to war for conventional reasons, but none of these seemed to apply to Amalek's war against the Jews. Were they looking to capture land? The Jews did not have a homeland. Were they looking to defend their own territory from attack? The Jews had no designs on Amalekite lands. Were they retaliating against a hostile nation? The Jews had never attacked or even threatened them. Was their intent to show off their military prowess? There was no military feat in attacking defenseless civilians. Did they do it for the glory of their gods? The Amalekites were a godless people.[52]

What did the Amalekites want to accomplish by this treacherous war? They wanted to challenge the Jewish faith in Hashem, to undermine His credibility and prove His ineffectiveness, and they wanted to vent their ancient hatred for the Jewish people and wreak their vengeance on them.[53]

The Amalekites had followed Bilam's advice. Their soldiers seemed invincible, especially since their victims were defenseless. Despite their great numbers, the Jewish people had no army, no soldiers to stand against the advancing Amalekite army. The situation was desperate. Something had to be done. And quickly.

Counterattack on Two Fronts

The Jewish people had reached a moment of truth. The Amalekite invasion was moving forward inexorably, and the casualties were mounting. They realized that their persistent lack of faith and trust had made them unworthy of having Hashem fight their battles, as He had done against the Egyptians; they could not rely on a pure miracle. Their

---

50. See *Rashi and Gur Aryeh* to *Devarim* 25:17-19. He did this only to the Jews who did not have a *bris milah* (*Yedei Moshe* to *Bamidbar Rabbah* 13:3). See *Tanna D'Vei Eliyahu Rabbah* 24 about how Amalek's ancestor Eisav deplored the very essence of *bris milah*.
51. See *Rashi* to *Devarim* 25:17-19.
52. *Malbim; Abarbanel,* end of *Beshalach*.
53. *Malbim; Beis HaLevi*.

only chance was to fight as any other army would fight, without resorting to the supernatural, while at the same time they would pray intensely to Hashem and reaffirm their faith in Him. Perhaps He would guide the battle so that its outcome would be in their favor.[54]

In addition, Moshe concluded that the war against Amalek needed to be fought on two fronts — on earth and in heaven. He would have to devise a strategy for a physical war of defense that would not rely on miracles. And he would have to mount a spiritual war of defense against the avenging angels that were taking the Amalekite side in heaven.[55]

Moshe summoned his disciple Yehoshua to his tent and explained his idea.[56] "You and I, Yehoshua, will divide the responsibilities between ourselves. I will conduct the battle above, and you must lead the battle below. Time is running out. We have to assemble an army right away. I will leave the generalship in your capable hands."[57]

Yehoshua wondered why he had been chosen for this position. Why not Aharon or Moshe's nephew Chur, the son of Calev and Miriam? Or why not one of the seventy elders of the Jewish people? Surely, he thought, any of these people was on a higher spiritual level and more qualified than he. But it did not occur to him to argue with his teacher and master. He simple nodded and remained silent.[58]

"You have to understand, Yehoshua, that although we are going to fight a natural war here on earth, we need to rely on Divine assistance. So it will not be enough to choose men adept at fighting. We need faithful, righteous men of good and noble lineage who fear Hashem and accept the vicissitudes of life without the kind of whining and complaining we have unfortunately seen the past few weeks.[59] Their merit and the merit of their ancestors will protect them in battle and bring victory to our people."[60]

---

54. *Abarbanel; Ramban* to *Bamidbar* 24:20.
55. See *Zohar* 65b; *Malbim; Levush Orah*.
   This angel, known as Sama-el, is known as the accusing angel of evil and death. Amalek and this angel have the same numeric value (240/241) (*Sifsei Kohen*).
56. See *Lekach Tov* to *Shemos* 24:13 and *Ramban* to *Shemos* 17:9 as to the reason why Moshe refers to him as Yehoshua when at the present he was called Hoshea and was not named Yehoshua until more than a year later.
57. *Zohar*.
58. See *Tanchuma Yashan Yisro; Zohar*.
59. See *Mechilta; Rashi* to *Beshalach*; R' *Avraham Ben HaRambam* to *Shemos* 17:9; *Shemos Rabbah* 26:3; *Zohar* 65b.
60. *Mechilta; Akeidah* to *Shemos* 17:9.

"I understand," said Yehoshua.

"At the same time," Moshe continued, "we cannot forget that we are fighting on the battlefield. We need strong, mighty warriors, men of bravery and courage.[61] We also need people with a good understanding of divination, witchcraft and sorcery so that they will be able to counter Amalek's occult powers, which are state of the art, according to what I hear. I would suggest we find people born in Adar Sheni, the supplementary month of leap years. They are not under the influence of any of the signs of the Zodiac and are therefore impervious to the Amalekite magic spells. I believe we have a total of 16,000 men born during Adar Sheni.[62] As for the total strength of the army, the number of defenders should be comparable to the number of attackers."[63]

"How will we find the men?" asked Yehoshua. "Is it my responsibility? I'm afraid that if I turn people down they will be offended, taking it as a judgment of their righteousness or their physical abilities, which it is. And what if I had judged them incorrectly?"

"Do not be concerned, Yehoshua," said Moshe. "I will choose the men for the army, and I will leave the fighting to you."[64]

"Thank you," said Yehoshua. "When will the battle be joined?"

"The battle will be joined tomorrow, not today," Moshe replied.[65] "Today, I will announce a day of fasting tomorrow for all the Jewish

---

61. *Mechilta; Lekach Tov; Rashi* to *Shemos* 17:9. See *Pirkei D'Rav Eliezer* 44.
62. *Mechilta; Rashi; Chizkuni* to *Shemos* 17:9; *Hashmatos* to *Torah Shleimah*.

The word *"bochar,"* meaning choose, has the same numerical value as the word *v'Adar*, 210/211 (*Yalkut HaEzuvi*). It is interesting to note that Haman, a descendant of Amalek, also believed in the powers that the month of Adar assumed to overpower the Jewish people.

63. *Chizkuni; Tosafos* to *Shemos* 17:9.

Although one source suggests that Amalek had an army of one million people, which the Jewish people clearly could not match, some suggest that the 16,000 applied to the people whose birthday fell on that day to counter this weapon Amalek used.

64. *Abarbanel*.
65. *Mechilta; Sifsei Chachamim; Maharal* to *Shemos* 17:9; *Yoma* 52b with *Rashi* and *Tosafos*. See *Abarbanel*.

Many question the Torah's use of the word "tomorrow." There is no question that Moshe indicated to Yehoshua that the following day he would ascend the mountain. The question however was if the battle would begin tomorrow or would begin immediately. The *Chasam Sofer* suggests, based on the *"esnachta"* (a punctuation mark used in the Torah, similar to a comma) placed in *Shemos* 17:9 preceding the word *"machar,"* that the war would begin today and that the ascension would take place tomorrow. Others as well use that logic, while others disagree by sighting proof that the *esnachta* is not a decisive factor in determining the interpretation of a specific text. As is the case in all my work, I offer objective views on all opinions, and I have chosen not to be decisive in this matter but rather offer the various opinions on the subject.

people. Today, it is too late, since many have already eaten. Tomorrow, we will fast and fight.[66] Also, the Amalekites have probably filled their ranks with people whose birthday is today. Tomorrow, they will not have that advantage.[67] Besides, I understand through *ruach hakodesh*, Divine inspiration, that Amalek will be vulnerable tomorrow but not today."[68]

"Where will you be during the fighting?"

"While you are fighting with Amalek," Moshe replied, "I will ascend Mount Chorev. From there, I will fight the spiritual battle above."[69]

The Perfect Choice

Yehoshua was 57 years old when Moshe appointed him to the generalship. Moshe had chosen well.[70]

A member of the tribe of Ephraim, the son of Yosef, Yehoshua was descended from a family with a military tradition. Yosef's descendants were not subjected to slave labor in Egypt, but they were nonetheless confined to the land and not permitted to leave. Thirty years before the exodus, the tribe of Ephraim tried to break out of Egyptian captivity, with disastrous results.

The word *machar* has the numerical value of 248, the same value as Avraham. In his merit, tomorrow they would prevail (*Tosafos*).

66. See *Mechilta*; *Targum Yonasan* to *Shemos* 17:9; *Mishnas R' Eliezer* 284; *Chemdas Yamim*; *Chasam Sofer*; *Midrash Biyur*.

It is interesting to consider what happened on a day of fasting regarding the falling of the manna. Some propose that it fell as usual because of those who were not fasting, such as the weak, the sick and children. In addition, the manna would have to be collected so that when the fast broke, they would eat their evening meal as usual.

67. See *Chemdas Yamim*.

The word *machar* has the same letters as the word *racheim*, which means mercy. Tomorrow would be a day that would be merciful for the Jewish people.

Others simply suggest that the Jewish people needed a full day to reach the Amalekite camp and attack them (*Abarbanel Ki Seitzei*).

68. See *Menoras HaMaor*; see *Rashi* to *I Shmuel* 30:17; *Yalkut Reuveni*.

When Esther wanted a party that would include Haman (leading to his eventual downfall), she chose to do it on the following day, "tomorrow," because she learned this from Moshe. Haman, a descendant of Amalek, was vulnerable on the morrow as Amalek would be now (*Panim Acherim*). (See *Let My Nation Live* p. 250 fn. 16.)

69. *Mechilta*.

70. *Yalkut Reuveni Beshalach*. See *Ibn Ezra* to *Shemos* 33:11 who writes that he was 56. All agree that Yehoshua was 110 when he died. (Add to 56 the 40 years he spent in the desert and the 14 years he led the people in the conquest and distribution of the land — and the total is 110.) Others suggest that he ruled for 28 years which would mean he was 42 at this time. Still others suggest he was a *"nuar,"* a young man of 35. See *Seder Olam Rabbah* 12; *Yalkut Shimoni Yehoshua*.

They mustered an army of several hundred thousand, but almost all of them were killed in battle with the Philistines. There were only ten survivors. According to some, the general of this Ephraimite army was none other than Nun, Yehoshua's father.[71]

Jewish tradition maintained that the descendants of Yosef are best equipped to combat the descendants of Eisav. Yosef is compared to a flame and Eisav to straw. Flame consumes straw. Therefore, Yehoshua would consume Amalek.[72]

Furthermore, the descendants of Yosef had inherited the birthright Yaakov had purchased from Eisav, and they were also the custodians of the blessings Yaakov had received from his father Yitzchak. It was only logical that Yehoshua, the rightful owner of the birthright, go up against the Amalekite usurper who was trying to reclaim it.[73] Also, Amalek had counted on having an advantage over the descendants of Yaakov because his sons had sold their brother Yosef into slavery. But Yosef, of course, did not share that guilt.[74]

Yehoshua, as a descendant of Yosef, also had another advantage over Amalek. Yosef had asked that his remains be removed from Egypt and transported to Canaan, indicating that he believed in the resurrection of the dead. Eisav, however, had readily sold his birthright, because he was afraid he might die and then his birthright would not do him any good.[75]

Astrologically, Yehoshua was also in an advantageous position. Having been born in Iyar gave him an advantage in a battle that would be fought in Iyar against witchcraft and astrological

---

71. See *Sifsei Kohen* to *Shemos* 14:3; *I Divrei HaYamim* 7:21; *Yalkut* on *Divrei HaYamim* 1077; commentaries to *Tehillim* 80:3. See *Let My Nation Go* pp. 97-98.
72. *Aggadas Esther*; *Sechel Tov Beshalach*; *Pesikta D'Rav Kahana* 3 p. 21. See *Anaf Yosef* to *Esther Rabbah* 7. See *Ovadiah* 1.
73. See *Bava Basra* 123b with *Maharsha*; *Yalkut Shimoni Shoftim* 51.
74. *Yalkut Shimoni Shoftim* 51.
   In addition to this, each of Yaakov's children had a shortcoming so they could not serve as a merit on behalf of the Jews. Reuven desecrated the bed of his father, Shimon and Levi were guilty for their attack on Shechem. Yehudah had the obstacle of Tamar standing in his way and the remaining children of Yaakov were guilty of selling Yosef. Binyamin, who did not sell Yosef, had the pending doom of *pilegesh b'Givah* looming. This left only the Tribe of Yosef who could stand tall to merit a defense against Amalek (*Tanchuma Ki Seitzei* 10).
   Further reasons included the fact that Yosef protected his mother when facing Eisav. Yosef wanted to know if his father was alive after revealing himself to his brothers, while Eisav, by thinking *"yikrevu yemei avel avi* — may the days of mourning for my father draw near,"indicated that he was waiting for his father to die.
75. *Yalkut Shimoni Shoftim* 51.

weapons. The astrological sign for Iyar is an ox, which is also the symbol for Yosef, further reinforcing the connection.[76]

Finally, despite his own humble opinion of himself, Yehoshua was a man of extraordinary righteousness and piety, and on this measure alone, he was an excellent choice.[77]

There was also a strong practical reason for the selection of Yehoshua as the commanding general of the army. Yehoshua was the heir apparent to Moshe's position as leader of the nation. He would eventually wage the war of conquest against the thirty kings of Canaan and annihilate them. Moshe therefore wanted to give him some valuable experience in the art of warfare.[78]

The choice of Yehoshua also shielded Moshe from direct confrontation with Amalek. Moshe was the greatest leader in the world, the one who had destroyed the Egyptians before the astonished eyes of the entire world, and Amalek would have liked nothing more than to defeat him. It would be a great boost to their pride and status among their neighbors and a blow to the honor of Hashem. By choosing Yehoshua to lead the army, Moshe was pulling the rug out from under the feet of the Amalekites. If they won, Heaven forbid, they would only have beaten a neophyte general, and if they should lose even to Yehoshua, their humiliation in defeat would only be that much greater.[79]

War on Two Fronts

With the battle raging on the outskirts of the encampment, Moshe sent out an urgent call to all the people to take it upon themselves to fast the following day in preparation for the great battle that loomed before them. The merit of the fast day and the repentance and faith it would inspire would stand the Jewish army in good stead in their struggle against the villainous Amalekites.[80] The people were in an uproar. Gone were the arro-

---

76. *Rokeach* to *Shemos* 17:10.
77. *Zohar* 65b; *Malbim*.
    See *Yaaros Devash* and his reasoning as to why Moshe felt he was unfit to battle Amalek.
78. *Pesikta Rabbah* 13; *Tanchuma Yashan Yisro*; *Shemos Rabbah* 26:3. See *Malbim*.
79. *Abarbanel*; *Sifsei Kohen*.
80. See *Zohar* 65b; *Ramban*.
    Victory or defeat had long-term effects beyond this war. Celestially speaking, the battle of merits between the children of Yitzchak was now being waged. A victory for Amalek would mean that the merit of Eisav overpowered the merit of Yaakov and would have great ramifications for the Jews throughout their history. (See *Ramban*.)

gant demonstrations and rebellious talk that had resulted from earlier crises. With the Amalekites on their doorstep, they knew that their backs were against the wall, that only Hashem could save them. Humbled and contrite, they gravely resolved to fast and pray for a speedy Jewish victory.[81]

By dawn the following day, the Jewish army was assembled and ready to join battle with the Amalekites. As they lined up in formation under the watchful eye of Yehoshua, their general, Moshe, accompanied by his brother Aharon and his nephew Chur, was already on his way to Mount Chorev, otherwise known as Mount Sinai, after speaking words of reassurance to Yehoshua.[82] It was Moshe's task to purify and enhance "the voice of Yaakov" so that it would triumph over "the hands of Eisav."[83]

Just days earlier, Moshe had climbed this selfsame mountainside and extracted water from a stone for the Jewish people. This was the selfsame mountainside where Moshe had witnessed the burning bush and spoken with Hashem. This was the selfsame mountainside where the Jewish people would receive the Torah.[84] It was an exceedingly holy place, the holiest place on the face of the earth. On this sacred site, Moshe would call on the merit of the great events that had taken place in the past and would take place in the future.[85] On this sacred spot, Moshe would pray in utmost purity for the deliverance of the Jewish people from their implacable enemies.

The presence of Aharon, the future Kohen, and Chur, the descendant of the royal line of Yehudah, would contribute additional merit to Moshe's spiritual battle.[86]

---

81. *Alshich* to *Shemos* 17:9.
82. This would act as a symbolic merit to prevail over Amalek. The Jewish people received three gifts through Moshe, Aharon and Miriam. Through Moshe they received the manna. Through Aharon they received the Clouds of Glory and through Miriam the Well of water. Chur was the son of Miriam. (See *Divrei HaYamim* 2:18 with *Targum*.) The end letters of Moshe, Aharon and Miriam — *hei, nun, mem* — spell the word Haman. This symbolized that they would triumph over the forefather of Haman — Amalek (*Maharal*).
83. *Alshich* to *Shemos* 17:9.
84. *Ibn Ezra; Aruch; Ibn Ezra HaKatzar; Abarbanel* to *Shemos* 17:9.
85. *Rokeach; Abarbanel*.
86. *Pesikta Rabbah* 12; *Ibn Ezra* to *Shemos* 17:9. See *Pirkei D'Rav Eliezer* 44.
   The team fighting Amalek consisted of Aharon, Chur, Yehoshua and Moshe. The first letters of their names spell the word *"achim"* (brothers). David HaMelech alludes to this in *Tehillim* when he states, "How good and how pleasant is the dwelling of (*achim*) brothers in unity" (*Tehillim* 133; *Yalkut Reuveni*).

Mount Chorev, as the eternal symbol for Torah, also served as a subtle reminder to the Jewish people that they had brought this calamity upon themselves by their indifference to the Torah. This would lead them to repent and strengthen their faith in Hashem.[87]

Moshe brought along with him his reliable staff, the one he had used to bring the plagues upon the Egyptians, to split open the sea and to extract water from the stone. The staff would serve a dual purpose on the mountaintop. He would brandish it aloft like a battle flag, a sign of confidence and assurance to the fighting men that the tide of battle was running in their favor. Like a fist raised in triumphant victory, it would bolster the morale of the soldiers, strengthen their faith and empower them in prayer and battle.[88] In a different capacity altogether, Moshe would use the staff as a supernatural weapon and rain down plagues, pestilence and destruction on the heads of the Amalekites.[89]

He began his spiritual campaign against the Amalekites by invoking the meritorious memory of Avraham, Yitzchak and Yaakov, the Patriarchs of the Jewish people, and Sarah, Rivkah, Rachel and Leah, the Matriarchs.[90] Then he raised his hands, one empty and one holding his staff, the right hand somewhat higher than the left.[91]

"Master of the Universe!" he cried out. "In the merit of these hands that performed miracles and wonders in Your honor and accepted nothing in return, let this staff that worked wonders in bringing the people forth from Egypt, this staff that split the sea, that brought the quail and manna from the heavens, that drew water from a stone, let this staff work wonders for the Jewish people and help them prevail in the battle today."[92]

Far below, the Jewish people in the encampment watched in awe as Moshe prayed on the mountaintop. Those in the thick of the battle found new reservoirs of courage and faith and were inspired to fight like lions. Those behind the lines were inspired to pray, following their leader step by step. When Moshe knelt, they

---

87. *Alshich.*
88. See *Chizkuni; Rashbam; Bechor Shor; Sforno; Sechel Tov; Tur; Abarbanel.*
    See *Let My Nation Go* p. 328.
89. *Ramban.*
90. *Zohar; Pesikta Rabbah* 12. This is explained in the context of the words "*Vayehi yadav emunah* — and he remained with his hands in faithful prayer."
91. *Mechilta; Zohar.* This was similar to the laws regarding the Kohanim raising their hands when blessing the people, in that the right hand must be raised higher than the left hand.
92. *Mechilta D'Rashbi.*

knelt, and when he prostrated himself, they did too.[93] The prayers of the people and their renewed faith made them worthy of miracles, and the tide began to turn in their favor.[94]

Many years earlier, Yitzchak had blessed Eisav, saying, "*Al charbecha tichyeh* — You will live by your sword." Now Eisav's Amalekite descendants were attacking the Jewish people with their swords to devastating effect. But Moshe's hands and the response they elicited from the Jewish people were a powerful weapon in their own right, a weapon of prayer strong enough to counteract the sword of Eisav.[95] The hands played a very important part in the composition of this weapon of prayer. Eisav had used his hands to serve his father Yitzchak, while Yaakov had disguised his hands with animal fur in order to secure the birthright. By using his hands for prayer, Moshe reclaimed the power of the hands, and the Jewish people could now use their hands to destroy Amalek.[96]

From time to time, Moshe's hands would tire slightly, and he would raise one hand and lower the other, laying the staff on the ground temporarily.[97] This fatigue, however, was not physical in nature. His strength ebbed and flowed with the level of faith among the Jewish people. Many Jews continued to be weak in their faith in Hashem, putting their future instead in Moshe's hands and causing them to become heavy. Other Jews of stronger faith put their future in Hashem's hands, easing the burden on Moshe's hands and allowing him to lift them up in prayer.[98]

As the day wore on, however, Moshe began to tire. He was fasting and standing on his feet since sunrise. His hands and feet grew heavy, and he felt as if he were holding heavy barrels or poles in his arms.[99] Although the level of the people's prayer was high at times, Moshe's fatigue persisted, because it was in retribution for his

---

93. *Pirkei D'Rav Eliezer* 44; *Ramban*.
94. *Mechilta; Chemas HaChemdah; R' Avraham Ben HaRambam* to *Shemos* 17:11.
95. *Alshich*. See *Mabit*.
   It would also be the merit of these hands holding up the *Luchos* that would allow the Jewish people to prevail.
96. *Tzeror HaMor Beshalach*.
   In addition, while Eisav honored his father, Yaakov did not do so for twenty-two years (*Meam Loez*).
97. See *R' Avraham Ben HaRambam; Lekach Tov; Alshich*.
98. *Zohar; Alshich; Malbim Beshalach; Menachem Meishiv Nefesh; Maharsha* to *Rosh Hashanah* 29a.
99. *Mechilta; Lekach Tov; Targum Yonasan; Pesikta Rabbah; Tanchuma Beshalach* 27. See

delaying the battle against the Amalekites until the following day. Despite his good motives, he should not have done so.[100] He also should not have distanced himself completely from the physical battle, leaving everything in the hands of Yehoshua.[101] Worst of all, Moshe had advocated for allowing the Erev Rav, who were a major cause of sinfulness, to accompany the Jewish people. In a sense, then, he bore some responsibility for the Amalekite attack.[102]

The fatigue that caused Moshe's hands to feel so heavy had significant consequences for the Jewish people. They controlled the ebb and flow of the spiritual battle. As long as he was able to keep his hands steady in the air, the Jewish people would be inspired to strengthen their faith and pray to Hashem, and they would be victorious. But when Moshe's hands sank with heaviness, the faith of the people would diminish, and the tide would turn in favor of the Amalekites.[103]

In order to help Moshe keep his hands aloft regardless of his fatigue as the battle raged below, Aharon and Chur took up positions on either side of Moshe, Aharon to his right and Chur to his left, to support his hands and keep them from dropping down.[104]

There was a slight problem, however. Since Moshe was ten cubits tall, Aharon and Chur could not reach Moshe's hands when he held them aloft.[105] There was also a second problem in that Moshe's legs were also tiring, and he was finding it difficult to remain standing.[106] Aharon and Chur solved these problems by bringing a large rock on which Moshe could sit. This immediately relieved the pressure on Moshe's legs, and it also lowered his hands so that Aharon and Chur

---

Ibn Ezra; Chizkuni.

Some suggest specifically three barrels of water. This was an illusion to the sin of the *Mei Merivah*, where the Jewish people complained about their lack of water.

See *Rabbeinu Bachya* and his reference to Kohanim not being allowed to bless the people for more than three hours.

100. *Zohar* 278b; *Mechilta; Sechel Tov; Targum Yonasan* to *Shemos* 17:12.

101. See *Mechilta; Targum Yonasan; Rashi; Lekach Tov* to *Shemos* 17:12.

Hashem judges the righteous with great exactness. No one would argue that all of Moshe's reasoning and decisions about how to fight Amalek were correct, but quite often, the righteous are judged with such minute detail that at times we cannot understand the wrongdoing of something that appears to be the proper path of action.

102. See *Meam Loez.*

103. *Mechilta; Ramban; Mishnah Rosh Hashanah* 3:8; *Rosh Hashanah* 29a with *Maharsha.*

Moshe's hands also symbolized the potential triumph or defeat of the Torah they would receive in just a few days (*Mechilta*).

104. *Rabbeinu Bachya; Radal* to *Pirkei D'Rav Eliezer* 44.

105. *Minchah Belulah; Kesef Mezukak* to *Shemos* 17:12.

106. *Ralbag; Tur; R' Avraham Ben HaRambam; Rokeach.*

could prop them up and keep them aloft.¹⁰⁷ Their help provided Moshe some relief, and at the same time, he prayed for additional stamina in the merit of the Patriarchs and Matriarchs.¹⁰⁸

It would have been more appropriate and respectful for a great leader such as Moshe to sit on a cushion or stool rather than on a bare rock.¹⁰⁹ But Moshe would not hear of it. Down below, the people were fighting for their lives, some dying and some falling wounded in the battlefield. Behind the lines, the people were fasting and overwhelmed with anxiety. Moshe wanted to share their pain and stress. Later, he would share in their redemption.¹¹⁰ In addition, the rock was a symbol of the *Luchos* Moshe would receive, and Moshe wanted this symbol to work in favor of the Jewish people.¹¹¹

The battle raged as the day drew to a close. Moshe had been successful in thwarting the Amalekite onslaught, but they were far from destroyed. A whole phalanx of Amalekite wizards, sorcerers and astrologers worked feverishly in the rear echelons to bring their powers to bear against the Jewish people, calculating the time they would be most vulnerable according to the alignment of the stars and constellations. They awaited the rapid approach of night with great eagerness, because the nighttime was more suited for astrological readings. In additions, the Amalekites with birthdays on that day were proving difficult to kill.¹¹²

Time did not seem to be on the side of the Jewish people. But Moshe was not to be denied. He raised his hands and waved them about in all directions until the sun stopped in its path, and the approach of night was postponed. All calculations of time and astrological readings were completely disrupted.¹¹³ Later Moshe told Yehoshua that he had blazed the way for him and that someday he too would halt the sun in its path. This would happen forty years later at Yericho, during the conquest of Canaan.¹¹⁴

---

107. See *R' Saadiah Gaon; Zayis Raanan; Rashbam; Chizkuni.* See *Maaseh Hashem* for his view.
108. *Mechilta; Hadar Zekeinim.*
109. *Mechilta; Rashi* to *Shemos* 17:12; *Pirkei D'Rav Eliezer* 44. See *Pesikta Rabbah* who writes that this would eventually be a merit for Esther to prevail over Haman.
110. See *Taanis* 11a; *Rashi; Mechilta; Tanchuma* 28.
111. *Tosafos* to *Shemos* 17:12. "*Even*" (stone) has the numerical value of 53, the number of *Parshiyos* in the Torah.
112. See *Midrash HaChefetz; Rashi* to *Shemos* 17:12.
113. *Tanchuma Tetzaveh* 9; *Beshalach* 28; *Mechilta; Rabbeinu Bachya; Yerushalmi Rosh Hashanah* 3:8; *Yalkut* 2:564; *Midrash HaChefetz* to *Shemos* 17:12; *Tosafos* to *Shemos* 17:9,11. See *Yehoshua* 10:12,13.
114. See *Yehoshua* 10:12,13.

The Amalekite wizards, sorcerers and astrologers were thrown into a panic. Desperately, they scribbled and scratched out new divinations and formulae to reactivate their spells, but they were ineffective. All they accomplished through their efforts was to levitate a few hundred Amalekite soldiers into the air beyond harm's way. But Moshe quickly counteracted these spells, and the floating Amalekites plummeted to the ground and were killed.[115] Then Moshe turned their powers on them and bombarded them with plagues, pestilence and destruction.[116] At this moment, the prosecuting angel in Heaven tried to come to the assistance of Amalek, but Moshe restrained it with his great powers.[117]

The battle was now turning decisively in favor of the Jewish people. The Amalekites were weakening. Moshe's spiritual battle was taking effect, but perhaps more important, the merit of his effort and suffering on behalf of the Jewish people would bring them ultimate victory.[118]

On the battlefield, Yehoshua followed Moshe's instructions and brought his forces out from the protection of the cloud pillars and into the open; no arrows or missiles were fired while they were still within the cloud pillars.[119] Since the Jewish army was outnumbered, Yehoshua realized that it would be best to concentrate his firepower on those Amalekites who were not destined to survive the battle for various reasons, but by just surveying the enemy he could not tell which soldiers were the most vulnerable to attack. Therefore, he cast lots to determine which Amalekites were to be killed and which were invulnerable to death but could be incapacitated.[120]

---

115. See *Taama D'Kra*.
116. *Ramban; Esther Rabbah* 7:13.
117. *Chemdas Yamim; Minchah Belulah Beshalach*.
  Some suggest this was the *yetzer hara*; others suggest that it was the angel Matat, or Sama-el. In either case, Moshe could not defeat him. The angel would torment the Jews until they would repent. His defeat would come in the time of Mashiach and would be followed by the defeat of Amalek once and for all.
118. *Pesikta Rabbah* 12.
119. *Mechilta; Targum Yonasan; Rashi; Ibn Ezra; Zayis Raanan* to *Shemos* 17:9.
  Depending on how one looks at it, Chorev and Refidim were very close. The Jewish camp was so big that the far end of one portion of the camp actually neighbored Refidim (*Ibn Ezra HaKatzar* 17:9).
120. *Pirkei D'Rav Kahana* 3; *Tanchuma Yashan Yisro; Yalkut* 265; *Zayis Raanan*.
  This was an allusion to the great miracle where lots played a major role in the destruction of Haman, a descendant of Amalek.

The assault began in an orderly fashion. The Jewish soldiers penetrated the Amalekite defenses and decimated the Amalekites. Assisted by the hands of Moshe high on the mountaintop, the Jewish soldiers methodically demolished the enemy, inflicting heavy casualties on the finest Amalekite battalions, leaving the Amalekites in disarray and essentially defenseless.[121]

The Jewish soldiers decapitated the mightiest Amalekite warriors, pulverizing their severed heads beyond recognition. They also slaughtered the soldiers from other nations who had joined the battle on the Amalekite side and all the women and children in the Amalekite camp. The only ones they spared from death or mutilation were the weakest derelicts among the Amalekite soldiers.[122] Despite the ferocity of the battle, however, the Jewish soldiers treated their enemies with dignity and humanity. Hashem did not allow them to kill with axes but rather with clean thrusts of their sharpened swords that bring a swift, relatively painless death and do not mangle the corpses.[123]

Among the Amalekite survivors were a number of soldiers who had wrapped themselves in spell-generated protective occult shields that could not be penetrated by Jewish swords. Hashem did not choose to perform miracles that would override the occult systems of the world.[124] Therefore, the Jewish soldiers could not kill these spell-protected Amalekites, but they did cut off their hands and feet, efectively putting them out of action.[125]

Ironically, the signature weapon of Eisav, the sword, was the weapon with which the Jewish people destroyed the Amalekite attackers. The war would remain an everlasting reminder to the nations of the world that an attack against the Jewish people would ultimately fail and lead to the destruction of the attackers.[126]

But in the end, although the Jewish people emerged victorious, Moshe's prayers and Yehoshua's fighters did not succeed in obliterating the Amalekites completely.[127] Remnants of Amalek survived to

---

121. *Sechel Tov; Rokeach; Abarbanel* to *Beshalach*.
122. *Mechilta; Rashi; Tanchuma Yashan; Lekach Tov; Rokeach* to *Shemos* 17:13; *Tanchuma Beshalach* 28; *Ralbag; Sforno* to *Shemos* 17:13, *Yalkut* 265; *Targum Yonasan*.
123. *Mechilta; Zayis Raanan*.
124. *Rabbeinu Bachya* to *Shemos* 17:13. See *Maaseh Hashem* and *Malbim*.
125. See *Daas Zekeinim; Moshav Zekeinim, Chizkuni; Rabbeinu Bachya; Bechor Shor* to *Shemos* 17:13.
  See *Bechor Shor* to *Shemos* 17:13 who defines the word *chalash* to mean death and not victory.
126. See *Mechilta*.
127. *Abarbanel*.

fight again another day. The time for the annihilation of Amalek had not yet arrived.[128]

Remember Amalek

In the aftermath of the battle, Hashem said to Moshe, "Inscribe this as a remembrance in the book and say it into the ears of Yehoshua — that I will surely obliterate the memory of Amalek from underneath the heavens."[129]

The treachery of Amalek was the essence of the remembrance. Amalek was the first nation to show that the Jewish people were vulnerable to attack. After all the wonders and miracles that had characterized the exodus of the Jewish people from Egypt, the other nations were too terrified to even contemplate war with them. Many gentiles were even considering conversion to the Jewish faith, just as the Erev Rav had done. But the Amalekites were prepared to absorb heavy casualties just to demonstrate to the world that the Jewish people could be bloodied in battle. The gentiles began to discount the stories of the miracles that had transpired in Egypt. Perhaps they were all happenstance or coincidence, since the Jewish people were obviously not invulnerable to attack.[130]

Had Amalek not attacked the Jewish people, no nation would ever have done so. But Amalek cooled off the fear of the Jewish people and gave their enemies the courage and the confidence to engage them in battle. It is like a steaming bath that everyone is afraid to touch, until one fellow came along and jumped in. He

---

128. *Alshich; Ohr HaChaim.*
 This is suggested by the Torah's use of the word *vayachlash* instead of the word *vayimach*, or *vayamusu*.
 One reason for this was that the Jewish people were not worthy at this time to earn the right to totally annihilate Amalek. They still had to repent for their previous sins. See *Alshich* for further discussion as to why Yehoshua was only allowed to weaken them.
129. *Shemos* 17:14.
 The reference to erasing the Amalekites from beneath the heavens alludes to the Amalekites who tried to escape via the spells that allowed them to suspend themselves in midair. This would also be a reference to Haman who would be hanged and would dangle from the air under the heavens (see *Sifsei Kohen; Taama D'Kra*).
130. *Kli Chemdah Beshalach; Tanna D'Vei Eliyahu Rabbah* 24. *Ibn Ezra; Chizkuni; Rashi; Be'er Yitzchok* to *Shemos* 17:14. See *Rashi* to *Bamidbar* 24:20.
 It is repeated in the name of R' Yosef Chaim Sonnenfeld in *Mara D'Ara Yisrael* (p. 199) that the Nazis were of Amalekite descent. Some suggest that the words "*Reishis Goyim Amalek*" mean that Amalek believed they were the "*Reishis*," the superior race of their time, no different than how the Nazis felt about themselves. (See *Shaarei Aharon*, end of *Ki Seitzei; Ramban* to *Shemos* 24:20.)

may have been scalded, but by showing he was still alive, he emboldened others to step into the bath.[131]

Amalek showed themselves to be the implacable enemies of the Jewish people. Their attack was unprovoked, since the Jewish people had no territorial or any other designs on Amalek. Their attack was cowardly, picking off the weakest stragglers outside the protective shield of the cloud pillars.[132] Their attack was corrosive, as it undermined the Jewish faith in Hashem and Moshe and planted seeds of doubt regarding future attacks.[133] And their attack was an all-out effort to eradicate the very memory of all things Jewish. When they castrated the Jewish bodies and waved the signs of circumcision in the air, they were symbolically declaring that they wanted to cut off all future Jewish generations.[134] Amalek also killed many Jews, preventing them from receiving the Torah at Mount Sinai and experiencing the radiance of the Throne of Glory. In essence, then, this was an attack on the Throne of Glory itself.[135] For these heinous acts, Amalek was condemned to extinction, but not just yet. The right time would come. In the meantime, no converts would be accepted from Amalek.[136] They had attacked the Throne

---

131. See *Zohar Beshalach; Zera Baruch Yisro; Tanchuma; Lekach Tov; Rashi; Targum Yonasan* to *Devarim* 25:17-19; *Rashi* to *Bamidbar* 24:20.
132. *Abarbanel.* See *Malbim* to *Shemos* 17:8.
133. See *Tanna D'Vei Eliyahu Rabbah* 24 and *Rimzei Eish.*
134. *Sechel Tov* to *Shemos* 17:14; *Targum Yonasan* to *Devarim* 25:17.
  Others suggest that the purpose of wiping out Amalek was to prevent his descendant Haman from doing the same to the Jewish people. In the end, Amalek was not entirely wiped out and Haman did in fact want to exterminate the Jewish nation entirely (*Pesikta Rabbah* 13).
135. *Kli Chemdah Beshalach.*
136. *Mechilta; Tanchuma Ki Seitzei* 11. See *Sanhedrin* 91b with *Maharsha.*
  The *Shevus Yaakov* questions how the *Gemara* in *Sanhedrin* can write that the children of Haman are learning Torah when Amalek was to be wiped out, or at the very least, unable to enter the Jewish faith. There are many solutions to this problem. One suggestion is that through assimilation and years, these further offspring would no longer be recognized or carry the lineage of an Amalek descendant. In fact it was through a prophetic vision that they were recognized to be Haman's descendants (*Tzitz Eliezer* 13). Furthermore, they were grandchildren through the daughters of Amalek and the law only applied to one who was a descendant through males. Some suggest that the woman who would become the grandmother of Haman was the maidservant of Agag, while others suggest that she was his concubine. In either case, she was not of Amalekite descent (see *Rambam* on *Esther* 3:1 footnotes). Others suggest that since Haman sold himself as a slave to Mordechai, he lost all legal claims to his ancestry. One's *yichus* is erased as soon as one becomes an *eved*. That being the case, by legal definition the children of Haman were not of Amalekite descent and were excluded from the law preventing Amalekites from converting (*Tzofnas Pane'ach Balak*). Others suggest that the laws of annihilating Amalek and disallowing

of Glory and therefore could never be allowed to receive its radiance. The sinfulness of Amalek was so deeply engrained in their souls that they could never be purified even through conversion. In fact, some suggest that the Jewish people had such horrendous problems with the Erev Rav because many of them were descended from Amalek.[137]

Hashem wanted the Jewish people to remember the full extent of the Amalekite treachery. He wanted their hatred for Amalek to smolder in their hearts forever without a diminution of intensity.[138] He also wanted them to remember that their own lack of faith had opened the door to the Amalekite attack. By questioning Hashem's presence in their midst, they had shown themselves unworthy of His protection.[139]

Moreover, the commandment to remember is expressed with the word *zachor*, the identical word used in the commandment to observe Shabbos. This was an everlasting reminder to the Jewish people that if they had not desecrated the Shabbos by going out to collect the manna, He would never have allowed Amalek to attack them.[140]

Therefore, He commanded that the story of what had transpired should be inscribed as a remembrance in "the book." Which book? Some suggest that this is a reference to the Torah, specifically to *Parashas Ki Seitzei*, where the Torah declares, "Remember what Amalek did to you on the way when you were leaving Egypt."[141] Others suggest that it a reference to the military archives of the Jewish people; these historical records have since

---

conversion applied only if they did not do *teshuvah*, but if they repented or kept the Seven Mitzvos of Noach, then an exception could be made (*Avnei Nezer Orach Chaim* 2:508). Others posit that although the law states that they were not allowed to be accepted, however, if one chose to convert on his own, the conversion would still be valid. Some simply say that no one knew they had converted to Judaism. (See *Rambam, Hil. Melachim* 6:4; *Kesef Mishneh*; *Shevus Yehudah*; *Ben Yehoyada* to *Gittin* 56b; *Sanhedrin* 96; *Berachos* 28a.) See *Pesach Einayim* to *Sanhedrin* who goes into further detail. He also writes that the *Gemara* simply argues with the *Mechilta* and that the *Rambam* sided with the *Gemara* (*Chida*).

See *Baal HaTurim* to *Shemos* 28:7 who eliminates this problem by reading the phrase as the "Children of **Naaman**" and not "Children of **Haman**" who are learning Torah.

137. *Zohar Bereishis* 169; *Zera Baruch* to *Yisro*.

138. *Abarbanel* to *Devarim* 25:18; *Sefer HaMitzvos* 189.

There are different views about to what extent one is commanded to remember what Amalek did — whether daily, yearly or once in one's lifetime. See *Minchas Chinuch* mitzvah 603; *Sefer HaMitzvos L'Rambam* and *Chasam Sofer* for some views.

139. *Rabbeinu Bachya* to *Devarim* 25:18.

140. See *Mechilta Beshalach*; *Sifri Ki Seitzei* and commentaries.

141. See *Ramban*; *Sforno*; *Ibn Ezra*; *Zohar* to *Shemos* 17:14; *Devarim* 25:17-19.

been lost.[142] In addition to inscription in "the book," Hashem also insisted that Moshe tell the details orally to Yehoshua, setting into motion a tradition of recounting the events from generation to generation and ensuring that they would never be forgotten.[143] The oral tradition would also ensure that all the specifics of the commandment to annihilate Amalek — such as the inclusion of women, children and animals — would not be forgotten.[144]

The Annihilation of Amalek

At the time of the Amalekite attack on the Jewish people, Hashem did not allow Yehoshua to destroy them completely, only to debilitate them severely in their arrogance and military might. Hashem wanted the Jewish people to live with the fear of another Amalekite attack so that they would refrain from sin and remain faithful to Him.[145] Others suggest that the total destruction of Amalek could only be accomplished if his ministering angel in Heaven was first destroyed. Since the Jewish people were not completely free of sin they could not effect the destruction of an angel. This would actually explain why Amalek still survives until this very day.[146]

The original intent was for the Jewish people to destroy Amalek immediately after the conquest of Canaan and the destruction of the seven Canaanite people that occupied it.[147] This task would fall to Yehoshua who would lead the Jewish armies in the War of Conquest. In effect, he would be expected to finish what he had

---

Accordingly, some suggest that this commandment was said in the fortieth year of the Jews in the desert. Since it was only then that the Torah was given, Hashem's commandment referenced the Torah that had already been written and not a Torah that was to be written in the future (*Ibn Ezra*).

142. See *Ibn Ezra; Chizkuni; Ralbag*. See also *Targum Yonasan; R' Saadiah Gaon*.

143. See *Ramban; Malbim; Sfas Emes* to *Shemos* 17:14; *Ramban; Sifri* to *Devarim* 25:18; *Megillah* 18a.

This was like everything else in which Moshe passed down all the laws and commandments to Yehoshua as stated in *Pirkei Avos*: "Moshe kibel Torah MiSinai umesarah l'Yehoshua — Moshe received the Torah from Sinai and transmitted it to Yehoshua."

144. *Gra* to *Shemos* 17:14. See also *Bava Basra* end of 21a; *Maharsha, Ritva, Rashba*. See *Pardes Yosef* for a complete discussion of this issue.

145. *Rabbeinu Bachya* to *Devarim* 25:18; *Chemdas Yamim*.

146. See *Mechilta; Tosafos Beshalach*.

147. See *Rambam, Sefer HaMitzvos* and *Hilchos Melachim* Ch. 6.

begun.¹⁴⁸ This arrangement also sent a subtle message to Moshe that Yehoshua rather than he would lead the Jewish people into the land; otherwise, the task of completing the destruction of Amalek would have fallen to Moshe.¹⁴⁹

Ultimately, the task of annihilating Amalek was delayed for several centuries. The commandment to annihilate Amalek was to be fulfilled after the conquest and distribution of the land and the appointment of a king. For various reasons, however, the appointment of a king was delayed. Consequently, the honor of annihilating Amalek fell to Shaul, the first king of Israel.¹⁵⁰ King Shaul was a descendant of Binyamin, Rachel's younger son. It fell to him to complete the task begun by Yehoshua, who was descended from Yosef, Rachel's older son. Thus, it was the merit of Rachel that facilitated the destruction of Amalek.¹⁵¹

The commandment to annihilate Amalek is so grave that Hashem promised to do it Himself if the Jewish people failed to do so.¹⁵² In the end, however, King Shaul did not complete the task either. He left a tiny remnant of Amalek, which then regenerated into a revitalized nemesis to the Jewish people. Nonetheless, the Torah assures us that in the end of days, when Mashiach comes and Hashem's glory is universally acknowledged, the eradication of Amalek will finally be completed.¹⁵³

---

148. *Ramban; Chizkuni.*
149. See *Rashi; Zayis Raanan.*
    Many question this hint since Moshe never made the slightest inquiry about the possibility of his not entering Eretz Yisrael till close to forty years later, despite the fact that Hashem told him that it would be Yehoshua's responsibility and not his. Some posit that as far as Moshe was concerned he thought he would enter Eretz Yisrael like anyone else, but that he would not live long enough to carry out that mission. Another alternative suggests that Moshe thought that his children would take over (see *Maskil LeDavid*).
150. See *Sanhedrin* 20b and *Maharsha; Sifri Ki Seitzei.*
151. *Pesikta Rabbah* 12; *Ramban.*
    Since they did not take part in selling Yosef they would not be vulnerable to Amalek's strength.
    The mitzvah to annihilate Amalek was to take effect only after every one of the seven nations was wiped out. Since during Yehoshua's lifetime this was not completed, it was Shaul and not Yehoshua who would be responsible to destroy Amalek (see *Ramban*).
152. *Midrash HaChefetz; Tanna D'Vei Eliyahu Rabbah* 24.
    In fact, this would be the case. After Shaul's failed attempt to destroy Amalek, the Jews would be threatened years later with their own destruction by Amalek's descendant Haman. See *Tanna D'Vei Eliyahu Zuta* 19 and its commentaries as to how removing the sins of Yaakov and transferring them to Eisav would increase the wickedness of the Edomite family and lead to their inevitable destruction.
153. *Mechilta; Pesikta Rabbah* 12; *Abarbanel.*

The commandment is to wipe Amalek off the face of the earth without a trace, as happened to the generation of the Great Flood in the times of Noach.[154] Men, women, children, animals, property, anything identified with Amalek that would call to mind this evil nation,[155] even an image engraved on a stone, all these were to be destroyed until the last trace was gone.[156] Hashem would also eradicate Amalek from the World to Come, to which they would have no entry. The door to Gehinnom and perdition would be opened to them because of their treacherous attack on the Jewish people.[157]

A Commemorative Altar

After the battle with Amalek, Moshe built a commemorative altar in Chorev and brought a thanksgiving offering upon it.[158] He named the altar Hashem Nissi, which means "Hashem is my miracle maker," memorializing the miraculous nature of the victory.[159] The altar reminded the people that, despite the great military feats of Yehoshua and the Jewish fighting men, the victory was the result

---

The prophet Shmuel told him, in the name of G-d, that he was to attack the Amalekite kingdom and wipe it out — men, women, children and every single animal. Shaul assembled an army of 200,000 men and attacked the Amalekite kingdom, killing the entire population, a total of a half million people. But he did not obey the prophet Shmuel's directions completely. He took pity on Agag, the Amalekite king, and his wife and imprisoned them until he could consult with Shmuel. He also failed to destroy all the livestock, which seemed wasteful to him. Because of this disobedience, Shmuel told Shaul that he had forfeited his kingdom (*I Shmuel* 15, *Sefer Yosefun*). When Shmuel arrived in the morning Agag was caught before he could make good his escape. His pregnant wife, however, got away. She would eventually give birth to a child who would be the ancestor of Haman. (See *Yerushalmi Yevamos* 2-6.)

154. *Tur* to *Shemos* 17:14.
The *Tur* makes this connection in conjunction with the word אמחה, *emche*, a root word used both in relation to the *mabul* and to Amalek.

155. *Mechilta; Midrash Tehillim* 89; *Rabbeinu Bachya* to *Beshalach; Rashi* to *Devarim* 25:19.
One reason for killing the animals was because Amalek used sorcery to turn themselves into animals. Killing the animals guaranteed that the Amalekite magicians would be slaughtered. See *Let My Nation Live* pp. 43-44.
Realistically, Haman would survive the eventual annihilation. In the end, he too was to be slain along with his entire family and relatives. The words אמחה מחה, *machoh emcheh*, total 107, the same numerical value as "*Zeh Haman*" (*Tosafos; Sifsei Kohen*).

156. See *Orach Chaim* 690; *Avudraham; Beis Yosef; Rama; Beur HaGra*.

157. See *Mechilta; Rashi; Abarnbanel; Tosafos; Zohar* to *Shemos* 17:16.

158. *Ibn Ezra; Aruch; Chizkuni; R' Avraham Ben HaRambam* to *Shemos* 17:15. See *Ibn Ezra HaKatzar* and *R' Avraham Ben HaRambam* who write that he built it in Refidim. The *Ralbag* suggests that Moshe built it on the mountain in which he stood, which we have accepted to be the mountain of Chorev or Sinai.

159. See *Rashi; Mechilta; Midrash HaChefetz Beshalach.*

of a *nes*, a miracle that Hashem in His mercy had performed for the Jewish people.[160] The altar also reminded the people to remember that Hashem is the "Man of War," that victory flows from His power, not from the strong arms of the fighters.[161] The altar, a symbol of the people serving Hashem, bore the message that by serving Hashem faithfully and praying with sincerity the Jewish people would be worthy of miracles. Otherwise, they would be at the mercy of their enemies.

The people had questioned the presence of the Almighty among them and had not deserved the victory on their own merits, but Hashem had performed a miracle for them purely out of mercy and love.[162]

It is like the king who one day was angered by his beloved queen. He left the palace in a rage and went for a stroll in the marketplace. He entered a jewelry store and asked to be shown the finest necklaces and bracelets. Then he chose the most beautiful pieces made of the rarest precious stones and brought them back to the palace as a gift to his queen. The king's ministers looked at each other in wonder. "If this is how he treats his queen when he is angry," they said, "imagine how he treats her when he is not."

Similarly, the commemorative altar reminded the Jewish people that if Hashem works wonders and miracles for them when He is angry with them, how much more He would surely do for them if they remained faithful, loyal and steadfast.[163]

There are also other interpretations of Hashem Nissi, the name Moshe gave the commemorative altar, but essentially the message is the same. Some suggest it means "Hashem is my banner."[164] This was a reminder of the staff that was raised in battle to rally the soldiers physically and spiritually and enable them to defeat Amalek.[165] Others suggest that it means "Hashem has lifted me up." Once

---

160. *Midrash Aggadah.*
 Many opinions suggest that Hashem in fact did it for His sake and not necessarily for the Jews. In order for His Name to be exalted, the world had to witness this great miracle (see *Midrash Tanchuma Beshalach* 28).
161. See *Pesikta Rabbah* 12.
162. *Gur Aryeh* to *Shemos* 17:15.
163. See *Pesikta Rabbah* 12.
164. *Rashbam; Bechor Shor; Akeidah* to *Shemos* 17:15.
165. *Maaseh Hashem; HaKesav VeHaKabbalah; Malbim* to *Shemos* 17:15.

again, this is a reminder that Hashem is responsible for the victory of the Jewish people over the Amalekite enemy. [166]

Once the altar was erected, Moshe declared to the people that Hashem had taken hold of the Throne of Glory and sworn to prosecute the war against Amalek until its final resolution. The war that had just begun would continue for generation after generation until the last chapter of history.[167] In the time of Shaul, Mordechai and all the way until the arrival of Mashiach, there would be recurrent battles with Amalek.[168] Each time, Amalek would be defeated and another step in his destruction would be accomplished.[169]

As long as Amalek, the sworn enemy of Hashem, still walked on the face of this earth, the Name of Hashem as the manifestation of His authority in the world would be incomplete. Only when Amalek would be wiped off the face of the earth without a trace would the Name of Hashem be completely manifested among all the people of the world in its fullest sense.[170]

---

166. *Sforno;* see *R' Saadiah Gaon.*
167. See *Mechilta; Rashi* to *Shemos* 17:16; *Pirkei D'Rav Eliezer* 44; *Tanchuma Ki Seitzei* 11.
    Using the throne as part of the oath was to symbolize the throne of Shaul and that it would be his initial responsibility to annihilate Amalek.
    It is common to take hold of something when making an oath; we see this when Avaraham made Eliezer swear. And so, in a manner of speaking, Hashem took hold of His throne to validate His oath.
168. See *Mechilta; Sechel Tov; Tosafos* to *Shemos* 17:16. See *Tur.*
169. *Abarbanel* to *Beshalach; Alshich; Malbim; Sforno* to *Ki Seitzei.*
170. See *Mechilta; Pesikta Rabbah* 12; *Abarbanel.*
    The symbolic reference of Hashem's incomplete Name is as though He is covering His face and will expose Himself only when Amalek is finally annihilated (*Pesikta Rabbah*).
    The commentaries offer various opinions of Hashem's incomplete Name, symbolized by the Torah's use of the first two letters of Hashem's Name — *yud* and *hei.*

6 Arrival at Sinai

Six weeks after the exodus from Egypt, on Rosh Chodesh Sivan 2448, the Jewish people broke camp in Refidim and encamped that same day at the foot of Mount Sinai four and a half miles away.[1] This was the place where Moshe had seen the *sneh*, the burning bush that was not consumed. Hashem had spoken to him from the burning bush and promised that the Jewish people would be redeemed from their bondage in Egypt. This was the place where the promise would be fulfilled and the redemption would reach its climactic culmination with the Giving of the Torah.[2]

The Jewish people had made a commitment to Hashem to accept the Torah in return for their redemption. The time to honor the com-

---

1. *Bechor Shor; Ohr HaChaim* to *Shemos* 19:1; *Seder Olam*. See *Tur* for his opinion. Some suggest it was Sunday while others say it was Monday. See *Rabbeinu Bachya, Seder Olam* 5; *Shabbos* 87.
   This is in agreement with the view that Moshe went two *parsahs* to Chorev (Sinai).
2. *Tanchuma Yashan Yisro.*

mitment had now arrived. They had gone through a number of ordeals after leaving Egypt — lacking food, lacking water on two occasions and being attacked by a treacherous Amalekite enemy. There were serious shortcomings in their approach to these crises, but in the end, they persevered and lived to face their moment of national truth at Sinai.

There was an electric expectancy in the air. The very sand and pebbles were aglow with holiness and sanctity. The Jewish nation, the last to be formed, represented the completion of the community of nations, paving the way for the introduction of the celestial Torah into the world below. This great event, the shining goal toward which history had been pointing for twenty-six generations since the creation of the world, was now about to take place.[3]

The first step toward the Giving of the Torah was their emancipation from the yoke of Egyptian bondage. By accepting the Torah, the Jewish people would be making a commitment to be subservient to Hashem. Therefore, they could not be in a condition of subservience to slavemasters. After the exodus, this obstacle was removed, but they were still not properly prepared to receive the Torah for another fifty-one days.[4]

What was the purpose for this delay? What was the significance of the Torah being given in the month of Sivan? And if there was a need to wait, why was the Torah given in the desert? Why didn't Hashem bring the Jewish people to Eretz Yisrael during this period of delay and give them the Torah there, right in their own homeland?

Sivan in the Desert

First, let us consider why there was a delay altogether. It can be explained with a parable. There was once a king who had an only son. The king arranged a wonderful marriage for the young prince, and the kingdom prepared for a gala wedding celebration. But there was one problem. The royal palace was old and decrepit, and its banquet hall was in serious disrepair. The king was prepared to build a new palace, but it did not seem right to postpone the wedding until the new palace was built. On the other hand, it would not have been fitting for the honor of the

---

3. *Tiferes Yisrael* Ch. 17; *Mabit, yesod* 21; *Pesachim* 118a; *Tanna D'Vei Eliyahu* 28.

4. See *Maharsha* to *Avoduh Zarah* 3a who writes that in fact it was 51 days since they left Egypt. In the future there would be 50 days from Pesach to Shavuos.

king to make the wedding in a ramshackle banquet hall. What did the king do? He summoned the finest builders and craftsmen in the realm and commissioned a complete renovation of the banquet hall. The prince's wedding took place in surroundings that were as good as new, and there was no reason to delay.

The Giving of the Torah to the Jewish people was like a wedding between Hashem and His people. But the Jewish people, newly emancipated from slavery, bruised and beaten, were not in a condition fit for a royal wedding. Some were lame, some blind, some deaf, some with broken or missing limbs. Hashem did not want the consummation of the bond to be delayed, so He sent an angel to heal them. Once the people were fully recovered physically, mentally and emotionally, they would be fit to receive the Torah.

Others offer a slightly different parable. A prince fell seriously ill, and he had to spend a considerable amount of time confined to his bed. In the meantime, he fell behind in his studies, which greatly concerned his father, the king. After a while, the prince recovered and returned to his full health. Nonetheless, the king did not send him back to his tutors right away. Much as the king was concerned about the interruption in the prince's education, he did not send him back to his studies for several months. He understood full well that even after returning to health, a long period of recuperation and convalescence was needed to restore the prince's former vigor and stamina so that he could resume his rigorous program of study.

Similarly, the Jewish people had recovered superficially from the deep wounds of bondage, but they were still physically and emotionally fragile. They still needed time to get back to themselves fully, to mend until they were without blemish, to be strong in body and spirit after being persecuted and oppressed in Egypt for so many years. That is why Hashem kept them in transit for fifty days, giving them the quail, the manna and water from Miriam's Well, before bringing them to Mount Sinai.[5]

There was also a spiritual reason for the delay in their arrival at Sinai. A *niddah*, a menstruant woman, must count seven clean days before she can return to a state of *taharah*, ritual purity. In the same

---

5. See *Tanchuma Yisro* 10, 8; *Zohar*; *Yalkut* 271; *Bamidbar Rabbah* 7:1; *Midrash Aseres HaDibros*; *Pesikta D'Rav Kahana* 12 (104); *Abarbanel* to *Shemos* 19:1; *Kometz HaMinchah, Shavuos*.

Symbolically, the Jews were to be "married" to Hashem in the very same manner. (See *Baal HaTurim* to *Shemos* 19:4 for his detailed explanation.)

way, the Jewish people, steeped in the spiritual contamination of Egyptian culture for many years, had to count seven weeks of purity and cleanliness before they could reach a level of *taharah* high enough to receive the Torah at Sinai.[6]

Moreover, according to the Torah, a female convert to Judaism or a female gentile slave who is emancipated and joins the Jewish people must wait three months before getting married. This is called the time of *havchanah*, determination of the identity of her child. If she waits fewer than the three months and has a child, we cannot be sure if it is a nine-month child conceived before she converted and therefore gentile, or a seven-month child conceived after she converted and therefore Jewish. Since the Jewish people at the time of their arrival at Sinai were in a status comparable to converts to Judaism, they were required to observe the laws of conversion and wait three calendar months.[7]

There was also a special significance in the Torah being given in the month of Sivan. The astrological sign for Sivan is Gemini, twins. The gentile nations would one day have to give an accounting for their rejection of the Torah when Hashem offered it to them, and Hashem wanted to anticipate the arguments they would offer in their own defense and refute them from the very beginning. He knew that gentile nations would say that they had thought the Torah did not relate to them. It was designed for the Jewish nation, a nation with which they had no kinship or connection.

Therefore, Hashem chose to give the Torah during the month of Sivan, a month characterized by the sign of the twins, as if to say, "The Jewish people are not, from their origin, a nation apart. They are descended from Yaakov, who had a twin brother Eisav, and the gentile nations, at least those descended from Eisav, cannot claim that the Torah is not destined for them."[8]

---

6. *Zohar* 78b; *Ohr HaChaim* to *Shemos* 19:1; *Sifsei Kohen*.
7. *Tanchuma Yashan Yisro; Yalkut.* See *Tiferes Yisrael* Ch. 25 for another approach to the necessity of a three-month interval.

Although it is supposed to be 90 days rather than 50, this was all just to symbolize that Hashem loved the Jews and could not wait until they would accept the Torah. (See *Chizkuni; Rosh; Zayis Raanan.*) See *Alshich*, who writes that when you add the 40 days till they received the *Luchos*, in total it would be 90 days of *perishah*. Others suggest that although it is only 50 days, it was still three calendar months that passed, more than enough to drive home this point.

The Jewish people were considered captives, having been imprisoned in Egypt until they were freed (*Sifsei Kohen*).

8. *Pesikta D'Rav Kahana* 12 (107).

The sign of the twins is also especially propitious for the Giving of the Torah. Hashem did not want to give it during Nissan, whose sign is Aries, the sheep, because the Egyptians worshiped sheep. He did not want to give it during Iyar, whose sign is Taurus, the bull, because the Jewish people would worship the Golden Calf, a young bull. Hashem did not want an everlasting association between the idol and the Torah. Therefore, He chose to wait until Sivan, whose sign is the twins, a symbol of fraternal love and solidarity. These are the virtues that qualified the Jewish people to receive the Torah.[9]

There was also a special symbolism in the Torah being given on 6 Sivan rather than on another day of the month. The original creation of humankind took place on the sixth day of creation. The Giving of the Torah would be the act of national creation for the Jewish people, and therefore, it too was to take place on the sixth day. Furthermore, that year 6 Sivan fell on a Shabbos, which was also significant. Just as Shabbos provided the spiritual protection of the newly created Adam, so did the Shabbos on which the Torah was given provide the spiritual protection for the newly created Jewish nation.[10]

This leaves us with the question of why Hashem chose to give the Torah in the desert rather than in Eretz Yisrael. There were a number of reasons.

As mentioned before, Hashem wanted to anticipate the argument of the gentile nations when they would be taken to task for rejecting the Torah. Had the Torah been given in Eretz Yisrael, the gentiles could have argued that they could not trespass in a foreign land. After the conquest, the Jewish people had evicted the gentiles already living in the land, so it was highly unlikely they would welcome gentiles from abroad to come and receive the Torah with them in their land. The desert, however, was in the public domain, open to all comers. No one would have prevented the gentiles from coming and joining the Jewish people had they chosen to do so.[11]

Furthermore, had the Torah been given in Eretz Yisrael, it would necessarily have been given in the territory of one of the tribes.

---

9. *Kometz HaMinchah, Shavuos;* see *Pesikta Rabbah* Ch. 20.
10. *Sifsei Kohen;* this is based on the view that it was given on the 6th and not the 7th of Sivan.
11. *Abarbanel.* See *Mechilta; Pirkei D'Rav Kahana* Ch. 12.

Afterward, this tribe could claim that they enjoyed special preference because of their selection as the venue for the Giving of the Torah. Therefore, Hashem chose the desert, a place where all the tribes are equal with no preferences.[12]

There was also a very practical reason for the choice of the desert over Eretz Yisrael. In their own land, the people would have been preoccupied with commerce, agriculture or just plain nation building. They would not have had the patience to devote themselves to Torah study for a long time in a very serious way. But in the desert, with all their needs provided miraculously, they were free of all worries and concerns and fully receptive to a heavy schedule of Torah study.[13]

In addition, had the Torah been given in Eretz Yisrael, Jews of meager faith and learning could someday claim that the laws of the Torah were specifically designed for that particular culture at that particular time in Jewish history. Different times would require different sets of rules. Therefore, Hashem gave the Torah in a desert, a place with no indigenous culture and no particular place in cultural history. Clearly then, the Torah was timeless and unaffected by cultural changes.[14]

Last but not least, the choice of the desert as the venue for the Giving of the Torah sent a subtle but powerful message to the Jewish people. If they wanted the Torah to take root and blossom in their hearts and minds, they had to see themselves as a desert, a place barren of luxuries and distractions. A person who pampers himself and is unduly concerned with the pleasures of life will not be successful in mastering the Torah.[15]

The Encampment at Sinai

The Jewish people arrived at Sinai six days before the Giving of the Torah, which was excellent timing. They did not have to wait there for long interminable weeks, chafing with impatience. Nor would they have to rush to receive the Torah in a matter of hours after their arrival. They would have six days to settle in and prepare

---

12. *Lekach Tov* to *Shemos* 20:2.
13. See *Mechilta; Moshav Zekeinim; Pane'ach Raza*.
14. *Tosafos*.
15. *Mechilta D'Rashbi* 19:2; see *Bamidbar Rabbah* 1:16; *Matnos Kehunah*. See *Tiferes Yisrael* Ch. 26.

themselves for the great event.[16] They would remain there, studying and reviewing the Torah, for 344 days, just short of one year.[17]

As soon as the cloud pillars came to a stop at Sinai and the people saw the mountain looming before them, they were overcome with joy and excitement. They immediately sought out a flat expanse suitable for habitation and established the encampment on the east side of the mountain facing west.[18] Although they did not know it at the time, the spot they chose was exactly the spot where Moshe had drawn water from a stone when the Jewish people had clamored for water at Refidim, otherwise known as Masah U'Merivah. This was also the spot from which Moshe had observed the *sneh*, the burning bush from which Hashem spoke to him.[19]

With the encampment on the eastern side of the mountain facing west, the Jewish people were looking directly at the spot where the *Shechinah*, the Divine Presence, had alighted on the mountain. Normally, they would have chosen a spot with an unobstructed view for their encampment, but on this particular occasion they wanted to be in full view of the holy mountain.[20]

The sight of the humble mountain dwarfed by the towering peaks that surrounded it had a powerful effect on the people. They understood that Hashem does not choose the arrogant but rather those who have humility and contrition in their hearts. They were also humbled by the utter desolation of the wilderness around them, and they realized that there was nothing more important than peace, harmony and serving Hashem.[21]

---

16. *Ohr HaChaim; Sifsei Kohen.* Once again it was symbolic of a marriage in that the Jews (the bride) did not have to wait too long for the groom (Hashem) to arrive.

17. *Mechilta, Lekach Tov* to *Shemos* 19:2. They would leave on the 20th of Iyar of the following year.

18. *Ramban; Abarbanel* to *Shemos* 19:1; *Mechilta; Panim Yafos.* See *Malbim.*

As was the case with the *Beis HaMikdash*, the *Shechinah* always rested on the western portion. The numerical value of the words *neged hahar* (facing the mountain) is the same as *zeh mizrach* (this is east) — 267 (*Rokeach*).

19. *Abarbanel.*

20. See *Mechilta; Rashi; Mizrachi; HaKesav VeHaKabbalah.* See *Malbim.* Some suggest that the Jews camped around the mountain in a manner similar to the way they would camp in their travels with the Mishkan: three tribes in each of the four directions. See *Bechor Shor* to *Shemos* 24:4; *Ibn Ezra* to *Shemos* 19:2.

21. *Chasam Sofer.*

This is why they also called it "Har Chorev," reflective of the fact that it was a place of desolation.

The arrangement of the encampment was by order of prestige. The elders and leaders were given the honor of pitching their tents closest to the mountain, with the common people behind them, pitching their tents as close to the mountain as possible.[22] Only the Erev Rav shied away from close proximity to the mountain, choosing instead to pitch their tents some distance out in the desert beyond the main encampment.[23]

For the first time since leaving Egypt, the Jewish people in the main encampment were unified as one nation, focused on the glorious destiny that awaited them. No longer were there incessant complaints, arguments and bickering. The dissension and sedition of Marah, Alush and Refidim-Masah U'Merivah were no more than painful memories. At Refidim, faced with the Amalekite attack, the people had finally repented for their negligence of Torah study, their lack of faith and their quarrelsome and insubordinate behavior. They had purified and cleansed their souls, and for the first time, they were truly worthy of receiving the Torah.[24] At last, they were a unified people treating each other with love and compassion, like the twins of Sivan's astrological sign.[25]

As that first day at Sinai drew to a close, the people felt tired but content, at peace with themselves and with each other. They were tired and rested comfortably for the rest of the day until they retired for the night.[26]

The Second Day

Early the next morning, on their second day at Sinai, Moshe ascended the mountain to receive instructions from Hashem.[27] The Clouds of Glory that blanketed the crest of the mountain bore witness that the Divine Presence had already descended.[28] A year earlier, Hashem had already told Moshe that the Jewish people would

---

22. *Ibn Ezra* to *Shemos* 19:2.
23. *Ralbag*.
24. *Zohar; Mechilta; Rashi; Riva; Tanchuma Yashan Yisro; Yonasan Ben Uziel* to *Shemos* 19:2. See *Meam Loez*.
25. See *Sifsei Kohen; Kli Yakar* to *Shemos* 19:2 The *Luchos* too were symbolic of this in that they were identical in size and shape, as twins.
26. See *Shabbos* 86b with *Maharsha*.
27. *Shabbos* 86b; *Rashi; Mechilta; Chizkuni; Yonasan Ben Uziel*.
   Some suggest this was Monday morning, while others suggest it was Tuesday morning. See *Zayis Raanan* to *Yalkut* 276.
28. *Mechilta; Sechel Tov; Lekach Tov; Ramban* to *Shemos* 19:3.

come to serve Him on this mountain after they left Egypt. Now Moshe needed further details and more specific instructions.[29] Some suggest that Moshe did not go up on his own initiative but was summoned by Hashem.[30]

The encounters between Hashem and Moshe took place in the nebulous domain between heaven and earth. Moshe rose no higher than nine handbreadths above the ground, while the *Shechinah* never descended lower than ten handbreadths above the ground. The two worlds never came into direct contact. Moshe never entered the heavenly domain, while the *Shechinah* never entered the earthly domain.[31]

Hashem waited until Moshe made a concerted effort to climb the mountain, and then He addressed him.[32]

"Moshe, Moshe!" He called out, using the affectionate form of addressing him twice by his name.

"*Hineni*," Moshe replied. "Here I am."[33]

"When you tell the women about the laws in the Torah," Hashem said, "speak to them softly and gently. Describe to them the wonderful rewards that await them. Then they will listen to you attentively.[34] Be more forceful when you speak with the men. Give them detailed instructions and make sure they understand you perfectly. Let them know that the laws of the Torah are not negotiable, optional or flexible. Impress on them that they are obligated to serve Me as a servant serves his master, without objections or debate.[35] Do not be concerned about being too authoritative. Just make sure they understand the laws and the consequences of disobedience.[36] Speak first to the Sanhedrin and the elders and afterward to the common people."

---

29. See *Ohr HaChaim* to *Shemos* 19:3; see *Shemos* 3:12 with *Rashi*.
   Others suggest that Moshe went up on his own to personally find out what to do next even though Hashem did not address him yet (*Chizkuni*). See *Yalkut* 269.
30. See *Mechilta; Sechel Tov; Ibn Ezra* to *Shemos* 19:3.
31. See *Succah* 5b; *Bava Metzia* 86b with *Maharsha; Devarim Rabbah* 10:2; *Shemos Rabbah* 12:3. See *HaKosev; Iyun Yaakov; Yad David* as to why this was so.
   It was the portion above nine cubits from the ground and beyond nine cubits from the heavens that Hashem spoke to Moshe.
32. *Ohr HaChaim* to *Shemos* 19:3; see *Zohar* 79b.
   Some suggest that the appearance of Hashem's voice came out from the crevices of the mountain with the letters of the words protruding from it (*Tosafos Al HaTorah*).
33. *Midrash Chadash Al HaTorah; Yalkut* 269.
34. *Mechilta; Rashi* to *Shemos* 19:3; *Shemos Rabbah* 28:2; *Matnos Kehunah*.
   In addition to this, Moshe was to teach them *mussar* and *derech eretz* (*Rabbeinu Bachya* to *Shemos* 19:3).
35. *Shemos Rabbah* 28:2; *Yefei To'ar; Rashi* to *Shemos* 19:3.
36. *Rashi*; see *Shabbos* 87a; *HaKesav VeHaKabbalah*.

Hashem told Moshe to speak with the women before the men. This was an acknowledgment of the central role of the women in raising the children in the way of the Torah. While the fathers are away working, the mothers spend time in the home with the children. They teach the very young children the most basic elements of the Torah in a kind but passionate manner, and they give the children rewards for assimilating the information. When the children grow a little older, it is the mothers who send them off to school and await them on their return. The main responsibility for the Torah of the children is borne by the women. Therefore, Hashem told Moshe to speak to them first.[37]

Furthermore, women are by nature more responsible, meticulous and diligent in their observance. Therefore, in recognition of their dedication to the mitzvos, Hashem honored them by having Moshe speak to them first.[38] The women also were deserving of special recognition, because it was in their merit that the Jewish people were liberated from Egyptian bondage.[39]

Some suggest that the women also needed to be told first because women reach legal adulthood at age 12, while men only reach it at age 13.[40] Others suggest that the women were told first to avoid a recurrence of the disaster in Gan Eden. Hashem had told Adam not to eat from the Tree of Life, and Adam then relayed the prohibition to his wife Chavah. Chavah was offended that Hashem had not told the prohibition to her directly, and she took a cavalier attitude toward it. She transgressed the prohibition and caused her husband to transgress it as well, bringing grievous harm to all of humankind for all time. Hashem did not want women to take offense again, so He told Moshe to speak to them first.[41]

The Chosen People

Hashem went on to describe to Moshe the manifestations of His love for the Jewish people. "With your own eyes," He said, addressing the people to whom Moshe

---

37. *Shemos Rabbah* 28:2; *Radal*; *Matnos Kehunah*; *Rabbeinu Bachya*. See *Sotah* 21a; *Kiddushin* 31a.
38. *Shemos Rabbah*; *Radal*; *Maharzav*. See *Radal* and *Yefei To'ar* regarding their explanation of the sources that say women are lazy in regard to mitzvos. See *Tiferes Yisrael* Ch. 28 for his interpretation.
39. *Tzeidah LeDerech*.
40. *Toldos Tzion*.
41. *Shemos Rabbah* 28:2; *Matnos Kehunah*; *R Efraim Al HaTorah*. See *Zeh Yenachmeni*.

would transmit these words, "you have witnessed the miracles and wonders I performed for you in Egypt. You did not hear about them from other people, nor did you learn of them from written reports or oral traditions. Your own eyes witnessed My glory when I brought down the Egyptians and elevated you as My chosen people.[42] Despite the transgressions of idol worship, adultery and murder, I did not wreak My vengeance on you until you harassed my servant Moshe.[43]

"I have treated you with high regard, carrying you on My wings like an eagle, the king of birds, from your places of bondage to Ramses so that you would depart from Egypt all the more quickly.[44] I led you across the Yam Suf so smoothly, like an eagle soaring across the sky, bringing you safely to the opposite shore while the Egyptians drowned behind you.[45] I protected you like an eagle protects his young. Most birds carry their young below their wings, gripping then with their feet, because they fear the predatory birds that fly above them. An eagle flies higher than all other birds, so he is not concerned with predators that will attack from above. Rather, he fears the arrows and missiles of the humans from down below, and therefore, he carries his young upon his wings rather than below them. Like an eagle, I carried you in the cloud pillars to protect you from the arrows and missiles of the Egyptians.[46] Like an eagle that separates itself from the rest of the birds and flies high into the sky, so did I separate you from among the nations of the world by performing wondrous miracles for you, and I elevated you above all others.[47]

"You were cornered, beset by bandits before you and by wolves from behind. But I was like the father who carries his son upon his shoulders to protect him from harm. So did I protect you from the Egyptians. Does a master carry his servant to protect him? Yet I

---

42. *Mechilta, Rashi* to *Shemos* 19:4; *Lekach Tov; Rabbeinu Bachya*. See *Devarim* 29:15-16.
43. *Mechilta; Rashi; Sechel Tov*.
44. See *Rashi; Mechilta; Chizkuni*. See *Rashi* to *Shemos* 12:37. See *Let My Nation Go* p. 312 fns. 49, 50.
45. *Rashbam; Chizkuni*. See *Mikra'ei Kodesh*.
46. *Rashi; Mechilta; Midrash Tehillim* 48. See *Rabbeinu Bachya; Targum Yonasan; Rokeach* to *Shemos* 19:4. See *Rashi* to *Devarim* 32:11.
47. *Sforno; HaKesav VeHaKabbalah*. See *Rashi* to *Devarim* 32:11.
   Hashem took them from the lowest depth of *tumah* to a level where they would be worthy of accepting the Torah. (See *Malbim*.)

carried you in my cloud pillars to protect you from Egyptians who tried to destroy you.[48]

"I have shown My love for the people through all the wonders and miracles I performed on their behalf. Now I will show My love by giving them the Torah. They must accept Me as their God and the yoke of My commandments as their obligation.[49] It will not be too difficult for them, although it may seem so in the beginning. Indeed, all beginnings are difficult. But once they become accustomed to the Torah, they will find it exceedingly pleasant.[50]

"I am not demanding this for Myself, as a reward for everything I have done for you. I do not need your rewards. I am doing this out of My love for the Jewish people. But much as I love you, I will treat you according to the way you act toward Me.[51]

"Think of all the great miracles I have performed for you and how many more I will perform for you in the future.[52] But first you must become My chosen people, the people I have selected from among all the nations of the world, by accepting the Torah in its entirety, the Written Law and the Oral Law, and safeguarding the covenants of Shabbos, *bris milah* and the rejection of idol worship.[53]

"You are My most precious treasure. I am like a king who has storehouses full of diamonds, jewels and precious stones, yet only one is dearer to him than all the rest. He does not allow anyone to touch it, not even his ministers and closest advisers. It stays hidden away in a separate strongroom to which only the king has the key. And if any flaw should affect it, the king would move heaven and earth to restore it to its original perfection. This describes My love for you, the Jewish people. Should you keep My covenants and commandments, then you will be like that precious treasure to Me. The entire world is My storehouse of treasures. All the nations of the world belong to Me. Yet I have chosen you from among all of them, because you are most precious of all to Me. I have brought you forth

---

48. *Shemos Rabbah* 25:6; see *Tzeror HaMor*; these were the words given first to the women before the men.
49. *Rashbam; Midrash HaChefetz* to *Shemos* 19:4.
50. *Mechilta, Rashi* to *Shemos* 19:5.
51. *Abarbanel* to *Shemos* 19:5.
52. *Mechilta; Netziv.*
53. See *Mechilta; Ohr HaChaim* to *Shemos* 19:5. See *Aggadas Bereishis* and *Peirush HaMishnayos L'Rambam* to *Chullin* Ch. 7 where it states that this is proof that *milah* was specifically given at Sinai. Until now we followed the commandment given to Avraham, but now it is the mitzvah of *milah* given at Sinai. See *Ramban* and *Ibn Ezra* who write

from slavery in Egypt, healed your wounds and restored you to perfect form. I love you as a father loves his son.[54]

"As long as you obey My laws, no one can harm you. Should I choose to bring plagues, epidemics and disasters to the world, you will be spared. I will raise you up above all other nations and exalt you before all the world as My chosen people. But first you must make Me your chosen one by accepting Me as your one and only God.

"I call on you to become My priests, to focus on My sovereignty and My unity when you perform the service in My honor. If you acknowledge that I am One, the one and only God, then I will acknowledge you as My one and only chosen people.[55] And in order to be united with Me, you must have unity among yourselves, care for each other and be responsible for each other. The Jewish nation is as one soul. When one Jew is hurt, all Jews feel the pain. When one Jew sins, all Jews fall from their high spiritual state. Treat each other with love and affection; then you will be worthy of My love. You will deserve to be the Almighty's chosen people.[56]

"Do this, and you will enjoy a glorious future. You will be a kingdom of priests, ministers and leaders, a holy nation.[57] You will enjoy national independence, ruled by a king chosen from among you; no other nations will rule over you.[58] You will be a free and distinguished people, never experiencing foreign domination or the destruction of war. You will enjoy the prestige of eminent priests, the respect of illustrious ministers and royal dominion over other nations. Your society will be prosperous and advanced.[59] Above all,

---

that this *bris* refers to the one they will accept after *Matan Torah*.
54. See *Mechilta; Rashi; Yalkut Midrash Teiman; Targum Yonasan; Rabbeinu Bachya; Ibn Ezra; Rashbam* to *Shemos* 19:5; *Pesikta Rabbah* 11 p. 47.
55. See *Tur; Tzeror HaMor; Abarbanel; Bechor Shor* to *Shemos* 19:5 6.
56. See *Vayikra Rabbah* 4:6; *Divrei Shalom*. See *Devarim* 32:9.
57. *Mechilta; Rashi; Rashbam; Bechor Shor; R' Avraham Ben HaRambam; Chizkuni* to *Shemos* 19:6.
Hashem's love for the Bnei Yisrael, His choosing them as His own, "Li," would last only forty days. The Bnei Yisrael were "Li," "Mine," for forty days — the numerical value of *Li*. It was after these forty days that they worshiped the Golden Calf (*Bamidbar Rabbah* 7:4). Others suggest that the Bnei Yisrael were close to Hashem for twenty-nine days and contemplated making the Golden Calf for 11 days, and after that they actually went through with their thought (*Shemos Rabbah* 42:7).
58. *Mechilta; Sechel Tov* to *Shemos* 19:6.
59. *Mechilta;* see *Horayos* 13a with *Rashi*. See *Pane'ach Raza; Moshav Zekeinim*.
The gifts given to the Bnei Yisrael — "treasure," "a kingdom of priests" and "holy nation" — were due to the fact that the they were going to accept the Torah. In

you will be a holy nation, unpolluted by the corruption and decadence of the nations of the world.[60]

"But if you do not follow the Torah or acknowledge Me as your one and only God, if you will not have faith in Me and pay homage to Me with your prayers, then I will not protect you from your enemies, and you will suffer great hardship and loss.[61]

"The choice is clear, and the choice is yours."

Hashem's message to the Jewish people was complete. Now all that remained was to give Moshe his final instructions.

"Moshe, transmit the message exactly as I told it to you. Do not add anything of your own or subtract anything from what I told you. Do not tell it to them with any undue duress and intimidation by dwelling at length on the punishments and repercussions for disobedience, because this will allow them in the future to claim they were frightened out of their wits and did not agree of their own free will. At the same time, do not exaggerate the rewards for obedience, because this will diminish the intrinsic value of the mitzvos. The greatest reward of a mitzvah is the mitzvah itself, because it brings them close to Me. The promised rewards are only of secondary importance. Tell them My message exactly as I told it to you."[62]

Moshe Speaks to the People

Moshe came down from the mountain that very same day[63] and went directly to the encampment to deliver

---

addition, by accepting the crown of the Torah, the Jews would be worthy of receiving the additional crowns of *Kehunah* and *Malchus* (*Bamidbar Rabbah* 14:10; *Rabbeinu Bachya* to *Shemos* 19:6; see *Chen Tov* brought down by *Meam Loez*).

60. *Mechilta; Sechel Tov* to *Shemos* 19:6.

When the Serpent offered fruit from the Tree of Knowledge to Chavah, a *zuhama*, defilement, entered into her. This defilement would be removed upon the acceptance of the Torah. The nations of the world, who did not stand at Mount Sinai, did not benefit from the ceasing of this defilement (*Shabbos* 15b).

61. *Mechilta; Lekach Tov; Tosafos Al HaTorah.* See *Devarim* 7:7-8.

Some suggest that Hashem's message to Moshe was split in two, as seen earlier. The section dealing with *"segulah"* referred to the general public, people who, through Hashem's love, are naturally held in high esteem. However, *"mamleches Kohanim"* and *"goy kadosh"* referred to the leaders and scholars (*Abarbanel; Maaseh Hashem*).

Others suggest that the first half referred to the women, and the second half was meant for the men (*Tzeror HaMor*). Others suggest that the second half referred to Moshe and Aharon (*Ohr HaChaim*). See *Malbim* for a different version. See *Tzeror HaMor* for his interpretation of *segulah*.

62. *Mechilta; Rav; Tzeror HaMor; Ohr HaChaim; Gur Aryeh; Zeh Yenachmeni.*

63. *Yonasan Ben Uziel* to *Shemos* 19:7. See *Shabbos* 87 and the *machlokes* between R' Yosi

Hashem's message without the slightest delay. He did not stop in his own tent or consider any other matter before he fulfilled his mission.[64]

As Hashem had instructed him, he went first to the women and spoke to them in a soft and gentle manner. Then he turned his attention to the men, to whom he would speak in much sterner tones.[65] First, he summoned the leaders of the people — the elders, scholars, judges and other officials — and addressed them in full view of the common people.[66]

It was important that the leaders hear the message first, not only because it gave them honor and respect, but also because their prior commitment would be an essential factor in the common people's making their own commitment.[67] Once the people saw that their leaders had accepted the obligations of the covenant, they would be less inclined to reject the proposal. Furthermore, the leaders themselves, once they made the commitment, would circulate among the people and persuade them that this sacred covenant with the Almighty was the greatest privilege possible.[68]

In addition, the leaders had a historical role to play in all matters spiritual. Prior to the exodus from Egypt, Moshe had assembled the leaders and addressed them before he had gone to the common people. Now, too, the leaders would be his supporters in delivering Hashem's message to the entire Jewish people.[69]

As Moshe prepared to address the elders, the common people gathered around them, eager to hear what had transpired on the mountaintop. Soon there was a vast audience listening to every word with bated breath.

---

and Rabbanan as to whether it was Monday or Tuesday. According to some, Moshe came down while it was still daybreak, soon after he went up to Hashem. This is based on the discussion of whether Moshe's ascents or his descents were at daybreak (see *Chizkuni* to *Shemos* 19:7).

64. *Mechilta D'Rashbi* to *Shemos* 19:7.

65. See *Be'er Yitzchok; Tzeror HaMor* to *Shemos* 19:3.

66. *See Mechilta, Ramban* to *Shemos* 19:7; *Rokeach; Ibn Ezra* to *Shemos* 19:3; *Shemos Rabbah* 28:2. See *Panim Yafos.*

67. *Mechilta.*
  Some suggest that when Hashem told Moshe, "*Ko somar leBeis Yaakov*" and "*sagid livnei Yisrael*," the *Beis Yaakov* referred to the *zekeinim*, and he would then say over the other things to the Bnei Yisrael. Others suggest that after relaying Hashem's message to them, the elders and not Moshe repeated it to the Jewish people (see *R' Avraham Ben HaRambam; Maaseh Hashem*).

68. See *Abarbanel; Ohr HaChaim* to *Shemos* 19:7.

69. *Midrash Shocher Tov; Abarbanel.*

Moshe relayed the message to the leaders exactly as Hashem had told it to him, and then he got straight to the point. "Do you, the leader of the Jewish people," he asked, "accept upon yourself the Torah with all its obligations and responsibilities?"

One of the leaders, an old sage with blazing blue eyes and a sparse white beard, stood up. "If my distinguished colleagues have no objection," he began, "I would like to respond on behalf of everyone."

He looked around at the assembled sages and dignitaries, and they all nodded gravely.

"I believe that what I have to say," he continued, "is in everyone's heart. If, when I am done, anyone wishes to disagree or to add something, feel free to speak your minds."

Again, everyone nodded in assent.

"As far as I am concerned," said the old sage, "the Torah is already part of our tradition and heritage for hundreds of years. Our forefathers accepted the Torah from Hashem, and we have inherited this incredible treasure from them. Avraham accepted the prohibition against coveting what other people have. Yitzchak accepted the commandment of honoring one's parents when he stretched out his neck and was willing to let his father sacrifice him on the altar. Yaakov accepted the first two of the Ten Commandments, and Yosef accepted the following two. Yehudah accepted the prohibition against murder and the commandment of conducting fair trials. Yosef accepted the prohibition against adultery, and all the brothers accepted the prohibition against stealing. The Torah is not new to us, and we embrace it with our arms and our hearts. We are fortunate that at long last, in our time, we will receive it as a gift from Hashem in its entirety. We are pleased, honored and indeed humbled to accept it. This is the greatest day of our lives."[70]

His impassioned words were greeted with a murmur of unanimous approval. No one offered even the slightest objection. The leaders were all committed. Now it was time for Moshe and the leaders to bring the message to the common people and persuade them to make the same commitment.[71]

---

70. See *Pesikta Chadata* p. 40; he brings the *pesukim* where they accepted the different *isurim* and mitzvos of the *Aseres HaDibros* (the Ten Commandments).
71. *Pesikta Chadata* p. 40.

Moshe and the leaders turned to the people and prepared to begin their presentation complete with an entire arsenal of persuasive arguments, but before they could even begin to speak, there was a startling turn of events.[72]

The people had heard everything Moshe had told the leaders and their positive response. The decision of the people was delivered immediately, with no hesitation, deliberation, consultation or further discussion. The decision was instantaneous and unanimous.

"We will do it!" they all shouted with joy and excitement. "We will do everything, just as Hashem has told it to you."

One young man asked his companions to lift him on their shoulders. "United as one people," he cried out, "we accept the Torah unconditionally, willingly and happily.[73] We want an equal part in the entire Torah, and by uniting as one, we embrace everything in the Torah. We want to hear everything in the Torah, including the tough laws, the rewards, the penalties, things that apply to the present, things that apply to the future, things that apply to women or to other Jewish groups. We want to learn and embrace the entire Torah on behalf of all the people united as one."[74]

His impassioned words were greeted with loud cheers. The excitement in the vast crowd was electric.

Another man jumped onto a rock and waved his arms for attention. "This is the highest point of my life. How fortunate we are to receive the Torah from the Almighty. I believe I speak for all of us

---

72. See *Ramban*.
73. *Mechilta; Lekach Tov; Ramban; Abarbanel*.
   Their acceptance here would be for the Written Law of the Torah. As for the Oral Law, that would be forced upon them later. Later on they would utter the famous words, "We will do and we will listen"; at this point, though, all they said was "We will do" (*Rabbeinu Bachya*; see *Midrash Tanchuma Noach*).
   Others suggest that the Jews accepted the yoke of all negative commandments (*Tosafos*). The *Rokeach* says that the numerical value of *"Naaseh"* and *"b'ksav"* are equal — 425.
   See *Pardes Yosef* who writes that it was at this point that Hashem was about to bury them under Mount Sinai.
74. *Tosafos Al HaTorah; Bechor Shor; Sifsei Kohen; Maaseh Hashem; Malbim; Meshech Chochmah* to *Shemos* 19:8.
   Their agreement to do what he said or agree to do what Hashem said would only be in the context of Hashem addressing them personally. As we will see later, the Jews would request to hear the Ten Commandments from Hashem Himself (*Alshich*).
   Whether it was laws of Kehunah or Levi'ah, laws that did not apply to everyone, they wanted to accept the Torah even if it meant that they could only learn the laws that did not apply to them, but not perform them; nevertheless they wanted to be equal in the rewards at the very least.

when I say that we want this moment to be etched into our souls forever. We want to hear the Torah directly from Hashem. No barriers, no separations. This time, we do not want Moshe to be the intermediary between Hashem and the people. This time, we want to hear His voice talking to us. Yes, even to humble me. This time, we want to see our King. We want to see the *Shechinah* with our own two eyes.[75] When we encounter Hashem in our own direct experience, we will forever serve Him with absolute assurance in our hearts."

Once again, the crowd cheered its approval. This was exactly what they wanted, a personal encounter with the Creator of the Universe for each and every Jew, even the common people, a chance to hear His voice and see the aura of the Divine Presence, something that had never happened before.[76]

The Third Day

Moshe was gratified with the response of the people. At daybreak on the third day of the Jewish encampment at Sinai, Moshe ascended the mountain to the resting place of the Divine Presence to tell Hashem about what had transpired with the Jewish people.[77]

Of course, Hashem did not need Moshe to inform Him of the people's response; nothing escapes His awareness. Nonetheless, Moshe followed the protocols of common courtesy in his relationship with Hashem. When a king sends emissaries on a diplomatic mission, his spies and agents usually keep him abreast of everything that is going on. Still, the king expects his emissaries to submit an official report when they return. Moshe knew that there was nothing Hashem did not know even before it happened, but he still understood his obligation to return and deliver a full report.[78]

Moshe felt obligated to deliver the response of the Jewish people to Hashem, but at the same time, he was ill at ease with the mission that had fallen to him. He felt the request was somehow presumptuous.

It can be explained with a parable. A king sent his emissaries to a noblewoman of great valor to ask for her hand in marriage.

---

75. See *Mechilta, Rashi* to *Shemos* 19:9.
76. *Shlah* on *Shavuos* p. 40.
77. *Shabbos* 87b.
 Some suggest this was Tuesday while others suggest it was Wednesday (see *Chizkuni*).
78. *Mechilta; Netziv; Lekach Tov.*

"I am astonished," the noblewoman said. "You see, I am unworthy of being his majesty's maidservant, let alone his wife. I find it hard to believe that such an offer of marriage could be genuine. Please tell his majesty that I would like to hear the offer directly from his lips."

The emissaries were taken aback by the audacity of the request, but their duty to the king compelled them to bring this response back to him.

When they returned to the royal palace, the king was already awaiting them eagerly. The emissaries approached the throne, but they found themselves stuttering and stumbling over their words.

The wise king understood what had happened.

"There is no need to explain," he told them. "I can see that this fine noblewoman wants to hear the offer directly from me, because she finds her good fortune incredible. Very well. That is how it shall be. Bring her to the palace, and I will tell her myself."

The Jewish people also found their good fortune almost too good to be true. They understood that they were a noble people, descended from the forefathers who were beloved to Hashem, and that they of all people were most suitable to enter into the Divine covenant. Nonetheless, they wanted to hear it directly from Hashem.[79]

Like the emissaries in the parable, Moshe began to speak in a tentative fashion, groping for the right words with which to articulate this audacious request of the Jewish people, but Hashem stopped him before he could get too far.[80]

---

79. *Shir Rabbah* 1:3; *Yefei Kol*; *Yalkut* 2:581.
80. See *Rabbeinu Bachya*; *Bechor Shor*; *Daas Zekeinim* 19:8-9.
    See *Shabbos* 87a; *Mechilta*; *Rashi*; *Yalkut Midrash Teiman*; *Chizkuni*.
    There is much discussion in regard to the Torah's use of the words "*vayashev*," and "*vayageid*." Some suggest that Moshe returned (*vayashev*), Hashem interrupted him, and after Hashem spoke, Moshe said (*vayageid*) what the Jews had decided earlier. This was all at the same time on the third day. Others suggest that Moshe went up and down again and "*vayageid*," he told Hashem what the nation responded to what he had *just* been told, on the fourth day. A major factor in this argument is when the Jews accepted the Torah. If they accepted it on the 6th day, then Moshe went up to the mountain one day less, and all this occured on one day. If the Jews accepted the Torah on the 7th day, Moshe had an extra day to ascend and descend the mountain and bring to Hashem the words of the Bnei Yisrael. See *Malbim* for his explanation of the terms *vayeshev* and *vaygeid*. See also *Midrash Even* and *Sho'eir*.

"I understand what has happened," He said to Moshe. "The Jewish people want to hear the commandments of the Torah directly from Me. I will honor their request.[81]

"I will come to you in a thick foglike cloud called *arafel*, which obscures the image. Since you are on a high spiritual level, I always speak to you from a cloud that is not as thick so that the radiance will come through for your benefit.[82] But the people are not on such a level. Therefore, I will speak to them from an *arafel*, which is so thick and dense that the radiance will not come through with such clarity. All the people will witness My glory and enjoy the gift of prophecy on this day, but the vision will be subdued.[83]

"It is a good thing that I will show Myself to them in some form. Until now, the Jewish people believed that you were My messenger because of the wonders and miracles you performed.[84] But such a faith is not absolute. It is based on logic rather than experience. In the back of their minds, they may have a suspicion that maybe you performed all those feats on your own, that perhaps you are privy

---

81. *Mechilta.*
Some suggest that initially the Jews told Moshe that they were not interested. It appeared to Moshe that they did not believe him and he was afraid to tell Hashem the answer of the Jews, especially in light of the fact that this would be the second time that Moshe would doubt the faith of the Jews. Hashem interrupted Moshe and told him that He understood what the Jews meant. "They do believe you," Hashem replied, "they just want to see My glory and receive the Torah personally, just not in the manner you presented it to them." (See *Midrash Aggadah; Ralbag* to *Shemos* 19:8; *Maharsha* to *Kiddushin* 30a.)
82. See *Mechilta; Rashi; Sifsei Chachamim; Rashbam; Kesef Mezukak* to *Shemos* 19:9. See *Midrash Tehillim* 104 as well. See *Rabbeinu Bachya, Ramban* to *Shemos* 24:2; *Maharsha* to *Yevamos* 49b based on the *Aruch's* definition of the word "*spaklarya.*" Like one unable to look directly into the sun, a blockage was necessary for one to view Hashem's spiritual holiness (*Alshich*).
The commentaries write that Hashem would not be communicating with Moshe through an *aspaklarya meirah*. There is question as to what this *aspaklarya* is and the extent of the vision of Hashem's *Shechinah* the people witnessed in the first place. I have chosen to remove myself from even attempting to explain the spiritual phenomenon that was taking place here. Although in the past I offered various views and opinions regarding complex subjects, I cannot even begin to write the opinions, let alone explain them, on subject matter that is beyond my comprehension. I have therefore chosen to relate the general result of the subject at hand and no more. In this case, the Jews would witness a vision of Hashem speaking with Moshe and this would leave an everlasting effect on the prophecy they experienced. For further discussion of the term *aspaklarya*, see commentaries on *Keilim* 30:2; *Rashi* and commentaries on *Succah* 45b. Some suggest it to be a mirror, others a window or screen, others a lens. Some refer to it as a barrier, while most believe it to be a window or glass. In any case, this vision was obscured and not seen with clarity.
83. See *Ramban; Ibn Ezra; Sechel Tov; Alshich; Sforno; Kesef Mezukak.*
84. See Introduction to *Smag; Ramban* in *Yisro.*

to some extraordinary form of magic or sorcery that can accomplish such things.

"And when they hear Me speaking from your throat, they may suspect that a demon has possessed you or that it is an act of ventriloquism.[85] The Egyptians and other Hamitic peoples contend that no human can communicate with a spirit that is superhuman, for to do so would kill him.[86]

"Therefore, it is important that right now the Jewish people hear the prophecy directly from me without an intermediary in between. With no devious middleman between us, the people will not need to worry about deception. They will be getting the Torah directly from Me, the Seller.[87]

"Then in the future, if anyone should perform wonders and miracles in the Name of Hashem and speak prophecies that contradict your prophecies or the laws of the Torah, the people will identify him as a fraud. Once the people witness My glory with their own eyes and ears the memory will endure forever. They will know that your prophecy is authentic and any alleged prophecy that contradicts yours is fraudulent.[88] Your message will be accepted for all time as undisputed and unquestioned; they will recognize you as My prophet, and know that you heard My word directly from Me even as you were awake, rather than in a dream or vision that needs interpretation.[89]

"They will see the heavens descend onto the mountaintop and perceive the *Shechinah* in its resting place, and they will see that it is I Who am giving them the Torah. When they hear My voice and see My glory, when they experience a taste of prophecy on their own, they will understand the true meaning of authentic prophecy, that it derives exclusively from Hashem and not from any natural sources. All the multitudes of the Jewish people — men, women and even the smallest children — will rise to the level of angels on this day. They will know the meaning of prophecy, and they will remember the experience for the rest of time.[90]

---

85. See *Tosafos Al HaTorah*; *Rambam, Hil. Yesodei HaTorah* 8:1; introduction to *Sefer HaChinuch*.
86. See *Ibn Ezra; Ramban* to *Shemos* 19:9.
87. See *Rashi* to *Devarim* 5:4.
88. *Sforno; Rambam, Hil. Yesodei HaTorah* 8:1.
89. *Mechilta; Rashi; Ramban; Ibn Ezra* to *Shemos* 19:9; *Abarbanel* 19:20.
90. *Meam Loez nes* 26.

"All the souls of the Jewish people will be present at Mount Sinai when I will give the Torah — the souls of those who are alive today as well as the souls of all the Jews who will be born in the future. Every one of these souls will have this prophetic vision, and it will remain engraved in their souls for all eternity. No one who stood at Mount Sinai will ever deny the events that will transpire here. Should anyone dare to deny them, you can be sure that neither he nor his forefathers were present at Mount Sinai on this day. [91]

"Go tell the Jewish people what I have told you here today. And tell them as well that if they are indeed to enjoy the privilege of prophecy and see My glory with their own eyes, they will have to make special preparations for it, as I will instruct you."[92]

---

91. *Mechilta; Midrash HaGadol; Tosafos; Malbim*; see *Nedarim* 20a and commentaries.

For an overview to this whole discussion, see *Rambam, Hil. Yesodei HaTorah* 8:1; Introduction to *Smag; Mechilta; Rashi; Sifsei Chachamim; Ramban; Rashbam; R' Yehudah HaChassid; Ibn Ezra, Sforno; Malbim* to *Shemos* 19:9.

92. As mentioned earlier, there are differing views as to what took place at this point. *Rashi's* view suggests that Moshe repeated these words to the Jews at this point on day three and then ascended back the following day, on the fourth, to tell Hashem of the nation's wish to see His glory personally.

7 A State of Preparation

The Jewish people were tremendously inspired when they encamped at Sinai. They wanted to draw close to the *Shechinah*. They wanted to receive the Torah directly from Hashem. They wanted to see the manifestations of the Divine Presence and hear His voice speak to them directly. They wanted to climb the mountain and let their spiritual essence absorb the holiness of the Divine Presence that rested there. But that was not such a simple thing.

Hashem warned Moshe that the people should not approach the mountain, because the level of holiness was too great for them to endure. If Moshe, who was on the highest spiritual level, could not approach the *sneh*, the burning bush in which the Divine Presence rested, the rest of the people would certainly be considered unfit to approach the mountain. Violation would result in death. Hashem, therefore, instructed Moshe to erect boundaries around the mountain to ensure that no one approached and was harmed.[1]

Furthermore, the Jewish people would have to prepare themselves to receive the Torah in purity and holiness. Even to stand behind the barricades at the foot of the mountain — to hear Hashem's voice and see the manifestations of the Divine Presence — would also require considerable preparation.[2]

Establishing Boundaries

While still on the third day of their encampment at Sinai, Hashem gave Moshe detailed instructions regarding the establishment of a restricted zone around the holy mountain for the duration of the presence of the *Shechinah* there. Although the boundaries were only to be set on the day the Torah would be given, which was still three days in the future, Hashem gave Moshe his instructions well in advance, in order to accustom the Jewish people to the idea of restraint.[3]

The boundaries were to encircle the mountain completely, each point on the perimeter being 2,000 cubits distant from the mountain. This would prevent the Jewish people from entering the restricted area from any direction.[4] All the Jewish people — male

---

1. *Zohar Emor* 106; *Abarbanel*; *Pnei Yehoshua* to *Shabbos* 87a.
   Some suggest that, on the contrary, the Jews needed to practice fear of and reverence for Hashem and distance themselves from a light and carefree attitude. It was for this reason that Hashem wanted to set boundaries — so that they should understand the impact of the *Shechinah's* holiness (*Ralbag*).
   Some add that Hashem wanted to give them a prohibition on something they specifically wanted to do. The more they wanted to get close, the more Hashem would tell them that they could not. This would teach them the practice of following laws in instances when it was hard and in instances when it went against their natural tendencies and desires (*Shem MiShmuel; Kli Chemdah*).

2. See *Rashi* to *Shemos* 24:3; *Ralbag*; *Abarbanel*; *Rashbam*; *Malbim* to *Shemos* 19:10.
   See *Sifsei Chachamim* and *Gur Aryeh* who write that according to R' Yosi this preparation would begin on Tuesday, the 3rd of the month. According to the Rabbanan, it took place on Wednesday, the 3rd of the month.
   Some say that sanctification indeed took place on the 5th day of the month, but that Hashem spoke to Moshe about the laws on the 4th day. See *Rashi* to *Shemos* 24:3 with *Mizrachi* and *Gur Aryeh*.
   Some suggest that an angel spoke with Moshe and not Hashem (*Rokeach; Rashbam*). See *Yonasan Ben Uziel* to *Shemos* 19:9.

3. *Rabbeinu Bachya; Ohr HaChaim* to *Shemos* 19:12.

4. *Mechilta; Chizkuni* to *Shemos* 19:12.
   This also conforms with the opinion that they were only camped on the eastern portion of the mountain. As mentioned earlier, there is a view that the Jews were camped around Mount Sinai with three tribes on each side. (See *Panim Yafos; Targum Yonasan*.)

and female, righteous and not so righteous, on foot or riding in an animal-drawn cart — were forbidden to ascend the mountain or even touch the base of the slope. They were also instructed to be vigilant and issue warnings should they see anyone else venturing near the boundary.[5] In fact, according to some opinions, the boundary itself called out to anyone approaching, "Halt! Do not cross this line. No unauthorized person may pass beyond this point."[6]

The large restricted zone around the mountain served as a buffer to keep people far away from the mountain itself. Unauthorized entry into the restricted zone carried no penalty. But there was a severe penalty for trespassing on the mountain itself or even touching it. All trespassers were to be stoned to death.[7]

It was the responsibility of the courts to administer this death penalty immediately, while the perpetrator was still on the mountain. The courts were not permitted to send one of their bailiffs to remove the perpetrator from the mountain and bring him to justice, since that would entail an unauthorized ascent on the mountain by the bailiff.[8] Therefore, the penalty by stoning was to be administered from a distance. The people were to throw stones at the perpetrator until he died. If he was too far to be reached by hand-thrown stones,

---

5. *Mechilta; Yalkut* 280; *Minchah Belulah; Rabbeinu Bachya* to *Shemos* 19:12-13. See *Netziv* and his interpretation of *Mechilta's* text. See *Yerushalmi Beitzah* 85.

Some suggest that this only applied to direct body contact, but if someone touched the mountain with a stick it did not apply (see *Be'er Yitzchok*).

Some suggest that it did not apply to birds since they can fly away and avoid retribution. See *Ibn Ezra; Bava Kamma* 54b. Many question the opinion of the *Ibn Ezra* since the *Gemara* clearly states that the law applied even to birds. Some offer an answer that even the *Ibn Ezra* agrees that the prohibition applied to birds as well, but birds were free of punishment because they could fly away and avoid capture. Others question how an animal who is unable to discern right from wrong should be punished like that, and answer that the death of the animal was punishment to its owner who was not careful in watching his animal (*R' Avraham Ben HaRambam*).

6. *Rashi; Mechilta; Gur Aryeh; Levush Orah*. There is discussion about *Rashi's* translation of the word *"leimor"* as "saying." Some have a different text of the words of *Rashi* because they feel that if, in fact, the boundaries actually spoke, it would have been too great a miracle to have gone unnoticed and not spoken of. See *Ibn Ezra; Be'er Yitzchok; Meam Loez; Divrei David; Maskil L'David*. For this reason, some suggest that *Rashi's* statement means nothing more than that when the boundaries were set, they gave the appearance as if to say, "Here is the line, do not pass," but they did not in fact talk. See *Sefer Zikaron*.

Others suggest that this was no different than when the lotteries were made to divide up Eretz Yisrael. In that case, the lot itself would call out which boundary it set for which *shevet* (tribe) (*Tzeidah LaDerech*). See *Bava Basra* 122a; *Rashi* to *Bamidbar* 26:54.

7. See *Mechilta; Rashi; R' Avraham Ben HaRambam*. See *Sanhedrin* 45a.

8. *Lekach Tov; Da'as Zekeinim; Bechor Shor; Rashbam*.

they were to use catapults, arrows, spears, javelins or any other projectiles that could be hurled at him with effectiveness.[9]

After the perpetrator died under a hail of stones, it was forbidden to go onto the mountain to retrieve the corpse for burial, since that would again entail an unauthorized ascent on the mountain. But this would present no problem, since the mountain would miraculously cast away the corpse that was defiling the holy environment.[10]

If the courts found it impossible to administer the death penalty to the perpetrator while he was still on the mountain, Heaven would administer it. This supernatural execution could take the form of hailstones, lightning bolts or an avalanche. It could also take the form of seismic tremors on the mountainside that would cast off the perpetrator and cause him to fall to his death.[11]

Should the perpetrator, for some reason, be spared execution by supernatural means, the courts were to arrest him when he came down from the mountain or when the restricted zone expired and a bailiff could be sent onto the mountain to take him into custody. After a proper proceeding, he was to be stoned to death.[12]

The expiration of the restricted zone was marked by the long blast of the *shofar*, which signaled the departure of the *Shechinah* from the mountain and the termination of its enhanced state of sanctification.[13] This state lasted into the following year when Moshe returned with the second Tablets on Yom Kippur. Until then no one was allowed to ascend the mountain except for Moshe. After that, Aharon, his sons

---

9. See *Rashbam; Chizkuni; Targum Yonasan; Minchah Belulah; Rosh; Rokeach.*
10. *R' Efraim Al HaTorah.*
11. See *Targum Yonasan; Peirush Yonasan; Chizkuni; Malbim.*
12. *Rashi; Midrash HaChefetz; Akeidah.*
13. *Shemos* 19:13. See *Rashi; Mechilta; Minchah Belulah; Chemas HaChemdah* to *Shemos* 19:13; *Rashi* on *Taanis* 21b; see *Beitzah* 5b.

The long blast represented the *tekiah gedolah* (long blast of the *shofar*) which signified the conclusion of Yom Tov.

Some suggest that the *shofar* was the horn of a goat. Much of the difference of opinion depends on whether or not this *shofar* was the representation of the ram which replaced Yitzchak at the *Akeidah*. See *Rashi; Tur; Ibn Ezra.*

Some contend that since that ram was completely sacrificed, not even its horn remained. Some suggest that the ashes of its horns were miraculously heaped or kneaded together and put back to use. Others suggest that the ram was reborn for this use. Still others suggest that the ram's parts were all used for specific purposes. The left horn was for the *shofar* used at Sinai and the right horn would be used for the "Great *shofar*" at the coming of Mashiach. Still others suggest that it was not the actual horn but that its spiritual power and metaphoric symbol and merit actually was the sound of the *shofar* heard at Har Sinai. This was a supernatural sound, appropriate for such a supernatural event. See *Pirkei D'Rav Eliezer* 31; *Radal; Rabbeinu Bachya; Ramban; Chizkuni; Gur Aryeh* to *Rashi* to *Shemos* 19:13.

and the elders were allowed to ascend. The rest of the people could not ascend until the month of Iyar of the following year. Once the Mishkan was built, the *Shechinah* took up residence, so to speak, in the Mishkan, and the people were allowed to ascend the mountain if they so chose.[14]

Our Sages derive an important lesson from the shift in the status of the mountain. Mount Sinai was an ordinary place until the *Shechinah* settled upon it, and it returned to being ordinary after the *Shechinah* departed. Honor and prestige, they point out, does not flow from a person's place or position. On the contrary, it is the person who honors his place or position. Once he leaves, the honor departs.[15]

Ascending to Arafel

On the morning of the fourth day of the Jewish encampment at Sinai, Hashem once again summoned Moshe to the mountaintop. According to some, He sent the angel Michael to deliver the summons.[16] The summons also included Aharon, his two eldest sons Nadav and Avihu, and the seventy elders of the Jewish people. They were to approach the mountain, and at a distance of 2,000 cubits, they were to prostrate themselves.[17] Then they were to continue toward the mountain in a formal procession in rank order. Moshe, being the greatest, would lead the way, followed by Aharon, then his two sons and then the seventy elders. This passage through the restricted zone would also familiarize them with the terrain and help them educate the people about the prohibition of trespassing.

---

14. See *Rashi* to *Taanis* 21b; *Beitzah* 5b with *Tosafos* there and *Rashi*; *Ibn Ezra* to *Shemos* 19:13; *Abarbanel*.
15. *Taanis* 21b.
16. *Yonasan Ben Uziel* to *Shemos* 24.1.
    There are others who suggest that another ministering angel called to Moshe to make his way to Sinai. See *Sanhedrin* 38b; *Ramban*; *Rabbeinu Bachya*; *Sifsei Kohen* to *Shemos* 24:1; *Abarbanel*.
17. *Lekach Tov* to *Shemos* Ch. 24. See *Midrash HaChefetz*.
    There is a dispute as to the time this event took place. Some suggest that it happened after *Matan Torah* on Shabbos (the 6th or 7th day) (*Ramban*; *Rashbam*; *Ibn Ezra*; *Ralbag*; *R' Avraham Ben HaRambam*; *Ohr HaChaim*; see *Chazon Ish, Orach Chaim* 125).
    Others suggest that although this is mentioned in *Mishpatim*, it took place before *Matan Torah* (*Rashi* to *Shemos* 24:1; *Sifsei Chachamim*; *Lekach Tov*; *Bechor Shor*; *Sifsei Kohen* to *Shemos* 24:1; *Gitin* 88b with *Rashi*).
    See *HaKesav VeHaKabbalah* to *Mishpatim* who offers an explanation of the dispute in the *Mechilta* if this was before or after *Matan Torah*. See *Abarbanel* who explains the sequence of events very clearly.

Only Moshe, however, would be allowed to enter the spiritual *arafel* cloud that sat atop the mountain. The others would be permitted to approach the mountain, but they would have to wait at a distance when Moshe entered the *arafel*.[18]

The elders, to their displeasure, were relegated to bringing up the rear of the procession, because they were not on the same level as Moshe and Aharon. There was also a significant element of symbolism in their being directed to lag behind. When Moshe went to Pharaoh's palace for the first time, to demand the emancipation of the Jewish people, he was accompanied by Aharon, the elders and many of the common people. As they drew closer, they encountered the fearsome symbols of Pharaoh's power — fierce, heavily armed guards and snarling lions. The common people were the first to slip away and flee. The elders accompanied Moshe into the palace, but soon, they too made a quick getaway. Only Aharon accompanied Moshe all the way to the audience with Pharaoh. Hashem now repaid, measure for measure, those who showed the most dedication to Moshe's Divine mission. The common people were asked to stay behind the boundaries. The elders could enter the boundaries but still had to remain a distance from the mountain. As for Aharon, he was now invited to accompany Moshe the furthest of all.[19]

As the procession passed through the boundaries and approached the mountain, Nadav and Avihu, Aharon's sons, were having a disdainful and inappropriate conversation. Nadav and Avihu had reached very exalted spiritual levels, and in certain aspects, they surpassed all of the Jewish people, bar none.

"My brother," one of them said to the other, "why do you think we have been assigned to the third position in this procession? Shouldn't our hard-earned spiritual achievements have warranted a higher rank?"

"I agree with you, my brother," said the other. "I suppose that the older generation is given preference regardless of personal merit."

"Yes, I suppose you're right. Sometimes, I am impatient for these two old men to move on to a higher world, so that we can assume the mantle of leadership already."

---

18. *Mechilta D'Rashbi; Rashi* to *Shemos* 24:2; *Moreh Nevuchim* 2:32. *Bechor Shor; Rabbeinu Bachya; R' Samson Rafael Hirsch.* See *Ramban* here.
19. *Midrash HaGadol; Rashi; Pane'ach Raza* to *Shemos* 5:1; *Shemos Rabbah* 5:24.

Although there may have been a small measure of justice to their claims of superior achievement, their lack of humility certainly left them far short of Moshe and Aharon in overall greatness.

Hashem responded to their presumptuous conversation with the popular saying that "the mother animal wears the flesh of its young." In other words, Aharon would outlive his two sons. This would take place in the not-too-distant future.[20]

When the procession reached the mountain, a path opened in the cloud covering the peak, and Moshe went forward himself.[21] The cloud was comprised of three chambers within chambers. The outer cloud is called *choshech*, the middle cloud *anan* and the inner cloud *arafel*.[22] According to some, *arafel* is the darkest of the three; its transcendent spirituality makes it almost impossible to perceive, impenetrable even to angels. Others suggest that the *arafel* is not dark at all, but clear and gleaming, a manifestation of the radiance of the *Shechinah* — so bright that the human eye cannot look at it, just as one cannot look at the sun for more than a moment or two. Yet, although no being can presume to enter this holiest of domains, this inner sanctum of the celestial world, Moshe was granted entry.[23]

Sanctification and Purification

Back on the mountaintop in the presence of the *Shechinah*, Moshe articulated the yearning of the Jewish people to see the manifestations of the *Shechinah* and to hear Hashem's voice. Hashem granted their wish, but He told Moshe that the people would have to perform a process of ritual cleansing as a preparation. Only after they had properly sanctified and purified their bodies and souls

---

20. See *Vayikra Rabbah* 20:10; *Maharzav*; *Yefei To'ar*; *Sanhedrin* 52a with *Rashi*; *Tanchuma Acharei* 6. See *Yalkut Shemos* 361, *Tur* to *Shemos* 24:1. See *Mishlei* 27:1.

Aharon, in fact, had two more children (Elazar and Isamar) who were not included in this march before Har Sinai. Hashem knew that transgressions were going to take place during this time, and punishment would be meted out. As it turned out, Nadav and Avihu would later be sentenced to death for their transgression and Hashem wanted to leave Aharon with a legacy of Kehunah by keeping Elazar and Isamar away — and alive (*Tur*). We later discuss the fact that Aharon was deserving of punishment for having an indirect part in the Golden Calf. As retribution, his two older children, Nadav and Avihu, would be sentenced to death.

21. *Yoma* 4b; see *Maharsha*.

22. See *Rashi*; *Rabbeinu Bachya*; *Abarbanel*; *Malbim* to *Shemos* 20:18; commentaries to *Tehillim* 18:10,12; *Iyov* 23:13; *Yalkut* 301; *Lekach Tov*; *Rokeach* to *Devarim* 4:11. See *Ramban* to *Devarim* 5:19.

23. See *Rabbeinu Bachya*; *Malbim*; *HaKesav VeHaKabbalah* to *Shemos* 20:18. See *Malbim* to *Devarim* 4:11.

could they be considered worthy of such a close encounter with the *Shechinah*.[24]

"Tell these words to the Jewish people," Hashem said to Moshe. "Prepare yourselves properly today and tomorrow and then, on the third day, you will be ready to see Me descend and reveal My presence on Mount Sinai. I will descend in a manner that will allow you to perceive My presence."[25]

After Hashem finished speaking to him, Moshe left the *arafel* and descended the mountain. As a scrupulous intermediary between Hashem and the Jewish people, he wasted no time in delivering the message with which Hashem had entrusted him;[26]

---

24. This is based on the discrepancy between the words *vayashev* (brought back) and *vayageid* (told) in *Shemos* 19:8-9. There were two issues here. One was that the Jews wanted to experience direct vision and the radiance of Hashem. In that aspect, Hashem responded with verse 9 that He would come in a thick cloud. As to their wish to see and hear Hashem, He responded by giving them the laws of *perishah* (separation).

25. *Rashi* to *Shemos* 19:10,11; *R' Saadiah Gaon*; *Malbim*. See *Sefer HaParshiyos*. See *Chidushei HaRan*; *Ritva* to *Shabbos* 87a.

There is a dispute in the *Gemara* regarding the days of preparation. According to R' Yosi, who believes that the Torah was given on Shabbos, the 7th day of Sivan, the days included in the above phrase were three. Accordingly, it was on Wednesday, Thursday and Friday that the Jews prepared, with the Torah being given on the 7th day, on Shabbos. The Rabbanan believe that there were no additional days, and that the preparations took place on Thursday and Friday, with the Torah being given on Shabbos. (See *Rashi*; *Yalkut Midrash Teiman* to *Shemos* 19:15; *Shabbos* 87a; *Chizkuni* to *Yisro*.)

Some suggest that Hashem used the term day "three" (three days from the day He was speaking to Moshe He would give the Torah), because the trees were created on the third day of creation. This would be a reference to the Torah being "*Etz Chaim*" (*Midrash Chadash Al HaTorah*).

26. Although, in the Torah, *perishah*, the command to separate themselves, appears before that of *hagbalah*, cordoning off the mountain, all agree that the cordoning took place first. The dispute in the *Gemara* is if *perishah* took place on Wednesday or Thursday. According to R' Yosi, as we will see, *perishah* took place on Wednesday, with Moshe adding a day. According to the Rabbanan it took place on Thursday. Both agree,

R' YOSI						
Sunday	Monday	Tuesday	Wednesday	Thursday	Friday	Shabbos
1	2	3	4	5	6	7
	Yom HaMeyuchas	hagbalah	perishah	perishah	perishah	

RABBANAN						
Sunday	Monday	Tuesday	Wednesday	Thursday	Friday	Shabbos
30	1	2	3	4	5	6
		Yom HaMeyuchas	hagbalah	perishah	perishah	

he did not stop anywhere else beforehand or tend to any personal matters.[27]

Moshe reported the words Hashem had said to him earlier in the morning. He explained to the people that after their preparations, they would all see a manifestation of the *Shechinah*. Every single one of them. Anyone blind, visually impaired or having any other handicap would be healed so that he could perceive the holy vision without any debilities.[28] Every single Jew would witness the image of the Almighty in a fiery cloud, a vision not granted even to the greatest prophets, such as Yeshayahu and Yechezkel.[29]

Moshe now considered Hashem's instructions that the Jewish people sanctify and purify themselves. What exactly did this mean? What cause of ritual impurity needed to be addressed? It could not mean circumcision, because the people were all circumcised. It could not be related to the food and water supply, because the people were living on the manna from Heaven and the water from Miriam's Well. It could not be related to defiled creatures or other ritual contaminants in the environment, because the cloud pillars did not allow any of those things into the encampment. Therefore, Moshe concluded, it could only mean that the Jews were to refrain from any intimate contact with their wives during this period of preparation.

Having reached this conclusion, Moshe added one full day to the period of preparation in order to ensure that everyone would be sanctified and pure in time to receive the Torah. Hashem had directed the people to prepare themselves properly on that day, the fourth of the encampment at Sinai, and the next day, which would be the fifth of their encampment. They would then receive the Torah on the following day, 6 Sivan, the sixth day of their encampment. Moshe added one more day of preparation, causing the Torah to be received on 7 Sivan.[30]

---

however, that it took place on day four. See *Rashi, Tosafos* and *Maharsha* to *Shabbos* 87a for their explanations on the subject. See *Chizkuni; Mechilta*.

27. *Rashi; Mechilta; Lekach Tov* to *Shemos* 19:14.
28. *Mechilta; Rashi* to *Shemos* 19:11.
29. *Mechilta; Bamidbar Rabbah* 7; *Ramban; Tur; Malbim*.
30. See *Pirkei D'Rav Eliezer* 41; *Radal; Yalkut* 279. *Rashi* and *Ramban* to *Shemos* 19:10. See *Shemos Rabbah* 46:3; *Vayikra* 15:11; *Moreh Nevuchim* 3:33; *Ramban; Chidushei HaRan* to *Shabbos* 86a. There are forms of ritual contamination which require more than three days of cleansing. Hashem could have also made a miracle that there would be no contaminating incidents in the first place, thus avoiding any necessity of purification. See *Avos D'Rav*

Some suggest another reason for the addition of a full day of preparation. Moshe knew that the words *"yom ha'shishi,* the sixth day" at the end of the story of Creation are a reference to the sixth day of Sivan, the day on which the Torah would be given to the Jewish people. This means that the entire world was created for the purpose that would be fulfilled that day. If it somehow failed, the world would cease to exist. Moshe was therefore concerned that the Jewish people might balk when the Torah would be offered to them and thereby cause the destruction of the world. This was not an unjustified concern, because on 7 Sivan, the people did indeed reject the Torah until the mountain was held over their heads and coerced them.

This was the problem facing Moshe — how to ensure that on 6 Sivan there would be only acceptance of the Torah without a whiff of rejection. Moshe's solution was to add a day of preparation and thus delay the actual receiving of the Torah until 7 Sivan.

Moshe knew that on 5 Sivan the people would say, "*Naaseh venishma* — We will do, and we will hear." This declaration would be considered a binding commitment to accept the Torah as long as they did not clearly renege. Then 6 Sivan would pass without incident as the people would still be in the midst of their preparations. In this way, there would only be acceptance on 6 Sivan with no hint of rejection, and the world would escape destruction. Although trouble would surface on 7 Sivan in the form of rumblings of rejection, it would be too late. The date of 6 Sivan would have passed without incident.[31]

Others suggest yet another reason for Moshe's addition of a third day of preparation, even though Hashem had only specified two days of preparation. The purpose of this period of preparation was to render

---

Nassan 2:3 for his view. See *Rabbeinu Tam; Tosafos* to *Shabbos* 87 on the discussion of Hashem agreeing with Moshe regarding his "added" day, and regarding Aharon and Miriam's objection to Moshe separating from his wife.

Moshe himself separated from his wife because he was always available for Hashem to speak with him. Some suggest that Moshe actually divorced his wife at this time since he could not live under normal marriage conditions. Although after *Matan Torah* the Jews went back to their wives, Moshe did not. (See *Shemos Rabbah* 46:3; *Riva.*)

Some suggest that Moshe added this day after the Jews had said *Naaseh venishma* ("We will do and we will hear"; *Shemos* 24:7) (*Chasam Sofer*). The apparent difficulty is that *Naaseh venishma* was said on the 5th day and Moshe's instruction to the Jews had already been given.

31. *Kometz HaMinchah, Shavuos.*

Some add that Moshe added a day so that the Bnei Yisrael would not have to accept the Torah on Friday. Since it was Erev Shabbos, it would be difficult for them to prepare properly (*Haamek Davar*).

them worthy of having a direct encounter with the *Shechinah*. In the end, they would find the experience unbearable and would plead for it to end after the first two Commandments. Such an abbreviated encounter would not have necessitated three days of preparation. Two days would have been enough. Moshe, however, did not know this would happen. He thought the people would hear all Ten Commandments directly from Hashem, and therefore, he prescribed for them the full regimen of preparation, which took three days. But Hashem did know this would happen and that the Jewish people would have only a brief encounter with the *Shechinah*. Therefore, He prescribed only two days of preparation.[32]

Stages of Preparation

The preparations first addressed the issue of *taharah*, ritual purity, by requiring *perishus*, the abstention from all physical contact between husband and wife. As an additional safeguard, the prohibition also included *yichud*, being alone together.[33] They were also required to purify their bodies and their garments from all ritual contamination by immersion in a *mikveh*.[34]

Furthermore, the Jewish people, as part of their preparations, were required to ensure that they would come to their encounter with the *Shechinah* in perfect cleanliness and hygiene. They were to spend the period of preparation bathing and scrubbing themselves until the last vestige of desert dust was removed from their bodies and clothing.[35]

---

32. *Kometz HaMinchah, Shavuos.*
33. See *Panim Yafos; Targum Onkelos* and *Targum Yonasan* to *Shemos* 19:10,15.
It was for this reason that the women were separated from the men at Har Sinai when receiving the Torah — so as to prevent even the slightest form of contact of any kind (*Pirkei D'Rav Eliezer* 41, see *Radal*).
Some suggest that "*Ko somar l'Beis Yaakov*" was a reference to telling the women to separate themselves from their husbands.
34. See *Mechilta; Ramban; Bechor Shor* to *Shemos* 19:10,15; *Rambam, Hil. Isurei Biah* 13:1.
35. *Ibn Ezra; Bechor Shor; Malbim; Sifsei Kohen; Yalkut* 282; *Midrash HaGadol* 10,14. The numeric value of *machar* (tomorrow) (*Shemos* 19:10) is 248 — the number of limbs in a man's body. See *Chizkuni* who writes that although washing did not require three days of preparation, because the Erev Rav were included as part of the Bnei Yisrael, and they had the tendency to postpone commandments given to them, three days were necessary.
Some question that in *Parashas Eikev* (8:4) *Rashi* suggests that the *ananei kavod* (cloud pillars) cleansed and pressed the clothing, renewing them. If that were the case, what necessity was there for washing clothing? See *Aderes Eliyahu* who writes that the well water was such that there was no perspiration, thus clothing never got worn out. Some offer a suggestion that the necessity to wash the clothing was nothing more than to do *hishtadlus* (endeavors) for *kavod HaTorah* in preparation for *kabbalas HaTorah*.

In addition, they were to purify and cleanse their souls as well as their bodies from all traces of contamination. It would not be enough to purify and cleanse the body, which is the outer garment of a person, and leave the soul, which is the inner essence, sullied and unclean. Drunkenness and gluttony were not issues at this time for the people, since they ate only the manna and drank the water from Miriam's Well. But there was concern about other sins that sat like blemishes on their souls; for instance, they were to collect every item in their possession to which they did not have legitimate legal claim and return it to its rightful owner. Purifying their souls also meant purifying their minds from evil and improper thoughts.[36]

During this period of preparation, as the Jewish people worked hard to cleanse, purify and sanctify themselves, they were also to refrain from work and other mundane tasks and concentrate on Torah study and strengthening their faith. This would bring them to the exalted spiritual level at which they would be worthy of the gift of prophecy. Only then could they hope to hear Hashem's voice and see the manifestation of the *Shechinah*.[37]

Moshe also told them that it would be entirely proper and worthwhile to stay awake and study for the entire night, so that they would be fully awake and receptive when Hashem spoke to them, instead of rubbing sleep from their eyes.[38]

The last step in the preparation process would take place on the fifth day of the encampment at Sinai when the Jewish people would bring special sacrifices in honor of the occasion.

The preparation for receiving the Torah, in a certain sense, paralleled the conversion process by following three distinct steps — circumcision, immersion and sacrifice. The first step had been accomplished when the Jewish people circumcised themselves while yet in Egypt. The immersion took place during the period of preparation at Sinai, and the sacrifices were brought on the fifth day of the encampment.[39]

---

36. *Tanna D'Vei Eliyahu* 18; *Sforno*; *R' Avraham Ben HaRambam*; *Sifsei Kohen*; *HaKesav VeHaKabbalah*; *Alshich*; *Kuzari* 1:87; *Malbim*; *Minchah Belulah*; *Abarbanel* to *Shemos* 19:10,14.
37. *Sforno*; *Abarbanel*; *Malbim* to *Shemos* 19:10,14.
38. *Ibn Ezra*; *Minchah Belulah* to *Shemos* 19:11.
    He further points out that this would be similar to a Kohen Gadol staying awake on Yom Kippur night in preparation for the next day's service.
39. See *Kereisos* 9a; *Rabbeinu Bachya*; *Mechilta D'Rashbi*; *Rashi* to *Shemos* 24:6; *Mechilta*; *Rambam, Hil. Isurei Biah* 13:1.

A State of Preparation

There was also an additional dimension to these preparations. The Giving of the Torah was the marriage between Hashem and the Jewish people. It consummated the bond and sanctified it in a state of matrimony. Such a royal wedding certainly called for meticulous preparation.[40]

Moshe finished giving the Jewish people detailed instructions about the period of preparation and he spent the rest of the day teaching them the Torah. He reviewed with them the *Sheva Mitzvos Bnei Noach*, the seven universal mitzvos that apply to all human beings. He then reviewed with them the mitzvos presented at Marah, given specifically for the Jewish people — such as Shabbos observance, honoring parents, basic civil and business law and the laws of the red heifer (*parah adumah*) — and added many more details than they had been given at first.[41]

After Moshe finished teaching them the laws, the people responded with a loud cry, "*Naaseh!* We will do it!" There was no need to ask each individual Jew if he agreed to embrace the Torah. The acceptance was by unanimous acclaim.[42] This was the prerequisite for the Giving of the Torah. Had even one Jew objected, Hashem would not have given it.[43]

Later, when the people went off to study on their own and take care of their families, Moshe sat down to put in writing the words of Hashem he had been given thus far — the Torah as we know it from the beginning of *Parashas Bereishis* until *Parashas Yisro*, which describes the events they were experiencing.[44]

---

40. *Bamidbar Rabbah* 12:8. See *Maharzav* and *Matnos Kehunah*; *Pesikta Rabbah* 5 p. 20. This is based on the term *"vekidashtam,"* an allusion to *kiddushin* (a marriage ceremony).

41. *Rabbeinu Bachya; Rashi; Tosafos Al HaTorah* to *Shemos* 24:3.
Moshe's teachings included the episodes and incidents involving Adam. Moshe taught the Jews that before Adam's sin, he was eligible to live in Gan Eden. It was only after he became contaminated by the *"zuhama"* (spiritual defilement that results from sinning) that he was evicted. The Jews would know that if and when they were purified and spiritually ready, they could accept the Torah and hear Hashem personally on the highest level (*Alshich*).

42. See *Midrash HaGadol Mishpatim; Lekach Tov; Ibn Ezra* to *Shemos* 24:3.

43. *Sefer Chassidim.*

44. *Rashi* to *Shemos* 24:4. See *Chizkuni*. According to *Mechilta D'Rashbi*, who writes that "he arose early" was on day four, after that is when day five began. Some suggest that according to R' Yosi's view, this occurred on day six, a day before *Matan Torah*, which occurred on the seventh day. (See *Lekach Tov* and commentaries below to *Shemos* 19:10 and 24:4.)

The Fifth Day

On the morning of the fifth day, Moshe rose early and went out to the mountainside to build the *mizbe'ach*, the altar, upon which the Jewish people would bring sacrifices later that day in preparation for receiving the Torah.[45] He also erected twelve monuments, representing the twelve tribes of Israel, and arranged them in a cluster that replicated the pattern of the encampment.[46] The close configuration of the monuments symbolized the unity and harmony of the Jewish people, a nation characterized by brotherly love and the common goal of serving Hashem.[47]

The work of construction completed, Moshe summoned the youths, among them firstborn Jews, and instructed them to bring the sacrifices.[48] At this time, the rights to perform the priestly services belonged to the firstborn. Moshe specifically chose the younger ones among them in order to give them an opportunity to gain some experience in the sacrificial service. In addition, he preferred the young innocent boys who had never known the flavor of sin. Their souls were still pure and untainted, and their service would be more pleasing to Hashem.[49]

The sacrificial service on that day consisted of an *olah*, a burnt offering, and a *shelamim*, a peace offering. They represented the covenant between Hashem and the Jewish people. The blood, as the blood of all sacrifices, represented the consequences of disobedience.[50]

---

45. *Shabbos* 88a; *Lekach Tov*; *Midrash HaGadol*. See *Rashi* and *Targum Onkelos* to *Shemos* 24:4.
    See *Mechilta* to *Yisro*; *Lekach Tov* to *Mishpatim* for a discussion of the day to which "*bo bayom*" ("on the very day") refers, and when this all took place (*Mechilta Yisro* 19:10). See *HaKesav VeHaKabbalah* and *Netziv* on *Mechilta*.
46. Some suggest that the *mizbe'ach* itself was built with twelve stones representing the twelve tribes (see *Bechor Shor*). According to those who suggest that the Jews camped around the mountain in a manner similar to the way they would camp in their travels with the Mishkan, three tribes camped in each of the four directions of Sinai with three monuments on the east, three on the west, three on the north and three on the south of the mountain (*Bechor Shor*).
47. *Bechor Shor*.
48. See *Rashi*; *Ramban*; *Onkelos*; *Tur* to *Shemos* 24:5. See *Lekach Tov* and *Rokeach* who write that they were *zekeinim* and not young. Some suggest it was because of their strength in handling the animals used for sacrifices that youths, rather than old people, were used (*Abarbanel*).
    Before the Mishkan was built, the firstborn were given the honor to do the *avodah* (service). It was only after the Sin of the Golden Calf that the Kohanim, beginning with Aharon, were inaugurated to officially do the service of Hashem. See *Targum Yonasan* to *Shemos* 24:5; *Zevachim* 112b, 115b; *Bamidbar Rabbah* 4:8, 12:6.
49. *Ramban*; *Chizkuni* to *Shemos* 24:5.
50. *Rokeach*; *Bechor Shor* to *Shemos* 24:4. See *Abarbanel*. Since the Jews were on a lower level than the Kohanim and *zekeinim*, they needed this covenant to reach the level of *Naaseh venishma* (*Maaseh Hashem*).

Moshe divided the blood of the two sacrifices into two separate but precisely equal parts and placed them in different basins. He sprinkled half of the blood onto the *mizbe'ach* and saved the second part to be sprinkled on the Jewish people later.[51]

How did he get an exact split of the blood to the last drop? Some suggest that the blood split miraculously by itself. Others suggest that the blood had divided itself into two halves, one red and the other black, making it easier for Moshe to effect the division. Some suggest that the angel Gavriel appeared in the guise of Moshe and made the apportionment. Others say that Moshe used his own genius to determine the measurements of the division with the highest precision.[52]

The sprinkling of the blood of the sacrifices sealed the treaty between Hashem and the Jewish people. It signified the entrance of the Jewish people into a binding covenant between them and Hashem, just as the sprinkling of the blood of a convert's sacrifice signifies his entry into the holy covenant.[53]

There was additional symbolism in the division of the blood into two basins. If the people would remain loyal, steadfast and faithful, they would be protected like liquid in a basin, but if not, they would

---

51. *Mechilta; Yalkut; R' Avraham Ben HaRambam*. See *Onkelos* to *Shemos* 24:8. See *Ramban; Ibn Ezra; Tur* to *Shemos* 24:6 as to the types of basins used for this service.

Some suggest that the other half was not sprinkled on Bnei Yisrael, but on the twelve monuments representing the twelve tribes (*Abarbanel*). This is not meant to suggest that a couple of animal sacrifices had enough blood for the sprinkling of the whole Jewish nation. Rather, blood was sprinkled on the elders of the Bnei Yisrael and that represented the sprinkling on the whole of Bnei Yisrael (*Ibn Ezra; Abarbanel* to *Shemos* 24:7).

Some suggest that Moshe just sprinkled the blood on the elders and Jewish leaders, who represented the Jewish nation (*Ibn Ezra* to *Shemos* 24:8; *R' Avraham Ben HaRambam*). Others suggest that Moshe sprinkled the blood on the group of people that stood before him. They too were a representation of the entire Jewish community (*Ralbag; R' Avraham Ben HaRambam*). Some suggest that a miracle occurred and Moshe sprayed the blood into the air and, miraculously, it was able to reach each and every Jew and anoint him. This was similar to the plague of boils in Egypt, where Moshe threw the dust into the air and it miraculously reached every single Egyptian in the land (*Mechilta*).

Some posit that the blood was sprayed in front of them; others suggest that it actually was sprinkled onto their clothing; still others suggest that it was sprayed atop their heads (*Rabbeinu Chananel; Ralbag; Rabbeinu Bachya; HaKesav VeHaKabbalah*).

52. See *Vayikra Rabbah* 6:5; *Yefei To'ar; Maharzav; Rashi* to *Shemos* 24:6; *Midrash HaChefetz; Tosafos*. Some suggest that Moshe took a scale and divided the blood evenly (*Midrash Chadash*).

See *R' Saadiah Gaon* who has a different opinion on this matter altogether.

Rashi says one basin was for the *olah* and one for the *shelamim*.

53. See *Kereisos* 9a, *Tosafos* to *Yoma* 4a; *Midrash Aggadah Shelach* 111; *Rabbeinu Bachya* to *Mishpatim*.

be scattered like sprinkled blood.[54] If they would remain loyal, their blood would be guarded, but if not, their blood would be spilled, Heaven forbid.[55] Furthermore, the blood on the *mizbe'ach* represented atonement, and the blood sprinkled on the people represented national unity and allegiance to Hashem.[56]

Having completed the sacrifices, Moshe read numerous Torah texts to the Jewish people. He began by reading the part of the Written Torah already recorded at that time, placing strong emphasis on particularly relevant passages.[57] He read to them the commandments given to Adam, Noach and to the Jewish people in Egypt. He read to them the covenants Hashem had made with humanity over the years — with Noach never again to bring a great flood, the covenant of circumcision with Avraham and the covenants with Yitzchak and Yaakov. He read to them about the Generation of the Flood, the Generation of the Dispersion and the Generation of Enosh. He read to them about the Patriarchs and their trials and tribulations. All of these chronicles were meant to raise the people's awareness of their illustrious roots and bring them closer to Hashem.

After reading the chronicles, Moshe read to them from his own annotations of Torah-related subjects. He told them about the blessings they would receive as a reward for being faithful, and the curse that would be the consequences of disloyalty. He reviewed the mitzvos they had been given at Marah and elaborated on them in great detail. He also taught them the laws of *Shemittah* and *Yovel*, the Sabbatical and Jubilee years.[58]

When the reading was complete, Moshe took the remaining half of the blood and sprinkled it on the people.[59] As the blood showered down upon them, the people swore their allegiance to Hashem as their one and only G-d. They swore never to worship idols of any

---

54. *Midrash HaChefetz.*
55. *Rabbeinu Chananel; Rabbeinu Bachya; Midrash HaGadol; Hadar Zekeinim* to *Shemos* 24:8.
    Some add that Hashem wanted to show the Bnei Yisrael that one must bloody oneself, so to speak, for the sake of Torah (*Tosafos Al HaTorah* to *Shemos* 24:8).
56. *Lekach Tov.*
57. See *Rashi; Mechilta; Lekach Tov; Abarbanel* to *Shemos* 24:7.
    See *Pane'ach Raza* for his view on what Moshe read.
58. *Mechilta; Pane'ach Raza; HaKesav VeHaKabbalah; Pesikta Rabbasi; Lekach Tov; Ralbag* to *Shemos* 24:7.
59. See *Mechilta; Targum* to *Shemos* 24:8.

sort, and they made a commitment to abide by the Torah's civil and administrative laws, making the Jewish community a worthy domicile for the *Shechinah*.[60]

The bloodstains on their garments, left there by the sacred blood of the sacrifices, were a badge of honor for the Jewish people, a proud symbol of the covenant between them and Hashem. In fact, the red bloodstains miraculously turned white on their garments, signaling the atonement and purity of the Jewish people.[61]

These garments would accompany the Jewish people all through their years in the desert. They never wore out, and they always adapted to changes in the size of those who wore them. They were always clean, laundered by the cloud pillars that removed all dirt and residue. They never smelled of perspiration or other foul odors, because the waters of the Well endowed them with wondrous fragrance. All the Jewish people recognized these garments as the symbol of the miraculous bond with Hashem.[62] In the future, sadly, the Jewish people who worshiped the Golden Calf would remove these garments, symbolically casting off their bond with Hashem.[63]

---

60. *Bamidbar Rabbah* 9:54; *Mishnas R' Eliezer.*

Some suggest that the blood in question in making this treaty was related to circumcision. The blood of circumcision was to be the foundation of the Jewish people as a unified nation to Hashem, making the entire Torah dependent on it. Although the Jewish people had already performed circumcision, they had not yet done *pri'ah*, a second component of circumcision, which they completed before receiving the Torah. (See *Yerushalmi Nedarim* 3:9; *Zohar* 2:124; *Sifsei Kohen* to *Mishpatim*.)

61. *Midrash Ohr Afeilah* cited in *Torah Shleimah.*

62. *Devarim Rabbah* 7:11. See commentaries to *Devarim* 8:4.

63. *Rabbeinu Bachya; R' Chananel.*

8
We Will Do and We Will Listen

Before the covenant with the Jewish people was finalized, Hashem offered the Torah to the other nations of the world. Although Hashem knew full well that they would not accept, He offered it to them as a matter of protocol, a mere formality that would preclude any future grievances on the part of the gentiles for not having been given the choice.[1]

The Nations Reject the Torah

At first, Hashem offered the Torah to the people of Edom, who were descended from Eisav.

"What exactly is written," they asked, "in this Torah that You are offering to us? After all, you cannot expect us to accept it sight unseen."

"One of the laws," said Hashem, "is 'You shall not kill.'"

---
1. *Rashi* to *Devarim* 2:26.

"Oho! Wait a minute," the Edomites replied. "This is obviously not for us. Our ancestor Eisav received a blessing from his father Yitzchak that he should live by the sword. Eisav himself was a man of violence, who lived and died by the sword. That is the heritage and hallmark of our people. We are a nation of mighty warriors. We achieve our goals through bloodshed. In no way will we abandon the ways of our fathers and accept laws that will turn us into meek scholars. Without even looking into the rest of this package we know this is not for us. We have to decline Your offer."[2]

This conversation took place simultaneously in Heaven. Sama-el, the patron angel of Edom, was also expressing his regrets and declining the offer of the Torah. "It is simply impossible," he said. "My entire dominion in the world is built on bloodshed."[3]

"But you are the firstborn among the nations," said Hashem, "and as such, it behooves you to accept the Torah."

"That situation is no longer operative," said Sama-el. "We've sold the birthright many years ago. Edom is no longer the firstborn. Give it instead to the descendants of Yaakov. I'm sure they will be glad to accept it."[4]

"How do you know they will accept it?" asked Hashem. "Can you guarantee it to Me?"

"Just about," said Sama-el. "Here, take some of my light and offer it as a gift to the Jewish people. It will be my little bribe to induce them to accept the Torah."

After Edom, Hashem approached the nations of Ammon and Moav and offered them the Torah.

"What is written in this Torah?" they asked.

"One of the laws," said Hashem, "is 'You shall not commit adultery.'"

"Uh, we do not think this is for us then," they said. "After all, our very nation is the product of illegitimacy. Our two nations are named after our ancestors, the brothers Ammon and Moav, who were born from Lot and his two daughters. No, we don't think

---

2. See *Bereishis* 27:40.
3. He is also known as the Satan, evil inclination and angel of death (*Tikkunei Zohar* 69b).
4. *Zohar Balak*.
    Sama-el wasn't looking to be generous to the Jews; this "gift" was all part of a devious plan. He felt sure that the Jews would violate the Torah. Knowing this, he was convinced they would be destroyed because of it and, as a result, it would make him more powerful than ever. See *Rashi* to *Devarim* 30:1.

eliminating adultery from our lifestyles is something we care to do."[5]

After Ammon and Moav, Hashem approached the Ishmaelites and offered them the Torah.

"What is written in the Torah?" the Ishmaelites asked.

"One of the laws," said Hashem, "is 'You shall not steal.'"

"No stealing?" they said. "Then how are we supposed to make a living? Stealing is our specialty. Our ancestor Yishmael was a great expert at liberating money and property from other people. He was a famous highwayman, and we are very proud of him. No, this Torah doesn't seem to be a good fit for us. We will have to pass on it."[6]

Simultaneously in Heaven, Hashem was discussing the possibility of giving the Torah to the Ishmaelites with their patron angel.

"It is not the right thing for our people," said the angel. "Yishmael is described as a *pere adam*, a wild man, which essentially means that he was uncontrollable in his relationships with other people, taking what he liked and not particularly caring about the niceties of private property. So the Torah doesn't appeal to us because of this stealing issue. And there is also the issue of adultery that cannot be ignored; I've got problems with that as well. The bottom line is that I cannot, in good conscience as the guiding force of the Ishmaelites, accept rules that contravene the very nature of my people. Give the Torah to the Jews."

"But they are descended from Yitzchak," said Hashem, "and the Ishmaelites are descended from his older brother Yishmael. Shouldn't you have first rights to the Torah?"

"No problem," said the angel. "Yishmael forfeited his birthright to his younger brother Yitzchak. No, we will have to pass on it. Give it to the descendants of Yitzchak. They will take it."

"How do you know they will accept it?" asked Hashem. "Can you guarantee it to Me?"

"I can try," the angel said. "Take some of my light that I inherited with my birthright and offer it as a gift to the Jewish people. It will motivate them to accept the Torah."[7]

---
5. See *Bereishis* 19:31-38.
6. See *Bereishis* 16:12.
7. *Zohar Balak*.

As a result of their rejection of the Torah, the patron angels of both Eisav and Yishmael forfeited the spiritual light they carried as a mantle of honor, and it was given to the Jewish people. The infusion of this light transformed the Jewish people into a treasured nation and a kingdom of ministers who would triumph over their enemies and conquer their lands.[8]

Hashem continued to offer the Torah to one nation after the other, until every single nation in the world had been offered this opportunity. Yet each and every one rejected the offer. Each one found something in the Torah that would put an unacceptable crimp into its lifestyle. In fact, they even refused to make a commitment to the observance of the *Sheva Mitzvos Bnei Noach*, the seven universal mitzvos that apply to all human beings.

All the nations of the world had been given the opportunity to stand at Sinai and experience eternity, but they had chosen the pleasures of the moment. Their rejection of the Torah put into jeopardy the very existence of the world, which was created for the Torah. Hashem would have returned the world to its primordial water had it not been for the Jewish people, who accepted the Torah and allowed the world to continue to exist as it was.[9]

"Master of the Universe," the nations of the world argued, "just because the Jews accepted the Torah, it doesn't mean that they are better than we are. We turned it down, because we knew we could not fulfill it. But who is to say that they will do any better? Who will

---

The refusal to accept these individual commandments was symbolic of the rest of the commandments. These nations, regardless of their heritage, blessings and destiny were not capable of accepting any portion of the Torah because their very essence as a nation did not allow them to accept the sovereignty of Hashem. Their very beings were in contrast with everything the Torah teaches and thus they could not possibly accept the Torah (*Tiferes Yisrael* Ch. 1).

8. *Shlah*.

Some add that the mitzvah of *hagbalah*, cordoning off the mountain, was a prerequisite for the Jews to accept the Torah. Just as the gentiles had to go against their tendencies of killing, adultery and robbery, the Jews had to go against their tendency and refrain from nearing the mountain, despite their love for Hashem and the Torah. The gentiles refused; the Jews accepted (*Kli Chemdah Beshalach* 2).

9. See *Mechilta Yisro*; *Sifri Zos HaBerachah*; *Pesikta Chadata*; *Shemos Rabbah* 27:9; *Tanchumah Yisro* 14; *Pirkei D'Rav Eliezer* 31; *Zohar Balak* 193; *Shir HaShirim Rabbah* 1:9; *Avodah Zarah* 2b, 3a.

The condition for the world to continue meant that at no time could the world be silent from Torah. If, at any time, there would be a silence of Torah in the world, it would return to its desolate beginning. See *Nefesh HaChaim* 4:11.

testify on their behalf that they actually lived by the strict requirements of the Torah?"

"I will testify on their behalf," Hashem replied.

"But how can this be?" they asked. "The Jews are considered Your firstborn sons. Can a father testify on behalf of his children?"

"The heavens and the earth shall testify that they kept the Torah."

"But the heavens and the earth are not reliable witnesses," they objected, "because they would be destroyed if the Jewish people failed to keep the Torah."

"Then you yourselves, the nations of the world," said Hashem, "will testify on behalf of the Jewish people. Nimrod will testify to the faithfulness of Avraham. Lavan will testify about Yaakov. Potiphar's wife will testify for Yosef. And so on, throughout history. All the sworn enemies of the Jews will come forward and testify to the Jewish fortitude and faithfulness. They will testify that, despite all the difficulties the Jewish people encountered, they faithfully kept the Torah."[10]

The rejection of the Torah by the nations of the world can be explained with a parable.

A wealthy doctor invented a medicine so potent that it could cure the worst illnesses. Of all his great wealth, the doctor realized that this invention was the greatest treasure of all. He wanted to ensure that it would be passed on to his son after him, but he was concerned that his greedy servants would steal the invention and keep it for themselves.

What did he do? He placed the medicine in a container and applied an ointment to its mouth that gave off noxious fumes. Then he summoned his servants and gave them his final instructions.

"I have invented a miracle drug," he told them, "and I charge you with the mission of making sure that my young son inherits this potion and that no one steals it from him." He held out the container to them. "Here, you can examine my invention."

The servants took the container and lifted it to their noses. One whiff and they turned colors.

"A miracle drug?" one of them whispered to the other. "It smells like rat poison. The only miracle this stuff would accomplish would be to put the sick out of their misery quickly."

---

10. *Avodah Zarah* 3a; see *Tosafos* and *Rashi* there for commentary.

"Exactly right," his friend whispered back. "This is foul stuff. Let's give it to the doctor's son and put him out of his misery. Then we can divide the doctor's real treasures among ourselves."

Similarly, Hashem knew that if the nations of the world appreciated the deep secrets of the Torah they would have stumbled over each other in their rush to accept it, and they would have slaughtered the Jewish people in order to lay claim to the Torah that was rightfully theirs. And so Hashem concealed the inner core of the Torah under laws prohibiting bloodshed, adultery and theft. The nations of the world took one whiff of the outer shell of the Torah, and they wrinkled their noses as if they had smelled some noxious fumes.

"Let the Jews have the Torah," they declared. "There is nothing here but restrictions and trouble. It will surely destroy them and then we will take the treasures they leave behind."

The nations of the world stepped aside, and the Jewish people became Hashem's undisputed chosen nation.[11]

Some cynics contend that Hashem "tricked" the nations of the world into rejecting the Torah by highlighting for them the one prohibition they would find abhorrent, rather than giving them the Torah's hidden treasures. The fallacy of this argument can be explained by a parable.

The king appointed a guard to stand watch over his stockpiles of straw, hay and other animal feed. He appointed a second guard to watch over his treasure-house filled with gold, silver and precious stones.

The guard in charge of the feed was negligent in his duties, and a large amount of feed was stolen. The guard was brought before the king.

"What do you have to say for yourself?" said the king.

"I'm sorry, your majesty," said the guard, "but you have to understand that there were mitigating circumstances."

"Indeed?" said the king. "You have an excuse?"

"Yes, your majesty. I was upset that you appointed me to watch over your animal feed and not your storehouse of treasure."

"You silly fool," said the king. "If you cannot be trusted to take care of my animal feed, do you expect me to entrust my treasures to you?"

---

11. *Zohar.*

In the same way, Hashem said to the nations of the world, "How could you expect me to entrust you with the 613 mitzvos, when you cannot even keep the seven universal mitzvos that apply to all human beings?"[12]

No Questions Asked

Meanwhile, back at Mount Sinai, in stark contrast to the cynicism and rejection of the nations of the world, the Jewish people were actively preparing to receive the Torah from Hashem. The fifth day of the encampment at Sinai was drawing to a close. Moshe completed his reading of the portions of the Torah already committed to parchment and supplemented it with additional oral instruction, words of rebuke and words of encouragement.

"We are prepared to keep the Torah," the people said when he was finished. "We will observe and safeguards all of its mitzvos."[13]

The concept of the Torah was not new to the Jewish people. They had already received many mitzvos and related laws from Moshe over and above the mitzvos that had come down to them from earlier generations. The great event at Sinai they so eagerly anticipated would not be a beginning for them but the completion of a venerable process.

Adam had received six mitzvos, Noach a seventh, Avraham an eighth and Yaakov a ninth. Furthermore, although not specifically commanded, the Patriarchs and the early generations actually fulfilled the Ten Commandments.

Yaakov fulfilled the First and Second Commandments by telling his children to remove the alien gods they had plundered from Shechem. Avraham fulfilled the Third Commandment when he refused to swear to the king of Sodom in Hashem's Name. Yosef fulfilled the Fourth Commandment when he prepared a feast for his brothers in honor of Shabbos. Yitzchak fulfilled the Fifth Commandment when he honored his father by acquiescing to be offered as a sacrifice.

Yehudah honored the Sixth Commandment when he pleaded with his brothers not to kill Yosef, their younger brother. Yosef honored the Seventh Commandment when he spurned the advances of

---
12. *Mechilta Yisro* Ch. 20.
13. *Pirkei D'Rav Eliezer; Chizkuni; Abarbanel* to *Shemos* 24:7.

Potiphar's wife. Yosef's brothers honored the Eighth Commandment by renouncing theft in their statement to Yosef's messenger, "How could we have stolen any silver or gold from your master's house?" Avraham honored the Ninth Commandment by testifying truthfully to the world that Hashem was the Master of the Universe. Avraham also honored the Tenth Commandment when he did not covet the gifts offered by the king of Sodom.[14]

For the rest of the night, the Jewish people discussed among themselves all that they had learned and heard from Moshe, and when they went off to their own tents, their thoughts were still aflame with the magnitude of what they were discovering and experiencing.

On Friday morning, the sixth day of the encampment at Sinai, the day before they would actually receive the Torah, all the people — all the three million men, women and children — assembled and declared in unison, "*Naaseh venishma!* Everything Hashem has told us, we will do, and we will listen. We will do it, and we will obey."[15]

There were multiple layers of meaning to this historic statement. We will do what Hashem has already commanded us at Marah, what He tells us now and what He will tell us in the future. We will do the

---

14. *Yalkut* 1:276; *Tanchuma Nasso* 28; *Bereishis* 35:2; 44:8.

Many suggest that the Jewish nation received Ten Commandments but not as a completion of the previous nine given years earlier. Adam had been given six mitzvos: the laws of idolatry, cursing G-d, judges, murder, illicit relationships and stealing. Noach completed the series of the *Sheva Mitzvos Bnei Noach* with the law of not eating any portion of a "live" animal. The mitzvah of *milah* was given to Avraham; the prohibition of eating the *gid hanasheh*, the sciatic sinew, was given to Yaakov. These were obviously not part of the *Aseres HaDibros*. See *Bereishis Rabbah* 16:6; *Maharzav*; *Yalkut* 22. See *Tanchuma* which says that Noach was given six, not seven mitzvos, as mentioned in *Bereishis Rabbah*. See *Devarim Rabbah* 2:25; *Tiferes Yisrael* Ch. 19 for additional information on this subject.

Additionally, this was not a coordinated series of commandments, as evidenced by the fact that the Jews had received twenty-four documented mitzvos before this. It does not include the commandments given at Marah either.

15. See *Onkelos; Abarbanel* to *Shemos* 24:7; *Shemos Rabbah Ki Sisa*.

Much is written about the slogan of *Naaseh venishma*. The very foundation of its term is, in and of itself, in question. Some suggest that the Jews were ready and willing to **listen** to anything Hashem would command of them. Others clearly state that the Jews were willing to **obey** and accept anything Hashem wanted from them. It all related to the meaning of the word *nishma*. See *Rashi* to *Bereishis* 37:27.

The Jews, with their utterance of *"Naaseh venishma,"* merited many gifts and rewards with an assurance of peace among them. See *Bamidbar Rabbah* 14:10; *Maseches Derech Eretz Zuta, Perek Shalom*. See *Sifsei Kohen* who explains the secrets of what *Naaseh venishma* meant for the Jews on earth.

positive commandments, and we will listen to refrain from transgressing the prohibitions.[16] We will do everything Hashem tells us to do even if we do not understand the logic and the reasoning, and we will listen intently so that we can understand the essence of the commandments and perform them properly, as a servant would do for his master.[17]

It was, of course, not the first time they had declared, "*Naaseh!* We will do it." But the previous declaration had come after Moshe taught them specific laws and obligations, and their declaration was an acceptance of his words. Now, the Jewish people added the critical word *nishma*, we will hear, because they wanted to make a powerful commitment to all future commandments even before they were issued.[18]

This historic statement teaches us an important lesson. The key to growth in Torah knowledge is for one's deeds to forge ahead of one's knowledge.[19]

The Coronation of the Jewish People

The stunning declaration of the Jewish people, "We will do, and we will listen," caused a great stir in Heaven. A wonderful spiritual fragrance rose to the highest spheres to greet Hashem.[20]

---

16. *Lekach Tov; Rokeach; Panim Yafos* to *Shemos* 24:7; *Yalkut Shir HaShirim* 986; *Maharsha* to *Shabbos* 88a; *Maggid Meisharim* to *Yisro*.

The Jews accepted the Torah knowing full well what their predecessors had accepted. As mentioned earlier, their forefathers practiced the very laws mentioned in the Ten Commandments. Before the Jews would even listen to them they expressed their willingness to accept and "do" them as well (*Yalkut* 276).

17. *Bamidbar Rabbah* 14:10; 7:4; *Sforno; Malbim* to *Shemos* 24:7.

See *Yalkut Reuveni* who explains that the Jewish people said: We will do the mitzvos taught to our *neshamos* before we came into this world and listen to the future commandments given to us in this world.

As we will soon see in the following chapters, there are various opinions suggesting that the Jews did not initially accept the Oral Torah or difficult laws. Hashem forced the Jews to accept those when He held Mount Sinai over their heads, when He threatened them. See *Tanchuma Noach* 3; *Tosafos* and commentaries to *Shabbos* 88a.

Others suggest that some of the Jews made this declaration insincerely, thinking they could fool Hashem. This most likely applied to the Erev Rav, who never seemed to be united with the conventional Jews, and who soon led them in clamoring for the Golden Calf (*Yalkut Hoshea* 525; *Shemos Rabbah* 42:8).

18. R' *Avraham Ben HaRambam*. See *Meam Loez* for a different approach. See *Shemos* 24:3 and 24:7

19. See *Avos* 3:9; *Avos D'Rav Nassan* 22a. See *Shaarei Teshuvah* 2:10 who writes that a sincere resolution not to sin is considered as repentence. (See *Rabbeinu Yonah* to *Avos*; *Binyan Yehoshua* to *Avos D'Rav Nassan*.)

20. *Shir Rabbah* 1:12.

A heavenly voice rang out. "Who revealed to My children this secret that is known only to the ministering angels?" This is the nature of angels whose very essence is the instant unquestioned fulfillment of Hashem's will, to be ready and willing to do, even before they hear.[21]

Ordinary servants react differently to different commands. They obey certain commands with enthusiasm and try to extricate themselves from fulfilling others. Only the extraordinary servant is prepared to do anything his master wishes. Only the extraordinary servant will declare, "Your wish is my command." The Jewish people had shown themselves to be extraordinary servants of Hashem, similar to the ministering angels.[22]

In fact, they had reached an even higher level than the purely spiritual angels, who have no evil inclination. Human beings, however, do have an evil inclination. They do have to struggle with the inner conflict between their spiritual and material sides. Nevertheless, at Mount Sinai the Jewish people had, at least for the time being, overcome the evil inclination, ripped it loose and cast it away. At that point, free from the clutches of the evil inclination, they stood higher than the angels.[23]

At that moment, when the heavenly voice spoke out in praise of the Jewish people, 600,000 ministering angels descended to Sinai, each holding two crowns. These crowns were not material but rather spiritual in nature. They were constructed from the radiance of the *Shechinah*. The angels spread out among the people, one angel for each adult male, and placed two crowns on each Jewish head, one representing the crowning achievement of saying *naaseh* and the other the crowning achievement of saying *nishma*. In addition, one crown represented priesthood and was placed on the right side of the head, while the other represented kingship and was tied to the left side of the head.[24]

Then another 600,000 ministering angels descended and placed a suit of spiritual armor on all the Jewish people to protect them from

---

21. *Shabbos* 88a; *Tehillim* 103:20; *Yalkut* 246; *Tiferes Yisrael* Ch. 29. See *Griz* in *Mishpatim*.
22. See *Rashi* to *Shabbos* 88a; *Sforno* to *Mishpatim*.
23. See *Maharsha* to *Shabbos* 88a; *Etz Yosef*. See *Eliyahu Zuta* 12.
24. See *Shabbos* 88a; *Rashi*; *Maharsha*; *Pesikta D'Rav Kahana*. See *Kometz HaMinchah*, *Shavuos* for his views on this subject.
   Some add that one crown was for the positive precepts and the other crown represented the negative precepts they had accepted upon themselves (*Maharsha; Midrash Ohr Afeilah*).

illness, suffering and the angel of death.²⁵ The angels also touched the people's faces with a spiritual radiance that caused them to gleam with an otherworldly beauty.

Tragically, when the Jews sinned with the Golden Calf, 1,200,000 angels descended and withdrew the gift of the crowns and the armor from the Jewish people who had proven themselves unworthy. These gifts will be returned, however, when Mashiach comes.²⁶

Instant Rewards

Hashem rewarded the Jewish people as soon as they declared, "We will do, and we will listen." He granted them Eretz Yisrael, Mashiach and the World to Come.²⁷ He also officially ordained them "My firstborn nation," a confirmation of Eisav's sale of the birthright to Yaakov. They became His beloved nation, the elder among the nations of the world.²⁸

At the same time, Hashem healed the Jewish people of all illnesses and disabilities. The blind could now see, the deaf could hear, and the lame could walk. People with mental deficiencies suddenly became lucid and rational.²⁹ All blemishes were removed until the Jewish people became perfect physical specimens, the implicit message being that physical well-being depended on spiritual well-being. The people had purified and perfected their souls by their unquestioning commitment to the Torah, which in turn brought them physical perfection.³⁰

Furthermore, at that exalted moment, Hashem removed the Jewish people from under the rule of the angel of death.

"They are My children," Hashem said to the angel of death. "You are not to harm them in any way."³¹

---

25. See *Tanchuma Tetzaveh* 11; *Etz Yosef*.
26. *Shabbos* 88a; *Pesikta D'Rav Kahana*. See commentaries there who explain why, when the crowns were removed it was one angel per crown, but when they were given to the Jews, each angel carried two crowns. *Tosafos* writes that the angels of devastation do not have the same spiritual strength as the ministering angels.
27. *Rokeach* to *Shemos* 24:7.
28. *Shabbos* 89b; *Rashi* to *Shemos* 4:22. See beginning of introduction to *Ruth Rabbah*. See Prologue.
29. *Vayikra Rabbah* 18:4; *Shir Rabbah* 4:7; *Mechilta*; *Rashi* to *Shemos* 19:11; *Pirkei D'Rav Kahana* 12. There were no Jews who were at all impure; they all were prepared to accept the Torah in purity.
30. *Kometz HaMinchah, Shavuos*. See *Shemos* 15:26 for a discussion of this concept.
31. *Vayikra Rabbah* 18:3; *Yalkut Yeshayah* 419. See *Avodah Zarah* 5a.

"So what am I supposed to do?" asked the angel of death. "Why was I created? To do nothing?"

"You still have power," said Hashem, "over the nations of the world. Just the Jewish people have been removed from your jurisdiction. They have been liberated from slavery and hardship, and now they have also been liberated from death. I have enclosed them in a cloak of My radiance, which you will not be able to penetrate. But don't worry, you will have your hands full with the other nations."

"And what if they should all decide to convert and become Jewish? What will I do then?"

"You needn't worry," Hashem reassured him. "They rejected the Torah when I offered it to them. They will not merit conversion en masse."

Tragically, the angel of death would not be separated from the Jewish people for very long. When they sinned with the Golden Calf, Hashem removed His protective radiance from them, and the angel of death was back in business.[32]

Visions of the Shechinah

On this fifth day as well, the Jewish people approached Mount Sinai in the order of rank prescribed on the previous day. Moshe led the procession, followed by Aharon, then Nadav and Avihu, and then the elders. The common people did not enter the restricted zone but remained 2,000 cubits away.[33] Moshe went up to the top of the mountain and Aharon stopped halfway up the mountainside. Nadav and Avihu stayed at the foot of the mountain while the elders remained a short distance from the mountain.[34]

---

32. See *Shemos Rabbah* 32:7, 51:8, *Meam Loez*.

The Jews had become like angels, holy and pure as Adam was before he ate the forbidden fruit. It only stands to reason that they would become immune from death just as he was before he sinned (*Yefei To'ar*).

33. See *Sforno; Lekach Tov; Abarbanel; Maaseh Hashem* to *Shemos* 24:9.

Included among the elders were Aharon's two younger sons, Elazar and Isamar, as well as Chur, Pinchas, Yehoshua, Kalev, Betzalel and Eliav (*Abarbanel*).

There is a difference of opinion as to when this actually took place. Some even say that this took place on day four, the time when Moshe himself separated himself from the others through the cloud of *arafel*. Others suggest that this took place in its proper sequence after the spraying of the blood and sacrifices to Hashem honoring the covenant made between them.

34. *Midrash HaGadol*.

Some views suggest that not even Aharon was able to approach the mountain.

Because they had entered into a covenant with Hashem, the Jewish people were now granted the singular privilege of perceiving the *Shechinah*. Each person, from his particular vantage point and according to his particular spiritual level, saw a prophetic vision of the *Shechinah*.[35] Moshe, being on the highest level, attained the highest level of prophecy as well.[36] The others saw the vision with varying degrees of haziness. For some it was actually very cloudy, like something seen through a fog. Some people saw it as a distorted vision, jumbled and confusing. Others saw it as a blurred image with poor definition of depth and distance. But they all saw something spectacular that ordinary mortals cannot ever see.[37]

Common to all the visions, the people saw Heaven and the Throne of Glory.[38] Below the Throne was a sapphire brick and brick-making tools. This brick symbolized Hashem's compassion for the

---

35. See *Moreh Nevuchim* 1:5. R' *Avraham Ben HaRambam*; *Ibn Ezra*; *Rashbam*; *Rashi* to *Shemos* 24:10.
    Some suggest that they saw a more direct essence of Hashem's holiness. Others suggest that it was more a feeling "seen" by the heart, which can grasp much more than the eyes. See *Maharsha* to *Yevamos* 49b; *Lekach Tov*.
    Others suggest that they saw the "*Chayos*" and "*Ofanim*" angels, but not Hashem's glory.
    Although the Torah writes that they "saw" Hashem, it cannot be taken literally, for no one is able to "see" Hashem. Even Moshe, who did have close contact with Hashem, only "saw" Hashem in a euphemistic sense, from the back (*Tosafos* to *Kiddushin* 49a; see *Maharsha* to *Yevamos* 49).
    When we describe a vision of someone "seeing" Hashem, it must be understood that these are just words that we use to explain it to the best of our capabilities. The reality though is that any form of sight or vision, any form of shape or substance used to describe anything relating to the *Shechinah*, is just human down-to-earth words we use to give the smallest level of understanding. In fact, there is no true realistic way to describe the *Shechinah* or Hashem's aspect, in any true sense (*Rambam*, *Hil. Yesodei HaTorah* 1:9). I do not in any way intend to suggest that I have a true understanding of the meaning of this subject. I am only presenting what the commentaries write.
36. See *Ramban* to *Shemos* 24:7. See *Chemas HaChemdah*; since Moshe showed constraint by not looking at the burning bush, now he merited the opportunity to view the *Shechinah* in its purest form (see *Vayikra Rabbah* 20:10; *Yalkut*).
37. See *Maharsha* to *Yevamos* 49b based on *Aruch*, *os samech*, "*spaklarya*"; *Rabbeinu Bachya*; *Ramban* to *Mishpatim*. See *Midrash Ohr Afeilah*. This blockage was covered with the cloud of *arafel* as seen earlier. Like one unable to look directly into the sun, a blockage was necessary to view Hashem's spiritual holiness (*Alshich*). See *Lekach Tov* to *Shemos* 32:4; *Tur*; *Rokeach Mishpatim* for their comments on the vision the Jewish people saw.
38. *Lekach Tov*; *Rabbeinu Bachya*. See *Maharsha* to *Chullin* 89a.
    There are various opinions as to the color of this sapphire-type throne. Some suggest that it was transparent like a diamond or crystal; others say it was granite or a ruby and was red, as the image of the throne or brick under it; still others suggest it was blue like the clarity of the cloudless sky. (See *Lekach Tov* to *Mishpatim* and *Tetzaveh*; *Ibn Ezra*; *Bechor Shor*; *Hadar Zekeinim*; *Chizkuni*; *Alshich*.)

Jewish people, who had suffered so much when they had been forced to make bricks, under the whip of the Egyptians.

There was a story of a pregnant woman who was laboring with the mortar. She miscarried. The fetus eventually fell into the liquefied mortar before it hardened into brick, and the mother's outcry penetrated the heavens. The angel Michael took the brick in which the fetus was sealed and placed it underneath the Throne of Glory as a symbolic reminder of the Jewish suffering.[39] It remained there until the Jewish people were liberated. Then it was removed and, in its place, the clarity of the sky and the heavens was clearly visible.[40]

Some of the elders strained to receive a level of prophecy and perceive aspects of the *Shechinah* of which they were unworthy, but they were unsuccessful. Since these attempts were fruitless, Hashem did not hold their attempts against them.[41]

Other unworthy people, however, did look at what they had no right to look at. They drank in the visions of spiritual holiness until their eyes were satiated with the visions, even though they did not really understand what they were seeing.[42] These unauthorized visions had a deleterious effect on them, filling them like gluttons with arrogance, conceit and an inflated sense of their

---

39. See *Chizkuni; Hadar Zekeinim* to *Shemos* 24:10. See *Rashi, Targum Yonasan; Pane'ach Raza* to *Mishpatim; Yerushalmi Succah* 4:3; *Korban HaEidah*. See *Vayikra Rabbah* 23:8; *Maharzav; Matnos Kehunah*. See *Let My Nation Go* p. 163 and the footnotes for a variation of this episode.

Others suggest that it remained there until the destruction of the Temple, when it was thrown down as a symbol of Hashem's anger and the lack of compassion for the Bnei Yisrael (see *Zohar; Pane'ach Raza*).

It was specifically for the elders that this brick had deeper meaning. It was these elders who took the brunt of the Egyptians' wrath, by being struck and beaten. They were the Jewish police and, rather than identify the Jews who could not keep up with the workload, they remained quiet and took the beatings instead. It was for this that the elders were elevated to become part of Jewish law enforcement and merited to be able to see aspects of the *Shechinah*. See *Rabbeinu Bachya*.

Some suggest that it was from this very brick that the Tablets would be carved. See *Yalkut* 854.

40. See *Yerushalmi Succah* 4:3; *Korban HaEidah; Rashi* to *Mishpatim; Vayikra Rabbah* 23:8.

Others suggest a transparent clear vision of a cloudless sky. See *Ibn Ezra; Rashbam; Rabbeinu Bachya*.

41. See *Lekach Tov; Midrash Ohr Afeilah*.

42. *Midrash HaGadol* to *Shemos* 24:11; *Vayikra Rabbah* 20:10. See *Rashi* to *Berachos* 17a with *Maharsha*; see *Lekach Tov*. It is with this mind-set that there is no food or drink in the World to Come. It is one's soul and spirit that indulge in consuming the high level of the Divine Presence and not one's earthly body and its physical necessities. Similarly, Moshe, when he went up to heaven, did not eat or drink, because his physical being did not rise, only his soul and spirit did. See *Rambam, Hil Teshuvah* 8:2.

own importance. Suddenly, they considered themselves residents in the royal palace, with no sense of reverence and awe.[43]

This insubordination should have earned them the penalty of immediate death, but Hashem did not want to dampen the great joy that suffused the Jewish people at this time. Instead, He postponed the reckoning for a later time. The elders among these people would receive their punishment when they complained about the food in the desert, and a spiritual fire consumed Nadav and Avihu during the consecration of the Mishkan.[44]

In the meantime, there was only joy and celebration over the momentous occasion of the establishment of the covenant and also the prophecies that everyone had seen without suffering any harm. The elders and the firstborn brought sacrifices near the mountain, and the rest of the people celebrated with food and drink.[45]

The fifth day was drawing to a close. Tomorrow they would stand before the mountain to hear Hashem's voice and receive the Torah. The preparations were nearing completion. The people were circumcised, purified, cleansed and well informed. Hashem wanted the Jewish people to resemble Him in the sense of having attained a high level of holiness like that which existed before the creation of the world. The Jewish people had accomplished this, and now they were ready for the great day.[46]

---

43. *Midrash HaGadol*. See *Rashi; Vayikra Rabbah* 20:10; *Yefei To'ar; Riva; Tanchuma Acharei.*
44. See *Rashi; Sifsei Chachamim; Yonasan Ben Uziel* to *Shemos* 24:11; *Tanchuma Beha'aloscha* 16, *Acharei* 6; *Etz Yosef*. The *zekeinim* would be punished later, when the Jews complained against Moshe. Some question that if, according to *Ramban's* view, this took place after *Matan Torah*, it was no longer a joyous occasion, and if we are to conclude that this occurrence had negative implications, why didn't they die immediately?
45. See *Rashi; Onkelos; Lekach Tov; Ramban; Ohr HaChaim; Bechor Shor; Chizkuni* to *Shemos* 24:11.
46. *Tanchuma Kedoshim* 2; see *Etz Yosef; Midrash Aggadah; Alshich.*

9 The Great Day Arrives

It was the day on which the covenanted relationship between Hashem and the Jews would be formalized. The Jewish people would become Hashem's nation for all eternity.[1] The people had made their meticulous preparations and reached the highest levels of purity and holiness. Adorned with their celestial crowns, the Jewish people were welcomed by the ministering angels of Heaven as their brethren and perhaps even superiors.[2]

Twenty-six generations had come and gone since the creation of the world before the Torah entered at center stage. The existence of the world without Torah had been tenuous for all this time, surviving solely by the mercy of Hashem Who waited patiently until the age of Torah would arrive. And now, at long last, the Jewish people

---
1. See *Seder Olam Zuta* 4:21.
2. *Zohar Shemos* 2:81.

stood at the foot of Mount Sinai, a free and complete nation ready and eager to receive the Torah and bring it into the world.[3]

The Jewish people were like a beautiful rose, and the pagan nations were like evil thorns. Hashem had preserved His garden for the sake of the rose among the thorns. Now that the Jewish people were about to receive the Torah, the survival of the worlds was assured. It was a moment of monumental historic proportions.[4]

The day on which the Torah was to be given, 6 Sivan, was a Shabbos that year, which is exactly what Hashem wanted. Hashem had blessed and sanctified the Shabbos, the seventh day of creation. Now that He was going to imbue another day with the transcendent spiritual blessing of the Giving of the Torah, He deemed no other day as worthy of this blessing as Shabbos. Moreover, the world had been incomplete for thousands of years until the appearance of the Torah brought it to completion. Therefore, it was only appropriate that Shabbos, the day that brought the creation of the world to physical completion, should bring it to spiritual completion as well.[5]

The Jewish encampment was abuzz with almost unbearable excitement that Friday night, and then everyone went to sleep. Earlier in the week, Moshe had urged them to stay up this night with eager anticipation and be prepared to receive the Torah with full awareness and concentration rather than to be rubbing sleep from their eyes. But the people deemed it better to go to sleep and be fully rested instead of risking fatigue and drowsiness during the great event.[6]

They slept soundly and peacefully through the night, undisturbed by mettlesome insects.[7] The short spring night slipped away,

---

3. *Pesachim* 118a,13a; *Shir Rabbah* 2:3; *Midrash Aseres HaDibros*; Rashi to *Shabbos* 88b; see Rashi to *Devarim* 30:15. See *Yedei Moshe* to *Shir Rabbah* 5:8; Rashi to *Chagigah* 13b.

Others suggest that it was 2,000 years before the world came to be that the Torah was created.

4. *Shir Rabbah* 2:3.

See *Bnei Yissaschar Sivan* 4:7 that this is one reason for the custom to decorate shuls and homes with roses and flowers on Shavuos. See *Orach Chaim* 494:2 with *Rama*.

5. *Tiferes Yisrael* Ch. 27.

The Torah was specifically given on Shabbos to teach us that since people are working and busy during the week, Shabbos is to be set aside as a day of learning (*Sifsei Kohen; Mikra'ei Kodesh* 8).

6. *Zohar Shemos* 2:81.

7. *Shir Rabbah* 1:12; *Pirkei D'Rav Eliezer* 41; *Radal* 65.

and the sun's first rays crept over the horizon and heated up the desert, and still, the Jewish people slept.⁸ The desert was silent. Day was about to break. The Jewish people had overslept and would not be ready to receive the Torah at the designated time.⁹

According to some opinions, Hashem responded to the lethargy of the Jewish people by slowing up the sun in its heavenly pathway so that the day would last seventy-two hours, three times the length of a normal day.¹⁰ In this way, the Jewish people would accept the Torah at the proper time — at daybreak, right after the reading of *Krias Shema*. Others contend that the revelation lasted all morning and that the actual Giving of the Torah took place at high noon. Thus, if we assume that daybreak was at 6 a.m., the people awoke at 8 a.m. and received the Torah at 12 o'clock.¹¹

A Rallying Cry

The prelude to the Giving of the Torah began with a spectacular display of meteorological disturbances. At first, the desert was still and calm, with only a dry breeze stirring the loose sands, but, gradually, it became the scene of a mighty maelstrom.

A diaphanous mist rose from the mountaintop, and soon it was surrounded by immense cloudbanks that congregated over Mount Sinai, as if all the heavens had come together to form a single thick blanket.¹² A stiff wind whipped through the Jewish encampment, and a light rain began to fall, taking the edge off the desert heat and washing the mountainsides of debris until they gleamed spotless.¹³ The winds gathered force, coming in from every direction, a miraculous phenomenon that was only a harbinger of greater miracles to come.¹⁴

---

8. See *Mechilta*; *Pirkei D'Rav Eliezer* 41; *Radal*; *Tosafos*; *Ibn Ezra HaKatzar*; *R' Saadiah Gaon* to *Shemos* 19:16.
   It was just a little after *amud hashachar* (pre-dawn), the exact time when the three days of *perishah* (separation) would expire (*Panim Yafos*).
9. See *Shir Rabbah* 1:12.
   See *Pirkei D'Rav Eliezer* 41 who writes that the Jews slept two hours into the morning.
10. *Rabbeinu Bachya*; *Yalkut Reuveni*; see *Meam Loez nes* 32; *Avodah Zarah* 25a.
11. *Pirkei D'Rav Eliezer*; *Radal* 41,46.
    According to *Pirkei D'Rav Eliezer*, the Jews accepted the Torah on Friday and the revelation concluded at 3 p.m. so that they could prepare for Shabbos. See *Tosafos* to *Avodah Zarah* 3a.
    See *Shibbolei HaLeket* 76 who writes that the Jews received the Torah early in the morning.
12. *Yefei Kol* to *Shir Rabbah* 1:12; *Rabbeinu Bachya*; *Ralbag* to *Shemos* 19:16.
13. *Mechilta D'Rashbi*; *Rokeach*; *Zohar* 2:81b. See *Shoftim* 5:4.
14. *R' Saadiah Gaon*.

Suddenly, a brilliant flash of lightning, crackling with an earsplitting, heart-pounding shower of flames and sparks, rent the morning sky, its light so dazzling it could be seen to the ends of the earth.[15] The image of the lightning bolt was followed immediately by a mighty crash of thunder that rattled the encampment and reverberated to the ends of the earth.[16]

No one in the desert watching this spectacular display had ever seen sights and sound such as these,[17] and, as they stood there transfixed, a new and powerful sound emanated from the mountaintop — the sounding of a *shofar*, which had once been the left horn of the ram at the *Akeidah*. The blasts of the *shofar*, on a gargantuan scale that struck fear into all hearts, followed the long and staccato pattern of *tekiah, shevarim, teruah*.[18]

Paradoxically, unlike human sounds that grow weaker once they are emitted, the sounds of this celestial *shofar* grew more intense and powerful as they flowed away from the mountaintop and spread across the desert.[19] In His infinite kindness, Hashem did not want to subject the people to the full intensity of the sounds right away. Instead, he let the sounds begin softly and grow with intensity as the people became accustomed to each new level.[20]

The people realized that these blasts of the *shofar* were an otherworldly, spiritual sound. They recognized it as a rallying cry, a call for preparation, and they trembled with awe and fear.[21] They realized that

---

15. *Tosafos; Alshich* to *Shemos* 19:16.
16. See *Ibn Ezra; Rabbeinu Bachya; Tosafos* to *Shemos* 19:16.
   There is a question as to the order of events that took place. The *Malbim* suggests that, unlike the usual form of stormy weather, this time sounds of lightning preceded the thunder (contrary to the normal order).
17. *Ralbag* to *Shemos* 19:6; *Maharsha* to *Shabbos* 88b.
18. *Tosafos Rid; Rokeach; Ralbag; R' Avraham Ben HaRambam* to *Shemos* 19:16; *Zohar* 81b; see *Pirkei D'Rav Eliezer* 31.
   It isn't clear if the name of the sound was "*shofar*" or if the *shofar* and the sound were two separate entities (*Zohar*).
   The Torah's use of the word *shofar* is only to the extent that it mirrored the sound of a *shofar*.
   On Rosh Hashanah we memorialize the sounds of the *shofar* heard at Har Sinai when we blow the *shofar* (*Avudraham Rosh Hashanah*).
19. See *Tikkunei Zohar* 21:57b; *Mechilta; Abarbanel; HaKesav VeHaKabbalah* to *Shemos* 19:16.
   See *Ramban; Rashi* to *Devarim* 5:19.
   These sounds were in the merit of "*Hakol Kol Yaakov*" (*Chasam Sofer*).
20. *Rashi; Mechilta; Ibn Ezra* to *Shemos* 19:19.
21. *R' Saadiah Gaon*.

they were witnessing the descent of the *Shechinah* onto the mountaintop. Hashem had clearly accepted Moshe's addition of another day of preparation and was now descending on the seventh day of Sivan.²²

Sounds and images bombarded the people from every direction. The crackle and flash of lightning and the booming crash of thunder were more intense than had ever been experienced before. The Jewish people were all deeply moved, impressed and inspired, each according to his level of spiritual achievement.²³

The Heavens Part

Amid all these astonishing manifestations of sight and sound, a huge pillar of flame, a symbol of the *Shechinah* and the Torah, erupted from the base of the mountain and pierced the very heavens.²⁴ The flames were fiercer than the fire of a furnace, and their intense spiritual light obliterated all signs of day and night and could not be viewed with the naked human eye.²⁵

The fire emanated from the mountaintop in seven concentric circles, rising in intensity as they came closer to the *Shechinah*.²⁶ On the mountainsides the fires dried any wetness left by the rainfall and

---

22. *Mechilta; Rabbeinu Bachya* to *Shemos* 19:16, 24.
   Hashem brought the three foundations of the world to the fore:: Water, Air, fire and water all brought with them their unique sounds. Thunder was from the air, lightning was from the fire and the clouds and rain were from the water. (See *Abarbanel; Maharal; Malbim.*) Others add that the Torah was prepared to be given with four items that included water, fire, air and desolation. It was given in the desolate desert to show that just as the desert is humble, free and open, so too is the Torah free to all who choose to accept it and show humility before it. It also showed that the Torah encompasses every nuance and aspect of the entire world, just as the world is made up of these entities. (See *Tanchuma Bamidbar* 6; *Bamidbar Rabbah* 1:7; *Matnos Kehunah; Tiferes Yisrael* 30.)
23. See *Mechilta, Netziv* to *Shemos* 19:16; *Rokeach; Pesikta Chadata; Rashbam* to *Devarim* 5:19.
24. *Mechilta; Rabbeinu Bachya* to *Shemos* 19:18; see *Targum Yonasan; Ohr HaChaim* to *Shemos* 19:18, *Devarim* 4:11. See *Zohar; Ramban* to *Shemos* 20:15 for a different view.
   Just as one who gets too close to fire will be burnt and one who distances himself becomes cold, similarly one must get close enough to the Torah to get warm, but not examine the depth of Torah beyond his means lest he get scorched. (See *Avos* 2:15 and commentaries.)
25. See *Mechilta; Rashi* to *Shemos* 19:18; *Tanchuma Yisro* 13; *Etz Yosef* 20; *R' Avraham Ben HaRambam* on *Yisro; Panim Yafos.* See *Yeshayah* 60:19.
   It also symbolized that one must throw oneself into a furnace like Avraham to sanctify Hashem's Name (*Sifsei Kohen* to *Shemos* 20:1).
   It was so bright that one could not distinguish whether the fire had lit up the night or if day had arrived (*Panim Yafos*).
26. *Yalkut Tehillim* 795. See *Pesikta Rabbah* Ch. 20; *Ramban* to *Devarim* 5:19; *Rabbeinu Bachya* to *Shemos* 19:18.
   When Hashem would give the Torah, His voice would travel through these seven partitions (manuscript of *Shir HaShirim* as mentioned by *Maamad Har Sinai* p. 95).

completely incinerated the stones and rubble that the rain did not wash away. The mountain shook and trembled as fire roasted its flanks.[27]

A mysterious purple vapor with a fragrant scent then rose from the mountaintop and enveloped the entire mountain in a purple mist[28] — even the parts untouched by fire, a clear indication that the vapor was not smoke produced by the fires. Instead, it was a special miraculous vapor that emanated from the depths of the mountain, to cool it from the intense heat of the flames and allow the Jewish people to approach.[29]

The *anan* and *arafel* clouds now spread across the heavens so that the brilliant day was plunged into deep shadow. It was as if a curtain had descended to filter and obscure the images as the revelation of the *Shechinah*, as a retinue of heavenly angels drew closer.[30]

The obscuring of the fires and the darkening of the sky were also making the symbolic statement that the Jewish people, should they obey Hashem, would be spared the fires of Gehinnom while the pagan nations of the world would suffer darkness.[31] The darkness also symbolized the gloom that would descend on the Jewish people after they worshiped the Golden Calf. In the midst of all the joy and jubilation of the Giving of the Torah, Hashem was expressing His sorrow over what lay in store.

"Why do You show signs of sorrow," the angels asked Hashem, "on such a happy day?"

"A terrible thing," Hashem replied, "is about to occur. The Jewish

---

27. See *Targum Yonasan; R' Avraham Ben HaRambam; Ohr HaChaim* to *Shemos* 19:18; see *Yeshayah* 64:1, *Mahari Kra* and commentaries.

28. *Zohar Yisro* 84.

It is suggested that it originated from the colors black, red and white that the fire appeared to resemble. Fire in itself originates from darkness that is called *choshech*. See *Zohar Yisro* 89; *Ramban*, end of *Bereishis* 1:1.

The scent of this smoke was from the fragrance and spices of Gan Eden (commentary to *Zohar*). See *Rashi* to *Bereishis* 27:27.

29. *R' Saadiah Gaon;* see *Mechilta; Rabbeinu Bachya* to *Shemos* 19:18.

A spiritual fire is not accompanied by smoke (see *Lekach Tov*). See *Ramban; Malbim* to *Shemos* 19:20; *Shev Shemaatsa* 30 for their explanation; *Rabbeinu Bachya; Malbim; HaKesav VeHaKabbalah* to *Shemos* 19:18.

The word *ashan* (smoke) and *onesh* (punishment) have the same letters. This suggests that if the Jews would not accept the Torah, they would be punished and burn in the furnace of Gehinnom (*Tosafos*).

30. *Alshich; HaKesav VeHaKabbalah; Rabbeinu Bachya* to *Shemos* 19:16; *Abarbanel* to *Shemos* 20:1; *Lekach Tov* to *Devarim* 4:11; *Ramban* to *Devarim* 5:19. See *Malbim* to *Devarim* 4:11.

31. *Zohar Yisro* 83.

people will violate the Commandment against worshiping false gods."

It is like a king who knows the marriage of his daughter will last only forty days. He does not call off the wedding, but he hangs black curtains at the celebration as a symbol of the impending tragedy. The wedding of Hashem and the Jewish people would last in its purest form for only forty days, and then the relationship would be adulterated by the worshiping of the Golden Calf. In the meantime, however, it was a time for celebration, but the ominous clouds symbolized the looming tragedy.[32]

As the *Shechinah* descended onto Mount Sinai, the heavens draped themselves like a sheet over the mountaintop.[33] The mountain shuddered, then lifted itself up into the cloudbank, like a servant running out to greet his returning master.[34]

The heavens and earth came toward each other and embraced, and in this embrace the *Shechinah* made its abode.[35] It was as if the heavens were lamenting the transfer of the Torah from its spiritual realm to the physical realm of the earth, and as if the earth were smiling with pleasure as it gathered the Divine gift into its possession.[36] The seven heavens parted and revealed the glory of the *Shechinah* in all its majestic beauty.[37]

The Jewish people watched with bulging eyes as 22,000 chariots of angels clothed in fire accompanied one side of the *Shechinah*. In

---

32. *Pirkei D'Rav Eliezer* 41; *Radal*; *Hadar Zekeinim*; *Moshav Zekeinim* to *Shemos* 20:18; *Midrash HaChefetz* to *Devarim* 5:20; *Pesikta Rabbah* Ch. 20 p. 96b.

33. See *Mechilta*; *Rashi*; *Onkelos*; *R' Saadiah Gaon*; *Rabbeinu Meyuchas* to *Shemos* 19:20.

Great attention is placed on the Torah's use of the word *"vayeired"* (and he descended) as it pertains to how the *Shechinah* made its presence at Sinai. *Targum* translates it to mean that the *Shechinah* showed Itself on Mount Sinai. Many commentaries suggest that the Torah's usage of the word is nothing more than a metaphor to help us understand what the *Shechinah* was doing. The Jewish people on earth would be considered a decline of sorts when placed in the context of Hashem, the heavens and the spiritual world. The end result was that Hashem made his presence above Mount Sinai. For a detailed explanation on the subject, see *Ibn Ezra*; *Rabbeinu Bachya*; *Meor Einayim* on *Yisro*; *Ramban* to *Bereishis* 46:1; *Moreh Nevuchim* 27; *Tiferes Yisrael* Ch. 33.

34. See *Pirkei D'Rav Eliezer* 41; *Midrash Shocher Tov* 68; *Hadar Zekeinim*; *Ohr HaChaim* to *Shemos* 19:20.

See *Radal* for his commentary relating to the extent to which Mount Sinai raised itself toward the heavens.

35. See *Mechilta Shemos* 19:20; *Tanchuma Va'eira* 15; *Shemos Rabbah* 12:3.

See *Hadar Zekeinim* who writes that since the sin of Adam HaRishon, Hashem had distanced Himself from this world and ascended seven firmaments. Over time the Jewish people merited His return because of their unified acceptance of the Torah.

36. *Pesikta Rabbah* Ch. 20. See *Shoftim* 5:4.

37. *Pesikta Rabbah* Ch. 20 p. 98b; *Midrash Aseres HaDibros*; *Rashi* to *Devarim* 4:35.

their hands, they held crowns for the Leviim to be placed on their heads during the Giving of the Torah. The angels cried out paeans of praise and tribute to Hashem that could be heard throughout the encampment, but the *arafel* cloud shielded the people from the fearsome sight.[38]

On the other side, the *Shechinah* was accompanied by myriads of other angels. Despite the scarcity of space and the abundance of angels, there was room on the mountaintop for every angel. Hashem had commanded the mountain to expand and receive all the angels.[39]

The Earth Quakes

The earth responded to the great manifestations and the parting of the heavens with a churning seismic outcry that rolled and echoed across the desert.[40] Mount Sinai itself roared, trembled and smoldered as if it were consumed with rage at the pagan nations for rejecting the Torah. Its very name Sinai, related to *sinah*, hatred, memorialized the antipathy of the mountain to the pagan rejectionists.[41]

The heavens above and the surrounding terrain, as if it could see the spectacle at Sinai, quaked and trembled.[42] Rocks and stones were pulverized in the seismic upheavals.[43] It was as if mountains were uprooted and retreated in fear.[44] It was as if the earth feared the

---

38. *Tanchuma Vayishlach* 2; *Tanchuma Yisro* 16; *Mechilta*; *Rabbeinu Chananel*; *Rabbeinu Bachya*; *Tos Rid*. See *Bamidbar Rabbah* 2:3; *Shemos Rabbah* 29:2; *Eliyahu Rabbah* 22; *Pesikta Rabbasi* 21; *Toldos Yitzchok*.

Some add that there were 60 myriads (603,550) of angels present in another direction to correspond to the amount of Jews that were there.

The 22,000 angels corresponded to the amount of people in the tribe of Levi. They were rewarded with these special crowns because they would not worship the Golden Calf. (See *Bamidbar* 3:39.)

See *Sifsei Kohen* who writes that the angels were actually lamenting the fact that the Torah was being given to the inhabitants of the earth rather than the dwellers in the heavens.

39. *Pesikta D'Rav Kahana* 12 p. 108; *Shemos Rabbah* 29:8.

This was similar to the *Azarah* in the *Beis HaMikdash* which was able to miraculously expand to receive the Jews who came to serve there. See *Rashi* to *Yoma* 21 (*Maamad Har Sinai* p. 73).

40. See *Pesikta Chadata*; *Tehillim* 68:9; *Rashi*, *Radak* to *Berachos* 6b. See *Maharsha*.

See *Abarbanel*; *HaKesav VeHaKabbalah* for their interpretation of the various sounds and visions that took place at Mount Sinai and their meanings.

41. See *Shabbos* 89b; *Lekach Tov*; *Rashi*; *Sifsei Kohen* to *Shemos* 19:18; *Zohar* 84.

This was one of the six names of this mountain.

42. See *Bechor Shor* to *Shemos* 19:18.

43. See *Tehillim* 68:9 and commentaries; *Pesikta Chadata*.

44. See *Mechilta*; *Zohar* 149; *Tanchuma Bamidbar* 2; see *Radak*; *Metzudas* to *Tehillim* 114; *Shoftim* 5:5 with *Ralbag* and *Metzudas*. See also references to this in *Tehillim* 29:6; *Zohar* 82a.

world was coming to an end, that the dead would be resurrected and the earth would be called to account for the blood of the slain that it had absorbed and concealed.[45]

Gradually, the vast terrain around Mount Sinai, the mountains and the desert, realized that the world was not coming to an end, that the apocalyptic phenomena were in honor of the Giving of the Torah. The mountains stabilized in their places and began to compare themselves, so to speak, with Mount Sinai.

"What a relief," said one mountain. "The whole thing was a false alarm. The world is not coming to an end. In fact, it is coming to a beginning. Today, Hashem is giving the Torah to the Jewish people. But why on Mount Sinai of all places?"

"My question exactly," said another mountain. "Mount Sinai is such a small, humble, insignificant mountain. Why does it deserve such an honor? I don't think it is fair that this pipsqueak of a mountain gets the honor."

"I agree," said Mount Tavor, which is located in northern Canaan. "Look at me. I'm the tallest, too tall to be submerged even by the waters of the Great Flood. I should get the honor."

"Well, I think I deserve the honor," said another mountain. "After all, I am the most beautiful mountain of all."

"Not so fast," said Mount Carmel. "I stand as a bulwark between the land and the sea. I think that makes me the most important."

More and more mountains put in their claims for the honor of being the venue of the Giving of the Torah, until Hashem decided to resolve the dispute by Himself.

"Why are all of you humpbacked mountains complaining?" He declared. "You are all tainted by idol worship, sin and just plain arrogance. Only Mount Sinai is completely pure. It is also the humblest and therefore the most deserving of the honor."[46] This was also why Moshe was most deserving of being the Divine messenger to

---

45. See *Peskita Rabbah* 21; *Pirkei D'Rav Eliezer* 41.
46. See *Bereishis Rabbah* 99:1 and commentaries; *Rashi* and *Maharsha* to *Megillah* 29a; *Midrash Aseres HaDibros*; *Tehillim* 68:17 with *Rashi* and commentaries; *Yeshayah* 63:19 with *Radak*; *Pesikta Rabbah* 17 (27b); *Arugas HaBosem* 1; *Sotah* 5a with *Rashi*; *Meam Loez nes* 2; *Yirmiyah* 46:18; see *Meam Loez nes* 13; *Lekach Tov* to *Shemos* 20:2 for a variation of this occurrence.

Sinai was only 500 cubits high, not close to the height of other eligible mountains such as Mount Tavor, which was 32,000 cubits high. See *Bava Basra* 73b; see *Taanis* 16a where it states that this was Har HaMoriah.

It is only logical that the Bnei Yisrael, who were the smallest of nations, joined by Moshe, who was the most humble of leaders, would receive the Torah on the most humble of

the Jewish people. His extraordinary humility was his greatest qualification.[47]

Before the Giving of the Torah, Mount Sinai was already known by a number of other names. It was called "Har Hashem," because Hashem chose to sit there in judgment. It was called "Bashan," a variant spelling of the phrase meaning that Hashem "came there." It was called "Chemed," because Hashem found it desirable. It was called "Chorev," because it would be the source of the destructive sword, if the Jewish people disobeyed the Torah. It was called "Sinai," because it sparked hatred against the idolaters. And now it was also called "Gavnunim," because it disqualified the other mountains from the honor of being the venue for the Giving of the Torah.[48]

The pagan nations of the world were thunderstruck by the terrifying events taking place at Mount Sinai. Breathless with fear, they ran to seek Bilam's advice.[49]

"Bilam, what is going on here?" they shouted. "Is the earth being torn apart? Is Hashem cracking open the abyss and sending another flood to wipe out civilization?"

"Don't be such fools," said Bilam. "Hashem has promised never to send another flood such as He sent in the days of Noach."

"He only promised not to send water," they said. "But look at all the fire in the atmosphere. We may be on the verge of a global conflagration. A deluge of fire is all around us."

"All right, all right, calm down, everyone," said Bilam. "No need to panic. Hashem promised not to destroy the world again in any way, shape or form, not by water and not by fire."

"So what are all these sounds?" they asked. "What about all these shakes and quakes?"

---

mountains, Har Sinai. From here we see that someone conceited and haughty is considered to be blemished.

Some question why Hashem did not choose a lowly valley which would seem to be the humblest of landscape. The Kotzke Rebbe answers that it is not much of a compliment to say that a valley is humble as compared with a mountainous region, but for any mountain to remain reserved and humbled is a compliment and a special quality.

47. *Midrash Aseres HaDibros*; see *Tiferes Yisrael* Ch. 23.

When Moshe looked away from seeing the *Shechinah* as It appeared to him at the burning bush, he showed humility and fear, traits that made him worthy of receiving the Torah on behalf of the Jews.

48. See *Tanchuma Bamidbar* 7.

49. *Pesikta Rabbah* Ch. 20.

In fact, many of them fainted and died from the fear and dread they were experiencing (*Shemos Rabbah* 5:9).

"Nothing to worry your little heads about," said Bilam. "Hashem is descending onto Mount Sinai and is about to give the Torah to the Jewish people. We all turned it down, remember? Well, the Jews did not. Take a good look at my face. What do you see? Do you see 'nervous'? Do you see 'upset'? No, you see 'calm, cool and collected.' Take a page from my book."[50]

A Thunderous Awakening

By this time, all the Jewish people who had overslept were already wide awake. The earth under their beds was literally shaking, and the air was filled with uproarious sounds. The deepest sleeper could not have slept through such a tumult. The sleepers awoke startled and disoriented. They did not have the presence of mind to leap from their beds with joy and run to their designated places.[51] They knew the *Shechinah* awaited them, but they were paralyzed with fear, cowering in small groups before the onslaught of the thunder and lightning.[52]

"What have we done?" some of them whispered to each other. "Yesterday, we said, '*Naaseh venishma* — We will do and we will listen.' But right now, I'm not sure it was such a good idea. We could get killed here!"[53]

"I think maybe we should go already," said others. "Hashem is testing us with these frightening sounds. He wants to see if we have the courage of our commitments."[54]

The talk went back and forth. Some people pulled themselves from their tents and went off to Mount Sinai. Others remained, terrified and bewildered, in the illusory safety of their tents.[55]

---

50. See *Zevachim* 116a; *Mechilta D'Rashbi* to *Shemos* 19:17; *Yalkut* to *Shoftim* 2:48; *Sifri Zos HaBerachah*; *Pesikta Rabbah* Ch. 20; Ibn Ezra to *Tehillim* 68:8. See *Tanchuma Yisro* 14 for a variation.
   As for the worries of the Egyptians that Hashem would destroy them with fire, Hashem only swore not to burn the entire world, but not in regard to one nation (*Maharsha*).
51. *Chizkuni*; *Malbim* to *Shemos* 19:16; *Mechilta*; *Eliyahu Rabbah* 22.
52. *Mechilta D'Rashbi*; *Zayis Raanan* to *Shemos* 16:17.
53. *Tosafos* to *Shabbos* 88a.
54. *Shemos Rabbah* 42:9.
   Under normal circumstances, Hashem would have preferred giving the Torah in a warm and mild-mannered fashion, since "*Divrei chachamim benachas nismaim* — The words of scholars are received through pleasant speech," but under these circumstances, this was not an option (*Yefei To'ar*; *Radal*).
55. See *Yerushalmi Shekalim* 1:1, *Korban HaEidah*; *Chizkuni*; *Ohr HaChaim* to *Shemos* 19:17.

Moshe saw what was happening and circulated throughout the encampment, urging the people to hurry and congregate at the foot of the holy mountain.[56]

"My people, there is nothing to fear," he shouted. "Everyone, to Sinai! Right now! Hashem, our Bridegroom, awaits us, His bride. Hashem, our Teacher, awaits us, His disciples. We dare not keep Hashem waiting. Quickly, to the mountain!"[57]

Like a small-town mayor waking his townspeople to greet the arrival of the king, Moshe woke the Jewish people who overslept in the desert.[58] He hurried them off to Mount Sinai and advised them to find their designated places from which they would hear Hashem speak. Although they had overslept, they were still eligible to receive the Torah in the merit of their forefather Yitzchak who awoke early to go to the *Akeidah*.

Then Moshe set off for the mountaintop, followed in the procession by Aharon and his sons, the firstborn Jews, the elders, the princes, the officials, the general population, their families and the converts.[59]

---

56. *Eliyahu Rabbah* 22. See *Shir Rabbah* 1:12.

57. See *Zohar Shemos; Shir Rabbah* 8; *Mechilta* and *Rashi* to *Shemos* 19:16; *Pirkei D'Rav Eliezer* 41.

Some add that the clouds signified the *chupah* at this wedding while the future *Luchos* would symbolize the *kesubah* (R' *Efraim Al HaTorah*).

See *Mahari Kra to Hoshea* 2:21 for an additional source to this concept.

The *Radal* in footnote 45 of *Pirkei D'Rav Eliezer* 41 says that all the customs relating to a wedding are learned from *Matan Torah*.

Some add that the Second Commandment, "You shall not follow the gods of others," is symbolic of Hashem saying in effect that I am married to you and you shall not have any other husbands (*Zera Baruch*).

58. See *Shir Rabbah* 1:12.

59. See *Ibn Ezra; Rabbeinu Bachya; R' Avraham Ben HaRambam; Bechor Shor* to *Shemos* 19:17,22; *Mechilta; Rashi; Midrash HaChefetz* to *Shemos* 19:24.

Mount Sinai symbolically resembled the holiness of the *Beis HaMikdash*. The thickest cloud-covered area atop the mountain was the holiest and resembled the *Kodesh HaKodashim*. The rest of the clouded area resembled the *Heichel*. The top of the mountain, which was a decrease in holiness, resembled the *Azarah,* and the bottom of the mountain resembled the gates of the *Azarah*. Moshe could enter the most clouded area, while the Kohanim and the *zekeinim* remained further back, depending on their level of holiness. See *Rabbeinu Bachya*; and *Peirush* on *Sefer Zechirah* 52.

Some suggest that the women were completely separate from the men, as part of the extension of separation of men and women (*Pirkei D'Rav Eliezer* 41).

Some add that the converts refer to the Erev Rav who were in fact outside the camp. Some suggest that they did not even receive the Torah. Others comment that this source does not take into account who stood at the foot of the mountain and who stood on portions of the mountain itself. See *Zohar Yisro* 82; *Bamidbar Rabbah* 15:21.

Even though Moshe had shepherded them to the mountain and reassured them that they would not be harmed, some of the people still trembled with trepidation and hung back, afraid to approach the mountain, afraid that they would not be able to withstand the revelation.[60]

There was, of course, nothing to fear, just as Moshe had told them. On the contrary, there was only a shower of blessings for those who stood at Mount Sinai, even before they received the Torah. All in attendance were healed of any physical, mental or emotional disabilities they might have. The blind could see, the deaf could hear and the lame could walk. People with mental deficiencies were lucid and rational.[61] The Jewish nation was complete and healthy, fully capable of coming, seeing, hearing and understanding everything at Mount Sinai. No one could say he could not attend because of illness.[62]

In addition, they were cleansed of all defilement and impurities so that they became as spiritually pure as angels. When the Serpent had coerced Chavah to eat from the Tree of Life in Gan Eden, he had injected her with a *zuhama*, a spirit of defilement, which she then passed on to all humanity throughout the generations. The Jewish people, by standing at Mount Sinai and receiving the Torah, finally rid themselves of this *zuhama*, while the pagan nations still retain it. Tragically, this *zuhama* would return to the Jewish people when they worshiped the Golden Calf.[63]

The blessings that the people enjoyed at Mount Sinai taught them a lesson for the ages. The Torah, they realized, is the most potent cure for all illnesses. Rejection of the Torah, on the other hand, can cause illness. The Torah is a two-sided blade.[64]

---

60. See *Rabbeinu Bachya*; *Ramban* to *Shemos* 19:22; 20:1.
  The events in verses 20:15-16 took place before the Torah was given even though they are mentioned afterwards.
61. *Vayikra Rabbah* 18:4; *Shir Rabbah* 4:7; *Mechilta* and *Rashi* to *Shemos* 19:11, 20:15; *Pesikta D'Rav Kahana* 12; *Zohar* 82b.
  See *Maharal Diskin* who writes that the reason *Rashi* repeats this twice is to teach us two different lessons. The first time is to teach us that the Jews were healed by the miracle of Hashem's hand as a means to be ready to accept the Torah. The second time was to teach us that as long as the fire remained on Mount Sinai, they stayed healthy and did not return to their illnesses. See *Bamidbar Rabbah* 7:1 who writes that after the Jews worshiped the Golden Calf, their illnesses returned.
62. *Zeh Yenachmeni*.
63. See *Shabbos* 145b; *Zohar Yisro* 94b.
  For further discussion on this subject, see *Nefesh HaChaim Shaar* 1, 6:2.
64. *Shabbos* 88b; *Taanis* 7a; *Yoma* 72b; see *Rashi* to *Devarim* 30:15.
  Just as many of the people in the non-Jewish world died from the dread and fear

A Case of Compulsion

The Jewish people had made a strong commitment the day before when they said, "*Naaseh venishma* — We will do and we will listen." But Hashem still did not consider it sufficient. There were still latent reservations among the people.

Did this blanket commitment encompass every single one of the laws in the Torah? Did it encompass all the laws of the Oral Torah? Did it encompass the strict laws whose violation resulted in severe punishment? Did it encompass an acceptance of only the laws themselves or also all the penalties for violation? This was not so simple. According to some opinions, the acceptance did not really extend this far.[65]

Furthermore, numerous Jews were not very excited about standing at Mount Sinai in the midst of a maelstrom of thunder, lightning and deafening noise. They were frightened, and in their panic, they had second thoughts about the commitment they had made the day before.[66]

Hashem, however, would see to it that the commitment of every Jew was total, absolute and unconditional.[67]

As the Jewish people congregated around the mountain, the mountain itself was suddenly uprooted from the ground. It rose into the air high above the heads of the people, who saw it as a sparkling glass disc suspended above them.[68] It then slowly lowered itself, expanding its circumference as it neared the ground, until it hovered over all the people.[69] According to some opinions, the people understood that Hashem was about to use the mountain as a means of compulsion, and they actually clustered together under the mountain to accept this compulsion upon themselves.[70]

---

they had from the revelation at Sinai, the Jews remained standing and well (*Shemos Rabbah* 5:9).

65. Some suggest that this contrasts with the view stated in Ch. 6 fn. 74 and Ch. 8 fns. 16-17.

66. *Tosafos*; *Ein Yaakov* to *Shabbos* 88a.
   See *Kometz HaMinchah, Shavuos* as to why the *yetzer hara* approached the Jewish people to retract their statement after they said *Naaseh venishma*, as opposed to preventing them from saying it in the first place.

67. See *Tanchuma Noach* 3, *Reav Al HaTorah*; *Tur Al HaTorah*.

68. *Yonasan Ben Uziel* to *Shemos* 19:17; *Shir Rabbah* 8:5.
   See *Sefer HaMiknah* to *Kiddushin* (*Pesichah*) for the natural cause of this phenomenon.

69. *Rokeach*; *Pirkei D'Rav Eliezer, Radal*; *Yalkut Shimoni*.

70. See *Rashi* to *Devarim* 33:3; *Panim Yafos* to *Yisro* p. 125.

The descending mountain gave the appearance of an inverted vat that was about to trap and bury everyone standing under it. There was nowhere to run, nowhere to hide. Fear gripped all hearts. Death loomed over them.

Suddenly, Hashem's mighty voice rang out, "If you accept the Torah, everything will be fine. If you do not, this will be your burial place."

There was no way out. Those among the Jewish people who had harbored reservations or second thoughts about their commitment to the Torah burst into tears. They repented and resolved, then and there, to make a complete commitment.

"We accept it," all the Jewish people cried out with full sincerity. "We will do and we will listen."

Hashem was not satisfied. "I want guarantors," He said. "Who will guarantee that your commitment is genuine?"

"Master of the Universe," the Jewish people cried out, "the Patriarchs will be our guarantors."

Hashem was not satisfied.

"Then our prophets," the Jewish people said, "will be our guarantors."

Hashem was still not satisfied.

"Then our children," they offered, "will be our guarantors."

"I accept these guarantors," Hashem replied. "For their sake, I will give you the Torah."

Hashem turned to the children, including the unborn children still in their mothers' wombs, and asked them, "Will you be guarantors for your parents, should they refuse to keep the Torah?"

"Yes, we will," the children responded.[71]

Satisfied with the guarantee, Hashem allowed the mountain to return to its original place.

This form of compulsion may have solved the problem of some of the Jewish people having reservations about accepting the Torah. But it raises other issues. Hashem had offered the Torah to the other

---

71. See *Mechilta; Lekach Tov* to *Rashi* to *Shemos* 19:17; *Shabbos* 88a; *Tanchuma Noach* 3; *Midrash Shocher Tov* 1; *Midrash Aseres HaDibros*; *Shlah* to *Shavuos* p. 39; *Kometz HaMinchah, Shavuos*. See *Malbim* for his in-depth explanation of this subject.

Using the analogy of marriage, the Jewish people were under a canopy ready to be married (*Meam Loez nes* 15).

Others add that when Hashem saw their yearning of love and affection toward Him, only then did He begin to give the Torah to the Jewish people (*Pesikta Rabbah* 21).

nations so that they would never be able to argue that they too would have kept the Torah had they been given the opportunity. But then they rejected Hashem's offer, which supposedly laid to rest any defense they might present in the future. But now that Hashem had held a mountain over the heads of the Jewish people and threatened to bury them, then and there, if they didn't accept the Torah, the other nations could argue once again that they had never been threatened and forced to accept the Torah. Had they been forced to accept it, they would have enjoyed an entirely different destiny.

There are rebuttals to this hypothetical argument. First of all, the Jewish people did make a real concerted effort to embrace the Torah. The final act of compulsion was just to remove any residual reservations and doubts. The principal commitment had been made voluntarily in the most enthusiastic form possible. The other nations, however, had rejected the Torah out of hand. Furthermore, the other nations had shown that they could not even keep the basic seven universal mitzvos. How then could they be expected to keep all 613 mitzvos of the Torah?[72]

Another problem arising out of this act of compulsion relates to Jewish people in later times who abandon observance with the argument that they never accepted it of their own free will. It was just because of people like this that the Jewish people rededicated themselves to the Torah during the time of Purim with a new, entirely voluntary commitment, accepting both the Written Law and the Oral Law with full obligation.

Just as they had accepted the Written Law after the attack of Amalek at Refidim, they accepted the Oral Law after the attack of Amalek, in the form of Haman, at Shushan.[73]

---

72. See *Avodah Zarah* 2b; *Tanchuma Mishpatim* 9; *Ein Yaakov*.

73. For a full discussion on this issue see the following: *Shabbos* 88a with *Rashi*; *Rokeach*; *Menos HaLevi*; *Chidushei HaRim*; *Midrash Eliyahu*; *Sfas Emes*. *Ramban* to *Shabbos* 88a; *Rashba* to *Shevuos* 39a; *Tosafos* to *Shabbos* 88a.

True, the Jews did assemble of Mount Gerizim and Mount Eival to swear an oath to fulfill the Torah, but that too, according to some opinions, may have been under compulsion. Others suggest that the oaths on the mountains were made conditional on the Jewish possession of Eretz Yisrael. Once they were exiled, the oaths were no longer in effect. Some say that the acceptance of *Naaseh venishma* was a verbal one, stemming from fear, but was not meant in the heart. This behavior was typical of Eisav, who spoke with his mouth but not with his heart. Thus Haman, a descendant of Eisav, had the power to decree death to the Jews, for their behavior did not render them special in any way. When the Jews accepted the Torah with all their hearts on Purim, this elevated them to a higher level than the Amalekites, and they could then prevail over Haman (*Yaaros Devash*). See *Let My Nation Live* Ch. 26 p. 349.

Some suggest that the act of compulsion was not designed to extract a commitment that would otherwise not have been forthcoming. According to these opinions, the Jewish people were perfectly willing and ready to make a full commitment with no duress whatsoever. Hashem, however, wanted to seal the "wedding" covenant in such a way that it would last forever. Just as a man who forces himself on a woman is required to stay married to her forever, Hashem forced the Jewish people to commit to Him so that His commitment would endure forever.[74]

Others suggest that the act of compulsion was only symbolic and completely unnecessary with the Jewish people already having said, "*Naaseh venishma* — We will do and we will listen." Hashem just wanted to impress upon the people the idea that there is no life without Torah.[75]

The entire event can be explained with a parable.

A princess reached marriageable age, and the king set about to find her a suitable match. The greatest nobles in the land vied for the princess' hand in marriage, but she turned them down, one after the other. None of them measured up to what she was seeking.

One time, the princess was riding on a country road, and she stopped to ask some questions of a peasant wearing tattered clothing and walking barefoot on the road. The man answered all her questions with a gentle grace and humility that deeply impressed the princess.

When she returned to the palace, she told her father to seek out this peasant. He was the one she wanted for her husband. The king tried to argue with her, but there was no use. She had made up her mind.

The king sent off his emissaries to summon the peasant to the palace to become the husband of the princess.

The peasant was overwhelmed by the opportunity to become a prince, something beyond his wildest dreams, and he instantly answered, "Yes! I accept. I will come with you."

But then he had second thoughts. Why would the princess choose him over all the illustrious nobles with their fancy clothes and fancy pedigrees? What did she see in him that was so special?

---

74. See *Minchah Belulah*; R' *Yosef Kimchi* in *Tosafos Al HaTorah*; *Sifsei Chachamim* to *Shemos* 19:17; *Maharal* in *Tiferes Yisrael* Ch. 32, and introduction to *Ohr Chadash*.
75. *Gur Aryeh* to *Rashi* to *Shemos* 19:17. See *Alshich* to *Shemos* 20:1 for a different view. See *Meshech Chochmah* to *Shemos* 19:17 for his view.

What was she really after? And then a thought occurred to him. Control! She wanted to control her husband totally and absolutely. She knew that the highborn nobles would not be so easily manipulated, but a peasant? What could be easier? He would have to jump at every word she said and fulfill her every whim. Otherwise, off with his head! And what would he be able to do about it? Nothing. So maybe accepting the royal offer of marriage was not such a good idea after all.

But then again, maybe the offer was genuine. Maybe the princess was disillusioned by all the airs and foppery of the aristocracy. Maybe she had really seen sterling qualities in the poor peasant that had appealed to her.

The peasant concluded that there was only one way to find out. He would travel to the palace with the royal emissaries, and when he got there, he would agree to the marriage depending on certain conditions and rules. If the princess laughed in his face, then she was really interested only in total control of her husband. But if she agreed to the terms, she was genuinely interested in him for himself.

When he arrived at the palace, he set his conditions, and the princess gladly accepted them. A stone rolled off the peasant's heart. It was indeed a dream come true, and he would be rich and happy for the rest of his life.

When the Jewish people were offered the wondrous Torah, they immediately uttered the famous statement, "*Naaseh venishma* — We will do and we will listen." But then a day or two passed, and they had time to think about it.

How could they have made such a commitment to a difficult Torah when one deviation from the straight and true path would bring down on their heads the wrath of the Master of the Universe?

And so the Jewish people hesitated and reconsidered. Hashem raised the mountain over their heads and gave them another opportunity to accept without reservation. When the Jewish people realized that there was always the open door of repentance and reconciliation, they knew they would be able to keep the Torah. It would not be too difficult.[76]

---

76. *Kometz HaMinchah, Shavuos.*

Final Instructions

After the Jewish people made their final commitment and the mountain returned to its place, Moshe remained by himself off to the side at the foot of the mountain as he awaited further instructions from Hashem.⁷⁷ Presently, Hashem called out to him and summoned him to the mountaintop where the *Shechinah* was resting.⁷⁸

Since the heavens had come down to embrace the earth, Moshe was partly in the heavens when he ascended to the mountaintop.⁷⁹ The Jewish people were about to see and hear what they had requested — Hashem and Moshe conversing face to face, like two friends.⁸⁰

"Go down and warn the people," said Hashem, "that despite their desire to see My glory they should not trespass in the forbidden zone.⁸¹ Their eagerness and zeal could lead them to penetrate, break or cross the boundaries you have set around the zone.⁸² This would result in great destruction. People will die, and once the destroyer is released among the people, there is no telling what he will do — to both the guilty and the innocent.⁸³ Should even one person die, I would consider it a great tragedy, as if many had fallen, because each one is precious to Me.⁸⁴ Moreover, if the numbers of the Jewish people ready to accept the Torah are diminished, I may not reveal My glory to them. That would certainly be a great tragedy. So warn the people! And tell them to warn each other!⁸⁵

"Also, you must warn the Kohanim, the firstborn, the elders and the officials to respect the boundaries that restrict them.⁸⁶ In fact, should they breach their boundaries and come right up to the

---

77. *Abarbanel* to *Shemos* 19:20.
78. See *Mechilta*; *Abarbanel* to *Shemos* 19:20; *Tanchuma Va'eira* 15; *Shemos Rabbah* 12:3.
    Some suggest that an angel called to Moshe to inform him that Hashem would like to speak to him (*Rokeach*).
79. *Pirkei D'Rav Eliezer* 41; *Midrash HaChefetz* to *Devarim* 4:36.
80. See *Sifsei Kohen*; *Malbim* to *Shemos* 19:20; *Pirkei D'Rav Eliezer* 41; *Bechor Shor*; *Ralbag* to *Shemos* 19:19.
81. See *Rashi*; *Mechilta D'Rashbi* to *Shemos* 19:21.
82. *Minchah Belulah*; *Tur* to *Shemos* 19:21. See *Bechor Shor* for his view.
83. *Zayis Raanan* to *Mechilta*; *Ohr HaChaim* to *Shemos* 19:21; *Rashi* to *Bereishis* 43:3.
84. See *Rashi*; *Mechilta*; *Zeh Yenachmeni* to *Shemos* 19:21.
    The end letters of the Hebrew words ונפל ממנו רב וגם (many of them will fall and also) spell the word *mabul*. This is to suggest that if one person falls, it is as though the Jews were wiped out by the great Flood (*Tosafos*).
85. *Shemos Rabbah Ki Sisa*.
86. See *Rashi*; *Mechilta*; *Chizkuni* to *Shemos* 19:22; *Zevachim* 115a.

mountain, it would be far more destructive than the common people breaking through their boundaries. You must be especially careful to warn them, because since they are on a higher spiritual level, they may rationalize and think that they are worthy enough to cross the boundaries if they consider themselves spiritually fit.[87] So give these elite people a special warning and tell them to purify themselves physically and spiritually in preparation for My giving the Torah. Their close proximity to the mountain obligates them to a higher degree of awe and trepidation."[88]

"I don't understand," Moshe replied, "why I need to descend the mountain and warn the people again about their not breaching the boundaries. They've already been told three days ago. They know the rules already. They know that violators will be stoned. So why can't I remain here on the mountain with You?"[89]

"You have asked well and properly, Moshe," said Hashem. "But your question reveals that you have misunderstood Me. Let me explain to you the basis for My instructions. True, the Jewish people have been given full and ample warning about the boundaries, but it is still better to warn people twice — once well in advance and again when the actual situation arises.[90]

"There is also another problem. The people in the back of the crowd, well away from the boundaries, may push forward to get a better view and inadvertently push the people ahead of them across the boundaries. Although they will only have crossed by accident, their unauthorized presence in the forbidden zone will be harmful to them. The additional warning I want you to issue is, therefore, of special importance to those people who are nowhere near the boundaries.[91]

"Now here is the part you have misunderstood. There is an additional element in this warning that was not in the previous one. All the Jewish people, both the elite and the common people, are not to gaze at the fiery vision that represents the *Shechinah* at the top of the mountain. This would stimulate others to want to trespass the boundaries."[92]

---

87. See *Mechilta; Rashi; Sforno; Bechor Shor; R' Avraham Ben HaRambam* to *Shemos* 19:22.
88. *Bechor Shor; Ibn Ezra* to *Shemos* 19:22.
89. See *Mechilta; Rashi; Ralbag; Alshich* to *Shemos* 19:23; *Pirkei D'Rav Eliezer* 41.
90. See *Mechilta* to *Shemos* 19:21.
91. *Panim Yafos.*
92. See *Mechilta; Yonasan Ben Uziel; R' Saadiah Gaon* to *Shemos* 19:21; *Pesikta Chadata.*
    See *Rashbam; Chizkuni; Hadar Zekeinim; Imrei Noam* for a different opinion.

"But how would it make a difference?" asked Moshe. "They know they cannot ascend the mountain, and they cannot really see anything anyway because of the *arafel* cloud and the dense smoke that is blanketing the mountaintop."[93]

"This warning, which applies to Kohanim as well as the common people," explained Hashem, "is primarily for what goes on inside the mind.[94] I do not want them to visualize, contemplate, reflect or meditate on the *Shechinah* on a spiritual level. The vision conjured up in the mind is likely to be no more than an illusion and would lead to distortions of the truth and faulty decisions. Any attempt to perceive the *Shechinah* on a level beyond one's spiritual reach can only cause damage both physically in the form of death by plague and spiritually in the form of loss of faith.[95]

"There is also another reason for you to descend the mountain. When you return, I want you to stop halfway up the mountainside, well below the *arafel* cloud on the mountaintop, and remain in full view of the people. Should you enter the *arafel* cloud, some people may suspect it is you talking to them and giving them the Torah rather than I.[96] You must remain in a place where you are separated from the rest of the people because of your elevated status but close enough to give them comfort and reassurance."[97]

---

93. *Abarbanel; Sifsei Kohen; Malbim* to *Shemos* 19:23.
94. See *Rabbeinu Bachya; Minchah Belulah; R' Avraham Ben HaRambam* to *Shemos* 19:21.
95. *Bechor Shor; Ralbag; R' Avraham Ben HaRambam; Abarbanel* to *Shemos* 19:24.
 One of the deaths would include *misah b'yedei Shamayim* (death by the hand of Heaven). Since only Hashem knows what a person was looking at and contemplating, only Hashem could impose a punishment for this violation (*Yefei Einayim*).
 Nadav and Avihu would once again sin in this manner in trying to perceive the *Shechinah* beyond their spiritual level (*Tosafos*).
96. *Pirkei D'Rav Eliezer* 41; *Radal; Zayis Raanan; Abarbanel; Akeidah; HaKesav VeHakabbalah; Ohr HaChaim* to *Shemos* 19:22,24.
 When the Jews would then hear "*Anochi*," people would possibly think that it was Moshe who took them out of Egypt and not Hashem, Who in fact was the One saying *Anochi* (*Alshich*).
 Another opinion suggests that Moshe descended the mountain with the intention of returning before the Torah was given. However, as soon as Moshe descended and completed his warnings, Hashem immediately began giving the Torah (*Shemos Rabbah* 28:3).
97. See *Tur; R' Avraham Ben HaRambam; Akeidah; R' Chaim Paltiel Al HaTorah* to *Shemos* 19:24. See *Tiferes Yisrael* 32 to *Maharal* which states that Moshe was on the bottom of the mountain. See *Yefei Kol* to *Shir HaShirim* 1:52 which states that Moshe was actually closer to the top of the mountain.
 When it would be time for Moshe to complete the *Aseres HaDibros*, he would already be on the mountain to address the Jewish people (*HaKesav VeHakabbalah*).

After Hashem gave Moshe his final instructions, Moshe immediately descended the mountain and conveyed the instructions to the Jewish people.[98] Then he went back up the mountain part of the way, as Hashem had instructed him. Aharon assumed his position further down the mountain.[99]

Then Hashem began to speak.

---

98. See *Mechilta; Rashi; Ibn Ezra; R' Avraham Ben HaRambam* to *Shemos* 19:25.

99. See *Malbim*, that Moshe stood together with the Bnei Yisrael when the *Dibros* were given. This was to prevent the Jews from following him up the mountain.

Others suggest that the ascension on the mountain mentioned in verse 24 was meant for *after Matan Torah* and not before. It is their opinion that Moshe and Aharon remained below throughout the Giving of the Torah to make sure the Jews did not pass those boundaries. See *Tur; Tosafos; Abarbanel; Sifsei Kohen; Alshich* to *Yisro*. See *Devarim* 4:11; and *Ramban* to *Devarim* 5:5.

10 The Giving of the Torah

The entire world trembled and quaked, its very material existence on the verge of being dissolved as the *Shechinah* descended upon it. In the background, the long tremulous wail of the *shofar* gave an air of supernal spirituality to the seismic upheavals.

The earth shook to its very core so that the reservoirs in the bowels of the earth nearly ruptured and flooded the entire world; only the imminent acceptance of the Torah prevented a catastrophic rupture.[1] Mountains shivered and tottered. Hills collapsed. Seas and rivers receded. Trees shattered and fell. Forests were devastated. Animals miscarried in their panicked scamper for safety.

In the spiritual realm there were upheavals as well. The dead consigned to *Sheol* were resurrected, and the angels shrank back, frightened that they would be consumed by the *Shechinah's* radiance.

---

1. See *Yerushalmi Sanhedrin* 10:2; *Peirush Ri* to *Sefer Yetzirah* 73.

The world continued to shake and quake until Hashem's voice rang out.

Just before Hashem spoke the Ten Commandments, the Jewish people recited *Krias Shema*.

"*Shema Yisrael*," Hashem said. "Hear, O Israel."

"*Hashem Elokeinu Hashem Echad*," the Jewish people responded. "Hashem is our L-rd. Hashem is One."

"*Baruch Sheim kevod malchuso le'olam va'ed*," Moshe concluded. "Blessed is the Name of His glorious kingdom forever and always."[2]

At this point, Hashem began to speak the Ten Commandments.

"*Anochi Hashem Elokecha!*" Hashem declared. "I am Hashem your L-rd."

Hashem spoke in the startling voice that the people had heard when He spoke to Moshe earlier, and they instantly recognized it as belonging to the *Shechinah*.[3] In fact, the entire world heard the voice emanating from Sinai.[4]

Immediately, the clamor of the environment stopped, and the world stopped and listened, as if with bated breath, to the *Shechinah* speaking. The seismic tremors and the atmospheric disturbances subsided. The sun stopped in its path, and the waters ceased to flow. The birds ceased their chirping, and the cows did not low. In the realm of Heaven, the ministering angels fell silent, and the angels of the Divine Chariot known as Ofanim interrupted their celestial movements.

The entire world, informed through prophecy that the *Shechinah* was speaking, fell utterly silent. No creature or entity dared emit a sound lest it be thought that there was another god, and it was speaking at the same time and competing with the *Shechinah*.[5]

According to some, all the idols and icons of the world were brought to Sinai on that day, where they bowed to Hashem's glory. When they were returned to the temples and shrines they normally occupied, they oozed body fluids and vomit, as if to proclaim, "How

---

2. *Devarim Rabbah* 2:31; *Maharzav*; *Pesikta Chadata*.
3. *Abarbanel* to *Shemos* 20:1.
4. *Zohar*.
5. *Pirkei D'Rav Eliezer* 41; *Radal*; *Shemos Rabbah*; *Yefei To'ar*; *Maharzav* 29:9; *Yalkut Shimoni*. See *Meam Loez nes* 14; *Berachos* 58a with *Maharsha*; *Reishis Chochmah*, *Yirah* 1:5.
    This was the meaning of the verse, "The earth became afraid and grew calm." See *Tehillim* 76:9, 68:9; *Shoftim* 5:4.

can you abandon Hashem and worship worthless statues that cannot speak or keep themselves clean?"[6]

The message to the world in these miraculous manifestations was clear. Only Hashem was worthy of being acknowledged and served. The world was created only because of the Torah, without which the world would be a desolate ruin.[7]

Simultaneous Commandments

Even before He had uttered those first words, *"Anochi Hashem Elokecha,"* Hashem already spoke all Ten Commandments. It was impossible, however, to understand what He was saying, because He said them all simultaneously, something that a mortal cannot do or comprehend. The assembled people heard it as a muffled, indecipherable cacophony. Nonetheless, even though they could not process what they heard, they did hear the entire Torah as one unit directly from Hashem.[8] From this they could infer that the violation of any one Commandment was tantamount to the violation of the entire Torah.[9] Now it was time for Hashem to repeat all Ten Commandments, one at a time, so that the people could understand what He was saying.

As it would turn out, Hashem spoke only the first two Commandments directly to the people. The rest of the Commandments were transmitted to the Jewish people through Moshe.[10] There is a hint to this in the *gematria*, the numerical value,

---

6. *Yalkut Tehillim* 714; *Midrash* in *Torah Shleimah*.
7. *Shir HaShirim Rabbah* 1:9; *Kesef Nivchar*.
8. See *Mechilta; Mechilta D'Rashbi; Tanchuma Yisro* 11; Rashi; Chizkuni; R' Avraham Ben HaRambam to *Shemos* 20:1. See *Alshich* to *Devarim* 5:19.
9. *Gur Aryeh*.
10. See *Mechilta; Mechilta D'Rashbi; Tanchuma Yisro* 11; Rashi; Chizkuni; R' Avraham Ben HaRambam to *Shemos* 20:1. See *Alshich* to *Devarim* 5:19.
  The purpose of uttering the Ten Commandments at one time was to symbolize that the Torah is one unit and not a composition of assorted laws. One is to accept the Torah as a whole, and not selectively choose the laws based on preference (*Ohr HaChaim; HaKesav VeHaKabbalah; Gur Aryeh; Tiferes Yisrael* Ch. 34).
  Another reason for this was to convince any doubters that the Torah was given by Hashem and not an angel or demon. Uttering the Ten Commandments would be impossible by any living being other than Hashem (*Rokeach*).
  There are numerous reasons given for the emphasis placed on the first two Commandments. One view suggests that the First Commandment represented all positive commandments while the second one represented all negative commandments in the Torah (*Ohr HaChaim* to *Shemos* 20:1).
  Some suggest that Moshe repeated the *Dibros* written in *Va'eschanan* as well (*Mishnas*

of the word Torah. Our Sages tell us (*Avos* 1:1) that "Moshe received Torah from Sinai and transmitted it to the Jewish people." The *gematria* of Torah is 611, representing all the mitzvos, except for the two that the Jewish people heard directly from Hashem.[11]

The first two Commandments, which deal with Hashem's sovereignty and dominion, were the only ones the people really had to hear directly from Hashem as one unified community, from Moshe to the humblest person. The other Commandments could be transmitted to the people through Moshe with each individual hearing them on his own level.[12]

R' Eliezer; see *Ibn Ezra*).

See *Ibn Ezra* to *Shemos* 20:1 for a detailed explanation as to the differences between what the *Dibros* in *Yisro* represented and what the *Dibros* in *Va'eschanan* represented.

Some say that the fact that the first two Commandments were stated at one time suggests that it was done as one song, one segment or one paragraph (*R' Chaim Paltiel* to *Shemos* 20:1).

There are a number of opinions as to how the Commandments were given by Hashem and retold by Moshe. Some suggest that the Jewish people heard only the first two Commandments, and even those they could not decipher or understand. They never even heard the sounds of the remaining eight Commandments. Moshe translated all Ten Commandments for the Jewish people, including the first two which they heard but could not understand. (See *Moreh Nevuchim* 2:33; *Daas Zekeinim* to *Shemos* 20:1.) Others suggest that the Jewish people, understood all Ten Commandments given by Hashem in a general sense, but they needed to be repeated in order for the people to understand the depth and detail of each Commandment (*Tzeidah LaDerech*).

Another view suggest that the Jews did comprehend the jumbled sounds that entailed the first two Commandments the very first time; the rest, which they could not understand, Moshe had to explain. (See *Shir HaShirim Rabbah* 1:2; *Shemos Rabbah* 42:8; *Ramban* to *Devarim* 4:12, *Shemos* 20:7; *Moshav Zekeinim* to *Devarim* 4:12 and 5:5; *Lekach Tov* to *Devarim* 5:25.) See *Ohr HaChaim* to *Devarim* 4:12 and *Shemos* 20:1 for a different view.

Some suggest that the Jews heard the eight remaining Commandments from both Hashem and Moshe. See *Abarbanel* in *Va'eschanan* p. 69; *Shlah* to *Shavuos* p. 39 for added opinions and discussion on the subject.

Another view suggests that only the first two were said in one utterance; the rest were said separately by Moshe (*Hadar Zekeinim*; *Abarbanel* to *Shemos* 20:1).

Another view suggests that the Jews did in fact hear and understand all Ten Commandments from Hashem. (See *Shemos Rabbah* and the dispute on this issue.)

11. *Makkos* 23b; *Shemos Rabbah* 33:7; *Shir HaShirim Rabbah* 1:2; *Pirkei D'Rav Eliezer*. See *Bamidbar Rabbah* 13:16.

This is a point of contention since many views suggest that Moshe and the Jews received 613 mitzvos. In fact, the numerical value of Moshe "Rabbeinu" is 613 (*Yalkut Reuveni* to *Shemos* 20:1). Others suggest that Moshe transmitted 603 mitzvos (the value of the word "Rabbeinu" without the *yud*) and the Jews received ten. See *Maamad Har Sinai* pp. 166-167 for further discussion.

See *Pane'ach Raza* to *Devarim* 5:24 which explains that the word אֵת, *you*, has the same numerical value as the word *shemoneh*, which is 401. The allusion is that "you" Moshe should complete the remaining "eight" Commandments.

See *Mabit* in *Shaar HaYesodos* 11; see *Bamidbar Rabbah* 13:16 which states that there are 613 letters in the *Aseres HaDibros* to correspond to the 613 mitzvos that are symbolically referenced there.

12. *Tiferes Yisrael* Ch. 21.

One other Commandment stands out from among the rest in the mode of its delivery. The Commandment to keep Shabbos appears in slightly different language in the two places in the Torah where the Commandments are presented. In *Shemos* (20:8), the command is "*zachor* — remember" the Shabbos day, while in *Devarim* (5:12), it is "*shamor* — safeguard" the Shabbos day. Both are correct, because Hashem spoke both versions of the Commandment simultaneously. According to some opinions, the two forms of the Commandment represented the Divine characteristics of mercy and strict judgment. Hashem combined them and spoke them simultaneously in order to create a proper balance in the Torah.[13]

This certainly holds true for the two forms of the Commandment to keep Shabbos. The first, *zachor*, a positive commandment, represents Divine love and mercy. The second, *shamor*, a prohibition, represents fear and awe. By seeing the two of them together, Hashem showed that He wants the observance of Shabbos to be rooted in both relationships simultaneously.

Perfectly Clear Commandments

As the First Commandment issued forth from the mountaintop, most of the Jewish people found the words incomprehensible. The image of the *Shechinah* was represented by a flaming vision, and the sounds in the immediate vicinity of Mount Sinai assumed five different forms.[14]

---

13. *Rabbeinu Bachya; Ohr HaChaim* to *Shemos* 20:1. See *Sefer Etz Daas* to *Devarim*.
   It too was said in one utterance only to Moshe and later translated to the Bnei Yisrael (*Gur Aryeh*).
   With this thought, the *Kli Yakar* explains why the Torah uses two different words to express speech — *amirah* and *dibbur*. *Dibbur* is used for speaking harshly, while *amirah* is used for speaking softly. In *Yisro* the term *dibbur* is used.
   Although different in meaning, one depended on the other. Hashem wanted the Jews to "remember" the Shabbos so that they could honor and "keep" it properly (*Ibn Ezra*).
   In fact, this opinion suggests that on the *Luchos* the word *Shamor* is chosen over *Zachor* to represent the commandment of Shabbos, to signify that it too was mentioned at this time (*Meam Loez nes* 29). (See Ch. 12 fn. 82.)
   The Torah is either a potion of life or of death. How one chooses is how he will be treated. This adds another meaning to the Torah's two extremes of mercy and judgment (*Sifsei Kohen* 20:1).
14. See *Rashi* to *Shemos* 20:19; *Midrash Tehillim* 119; *Berachos* 6b.
   Despite the use of *lashon hakodesh* (the sacred tongue), Hashem began the Ten Commandments with the word *Anochi*, which is part of the Arabic dialect of the word "I" (*Yalkut* 286).
   See *Ramban* to *Devarim* 4:12 and *Rashash* to *Shemos Rabbah* 5:9, which explain the five sounds.
   See *Rabbeinu Bachya* to *Shemos* 20:1 for an extensive and detailed description of the revelation.

Presently, the words coalesced and began to take on forms all the people could understand. In fact, there were seven forms of the sound adapted to the different levels of understanding among Moshe, the elders, men, women, teenagers, children and infants. Even fetuses inside their mothers' wombs received the Torah in a form they could absorb.[15]

Each of these seven sounds was translated into seventy languages so that the Torah would exist in all languages and be accessible, in the future, to all Jews — no matter where they would live and which language they would speak.[16]

Every single Jewish soul — past, present and future — was present at Mount Sinai on that fateful day. Departed souls and the souls of the unborn joined the living, so that every Jew — until the end of time — would be personally committed to the Torah.[17]

Moreover, the seventy pagan nations would not be able to claim ignorance as an excuse for their flagrant violation of the principles of the Torah.[18]

An Extraordinary Delivery

At the splitting of the sea, even the humblest among the Jewish people saw prophetic visions that even the great prophet Yechezkel had never seen.[19] Now again, the people saw visions that no mortal had ever seen or would ever see again. They were actually able to see

---

See *Zohar Yisro* 90a which explains that the five sounds represent the pair of five Commandments lined up side by side on the *Luchos*.

15. See *Tanchuma* 11, 25; *Shemos Rabbah* 5:9; *Yefei To'ar*; *Rashash*; *R' Avraham Ben HaRambam* to *Shemos* 20:1; *Pesikta Chadata*; *Midrash Aseres HaDibros*; *Tiferes Yisrael* Ch. 31. See *Tehillim* 29 and commentaries; *Berachos* 6b; *Ramban* to *Shemos* 19:20 for additional discussion on this subject.

Some suggest that infants heard the Torah in a lullaby-type sound and, accordingly, others heard based on their age and understanding. The sounds too were sensitive to the needs of the pregnant women so that they should not miscarry from fright (*Abarbanel*).

This was similar to the manna which tasted unique to each individual, according to that individual's age and preference.

See *Zohar* which states that the Jews actually saw the words and perceived them according to their level.

16. *Shabbos* 88b; *Tanchuma* 11; *Zohar* 146a; *Sifsei Kohen* to *Shemos* 20:1; *Tiferes Yisrael* Ch. 31.

17. *Zohar* 82a; *Shemos Rabbah* 28:6; *Pirkei D'Rav Eliezer* 41; *Radal*; *Tanchuma Yisro* 11.

18. *Maharsha* to *Shabbos* 88b; *Shemos Rabbah* 5:9.

19. See *Mechilta D'Rashbi*; *Zohar* 93b.

This applied to the fetuses in their mothers' wombs; they too witnessed the revelation. Just as they witnessed the splitting of the sea, they were able to see it as though their mothers' wombs were as transparent as crystal.

sounds.[20] First, they saw the thunder and heard the lightning, penetrating, with the power of prophecy, to the essence of these phenomena.[21] As Hashem began to speak, they saw the blazing vision of the *Shechinah* pierce through the dense darkness of the *arafel* clouds.

Then they perceived the words, in their sound waves. The words also emanated from the *Shechinah* in fiery sparks that formed into letters. The letters rose high into the sky so that everyone could see them.[22] The First Commandment, "I am Hashem your L-rd," streaked across the sky in a tangible form within sight of all the Jewish people congregated at the foot of the mountain. The letters of the first word of the Commandment, *"Anochi"* — *aleph, nun, chaf* and *yud* — shimmered in fire before their eyes in all directions.[23] The people reached out for them, as if to grab hold of them, but the letters eluded their grasp. They understood, however, that Hashem was demonstrating to them that He was everywhere, not only above them.[24]

---

20. See *Mechilta; Rashi* to *Shemos* 20:15; *Devarim* 4:12.
　See *Berachos* 6b; *Shitah Mekubetzes* and *Ramban* to *Shemos* 20:15 as well. See *Rashbam* for a different view.
21. *Lekach Tov* to *Shemos* 20:15. Light travels faster than sound; thus when lightning and thunder strike at the same time, lightning is seen before thunder is heard. Yet they were actually able to see the waves of the thunder sounds and hear a vision of the lightning. (See *Yalkut Yisro; Pirkei D'Rav Eliezer* 41; *Maaseh Hashem.*)
　They were able to perceive and identify with their heart and with prophecy the depth and secrets of what the thunder and lightning represented. See *Moreh Nevuchim* 1:46; *Rabbeinu Bachya; Bechor Shor* to *Shemos* 20:15.
22. *Sefer Yetzirah* 273; *Midrash Aseres HaDibros; Targum Yonasan* to *Shemos* 20:2. *HaKesav VeHaKabbalah* to *Devarim* 4:12.
　Just like the moon, visible against the night sky, some suggest that the perception of this vision was similar to the smoky-looking frosty air that comes out of one's mouth in the cold. As the *Shechinah* spoke, the Jews were able to see the letters and words appearing in this manner (R' *Saadiah Gaon; Pane'ach Raza*).
23. See *Zohar* 81a; *Mechilta; Midrash Aseres HaDibros; Hadar Zekeinim; Kli Yakar* to *Shemos* 20:15; *Targum Yonasan* 20:2; *Rashi* to *Shabbos* 88b; *Shemos Rabbah* 5:9; *HaKesav VeHaKabbalah; Malbim* to *Devarim* 4:12. See *Pesikta Chadata; Berachos* 6b; *Shlah* to *Shavuos* p. 38. See *Maharsha*.
　See *Rabbeinu Bachya; Tur; Ralbag; Pane'ach Raza; Maaseh Hashem; Yalkut* 2:709 for additional opinions and views on this matter.
　The words *temunah einchem ro'im (Devarim* 4:12) clarify this very point. This means that they did not see Hashem's image but they did see the sounds. The word *einchem* includes in it the word *Anochi (HaKesav VeHaKabbalah).*
24. See *Zohar* 82a; *Tanchuma Yisro* 25; *Shemos Rabbah* 5:9; *Etz Yosef; Sifri Zos HaBerachah; Midrash Aseres HaDibros.*
　One purpose for this was to show that Hashem fills the world and its every direction with His glory.

The letters that hovered all around them suddenly cried out, "I am Hashem, your L-rd, Who took you out of Egypt." The delivery of the Ten Commandments had begun.[25]

Each Commandment took on the form of an angel flying over the assembled Jewish people and asking every man, woman and child, according to their respective levels of understanding, "Do you accept upon yourself the obligations of the Commandments? Do you accept upon yourself the laws, penalties and rewards that come with the Commandments?"

"Yes!" they all replied. "We accept."

"Do you accept upon yourself the 248 commandments, corresponding to your limbs and organs?"

"Yes! We do!"

"Do you accept upon yourself the 365 prohibitions, corresponding to the days of the solar year?"

"Yes! We do!"

"Will you worship idols?" the angel asked when that Commandment was delivered.

"No!" they replied.

The same pattern followed every successive Commandment. The angel formed by that particular Commandment would ask each Jew individually if he or she accepts the Commandment, and each one would say, "Yes!"[26]

---

25. *Targum Yonasan* to *Shemos* 20:2.
26. See *Zohar* 146a; *Shir Rabbah* 1 (s.v. *yishakeini*); *Midrash Aseres HaDibros*; *Midrash HaChefetz*; *Mechilta*; *Zayis Raanan*; *Alshich*; *Yalkut Tehillim*; *Midrash* in *Torah Shleimah Yisro* 20:1,15; *Ohr HaChaim* to *Devarim* 4:12.

See *Midrash HaGadol Yisro*; *Pesikta Rabbah* p. 155, *Rabbeinu Bachya* to *Devarim* 5:4; *Shemos Rabbah* 29:2; *Yalkut Yisro* 286; *Zohar Yisro* 80; *Rashi* to *Shemos* 20:2 which states that Hashem appeared to the Jewish people in many facets throughout time. To some He was old, to others young, to some sitting and to others standing. During the splitting of the sea His appearance was of a warrior. During the revelation at Sinai and as well in the time of Daniel He had the appearance of an elderly compassionate man full of mercy. There are many views and opinions as to what this Midrash means, but needless to say it was all part of the prophetic revelation. With so many image-oriented visions, it was important for Hashem to tell the Jews in the First Commandment that He is Hashem and there is only one G-d and they should not think that all these images were part of a celestial world of many deities.

The event mentioned above applies to all views, irrespective of in what fashion the Jewish people received the Commandments from Hashem. (See *HaKesav VeHaKabbalah*; *Yefei Kol* to *Shir HaShirim* ibid.)

Others add that when Moshe relayed the words of the *Aseres HaDibros* to the Jews, Hashem would add a phrase that pertained to that subject. When Moshe would say, "You shall not say Hashem's Name in vain," Hashem would respond, "Do not swear in My Name falsely." When Moshe would say, "Remember the

Even fetuses in their mothers' wombs were included. They were able to watch the revelation through miraculous crystal windows in the wombs. The angels asked them the same questions they asked the others, and they responded as the others had.[27]

After surveying the people, each angel would kiss the people and return to Heaven where it would engrave itself into the *Luchos*, in the letters of its respective Commandment.[28]

This penetrating look into the heart of every Commandment revealed to the Jewish people that they were hearing the entire spectrum of the Torah. Not only did they learn the Written Torah and its 613 mitzvos, but also every word and iota of the Oral Torah, Mishnah, Gemara, Halachah and Aggadah. They also discovered the hidden aspects of Torah and all the prophecies that would be told to the Jewish people in future times.[29]

The Torah the Jewish people received in this manner remained etched in their memories forever. They did not forget a single word or letter of it. They also rid themselves of their *yetzer hara*, their evil inclination, leaving them in a sublime, angelic condition.[30] According to some opinions, this exalted state did not extend to the Erev Rav, and being relegated to the outskirts of the

---

Shabbos day," Hashem would respond by saying, "You shall heed the Shabbos" (*Rokeach; Moshav Zekeinim* to *Shemos* 19:19).

27. *Shlah* to *Shavuos* p. 39; *Midrash Aseres HaDibros*.

28. *Zohar* 146; *Shir Rabbah* 1:2; *Midrash Aseres HaDibros*.

Some say the words themselves kissed the Jews and there was no angel within the words. According to most authorities and commentaries to these Midrashic sources, all nonlifelike miracles that took place emanated from angels that were created to perform these miracles. See *Ohr HaChaim* to *Devarim* 4:36; *Tikkunei Zohar* 22:64.

29. See *Zohar* 81a, 92b; *Shemos Rabbah* 28:6, 47:1; *Vayikra Rabbah* 22:1; *Tanchuma Shemos* 11; *Yerushlami Shekalim* Ch. 6; *Tur Al HaTorah*; *Sifsei Kohen* to *Shemos* 20:1; *Rashi* to *Devarim* 4:14, *Shemos* 24:12; *Rokeach* 5:9; *Shlah* to *Shavuos* p. 39.

See *Zohar Yisro* 90a that the entire Torah and world's knowledge could be understood from within the engraved letters of the Torah in the *Luchos*.

This included the first prophecy till the last one given to Malachi (*Yefei To'ar*).

30. *Zohar* 261; *Devarim* 5:28; *Shir HaShirim* 1:4; *Yalkut Shir HaShirim* 2:98; *Midrash Chazis*.

These miracles would not last when Moshe relayed the commandments. As we shall see in fn. 79, the Jews only merited this miracle of not forgetting and losing their evil inclination while the roots of these words came from Hashem and not from Moshe. See *Etz Yosef* who writes that (as we have written earlier) the first of the Commandments, *Anochi*, includes all the positive commandments and therefore the Jews would remember all of the positive commandments. The Second Commandment includes all of the negative commandments, and the evil inclination is also included, as it lost its power to block their spiritual growth and prevent them from keeping the Torah.

encampment beyond the cloud pillars, they did not hear the voice of Hashem speaking to the Jewish people.[31]

The People Expire and Are Revived

The Jewish people had clamored for the singular privilege of seeing the *Shechinah* and hearing the Commandments directly from Hashem. But the experience was far more frightening than they had anticipated. The sight of the blazing fires, the wail of the *shofar* and the terrifying sound of the First Commandment spoken by the Divine voice were too overwhelming to endure.[32] The people were gripped by a mighty fear. Their bodies and souls trembled with awe and dread.[33]

Many people regretted their desire to experience the *Shechinah* directly.[34] The weaker ones fainted, and the weakest of all, unable to endure the visions and the sounds, simply expired. The stronger ones retreated warily.[35] Those closest to the mountain retreated twelve *mils*, so that they were beyond the entire encampment, assuming that the distance would protect them from harm.[36] Those furthest from the

---

31. *Sifsei Kohen*.

It then follows that the Erev Rav never received the qualities of humility and modesty that the Jews received upon hearing the Commandments straight from Hashem. Thus it is clear why *Chazal* tell us that one who is brazen faced surely was not present at Mount Sinai. (See *Sifsei Kohen* in *Parashas Tetzaveh* on the *Tzitz*.)

It is interesting to note that while the whole world had the choice and opportunity to hear the Torah, the Erev Rav did not. This leads to the question: If they in fact accepted it with the Bnei Yisrael, would they be able to defend themselves by claiming they never heard the Torah?

32. See *Ramban* to *Shemos* 20:15.

33. *Zohar* 2:82; *Mechilta D'Rashbi*; *R' Avraham Ben HaRambam* to *Shemos* 20:15; *Tanna D'Vei Eliyahu* 22; *Panim Yafos* to *Devarim* 5:25.

Some suggest that because of the shaking that took place at Mount Sinai, it has become customary to shake while one prays and learns Torah (see *Minchah Belulah*; *Tur* to *Shemos* 20:15).

34. *Abarbanel* to *Shemos* 20:15.

Despite their high level of purity and preparation for this revelation, the faith of the Jewish people was not up to the level necessary to be able to withstand this revelation (*Panim Yafos* to *Devarim* 5:25).

35. *Maharsha* to *Shabbos* 89a.

36. See *Mechilta*; *Rashi*; *Abarbanel*; *Kli Yakar* to *Shemos* 20:15; *Shabbos* 88b; see *Panim Yafos* to *Devarim* 5:12.

The camp size was approximately 7-9 miles long (a *mil* = 1028 - 1269 yards), 3 to 4 hours of walking time. (See *Pesachim* 93b with *Rashi*.) Others suggest that the size of the camp was 18 *mil* (*Shir Rabbah* 1:2).

mountain were forced to retreat simply to make room for the front ranks of the retreaters.[37]

The angels Michael and Gavriel revived the ones who had expired and fainted and went out to the Jews who had fled and gently spoke words of comfort and encouragement to them, like a mother to a frightened child. "You, the Jewish people, are fortunate," they said. "Your pain and sorrow are all in the past. Goodness and greatness await you in the future."

Then, swift as eagles, they carried them back to their stations.[38] After the Second Commandment, it started all over again.[39] Most of the people shuddered and fainted away. The dread was unbearable.[40] Some of them expired from fear. Others expired from love and yearning; the revelation was like a magnet drawing their souls from their bodies and pulling them to approach and cling to their Heavenly Source.[41]

They feared the sounds more than they feared the vision. Thinking they could still witness the revelation from afar, they backed up to avoid the tumultuous sounds and yet benefit visually (*Kli Yakar*).

37. Alshich.

38. See *Rashi* to *Shabbos* 88b; *Mechilta*; *Rashi*; *Pane'ach Raza*; *Alshich* to *Shemos* 20:15; *Mechilta*; *Zayis Raanan* to *Shemos* 19:4; *Midrash Aseres HaDibros*; *Yalkut Tehillim* 795.

The Jews traveled six times the normal daily walking distance (*Zayis Raanan*).

Some suggest that this pertained only to the Erev Rav, who had every reason to fear the revelation and potential death (*Midrash HaChefetz*).

39. *Tosefta Arachin* 1:4.

Some opinions suggest that this occurred during each and every Commandment and that Hashem relayed to the Jews all Ten Commandments. Thus, miraculously the Jews would travel to and from the campsite 240 *mil*, a total of close to 100 miles on this day when one can normally only travel 40 miles a day. At the minimum, the Jews traveled 24 *mil* during each Commandment, 12 backwards and 12 forwards. How was it physically possible to do that? Some suggest it was all a miracle; others add that with the angels literally carrying the Jews in a manner of flying, neither time nor strength were an issue. (See *Mechilta D'Rashbi*; *Maharsha* to *Shabbos* 88b; *Yefei To'ar*; *Pesachim* 93.) See *Zayis Raanan* above for his difference of opinion.

According to most authorities who suggest that Hashem only delivered two specified Commandments to the Jews and that Moshe completed the remaining eight, this set of sequences only took place for the first two Commandments and stopped once Moshe took over. Some question why the Jewish people did not want it to stop after the First Commandment rather than after the Second Commandment. According to the *Gra*, who suggests that the first two Commandments were stated in one utterance and understood by the Jewish people, there is no problem. According to the *Pirkei D'Rav Eliezer*, they died after the First Commandment and were revived after the Second Commandment and that is when they asked that Hashem stop. Others suggest that this took place after the Ten Commandments. Some suggest that this view holds that the Jewish people heard all Ten Commandments from Hashem in their entirety. (See *Alshich*; *HaKesav VeHaKabbalah*; *Malbim*.) See fns. in *Maamad Har Sinai*, pp. 120, 121, 124 for further discussion.

40. *Shabbos* 88b with *Maharsha*; *Pirkei D'Rav Eliezer* 41; *Malbim*.

41. *Zohar* 82a; *Moreh Nevuchim* 1:46; *Sifsei Kohen* to *Shemos* 20:1; *Yefei To'ar*.

The Torah came to advocate on behalf of the Jewish people. "Does a king marry off his daughter," asked the Torah, "and kill off his family during the celebration? You created me 2,000 years before You created the world and filled me with laws that refer specifically to the Jewish people. What will happen to me now if the Jews will die? Will I be forced to lie dormant again?"[42]

The angels created from the words of the Commandments came to advocate on behalf of the Jewish people. "Master of the Universe, You are eternal and the Torah is eternal. Are You sending us to dead people?"

Hashem took mercy on the Jewish people and softened the Divine utterances so that the people should be able to tolerate them and taste the sweetness of the Torah they were hearing.[43] He also surrounded them with fragrant spices, perfumes and incense to revive them. A cool light dew came down and bathed the feverish bodies of the people who had fainted from the heat of the day and the blaze of the fire on the mountaintop. For many of the people who had fainted, the life-giving words of the Torah itself revived them.

Then Hashem sent down angels to kiss and embrace the people, to revitalize and reassure them, "You have nothing to fear," they said. "You are Hashem's children."[44]

Two angels attended each Jew and helped him stand upright, one angel caressing his heart and the other supporting his neck and helping him face the *Shechinah*.[45]

It is like a king who spoke harshly to his son. The son was so overwhelmed that he fainted. The king gathered up the young

---

Some suggest that it was the frightening sound of the Ten Commandments uttered as one that made them succumb to their fears and they died on the spot (*Rabbeinu Bachya* to *Shemos* 20:1).

42. *Zohar* 84b; *Shemos Rabbah* 29:4; *Midrash Aseres HaDibros*.

43. *Shir Rabbah* 6:3; *Yefei Kol*.

44. *Zohar* 84b; *Shir Rabbah* 6:3; *Pesikta Rabbah* Ch. 20; *Shabbos* 88b with *Maharsha*; *Rif* in *Ein Yaakov*; *Mechilta*; *Tosefta Arachin* 1:4; *Tehillim* 68:10; *Pirkei D'Rav Eliezer* 41. See *Maharsha* to *Kesubos* 111b (*hahu*). This brings meaning to the words "*Toras Hashem temimah meshivas nafesh* — the Torah of Hashem is perfect, restoring the soul" (*Tehillim* 19:8).

Some suggest that the Jews were simply tired and weak and that the cool dew refreshed them, giving them strength to continue to withstand the revelation (*Minchas Bikkurim*).

These fragrances would be placed in Gan Eden set aside for the righteous (*Rashi*).

45. *Pesikta Rabbah* 20 p. 98.

prince in his arms, kissed him and said, "My beloved son, my only child, I love you dearly." The child, feeling his father's warmth and love, was revived.

In the same way, the Jewish people were so overwhelmed by the awesome experience of hearing Hashem's voice that their souls left their bodies and they fainted. But, when Hashem responded with kindness, mercy and love, they were revived.[46]

After they were revived, the Jewish people immersed themselves, so to speak, in the Dinur River, a stream of spiritual fire that purified and cleansed their souls of the last vestiges of Egyptian corruption.[47]

They then resumed their positions in front of the mountain, healthy and strong as before. The traumatic experiences of their expiration and revival left no ill effects on them. Their vision and hearing were not impaired, nor did they suffer any other disabilities.[48] In fact, not one Jew, among the millions present, became impure during the Giving of the Torah.[49] The added holiness the Jewish people absorbed during this time of revelation would endure for their entire stay in the desert. It would protect them from illness and keep them robust. They never suffered infestation by vermin, and even after death, their corpses remained free of worms and insects.[50]

---

46. *Shir Rabbah* 6:3. It is interesting to note that the conclusion of this Midrash suggests that Hashem uttered the First Commandment of *Anochi* as a means to pacify the Jews, just as the parable alludes to with the king and his son. This suggests that the Jewish people died *before* they heard the words of *Anochi*. Some suggests that it is nothing more than an allegorical parable referencing the events that took place at Sinai, but is in fact not a reflection of the sequence of events that took place there.

47. See *Meam Loez nes* 33; *Daniel* 7:10 with commentaries. See *Chagigah* 13b.

Hashem wanted to imbue the Jewish people with *mesiras nefesh* (self sacrifice) in accepting the Torah. Hashem wanted to teach the Jewish people that one must risk his life for the Torah, similar to Avraham throwing himself in the furnace to declare Hashem's sovereignty. It was from this revelation that the Jewish people had it etched in their hearts to give away their lives for the Torah. Some suggest that it was necessary for their souls to part so that they would be cleansed from the impurities that they had received in Egypt. When Hashem would reincarnate them, their souls would return pure, fresh and untainted (*Sifsei Kohen* to *Shemos* 20:1; *Kedushas Levi*).

48. *Sifsei Chachamim; Gur Aryeh* to *Rashi* to *Shemos* 20:15.

This is based on the question of the *Riva* asking why *Rashi* had to repeat something that had already been mentioned in *Shemos* 19:11.

49. *Tanchuma Metzora* 9.

50. *Pirkei D'Rav Eliezer* 41.

The Mass Revelation Ends

Once again, the Jewish people stood before the mountain whole in body and soul, but their troubles were not over. They still quaked with fear that they would not be able to tolerate the extreme spiritual power of Hashem's voice speaking directly to them. They were terrified that it would tear their souls from their bodies irrevocably, and leave them permanently dead.

The elders and Kohanim standing close to the mountain sensed the fear of the people and shared it themselves.[51]

"Please, Moshe," they pleaded. "Ask Hashem to stop. Ask Him to let you speak to us in His stead. This experience is too much for us, far more than we have the strength to endure. We are afraid that we will die if we continue to experience this revelation, hearing the sounds and listening to Hashem speaking to us directly.[52] We are concerned that we may have sinned by asking for this revelation; our brushes with death bear this out.[53]

"It is better that we hear the rest of the Commandments from you, Moshe. First, because we will survive this day. Moreover, it will help us in the long run. Should we ever transgress the Commandments we will not be punished as severely having heard them from you, as we would had we heard them from Hashem.[54]

"We need you to do this for us, Moshe. Our lives are at risk if we continue to listen to Hashem's voice directly. Who knows if we can be revived again and again? And for the future, we are also at great risk. If we die just from listening to Him, can you imagine what will happen to us if we get Him angry?[55] Moshe, we need you to give us

---

51. *Mechilta; Ibn Ezra; Chizkuni* to *Shemos* 20:16; *Haamek Davar* to *Devarim* 5:20; *Alshich* to *Devarim* 5:22.
52. *Mechilta* to *Shemos* 20:16; *Yalkut Tehillim* 301.
  Some suggest the Jews said this after they heard the first two Commandments (*Lekach Tov* to *Shemos* 20:2; *Tur* to *Devarim* 5:24); others suggest that this took place after they heard the Ten Commandments (*Rashbam; Ibn Ezra*). According to the view that it took place after the Ten Commandments, the Jews were worried that Hashem would continue with the entire Torah. They wanted Moshe himself to continue and not Hashem (*R' Avraham Ben HaRambam; Tosafos Al HaTorah* to *Shemos* 20:17).
  See *Panim Yafos* to *Devarim* 5:12 which states that the Jews were afraid they would be burned by the fire ever-present at Sinai.
53. *Maaseh Hashem* 20:17.
54. *Minchah Belulah* 20:16.
55. *Akeidah.* See *Rashi* to *Devarim* 30:15; *Alshich* on *Va'eschanan.*

the Commandments in a soft and gentle voice."[56]

Moshe was dismayed. "My people," he said. "I am your advocate before Hashem. I plead for you, but now you have stripped me of my arguments. I told Hashem you wanted to hear Him directly because of your great love for Him. But now you say you prefer to hear the Commandments from an intermediary rather than from Hashem. You are showing that your love is not so strong anymore."[57]

Hashem called out to Moshe, "It is not so. The Jewish people have not lost any of their love for Me. It is the fear in their hearts that prevents them from listening to Me directly.[58] And they are also right in that if they hear directly from Me, the consequences of disobedience will be greater."[59]

Having heard the words of Hashem, Moshe proceeded to reassure the people and calm them down.[60] "First of all," he said, "you have not sinned by asking to hear Hashem directly. The sounds and feelings may have been fearsome, but He would never have hurt you.[61] Hashem spoke to you directly in response to your request, but He had other reasons as well.

"He tested you to see if you could withstand the intense spirituality. Unfortunately, you did not.[62] He also wanted you to have the fearsome experience that no other human being ever experienced, because this would make you an exalted nation and establish your fame and reputation among the nations of the world.[63]

"The revelation is also a test of your gratitude toward Him. After seeing His glory revealed, would you give your everlasting allegiance to me as His emissary or would you blot out your memories and lapse into idol worship?[64] These sights and sounds will etch the

---

56. *Tur; Divrei David* to *Devarim* 5:24; *Ralbag; Ohr HaChaim* to *Shemos* 20:16.
   In fact, on this basis the Jews wanted *neviim* (prophets) to intercede for them in the future and deliver any messages that Hashem had for them. See *Ramban* to *Devarim* 5:25. See *Devarim* 18:15-16.
57. *Rashi; Sifsei Chachamim* to *Devarim* 5:24; see *Panim Yafos; Zohar* to *Devarim* 5:24.
58. *Rashi; Sifsei Chachamim* to *Devarim* 5:24; see *Panim Yafos; Zohar* to *Devarim* 5:24.
59. *Kometz HaMinchah, Shavuos.*
60. *Mechilta; Lekach Tov* to *Shemos* 20:17. See *Pirkei D'Rav Eliezer* 41 for a different view.
61. *Bechor Shor; Ohr HaChaim; Maaseh Hashem* 20:17.
62. See *Abarbanel; Akeidah; Alshich; Malbim* to *Shemos* 20:17. See *Shemos* 19:9.
   As we will see shortly, despite the fact that Hashem knew all along that the Jewish people would not be able to withstand the revelation, Hashem did so to quiet the future arguments of the Jews.
63. *Mechilta; Rashi; Tosafos Al HaTorah* to *Shemos* 20:17.
64. See *Moreh Nevuchim* 3:24; *Ramban* to *Shemos* 20:17.

Oneness of the Almighty into your hearts and minds forever and inspire within you a powerful faith and belief in Hashem's existence and in me as His sole messenger.[65] You will be ashamed to sin and transgress against the Commandments of Hashem.[66]

"It was important that you went through this experience. It humbled you and brought you to a profound recognition of Hashem's ultimate mastery of the universe. The only way you will remain attached to the Torah for all time is through humility and subservience. This could not have been accomplished fully without the degree of revelation you have experienced here today.[67]

"One final thing. You have enjoyed the gift of prophecy here today. You have seen what the greatest prophets will never see, and you will remember it as a nation for all future generations. Should any self-proclaimed prophet ever deny that these events took place, you will know that he is a false prophet, because you have seen these things with your own eyes and told them to your children and grandchildren. All the people who were, are and ever will be part of the Jewish people are here today and have seen the revelation of the *Shechinah*.[68] If anyone in the future expresses doubt about this revelation, it will be obvious that neither he nor his forefathers stood here with us at Mount Sinai on this day. He will not have a share in the World to Come."[69]

There was also another reason why Hashem granted the request of the Jewish people to experience revelation directly. Hashem knew that within forty days the Jewish people would worship the Golden Calf. He did not want them to excuse themselves by saying, "We asked to see the *Shechinah*, but You did not allow it. Had we seen the *Shechinah* our faith would have been

---

65. *Mechilta D'Rashbi; Rashi; Ramban; Kli Yakar; Abarbanel* to *Shemos* 20:17.
   The numerical value of the word *Torah* (611) is the same as the word *Yiras* (*Tosafos*).
66. See *Nedarim* 20a with *Maharsha; Ramban; Malbim* to *Shemos* 20:17; *Sifsei Kohen* to *Tetzaveh; Devarim Rabbah* 3:4.
67. *Kad HaKemach, Anavah; Yichud Hashem* 39; *Bechor Shor* to *Shemos* 20:17.
   There are three attributes that demonstrate that someone is Jewish. He must be charitable, merciful and humble. Humility is the root of fear; one cannot fear Hashem without first being humble. In fact the word "*gever*," which means man, is an acronym for the words *gomel* (*chassadim*), *bushah*, *rachum*, which mean charitable, humble and merciful. Also see *Yevamos* 79a and commentaries; *Chovos HaLevavos, Shaar Ahavas Hashem* 6; *Shaar Hachnaah* 5, *Tur* to *Shemos* 20:17.
68. *Moreh Nevuchim* 3:24; *Sforno* to *Shemos* 20:17; *Pesikta Rabbah* 20 p. 98b.
69. See *Nedarim* 20a and commentary; *Sanhedrin* 99a. See *Peirush HaMishnayos* of *Rambam, Sanhedrin* Ch. 10 Principles 7 and 8.

stronger and we would never have sinned." Now, there would be no excuses, and the Jewish people would have to face the consequences of their choices.[70]

Moshe Completes the Commandments

As the Jewish people had requested, the voice of Hashem stopped talking to them directly.[71] Moshe was still at the foot of the mountain, from where he had addressed the people, who had remained just where they had been revived, some being as far as twelve *mils* away.[72] Instantly, the angels Michael and Gavriel took Moshe by the arms and brought him, flying like a bird, straight up to the mountaintop and right into the *arafel* cloud, the inner ring of the *Shechinah* from which even angels were barred.[73] A pathway opened for Moshe in the *arafel* cloud, and he approached the *Shechinah*.[74]

The difference in location between Moshe and the Jewish people underscored the difference in their spiritual level. The Jewish people, who had declined the gift of prophecy, now stood far from the mountain, while Moshe, the intermediary who would deliver the Torah from Hashem to the people, reached heights beyond those that any other person would ever reach.[75] He entered the *arafel* cloud and approached the *Shechinah* without being scorched or otherwise harmed by the intense radiance.[76]

It was now time for the Commandments to continue, with Moshe hearing them from Hashem and relaying them to the people. From his location on the mountaintop, however, Moshe would have to speak very loudly for all of the several million Jewish people to

---

70. See *Shemos Rabbah* 29:4, 41:3; *Shir HaShirim Rabbah* 1:2; *Tzeidah LaDerech; Abarbanel; Alshich; Akeidah* to *Shemos* 20:17.
71. See *Radal* 77 to *Pirkei D'Rav Eliezer* 41; *Ralbag; Akeidah* to *Shemos* 20:18.
72. *Malbim* to *Shemos* 20:18.
73. *Pirkei D'Rav Eliezer* 41; *Mechilta; Rashi* to *Shemos* 20:18; *Rabbeinu Bachya; HaKesav VeHaKabbalah* to *Shemos* 20:18; *Tanchuma Ki Sisa* 32; *Yalkut* 301. See *Mechilta D'Rashbi* which states that this was done by force, because due to Moshe's humility, he did not want to be singled out for this honor in front of the Jewish people (*Radal* fn. 58).
  Some suggest that this is a reference to the Torah's use of the word "al kanfei nesharim — on the wings of eagles" (*Shemos* 19:4).
74. *Yoma* 4b; see *Maharsha; Rashi* to *Shemos* 24:18.
75. See *Ibn Ezra; Rabbeinu Bachya; R' Avraham Ben HaRambam; Ralbag; Akeidah; Abarbanel* to *Shemos* 20:18.
76. *Tanchuma Terumah* 11.

hear him. Some of them were as far away as twelve *mils*, which is more than eight miles. Hashem helped Moshe, boosting the power of his voice until the most distant Jew in attendance could hear him clearly.[77] Furthermore, Hashem followed each Commandment with a blast of the *shofar*, which convinced the people that Moshe was speaking in the Name of Hashem rather than on his own.[78]

Although they had asked Moshe to serve as an intermediary, the Jewish people now began to have misgivings. They realized that had they persevered and heard the Torah directly from Hashem, it would have been etched into their hearts and minds forever. They would have attained an angelic level of spirituality, forcing the evil inclination to abandon them forever. They would have been cloaked with a mantle of impregnable protection from the hostile nations around them. But now that they were receiving the Torah from Moshe, himself a mortal prone to forgetfulness and vulnerable to the evil inclination, the Jewish grasp of the Torah would only be tenuous. They would learn and forget, and they would struggle endlessly with their evil inclinations.[79]

---

77. See *Mechilta; Netziv; Rashi; Rabbeinu Bachya* to *Shemos* 19:19; *Alshich* to *Shemos* 20:16 and *Devarim* 5:19. See *Midrash Tehillim* 4.

Hashem would send out the Commandments in one word and sound. Moshe, who understood the content, broke up the sounds into words so they could be understood by the Jewish people. See *Moreh Nevuchim* 2:32.

78. See *Rabbeinu Meyuchas; Moreh Nevuchim* 2:33; *Maaseh Hashem* to *Shemos* 19:19.

See *Ohr HaChaim* who writes that in welcoming the *Shechinah*, Moshe sang praises to Hashem, and Hashem replied with the blowing of the *shofar*. See *Tur* for his explanation.

Some suggest that this exchange is symbolic of Rosh Hashanah. Moshe represented the community (*shaliach tzibbur*), and when the *shofar* responded, it was a sign that the sins of the Jewish people had been forgiven (see *Tosafos Al HaTorah*).

The instructions Hashem gave to Moshe were actually louder than Moshe's voice, because as interpreter of Hashem's words, Moshe's voice could not exceed the pitch of Hashem's voice (see *Berachos* 45a with *Tosafos, Maharsha; Panim Yafos*). Some suggest that Hashem had to speak louder so that his voice could be heard over the sounds of the *shofar* in the background. See *Rashbam* and *Chizkuni* to *Shemos* 19:19. See *Maaseh Hashem* for a different view.

Some suggest that the Jews requested that Moshe deliver the Torah alone without the assistance of Hashem.

79. *Zohar* 261; *Devarim* 5:28; *Shir HaShirim* 1:4; *Yalkut Shir HaShirim* 2:98; *Midrash Chazis; Kometz HaMinchah, Shavuos*.

Had Hashem been the one to give them the entire Torah, the Jews would have reversed the sin of Adam and the Serpent and would have exchanged the tree of death for the tree of life.

See fns. to *Maamad Har Sinai* p. 128 for his discussion on what seems to be a contradiction in sources as to when the evil inclination returned to the Jewish people and the circumstances that brought it back.

"Moshe, we've changed our minds," many of them cried out. "We want to retain the Torah forever, and therefore, we don't want to hear it through you. Great as you are, you are nevertheless only a mortal human being. We want to hear it again from Hashem as before."

"Too late," said Moshe. "Your request was granted once. It will not be granted a second time. But do not despair. Even if you forget what you learn, it will always be with you. In the World to Come, you will have at your fingertips everything you have ever learned, and you will gaze at the *Shechinah* and reach once again the angelic levels of prophecy and spirituality."[80]

Moshe completed his pronouncement of the Commandments, yet the heavens still remained open over the mountain. The revelation faded away, but the fire, a symbol of the *Shechinah* that resided there, still burned on the mountaintop, as it would for the forty days Moshe would spend in Heaven receiving the entire Torah. The sounds reverberating through the desert would also continue for these forty days.[81]

The Jewish people looked up at the heavens and recited *Shema Yisrael*. Then they added, "Just as no one resides in Heaven other than Your radiant glory, so too do You reign alone on this earth." The Jewish people accepted, without reservation, Hashem's sovereignty over the earth and all its inhabitants, the heavens and all the host of angels.[82]

This day was a greater and happier occasion for Hashem than the day He created the world. On this day, the master plan of the creation of the universe was completed. The Giving of the Torah was the justification for the existence of humanity and the ultimate destiny of the world.[83]

It is interesting to note that of all the holidays celebrated, Shavuos is the only one with an arguable date of occurrence. Some suggest that the basis for this argument is the forgetfulness that took place when Moshe interceded. Had the Torah never been forgotten, there would never be disagreements or arguments about laws. However, with the Torah now being lowered to a mortal standard and forgetfulness reigning in every facet of the Torah, all its portions are filled with arguments, disagreements and differences of opinions. Because of this, the foundation of the Yom Tov of Shavuos is based on an argument between R' Yosi and the Rabbanan as to when it actually takes place (*Kometz HaMinchah, Shavuos*).

80. *Shir Rabbah* 1:4; *Yedei Moshe, Yefei Kol*.
81. See *Pirkei D'Rav Eliezer* 41; *Chizkuni* to *Devarim* 5:19.
82. See *Devarim Rabbah* 2:32; 2:34. See *Berachos* 21a.
83. *Pesachim* 68b; *Zohar* 92b; *Midrash Chadash Al HaTorah* to *Shemos* 20:1.

Moshe Remains With Hashem

It was midafternoon. The delivery of the Ten Commandments was complete. Hashem told Moshe to send the Jewish people back to their tents and their families and resume a regular existence. When they returned home they realized that they were now bound by dietary laws and did not have any meat dishes that were properly koshered. Instead, they ate only dairy dishes. According to some opinions, this is the source of the custom to eat dairy foods on Shavuos.[84]

Moshe, however, did not return to his tent. Hashem commanded him to remain with the *Shechinah*, in constant contact with Him, always on call, should He appear to him at a moment's notice. Such a man had to live a life of utmost purity, like an angel; he could not conduct an ordinary family life.[85]

As Moshe stood at the threshold of the *arafel* cloud, Hashem gave him another message for the Jewish people.[86] "You, the Jewish peo-

---

84. See *Orach Chaim* 494:12.

Many ask an obvious question: Why was this a big deal, when the Jews had the manna to eat? As we know, the manna's two *omers* were more than ample for a person for a full day.

There are various answers to this problem. Some suggest that the Jews who had woken up late to receive the Torah had missed their chance to collect the manna. As a result, by this time of the day it had melted and there was no food available. The problem with this view is that it was Shabbos and the manna did not fall on Shabbos. In fact, the Jews had already gathered their Shabbos portions on Friday, the day before. See *Radal* to *Pirkei D'Rav Eliezer* 41 who suggests that based on the view that the Torah was given on Friday and that the Jews received the Torah at noon, they did collect the manna before they stood at Mount Sinai. Others suggest that along with the manna, there were livestock available and there was consumption of meat in the desert. Therefore *kashrus*, utensils and meat preparation became an issue at this time. Others suggest that since it was Shabbos, all the Shabbos laws already applied and thus, irrespective of *kashrus*, they could not slaughter meat on that day. This leaves one last opinion, that the meat had already been slaughtered the day before and that they had no utensils or dishes in which to serve it.

85. See *Zohar* 261 to *Devarim* 5:24,28; *Lekach Tov* to *Devarim* 5:27; *Rambam, Hil Yesodei HaTorah* 7:6.

86. There is some question as to the sequence of events that took place following *Matan Torah*. *Shemos* 20:18 states that Moshe entered the *arafel*. This is definitely after the giving of the Ten Commandments. *Shemos* 24:2 again states that Moshe entered the *arafel*. *Ramban* disagrees with *Rashi*, and maintains that this ascension took place after the giving of the Ten Commandments. *Shemos* 24:15 states that Moshe ascended Mount Sinai. In between all these verses are Hashem's directives about not worshiping idols (20:20) and the laws of *mishpatim* (21:1). The *Ramban* cites *Shemos* 24:3 as Moshe following Hashem's directives to relay the words told to him. After that, Moshe ascended the mountain for forty days. *Rashi* recognizes 24:1-11 as taking place before the Torah was given, so we are unsure what the entrance to *arafel* in 20:18 represents. *Shalsheles HaKabbalah* suggests that Moshe left the *arafel*, spoke to the nation and ascended again to Mount Sinai.

ple, did not receive the Commandments secondhand at Mount Sinai," said Hashem. "It is not as if you heard about them from someone else or saw the events through someone else's eyes. You were all there. I opened the heavens for you and showed you My glory, something I have never shown any other nation.[87] I was ready to give you the Torah without any intermediaries. At the last moment, you needed Moshe to relay My words to you, but I was speaking to you directly. It is part of your experience and your memory for always, and no self-proclaimed prophet will ever be able to deny it to you. There should be no doubts or reservations in your minds.[88]

"Now that you know so clearly that I alone am Hashem, that I am the only worthy object of your faith and your prayers, then you must be careful not to make any images, statues or other representations of Me to serve as intermediaries in your relationship with Me.[89] They will not help you. I will only answer you if you come directly to Me. Wherever you are, whenever it is, I will be accessible to you.[90]

"In addition, do not create images that represent the constellations, animals or anything else that might be construed as an intermediary between Me and the people.[91] Just as there were no images or representations during the revelation earlier today, so shall there never be any intermediaries between us.[92] You know that I am entirely Divine and spiritual. Do not disgrace Me by making physical images to represent Me."[93]

Having already followed *Rashi's* approach regarding the chronology of events that took place during the revelation, I hesitate to choose the *Ramban's* view despite its offering a clearer timeline. For the purposes of this book, I have therefore chosen to consolidate Moshe's ascension and Hashem's dialogue with him in one grouping, and present the events in the order in which they are written in the Torah. See *Shemos* 24:1-2; *Rashi* and *Ramban* to *Shemos* 24:12.

87. See *Mechilta*; *Rashi* to *Shemos* 20:19; *Midrash Aseres HaDibros*.

88. *Rashi* to *Shemos* 20:19; *Sefer HaIkrim*.

89. See *Ibn Ezra*; *Ramban*; *Sforno*; *Bechor Shor*; *Akeidah*; *Sifsei Kohen*; *Alshich* to *Shemos* 20:19-20; *Tiferes Yisrael* 46.

It is interesting to note that the first laws after the Ten Commandments were that the Jewish people should not make silver and gold images to worship. It was as though Hashem were warning the Jewish people about not erecting the Golden Calf, which would take place forty days later (*Sifsei Kohen*).

90. See *Tanchuma Bechukosai* 2.

91. *Malbim* to *Shemos* 20:19; *Devarim* 4:15-16.

92. See *Ibn Ezra*; *Ramban*; *R' Avraham Ben HaRambam*; *Sforno*; *Bechor Shor*; *Akeidah*; *Alshich* to *Shemos* 20:19-20; *Sefer HaIkrim* 3:13.

93. See *Chizkuni and Ralbag* to *Shemos* 20:19-20; *Rashi*; *Ramban*; *Rabbeinu Bachya*; *Chizkuni*; *Ohr HaChaim* to *Devarim* 4:12,15-16; *Panim Yafos*.

Having given Moshe these messages, Hashem went on to teach Moshe the civil laws governing interpersonal relationships among the people, as outlined in *Parashas Mishpatim*.[94] Even before the instructions for building a Mishkan, an Abode for the *Shechinah*, Hashem wanted to establish the pathways of justice and righteousness in the Jewish encampment. Only then would the *Shechinah* enter the encampment.[95]

Moshe Ascends the Mountain

Moshe relayed Hashem's messages to the Jewish people, and then returned to the mountain. Yehoshua, his closest disciple, followed close behind until they reached the boundary closest to the mountain, where he would remain for the entire forty days that Moshe was up in Heaven.[96] Aharon, Chur and the elders, not permitted to enter this far into the forbidden zone of sanctification, remained on the other side of a boundary much further away.[97]

For these forty days, during the absence of Moshe and Yehoshua, the mantle of leadership would fall on the shoulders of his brother Aharon and his nephew Chur. Aharon would stand in for Moshe, and Chur for Yehoshua.[98] They would remain within the boundaries of the encampment, and together with the elders, who were all qualified sages and scholars, they would settle any disputes that arose among the people.[99]

Before Moshe made his final ascent, he addressed the people. "I am about to ascend the mountain," he said, "where I will remain for

---

94. *Akeidah* to *Shemos* 20:19; *Tanna D'Vei Eliyahu* 22.
See *Shemos Rabbah* 30:11 which states that although the Torah was destined to be given by day, the laws and *mishpatim* would be given by night

95. *Tiferes Yisrael* 46.
Once the Jews said *Naaseh venishma*, Hashem felt welcome to live among the people who proclaimed His sovereignty (*Abarbanel* to *Shemos* 24:16).

96. *Ramban*; *Rabbeinu Bachya* to *Shemos* 24:13-14; *Rashi* to *Shemos* 24:13-14; *Rashi* to *Yoma* 75b; *Midrash Aggadah*; *Bechor Shor*.
Yehoshua would erect his tent there and eat from the manna that fell in the area (*Yoma* 75b; *Ibn Ezra*).
Having just completed the dialogue between Hashem with Moshe recorded in *Shemos* 20:18-23, the Torah now begins the description of Moshe's ascension to the mountain mentioned in *Shemos* 24:12.

97. *Ramban*; *Abarbanel*; *Malbim*; *Midrash Aggadah* to *Shemos* 24:13-14.

98. *R' Avraham Ben HaRambam*.
Chur was the son of Miriam and Calev.

99. See *Rashi*; *Targum*; *Malbim* to *Shemos* 24:13-14; *Yalkut Shimoni Shemos* 362.

forty days. I will return within a span of six hours exactly forty days from this moment, and I will bring with me the *Luchos*, the stone Tablets on which the Ten Commandments will be engraved."

Moshe now faced his mission with fear and awe. He was about to go into Heaven, to walk among the angels and advocate for the Jewish people. It would be a difficult task, and he asked the elders to pray and fast for his success and for his safe return.[100]

Many add that from this very verse the foundation of the first mishnah in *Avos* is formed. Moshe would ascend the mountain and would first relay all that he learned to Yehoshua who would pass it on to the *zekeinim* (elders) and eventually teach the *neviim* (prophets). (See *Tanchuma Noach* 3,14; *Tosafos* to *Shemos* 24:13; *Midrash* in *Torah Shleimah* 117.)

Many authorities learn from the word "*lehorosam*" in *Shemos* 24:12 that the Torah was purposely left obscure and incomplete so that the sages and scholars would be able to dispute and challenge the various opinions and laws created through the Oral Torah (see *Midrash HaGadol*).

100. *Midrash HaGadol;* see *Yoma* 4b; *Yalkut* 2:842.

11 The Ten Commandments

A great warrior once arrived in an embattled country and offered the people his services as their king. "I have come to deliver you from your troubles," said the warrior. "I will rule over this country and make it strong and prosperous. You will become a great nation, honored among the family of nations."

"Why should we accept you?" said the people. "Why should we submit to your authority and leadership?"

The warrior did not argue with the people. Instead, he organized and trained an army and deployed it along the borders. He also marshaled the resources of the country and built roads, aqueducts and reservoirs. The economy boomed, and the country's security was never better.

The warrior called for a public assembly.

"Now, I will make you my earlier offer again," he said. "I want to rule over this country as its king. I have shown you what I can do for you. Now that you have seen what I can do, you know it is for your own benefit."

The people saw the justice of his words and accepted him by acclaim.

In the same way, Hashem did not declare His kingship over the Jewish people immediately. First, He brought them forth from Egypt with a great show of miracles and wonders. Then He split the sea for them, sent them manna from the heavens and defended them in the war against Amalek. Having demonstrated the extent to which He would go for His people, Hashem decided that the time was right to declare His Kingship by giving the Jewish people the Torah. They would now be ready to accept Him and serve Him faithfully.[1]

Furthermore, the Torah itself would become a stronger motivation for Jewish loyalty and faithfulness than the miracles and wonders in Egypt. It can be explained by a parable.

A great king asked a young princess for her hand in marriage. The princess accepted, and the king sent her a shipment of the most spectacular gifts. The princess was delighted with her marriage gifts, even more so because they carried the promise of a fabulous life together with the king.

A few days before the wedding, the king was called away on an overseas mission, and the royal wedding had to be postponed. Years went by. The princess waited for the return of her future husband, but still the king did not return. The friends of the princess began to whisper in her ear.

"How long do you intend to wait, your highness?" they said. "You are wasting away the best years of your life. Find yourself a different husband. You can choose from among the finest gentlemen, the most eligible bachelors in the realm. Marry and enjoy the good life you deserve. Why do you insist on pining away the years?"

The princess did not know what to do. She wanted so much to marry the king, but how long should she wait? When would it be time to look elsewhere?

She was about to give in to the entreaties of her friends when she stepped into the strongroom and looked once again at the gifts the king had sent her. Once again, the gifts conjured up in her mind the wonderful life she would share with the king if she would only be patient and wait for his return. With renewed resolve, she decided to wait for the king no matter how long it would take.

---

1. See *Mechilta D'Rashbi; Shemos Rabbah* 29:6; *Lekach Tov.*

Finally, the king returned and was somewhat surprised to discover that the princess had loyally waited for him for such a long time.

"Tell me," he said to the princess, "why did you wait so long?"

"It was because of the beautiful and thoughtful gifts you sent me," she said. "When I looked at them, I knew that no one could give me the happiness and fulfillment you would."

The history of the Jewish people is characterized by long-suffering patience in the face of incredible adversity. During all these terrible times, the nations of the world try to undermine the loyalty of the Jewish people to Hashem.

"How long must you endure so much suffering and pain?" they ask. "What has Hashem done for you that you insist on being so loyal to Him? Come and join us. We will help you and support you. We will appoint you as leaders and officers of our societies. All you have to do is abandon your allegiance to Him.

These offers are appealing to the Jewish people in their times of trouble. But then, they look into the Torah and see the blessings that await them if they remain loyal to Hashem. Hashem promises to make them healthy, strong, fruitful and prosperous, and even more important, the spiritual rewards are limitless. And so they reject the offers of the nations of the world and remain loyal and faithful to Hashem.

In the end of days, Hashem will ask the Jewish people, "Why did you endure all the suffering and sorrow in order to remain loyal to Me?"

"If not for the Torah and its treasures," they will answer, "we would long ago have joined the other nations and blended into their societies."[2]

A Microcosm of the Torah

The Ten Commandments contain far more than Ten Commandments. They also contain allusions to the entire Torah. Furthermore, they are comprised of 620 letters, which are an allusion to the 613 mitzvos and the seven days of creation. Others suggest that they are an allusion to the 613 mitzvos and the seven universal mitzvos that apply to all human beings. According to both views, the implication is that all of creation is

---

2. *Pesikta Rabbah* Ch. 21 p. 106.

dependent on the Torah.³ The letters are also an allusion to the 365 limbs and the 248 veins of the body. The Ten Commandments themselves correspond to the ten principal organs — heart, brain, mouth, eyes, ears, hands, feet, liver, kidneys and *milah*.⁴

Just as the plagues in Egypt followed the systematic subjugation of a rebellious city, the order of the Ten Commandments follows the systematic establishment of royal sovereignty over a province newly wrested from an evil empire.⁵

First, Hashem demanded that the Jewish people accept His rule over them (*Anochi*). Second, He demanded that they disavow loyalty to any other deities (*lo yihyeh lecha*). Third, Hashem demanded that the people respect His Name by not taking it in vain (*lo sisa*). Fourth, Hashem gave the people a day of reflection on the seventh day of the week, during which they should contemplate His greatness and recall the wonder of His works (*zachor*).

Fifth, Hashem commanded that people honor their parents, thereby establishing a strong connection with the earlier generations that saw the miracles He performed and ensuring that the memories will be passed on to the next generations (*kabed*).

Sixth, Hashem forbade bloodshed, because it would decimate the population over which He chose to rule (*lo sirtzach*). Seventh, since people might think population is so important that any means of procreation are acceptable, Hashem forbade adultery (*lo sin'af*). Eighth, since a stable society protects private property and personal rights, Hashem forbade abduction, theft and robbery (*lo signov*). Ninth, in addition to physical assaults on other Jews, Hashem forbade verbal assaults in the form of false testimony (*lo saaneh*). Tenth,

---

3. *Bamidbar Rabbah Nasso* 13:16; 18:21; *Tur* to *Yisro*. See *Rashi* to *Shemos* 24:12.

This is also symbolized by the words *Keser Torah*. *Keser* (crown) has the numerical value of 620. If one keeps the Torah it becomes a crown for him; if not, then it is reversed to become *kares* (which also equals 620), meaning that one will be cut off from this world (*Minchah Belulah*; *Tur* to *Shemos* 20:14).

See *Pesikta Chadata*; *Pesikta Rabbah* 21; *Lekach Tov* to *Va'eschanan* where it states that the Ten Commandments correspond to the ten statements with which Hashem created the world, and to the ten plagues in Egypt.

See *Yalkut* 276; *Eliyahu Rabbah* 26 about how the Patriarchs and the ten tribes kept the Ten Commandments. See *Mechilta D'Rashbi Beshalach* about how Yosef kept the commandments.

4. *Rabbeinu Bachya*.

The 248 positive commandments are symbolized by the 248 letters in the three positive commandments of *Anochi*, *Zachor* and *Kabed* (*Midrash HaChefetz*). See *Panim Yafos* who suggests that the entire Torah is contained within the word *Anochi* alone.

5. See *Let My Nation Go* p. 192.

since people might think that simply having evil thoughts is harmless, Hashem forbade coveting the possessions of other people, which is equally damaging to others (*lo sachmod*).⁶

Originally, the Sages had wanted to institute the practice of daily recital of the Ten Commandments, just as the *Shema* is recited every day. They did not do so, because they were concerned that heretics would claim that these Commandments alone comprise the entire body of the Torah. Nonetheless, their intent was accomplished in an oblique way through the daily recital of the *Shema*, which contains allusions to the Ten Commandments.⁷

The words "*Hashem Elokeinu*" (Hashem our L-rd) recall the First Commandment, which establishes Hashem's sovereignty. The words "*Hashem Echad*" (Hashem is One) recall the Second Commandment, which forbids the worship of any other deities. The words "*ve'ahavta es Hashem*" (and you shall love Hashem) recall the Third Commandment, which forbids taking His Name in vain; if a person truly loves Hashem he would never do such a thing. The words "*lemaan tizkeru*" (in order that you remember) recall the Fourth Commandment, which commands us to remember Shabbos. The words "*lemaan yirbu yemeichem*" (in order that your days be many) recall the Fifth Commandment, which commands us to honor parents, a mitzvah rewarded by long life.

The words "*va'avadetem meheirah*" (and you will quickly be destroyed) recall the Sixth Commandment, which forbids bloodshed under pain of death. The words "*lo sasuru*" (do not be tempted) recall the Seventh Commandment, which forbids adultery. The words "*ve'asafta diganecha*" (and you shall harvest your grain) recall the Eighth Commandment, which forbids the use of anyone's property other than one's own. The words "*Hashem emes*" (Hashem is true) recall the Ninth Commandment, which forbids testifying falsely, a denial of Hashem's truthfulness. The words "*al mezuzos beisecha*" (on the doorposts of your house) recall the Tenth Commandment, which forbids coveting someone else's house.⁸

---

6. *Meam Loez*.
7. See *Berachos* 12a; *Rashi*; *Maharsha*; *Iyun Yaakov* there; *Yerushalmi Berachos* 1:5.
    Heretics could not use this argument once the Ten Commandments are alluded to in the *Shema*, since it contains references to *tefillin*, *tzitzis* and *mezuzah*, which are clearly not included in the Ten Commandments.
8. See *Yerushalmi Berachos* 1:5; *Pesikta Chadata*.

The First Commandment[9]

The First Commandment is a positive commandment that is incumbent on everyone. It is the basis of all the Ten Commandments and the entire Torah. It commands the sincere belief that Hashem is the essence of all existence, that nothing in the world has any being or existence external to Him. Hashem alone is the Supreme Being, Creator and Master of the Universe. He is One, everything is unified in Him. He is therefore infinite, omnipotent, omniscient, timeless and eternal. He is the Source of all physical and spiritual existence, and the ruler, supervisor and master of all.[10]

These thoughts, in concentrated form, must be implanted deep in one's heart. They must inspire and motivate everything a person does in life. Any action a person does or word he utters that belittles Hashem's honor and sovereignty is considered a violation of this Commandment, since it indicates a lack of appreciation for Hashem's infinite greatness.[11]

There are a number of reasons for this being the first of the Commandments in addition to its being the fundamental tenet of the Jewish faith and religion. During the revelation at Mount Sinai, the Jewish people witnessed a multitude of manifestations. They saw great fiery visions and crackling lightning and heard thunder and other frightening sounds. Someone might have thought that a pantheon of gods sat astride the mountain performing these different feats. Therefore, Hashem immediately announced: "I am Hashem your L-rd! I am the Source of everything you have witnessed. Let anyone dare come forward and deny it."[12]

Furthermore, Hashem takes on many guises in His conduct of the world. The Jewish people saw Him at the splitting of the sea as a Mighty Warrior, while at Mount Sinai they saw Him as a Merciful

---

9. I have chosen selected sources of information that apply to each of the Commandments. It is incumbent upon the reader to understand that in no way is this book a source from which any judgment should be made regarding each Commandment.

10. *Ramban; Ibn Ezra; Rabbeinu Bachya; Sforno* to *Shemos* 20:2; *Sefer Mitzvos Katan; Sefer Mitzvos Gadol; Sefer Charedim; Rambam, Hil. Yesodei HaTorah* 1:1; *Peirush Mishnayos L'Rambam, Sanhedrin* 10:1; *Sefer HaChinuch Mitzvah* 25; *Devarim* 4:35,39; *Tiferes Yisrael* 36.

11. *Ibn Ezra.* See *Chovos HaLevavos,* beginning of *Shaar HaYichud.*

When one multiplies each letter of the word *Echad* by itself (1x1 plus 8x8 plus 4x4) it totals 81, which is the same numerical value as *Anochi,* suggesting that the precept of *Anochi* is to recognize that Hashem is one (*Yalkut Reuveni*).

12. See *Tanchuma Yisro* 15; *Rashi* to *Shemos* 20:1; *Lekach Tov.*

Sage. There are also many other aspects and facets of the Divine Presence. Therefore, Hashem immediately informed the Jewish people that these various guises were all different facets of the one and only Hashem. "I am Hashem your L-rd," He declared. "I am the very same One about Whom you said, 'This is my L-rd,' at the splitting of the sea.[13] The Torah you have received comes from Sinai, and I, Hashem, have given it to you."[14]

Another reason for this being the first of the Commandments can be illustrated with a parable. A great and wise king entered a city he had just conquered and added to his kingdom. The people greeted him with pomp and rejoicing.

"Your majesty, we are eager to have you rule over us," they told him. "Issue some of your wise decrees for our city so that we may benefit from your great wisdom."

"Not quite yet," the king replied. "I have just come into the city. First, you must show me that you accept my sovereign rule over your city. Only then will I tell you my laws."

In the same way, before Hashem issued laws for the Jewish people, He first declared His sovereignty and unity. Only when the Jewish people accepted this Commandment would He go on to give them the rest of the Commandments.[15]

The first word of the First Commandment is *Anochi*, "I." This word begins with the letter *aleph*, the first letter of the *aleph-beis*. The entire Torah opens with the word *Bereishis*, "in the beginning," which begins with the letter *beis*, the second letter of the *aleph-beis*. Hashem chose to bypass the *aleph*, because it is reminiscent of the word *arur*, "accursed," which also begins with an *aleph*. The *aleph* considered itself unworthy, since its numerical value is 1, the least among all the letters. Therefore, it accepted Hashem's decision with humility and without complaint.

Hashem rewarded the *aleph* by saying, "You are really the king of the letters. You are the first, and you represent the number 1, just as I am one and the Torah is one. Nonetheless, you were silent and humble when I passed over you to begin the Torah with a *beis*. Therefore, you will be the first letter of the Ten Commandments."[16]

---

13. *Rashi; Sifsei Chachamim* to *Shemos* 20:2.
14. *Smag.*
15. See *Mechilta; Ramban* to *Yisro.*
16. *Osios D'Rav Akiva; Tiferes Yisrael* Ch. 34; see *Bereishis Rabbah* 1:10; *Shir Rabbah* 5:8; *Midrash Aseres HaDibros.*
  Some suggest that the dialogue that took place was an allegory only to show that every facet and nuance of the creation was done with purpose and reason (*Yefei To'ar*).

Others suggest that the Torah begins with the letter *beis* as a symbol of the first two Commandments, which declare His sovereignty and His supremacy over the entire world.[17] Furthermore, beginning with the letter *beis* makes the statement that, just as nothing precedes the *beis* but the *aleph*, so too, did nothing precede the world but Hashem, who is One.[18]

The word *Ani* also means "I" and begins with the letter *aleph*, but Hashem preferred to use the word *Anochi* to begin the Commandments. The word *Ani*, when written without *nekudos*, vowelization marks, can also be read as *Aini*, which means, "I am not." The word *Ani* could be misread as saying, "I am not Hashem your L-rd," Heaven forbid. The *Anochi*, however, poses no such danger.[19]

The word *Anochi* is also full of mystical meaning, symbolism and numerical significance in its individual letters — *aleph, nun, chaf, yud*. The *aleph*, with a numerical value of 1, represents Hashem's unity and sovereignty. The *nun*, which has a value of 50, and the *chaf*, which has a value of 20, collectively represent the 70 nationalities of the world over which Hashem rules. The *yud*, with a value of 10, represents the Ten Commandments.[20] The word *Anochi* is also an acronym of the Aramaic statement, "*Ana nafsahi kesavis yehavis* — I alone wrote and gave it"; the authorship and authenticity of the Torah are not to be questioned.[21]

---

17. *Tikkunei Zohar* 32 p. 76a.
18. *Mishnas R' Eliezer* to *Yisro*.
19. *Shlah.* See *Malbim.*
20. See *Pesikta Rabbah* Ch. 21 p. 105; *Pesikta Chadata.*
21. *Shabbos* 105a.

The Torah could easily have used the word *Ani*, which is a far more common word for "I" than the word *Anochi*. The Torah's use of the word *Anochi* is therefore intended to send a message (*Maharsha; Rashi*).

Another opinion suggests that the use of the word *Anochi* had another purpose as well. The Arabic word for "I" is the word *Anuch*. The Jews, having lived in Egypt for so long, were familiar and comfortable with that language. Hashem preferred to speak to them in a familiar language to which they found it easy to relate (see *Yalkut* 286 who explains this with a parable).

See *Torah Shleimah* to *Yisro* Ch. 20 fn. 30 that in the Egyptian hieroglyphics they indeed found a word similar to *Anochi* that means "I."

Some find this Midrash difficult to understand, for it was a known fact that one of the reasons the Jews merited the exodus of Egypt was because they did not change their language. They distanced themselves from the Egyptians by speaking *lashon kodesh* (the holy tongue) as opposed to the native Egyptian language. It stands to reason therefore that there was no emotional benefit to be gained by speaking to the Jewish people in an Arabic tongue.

The word *Elokecha*, "your L-rd," denotes a special relationship between Hashem and the Jewish people, who accepted His sovereignty, to the exclusion of the pagan nations, who rejected His sovereignty.[22] Furthermore, the use of the second person possessive singular rather than plural indicates a direct personal relationship between Hashem and every individual Jew. Each and every Jew must believe that he alone was worthy of the Torah being given, that Hashem is speaking in the Torah directly to him, that he alone is responsible for his own destiny as a Jew and that his actions or lack of them will determine his degree of reward or retribution.[23]

The singular also implies that the acceptance of the Torah by the Jewish people is dependent on its individual acceptance by each and every Jew.[24] All Jews are responsible for one another, and their behavior impacts on the entire Jewish people. This can be explained with a parable.

A king decided to give away one of the royal fields to one of his subjects. He offered it to different individuals throughout his kingdom, but all of them declined the honor. "The responsibility of caring for this field is just too great," they said. "If it is not kept up in a proper way, it will be a show of disrespect to the king."

The king continued to offer the field to his subjects until finally one man accepted the offer. In the beginning, he took good care of the field, but after a while, he neglected it. Weeds began to cover the once lush surface. Worms and insects gnawed at the vegetation, and plant disease destroyed whatever was left.

One day, the king rode by in his royal carriage and saw the land he had gifted to his subject. He was outraged. "What have you done?" he said. "At least the others had the good sense and the respect to decline my offer. At least the others did not ruin the field. But you accepted my gift, and then you let it go to ruin. Not only did you ruin this field, you also ruined all the fields around it, which are now afflicted with weeds and infestation."

In the same way, when Hashem offered the Torah to the nations of the world, they at least turned it down. But the Jewish people

---

22. *Mechilta D'Rashbi.*
23. See *Lekach Tov; Ramban.*
24. *Peskita Rabbah* Ch. 21 p. 100b.
    By telling the Jewish people I am "your" G-d, Hashem in essence was saying that even if one Jew rejects Him, it is as though the entire nation rejected Him (*Midrash HaGadol*).

accepted it, and by doing so, they also accepted the responsibility to safeguard and uphold it. Moreover, should they neglect to do so, they would be doing damage to all the Jewish people, spoiling not only their own fields, so to speak, but also the fields of their family, friends and neighbors.[25]

The use of the words *Hashem Elokecha*, "Hashem your L-rd," brings to mind both the Attribute of Strict Justice, represented by the Name Elokim, and the Attribute of Merciful Justice, represented by the Name Hashem. In effect, Hashem was telling the Jewish people, "If you abide by My laws and do my will, I will treat you with mercy and protect you. But if you rebel, I will treat you with merciful justice."[26]

With the words *"asher hotzeisicha mei'eretz Mitzrayim*, Who brought you forth from the land of Egypt," Hashem did not mention the creation of the universe in this context but rather the exodus from Egypt. Since the Jewish people had never seen the miracles of creation, these were an inadequate foundation for their belief and faith in Hashem. They did, however, witness His magnificent miracles and wonders during the exodus from Egypt and were the beneficiaries of the display of His awesome power. Therefore, Hashem expected them to recognize Him as their sovereign ruler.[27]

Furthermore, Hashem was saying that the exodus itself was reason enough for the Jewish people to worship and serve Him.[28] He had saved their lives. He had extricated them from bondage to a nation descended from Cham, a race of slaves, and made them the servants of the Master of the Universe. The basic requirements of appreciation and gratitude demanded that they accept His sovereignty.[29]

The events of the exodus also underscore the special relationship between Hashem and the Jewish people. Not only is He the G-d of all creation, He is also the specific national G-d of the Jewish people, Who came to their rescue when they were slaves in Egypt. The Ten

---

25. *Shemos Rabbah*, 25 cited by *Meam Loez*.
   This is similar to when one part of a person is in pain and the whole body feels it (*Yalkut* 276).
26. See *Mechilta D'Rashbi*; *Pesikta D'Rav Kahana* 12 p. 108b; *Rabbeinu Bachya*; *Lekach Tov*; *Bechor Shor*.
   See *Tiferes Yisrael* 37 for further discussion of this First Commandment.
27. See *Ibn Ezra*; *Rabbeinu Bachya*; *Ramban*; *Bechor Shor*; *Shlah* to *Yisro*; *Meam Loez*.
28. *Mechilta D'Rashbi*; *Rashi* to *Shemos* 20:2; *Shemos Rabbah* 29:3; *Meam Loez*.
29. See *Pesikta Rabbah* end of Ch. 21; *Rabbeinu Bachya*; *Yerushalmi Succah* 4:3; *Mishnas R' Eliezer* 7:138; *Lekach Tov* 20:2.

Commandments and the Giving of the Torah would now confirm and eternalize this special relationship.[30]

The Second Commandment

The Second Commandment is the immediate outgrowth of the First in a number of ways. Once it is established that the Jewish people must believe in Hashem, it follows that "gods of others" — the false and non-existent products of the fertile imaginations of "other" people — should play no role whatsoever in their spiritual lives, either as objects of worship or as intermediaries with Hashem.[31] Furthermore, not only substituting idols for Hashem but also any form of denial or rejection of the Kingship of Hashem is considered a violation of this Commandment and a denial of the entire Torah.[32]

If the situation arises in which a Jew is presented with the choice of denying Hashem or death, he is required to accept death rather than deny Hashem. It is better to suffer a little pain in this world and gain the eternal pleasures of the next world.[33]

The Second Commandment encompasses three other prohibitions as well. It is forbidden to construct or acquire an idol.[34] It is forbidden to serve an idol in its prescribed manner of worship, even if one does not do so with the intent of accepting the idol as a god.[35] It is forbidden to declare allegiance to an idol or even to have such thoughts, even if they are not accompanied by a concrete physical act.[36]

---

30. *Meam Loez.*
    Some add that since one of the Egyptian idols was the sheep, as preparation to accepting Hashem's sovereignty over them, they had to kill the Egyptian idol. Thus the concept of the days of *sefirah* connecting Pesach and Shavuos can be understood. On Pesach they slaughtered the deity worshiped by the Egyptians and on Shavuos they accepted Hashem as their sole focus of worship.
31. *Mechilta; Rashi* to *Shemos* 20:3.
32. See *Rashi; Meiri* to *Horayos* 8b; see *Sefer HaChinuch* 26; *Rambam, Hil. Yesodei HaTorah* 1:6; *Smag.*
33. *Rashbam* to *Shemos* 20:3.
34. See *Rashi* to *Shemos* 20:3; *Rambam, Hil. Avodah Zarah* 3:9.
    The principal acts of worship included prostrating and bowing before the idol, slaughtering animals, bringing offerings, libation of wine or other liquids and bringing incense before it (*Rambam, Sefer HaMitzvos* 5; *Avodah Zarah* 3:3). Still forbidden, but not rendering one liable to the death sentence, are kissing, embracing, clothing or any show of respect in honor of the idol. (See *Rambam, Hil. Avodah Zarah* 3:3; *Sanhedrin* 60b; *Yerushalmi Nazir* 6:1.)
35. See *Rashi* to *Vayikra* 19:4; *Rambam, Hil. Avodah Zarah* 3:9.
36. See *Smag; Midrash HaGadol* to *Devarim* 5:7; *Ramban; Rabbeinu Bachya; Ibn Ezra* to *Shemos* 20:3.

Even the inadvertent appearance of worshiping idols is forbidden. For instance, it is forbidden to bend down and pick up coins that have fallen to the ground near an idol, if doing so would give the appearance of a worshipful bow.[37] It is, however, permitted to bow to a human being out of respect, unless he is someone like Haman who has declared himself a god.[38]

Belief in luck, higher powers or superstitions is also considered a form of idolatry, since they are based on the denial of Hashem's specific supervision of the world.[39]

It is also forbidden to have images or likenesses — whether made of wood, metal, stone or any other material — of entities that pagans worship, including the constellations or any heavenly body.[40] Although some people might consider it acceptable to have an image of a fish as a reminder of the splitting of the sea or an image of a lamb as a reminded of the Pesach miracle, Hashem considers them as forms of idol worship.[41] Any image that reproduces a shadow, reflection or silhouette of any living creature, from a bull to a reptile to a lowly worm, for the purpose of idol worship or even to represent Hashem, is considered a violation of the Second Commandment. These images cut Hashem off from His role in the world, so to speak. In retribution, He will cut off the violators from both this world and the next.[42]

Many of the people in ancient times actually believed in Hashem, but they thought it would be presumptuous to approach such an exalted Deity directly. They also felt that Hashem would not concern Himself with the day-to-day affairs of the world and that He had relegated much of the control of the world to lesser deities and intermediaries. They believed He had established the sun, moon, stars and constellations and imbued them with special powers to govern the affairs of mankind. It seemed logical to them, indeed preferable, to worship these lesser deities, because honoring Hashem's ministers is a high form of giving honor to Him. It also seemed logical to

---

37. *Sanhedrin* 61a. See *Let My Nation Live* p. 161 fn. 28.
38. *Sanhedrin* 63a with *Yad Ramah*.
39. *Shlah*.
40. *Mechilta; Lekach Tov; Rashi; Ibn Ezra* to *Shemos* 20:3-5.
41. *Rabbeinu Bachya* to *Shemos* 20:3.
42. *Mechilta; Midrash HaChefetz* to *Shemos* 20:4-5; *Pirush Ri* to *Sefer Yetzirah* 14; *Zohar* 87a.
   The Torah refers to a carved image as *"pesel,"* a reference to the Hebrew meaning for cutting. Hashem says: Just as you cut me off from your world, I will cut you off from this world.

them, if not preferable, to construct images and symbols that would help them relate to the invisible Hashem. All of this is, nonetheless, considered absolute idolatry, because it assigns mastery of the world to entities other than Hashem and it takes the love, devotion, attachment and fear that are Hashem's due and diverts them elsewhere.[43]

Others may have thought that angels or demons are deserving of worship, as they are Hashem's spiritual messengers. This too is idolatry and a violation of the Second Commandment. In fact, angels are sometimes called *elohim*; this only means that they are powerful, just as the courts are also called *elohim*. It does not mean that they have any G-dlike qualities or their own will in the execution of their actions.[44]

The prohibition against idolatry in all its forms applies in all places and at all times. Hashem said, "Do not have any gods in front of Me." Idolatry is forbidden in His presence, and since Hashem is omnipresent, it is forbidden everywhere.[45] The prohibition also applies to all future generations and is not limited to those who came out of Egypt. Hashem said, "In front of Me." Since Hashem is eternal, the prohibition is perpetual.[46]

The Roman philosophers once asked the Sages, "Since Hashem despises idols so much, why doesn't He simply rid the world of them?"

"It would be impossible," said the Sages. "Some of the worst objects of worship are the sun, the moon and the constellations. Hashem did not want to destroy them, because doing so would devastate the universe."

"So why doesn't He leave the heavenly bodies," they asked further, "and destroy only the useless idols?"

"Good question," said the Sages, "but you realize that doing so would reinforce the beliefs of the foolish people who see these bodies as gods and would claim that they were obviously very strong. Otherwise, why would Hashem destroy all the other idols and leave the heavenly bodies intact?"[47]

---

43. See *Ramban; Sforno; Malbim; Onkelos; Bechor Shor* to *Shemos* 20:3. See *Rambam, Hil. Avodah Zarah* 1:1, 2:1; *Ikrim; Sanhedrin* 63a; *Tiferes Yisrael* 36; *Midrash* to *R' Moshe HaDarshan.*
44. See *Ramban; Ibn Ezra; Rabbeinu Bachya* to *Shemos* 20:3; *Rosh Hashanah* 24b; *Racanati* as quoted by *Torah Shleimah.*
45. *Ramban; Ibn Ezra; Lekach Tov* to *Shemos* 20:3; *Rashi* to *Devarim* 5:7.
46. *Mechilta; Rashi* to *Shemos* 20:3; *Zeh Yenachmeni.*
  See *Tiferes Yisrael* 38 for further discussion of this commandment.
47. *Avodah Zarah* 54b; *Midrash HaChefetz* to *Shemos* 20:3.
  See *Yalkut Reuveni* in the name of *Zohar* that if someone doesn't teach his son Torah,

A philosopher once asked Rabban Gamliel, "Why does Hashem punish the idol worshiper so severely? Shouldn't He rather wreak His vengeance on the idols, which are the root cause of idolatry?"

Rabban Gamliel responded with a parable. "A king gave his son a dog, and the son named the dog after his father. From then on, the son would swear by the dog. The king was humiliated and furious. With whom was he furious, his son or the dog?"

"His son, of course," said the philosopher. "The dog is innocent."

"Exactly," said Rabban Gamliel. "In the same way, Hashem is furious with the fools who worship the idols rather than with the meaningless idols themselves."[48]

Agrippas, the Roman general, once asked Rabban Gamliel, "Hashem declares that although He is ordinarily merciful, He is jealous of idols and promises to utterly destroy their practitioners. How can Hashem be jealous of idols made of metal and stone? These are meaningless pieces of rubble. They are not a threat or a competition to Him."

Rabban Gamliel responded with an analogy. "A man marries a second wife in addition to his first wife," he said. "Is his first wife angry at him for doing so?"

"Probably," said Agrippas.

"Would she be angrier if the second wife had more qualities than she does or if she had fewer qualities?"

"I would say," said Agrippas, "that she would be angrier if he took a lowly wife."

"Why?"

"Because it dishonors her more if he takes from her time and gives it to a lowly woman."

"Exactly," said Rabban Gamliel. "That is why Hashem is furious with idolaters. They take away His time and share it with worthless sticks and stones."[49]

The sin of idolatry is so severe that Hashem declares He will "recall the sins of the fathers for the sons, grandsons and great-grandsons." Hashem will punish great-grandchildren for the idolatry of their

---

it is as though he has built an idol image. The child eventually will become a *ben sorer u'moreh*, a wayward and rebellious son.

48. See *Avodah Zarah* 54b with commentaries.

49. See *Mechilta; Avodah Zarah* 54b; *Maharsha* and commentaries to *Ein Yaakov*. See *Rashi* to *Shemos* 32:11.

great-grandfathers, but only if the great-grandchildren themselves follow in the same idolatrous path. Hashem gives them the opportunity to repent, and if they don't, he gives them all the accumulated punishment.[50]

Moshe was startled when he heard that the sins of the ancestors are visited upon their descendants. Did that mean that Avraham would have suffered for the sins of Terach? Hashem reassured him that the rule did not apply to Avraham, who had not practiced idolatry. On the contrary, he had rejected it courageously.[51]

The Second Commandment concludes with Hashem's assurance that the rewards of compliance are many times as great as the punishment for violation. Hashem says that He "performs kindness for 2,000 generations for those who love Me and safeguard My commandments." Retribution follows the family line for four generations, but reward endures for 2,000 generations, 500 times as long, for who love Hashem and safeguard His commandments.[52]

The Third Commandment

The Third Commandment — the first delivered by Moshe to the Jewish people — is a fitting complement to the first two Commandments.[53] Having recognized Hashem as the one and only G-d and having acknowledged that recognition, by spurning idol worship in any of its numerous forms, it is incumbent upon every Jew to honor and respect the

---

50. *Mechilta; Rashi; Targum; Ibn Ezra* to *Shemos* 20:6; *Sanhedrin* 27b.

A son is the flesh and blood of his father and thus a part of him. By continuing in the path of his father, he only reasserts his connection to his predecessors and so, even though he may not have actually committed a specific transgression that makes him guilty, nevertheless he is guilty by association. Rejecting the father's path makes it clear that he is separating himself from his father's ways and therefore he is judged as an individual (*Nesivas Olam*).

Others suggest that it is four generations of *children*, and including the father it totals five generations of the family. It works the other way around as well. If someone was perfectly righteous, his descendants will be spared Hashem's wrath, despite their sins, in the merit of their righteous ancestor from four previous generations.

Some suggest that the reason why it is four generations is because they can technically all be alive at the same time and thus be smitten together as one family (*Tiferes Yisrael* 38).

51. *Bamidbar Rabbah* 19:33; *Devarim* 24:16.

52. *Mechilta; Rashi; Ibn Ezra; Ramban; Rokeach* to *Shemos* 20:6; *Makkos* 23a with *Rashi; Tosefta Sotah* 3:4. Others don't interpret the word *alafim* to mean 2,000 (*alpayim*), but thousands (*Mechilta; Rashbam; Ibn Ezra*).

53. *Ramban* to *Shemos* 20:7.

Name of Hashem and never to trivialize it by taking it in vain.[54] Invoking the Name of Hashem while making a meaningless oath denies the truth of His sovereignty in this world.[55]

In a certain way, violation of the Third Commandment is a more serious offense than idolatry. When a person worships idols, he essentially turns away from Hashem and seeks other avenues of divinity. But when a person makes a meaningless oath in the Name of Hashem, he retains his relationship with Hashem, but humiliates and belittles Him.[56] That is why the spiritual retribution for taking the Name of Hashem in vain is similar to the retribution for idolatry and *chillul Hashem*, desecration of the Name. In the courts, however, the physical punishment is flogging as opposed to the death penalty for idolatry.[57]

What is a "meaningless oath"?

It is an oath that serves no purpose,[58] for instance, an oath that denies or confirms the obvious. There are four variations. One, if someone swears that the day is, in fact, night or that a stone is, in fact, gold, it is a purposeless and meaningless oath, since no one will believe it. Two, if someone swears that the day is indeed day or that a piece of gold is indeed gold, it is also a purposeless and meaningless oath. Due to its obvious nature, what can such an oath accomplish? Third, if someone swears that he can go for more than three days without sleep or that he saw a snake as large as a tree, everyone knows this is a physical impossibility, and the oath accomplishes nothing at all. Finally, if someone swears to transgress a mitzvah in the Torah, it is an oath that accomplishes nothing, since the Jewish people have already made an irrevocable commitment at Mount Sinai to fulfill all the mitzvos.[59]

It is also possible to violate the Third Commandment without making an oath. If a person only intends to make such a meaningless oath in the Name of Hashem or if he accepts such an oath from someone else, he is also in violation of the Commandment.[60]

---

54. *Midrash Aseres HaDibros*; *Ramban* to *Shemos* 20:7.
55. *Ibn Ezra*; *Sforno* to *Shemos* 20:7; *Sefer HaChinuch* 30; *Yad Shavuos*.
56. *Tiferes Yisrael* 39.
57. See *Eliyahu Rabbah* 26; *Vayikra* 19:12. See *Reishis Chochmah Kedushah* Ch. 14; *Tiferes Yisrael* 36.
58. *Mechilta*; *Rashi* to *Shemos* 20:7; *Sefer HaChinuch* 30.
59. See *Rashi*; *Midrash HaGadol* to *Shemos* 20:7; *Pesikta Rabbah* 22; *Shevuos* 29a; *Rambam*, *Hil. Shevuos* 1:4-7.
60. *Mechilta*; *Sefer Charedim*, "Prohibitions of the mouth."

Moreover, the prohibition is not dependent on making an oath at all. The Commandment states, "Do not bear (*lo sisa*) the Name of Hashem in vain." It makes no specific mention of an oath. Therefore, if a person simply utters the Name of Hashem in vain, he has transgressed.[61] If he makes a superfluous blessing, he has transgressed; he would be better off, writes the *Zohar*, had he never been born.[62]

The possibilities extend even further. If a person represents himself as a holy person and as such is treated with honor and respect, he has transgressed the Third Commandment. A person's spiritual stature derives from Hashem, and anyone representing himself falsely as being on a high spiritual level is taking the Name of Hashem in vain.[63]

There are dreadful consequences for taking the Name of Hashem in vain. The earth trembled when Moshe delivered this Commandment, which states that Hashem "will not absolve (*lo yenakeh*) anyone who takes His Name in vain."[64] The stain of this sin cannot be cleansed and absolved by *teshuvah* alone. Only death and suffering can bring atonement for a sin that undermines the honor and glory of Hashem in this world. "His glory fills all the earth," says David HaMelech in *Tehillim* (72:19), but the one who takes the Name of Hashem in vain reduces His glory in the world and cannot expiate his sin with *teshuvah* alone.[65]

Some suggest that the earth trembled because it felt endangered. There are deep subterranean reservoirs that would inundate the entire earth if they were released, but they are sealed by a stone engraved with the Name of Hashem. When a person takes the Name of Hashem in vain, the letters of the Name engraved on the stone drift apart and the seal loosens, threatening to come completely loose under the pressure of the subterranean waters. Hashem mercifully sends down an angel to engrave the holy Name

---

61. See *Rabbeinu Bachya*; *Ramban* to *Shemos* 20:7; *Rambam, Hil. Shevuos* 12:11. See *Onkelos*; *Lekach Tov* to *Shemos* 20:7.
62. *Zohar Yisro* 87b; *Midrash HaGadol* to *Shemos* 20:7; *Temurah* 4a; *Berachos* 33a; *Rambam, Hil. Shevuos* 12:9; *Berachos* 1:15. In conjunction with this Commandment, one is guilty of transgressing the positive commandment of fearing Hashem. Uttering Hashem's Name needlessly minimizes one's fear and awe of Hashem. See *Devarim* 6:2.
63. See *Pesikta Rabbah* 22; *Midrash Aggadah*. See *Reishis Chochmah, Kedushah* 12:46.
64. *Shevuos* 39a.
65. See *Rambam, Hil. Shevuos* 21:1; *Shevuos* 39a with *Maharsha*; see *Shemos* 34:7,14; *Mechilta*. See *Yoma* 86a; *Tiferes Yisrael* 39; *Maharsha* to *Shevuos* 39a.

on the stone once again and prevent the waters from gushing forth and flooding the earth. That is why the earth trembled. It trembled in fear.[66]

The punishment for the violation of the Third Commandment can take many forms. The violator may lose his portion in the World to Come.[67] He may lose his children or his entire family.[68] He may be attacked by wild beasts or the sword of the invader; his livestock may perish or he may lose his wealth to criminals.[69] King Yannai often uttered the Name of Hashem in vain. Although he did so to support true statements, 2,000 of his towns and villages were destroyed.[70]

The Third Commandment, unlike the others, is the easiest to violate. It does not require that the opportunity arise or that the conditions or circumstances be just right. The Name of Hashem can be uttered in vain anywhere and anytime, with the greatest of ease. It is possible to rationalize that it is not such a serious thing, and whom does it harm? With this type of thinking, after a while it can become a barely noticed habit. Thus, it is possible to accumulate hundreds of terrible sins without even being aware that it is happening. This leads to swearing meaningless oaths while taking the Name of Hashem in vain, and eventually swearing falsely, blatant lies told in the Name of Hashem.[71]

The Gemara tells the story of a man who gave a widow a gold coin for safekeeping. She kept the coin in her apron, and while she was baking, the coin slipped out of her pocket and fell into the dough and was baked into the bread. A hungry beggar appeared on the doorstep and asked for a crust of bread. The widow gave the beggar a piece of the freshly baked bread. Unknown to her, the gold coin was in the piece of bread that she gave to the beggar but, by this time, she had completely forgotten about the coin.

Presently, the owner returned and asked the widow for the coin. She had no idea where the coin was, but she was sure she had not used it for herself.

---

66. *Zohar Yisro* 91b.
67. *Eliyahu Rabbah* 26.
   The word *sheol* (the underworld; a reference to Gehinnom) contains the same letters as the word *lashav* (in vain) (*B'Shem Omro*).
68. *Pesikta Chadata; Shevuos* 39a. See *Tiferes Yisrael* 39; *Eliyahu Rabbah* 26.
69. See *Midrash Mishlei* 6; *Shabbos* 33a.
70. *Tanchuma Vayikra* 7.
71. See *Chizkuni; Ibn Ezra; Rabbeinu Bachya* to *Shemos* 20:7; *Rashi* to *Shevuos* 45a.

"I cannot find the coin at the moment," she told the man, "but I did not steal it. May death overtake my child if I used the coin for myself."

Before long, the child passed away.

"If such a tragedy occurs," said the Sages, "when a mother swears truthfully, how much greater would the punishment be if she had sworn falsely."[72]

The only time it is permitted and honorable to swear in the Name of Hashem is to bolster oneself in defense against the evil inclination. Otherwise, truthful oaths that invoke the Name of Hashem are not much better than false ones.[73]

A businessman made a commitment never to make an oath. Eventually, he became very wealthy. On his deathbed, he told his son about his commitment and advised him to do the same.

"I am firmly convinced," he told his son, "that Hashem gave me all my success as a result of my commitment never to make an oath. It goes without saying that I wouldn't lie, but even to tell the truth, it has to be without making an oath."

"I will do the same," said the son.

After the father died, a number of swindlers made false claims against the estate, contending that the father had owed them large sums of money. The son denied their claims categorically, and they sued him in court. The court demanded that the son make an oath to verify his position, but the son would not break the word he had given his father. Rather than make an oath, he paid off most of their false claims until he had nothing left. The swindlers insisted that he make an oath that he had no other funds hidden away. The son refused, and he was thrown into debtor's prison.

In the meantime, his wife, a proud and modest woman, refused to accept charity from the community. Instead, she took in laundry to put bread on the table for her children.

---

72. See *Gittin* 35a with *Rashi* and commentaries as to the reasoning behind the events that took place.
 In reality it was an unintended false oath since she really had benefited from the coin. As minute as it was, the space taken up by the coin saved her that amount of flour, and thus despite her belief that she hadn't benefited, the widow did benefit.
73. *Zohar Yisro* 91b.
 See *Reishis Chochmah, Kedushah* 12 who writes that this only applied in those times, but today people's resolve is not as strong, and making an oath does not guarantee that one will not transgress. In fact it may lead to added sin because not only will he have been overcome by the temptation of the *yetzer hara*, but now he has a false oath to contend with.

One day, she was washing clothes by the river when a seafaring captain called out to her, "Madam, would you come on board and do my laundry please? I will give you a golden *dinar* if you do."

The woman accepted the offer, excited that she would have money to redeem her husband from prison. He gave her the money, which she handed to her children, and she went aboard. As soon as she stepped on board, however, the captain set sail with her as his prisoner. Her children were left with neither father nor mother.

Crying with despair, the children used the *dinar* to secure their father's release from prison and told him the sad news of his wife's abduction.

The father took his children and went off to search for his wife. They reached a certain seaside town. The father had the children wait while he went into the town to seek information. When he returned, the children were gone. They, too, had been abducted.

The father sat down by the riverside and put his face in his hands. This once-wealthy man, head of a proud family, was now penniless and alone. "Hashem, please let me die," he cried out. "I have nothing to live for."

In his head, he heard a voice saying, "Because you kept your word to your father and scrupulously avoided oaths, your plight will come to a happy ending. You will recover your wealth and your earlier stature."

He looked up and saw a tangle of snakes and scorpions in the swampy water. Suddenly, he saw a glint among them. He investigated and discovered a fabulous treasure. His wife and children were miraculously returned to him. He used the treasure to build great cities. He became a king, and his children grew up as princes. Because he endured his ordeals without uttering an oath, Hashem rewarded him with enormous success.[74]

The Fourth Commandment

The Fourth Commandment continues the theme established by the first three Commandments, adding a new dimension. The first three are focused on Hashem's sovereignty and glory as King of the Universe. The fourth focuses on Hashem as the Creator of the Universe.

---

74. *Otzar Midrashim, Midrash Aseres HaDibros.*

The Commandment requires us to remember and safeguard the seventh day of the week as Shabbos, a day of rest. It is an acknowledgment that Hashem created the world in six days and rested on the seventh. During the six days of creation, Hashem created everything that exists in the world. Only "rest" was missing. Shabbos provided the final missing element, and the world was truly complete. Failure to keep Shabbos, therefore, is a denial of Hashem as the Creator. It is also a denial of the completeness of creation.[75]

In addition to its role as a recognition of Hashem creating the world, Shabbos is also closely connected to the exodus from Egypt, for a number of reasons. First of all, the recollection of the miracles Hashem performed for the Jewish people in Egypt bear testimony to His being the absolute Master of the Universe and, by logical extension, its Creator. Furthermore, the abstention from work is a powerful declaration of independence. No longer were the Jewish people under the control of Pharaoh who could decide when they worked and when, if ever, they rested. By resting on Shabbos, therefore, the Jewish people were recalling and memorializing their release from bondage in Egypt.[76]

The Sages tell us that the spirit of Shabbos protested to Hashem. "Why am I alone among all the days of the week? Each day has a partner. Sunday has Monday, Tuesday has Wednesday, and Thursday has Friday. But I am alone. Who is my partner?"

"The Jewish people are your partners," Hashem replied. "They will honor and safeguard your holiness, and, in the process, the two of you will be joined together forever.[77] The Jewish people are a nation unto themselves among the nations of the world; they have no partner. You are a day unto yourself among the days of the week; you have no partner. The two of you are made for each other."[78]

---

75. See *Ramban; Rabbeinu Bachya; Tosafos Al HaTorah; Lekach Tov; Ibn Ezra; Abarbanel; Rashbam* to *Shemos* 20:8; *Tiferes Yisrael* 36,40; *Bereishis* 2:1; *Menoras HaMaor*.

It stands to reason that if someone desecrates the Shabbos it is as though he has worshiped idols (*Rambam, Hil. Shabbos* 30:15).

This commandment corresponds to the Ninth Commandment on the *Luchos*. Someone who desecrates Shabbos is bearing false testimony that Hashem created the world in six days and rested on the seventh (*Rosh*).

76. *Tiferes Yisrael* 44. See *Ramban; Kli Yakar*. See *Ramban* to *Devarim* 5:15.

Although Moshe convinced Pharaoh to allow the Jews to rest on Shabbos, it does not take away the concept that the Jews were not free to make that choice. See *Let My Nation Go* p. 88.

77. See *Bereishis Rabbah* 11:8 with *Maharzav* and *Rashi* there. *Akeidah Bereishis* 78; *Tiferes Yisrael* 44.

Before giving the Jewish people the Torah, Hashem said to them, "I have a great gift for you if and when you accept the Torah."

"What is the gift?" they asked.

"It is *Olam Haba*, the World to Come."

"Oh," said the Jewish people. "How wonderful, but what is the World to Come?"

"I will give you a taste of it," said Hashem. "It is called Shabbos. Its pleasures are one-sixtieth of the pleasures of the World to Come."[79]

The holiness of Shabbos is so great that, in a sense, the *Shechinah* rests on a person who keeps Shabbos, just a king sits on his throne.[80] In deference to the holiness of Shabbos, there is no judgment or punishment of souls on Shabbos. When Shabbos starts, the gatekeeper of Gehinnom, whose name is Dumah, releases all the residents of purgatory, and as soon as Shabbos is over, he summons them to return.[81]

The work of remembering Shabbos begins with the first day of the week. Just as it is a mitzvah to rest on Shabbos, it is also a mitzvah to work during the week, because idleness leads to sin and derangement.[82] Nonetheless, Hashem wanted the Jewish people to be busy with Shabbos all week. Although Hashem forbid making images and other forms of representation to help people relate to Him in a personal way, he did give them one opportunity to have a symbolic representation of Himself. It is called Shabbos. By experiencing Shabbos, the Jew keeps Hashem in his mind. Therefore, by remembering Shabbos all week and preparing for it, he keeps the image of Hashem, so to speak, and His role as the Creator before his eyes. In effect, we fulfill a positive commandment each day of the week.[83]

The fundamental form of remembering Shabbos all week is by studying its *halachos* (laws) and becoming familiar with the thirty-nine *melachos*, the labors forbidden on Shabbos.[84] In fact, studying these *halachos* is so important that it is comparable to the study of the entire Torah.[85]

---

79. See *Osios D'Rav Akiva Alef*; *Berachos* 57b.
80. *Yalkut Reuveni*.
81. *Midrash Aseres HaDibros*.
82. *Avos D'Rav Nassan* 11; *Binyan Yehoshua*.
83. *Midrash Aseres HaDibros*.
84. *Sefer Chassidim*.
85. *Chullin* 5a; *Zohar* 88; Introduction to *Eglei Tal*.

It is also important to think about Shabbos all week and take it into account when making business, travel or any other arrangements.[86] In addition, it is important to make sure that everything is properly prepared and cleaned for Shabbos. The best food, clothing, dishes and utensils should be set aside for Shabbos use. Making Shabbos enjoyable for oneself is comparable to giving pleasure to Hashem.[87] The Gemara tells us that when Shammai the Elder came across a delectable morsel, he would set it aside for Shabbos. If he found something better, he would use the previous morsel and set aside the new and better one for Shabbos. In this way, the Gemara concludes, Shammai was always eating in honor of Shabbos.[88]

One way to remember Shabbos all week is by identifying the weekdays by their relationship to Shabbos. Sunday becomes *Rishon LeShabbos*, the first day that leads to Shabbos, and so forth.[89] This also recalls the daily renewal of the world and brings to mind Hashem directly, as the Creator of the Universe.[90]

On Shabbos itself, the mitzvah of "remembering" requires that we always be aware that it is Shabbos and that this day is different from all other days. We are required to sanctify the Shabbos by honoring it properly. The subjects of conversations should not be about weekday matters such as business but rather about Torah and the greatness of Hashem.[91]

A ceremonial remembering in the form of *Kiddush* (Sanctification) marks the beginning of the day, and *Havdalah* (Disengagement) marks its end. Both are made over wine, as a symbol of their importance.[92] Just as Hashem created the world by speaking, we sanctify

---

86. *Sforno*.
87. See *Mechilta; Rashi, Ramban* to *Shemos* 20:8; *Eliyahu Rabbah* 26.
88. *Beitzah* 16a; *Pesikta Rabbah* 23.
   See *Mizrachi* and *Sifsei Chachamim* who comment that *Rashi* did not mention food as a means to sanctify Shabbos, because that was the manner in which Shammai honored the Shabbos, and Hillel disagreed with that approach. *Rashi* mentions an article (*cheifetz*) because Hillel agrees that one's best articles should be set aside for Shabbos. See *Rambam, Hil. Shabbos* 30:7; *Mechilta* to *Shemos* 20:8; *Tanchuma Ki Seitzei* 7; *Eliyahu Rabbah*. 26. See commentaries as to the root of the differing views of Shammai and Hillel and how it involved the root of faith and trust in Hashem.
89. *Mechilta* to *Shemos* 20:8.
90. *Abarbanel; Ramban.*
91. *Pesikta Chadata; Shabbos* 113a; *Ramban; Rabbeinu Bachya.*
92. See *Pesachim* 106a; *Sefer HaChinuch* 31; *Rambam, Hil. Shabbos* 29:1; *Pesikta Chadata; Zohar Yisro* 95.

the Shabbos by speaking the words of *Kiddush*.[93] Remembering Shabbos also mandates that we add a little margin of time (*tosefos Shabbos*) both at its beginning as a sign of eager anticipation, and at its end as a sign of reluctance to part.[94]

During Shabbos, there is a positive commandment to rest in addition to the prohibition against forbidden labors. Just as Hashem rested on Shabbos, so to speak, by desisting from the work of creation, we are required to desist from the weekday toil.[95] Even a person who has no job and is idle all week must rest by desisting from his weekday activities.[96] Furthermore, it is only considered true Shabbos rest if it is done for the sake of Heaven. A person who sleeps through Shabbos has only avoided forbidden labor. He has not fulfilled true Shabbos rest.[97]

Rest has different meanings for different people. People steeped in Torah can take the opportunity to relax and enjoy the radiance of Shabbos. People who are busy working during the week should devote substantial time on Shabbos to learning Torah.[98]

When Shabbos comes, a person should view the week that just passed as being complete and sealed shut.[99] By coming to the realization that what is done is done and his weekday affairs are completely out of his hands, he will feel immense relief. He will free himself from stress and set his mind to rest.[100] Rest also takes the form of

---

93. *Panim Yafos Yisro*. See *Tehillim* 33:6; see *Moshav Zekeinim*.

94. *Rambam, Hil. Shabbos* 29:1; *Pesikta Rabbah*; *Mechilta Yisro*; *Chizkuni*; *Menoras HaMaor*.

The word *Shamor* in reference to Shabbos can also mean wait/anticipate, as in *Bereishis* 37:11.

See *Meam Loez* for his lengthy description of these laws.

Hashem commands the Jewish people to remember to guard the Shabbos so that they do not transgress its laws. Remembering the Shabbos is a positive commandment, while the law of guarding the Shabbos is a negative precept telling us not to transgress the laws that are prohibited on Shabbos. Positive commandments are a source of love, while refraining from a prohibited act is something done out of fear of judgment. Hashem wanted the laws of Shabbos to be observed in both senses. Remember the Shabbos with love and be fearful of transgressing its prohibitions. It is for this reason that Hashem used both terms, *Zachor* and *Shamor*, in relaying the commandment of Shabbos (*Midrash Aseres HaDibros*; *Ramban* to *Shemos* 20:8; see *Rambam, Hil. Shabbos* 30:1; see *Mechilta*; *Rashi*; *Moshav Zekeinim* to *Shemos* 20:8; *Rashi* to *Devarim* 5:12; *Tehillim* 62:12).

95. See *Mechilta D'Rashbi*; *Midrash HaGadol Yisro*; *Rashi*; *Sifsei Chachamim*; *Tosafos Rid* to *Yisro*; *Sefer HaChinuch* 32.

96. *Mabit*.

97. *Ohr HaChaim* to *Yisro*.

98. *Midrash HaGadol*.

99. *Mechilta*; *Rashi* to *Shemos* 20:9.

100. *Panim Yafos* to *Yisro*.

One can look upon Shabbos as "a taste of the World to Come." Just as one

limiting all conversations to Shabbos-related or other spiritual matters and avoiding talk of business and other stressful concerns.[101] One should not go out to inspect his fields or place of business to determine what might be needed.[102]

A man once went out of the town on Shabbos to inspect his fields. He noticed a breach in one of the fences and made a mental note that he would have to repair it after Shabbos. Suddenly, he realized that he was doing something forbidden on Shabbos, and he resolved never to repair that breach, as a sign of his remorse. Hashem took note of his repentance and his righteous decision, and He caused a tree to grow next to the fence at the point of the breach. The tree grew so large that it filled the breach. It also provided the man with delicious fruits that he was able to enjoy for the rest of his life.[103]

The responsibility to keep Shabbos extends to making sure it is honored in one's household. The Commandment is directed at adults, but parents are required to supervise their minor children and prevent them from violations of the Shabbos. Parents may not derive any benefit from a forbidden labor their children perform for them.[104] Nor may they benefit from labors performed by their non-Jewish servants or even their animals on their behalf. The entire household is supposed to rest.[105] Furthermore, Jews may not benefit from labors gentiles outside their households do on their behalf.[106]

A Jewish man once sold his ox to a gentile. The ox, accustomed to the patterns of the Jewish family, did not work on Shabbos. The

---

who dies and enters the World to Come with his life's work complete, so too one should see his work as fully completed upon the entrance of Shabbos. See *Mechilta*; *Sefer Yetzirah* 191.

101. See *Pesikta Rabbah* 23; *Yerushalmi Shabbos* 15:3; *Shabbos* 150a.

See also *Pesikta Chadata*; *Shabbos* 113a; *Ramban*; *Rabbeinu Bachya*; *Sforno* to *Shemos* 20:8.

In fact, the Sages shortened the *Amidah* prayer from eighteen *berachos* to seven on Shabbos because a majority of the weekday prayer deals with concerns about life and the future. This is appropiate during the week, that one knows to whom to turn to have all his prayers answered. On Shabbos, however, one should only concentrate on the Creator and His awesome sovereignty in this world (*Midrash Yelamdenu*; *Ibn Ezra* to *Yisro*).

102. *Midrash HaGadol*.

103. See *Pesikta Rabbah* 23; *Yerushalmi Shabbos* 15:3; *Korban HaEidah*; *Shabbos* 150a; *Vayikra Rabbah* 34:16; *Rashi* and *Matnos Kehunah* there.

104. *Mechilta*; *Rashi*; *Ramban* to *Yisro*; *Be'er Yitzchok*; *Shabbos* 121a.

Most authorities suggest that this applies even to a child who is under the age of *chinuch* but is old enough to understand the needs of his parents.

105. See *Chagigah* 4a; *Ramban* to *Yisro*; see *Pesikta Rabbah*.

106. See *Ramban*; *Rosh Al HaTorah* to *Yisro*.

gentile thought there was something wrong with the ox, and he brought him back to the Jewish man.

"This ox doesn't work one day a week," he said. "There is something wrong with him, so take him back."

"There is nothing wrong with him," said the seller. "Give me a minute."

He whispered in the ear of the ox. "You do not belong to me anymore. Now you belong to this gentile. He doesn't have Shabbos, so you must abide by his rules. From now on, you will have to work on Shabbos."

The ox began to work seven days a week. The gentile was so impressed that he converted and eventually became a Torah scholar, and the ox was once again able to rest on Shabbos.[107]

Shabbos is a day of blessing and sanctification. Hashem blessed it by having a double portion of manna fall on Friday, and He sanctified it by having no manna fall on Shabbos.[108] It is a day of spiritual radiance that elevates the soul and provides spiritual and material blessings to the world. It is the foundation and the source of energy and vitality for the coming week. Therefore, the more effort one invests into honoring and sanctifying Shabbos, the more blessings one will accumulate for the coming week and the more merit one will gain for the World to Come.[109]

The Fifth Commandment

The first five Commandments address the relationship between a person and Hashem. The second five Commandments address the relationship between a person and his fellow human beings. The Fifth Commandment, honoring parents, rounds out the first five, even though it seems to address relationships with other people. In fact, however, it is a critical element in serving Hashem properly.[110] People are trained to have proper

---

107. *Pesikta Rabbah.*
 His name was R' Yochanan or Yehudah ben Torsah. See *Tosafos Yeshanim* to *Yoma* 9a.
108. *Mechilta; Rashi* to *Yisro.*
109. *Rambam, Hil. Shabbos* 30:15; *Lekach Tov; Ramban; Ibn Ezra* to *Yisro.* See *Rabbeinu Bachya; Zohar; Ohr HaChaim.*
 This is so because by differentiating between the workweek and Shabbos he has put more value into his workdays by associating them with — though distinguishing them from — Shabbos. As a result the person's Shabbos is holier and he is blessed with a more productive workweek. However, when one devalues the Shabbos he has in essence associated Shabbos with the rest of the week.
110. *Ramban* to *Yisro; Pesikta Rabbah* 21.

gratitude to Hashem for all His kindness by honoring their parents who brought them into this world and nurtured and raised them.[111] Also, as each generation honors the previous one, the chain of transmission will be secure, and the younger generation will follow the teaching of the older generation. Therefore, Hashem equates honoring parents with honoring Him.[112]

In a sense, the Commandment to honor parents mirrors the first four Commandments as well. Just as we have to recognize Hashem as the Creator, we have to recognize our parents for what they are. Just as we are forbidden to worship idols, we are forbidden to substitute anyone else as our parent figures. Just as we may not take the Name of Hashem in vain, we may not swear in the name of our parents. Just as Shabbos is an acknowledgment of Hashem as the Creator, we must acknowledge the role of our parents in our lives.[113]

When we honor our parents, it is as if we are honoring the *Shechinah*. Hashem says, "When I see people honor their parents, I will consider it as if they honored Me, and I will dwell among them."[114] With this in mind, Rabbi Yosef used to say when he heard his mother approaching, "Let me rise in honor of the *Shechinah*." It follows, therefore, that disrespect to one's parents is comparable to rejecting the *Shechinah*.[115]

Three partners bring a person into this world — his father, his mother and Hashem. The father is the source of the child's bones, nerves, brain, nails and the white of his eyes. The mother is the source of the child's skin, flesh, blood, hair and the pupil of his eyes. Hashem is the source of the child's spirit and soul, eyesight, hearing, sense of touch, speech, walking, insight, understanding and intellect.[116]

Hashem wants each of the partners to be honored.[117] If, however, there is a conflict between the wishes of Hashem and the wishes of

---

111. Introduction to *Sefer HaChinuch* 33; *Ramban; Abarbanel* to *Yisro.*
    It is for this reason that despite the fact that this is a mitzvah that deals with people, it is found on the right side of the *Luchos* along with the mitzvos that deal with honoring Hashem properly.
112. *Ralbag.*
113. See *Zohar* 93a; *Ramban; Rabbeinu Bachya; Abarbanel* to *Yisro.*
114. *Kiddushin* 31a.
115. *Kiddushin* 31b.
    This applies to the mother more so than to the father because she is more likely to be home with her children while the father is out of the house (*Tiferes Yisrael* 41).
116. See *Zohar* 93a; *Niddah* 31b; *Pesikta Chadata.*
117. *Eliyahu Rabbah* 26.

a parent, Hashem takes precedence. If a parent tells a child to commit a sin, he must disregard the wishes of his parent and obey the wishes of Hashem.[118]

When there is no conflict, the obligation to honor parents is very strong, in some ways stronger than the obligation to honor Hashem. For instance, Hashem expects to be honored through monetary contributions, such as giving *terumah* to the Kohanim, but the obligation to parents is not fulfilled by monetary contributions alone.[119] One is required to provide comfort for parents by any means whatsoever. Furthermore, if a person cannot afford the cost of fulfilling certain mitzvos, Hashem releases him from his obligation. For instance, if a person has no money, he does not have to beg or borrow to buy *tefillin* or build a *succah*, but he must go from door to door and beg, in order to provide for the needs of his parents.[120]

The obligation to parents has two parts. One is called honor, the other reverence. In order to honor parents properly, one must feed, clothe and clean them and assist them in their walking.[121] Reverence calls for standing when a parent enters the room, not sitting or standing in a parent's designated place and not contradicting the parent's statements. One should treat parents with the reverence one would accord to a king.[122]

The obligation to honor parents does not end when they pass away. The behavior of a child reflects upon the parents even when they are no longer alive. A child who sins humiliates his parents in Heaven and violates the Fifth Commandment. On the other hand, when a child learns Torah and does mitzvos, he honors his parents in Heaven.[123] In a certain sense, there is a greater fulfillment of honoring parents when they are no longer alive. As long as the parent is alive, it possible that the child who honors his parents is motivated by fear of retaliation or disinheritance, but when he honors parents who have passed away, he is clearly motivated by a desire to fulfill the mitzvah.[124]

---

118. *Mechilta; Rambam, Hil. Mamrim* 6:2,14; *Mishnah Kereisos* 6:9; *Kiddushin* 31b; *Meiri*.
119. See *Mishlei* 3:9; *Ramban* to *Yisro*; *Tosafos* to *Kiddushin* 31a.
120. *Yerushalmi Kiddushin* 1:7; see *Kiddushin* 32a; *Lekach Tov* to *Yisro*.
121. *Mechilta; Kiddushin* 32a; *Tosefta Kiddushin* 1:11; *Pesikta Rabbah* 23.
122. *Kiddushin* 32a.
123. *Zohar* 90a; *Nachal Kadmonim*.
124. *Semachos* 9:21.

The obligation to honor parents extends to the spouse of parents that remarry, the parents of one's spouse, grandparents and older siblings, as well as scholars and sages who are considered spiritual fathers.[125]

The reward for honoring parents, promised in the Commandment itself, is long life.[126] Some suggest that this reward is measure for measure. Children effectively lengthen the lives of their elderly parents by taking them in and caring for them. Measure for measure, they are rewarded with long life. Moreover, since caring for parents may impinge on the children's quality of life, Hashem rewards them twofold. First, their own children will care for them in the same manner when they are old. Second, Hashem gives them additional life to make up for their inconvenience.[127] Some also suggest that parents pray for the well-being of children who care for them, and Hashem answers these prayers by granting the children longevity.[128]

Hashem also rewards those who honor parents by protecting them from sin, especially from the desecration of the Shabbos, which is mentioned immediately preceding this Commandment.[129] In addition, He rewards them with wealth and honor in this world and a greater share in the World to Come.[130]

Conversely, those who do not honor parents risk a shortened life and a poorer quality of whatever life they do have.[131]

---

125. See *Kesubos* 103a; *Rambam, Hil. Mamrim* 6:15; *Lekach Tov; Charedim, Peh; Abarbanel*.
   There is a question if the law regarding honoring one's older brother applies to any older brother or only the oldest brother of the household.
126. See *Mechilta; Rashi; Ibn Ezra; Zayis Raanan* to *Yisro*.
127. See *Rabbeinu Bachya; Abarbanel; Shaarei Aharon*.
128. *Hadar Zekeinim* to *Yisro*. See *Tiferes Yisrael* 41 for another approach as to why one gets *arichas yamim* (longevity) for honoring one's parents.
129. *Eliyahu Rabbah* 26.
   Just as Shabbos is a day to reflect that Hashem is our creator, this precept primarily is one that says one must honor and recognize one's creator (*Tiferes Yisrael* 45).
   Both the mitzvos of Shabbos and honoring one's parents were taught at Marah so it makes sense that they follow one another.
130. See *Eliyahu Rabbah* 26; *Bereishis Rabbasi*. For further discussion on this subject, see *Megillah* 16b; *Pe'ah* 1:1; *Kiddushin* 31a. See *Midrash Aseres HaDibros; Kiddushin* 31 on the various historical accounts of people who honored their parents appropriately.
   In the repetition of the Ten Commandments cited in *Devarim*, the Torah writes that if one honors his parents it will be "good" (*yitav*) for him. This was not written in the first set of Commandments because Hashem knew that the *Luchos* would be broken and he did not want "goodness" to be shattered in this world (*Bava Kamma* 54b). It is interesting to note that in the second version of the Ten Commandments there are an additional 17 letters. The numerical value of the word "*tov*" (good) is also 17 (*Baal HaTurim*).
131. See *Rashi; Ramban* to *Yisro; Eliyahu Rabbah* 26.

There is also a collective reward for the Jewish people when they honor their parents. They are protected from exile and enjoy their own land in peace, tranquility and prosperity. The lesson can be learned from Cham and his son Canaan, who humiliated Noach. As a result, Hashem condemned them to servitude and exile and gave their land to the Jewish people.[132]

When the Commandments were given, the kings of the nations listened to them with skepticism. They heard Hashem demand faith, loyalty and respect and a day to commemorate His great power.

"Listen to this G-d of the Jews," they mocked. "He is no different from any of us. He cares only about Himself and His honor and respect. Why shouldn't we demand the same things for ourselves? We want to be recognized as supreme. We want special commemorative holidays in our honor."

Then they heard the Fifth Commandment, and they were stunned.

"What is this?" they exclaimed. "We demand of our subjects that they turn away from their parents and relatives and pledge their undivided allegiance to us. Yet the G-d of the Jews humbles Himself for the sake of an ethical ideal. If so, we must ourselves pay homage to Him."[133]

The Midrash relates a story about an emperor who decreed that anyone who spent his time in idleness would have his hands and feet cut off. There was a weak man who used to rest in his bed all day while his son worked the millstone. One day, the emperor's soldiers came, found the man lying in his bed and arrested him.

"Wait!" said the son. "You are making a mistake. My father works the mill all day, while I sit in idleness. I just took over at the millstone to give him a few minutes of rest."

The soldiers released the father and took the son in his stead. In accordance with the emperor's decree, the son's hands and feet were cut off.

The Midrash declares that this son was destined for Olam Haba.[134]

---

132. See *Rashi* in *Noach*; *Ibn Ezra*; *Abarbanel*; *Maaseh Hashem*; *Tzeidah LaDerech*; *R' Eliezer Ashkenazi* to *Yisro*.
133. See *Kiddushin* 31a; *Bamidbar Rabbah* 8:4.
134. *Midrash Aseres HaDibros*.

The Sixth Commandment

The Sixth Commandment prohibits the murder of another human being, who was formed on the sixth day of creation.[135] Hashem wanted the population to multiply so that the world would be inhabited by its people. Killing will decrease and minimize that very potential.[136] It follows immediately after the Commandment to honor parents, because it implies that one who neglects his obligation to support his parents is considered a murderer.[137] It also tells us that there are limits to the defense of a parent's honor; it is forbidden to kill someone who has dishonored one's parent.[138]

On the *Luchos*, the Sixth Commandment sits atop the second column, level with the First Commandment, which demands the acknowledgment of Hashem's greatness. Man is created *betzelem Elokim*, in the image of the L-rd, and anyone who spills a man's blood is considered, in a sense, to have shattered the image of the L-rd Himself.

It can best be illustrated with the following parable. A king conquered a province and added it to his realm. In honor of the occasion, he erected statues of himself in the public squares and minted coins with his likeness on them. The conquered people were not happy with the new situation, but they did not dare stand up against the king. Instead, they toppled the statues and destroyed the coins, symbolically attacking the king. In the same way, killing a person is tantamount to an attack on the King of the Universe.[139]

When a person commits murder, the soul of the victim cries out to Hashem. "Hashem, look what has happened," it says. "You created me. You kept an eye on me in my mother's womb to make sure the birth was uneventful. In Your great mercy, You guided me and supported me through my life. You constructed me. And now this murderer comes along and destroys what You have built. You made the world so that it should be populated, and this person comes along and depopulates it? Hashem! Avenge Yourself on him."

At that moment, Hashem's fury rises. He consigns the murderer to the fires of Gehinnom, and the victim is mollified.[140]

---

135. *Rambam, Hil. Rotze'ach* 1:1; *Rashbam*; *Tur* to *Yisro*.
136. *Sefer HaChinuch* 34.
137. *Eliyahu Rabbah* 26.
138. *Midrash Aseres HaDibros*.
139. *Mechilta Yisro*. See *Avos* 3:14; *Bereishis Rabbah* 34:14.
140. *Midrash Aseres HaDibros*.

Furthermore, a murderer denies Hashem. He lurks in the shadows and hides from people so that they should not see him commit his crime. But he is not concerned that Hashem is watching him. Once again, we see the correlation between the First and Sixth Commandments.[141]

The prohibition against murder also includes suicide. A person who takes his own life or puts himself in harm's way without regard for his life is guilty of murder and will lose his place in the World to Come.[142]

There are many ways to commit murder in violation of the Sixth Commandment, although only actual physical murder is punishable by death in the courts. Bearing false witness, spreading slander and offering bad advice that result in death are also considered forms of murder. Remaining silent about a potential danger is also considered a form of murder.[143] In addition, embarrassing or humiliating someone and causing his face to turn colors is considered a form of murder.[144]

Hashem warned the Jewish people that a disregard for human life would bring down upon them murderous invaders.[145] Because of bloodshed, the First *Beis HaMikdash* was destroyed, and the *Shechinah* departed from the Jewish people.[146]

The Seventh Commandment

The Seventh Commandment, whose intent is to protect the purity of the Jewish lineage, specifically prohibits adultery with a married woman.[147] Nevertheless, it also includes other forms of illicit relationships, including being alone with a forbidden person, extramarital relations, as well as acting as facilitating such relations.[148] People who act in this way should be shunned, ostracized socially and in the

---

141. *Midrash Aseres HaDibros.*
142. *Pesikta Rabbah* 23; *Midrash Tehillim.* See *Sefer HaChinuch* 34 for a different view.
143. See *Ibn Ezra; Chizkuni* to *Yisro; Ibn Ezra* to *Vayikra* 19:16.
144. See *Bava Metzia* 58b with *Tosafos* and *Maharsha; Charedim.*
145. *Midrash Aseres HaDibros; Targum Yonasan.*
   So great is the sin of committing murder that the only remedy for obtaining justice is by the loss of the murderer's life (*Pesikta Rabbah* 23).
146. See *Shabbos* 33.
147. *Sefer HaChinuch* 35.
148. *Sforno* to *Yisro;* see *Shevuos* 47b; *R' Saadiah Gaon; Ibn Ezra; Rabbeinu Bachya; Sifsei Kohen* to *Yisro.*
   This is the Seventh Commandment, and there are seven forbidden relationships included in this prohibition.

marketplace, so that children will not be influenced by their immoral behavior.[149]

Hashem deals very harshly with adulterers. The Great Flood was caused by adultery and theft. Hashem punishes adultery with destruction, plagues and exile.[150]

This Commandment immediately follows the prohibition against murder, which attempts to ensure that the world is populated. One might think, therefore, that for the sake of procreation, all relationships are permitted. Therefore, the very next Commandment prohibits adultery.[151]

On the *Luchos*, the Seventh Commandment sits in the second position of the second column, level with the Second Commandment, which prohibits gods of other people. Turning away from one's own spouse and seeking others is tantamount to turning away from Hashem and seeking gods of other people.[152]

The Eighth Commandment

The Eighth Commandment prohibits stealing.[153] The primary intent of this prohibition is to forbid abduction of people,[154] either adults or children; it is a capital offense when the abducted person is forced to work as a slave and then sold. This follows the previous two Commandments, prohibitions against murder and adultery, whose primary form of violation are also capital offenses.[155]

According to many opinions, theft of property, cheating, using inaccurate weights, measures or scales, withholding wages, not

---

See *Hadar Zekeinim* who writes that a casual relationship with a single woman does not fall under this particular prohibition, but under the prohibition of causing the promiscuity of women among the Jewish people (*Devarim* 23:18).

149. *Targum Yonasan*.
150. See *Yechezkel* 16:32-42 and commentaries; *Midrash Aseres HaDibros; Shabbos* 33; *Targum Yonasan; Meam Loez*.
151. *Rabbeinu Bachya; Chizkuni* to *Yisro*.
152. *Mechilta*.
The Torah also compares interfering in a neighbor's livelihood to defiling his wife. Both stem from the disregard for another person's possessions (*Sanhedrin* 81a; see *Yechezkel* 18:6).
Hashem will bring death, fire, poverty and destruction to the society that allows adultery to permeate the land (see *Yechezkel* 16:32-42 and commentaries; *Midrash Aseres HaDibros*).
153. See *Rambam, Hil. Geneivah* 1:1; *Hil. Melachim* 9:9.
154. *Mechilta; Rashi* to *Yisro*.
155. See *Sanhedrin* 85b, 86a; *Shemos* 21:16; *Rambam, Hil. Geneivah* 9:2; *Ibn Ezra* to *Shemos* 21:16.

returning lost items and misrepresentation (*geneivas daas*) are also included in this Commandment, although these are not capital offenses.[156] Even if the person from whom the money was stolen is so wealthy that he will not feel the loss, it is still a violation of the Eighth Commandment.[157] According to some, adultery can also be considered theft of someone else's wife.[158] Stealing from a gentile can be worse than stealing from a Jew, because it can cause a *chillul Hashem*, a desecration of the Name of Hashem.[159]

The prohibition against stealing, the third in the second column on the *Luchos*, is parallel to the prohibition against taking Hashem's Name in vain, because the thief swears in the Name of Hashem that he is innocent.[160] Therefore, someone who buys stolen goods or gives any sort of aid and comfort to the thief is considered a self-hater. By accepting the thief's protestations of innocence, knowing full well they are lies, he is sending a message to the thief that he is a ready customer for the contraband and is tacitly encouraging the thief to steal again. A person who does this destroys his own life and shows that he hates himself.[161]

Robbery and theft defile the land, cause the *Shechinah* to depart and lead to famine, hunger, pestilence and other disasters. The pervasiveness of robbery brought on the Great Flood in the time of Noach.[162]

Robbery and theft are never permitted. Misrepresentation, however, is permitted in the case of a student who pretends he does not understand because he wants his teacher to review the lesson yet another time. It is also permitted to swindle a cheater in order to recover the stolen property and return it to its rightful owner.[163]

---

156. See *Rabbeinu Bachya; Ibn Ezra* to *Yisro; Maseches Derech Eretz* 2; see *Chullin* 94b; *Sifsei Kohen* to *Yisro*.
157. See *R' Saadiah Gaon; R' Avraham Ben HaRambam; Ibn Ezra* to *Yisro*.
158. *Malbim*.
159. *Kad HaKemach*.
160. *Mechilta*.
161. See *Mishlei* 29:24 with *Rashi, Ralbag and Metzudas David; Choshen Mishpat* 356:1; *Yerushalmi Sanhedrin* 1:5.
162. See *Targum Yonasan* to *Yisro; Shabbos* 33; *Kad HaKemach; Midrash Aseres HaDibros; Zechariah* 5:4; *Vayikra Rabbah* 22:7; *Maharzav; Matnos Kehunah*. See *Mishlei* 30; *Yechezkel* 20; *Yalkut Reuveni*.
  Someone who steals in secret is arrogant, for his actions show that he is only afraid of people seeing him and has no fear of Hashem.
  Even Rachel the Matriarch lost the merit of being buried with Yaakov for stealing the idols of her father Lavan (*Midrash Aseres HaDibros*).
163. *Zohar*.

The Ninth Commandment

The Ninth Commandment prohibits bearing false witness. According to most opinions, this applies only to testimony in a *beis din* (court of law). Others say that it also includes slanderous remarks made out of court.[164]

The prohibition against false testimony, the fourth in the second column on the *Luchos*, is parallel to the Commandment to keep Shabbos, because one who bears false witness is considered to have denied the testimony of the Shabbos day that Hashem created the world in six days and rested on the seventh.[165]

It is forbidden to testify to anything one has not witnessed oneself; hearsay is not valid testimony.[166] It is also forbidden to intimidate a litigant by giving the impression that one is ready to testify when, in fact, this is not so.[167] False testimony is forbidden even when it is irrelevant and will not cause anyone financial damage.[168] It is also forbidden to arrange or suborn false testimony.[169] Bearing false witness against a gentile can be worse than stealing from a Jew, because it can cause a *chillul Hashem*, a desecration of the Name of Hashem.[170]

Hashem abhors falsehood. The first question posed to a deceased person on Judgment Day is, "Were you faithful in your dealings?"[171]

---

164. *Smag* 216, 235; *Sforno*; *Abarbanel*.
See *Sefer Chassidim* who adds that Yosef guarded this law when he did not divulge to his father Yaakov what his brothers did to him.

165. *Midrash HaGadol*.
People stand during *Kiddush* on Friday night because when someone testifies in court he must stand, and during *Kiddush* one is in fact testifying that Hashem created the world in six days and rested on the seventh (*Rosh Al HaTorah*).

166. *Yere'im* 178; *Sefer HaChinuch* 37; *Midrash HaChefetz*; *Midrash Ohr Afeilah*; see *Rambam, Hil. Eidus* 17:1; *Meshech Chochmah*; *Haamek Davar*.

167. See *Shevuos* 31; *Rambam, Hil. Eidus* 17:5; *Ibn Ezra* to *Yisro*.

168. See *Mishlei* 24:28; *Ibn Ezra*; *Metzudas*; *Chizkuni* to *Yisro*; *Ramban* to *Devarim* 5:18.
See *Minchas Chinuch* 37 for his discussion on this matter.
In the second version of the Ten Commandments the Torah uses the phrase *shav* (vain) instead of *sheker* (falsehood). This is to say that it makes no difference if the testimony is false or meaningless, where no losses occur; if it is false, it is prohibited. Both the words *sheker* and *shav* were uttered at the same moment, similar to *zachor* and *shamor* (*Yerushalmi Nedarim* 3:2).

169. *Rabbeinu Bachya* to *Yisro*.

170. *Rabbeinu Bachya*.
This is so from the Torah's use of the word neighbor (*rei'acha*) instead of brother (*achicha*).

171. See *Shabbos* 31a; *Midrash Aseres HaDibros*.
Falsehood in itself carries with it its own wickedness. It is the only thing that Hashem did not create. *Sheker* (falsehood) is something developed by man, created from his heart (*Pesikta Rabbah* 21).

Entire societies have been destroyed because of corrupt laws and legal systems.[172]

Just as it is forbidden to bear false testimony, it is also forbidden to withhold true testimony. Silence when one should speak out is another form of falsehood and is tantamount to false testimony.[173]

The Tenth Commandment

The Tenth Commandment prohibits coveting someone else's house, wife, servants, livestock or anything else desirable that he possesses.[174] Here the Torah teaches a person that, even if he refrains from forbidden actions, it does not mean that he may think whatever he wishes in the privacy of his own thoughts. Coveting someone else's possession may seem harmless, but it is actually destructive and sinful.[175] Nonetheless, since it does not involve an action, the Torah prescribes no punishment to be administered by the courts.[176]

The prohibition against coveting, the fifth in the second column on the *Luchos*, is parallel to the Commandment to honor parents. According to some opinions, this implies that coveting another man's wife may lead to adultery and the birth of a child who does not know his true parents. Others suggest that a parent who covets sets a poor example for a child and leads him to disrespect his parents.[177]

This final Commandment also rounds out the Ten Commandments as the extreme opposite of the First Commandment, which demands faith in Hashem. A person who has faith will never covet what Hashem has given to another person. The First Commandment represents all that is positive in the human heart, while the Tenth represents all that is negative.[178]

In *Shemos* the word used for coveting is *lo sachmod*, while in *Devarim* it is *lo sisaveh*, which is more accurately translated as "you shall not desire." Desire is a feeling in the heart, while coveting

---

172. See *Sefer HaChinuch* 37, *Targum Yonasan*.
173. See *Yefei To'ar* 6:1; *Vayikra Rabbah*.
174. *Rambam, Hil. Gezeilah* 1:10.
175. *Rabbeinu Bachya* to *Yisro*.
176. *Meshech Chochmah*.
177. See *Mechilta; Kli Yakar; Rashi* to *Shir HaShirim* 4:5; *Zohar* to *Yisro* 90a.
178. *Kad HaKemach*.

involves manipulation to fulfill the desire.[179] If someone coerces a sale, even if it is voluntary in the end and even if he makes payment in full, it is still considered coveting.[180] If someone convinces his neighbor to divorce his wife and marries her himself, he is guilty of coveting.[181] Others suggest that coveting emanates from the eyes and involves tangible things, while the abstract desire for wealth or hunger is borne in the heart.[182]

The prohibition against coveting, the last of the Commandments, affects the entire Torah. Once a person allows himself to be taken over by his desires, there is no end to what he might do and nothing in the Torah he would not violate in order to satisfy the hunger of his heart.[183] King Achav coveted the vineyard of Navos, and he killed him to acquire it.[184] On the other hand, a person who does not covet will always be good to his friends and family, because the usual points of contention will not be there.[185] It is acceptable, however, for a person to be jealous of Torah scholars for their knowledge, since this will stimulate and inspire him to learn more Torah himself.[186]

---

179. *Mechilta D'Rashbi*; *Sefer HaMitzvos L'Rambam* 266; *Rambam, Hil. Gezeilah* 1:9-10; *Maggid Mishneh*; *Sefer HaChinuch* 38.

Others are in disagreement and suggest that they are one and the same and equal in their prohibition. See *Rashi* to *Devarim* 5:18; *Smag* 158.

180. See *Sefer HaMitzvos L'Rambam* 266; *Rambam, Hil. Gezeilah* 1:9-10.

See *Sefer HaMitzvos L'Rambam* 266; *Choshen Mishpat* 359:10-12; *Yere'im* 115; *Midrash HaGadol* to *Devarim* 5:18; *Ramban* to *Yisro*.

Others suggest that one is only in violation of this Biblical prohibition if he does not pay. See *Tosafos* to *Bava Metzia* 5b; *Sanhedrin* 25b; *Moshav Devarim*; *Ravad* to *Rambam*.

R' Avraham Ben HaRambam suggests that one is only in violation of coveting if the object he desires is exactly what his neighbor has, not something similar or comparable.

181. See *Charedim*; *Ralbag*. See also *Gittin* 58a; *Iyun Yaakov*.

182. *Malbim*.

In the repetition of the Commandments, Moshe uses the word *tisaveh* as opposed to *tachmod*. *Tachmod* is a type of want that necessitates an action, while *tisaveh* is a desire from the heart without any further intent. In the repetition, directed to the Jewish people, Hashem could tell them that they should not desire even just in their hearts. However, in the first *Dibros*, which were intended for the nations of the world as well, He could not expect them not to desire at all. However, it is conceivable to stipulate to them that one should not covet something with the intention of getting what he coveted.

183. See *Rambam, Hil. Gezeilah* 1:11; *Choshen Mishpat* 359; *Sefer HaChinuch* 38; *Michah* 2:2 with *Radak* and *Ibn Ezra*; *Rabbeinu Bachya* to *Yisro*; *Yehoshua* 7:21.

184. See *Rambam, Hil. Gezeilah*; *Choshen Mishpat*; *Sefer HaChinuch* 38; *I Melachim* Ch. 21.

185. *Ramban*.

186. See *Zohar*; *Bava Basra* 21a; *Rabbeinu Bachya*.

Coveting also leads to an unnatural attachment to one's own possessions and a strong reluctance to part with them, even for the purposes of giving charity. The one who violates the Tenth Commandment will not want to give *maaser*, the tenth of his income he must give to charity.[187]

Coveting leads to theft and eventually to exile and to governments confiscating their wealth. Just as they coveted what was not theirs, the government will take what is not theirs, as well.[188]

One might wonder how the Torah can legislate against a natural human emotion such as coveting something desirable. Actually, however, these emotions only surface when the object of desire is accessible. A peasant does not covet a princess, since she is far beyond the realm of his possibilities. If a person has faith in Hashem and believes that Hashem gives every person what is right for him, then the other person's possessions are beyond the realm of his possibilities, and he will not covet them.[189]

Others offer an additional insight. In *Shema*, we say "to love Hashem with all your heart." If a person truly loves Hashem with all his heart then there will be no room in his heart for coveting.[190]

Yet others point out that when a person has true *yiras Shamayim*, fear of Hashem, he will not covet. A person going to a place to indulge his desires will quickly turn back if he encounters a lion on the road. In the same way, a person who lives with a constant awareness of Hashem will be able to banish covetous thoughts from his mind and heart.[191]

The first five Commandments express the fundamental belief system of the Torah. If a person is scrupulous in his observance of the first five Commandments, he will never even consider violating any of the second five, because he would be keenly aware that the Creator and Master of the Universe is watching his every move.[192]

The Serpent in Gan Eden transgressed all of the second set of five Commandments. He gave false testimony to Chavah when he told her that Hashem had forbidden them to eat from all the trees in Gan

---

187. *Kad HaKemach.*
188. *Targum Yonasan; Pesikta Rabbah* 24.
189. See *Ibn Ezra; Sforno; Kad HaKemach.*
190. *HaKesav VeHaKabbalah.*
191. *Beis HaLevi;* see *Sefer HaChinuch* for his approach.
192. *Tosefta Shevous.*

Eden. He was guilty of misrepresentation. He attempted to defile her. He caused mankind to suffer a decree of death for all time, which makes him a murderer. And all this, because he coveted Chavah.[193]

---

193. *Yalkut Reuveni.*

Someone who covets something will not only fail to gain the object of his desire but will eventually lose what he already has. This concept is seen in regard to the Serpent. When the Serpent coveted Chavah, not only was he unsuccessful in procuring his desire, but, as king of the beasts, he lost his prominence over all the beasts and lost his legs on which he stood above all, leaving him humbled and crawling on the ground (see *Sotah* 9b; *Rabbeinu Bachya* to *Yisro*).

Hashem's Name is not found in the Commandments on the left side of the *Luchos* because He does not want to associate with murderers, thieves and the like. It is as though one would consider placing the King's Image or Name in a place of defilement. Such an act would create great humiliation and dishonor for the King (See *Chizkuni* to *Devarim* 2:12; *Tosafos* to *Taanis* 3a s.v.*Vehilu*).

The second set of Commandments mentioned in *Parashas Va'eschanan* are, in general, only additions rather than changes to the Commandments in *Parashas Yisro*. Although there are minor differences, they only add to the lessons learned from the Commandments but do not change the basic premise of the laws. In three instances, however, there are actual changes which in fact create differences in the Commandments. While in the first set of Commandments the Torah writes **Zachor**, remember the Shabbos, in the latter *Dibros* the Torah writes **Shamor**, keep or wait for the Shabbos. In the first *Dibros* the Torah writes **sheker** that one should not bear false witness, while in the second *Dibros* it says one should not utter **shav**, vain testimony. Additionally **tachmod** and **tisaveh** are another difference between the two sets of Commandments. *Zachor* and *shamor* were actually said at once at Sinai, as were *sheker* and *shav*. (see *Gur Aryeh*; *Tiferes Yisrael* 43, 45; *Ramban* to *Yisro* 20:8; *Devarim* 5:6.)

See next chapter as to how these words were used in the first and second *Luchos*.

Others add that the first *Dibros* were intended for all nations who chose to hear and listen to them, while the second set of *Dibros* repeated by Moshe were intended only for the Jewish people (*Kil Yakar* to *Yisro* 20:8).

Besides the repetition of the Ten Commandments mentioned in *Va'eschanan*, the Torah also has a series of laws that correspond to the Ten Commandments in *Parashas Kedoshim* (19:2-16) (*Tanchuma Yashan Kedoshim*): In verse 19:1 *Rashi* makes reference to holiness and refers to **adultery**. 19:2 corresponds to the first Commandment of **Anochi**. 19:3 refers to keeping **Shabbos** and fearing one's **parents**. 19:4 refers to not following **idol** worship. 19:6 corresponds to not **killing**. 19:11 or 19:15 addresses the Commandments of **stealing** and **false** testimony. 19:12 refers to the Commandment of **swearing** falsely. 19:13 refers to not **coveting**.

12 Forty Days in Heaven

After Moshe delivered the Ten Commandments to the Jewish people, Hashem summoned him to return to the mountaintop. This time, the ascent would also be spiritual, elevating him to a spiritual level no human being had ever achieved before.[1] In this altered state, he would spend forty days in Heaven, receiving the *Luchos* upon which the Ten Commandments were engraved. He would also learn the entire Torah, the Written Law and the Oral Law, which he would teach the Jewish people after his descent from the mountain.[2]

---

1. *Recanati; Abarbanel; Alshich* to *Shemos* 24:12.
   As noted, Moshe's body never ascended beyond 10 cubits above the mountain. His ascension was that of a spiritual one, greater than any of the previous ascensions.
2. See *Berachos* 5a; *Rashi; Iyun Yaakov; Ibn Ezra; Midrash HaGadol; Lekach Tov* to *Shemos* 24:12.
   The *Luchos* are comprised of the Ten Commandments, the Written Torah is comprised of all of Scripture, while the Oral Torah includes the Mishnah and Gemara, which together are known as the Talmud. There are various opinions as to the definitions of the words Torah and mitzvah written in the *pasuk*. While Moshe committed the Written Torah to writing, as we will discuss later, Hashem Himself wrote the Commandments on the *Luchos* (*Mizrachi; Gur Aryeh*). See *Miluim* to *Torah Shleimah Mishpatim* Ch. 2.
   See *Sforno*, who writes that Hashem would have written the Torah as well if not for the fact that the Jewish people sinned with the Golden Calf.

The Divine summons took the form of a king extending his scepter to his subject.³ As Moshe reached the upper slopes of the mountain, the cloudbank bent down toward him and wrapped itself around him, beckoning to him to enter the presence of Hashem. From this point on, Moshe was obscured from the sight of the people at the base of the mountain. He had left the terrestrial domain and stepped across the threshold of Heaven.⁴

Six Days of Preparation

Moshe was wrapped in these clouds for six days, during which he was purged of all earthly matter (*chomer*) and prepared for his ascent to Heaven until he reached the level of the angels. The people could no longer see him; all they saw, those that were worthy, was a fiery manifestation of the *Shechinah*.⁵ Isolated from the world and from his people, he attained new depths of awe and reverence for the *Shechinah*. During all this time, he did not eat nor drink. Every last scrap of food was eliminated from his stomach and intestines. All his normal bodily functions ceased; he no longer had any need to relieve himself.⁶

Some suggest that these six days were the first six days of the forty that he spent in Heaven. Others suggest that they coincided with the first six days of Sivan, immediately prior to the Giving of the Torah and that, on the seventh day of Sivan, he went directly to Heaven and began his forty-day encounter with Hashem.⁷

---

3. See *Abarbanel* to *Shemos* 24:12. See *Let My Nation Live* Chs. 16 and 17.
4. *Midrash HaGadol*; *Lekach Tov*; *Ibn Ezra* to *Shemos* 24:15-17; *Zohar* 197. See *Malbim* for a different view.
5. See *Kuzari* 2:7, 4:3; *Ramban* to *Bereishis* 15:17; *Rabbeinu Bachya*; *Abarbanel*; *HaKesav VeHaKabbalah* to *Mishpatim*.
  Just as the rate at which fire will consume an item depends on its level of flammability, so too the Jewish people saw this fire and its traits according to the level of spirituality and understanding they could absorb (*HaKesav VeHaKabbalah Mishpatim*). See *Malbim* to *Shemos* 24:17.
6. *Abarbanel*; *Midrash Aggadah*; *Midrash HaGadol* to *Shemos* 24:12; *Lekach Tov*; *Avos D'Rav Nassan* 1:1; *Rashi* to *Yoma* 4b.
  See *Shlah* who writes that because of the spiritual essence of the manna, there was really no need for this six-day period of isolation.
  Others add that the miracle was not so much that Moshe did not eat for forty days, but that he did not even sustain himself from the food that he had previously eaten. He was totally empty when he ascended the mountain (*Panim Yafos*).
  Some suggest that Moshe was unaware that he would remain on the mountain for forty days, originally anticipating returning within two or three days (see *Kuzari* 1:97; *Ralbag*).
7. This would either be the 7th or the 13th day of Sivan. According to R' Akiva the 7th day of Sivan began the forty-day period in which Moshe was in the heavens, while

There is also a difference of opinion regarding the time of his ascent. According to some, it took place at daybreak (*alos hashachar*), while according to others it took place in the afternoon.[8]

After the six days of preparation, Hashem directed Moshe to enter further into the clouds.[9] As Moshe looked at the smoky denseness of the clouds, unsure of which direction to take, a brightly illuminated path, four cubits wide, opened through the cloudbank.[10] Still, Moshe remained frozen in place by fear. The angels took him and transported him to the designated place at the edge of the *arafel* cloud, the inner ring around the fiery *Shechinah* from which even angels were restricted.[11] Moshe had reached a level of spirituality that allowed him to go where angels feared to tread.[12]

The Angels Challenge Moshe[13]

Moshe walked through the clouds on the firmament of Heaven as if he were walking on the earth. The first angel he met was Kemuel.

"What are you doing here, son of Amram?" asked Kemuel. "This is a place designated for fiery angels."

---

according to R' Yosi the forty days started on the 7th of Sivan, but Moshe's true ascension to the *Shechinah* took place on the 13th.

According to R' Yosi, who says the Torah was given on the 7th day of Sivan, Moshe rose to Sinai that afternoon. For a full discussion on this subject see *Yoma* 4a with *Rashi*; *Avos D'Rav Nassan* 1:1; *Yerushalmi Yoma* 4:5; *Korban HaEidah*; *Tosafos* to *Bava Kamma* 24a; *Rashbam* to *Bava Basra* 121a; *Seder Olam* 6; *Lekach Tov* to *Shemos* 24:16. See *Torah Shleimah* to *Mishpatim* 24:141, 152 for further discussion.

8. See the following chapter for further discussion of this matter.
9. *Rabbeinu Bachya* to *Shemos* 24:18.
10. *Yoma* 4b with *Rashi*; *Midrash HaGadol*; *Lekach Tov*; *Abarbanel* to *Shemos* 24:18; *Maharam*.
11. *Netziv*; see *Rashi*; *Rabbeinu Bachya*; *Abarbanel*; *Malbim* to *Shemos* 20:18; commentaries to *Tehillim* 18:10, 12; *Iyov* 23:13; *Yalkut* 301; *Lekach Tov*; *Rokeach* to *Devarim* 4:11. See *Ramban* to *Devarim* 5:19.
12. See *Rabbeinu Bachya*; *Malbim*; *HaKesav VeHaKabbalah* to *Shemos* 20:18. See *Malbim* to *Devarim* 4:11; *Alshich* to *Shemos* 24:18.

See *Sifsei Kohen* as to the reason why the Torah refers to this period as forty days and forty nights. Usually the calendar day begins at night. One reason for this change is that Moshe ascended the mountain by day instead of at night. This was, in fact, the very premise which caused the Jewish people to err, leading them to the worship of the Golden Calf.

13. See *Radal* to *Pirkei D'Rav Eliezer* 46 about the sequence of events. Some simply suggest that this dialogue took place during one of Moshe's ascensions before receiving the Torah. Others suggest that this took place later, when Moshe went to receive the *Luchos* during his forty-day stay. Cognizant of the different opinions, I have chosen to place

"I have not come here of my own accord," Moshe replied. "I am here by the will of the Almighty. He has summoned me to receive the Torah and bring it to the Jewish people."

Kemuel refused to budge, and Moshe pushed him aside.

He continued on until he met a fierce angel named Hardarniel.

"You have no business here," roared Hardarniel. "This is the territory of Heaven. You belong on the earth."

As Hardarniel spoke, his mouth emitted flashes of lightning. Moshe recoiled in fear and almost fell. Tears fell from his eyes.

Hashem had mercy on Moshe and said to Hardarniel, "Leave him be. You angels are always quarreling since the day you were created. You complained when I formed mankind, and now you protest the appearance among us of my faithful and loyal servant Moshe who has come to receive the Torah. The world cannot exist without the Torah. If he does not receive the Torah, everything will cease to exist, including you angels."

Hardarniel accepted Hashem's rebuke and escorted Moshe as he continued on his way.

Presently, the angel Hardarniel said to Moshe, "We have to move away from here. If we don't move right away, we will be scorched by the fires of Sandalfon, the giant among the angels."

One glance at that powerful angel was enough to intimidate Moshe. Feeling faint and on the verge of falling, he pleaded with Hashem for mercy. Hashem responded by leaving the Throne of Glory, so to speak, and positioning Himself between Moshe and Sandalfon to protect Moshe from the fire until he passed.

A short distance further, Moshe came upon a stream of fiery coals named Rigion. Here again, Hashem helped Moshe pass without being scorched by the fires.

Then Moshe encountered the angel Gallizur, otherwise known as Raziel, the angel who discloses Hashem's decrees to the world. Once again, Hashem personally helped Moshe to pass without incident.

As Moshe drew near the Throne of Glory, where he would receive the Torah, the angels gathered to complain that a mere

---

this exchange here for the simplicity of events that will lead to the Golden Calf, using the view of the *Pesikta Rabbah* and *Yalkut Reuveni*.

I have chosen to consolidate and paraphrase these Midrashim, to simplify for the reader this very complex and difficult Midrash which is so hard to comprehend and understand.

mortal would have such a meeting with Hashem and, even worse, that he sought to take the Torah and bring it down to earth, to the Jewish people.

"Why is a man of flesh and blood coming here?" they wanted to know. "We are angels, purely spiritual beings. We are worthy of receiving the purely spiritual Torah, which existed before the material world was created. How can the Torah be given to material creatures in a material world? The Torah has waited for twenty-six generations. Should it now be given to mere mortals? And why should this Moshe be given the great privilege of coming into Your presence?"[14]

The angel of terror, mightiest among the Heavenly host, rose up and tried to immolate Moshe with his fiery breath.

"Answer them," Hashem said to Moshe.

"I am afraid they will destroy me," Moshe replied to Hashem. "They will consume me with their fiery breath. Their dislike for me is intense. How can I, a simple human being, withstand their spiritual fire?"

Hashem caused Moshe to take on the appearance of Avraham.

"Look at him," Hashem said to the angels. "Do you recognize him? Isn't he the one who fed you when you were guests in his home? Aren't you embarrassed to treat him with such hostility?"

The angels were rendered speechless.[15]

"Grab on to My Throne," Hashem said to Moshe. "That will protect you from harm. It will show them that you have attained the spiritual level to approach My Throne, while they are still restricted."

Moshe held on to the Throne of Glory and, enfolded by Hashem's radiance, he responded to the angels.[16]

---

14. The Torah was supposed to be given after a hundred generations, but Hashem saw that the world could not survive without Torah, so He gave it after only twenty-six generations (*Rashi* to *Shabbos* 88b, *Chagigah* 13a). See commentary on *Rashi's* use of the word "years" rather than the word "generations." See *Bereishis Rabbah* 1:1; see *Midrash Aseres HaDibros* for his version. For further information on the angel Sandalfon see *Chagigah* 13b.

15. The angels were speechless because they felt that they needed to reciprocate the goodness and kindness shown to them by Avraham. When Hashem made Moshe's image resemble that of Avraham, the angels found themselves unable to harm that image (*Tiferes Yisrael* Ch. 25).

Many suggest that the image Moshe took was not in the features of his face, but in the characteristics of Avraham's nature.

16. See *Zohar Beshalach* 58a; *Shabbos* 88b with *Maharsha; Rif; Anaf Yosef* to *Ein Yaakov; Pesachim* 118a; *Meam Loez; Midrash HaGadol; Yalkut Reuveni Mishpatim; Pesikta Rabbah* 20 (*Magen*

"You say the Torah should go to you," he said to the angels. "Let us look into the Torah and see if that would be appropriate. The Ten Commandments begin with the law of *Anochi*, which requires us to recognize Hashem as the one and only G-d Who took us out of Egypt. The next Commandment prohibit worshiping any other deity or making oaths in Hashem's Name. And so on. So tell me, esteemed angels, were any of you ever enslaved in Egypt? Do you have idol worshipers among you? Do you have business and financial dealing that might require you to take oaths? Do you have fathers and mother to honor? Do you have evil inclinations that might lead you to steal, kill and covet? Clearly, none of these laws apply to you, so how can the Torah be given to you?

"Although the Torah is exceedingly holy, it was not meant for superior beings such as angels. The Torah is full of laws designed for mortals with flaws, deficiencies, hungers and appetites and it was given to them to overcome their shortcomings. Indeed, those who succeed reach levels higher than those of the angels. So you see, angels are not legitimate claimants for the Torah."

At that moment, Moshe himself, holding onto the Throne of Glory which the angels could not approach, was the living proof of his arguments that human beings could surpass the angels in sanctity. In fact, Moshe had reached such a level of holiness that the angels could not look directly at the sacred radiance of his face.

The angels conceded defeat and became more conciliatory toward Moshe. They took him into their confidence and revealed to him certain esoteric knowledge of the world and deep secrets about the relationship between Hashem's Names and the Torah. Moshe eventually passed on these secrets to his nephew Elazar, Aharon's son, who would one day be Kohen Gadol (High Priest). Elazar passed the secrets on to his son Pinchas. The angel of death had a

---

David there); *Binah LeItim*. See *Yalkut Tehillim* 795; *Shemos Rabbah* 28:1; *Midrash Shocher Tov* 8. See *Maharsha*; *Pirkei D'Rav Eliezer* 46 and *Radal*; *Tiferes Yisrael* Ch. 24. See *Kometz HaMinchah, Shavuos*.

By grabbing on to the Throne and wrapping himself in Hashem's spiritual radiance, Moshe knew that, indeed, a mere mortal can reach even a higher spiritual level than an angel. Hashem sent a signal to Moshe indicating that his response would have to be one that proved man's ability to reach a higher level than the angels. Moshe would indeed succeed by explaining that one who conquers his *yetzer hara* is far greater than an angel who has no evil inclination to overcome.

See *Radal* regarding the sequence of events.

special gift for Moshe. He gave him certain incense that could prevent or cure plagues.[17]

"You asked why Moshe should be allowed to come here," Hashem said to the angels. "The willingness of Moshe and the Jewish people to accept the Torah, even though they are human beings full of temptations and desires, shows that they are greater and more spiritual than the angels who have no evil inclination, whose natural impulse is to be obedient and choose correctly."[18]

Moshe ascended higher into Heaven, and Hashem opened the seven firmaments of Heaven for him. Moshe saw a shimmering facsimile of the Mishkan that he would later build and the four primary colors of its fabrics. Hashem also taught him the laws pertaining to Eretz Yisrael, which would become the homeland of the Jewish people.[19]

Moshe now saw Hashem adorning the letters of the Torah with tiny coronets. He watched without uttering a word.[20]

"Do people offer greetings in your home town?" Hashem asked him.

"Is it proper for a servant to address his master?" Moshe replied. "Should he not stand silently, in fear and reverence, until he is called upon to speak?"

"You should have wished Me success in My work," Hashem said.

"May My L-rd's power increase," said Moshe, "as You have spoken."[21] Moshe paused. "If I might ask a question — what is the sig-

---

17. *Shabbos* 89a; *Pirkei D'Rav Eliezer* 46; *Kometz HaMinchah, Shavuos*; *Midrash Aseres HaDibros*. See *Eliyahu Zuta* 12; *Meam Loez*.

18. *Shabbos* 89a; *Binah LeItim*. See *Tosafos* to *Shabbos* 3a s.v. *Gadol*. Some commentaries note that *Ezekiel* 1:26 alludes that man is greater than an angel, since it is an image of man that appears, as it were, above the Heavenly Throne.

19. *Pesikta Rabbah* 21; *Shemos Rabbah* 40:2; *Abarbanel*; *Chemas HaChemdah*; *Chizkuni*; *Tosafos Al HaTorah* to *Shemos* 24:18.
   There is some question as to the sequence of events that took place. Some suggest that when Moshe ascended to Hashem he was taught all of the necessary laws contained in the Torah portions from *Yisro* through *Ki Sisa*. This included the civil laws, the laws and construction of the Mishkan and laws relating to the clothing of the Kohanim (see *Sifsei Kohen*; *Abarbanel*; *Mizrachi* to *Rashi* 31:18). Others suggest that the Torah is not written in chronological order and, despite the mention of the Mishkan and Kehunah laws, the episode of the Golden Calf preceded them (see *Rashi* and *Mizrachi*).

20. These are small strokes appearing like crowns placed on top of seven letters, *shin*, *ayin*, *tes*, *nun*, *zayin*, *gimel* and *tzadik*, the letters "שעטנז גץ."

21. See *Shabbos* 89a; *Tosafos* to *Bava Kamma* 73 s.v. *Kdei*. See commentaries to *Bamidbar* 14:17-18.
   Hashem did not need the blessing of success from Moshe, but Hashem was looking

nificance of these coronets on the letters? Why add crowns to letters that already exist?"

"Someday there will be a great man," said Hashem, "by the name of Akiva ben Yosef. He will expound on these crowns and derive mountains of laws from them."

"Please show me the secrets meanings of these crowns," said Moshe.

"First you must learn the meaning of the letters in their normal order and also in their reverse order."[22]

Moshe went into the Yeshivah of Heaven and sat in the eighth rank. He saw Rabbi Akiva teaching his disciples, but he could not follow what they were saying. Moshe was mystified and greatly aggrieved.

Then he heard one of the disciples say to Rabbi Akiva, "What is the source for this law?"

"This law," replied Rabbi Akiva, "was given to Moshe at Sinai."

Moshe was comforted. But he was still puzzled.[23]

"If you have a great man such as Rabbi Akiva," he asked Hashem, "why do you choose to give the Torah through me?"

"Do not question My decisions and decrees," Hashem replied. "Just as you don't understand the letters and their secret meanings, you also do not understand My ways. You just have to accept them."[24]

"May I see the reward in store for Rabbi Akiva?" Moshe asked.

Hashem let Moshe see that, in the marketplace, they were selling the flesh the Romans had scraped off Rabbi Akiva with their iron combs. Moshe was shocked.

"Is this the reward for Torah?" he asked Hashem.

---

to teach Moshe that among humans, upon seeing work being done, it is a kind gesture to wish someone success in his work.

Rashi suggests that this statement was said at a different time, when Moshe ascended to the heavenly realm to receive the Second *Luchos*.

22. *Rashi and Maharsha* to *Menachos* 29a.

There is meaning to the order in which the *aleph-beis* is set from *aleph* to *taf*. Hashem wanted Moshe to learn the meaning of the order as it is set up from *taf* to *aleph* as well.

One cannot question how or to what extent R' Akiva existed at this time. Moshe was in a supernatural and spiritual world. I, for one, am not qualified to offer any thoughts on subjects beyond the realm of my comprehension.

23. Despite the fact that Moshe had not learned the information being discussed, he was relieved that the very thing they were discussing had its source in what he would eventually teach the Jewish people (see *Rashi; Maharsha*).

24. *Maharsha*. See *Let My Nation Go* p. 138 fn. 154.

"You cannot understand My ways," Hashem replied. "The human mind does not have the capacity to grasp everything."[25] Moshe saw that Hashem was inscribing His Attribute of being "Slow to Anger."

"This refers to Your dealing with the righteous people, does it not?" Moshe asked.

"It is also for the sinners," Hashem replied.

"Let the sinners perish!" said Moshe.

"One day soon," said Hashem, "you will think otherwise. To defend the Jewish people you will need the words I have spoken."

Later, when the Jewish people worshiped the Golden Calf, Hashem would be prepared to destroy them. Moshe would intercede on their behalf and plead for mercy.

"But didn't you say," Hashem would remind him, "that I should be slow to anger only with the righteous?"

"And didn't You say you would be forbearing with the sinners as well?" Moshe would reply. "May My L-rd's power increase, as You have spoken. Please act according to the words You spoke Yourself and show tolerance toward the sinners as well."[26]

When Moshe was almost ready to descend from Heaven, Satan begged Hashem to tell him where the Torah was being kept.

"The Torah needs to be in a simple and humble environment," Hashem told Satan. "I have given it to the earth."

Satan approached the earth and asked, "Where is the Torah?"

"Hashem understands its way," the earth replied. "He knows its place. He looks to the ends of the earth and sees what is under the heavens."

Satan decided to pursue his investigations by approaching the sea.

"Where is the Torah?" he asked the sea.

"It is not with me," the sea replied.

"Where is the Torah?" he asked the abyss.

"It is not with me," said the abyss.

Satan finally approached Gehinnom and asked about the Torah.

---

25. See *Menachos* 29b with *Rashi; Maharsha; Iyun Yaakov.*
   This was all part of the learning process during Moshe's forty-day stay with the *Shechinah*. Moshe was not only learning the Torah, but also the ways of Hashem and the limitations of what can and cannot be understood.

26. See *Sanhedrin* 111 with *Rashi* and commentaries; *Bava Kamma* 50a with *Rashi, Tosafos* and *Maharsha; Pesikta D'Rav Kahana* 26:166; see *Shemos* 32:12; 33:19; 34:6.

"We have not received the Torah," he was told, "but we have heard it with our ears."

Discouraged, Satan returned to Hashem. "Master of the Universe," he said. "I have scoured the entire earth, but I have not found the Torah."

"Seek out the Torah," Hashem told him, "with the humblest of all men, who is the son of Amram."

Satan approached Moshe and asked, "Where is the Torah that Hashem has given to you?"

"Why would Hashem give the Torah to me, of all people?" Moshe replied.

Hashem interrupted, "Moshe! You are speaking falsehood."

"Hashem, You have in Your possession a hidden treasure that delights You," said Moshe. "Dare I take credit for it and declare that it is in my possession?"

"You have responded with humility," said Hashem, "and I will reward you, by naming the Torah for you. It will henceforth be called *Toras Moshe*, the Torah of Moshe."[27]

Telling Day From Night

Moshe was to spend precisely forty days and nights in Heaven. Therefore, it was necessary for him to keep track of day and night. He also needed to know this information so that he could recite *Krias Shema* every morning and night in its proper time.[28] On the earth, day is easily distinguishable from night as is light from darkness. But in the heavens, there is no distinction in the illumination of day and night. Nonetheless, Moshe had a number of ways to determine when day flowed into night and night into day.[29]

---

27. See *Shabbos* 89a with *Maharsha and Ein Yaakov*; *Tiferes Yisrael* 23; *Iyov* 28:14, 23, 24; *Sanhedrin* 26b; *Tanchuma Ki Sisa* 35.

The Satan was unaware that the Torah had already been given. Hashem had sent him away so that he would not speak up and accuse the Jewish people of being undeserving of the Torah due to their eventual worshiping of the Golden Calf (see *Tosafos* s.v. *Torah*).

Others suggest that all were aware that the Torah was given at Har Sinai. But the Satan assumed that it would remain in the heavens and just be shared with the Jewish people on earth, as opposed to be given exclusively to the Jewish people on the earth (*Chasam Sofer*).

28. *Etz Yosef*; *Tanchuma Ki Sisa* 36

29. See *Tehillim* 139:12; *Tanchuma Ki Sisa* 36; *Pirkei D'Rav Eliezer* 46; see *Pane'ach Raza* to *Shemos* 13:21; *Shir Rabbah* 5:11.

Others add that the angel of death carries the attribute of mercy on the front of his shoulder and, at night, which is a time of judgment, he places it on the back of his shoulder.

First, the *Shechinah* only learned Torah with him during the day. Therefore, when the *Shechinah* departed, he knew that night had arrived, and he sat down to review what he had learned that day.[30] Furthermore, the angels reciting the *Kedushah* prayers gave him strong clues to the time of day. He knew it was day when the angels said, "*Kadosh, kadosh, kadosh* — Holy, holy, holy." He knew it was night when they said, "*Borchu es Hashem HaMevorach* — Blessed is Hashem Who is the source of blessing." He knew it was day when he saw the moon and the stars prostrate themselves before His feet. He knew it was night when he saw the sun prostrate itself before His feet. He knew it was day when he saw the angels preparing the manna to send down to the Jewish people. He knew it was night when he saw the angels sending the manna down to the earth for the people to eat.[31]

During these forty days that Moshe spent in Heaven, he did not sleep, eat or drink in the ways we know.[32] Instead, he sustained himself as the angels do, deriving nourishment from the radiance of the *Shechinah*, the honeyed sweetness of the Torah and his sheer attachment to Hashem.[33]

During these forty days, Moshe learned the entire Torah, its depths, its intricacies and its details. By day he learned the Written Law, and by night he learned the Oral Law.[34] He also learned all the

---

30. *Midrash HaGadol* to *Shemos* 24:18; *Tanchuma Ki Sisa* 36 ; *Shemos Rabbah* 47:8; *Yefei To'ar*. See *Rashi* to *Megillah* 21a.

31. See *Yalkut Tehillim* 673; *Tanchuma Ki Sisa* 36; *Pirkei D'Rav Eliezer* 46; *Moshav Zekeinim*.

32. *Ibn Ezra* 24:18.

Moshe could not ignore the fact that the opportunity to dwell with the *Shechinah* and learn Torah was limited to just forty days. He could not imagine himself wasting time with sleep (*Shemos Rabbah* 47:7; *Abarbanel* to *Shemos* 34:28).

33. *Minchah Belulah*; *Abarbanel*; *Sifsei Kohen*; *Shemos Rabbah* 47:5,7; *Yefei To'ar*; *Radal*. See *Devarim Rabbah* 11:4; *Ohr HaChaim*; *Sifsei Kohen* to *Shemos* 34:28. See *Radak* to *I Melachim* 19:8; *Otzar Midrashim* 373; *Moreh Nevuchim* 3:1; *Rabbeinu Bachya* to *Shemos* 34:28.

Just as the Torah itself is a merit for one to survive and sustain oneself, here too Moshe was able to sustain himself in the spiritual realm of eating.

Just as Moshe accustomed himself to the sustenance offered in the heavens, similarly, when the angels came down to earth, they acted according to the surroundings in which they were. This was evident when they went to Avraham and acted as though they were eating food usually eaten on earth (*Bava Metzia* 86b).

34. See *Targum Yonasan* 24:18; *Midrash Aggadah*; *Lekach Tov* to *Shemos* 24:18; *Tanchuma Ki Sisa* 36; *Shemos Rabbah* 47:8; *Midrash Tehillim* 19:7; *Rabbeinu Bachya*; *Chizkuni*; *Sifsei Kohen* to *Shemos* 34:28.

Since it was forbidden to review the Written Torah orally, he could not do so at night, when he could not see. On the other hand, once forbidden to write down the Oral Torah, Moshe learned it by heart. *Radal*; *Pirkei D'Rav Eliezer* 46.

doctrines that would be expounded from the Torah by later generations, taking special pleasure in the opinions of his descendant, the Tanna Rabbi Eliezer.[35] Moshe also studied all the words in the Torah with variant spellings, some with missing letters and some with supplementary letters, and the information to be derived from these variations in spelling.[36]

According to some opinions, the expanses of the Torah are so infinitely vast that Moshe would not have been able to absorb so much information in a mere forty days. According to others, Moshe learned the general principles during these forty days and only fleshed out his studies after his descent from the mountain.[37]

In the beginning, Hashem taught Moshe the Torah as a rebbi teaches his student. Toward the end of the forty-day period, the relationship changed, and Hashem learned with Moshe as an older *chavrusah* (learning partner) would learn with a young prodigy.[38] During most of this time, Moshe forgot most of what he learned by day when evening fell. It was simply impossible for a human being to retain such a mass of information without forgetting.[39]

Frustrated, Moshe pleaded with Hashem, "I have toiled so hard for forty days, but I have virtually nothing to show for it. Please help me have some benefit from everything I've learned."

In the end, Hashem rewarded Moshe by granting him the basic knowledge of the entire Torah as a gift, like a bride given to the groom at her wedding. According to others, it was like the gift a groom gives his bride on their wedding night. From that point on, Moshe found that any area of the Torah that he learned came easily to him.[40]

---

35. *Yerushalmi Pe'ah* 2:4; *Peskita D'Rav Kahana* p. 40.
36. *Pirkei D'Rav Eliezer* 46.
37. *Shemos Rabbah* 41:6; *Rabbeinu Bachya*.
38. *Shemos Rabbah* 41:6; *Tanchuma Ki Sisa* 16; *Rashi* to *Shemos* 31:18.
   It would take a full forty days for Moshe's learning to be grasped and comprehended (*Rabbeinu Bachya*; see *Pesachim* 72a).
39. *Maharsha* to *Nedarim* 38a.
40. *Maharsha* to *Nedarim* 38a; *Shemos Rabbah* 41:6; *Rashi*; *Lekach Tov* to *Shemos* 31:18; *Tanchuma Yashan Ki Sisa*; *Tosafos Al HaTorah* to *Shemos* 24:18. See *Yerushalmi Horayos* 3:5; *Pnei Moshe*.
   The Torah's use of the word *"vayitein"* (and He gave) is symbolic of his receiving the Torah as a gift, as its root stems from the word *matanah* (gift) (*Yefei To'ar*; *Bereishis Rabbah* 6:5).
   See *Maharsha* and commentaries for their explanation of the differences of opinion between *Rashi* and *Maharsha*. At Mount Sinai Hashem, the groom, presented Himself before the Jewish people, His bride. According to *Rashi*, Moshe is the groom and the

According to another version, Hashem presented the Torah to Moshe on the day of his descent from Heaven. As he started down, he encountered the angel of terror and was frightened so badly that he forgot all the Torah that he had learned. Hashem dispatched Yefifiah, the prince of the Torah, to give Moshe the Torah in a form that would always remain with him. This was the nature of the gift.[41]

One may wonder why Hashem put Moshe through such a grueling forty days when He could have given him the Torah as a gift immediately, as He did in the end anyway. Some suggest that He did so to provide a lesson for the future — that success in learning requires effort and exertion. Only after a person invests tremendous effort in learning Torah — eating and sleeping only the minimum necessary to sustain himself — will Hashem bless him that he will retain what he has learned.[42] Others suggest that Moshe, by his constant and tenacious review, was setting an example for people not to be discouraged if they forget what they learn.[43] Moshe also taught us that, in order to remember what one learns, prayer is required.[44]

Hashem could have given the Torah to Moshe in any number of days that He would have chosen. Why did He choose the specific duration of forty days for this process? Some suggest that it is meant to parallel the early gestation period of a fetus (*yetziras havelad*), which is forty days. During these forty days, Moshe was transformed into a higher being, undergoing a metamorphosis and emerging like a newborn in a form that could live and learn in Heaven and, like an angel, never forget what he learned.[45] The number forty also recalls

---

Torah is the bride. According to the *Maharsha*, the Torah is the gift to the Jews, who continue to play the symbolic role of the bride. In any case, the symbolic reference of the bride is hinted at in the Torah's use of the word *k'chaloso* (when He finished), an allusion to the word *kallah* (bride).

41. *Pesikta Rabbah* 21.
42. *Iyun Yaakov; Nedarim* 38a.
43. See *Pnei Moshe; Yerushlami Horayos* 3:5; *Avodah Zarah* 19a.
44. *Radal; Shemos Rabbah* 41:6.
45. See *Sforno; Rokeach; Abarbanel; Sifsei Kohen; Chomas Anoch Mishpatim*.
    See *Alshich* for his detailed explanation of this subject. See *Menachos* 99b.

Another similarity to a fetus in the mother's womb is that it does not eat in a conventional way. Just as a fetus of forty days sustains itself off the nutrients of the mother, so too Moshe sustained himself, so to speak, off the nutrients of the *Shechinah* (*Abarbanel; Sifsei Kohen*).

From this period onward, Moshe's level of prophecy would reach its highest point, never to need a period of six days of preparation. The *Shechinah* would reveal Itself to Moshe at any time, and any place, without need of readiness on Moshe's part (*Abarbanel*). See last chapter for a different opinion.

the forty *se'ah* measures of the *mikveh*. During these forty days, Moshe was cleansed, purified and transformed into a spiritual being.[46]

The Luchos

Just as a child is first taught on a tablet or blackboard, and only afterward given books, the Torah was also introduced to the Jewish people in the form of *Luchos*, tablets, before they were given the *sefarim* of the Torah.[47]

The *Luchos* that Moshe brought down from the mountain were two separate square blocks of stone[48] six *tefachim* tall, six *tefachim* wide and three *tefachim* deep. According to some opinions, they were six *tefachim* tall, three *tefachim* wide and three *tefachim* deep.[49] Both *Luchos* were exactly identical in size and measurement to signify that the laws pertaining to the relationship between Hashem and His people, which appear on the right side of the *Luchos*, and the laws pertaining to relationships among people, which appear on the left, are of equal importance.[50]

The *Luchos* were created and prepared for inscription at twilight on the sixth day of creation. This required the additional creation of the Hebrew alphabet, including the shapes of the letters and their designated names. Although the Torah had existed long before the creation of the world, its ideas and concepts existed in pure spiritual form without connection to any language or letters.[51]

---

46. *Rokeach*.
There are 960 *lug* in forty *se'ah*. Moshe, over a forty-day period, was in the heavens for 960 hours. See *Malbim* to *Shemos* 31:18 for his view.

47. *Midrash HaGadol* 31:18.

48. *Zohar Shemos* 84a.

49. *Bava Basra* 14a; *Nedarim* 38a; *Tosafos* to *Menachos* 99a; *Yerushalmi Shekalim* 6:1; *Taanis* 4. See *Shemos Rabbah* 47:6; 45:1. See *Gra* to *Shekalim*; *Rabbeinu Bachya* to *Shemos* 32:15.
See *Yalkut Reuveni* who says that the *Luchos* were 108 square cubits.

50. *Shemos Rabbah* 41:6; *Yefei To'ar*.
It was miraculous that the measurements of the *Luchos* were exact (*Maharzav*).
See *Rabbeinu Bachya* who writes that although Hashem's Name is not found on the left side of the *Luchos*, there are twenty-six letters on it representing Hashem's Name.
The numerical value of the word *Luchos* is the same as that of the word *teomim* (twins) — 491 (*Tosafos*).

51. See *Rambam*; *Rashi*; *Rabbeinu Yonah* to *Avos* 5:6; *Rashi* to *Pesachim* 54a; *Zohar Mishpatim* 113a.
Another opinion is that the "pen" that wrote and carved the letters onto the *Luchos* was created at this time.
See *Malbim* for his opinion and interpretation of this *Chazal*.

Just as the manna was spiritual in nature, so were the *Luchos* spiritual in nature. They were made of sapphire stone hewn from the Throne of Glory.[52] Others suggest that the *Luchos* were made of terrestrial materials but that the writing on them was spiritual.[53]

The *Luchos* were originally of solid, impenetrable material, but Hashem blew on them, so to speak, making room for letters to penetrate.[54] The letters that appeared on the *Luchos* were actually those selfsame fiery letters that emanated from the mountaintop when Hashem spoke the Commandments. They alighted on the sapphire stone, white fire on black fire. Hashem outlined the letters with His finger, so to speak, and pressed them into the indentations of the stone.[55] According to some opinions, Hashem actually drew the letters onto the stone, like acid pouring onto metal, then the letters burned through the stone walls of the *Luchos* and emerged on the other side.[56] Others suggest that the letters were not only engraved onto the stone but they also protruded outward.[57]

The choice of sapphire, the hardest of stones, as the material on which the *Luchos* were engraved, was to signify that the Torah cannot be forged or counterfeited. For this reason, they are called the *Luchos HaEidus*, the Tablets of Testimony, because they attest to the integrity of the Torah in that it cannot be reproduced, changed or falsified.[58]

---

52. *Shir Rabbah* 5:14; *Yefei Kol*; *Pirkei D'Rav Eliezer* 46; *Radal*; *Lekach Tov*; *Sifri Beha'aloscha* 101; *Targum Yonasan*; *Rabbeinu Bachya* 31:18.
  In the system of *gematria* known as *a"t ba"sh*, the word *Luchos* is the same as *kisei*, throne (*lamed* is replaced by *chaf*; *ches* by *samech* and *taf* by *aleph*) (*Rabbeinu Bachya*).
53. *Midrash HaGadol* 31:18; *Zohar Shemos* 84a.
  See *Malbim*; the *Luchos* were carved from the brick that lay below Hashem's Throne, which was serving as a reminder of the Jews' enslavement in Egypt.
54. *Zohar Shemos* 84a.
55. See *Shir Rabbah* 1:13; *Maharzav*; *Matnos Kehunah*; *Malbim*. See *Tehillim* 29:7; *Zohar* 84a. See *Yerushlami Shekalim* Ch. 6; *Korban HaEidah*. This opinion would seem to disagree with the opinion stating that the body of the *Luchos* was bright and glaring like the sun.
  Others suggest that the letters were black fire etched over white.
  The fingers represented the number ten, as seen in the plague of lice. It suggests that on it were the Ten Commandments (*Zohar Shemos* 84a).
  See Ch. 17 for a discussion on the making of the Second *Luchos*.
56. See *Ohr HaChaim* 31:18; see *HaKesav VeHaKabbalah* for his opinion.
57. *Alshich* to *Shemos* 32:16.
  Given the total spiritual and heavenly nature of the *Luchos*, they were referred to as the handiwork of Hashem (*Rabbeinu Bachya* to *Shemos* 31:18).
58. *Rokeach* to *Shemos* 24:12.
  Others add that the fact that the *Luchos* were written with the "finger" of Hashem symbolizes that just as Hashem's glory cannot be erased, so too the Torah can never be

The *Luchos* were massive pieces of stone, weighing as much as forty *se'ah* measures of water, the equivalent of 700 pounds. Moshe would not have been able to lift such heavy stones, but the fiery letters miraculously bore the weight of the *Luchos*. When the Jewish people worshiped the Golden Calf, the letters forsook the stone, and Moshe could no longer carry their weight.[59] Since the *Luchos* were carried miraculously, they could just as easily have been made of one double-sized piece of stone instead of two separate stone tablets. They were made of two stones to symbolize heaven and earth, which were created for the sake of Torah. They also symbolize this world and the World to Come, since those who learn Torah in this world will merit the World to Come. Finally, they symbolize bride and groom, since Hashem gave the Torah to the Jewish people as a gift from the Groom to His bride.[60]

Moreover, since the *Luchos* are called *Luchos HaEidus*, the Tablets of Testimony, there should symbolically be two of them, paralleling the requirement for two witnesses.[61]

The Luchos Inscriptions

The Ten Commandments were inscribed on the *Luchos*, the first five on the right one and the second five on the left one. The first set dealt with spiritual issues and represented the Attribute of Mercy while the second dealt with mundane issues and represented the Attribute of Strict Justice.[62]

The letters were etched into the stone and penetrated to the other side. This meant that the center island formed by the two circular letters, the (final) *mem* and the *samech*, having no connection to any

---

erased or tampered with. It will remain in its perfection forever (*Bechor Shor*).

As explained earlier, the word *Luchos* is related to *kisei* (throne). It also has the same numerical value as the word *Anochi* — 81. This is to show that the *Luchos* are a testimony to the authenticity of the *Aseres HaDibros*.

59. *Yerushalmi Taanis* 4:4; see *Shemos Rabbah* 41:5; *Maharzav*; *Tanchuma Ki Sisa* 26.

This opinion plays a role in the discussion as to whether Moshe received the *Luchos* before or after the episode of the Golden Calf.

60. See *Shemos Rabbah* 41:6 and commentaries; *Tanchuma Ki Sisa* 16; *Devarim Rabbah* 3:16.

Some suggest that, in a sense, the *Luchos* brought finality to the wedding process. At Sinai, the Jews were betrothed to Hashem. With the giving of the *Luchos*, they were now, so to speak, married, with the *Luchos* representing a *kesubah* (see *R' Efraim Al HaTorah*).

61. *Midrash HaGadol*; *Lekach Tov*; *Rabbeinu Bachya*; *Abarbanel* to *Shemos* 31:18.

62. *Shir Rabbah* 5:14; *Maharzav*; *Shir Rabbah* 1:2; *Zohar* 82a; *Rabbeinu Bachya*; *Akeidah* to *Shemos* 20:1; *Midrash* in *Torah Shleimah*.

The first set had Hashem's Name in each while the second set did not have Hashem's Name at all.

of the surrounding stone, should have fallen out. Nonetheless, they were miraculously suspended in midair with no visible support.

In a further miracle, the inscriptions could be read from right to left on either side of the *Luchos*. For instance, the word *Anochi* was etched into the stone, going all the way through. From the other side, it also read *Anochi*, even though one would have expected the letters to be backward and in reverse order.[63]

Others suggest that the letters did not penetrate all the way through, but there was a different miracle. On the right side of the *Luchos*, in the very same space where the First Commandment was written, the Sixth Commandment could also be read.[64]

Some suggest that all Ten Commandments were written on each of the *Luchos*,[65] since Hashem had said them twice, once simultaneously and once sequentially.[66] Furthermore, some suggest that all Ten Commandments were written on each face of the *Luchos*, so that they were legible from any of the four directions.[67]

The Fourth Commandment, which commands that Shabbos be kept, appears in two versions in *Parashas Yisro* and *Parashas Va'eschanan*, the difference being that one uses the word *zachor*, remember, while the other uses the word *shamor*, which means safeguard. Hashem said both words simultaneously at Mount Sinai, but

---

63. *Shabbos* 104a; *Rashi*; *Midrash HaGadol*; *Rabbeinu Bachya* to *Shemos* 32:15-16 See *Ibn Ezra*; *Ralbag* to *Shemos* 32:15.
64. See *Zohar Yisro* 84b.
65. *Targum Shir HaShirim* 5:13.
66. *Zeh Yenachmeni*. See *HaKosev* in *Ein Yaakov* to *Shekalim* 6:1.
 Another reason for the necessity of the *Luchos* having the Ten Commandments written twice was that since the latter five *Dibros* did not have Hashem's Name in them, it would have seemed as a defect to the left side of the *Luchos* in relation to the right. By both *Luchos* having all Ten Commandments, they would be looked at as equals (*Yefei Mareh*).
 Others maintain that the Ten Commandments were repeated twice on each tablet. Others suggest that they were written only one time, but could be read on the other side as well, thus totaling twenty times.
67. According to this opinion, it is possible that the Commandments were only written twice but read four times. The ten in the front could be read in the back and the ten in the thickness of the right were miraculously able to be read through the *Luchos* on the left side.
 Others are of the opinion that the words were not engraved through the *Luchos* at all, the *mem* and *samech* were not standing by miracle and that, in fact, the Commandments were written four times. For a thorough understanding of the various opinions, see *Yerushalmi Shekalim* 6:1; *Peirush HaKosev*; *Yefei Mareh*; *Yerushalmi Sotah* 8:3; *Korban HaEidah*; *Shir HaShirim* 5:14; *Shemos Rabbah* 47:6; *Abarbanel*; *Tiferes Yisrael* 35. See *Radvaz* 3:549; *HaKesav VeHaKabbalah* to *Shemos* 32:16. (See *Miluim* 4:2,4 to *Torah Shleimah*, end of *Ki Sisa*, as to what script and language was used for the *Luchos*. See Schottenstein edition of Tractate *Megillah*, 8b note 42.)

what was written on the *Luchos*? According to some opinions, *zachor* was written on both the first and second *Luchos*. Others suggest that the word *zachor* was written on the first *Luchos* and *shamor* on the second *Luchos*. Others suggest that just as they were spoken simultaneously, they were also inscribed and read simultaneously.[68]

The Torah uses the word *charus*, engraved, to describe the inscription on the *Luchos*. This word can also be read as *cheirus*, freedom. The *Luchos* were the liberating force for the Jewish people. Had they not sinned, the *Luchos* would have released them from hunger, sickness, poverty, deprivation, pain, suffering and death. They would have been free forever of the yoke of exile among other nations. They also would never have forgotten any of the Torah they learned.

The angel of death complained to Hashem, "You have given me control of all the people on the face of the earth, but now I see that the Jewish people are beyond my reach. Why is this so?"

"Because they accepted the Torah," Hashem replied. "The spiritual *Luchos* protect them from your earthly forces and from your grim work."[69]

---

68. See *Haamek Davar*; *Pnei Yehoshua* to *Bava Kamma* 55; *Tiferes Yisrael* 35. R' Yaakov Kamenetsky writes that in the Shabbos morning *Amidah* we say, in regard to the *Luchos: vekasuv bahem shemiras Shabbos* (on which is inscribed the keeping of Shabbos). This suggests that *Shamor* — and not *Zachor* — was written on the *Luchos*.

The opinions vary if, in fact, the first *Luchos* represent the first *Dibros* and the second *Luchos* represent the second *Dibros*. Some suggest that Hashem did in fact repeat the Dibros twice, once reflecting what is found in *Yisro* and the other in *Va'eschanan*. Some are of the opinion that Hashem only said the *Dibros* once but that *Zachor/Shamor*, *Shav/Sheker*, *Tachmod/Tisaveh* were all said in one utterance. In order to reflect both utterances, they were separated into two written *Dibros*.

Some suggest that the reason why *Zachor* was written in the first *Luchos* and *Shamor* in the second was based simply on one's ability to honor Shabbos properly. Before the Golden Calf was worshiped, all the Jewish people had to be cognizant to remember Shabbos. Once they remembered it, it was a foregone conclusion that they would honor Shabbos. After the Golden Calf, however, when their status had been significantly lowered, the Jews needed to be warned that they must guard the Shabbos (*Pri Tzaddik Re'eh*).

Others add that once the *mekoshesh* (wood-gatherer) violated the Shabbos, it was necessary to put *Shamor* on the *Luchos*, to remind the Jewish people that one must guard the Shabbos (*Avudraham*).

69. Notwithstanding the difference of opinions as to how many Commandments were written on the *Luchos*, all 613 Mitzvos would be reflected within them. Just as in the sea, there are various amounts of smaller waves contained within the larger ones, so too, numerous mitzvos — divided into ten categories — are contained within the Ten Commandments, reflecting the entire Torah.

Commandment One had in it 80 mitzvos; Commandment Two had 60; Commandment Three, 48; Commandment Four, 75; Commandment Five, 77; Commandment Six, 50; Commandment Seven, 58; Commandment Eight, 59; Commandment Nine, 52; Commandment Ten, 54 — which total 613 (*R' Saadia Gaon*). See *Rashi* to *Shemos* 24:12. See beginning of following chapter for additional details.

But when the Jewish people worshiped the Golden Calf, they forfeited all these privileges and returned to the realm of ordinary human beings.[70]

The *Luchos* were also called *Luchos HaEven*, Tablets of Stone. The Torah and the evil inclination are both known metaphorically as stone. The symbolism of the *Luchos* was that the stone of Torah must be used to overcome the stone of the evil inclination.[71] Also, just as one can walk endlessly on stone without wearing it out, the Torah will never wear out for those who study and review it diligently.[72] Just as stone cannot be affected by *tumah*, ritual defilement, so too does the Torah reject anything or anyone that is defiled.[73] It also symbolizes that the gravest violations of the Torah are punishable by stoning.[74]

Some suggest that the Jewish people were fortunate that Moshe received the Torah before they worshiped the Golden Calf. Had they sinned first, Hashem would never have given the Torah to Moshe.[75] Others suggest that Moshe received the *Luchos* on the morning of 17 Tammuz, the day of his descent. At this point, the Jewish people had already sinned. Nonetheless, Hashem gave Moshe the *Luchos*, so great is His love for the Jewish people.[76]

The word *Luchos* has the numerical value of 438. The names Rochel, Leah, Bilhah and Zilpah also add up to 438. This is to symbolize that these four mothers, who gave birth to the twelve tribes, were the foundation of the Jewish people who would accept the Torah. Others suggest that they represent the Torah since they were married to Yaakov who was the representative of the Torah among the Patriarchs (*Tosafos* to *Shemos* 32:16).

70. See *Shemos Rabbah* 41:7; *Vayikra Rabbah* 18:3; *Maharzav*; *Yefei To'ar*; *Eruvin* 54 with *Rashi*; *Maharsha*; *Tikkunei Zohar* 146; *Zohar Mishpatim* 113a.

See *Iyun Yaakov* who writes that based on the dictum, "Someone who forgets his learning is worthy of death," it would stand to reason that since, at that time, no one would forget their learning, they would not die.

See *Eliyahu Zuta* 4,17; *Avos* 6:2 and commentaries.

71. See *Vayikra Rabbah* 35:5; *Shir Rabbah*; *Yefei Kol* 6:11; *Tosafos* to *Shemos* 24:12.

72. *Eruvin* 54a with *Rashi*; *Shemos Rabbah* 41:6; *Maharzav*.

Since the *Luchos* were actually sapphire, the Torah's use of the word stone is to teach a lesson (*Maharsha*).

73. *Rokeach* to *Shemos* 24:12.

74. *Shemos Rabbah* 41:6.

75. See *Maharzav*; *Rashash*; *Shemos Rabbah* 41:5; *Sifsei Kohen* 31:18.

76. *Chizkuni* to *Shemos* 31:18.

13 The Golden Calf

For nearly a full year, from the time Moshe had first come down to Egypt to bring them forth from bondage, the Jewish people had enjoyed the security and comfort of great leadership and a strong guiding hand. But now, as they awaited Moshe's return from his forty-day encounter with Hashem in Heaven, the people felt insecure and disconnected, alone in the inhospitable desert.

True, Moshe had appointed his brother Aharon and his nephew Chur to serve as interim leaders, but the people considered them a poor substitute for the great Moshe, Hashem's own emissary who would bring them to the Holy Land. So they waited anxiously, their nerves on edge, and counted the days until Moshe's return.

Moshe had given the people a precise timetable for his return. He would be away for forty days and return within the first six hours of the forty-first day. But when did the forty days begin? He had not been clear on that point. Was 7 Sivan, the day of his ascent, the first of the forty days? The people assumed that it was, and therefore, 16 Tammuz would be the forty-first day, the day of his projected return. They fully expected Moshe to return during the first six hours of the day on 16 Tammuz, as he had promised.[1]

But the people were mistaken. Moshe's ascent took place during the day of 7 Sivan. He did not spend the previous night, the beginning of 7 Sivan, in Heaven, and therefore, his first full day in Heaven was actually 8 Sivan. The forty-day period thus began on 8 Sivan, and he was not scheduled to return until the first six hours of the day on 17 Tammuz, the forty-first day after his departure from the encampment for Heaven. In other words, Moshe was not scheduled to return for a full day after the Jewish people expected him to return. The lack of communication between Moshe and the Jewish people on this critical point would lead to disastrous results.[2]

Moshe Does Not Return

On the morning of 16 Tammuz, the people were already buzzing with excitement as they awaited his return momentarily. Their illustrious leader had actually gone up into Heaven itself to bring down the Torah for them, and they stared anxiously at Mount Sinai for early signs of his return. At any moment, he would come down the mountainside, his face aglow after having encountered the Divine Presence for forty days.

The crowds that came out to greet Moshe swelled as the morning wore on. An hour passed, then another, with no sign of Moshe. But there was still no cause for panic. Moshe had said he would

---

1. See *Rashi* to *Shemos* 32:1; *Shabbos* 89a with *Rashi*; *Shemos Rabbah* 41:7.

The forty-day period began during the 7th day of Sivan. Adding an additional 24 days remaining in the month of Sivan, and 16 days of Tammuz, totals 40 days. Moshe came down on the 17th of Tamuz, during the day when the forty full days were completed. The Jews expected Moshe's descent from the mountain on the 16th day of Tammuz. (See *Rashi* to *Taanis* 28b; *Seder Olam* 6; *Rashi* to *Yoma* 4b; *Rashi* to *Shabbos* 89a. See *Tosafos* to *Shabbos* 89a s.v. *Lesof*. See *Maharal* to *Shemos* 32:1 as to his thoughts regarding *Tosafos'* question on *Rashi*.)

Although there are differing opinions as to when Moshe ascended the mountain, it depends on when the Torah was given. For those who suggest that the Torah was given on the 7th, sometime after that period Moshe ascended. According to those who say that the Torah was given on the 6th, he ascended the following day, on the 7th at *alos hashachar* (sunrise). The basic view of Moshe's absence which promoted the creation of the Golden Calf is that the Torah was given on the 6th. See *Chizkuni; Rabbeinu Meyuchas; Tosafos; R' Efraim Al HaTorah* to *Shemos* 24:18; *Rabbeinu Bachya* to *Shemos* 32:1.

2. See *Shabbos* 89a with *Rashi* and *Maharsha; Rashi* and *Be'er Yitzchok* to *Shemos* 32:1.

return within the first six hours of the day. There was still a lot of time remaining.³

The sun rose higher in the eastern sky, and the people grew more anxious by the minute. What could have happened to Moshe? It was not like him to be late, or even to wait until the last minute. Many thousands of fearful eyes followed the trajectory of the sun as it climbed across the last stretch of the eastern sky and reached its peak. It was high noon. The first six hours of the day had passed, and Moshe was nowhere in sight.

The people were at their wits' end, beside themselves with worry and apprehension. They gathered in small groups and spoke to one another in hushed tones.

"Do you have any idea where Moshe could be?" asked one fellow.

"I don't think anyone knows," replied another. "I've heard rumors that he decided to remain in Heaven to serve as Hashem's personal emissary. They say that he's finished with regular people. We'll have to find another leader."

"Nah," said a third. "I heard that he was attacked by the angels of destruction as soon as he passed through the gates of Heaven. That's been known to happen, you know. For all we know, Moshe could be seriously injured. In fact — I'm sorry for saying this — but do we even have any assurances that he is, you know, still alive?"⁴

"Well, I don't know what you all heard," said another man, "but I think Moshe is never coming back. Did you see the fire on that mountain? Something fierce, wasn't it? I don't think Moshe could have made it through that fire without being burned to a crisp."⁵

"I have to disagree," said another man. "I don't think that, after everything we have witnessed, Moshe just burned to death. It's just too ordinary. No, I say that when he stepped into those clouds over Mount Sinai, his soul separated from his body and he became like an angel. I think he decided to remain an angel and not return to human form."⁶

"That a nice theory," said another, "but it's too philosophical for me. I'm a practical person. I go by what I see. Or don't see, if you know what I mean. Did you ever see any manna fall on that mountain? I

---

3. *Shabbos* 89a.
4. *Midrash HaGadol* to *Shemos* 32:1.
5. *Targum Yonasan* to *Shemos* 32:1.
6. *Tzeror HaMor*; *Malbim* to *Shemos* 32:1.

haven't. So that means that Moshe has had nothing to eat for the entire forty days he has been away. You see? I think he starved to death. After all, how can a person live for forty days without any food?"⁷

Satan Makes Trouble

Satan saw an opportunity to exploit this volatile situation to undermine and gain control of the Jewish people. Of all the nations of the world, only the Jewish people were beyond Satan's grasp. And now it appeared that they would forever escape him. As soon as Moshe would come down from the mountain with the *Luchos* and deliver them to the Jewish people, they would gain their freedom from sin, suffering and even death. Satan would be helpless in affecting their destiny. Something had to be done before it was too late. And quickly.

The only solution, Satan decided, was to get the Jewish people to sin and thereby render themselves unworthy of the Torah. Only thus would they once again become vulnerable to Satan's power. In order to accomplish this goal, Satan needed to sow confusion and despair in the Jewish encampment. He had to make them doubt Moshe's assurances that he would return to them. Then Satan would implant sinful urges in their hearts and lead them astray until they succumbed to idolatry.⁸

Satan approached the Jewish people and told them, "It's time to move on. I believe Moshe is never coming back to you. It's time to make plans for a future without Moshe."

"You're wrong," they replied heatedly. "Moshe gave us his word that he was coming back, and we believe him. He always keeps his word."

"Is that really so?" said Satan. "Didn't he give you his word that he would return on the forty-first day during the first six hours of the day?"

"Uh, yes, he did," they replied.

"And haven't those six hours passed without his appearance?"

---

7. *Ibn Ezra; Chizkuni; Abarbanel* to *Shemos* 32:1.
8. *Shabbos* 89a with *Rashi; Alshich* to *Shemos* 32:1.
   Had the *Luchos* not been broken, the Torah would have been retained in the hearts and minds of the Jewish people forever. There was no evil inclination while the *Luchos* remained intact, due to its handiwork and spiritual nature. With the creation of the second *Luchos*, the evil inclination was brought back to life. This is symbolized by these *Luchos* being referred to as the *Luchos* of stone, an allusion to the *yetzer hara* which is compared to stone (*Chupas Eliyahu*).

"Well, technically you're right," the people replied, stubbornly refusing to accept that Moshe would never return. "But that doesn't mean he isn't coming back. Perhaps he is ill or otherwise unavoidably delayed. Don't worry, he'll be back."[9]

Satan realized that he would have to resort to special visual effects to raise the level of doubt among the Jewish people. While Moshe was up in Heaven, his *chomer* and *gashmius*, the material aspects of his being, became dormant, and he became a creature of spirit and soul. Satan capitalized on the dormancy of Moshe's materiality, to conjure up a dark vision of a dead Moshe in the sky. He then directed their attention to this artful illusion.[10]

"Look!" he cried, pointing heavenward. "What is that in the sky?"

"I don't know," said one man. "It's hard to see clearly, what with all the clouds and fog."

"Wait a minute," said another. "I think I see a casket floating in the air."

"Yes, yes," said a third. "I see it, too. And there's a body in it. Wait, can it be? It looks like Moshe. He's lying there as if he were dead."

"I see it now," cried the second man. "Yes, it is quite clear. It is Moshe, and he is absolutely lifeless. I can't believe it! Moshe has passed away. Our great leader is no longer among the living. Heaven help us!"[11]

As the word spread in the encampment, more and more Jews looked up at the sky and saw the insidious vision. The sun was already starting its descent in the western sky. The deadline hour had passed, and Moshe had failed to return. The visual evidence in the sky attested to Moshe's death. The people were in an uproar, stranded in the desert without leadership and guidance. Something had to be done to fill the leadership void, and great crowds gathered around Aharon and the elders demanding a new direction.[12]

---

9. *Shabbos* 89a with *Maharsha* and *Ben Yehoyada*; *HaKesav VeHaKabbalah* to *Shemos* 32:1.
10. *Iyun Yaakov*; *Ben Yehoyada* to *Shabbos* 89a.
11. *Shabbos* 89a with *Maharsha*; See *Tanchuma Yashan Ki Sisa*; *Shemos Rabbah* 41:7.
12. See *Tanchuma Yashan Ki Sisa*; *Shemos Rabbah* 41:7; *Maharzav*; *Tanchuma Beha'aloscha* 14; *Midrash HaGadol* to *Shemos* 32:1.

Mutiny in the Desert

During this time of great crisis, a formerly insignificant element of the Jewish people rose to sudden prominence. When the Jewish people emerged from Egypt, they were accompanied by a mixed multitude of 40,000 converts known as the Erev Rav, among them the famous Egyptian sorcerers Ianus and Iambrus, both sons of the infamous Bilam.[13]

The Erev Rav were a motley group of disgruntled outcasts who did not enjoy full and equal status with the rest of the Jewish people. Having seen the futility of their magic and sorcery in the face of Hashem's power, these Egyptians decided it was more prudent to join the Jewish people than to fight them, and so they asked to be accepted as converts.

While Hashem did not command Moshe to accept the Erev Rav into the Jewish fold, He did give Moshe the latitude to do so, on his own initiative. Moshe accepted the Erev Rav as converts but, considering the circumstances of their conversion, they were excluded from some of the privileges enjoyed by the descendants of Avraham, Yitzchak and Yaakov. They did not live within the protective shield of the cloud pillars. Instead, they lived with the livestock on the outskirts of the encampment, exposed to attack by hostile forces as well as the hot days and cold nights of the desert. They also did not receive a share of the manna along with the rest of the Jewish people. Instead, they got their nourishment from the leftover scraps.

Despite all the restrictions under which they lived, the Erev Rav always felt a strong personal attachment and loyalty to Moshe who had welcomed them into the fold of the Jewish people and treated them with warmth and compassion. The prospect of Moshe never returning, therefore, struck fear in their hearts. Now that their hero and champion was gone, what would happen to them? Would they still be allowed to be part of the Jewish people? Or would they be expelled and sent back to the place from which they had come?[14]

Feelings of frustration and belligerence rippled through the Erev Rav encampment. They wanted to assert themselves, to define and secure their role in the future of the Jewish people, and so they sought a confrontation with Aharon, the de facto leader of the

---

13. *Midrash HaGadol* to *Shemos* 32:1; *Tanchuma Ki Sisa* 19; *Zohar* 191. See *Let My Nation Go* p. 314.
14. *Zohar* 191; *Tikkunei Zohar* 142; *Kli Yakar*; *Sifsei Kohen* to *Shemos* 32:1.

Jewish people for the time being. Joining together with angry disgruntled elements among the Jewish people, they talked and they argued until they finally formed a large crowd and set off toward Aharon and the elders.[15]

"What's going on here, Aharon?" shouted the hotheaded young Nagdor. "What happened to Moshe? How come he hasn't returned?"

"Be patient, young man," Aharon replied in a calm voice. "Give him a little more time. He'll be back."

"You can't fool us so easily," Nagdor shot back. "What do you think we are? Children? You're just playing for time, but we all know perfectly well that he is never coming back. We've seen the proof."[16]

"With all due respect," added the gray-bearded Kumiel, "we need to discuss this new situation very seriously. You have to understand that the people feel abandoned and adrift now that we will no longer have Moshe's guidance. Perhaps, even more important, we have also lost our special connection with Hashem.[17] We will be vulnerable to the perils of life in the desert and to the treacherous attacks of our enemies."[18]

"That's right," said Achiash. "What's going to be with our babies? Who will protect them? Who will lead us?"

"We need leadership," shouted Nagdor. "Someone has got to lead us out of this desert. It doesn't really matter if we go back to Egypt or to the land of Canaan, as long as we get out of this horrible desert."[19]

"This desert will kill us," added Achiash. "We cannot stay here."

Loud shouts from the rest of the crowd seconded these sentiments.

Aharon raised his hands for quiet.

"Look, dear people," he said. "Moshe is only a few hours late. Why are you all panicking? Go back to your tents. Take a nap. Try to relax. Let us deal with the situation. After all, what do you hope to accomplish with this impulsive demonstration?"

---

15. *Bamidbar Rabbah* 15:21; *Zohar* 191a; *Rokeach*; *Toldos Yitzchok*; *Malbim* to *Shemos* 32:1.
16. *Ohr HaChaim* to *Shemos* 32:1.
17. *Toldos Yitzchok*.
  This statement was quite reflective of the foolishness of their arguments. Clearly Moshe's powers were not the source of Hashem's guidance. Hashem was still with the Jews despite Moshe's absence, yet, predisposed to start a revolt, all logic would fall on deaf ears.
18. *Ohr HaChaim* and *Tosafos* to *Shemos* 32:1.
19. *Rokeach*.

Nagdor sprang onto a rock and shook his fist in the air. "I'll tell you what we want," he shouted. "We don't want to take a nap. We don't want to be patient. We want a solution, and we want it now! Some of us have ideas, and we don't want to waste any time in putting them into action."

"What are these ideas of yours, young man?" asked one of the elders.

"We want to make an image," said Nagdor, "a spiritual force to replace Moshe, to be our guide and leader, our mentor, our judge, to maintain our connection with Hashem so that the cloud pillar will continue to accompany and protect us."[20]

"An image?" said Aharon, horrified. "What do you mean by an image? Are you suggesting an idol, Heaven forbid?"

"No, we are not looking to make a god, I tell you," said Nagdor. "Do you think we want to deny Hashem after everything that has taken place?"[21]

"Let me explain," said his friend Peliav. "We are all convinced that Moshe was more than a mortal human being."

"Please don't speak of Moshe in the past tense," said Aharon.

"We're sorry," said Peliav, "but we are convinced that Moshe is now part of the past. We will remember him with awe and fondness, but he has no role in our future. We also do not believe an ordinary human being can replace him. He was an intermediary between Hashem and the human race. Hashem does not want to concern Himself with the picayune daily affairs of people, so he invested Moshe with Divine powers to serve as a demigod in His stead. We need an image, an entity that will also be invested with these Divine powers, an entity that can serve as an intermediate Divine power that leads us on this earth and consults with Hashem from time to time, just as Moshe did when he was our leader."

"This is preposterous," said Aharon. "Moshe is a man like any one of us, and he will soon be back among us. Go home and forget all this foolish nonsense."

"Look, we believe Moshe is never coming back," persisted Peliav. "That is why we have come up with this plan. But I can assure you,

---

20. *Bamidbar Rabbah* 15:21; *Rashi; Mizrachi; Ramban; Chizkuni; Abarbanel; Toldos Yitzchok* to *Shemos* 32:1.
21. *Ramban; Tosafos; Chizkuni; Bechor Shor; Ralbag; Ohr HaChaim* to *Shemos* 32:1; *Yaaros Devash*, *Derush* 8.

Aharon, that if we're wrong — and I sincerely hope we are wrong — and Moshe returns, we will gladly remove this new power we want to construct and give Moshe our allegiance as before. You can count on it!"

Shock and disbelief played across Aharon's face.

"Wait a minute, Aharon," shouted Achiash. "Don't be so upset. We're just concerned about the safety of the people, about who will protect our helpless babies. Be open minded about this. This plan can work. The *Shechinah* will rest on this entity that we will construct, and you, Aharon, a man who is skilled in performing miracles, will work together with this entity in a partnership of sorts, to provide leadership and guidance for the people, just as you collaborated with Moshe. What do think? Isn't this a good idea?"[22]

Peliav shook his head. "I'm sorry, Aharon, but I have to disagree with my good friend Achiash here. We've had enough with mortal men as our leaders. Look where it got us with Moshe. As soon as he went up to Heaven on our behalf, that was the end of him. No, we cannot rely on the leadership of frail human beings. We need an immortal power, an omnipotent entity that can lead us through fire and water without a second thought. We love you, Aharon, but we do not foresee a serious leadership role for you or for any other human being. With Hashem reserving His attention to the realm of Heaven and leaving us here to our own devices, we need a superhuman force to lead us to safety and protect us forever." Peliav turned to the crowd. "Do you all agree?"[23]

There were nervous murmurs of assent that grew rapidly into loud shouts of endorsement.

"My friends!" shouted Nagdor, waving his arms to quell the roar of the crowd. "I'm glad to see that we are all in agreement. I want to make a proposal. This image, in my opinion, should evoke the merit of the Jewish people in the eyes of Hashem. That is why I think we should make an image of a ram, to remind Hashem of the *Akeidah*, when Avraham was prepared to slaughter his own son in order to fulfill the will of Hashem.[24] What do you say about a ram? A good

---

22. See *Chizkuni* and *Rokeach* to *Shemos* 32:1; *Maharsha* to *Sanhedrin* 63a; *Yaaros Devash*, *Derush* 8. See *Abarbanel* for his view.

23. *Alshich*; *Abarbanel* to *Shemos* 32:1,5.

24. *Tosafos* to *Shemos* 32:1. See *Tanchuma* 26 that an ox was chosen because it represented one of the four animals of the *Merkavah*, the "Divine Chariot."

idea, isn't it? Maybe a young ram, a calf, and I think it should be made of pure gold."

The tall, dark-skinned Toltep, still dressed in his colorful Egyptian garb, stepped forward. "Wait a minute," he said. "Not so fast. I want to say something. I'm speaking not only in my own name but also in the name of my friends Dernak and Bubmose and all the other members of the Erev Rav. Hear me out!"

The crowd fell silent and waited expectantly.

"We of the Erev Rav," said Toltep, "have joined the Jewish people, but we have been treated as second-class citizens. How do you think this makes us feel? We want to be part of the people, to share in the benefits of all the miracles that are taking place and, I have to tell you, we are sick and tired of being excluded. No more discrimination! It is unfortunate that we have to raise this issue at such a tragic time, when we are mourning the demise of our great and beloved leader Moshe, but changes are going to take place as a result of this tragedy. We want to make sure that these changes correct the injustices of the past. We want equality! We want liberty! We want full citizenship in the Jewish people!"

"Why bring this up now, Toltep?" asked the gray-bearded Kumiel. "Why don't you wait until the issues of leadership are resolved and present your demands to the new leaders?"

"That is exactly my point," said Toltep. "You are all trying to figure out what kind of an image to make to serve as the new leader of the people. I have the best proposal. I say that we appoint this new entity as our god and that we worship it and sing its praises together as equals, as we did back when we were together in Egypt."[25]

"Toltep has given us a great idea," added his friend Bubmose, "but I think we should go a bit further, if you know what I mean. If we're going to make a special god for ourselves to lead us in the future, why should we be restricted to one god? After all, there are so many things that need attention. Why burden one god with the whole thing? Let's make a whole set of gods. Besides, we need gods for all tastes. Some of us may hit it off with one god, but others may form

---

25. *Pirkei D'Rav Eliezer* 45; *Zohar* 191a; *Toldos Yitzchok* to *Shemos* 32:1.

One must be cognizant of the fact that this is only forty days since the Jews received the Torah, forty days since the Jews accepted the yoke of recognizing Hashem as the true and only G-d.

See *Malbim* for his view.

better relationships with another god. Like my friend Toltep, I'm in favor of life, liberty and equality. But I'm also in favor of choice. We need choices, my friends. One flavor can't satisfy everyone."[26]

Aharon raised his hands for quiet. He looked around at the angry and sullen faces in the crowd, and a shiver ran down his spine. He took a deep breath and spoke. "My friends, my dear people, I think it is critical that we all calm down. Try to overcome your fear. If we're not careful, mass hysteria will spread among the people, and that would be dangerous. Don't you all agree? Look at what's happening. Moshe is a few hours late, and already the discussion is veering into setting up idols to worship. Don't you find this shocking? I do. But I understand your anxiety. I know how much you all love and admire my brother Moshe and how his absence has made you all so nervous. As for the Erev Rav, I understand how you feel, and I think it's a good thing that we should talk about it and air our grievances. But we cannot be irresponsible. We have to do this thing right."

Aharon paused. The crowd remained silent, hanging on his every word.

"My dear people," Aharon continued, "I want to offer you a compromise. Are you willing to listen?"

The people nodded and grumbled a grudging assent.

"Look," said Aharon, "I personally am convinced that you all miscalculated in your count and that Moshe will soon return to us. For your part, you all agree that if he does return, you will forget all these wild ideas about images and entities and resume your allegiance to him. So I suggest a moratorium. We wait one day. Let's all of us get together here again tomorrow at this time and assess the situation. If Moshe is back, our problems will be solved. Then we can use this assembly to discuss the status of the Erev Rav. If Moshe is not back, Heaven forbid, then the elders and I will seriously engage in a dialogue about the future leadership of the Jewish people. So go home to your tents, and let's wait until tomorrow."[27]

Instead of listening to the voice of reason, however, the crowd responded with anger and resentment.

---

26. See *Sanhedrin* 63a with *Rashi*.
   In fact, as will soon be seen, several sources suggest that thirteen golden calves were created.
27. *Zohar* 191a; *Bamidbar Rabbah* 15:21; *Pane'ach Raza* 32:1.

"What do think we are, silly children?" shouted Nagdor. "You think you can just pacify us with clever words?"

"That's right," shouted Peliav. "We want to deal with it now, not tomorrow, not later, but right now."

The crowd took up the chant. "Right now! Right now! Right now!"

"The same goes for us in the Erev Rav," declared Toltep. "Enough with the stalling. Tomorrow, tomorrow, always tomorrow. Don't tell us that we'll talk about our issues in the future. The future is now!"

One of the elders, a feeble old man with a sparse white beard, stood up and shook his fist at the crowd. "Shame on you," he declared in a tremulous voice. "Shame on all of you, you rebellious rabble. How can you present such blasphemy after all the miracles Hashem has performed for you? How can you just turn your backs on everything Moshe and Aharon have always stood for and suggest that we set up a golden ram or calf or whatever? It is nothing less than scandalous!"

Moshe's nephew Chur stepped forward. "With the permission of my esteemed uncle Aharon and with the permission of the elders, I would like to speak my mind to this crowd. I think you are all a pack of hysterical fools. You are being ridiculous. First of all, my uncle Moshe promised he would return, and Moshe always keeps his word. Always! Where is your faith and trust in our leader? But let's even assume for a moment that you're right and that Moshe is not returning, perish the thought. So is that the end of the glorious story of the Jewish people? Moshe is just a man, a great man, the greatest man, but still just a man. Don't you think Hashem can perform miracles for us without Moshe? Don't you think He can send us the cloud pillars to shield us and guide us through the desert without Moshe? The Almighty is our leader, but you are rejecting Him by your despicable and repulsive proposals. You are mocking everything Moshe stood for, and you are blaspheming Hashem. You disgust me!"

The crowd responded with outrage. Many of the people in the crowd had served as generals and advisers in Pharaoh's court and in other positions of prestige and responsibility. How dare this young fellow castigate them in such harsh terms?

"Boo!" they shouted. "Boo! Boo!"

"Who gave him permission to talk to us?"

"Who does he think he is, that he can insult us?"
"Get him out of there!"
"Get rid of him!"

Suddenly, a rock flew through the air and struck Chur on the forehead. The young man reeled back as blood flowed down to his eyes. In an instant, the air was filled with a fusillade of rocks and stones hurled by the crowd with great force, at the helpless Chur. Many of the missiles found their mark. Chur tried to head for safety, but the barrage overwhelmed him. He fell to the ground bleeding from numerous wounds, his body a mass of bruises and broken bones, his life ebbing away in the dust of the desert. Many of the elders also fell wounded during the barrage.[28]

The crowd now turned its attention to Aharon.
"So what's it going to be, Aharon?"
"Are you with us or against us, Aharon?"
"Make your choice, Aharon!"
"Join us or die, Aharon!"
"We have plenty of stones for you, too!"
"Take a good look at your nephew Chur, Aharon. We mean business!"
"Have we made ourselves clear?"[29]

Aharon's Solution

Aharon's gaze moved from the frenzied mob that confronted him to the bloody corpse of his nephew Chur and back to the mob. The specter of death stared him in the face and sparked fear in his heart.[30]

---

28. *Tanchuma Ki Sisa* 19; *Eitz Yosef* 14 to *Beha'aloscha*; *Bamidbar Rabbah* 15:21; *Pirkei D'Rav Eliezer* 45; *Midrash HaGadol*; *Malbim*. Others add that the elders too were killed along with Chur (*Rashash Vayikra Rabbah* 10:3).

Although Chur was justified in protecting Hashem's and Moshe's honor, he did so using strong, and what they deemed as abusive, language toward them (*Radal*). See *Yalkut* 393 which suggests that the elders were not killed.

29. *Bamidbar Rabbah* 15:21; *Midrash HaGadol*; *Sanhedrin* 7a with *Maharsha*. See *Yedei Moshe*; *Shemos Rabbah* 41:7 as to Aharon's feelings on this matter.

Although there is no direct reference to Chur's death, all authorities believe that he was killed in this revolt since he is not mentioned throughout the remaining portion of the Torah. This is seemingly strange, since Chur is mentioned in *Shemos* 24:14 as standing alongside Aharon for any civil questions or disputes which needed to be resolved. He is not mentioned anywhere after that. Based on this, the authorities deduce that Chur was killed (see *Maharsha*). *Ohr HaChaim* suggests that it was purposely left out of the Torah due to the shame caused by the Jews killing one of their own.

30. *Pane'ach Raza*; *Abarbanel*; *Alshich* to *Shemos* 32:1.

Maintaining his composure, Aharon quickly analyzed the situation and explored his options. What could he do? Should he stand against them and risk being killed, as was Chur? On the surface, that appeared to be the heroic position, but it was flawed. If the people were to kill their Kohen (High Priest), their sin would never be forgiven. Better that they build their idols and images and repent when the time would come. At least then they could gain atonement, especially since most of them claimed they weren't seeking to make a god, but a supernatural intermediary with Hashem. The crime of killing the Kohen of the Jewish people, however, was inexcusable and forever unforgivable.[31]

Clearly, Aharon believed, he was left with no other option but to accede to their demands, to stipulate that Moshe might not return and grapple with the problems of finding a replacement. Perhaps he should try to persuade them to accept one of the prominent Jewish leaders as a replacement for Moshe.[32] Ah, but which one? He could recommend that they consider either Nachshon or Kalev of the tribe of Yehudah, both illustrious and highly respected. But that would create problems when Moshe returned. Moshe would surely not step aside from his Divinely appointed position as leader of the Jewish people in favor of these men. Many of the people, however, might give their loyalty to them over Moshe. The result would be a terrible power struggle in which many people would probably die. No, this was not an option.

Perhaps then, thought Aharon, he himself should accept the mantle of leadership on his shoulders, but this too could lead to disastrous results when Moshe returned. He would see Aharon serving as leader and instantly assume that Aharon had usurped his position in his absence. He would suspect that Aharon's enthusiastic acceptance of his younger brother as leader had all been a charade, and that underneath he had always harbored deep feelings of jealousy and resentment. The seeds of suspicion, once planted, would never be fully uprooted, and the relationship between the two brothers would be forever poisoned. No, this too was not an option.[33]

---

31. *HaKesav VeHaKabbalah*; *Keser Shem Tov* to *Shemos* 32:1. See *Sanhedrin* 7a; *Rabbeinu Bachya*; see *Eichah* 2:20. As it was, the Jews would kill the prophet Zechariah, which would eventually be the cause of the destruction of the Temple (*Rashi*).

32. See *Ramban* to *Shemos* 32:1; *Rashi* to *Shemos* 32:5; *Sanhedrin* 63a with *Maharsha*; see *HaKesav VeHaKabbalah* for his reasoning as to why this would be permissible under these conditions.

33. *Daas Zekeinim*; *Chizkuni* to *Shemos* 32:3.

Reluctantly, Aharon reached the conclusion that he had no choice but to go along with the wishes of the mob, at least superficially. If he refused, they would kill him and build the idol immediately. If he consented, however, he would exercise a certain amount of control. He could stall and delay until Moshe returned and the whole issue would become moot. Yes, that was clearly the best option.[34]

The next step for Aharon was to formulate a plan. First, he would demand that the image be made of gold, the most precious of metals. He would endorse the idea of a calf instead of a sheep, because gold was needed to represent a calf, while a sheep could be represented with silver.[35] They would need a lot of gold to produce a solid gold calf, and that should give them a little pause. For the Jewish people themselves, the requirement to use gold did not present such an obstacle, since they had emerged from Egypt laden with gold beyond their wildest dreams. Rather, the requirement to use gold was directed specifically at the Erev Rav, for whom gold was quite a precious commodity.

Unlike the Jewish people who had slaved in bondage and therefore earned the compensation upon their exodus, the Erev Rav were recent converts who had never suffered enslavement. They did not receive all the gifts of gold and jewelry from their former Egyptian friends and neighbors when they left Egypt; they did not carry with them great stores of gold.[36]

Yes, Aharon decided, he would put a great emphasis on the accumulation of a large amount of pure gold before construction would begin. He would also add another wrinkle that would make the collection problematic. He would demand that the source of the gold be jewelry, and not just any jewelry but golden earrings specifically. The Egyptians had adopted the custom of the Arab descendants of Ishmael of wearing golden earrings. The Erev Rav placed great store in this custom and were very attached to the ornaments that dangled from their earlobes, without which they would feel naked.[37]

Furthermore, the earrings of the Erev Rav usually featured etchings of Egyptian gods. Although they had nominally abandoned these gods and embraced the Torah, the Erev Rav were reluctant to part

---

34. *Tanchuma; Rabbeinu Bachya; Abarbanel; Alshich* to *Shemos* 32:2.
35. See *Rokeach; Abarbanel* to *Shemos* 32:3 See *Ramban.*
36. *Zohar* 192; *R' Efraim Baal HaTosafos; Sifsei Kohen.*
37. *Pirkei D'Rav Eliezer* 45; *Radal; Sifsei Kohen.*

with their heirloom jewelry. By melting these earrings down for the construction of the calf, reasoned Aharon, these idolatrous images would finally be eradicated. It would be a nice bonus to the plan.[38]

The plan still needed a deft final touch, some element that would ensure delay and disruption, that would consume enough time to allow Moshe to return before any serious damage was done.

Aharon knitted his brows and thought hard. The answer came to him in a flash. The golden earrings would have to be special earrings. He would explain to the people that the earrings would have to be taken from the women and the children in order for the construction to be effective. That should present a fine obstacle. The women and children would not be so eager to relinquish their precious golden ornaments for some golden idol. They would scream and fight and cause uproarious mutinies in their homes. The domestic battle would drag on for a long time and, by the time the earrings were finally extracted and amassed, Moshe would be back.[39]

One more wrinkle. Aharon would demand that the owners deliver the golden earrings to him, themselves. They could not be brought to him by a few common messengers. The long lines of personal contributors would add more delay to the process, if any were needed. All these requirements would cause unavoidable delay, especially because the Jewish people and the Erev Rav would not find it easy to coordinate their efforts, even though they had made common cause in their desire to construct an image. In the end, Moshe would return, and all the people would return sheepishly to their tents. This entire ugly incident would pass as a bad memory, with the only lasting damage being the tragic death of the young Chur.[40]

Aharon was ready to address the people.

"My dear people, listen closely," said Aharon. "You want to make an image that will serve as your leader? I'm prepared to work with you. If you want this image to be effective, you will have to follow certain esoteric guidelines. Otherwise, you'll just be wasting your time and mine, and we'll all be worse off than before we started. The instructions are as follows. They are fairly simple, but you have to

---

38. *Maasei Hashem; Meam Loez.*
   See *Malbim* who writes that Aharon wanted to convince the people that, in order to create a guide and leader from this gold, it would be necessary for something precious and sentimental to be used, as opposed to something distant and detached.
39. *Rashi* to *Shemos* 32:2-3; *Pirkei D'Rav Eliezer* 45.
40. *Ohr HaChaim* to *Shemos* 32:2.

adhere to them closely. If you break the rules, the plan will fail, I assure you.

"Now, here's the plan. We will make a calf out of pure gold. The gold must come from the earrings of your wives and children. Insist that they give them to you. If they resist, take them by force. Each of you must bring the gold to me by himself. Do not, I repeat, do not, send it to me by messenger or through anyone else. When we have all the gold, we will begin."[41]

Aharon was also sending them a subtle message with these instructions. Removing the earrings symbolized removing the golden value of Torah from their lives. The ornaments of the ears with which they promised "to listen" would now be used to commit the greatest crime in Jewish history.[42] The earrings also symbolized idol worship because of the images engraved on them, as if to say that they were slipping back into idol worship, as they had done in Egypt.[43] Aharon hoped that the message would get through to those who were still somewhat open-minded and, perhaps, it might even have a subconscious effect on the others as well.

Following Aharon's instructions, the mob dispersed. Most of the people headed back to their tents to collect the golden earrings for the construction. Only the tribe of Levi refused to take any part in the proceedings.[44]

Within a short time, a cacophony of screams and shouts spread over the encampment. As Aharon had expected, the men were finding the task of removing the ornaments from their wives and children exceedingly difficult. The women were horrified at the plan to construct an idol, and they certainly had no intention of surrendering their jewelry to facilitate its construction.[45]

Achiash, who was always so vocal about his concern for his children, came home to find his wife Beruchah preparing dinner. He told her about the confrontation with Aharon and the elders and the plan that had resulted.

---

41. See *Ohr HaChaim; Alshich.*

By suggesting the use of force, Aharon was convinced that it would raise the level of hostilities in the home, which would slow the process down and add to further delay. This would be far better than politely and gently requesting that they offer the earrings.

42. *Midrash HaGadol; Zohar; Sifsei Kohen; Malbim; Chasam Sofer* to *Shemos* 32:2.
43. See *Sechel Tov* to *Shemos* 12:35; *Rokeach* to *Shemos* 32:3.
44. *Lekach Tov* to *Shemos* 32:3.
45. *Pirkei D'Rav Eliezer* 45; *Radal; Zohar* 192; *Tanchuma Yashan Pinchas.*

"So you see, Beruchah," he concluded, "I need you to give me your golden earrings."

"You must be joking, Achiash," she said and laughed.

"I'm perfectly serious, Beruchah. I need those earrings."

"If you're not joking, then you must be out of your mind. After all the wonderful miracles Hashem performed for us — taking us out of Egypt, splitting the sea, the revelation at Mount Sinai just a few weeks ago — after all of that you propose to build a silly, lifeless pagan god? What kind of a man are you? Where is your loyalty and gratitude?"[46]

"Just give me the earrings, Beruchah. Now is not the time for talking."

"Well, it's also not the time for taking. No way will I give you my precious jewelry so that you can run off and make golden animals from them. You want me to take the earrings off the ears that heard the commandment 'You shall not make gods of others before Me' and give them to you to help you make an idol? You can stand on your head, Achiash, but I will not give you my jewelry."[47]

"Don't be difficult, Beruchah. Your jewelry is not so important. In a little while, I'll get you new jewelry, much nicer jewelry than you have now. Just give me the earrings."

"You think I'm refusing because I'm so attached to the jewelry? You should know me better than that, Achiash. If you told me that you needed the earrings to marry off an orphan girl, do you think I would hesitate for a moment? Do you?"

Achiash was silent.

"Tell me!" she said. "Do you think I am refusing because I love my jewelry so much? Or perhaps it is because I want no part of this silliness that you and your friends have cooked up? It's disgusting! Maybe, I think it is important to be faithful to Hashem. Did that ever occur to you?"

In the future, Beruchah and all the thousands of women like her would show their faith and sincerity. When they were asked to donate their jewelry for the construction of the Mishkan, to build a domicile for the *Shechinah* among the Jewish people, they brought it quickly and gladly. In that way, they proved that their earlier resistance had been out of courage and valor, rather than an overly strong attachment to their jewelry. As a reward, the minor festival of Rosh

---

46. *Pirkei D'Rav Eliezer* 45; *Radal*; *Midrash Tanchuma Ki Sisa* 19; *Bamidbar Rabbah* 21:10.
47. *Chasam Sofer* 32:2.

Chodesh (the new moon) was dedicated in honor of the women, and the custom was instituted that women for all future generations did not work on Rosh Chodesh.[48] The women of that generation were also rewarded with the privilege of entering Eretz Yisrael. Although Hashem ordained that the men of that generation were to die in the desert and only their children would enter the land, the women were exempt from this decree.[49]

In the meantime, Achiash would not be deterred. "Listen, Beruchah," he said. "Stop with the questions, the accusations and the insults. I don't have any time for them right now. Just hand over the earrings, and everything will be fine. Don't get yourself too excited, or you'll burn the dinner. Just give me the earrings."

"I absolutely will not," she said and turned back to the pot on the fire.

Achiash turned red in the face. He saw he would get nowhere with her by arguing. It was time for action. He also reached into the cradle and took the earrings from his baby daughter. Then he walked up behind his wife stealthily, snatched the earrings from her ears and turned to go.

"Give those back to me, you thief," Beruchah screamed at him. But he was already out the door.[50]

Achiash soon discovered that the others had all had similar experiences. Some had torn the earrings forcibly from their wives and children; some of the earrings even had scraps of skin and blood on them. Others had given up on their families and substituted their own earrings.[51]

The people all ran to bring the gold to Aharon, who was not expecting them back so soon. Because of their zeal and enthusiasm, they had accomplished their new task in record time. The sheer volume of the gold they had collected, a veritable mountain of thousands and thousands of golden earrings, also overwhelmed Aharon. All in all, they had collected 125 talents of gold, and more was still being brought in.

---

48. *Pirkei D'Rav Eliezer* 45; *Radal*; see *Orach Chaim* 417.
49. *Midrash HaGadol* to *Shemos* 32:3.
   Others suggest that due to the fact that the men did not stand up to the Erev Rav but, in fact, the women stood up to their spouses, they merited the ability to have an assertive role in the household (*Yalkut Reuveni Ki Sisa* in the name of the *Arizal*).
50. *Lekach Tov; Rokeach; Minchah Belulah* to *Shemos* 32:3.
51. *Zohar; Pirkei D'Rav Eliezer* 45; *Midrash Tanchuma* 19; *Rashi; Midrash HaGadol; Abarbanel* to *Shemos* 32:3.

"Enough!" cried Aharon, shocked and angry. "Don't bring any more. We have everything we need."[52]

Dark visions of the future loomed before Aharon's tear-filled eyes. It was obvious that virtually the entire people, except for the tribe of Levi and the princes of the tribes, had participated in this collection drive. Even those among the tribes that had not participated were also guilty of not having tried to persuade their friends, relatives and neighbors to desist; they should have protested.[53] Only the tribe of Levi was blameless, and they would be rewarded by being appointed to perform the service in the Mishkan and the *Beis HaMikdash*. The princes would be rewarded with a measure of Divine inspiration.[54] But what about all the people who had sinned? How would the people ever gain atonement for such a terrible sin?

The Construction of the Calf

Once again, Aharon set out to delay the progress of the construction. The frenzied speed with which the gold had been accumulated had caught him by surprise, and he had to act quickly to slow down the momentum.

He began with a prayer to Hashem. "I raise my eyes to You, the One that dwells in the heavens. O L-rd, You know my thoughts and motivations. You know I am only involved in this in order to stall for time until Moshe returns. Help me. Please help me."[55]

He then turned to the people and declared, "All right. We have to do this very carefully now. All of you bring me your gold, one by one. Then we will begin to process it."

He took each donation, used an engraving stylus to mark it with the image of a calf and slowly and carefully wrapped it in a cloth. The people looked on appreciatively, convinced that Aharon was being so careful and meticulous for the ultimate good of the project.

---

52. *Shemos Rabbah* 51:8, 42:8; *Zohar* 192. See *Rashi* to *Shemos* 32:4.
53. *Lekach Tov* to *Shemos* 32:3; *Ramban* to *Shemos* 32:7; *Zohar*; *Ohr HaChaim* to *Shemos* 32:4; *Sforno* to *Shemos* 32:25; *Matnos Kehunah*; *Bamidbar Rabbah* 9:54.
  See *Maharal Diskin* who writes that they did not protest because each person thought he was alone in his indifference toward the Golden Calf and did not feel that he could go up against an entire nation.
54. *Pirkei D'Rav Eliezer* 45; *Radal*; *Bamidbar Rabbah* 4:6,8.
55. *Tanchuma Ki Sisa* 19; *Eitz Yosef*; see *Tehillim* 123:1.

They did not realize that he was merely stalling for time. Once all the gold was marked and wrapped, he was ready to smelt the gold by throwing it all into the fire.[56]

There are a number of other versions about what Aharon's intentions really were, and what eventually transpired.

Others suggest that Aharon intended the golden image to be of Cherubim, as was etched into the Throne of Glory and would one day straddle the Holy Ark in the Mishkan. He wanted that this golden image, if it became a reality, should at least mirror a connection to Hashem. In the end, however, the sorcerers prevailed and made it into a Golden Calf.[57]

Others suggest that Aharon actually molded the Golden Calf with his own hands. He took all the gold donated by the people and piled it into a large shapeless mass. Then he slowly molded and shaped it into a calf and prepared to smelt the figure into a permanent shape in the furnace.[58] According to others, the gold was first melted and then shaped.[59] In the heavens, the stone tablets were being carved into the *Luchos*, and on earth a pile of gold was being molded into a golden idol.[60]

According to another version, the Golden Calf came about because of an evil Jewish man named Michah. During the worst days of the Jewish bondage in Egypt, Pharaoh used to take Jewish babies, put them into the walls of buildings under construction, and plaster over them. Moshe was horrified by this practice and asked Hashem why He allowed it to continue. Hashem reassured him that these children were destined to become evil people, and that their demise was no great loss for the world or for themselves. To prove

---

56. *Yerushalmi Shabbos* 6:4; *Chizkuni; Rashi; Rashbam; HaKesav VeHaKabbalah; Ralbag; Daas Zekeinim; Bechor Shor* to *Shemos* 32:4; see *Maharzav* in *Shemos Rabbah* 41:1; see *Bava Basra* 99.

57. *Malbim* to *Shemos* 32:4.

58. See *Rashi; Targum Yonasan; Lekach Tov; R' Saadiah Gaon; Ibn Ezra; Rashbam; Akeidah; Abarbanel* to *Shemos* 32:4.

  This may have been some type of wax or earthenware mold that could be formed into any shape of choice.

59. *Ralbag* to *Shemos* 32:4.

  The word *"cheret"* means a cloth or mold, and is a reference to *"charatah,"* regret. Aharon tried to stall for time so that the Jews would regret what they were doing (*Sifsei Kohen*).

  See *Akeidah* and *Abarbanel* for additional reasons as to why the image of a calf had to be formed.

60. *Shemos Rabbah* 41:1.

His point, Hashem allowed Moshe to rescue one of these babies, before the wall was sealed over him. The baby was given the name Michah, because he had been "crushed" inside the wall.

Years later, when the Jewish people prepared to leave Egypt, Moshe went off to fulfill a longstanding promise to Yosef. The Jewish people had taken an oath that, when they would leave Egypt, they would take Yosef's body with them and bury him in Eretz Yisrael. During all the years of bondage, Yosef's coffin had lain submerged in the Nile River. Now Moshe came to raise up the coffin and transport it to Eretz Yisrael.

In his blessings to his children, Yaakov had compared Yosef to a *shor*, an ox. Moshe now used this metaphor to exhume Yosef's coffin from the river. He took a gold plate and inscribed on it the Name of Hashem and also the words, "*Alei, Shor*," which means, "Arise, O Ox." He held this plate over the water, and the coffin miraculously rose to the surface.

Michah was watching as all this happened. When he had the opportunity, he stole the gold plate. Now, when the golden earrings of the Jewish people were being thrown into the furnace, Michah tossed in the supernatural golden plate on which the words "Arise, O Ox," were written, and indeed, a Golden Calf emerged.[61]

In a slight variation of this account, some suggest that Moshe produced four golden plates, each of which had engraved upon it one of the four images that adorn the Throne of Glory — a lion, a man, an eagle and an ox. Moshe used the golden plate with the lion-image to roil up the waters of the river, until they were roaring like a lion. Then he used the golden plate with the man-image to gather together Yosef's submerged bones into one unified body. Then he used the golden plate with the eagle-image to levitate the coffin from the riverbed and bring it to the surface. Having successfully recovered Yosef's coffin, there was no longer any need for the fourth golden plate, the one with the bull-image, so Moshe stored it away along with the coffin. Michah stole this plate and used it to create the Golden Calf.[62]

According to another version, the two Egyptian sorcerers, Ianus and Iambrus, who had joined the Jewish people as part of the Erev

---

61. *Rashi; Midrash HaGadol* to *Shemos* 32:4; *Tanchuma Ki Sisa* 19; *Yalkut Reuveni; Pirkei D'Rav Eliezer* 45. See *Let My Nation Go* pp. 165, 308-309.
62. See *Midrash Shir HaShirim* 13a-13b.

Rav, had important roles in the creation of the Golden Calf. The most effective time of day for their sorcery was between the hours of 1 and 3 in the afternoon.

At precisely 1 o'clock, one of them shouted to the other, "The hour of sorcery has arrived. Let us begin. Let us say our incantations."

One of them took two-thirds of the gold and mumbled his incantations, while the other took the other third and said his incantations. Then they held the gold carefully, making sure that it did not fall to the ground and invalidate the incantations, and placed it into the hands of the unsuspecting Aharon, who tossed it into the fire.[63] A Golden Calf emerged. In fact, according to one version, thirteen golden calves emerged, one for each of the tribes and one in "honor" of Aharon, representing the nation as a whole.[64] According to yet another version, the image that emerged was part calf, part donkey; the donkey being symbolic of the gentile roots of the Erev Rav.[65]

According to another version, the inspiration for the idea of a Golden Calf originated in the time of an Egyptian pharaoh named Apis. At about when Yaakov was 92 years old, this Apis, an accomplished sorcerer, declared himself a god. He made a golden calf, and, every morning at 10 o'clock, he would have the calf emerge from the river and fly through the air, as the people sang its praises. According to others, this event took place only once a year, a festival celebrated as the Day of Apis. These events became part of the Egyptian lore, deeply impressed upon the consciousness of the Erev Rav. When the opportunity presented itself, they decided to make a calf that recalled the legend of Apis.[66]

Be all this as it may, the result of the episode was that a golden entity representing a 3-year-old calf emerged from the flames.[67] All of Aharon's efforts to forestall its creation had proved fruitless. The sorcerers had been victorious in their struggle to create the idol.

Satan insinuated himself into the molten body of the golden calf. He moved its legs as if it were galloping across a field, and he

---

63. *Zohar*.
64. See *Yerushalmi Sanhedrin* 10:2; *Yefei Mareh*; *Vayikra Rabbah* 5:3; *Sanhedrin* 63a; *Sifri Eikev* 43; *Yalkut Reuveni Ki Sisa*.
   Symbolic of this opinion are the thirteen letters in the words וַיַּעֲשֵׂהוּ עֵגֶל מַסֵּכָה (*Tosafos*).
65. *Yalkut Reuveni Ki Sisa*.
66. *Yalkut Reuveni Ki Sisa*.
67. See *Miluim* to *Torah Shleimah Ki Sisa* number 13, based on *Tehillim* 106:19-20.

bellowed, as an angry ox would bellow. The effect was totally realistic. The Golden Calf seemed alive. It seemed as if the new leader of the Jewish people had arrived.[68]

"These are your gods, O Israel," the Erev Rav declared gleefully, "the ones that brought you forth from Egypt. These are the gods to which you shall pray, if you want your prayers answered.[69] These gods will partner with Aharon to provide the leadership for the Jewish people in the future."[70]

At this moment, the Erev Rav transgressed the First Commandment. They declared the Golden Calf a god, and they gave it credit for taking the Jewish people out of Egypt, contradicting Hashem's assertion that He had done so.[71]

The angels in Heaven rose up in fury and abhorrence. "Look how quickly they have forgotten that Hashem saved them from the Egyptians. Look how quickly they have forgotten all the miracles and wonders He has performed for them. These people were on the verge of becoming like the angels, free from the yoke of death, but now they will all die for their sins like ordinary mortals."[72]

In a last desperate attempt to put an end to the madness of the Golden Calf, Aharon began to mock and ridicule the molten calf, and he hammered at its legs. He wanted to show the people that it was only a piece of metal that would break if he hammered at it. "If this thing is indeed a god," he jeered, "it will save itself from my assault." Much to his dismay, however, the molten calf proved impervious to his blows. The people looked on in amazement, the esteem of the calf rising in their eyes with every blow Aharon administered.

"What have you done, Aharon?" Hashem said to him from Heaven. "You have transformed the people from unintentional sinners (*shogeg*) into intentional sinners (*meizid*). You have convinced them that this calf has powers, and you have made their sin that much greater."[73]

Despite the terrible sin that had been committed, there were mitigating factors in defense of the Jewish people who had been involved in the construction of the Golden Calf. Most of them did not accept the

---

68. *Vayikra Rabbah* 7:1; *Maharzav*; *Shir Rabbah* 1:9; *Matnos Kehunah*; *Tanchuma Ki Sisa* 19; *Pirkei D'Rav Eliezer* 45; *Radal*; *Maaseh Hashem* to *Shemos* 32:4.
69. See *Rashi*; *Sforno* to *Shemos* 32:4.
70. *Bechor Shor* to *Shemos* 32:4.
71. *Alshich*.
72. *Tanchuma Ki Sisa* 19; *Sifri Haazinu*; see *Tehillim* 82:6-7.
73. *Vayikra Rabbah* 7:1.

calf as the "god that had brought them forth from Egypt."[74] They knew full well that Hashem had done everything, and they were not about to reject His Oneness. Rather, they believed that, just as Hashem had endowed Moshe with special powers in order to enable him to lead the Jewish people through the desert, He had also endowed this golden calf with similar special powers. Perhaps these powers in the possession of the calf were unholy powers, *kochos hatumah*, but they were granted by Hashem, the only One Who was omnipotent. This belief in a sharing of powers, rather than outright idolatry, saved the Jewish people from total annihilation, because deep in their hearts they were still faithful to Hashem.[75]

For the Erev Rav it was an entirely different story. They were determined to establish an idolatrous cult among the Jewish people, similar to what they had experienced in Egypt. They rejected Hashem in the fullest sense of idol worship, but they were not successful in subverting the Jewish people to do the same.[76]

The Choice of a Calf

Why did the idea of using a calf catch on so well? There are many answers, not always the same for the Jewish people and for the Erev Rav.

During the revelation at Mount Sinai, the Jewish people had caught a glimpse of the Heavenly Throne of Glory. The legs of the throne gave the impression of an ox. Thereafter, in their minds, the image of an ox was a representation of the *Shechinah*.[77]

For the Erev Rav, there were different associations. After the splitting of the sea, the Erev Rav saw footprints in the sand that appeared to them to have been made by an ox. This led them to believe that the *Shechinah* resembled an ox. In fact, the angels that had escorted the Jewish people through the sea had left those footprints.[78]

---

74. See *Rashbam; Ramban* to *Shemos* 32:4.
 The Jews did in fact believe in *Anochi*, that Hashem exists, but they rejected the Second Commandment, of not partnering gods of others with Hashem.
75. See *Rashi; Chizkuni* to *Shemos* 32:4; *Maharsha* and other commentaries to *Sanhedrin* 63a.
76. *Anaf Yoseif* to *Sanhedrin* 63a.
77. *Lekach Tov* to *Shemos* 32:4; *Yalkut Reuveni Ki Sisa.* See *Yaaros Devash, Derush* 8.
78. *Chizkuni; Pane'ach Raza; Sifsei Kohen* to *Shemos* 32:4.
 Others add that upon saying, "This is our G-d," they saw the Throne of Glory and distinctively saw the image of the bull. Thinking that this bull had taken part in their exodus from Egypt, they paid homage to it with the creation of the Golden Calf.

Others suggest that when the Erev Rav witnessed the destruction in Egypt of the power of the zodiac sign Aries, the sign of the lamb, the successor power would be the sign of Taurus, the sign of the bull, that followed right after it. In fact, the sign of Aries itself arrogantly tried to insinuate itself into the month of Nissan. Because of these impressions, the Erev Rav saw the bull as the new symbol of strength and power.[79]

Others suggest that, since their successful travels in the desert had taken place during the month of Iyar under the sign of the bull, they decided to create a permanent one to lead them all year round.[80] According to others, the Erev Rav believed that the sign of the bull always ruled over the desert, a belief reflected in the name "Midbar Shur," the Desert of the Bull.[81]

Still others suggest that the words "these are the gods that brought you forth from Egypt" were actually referring to Yosef, without whose body the Jewish people would not have been able to leave Egypt. Thus it was Yosef's zodiac sign — the sign of the bull — that they closely associated with the exodus from Egypt.[82]

More Delaying Tactics

Aharon was devastated. Despite all his efforts to prevent or, at least, delay the construction of the Golden Calf, he had failed miserably. Still, perhaps he could still salvage something. The people had violated the commandment against recognizing gods of others, but they had not yet worshiped these gods of others. Perhaps he could do something to prevent it from happening.[83] Standing up against them was not an option, because they would swat him aside and kill him, just as they had killed Chur. Once again, Aharon resorted to delaying tactics. Perhaps he could delay this further transgression until Moshe would return from the mountain. Perhaps he could somehow relieve the terrible darkness of this day in Jewish history.[84]

The Erev Rav were excited about the success of their plan.

"Take a good look at this calf, Aharon," they shouted. "Look how

---

79. See *Pesachim* 112b.
80. *R' Avraham Ben HaRambam* to *Shemos* 32:4.
81. *Yaaros Devash, Derush* 8.
82. See *Kli Yakar; Alshich* to *Shemos* 32:4.
83. *Daas Zekeinim; Chizkuni* to *Shemos* 32:5.
84. *Rashi; Yonasan ben Uziel; Rabbeinu Bachya; Lekach Tov* to *Shemos* 32:5.

alive it is, how it moves. Here is our new leader! We want to build an altar so that we can offer sacrifices to our new leader and worship it."

"Excellent idea," said Aharon. "But once again we must do it right.[85] Don't forget that I am the designated Kohen Gadol. It is my role and my duty to perform and supervise all sacrificial rites. It would only be fitting that I should be the one who conducts all rites in honor of our new leader. I will oversee the building of the altar and bring sacrifices to our G-d."[86]

The Erev Rav were duly honored and impressed that Aharon was prepared to take such a direct role in the cult of the Golden Calf. But Aharon had another plan. He knew full well that if the people were left to their own devices, the altar would be erected in a matter of hours, just as the gold had been accumulated in record time. Aharon's true intention was to raise impediments that would slow the pace of the construction of the altar in the hopes that he could delay long enough to have Moshe return before any further damage was done.[87]

Furthermore, the sacrifices he had offered to bring "to our G-d" were intended for Hashem, although the Erev Rav understood it to mean their new god.

Aharon thus lulled the Erev Rav into thinking that he had come around to their side. They no longer harbored any thoughts of killing him as they had killed Chur. Aharon was safe for the moment, and free to sabotage the construction of the altar.[88]

Aharon took it upon himself to build the altar with his own hands.[89] The people brought him stones, but he rejected most of them.

"This stone is inappropriate for the altar," he said. "Look, it is chipped."

---

85. Some suggest that Aharon's agreeing to allow the altar to be built was not in order to slaughter animals for sacrifices, but as a metaphor to Chur who became a slaughtered sacrifice while standing up for Hashem's honor (*Sanhedrin* 7a).
86. *Tanchuma Yashan Ki Sisa*; *Shemos Rabbah* 41:7; *Ralbag*.
87. *Rashi*; *Be'er Yitzchak*; *Rabbeinu Bachya* to *Shemos* 32:5; *Shemos Rabbah* 41:7.
88. *Vayikra Rabbah* 10:3; *Midrash HaGadol*; *Kli Yakar* to *Shemos* 32:5.
   See *Rabbeinu Bachya* who writes that Aharon believed this would fall under the violation of "You shall not make graven images" and thus did not require giving up one's life to prevent it. *Rokeach* suggests that Aharon regretted that he did not give his life to prevent building the altar. The *Alshich* suggests that Aharon recognized that they had already violated the First Commandment and wanted to prevent them from violating the Second Commandment (see *Kli Yakar*).
89. *Ohr HaChaim* to *Shemos* 32:5.

"This one has a crack."

"This one is oddly shaped."

"Take these away, people. Bring me good stones, whole, unchipped, unblemished stones."

Not unexpectedly, the building of the altar proceeded at a snail's pace.[90] The sun sank in the sky, and still the altar was not complete. Total darkness had fallen before the altar was finally completed. Aharon had succeeded in delaying until the night. But the danger had not yet passed.

"The altar is complete," said the leaders of the Erev Rav. "We want to bring offerings now in honor of our new god."

"But it is late already," protested Aharon.

"Nevertheless, we are prepared to bring the offerings right now," they insisted. "It is never too late to show our devotion."[91]

"But look up at the sky," said Aharon. "It is dark. It is night. You cannot bring sacrifices in the night. It would be dishonorable. Are we thieves?"

"We still want to bring the offerings now," they insisted.

"Impossible," said Aharon. "I declare that tomorrow afternoon there will be a festival. That will be the right time to bring the offerings."[92]

The leaders of the Erev Rav grudgingly accepted the appointed festival. They were convinced that Aharon had sincerely come over to their point of view and was now devoted to the new leader.[93] But Aharon in his heart was intent on delaying as long as possible. He hoped Moshe would be back by the next afternoon.[94] Moreover, perhaps Moshe would see a vision in Heaven of the completed altar, and that would prompt him to hasten his return. Perhaps the holiness of the altar would counteract the defilement of the Golden Calf.[95]

---

90. *Midrash HaGadol* to *Shemos* 32:5.
91. *Tzeror HaMor* to *Shemos* 32:5.
92. *Yonasan Ben Uziel; Ibn Ezra; Alshich; Tzeror HaMor; Malbim* to *Shemos* 32:5.
93. *Reav Al HaTorah* to *Shemos* 32:5.
94. *Rashi* to *Shemos* 32:5.
95. *Zohar; Abarbanel* to *Shemos* 32:5.
   He also hoped that, with the erection of the altar, they would pray that the *Shechinah* would rest upon it, signified by a heavenly fire. Upon bringing offerings on it, it would become holy before Hashem (*Moshav Zekeinim; Rokeach* to *Shemos* 32:5).

Deep down, Aharon was convinced that the festival on the next day would celebrate the destruction of the evil Erev Rav. The people would come to their senses and sacrifice to the honor of Hashem, even if Moshe had not yet returned. Perhaps they would slaughter and sacrifice the Golden Calf itself on the altar before Hashem.[96] This last thought was behind Aharon's emphatic proclamation that "tomorrow afternoon there will be a festival." Moshe would come down from the mountain and see the great festival of repentance, and all would be forgiven.[97]

Early Morning Antics

The night passed uneventfully. Before dawn on the morning of 17 Tammuz, while Aharon still slept, Satan roused the leaders of the Erev Rav from their slumber. They sprang awake, energized by the excitement of what awaited them that day.[98]

They went from tent to tent, waking everyone, except for Aharon. "Come, let us hurry and bring sacrifices at once. We don't want to wait for Aharon. Let us honor our new leader and god at once. Let us show our respect and our zeal."[99]

They chose the firstborn to officiate at the sacrificial rites, because the firstborn were designated for priestly duties. The firstborn complied and brought burnt offerings and peace offerings on the new altar.[100]

Many of the Jews who brought sacrifices indeed did so in a legitimate fashion, paying homage to Hashem and recognizing His omnipresence. The Erev Rav and their fellow travelers, however, worshiped the new idol.[101] They prostrated themselves before the Golden Calf, celebrating its inauguration as their god. Then they sat

---

96. *Yonasan Ben Uziel; Moshav Zekeinim; Sifsei Kohen* to *Shemos* 32:5; *Zohar*.

The word *machar* has the numerical value of 248, equaling the number of limbs on a person. Aharon hinted, " 'Tomorrow' (248) will be a festival, a celebration of the destruction of your limbs" (*Sifsei Kohen*).

97. *Vayikra Rabbah* 10:3; *Ramban; Alshich; Malbim; Midrash HaGadol; R' Tzadok HaKohen* to *Shemos* 32:5.

Others suggest that Aharon intended to build an altar to make a celebration, but it would be the slaughtering and sacrifice of the Golden Calf itself, annihilating its existence completely (*HaKesav VeHaKabbalah* to *Shemos* 32:5).

98. See *Rashi; Chizkuni; Tzeror HaMor* to *Shemos* 32:6. Some suggest that this took place Friday at midday (*Yalkut Reuveni Ki Sisa*).

99. *Abarbanel* to *Shemos* 32:5.

100. *Bamidbar Rabbah* 4:6; *Tur* to *Shemos* 32:6.

101. *Sifsei Kohen* to *Shemos* 32:6.

down to have a feast in its honor.[102] They ate and drank and even fed some of the manna to the Golden Calf.[103]

The feast soon turned raucous. The eating and the drinking increased, and the celebration degenerated into gluttony and drunkenness. Wild singing and dancing followed. Instruments were produced, and horns, tambourines, drums, cymbals and flutes serenaded the Calf.[104] The people cavorted and laughed in increasingly drunken revelry. It was not long before they turned to lewd and licentious behavior, practices familiar to them from the pagan cult celebrations of Egypt.[105]

They were now guilty of the three cardinal sins — murder, idolatry and adultery. They had killed Chur, worshiped the idol and now they had descended into lewdness.[106] The people had been endowed with an angelic radiance when they accepted the Torah, but now they lost it. Their faces were darkened forever.[107]

Assigning Blame

Despite all the delaying tactics, the deed was done. The people sinned grievously and were corrupted. Hashem cried out in disgust, "Look at these ungrateful people. It is not enough that they reject My sovereignty, they also feed My manna to this abomination!"[108]

Some suggest that the worst crime they committed on that day was to rise early to honor the Golden Calf. What was their rush? They were devoted to Moshe and were only acting in this way because they thought he had perished. Had they known he was alive and would return the next day, they would never have done anything of the sort. So why didn't they sleep normally and take their time? If they had done so, Moshe would have returned before they went any further, and a lot of grief would have been avoided. Their principal guilt lay in the haste with which they

---

102. *Shemos Rabbah* 41:7; *Targum Yonasan*; *Ibn Ezra HaKatzar*; *Ralbag* to *Shemos* 32:6; *Eliyahu Rabbah* 13.
103. *Shemos Rabbah* 41:1.
104. See *Rabbeinu Bachya* to *Shemos* 32:18; *Daniel* 3:5; *Midrash Ohr Afeilah*; *Meam Loez* to *Shemos* 32:10.
105. See *Midrash HaGadol*; *Lekach Tov*; *Ramban*; *R' Saadiah Gaon*; *Rokeach*; *Malbim* to *Shemos* 32:6; *Sifri* to *Devarim* 32:15; *Midrash Tehillim* 1:14.
106. See *Rashi*; *Kli Yakar* to *Shemos* 32:6; *Tanchuma Ki Sisa* 20; *Shemos Rabbah* 42:1.
107. *Yalkut Reuveni Ki Sisa*.
108. *Shemos Rabbah*; *Matnos Kehunah*; *Maharzav* 41:1.

acted, and for this, they would be severely punished.[109]

The firstborn suffered a particular retribution. Originally designated for priestly duties, they were now rejected, just as they had rejected His sovereignty. Eventually, all priestly and ceremonial duties would be transferred to the tribe of Levi, who had not participated in this event.[110]

As for Aharon, the Torah relates that he "made" the Golden Calf, but what exactly does that mean? Aharon had acted in good faith by going along with the Erev Rav in the hope that he could delay any significant action until Moshe returned.

He did make two errors, however, that gave him a measure of culpability. When Ianus and Iambrus gave him the gold, he should have placed it on the ground before throwing it into the fire. He should have suspected that these sorcerers had uttered incantations over the gold; placing it on the ground would have invalidated the incantations. He also erred by wrapping the gold in a cloth so well that it was protected from the evil eye. Had the evil eye been allowed to affect the gold, the incantations would have been invalidated in this way as well.[111] Because of these two errors in his dealings with the two sorcerers, Aharon would eventually lose two of his sons.[112]

There is further proof of his essential innocence in his survival in the aftermath of the episode when all the sinners were killed. Furthermore, although the Golden Calf was destroyed, the altar Aharon had built remained intact. Clearly, he was not a willing participant.[113]

All in all Hashem recognized the sincerity of Aharon's intentions and considered him blameless. Hashem also instructed Moshe not to be angry with Aharon or cast blame upon him. He had done his best and was totally innocent in the matter.

---

109. *Chasam Sofer Ki Sisa.*

It is interesting to note that while the Jewish people overslept and took their time in accepting the Torah, here at the sin of the Golden Calf they woke up early in haste to worship the Calf.

110. *Bamidbar Rabbah* 4:6,8; see *Shemos* 32:29 and commentaries.

111. See *Zohar; Yalkut Reuveni; Midrash HaGadol; Ohr HaChaim* to *Shemos* 32:4; *Daas Zekeinim; Chizkuni* to *Shemos* 32:5. See *Vayikra Rabbah* 7:1; *Eliyahu Zuta* 4; *Shemos* 32:35.

112. See *Vayikra Rabbah* 10:4; 7:1; *Tanchuma Achrei* 8; *Zohar; Yalkut Reuveni Ki Sisa; Midrash HaGadol* to *Shemos* 32:33.

Aharon should have lost all four sons, but through Moshe's prayer, the two younger children survived. Nadav and Avihu would perish for separate violations but Aharon's fate was already sealed (see *Rashi* and *Sifsei Chachamim* to *Devarim* 9:20).

113. *Zohar.*

This can be explained by the following parable.

There was a headstrong prince who was trying to bore through the wall of the palace and attack his father, the king, with a knife. One of the royal courtiers saw what the prince was doing and approached him.

"Let me help you, your highness," he said to the prince and took the tools and weapons from the prince's hands. "I will take care of these things for you. You don't have to exert yourself."

Just then the king appeared and saw the courtier with the tools and weapons in his hands. The courtier was flustered and began to stammer his excuses.

"Don't be afraid," the king reassured him. "I know exactly what you are doing. Your intentions are excellent. Therefore, I am promoting you to the position of royal chamberlain. You will eat from the royal table. You have shown yourself to be a trustworthy and conscientious servant of the crown."

Similarly, Hashem took note of Aharon's good intentions and his exertions on behalf of Hashem's honor, and He rewarded him with the high priesthood in the soon-to-be-built Mishkan. He also rewarded him and his descendants with the twenty-four priestly donations he wold receive from the people.[114]

The Absence of Intervention

A burning question emerges from this infamous episode. How is it possible that a people could do such a thing? Having just stood at Mount Sinai and seen the revelation of the Divine Glory and accepted the Torah, how could they create a Golden Calf just a few weeks later? And how could Hashem have let it go so far? Why didn't He send Moshe down earlier or stop it otherwise?

There are many attempts to resolve this question. The following is but one approach. The Gemara teaches that Hashem took note of the evil tendencies of the Erev Rav and decided to let events take their course. He would not interfere. He allowed the situation to deteriorate until it reached the dismal point that it did. Why? Because He wanted to show all future generations that no matter how vile the sin, there is always the possibility of repen-

---

114. *Shemos Rabbah* 37:2; *Vayikra Rabbah* 10:3.

tance. He wanted people, when they slip into sinful ways, to be encouraged to seek the way back. If the Jewish people could be forgiven for the sin of the Golden Calf, then no sin was beyond repentance and atonement.[115]

---

115. See *Avodah Zarah* 4b with *Rashi, Maharsha, Iyun Yaakov; Kiddushin* 30b; *Rokeach* to *Shemos* 32:5.
    See *Yaaros Devash Derush* 12 for his opinion and discussion on this matter.
    Despite the debauchery that was taking place, as previously noted, Moshe could not descend before a full forty days was completed *(Ohr HaChaim* to *Shemos* 32:6).

14 Uproar in Heaven

The events taking place in the Jewish encampment in Moshe's absence, the construction of the Golden Calf and the wild celebration, did not go unnoticed in Heaven. Hashem observed it all with a sharp eye.[1]

"You have been demoted from your exalted position," Hashem said to Moshe in a harsh tone. "You have risen to greatness in the merit of the Jewish people. Now the people have sinned and are on the verge of annihilation. There is no longer any need for your services."[2]

Moshe listened in shocked silence.

"Descend from the mountain at once," Hashem continued. "Your level of prophecy and your overall status are diminished. You are no longer exalted enough to remain here in the highest

---

1. *Rashi* to *Shemos* 32:7; *Shemos Rabbah* 42:1; *Tanchuma Ki Sisa* 20.
2. *Rashi; Abarbanel* to *Shemos* 32:7; *Berachos* 32a.

spiritual realms.³ The blame is yours, because you chose to allow the Erev Rav to accompany the people in the exodus from Egypt."⁴

"I am puzzled," said Moshe. "Just a short time ago, You told Aharon and me to ascend the mountain because we were on a higher level. Now You are telling me that I must descend? That I am on a lower level?"

"Your status depends not on you," said Hashem, "but on the people you represent. I told the patriarch Yaakov a long time ago that as long as his descendants would maintain his level of righteousness, their emissaries would enjoy an exalted spiritual status. But should they sin and fall from their former levels of righteousness, their emissaries would be demoted as well. The people have sinned grievously. They have fallen to the lowest levels and, therefore, you have also lost your standing."

Moshe understood what had happened. He realized that the sins of the people had greatly diminished his powers of leadership and prophecy and that he had been banned from the realm of Heaven. Overcome by weakness and disappointment, he remained silent. He had nothing to say.⁵

These developments can be explained by the following parable.

A king brought his bride to his palace for a visit and made a banquet in her honor. After the banquet, he appointed one of his courtiers to give the future queen a tour of the palace.

He handed all his keys to the courtier and said, "I am giving you the right of entry to every room in the palace so that you can show them to my bride. One day, she will be the mistress of this vast palace, and it is important that she become familiar with it as soon as possible."

The courtier took the keys and carefully planned an itinerary for the king's bride. While he was steeped in his preparations, he received a summons from the king.

"Please return the keys to me right now," said the king. "Unfortunately, I have discovered that my bride has been unfaithful to me. Since she will no longer be mistress of the palace, you will not

---

3. *Alshich; Ohr HaChaim; Malbim* to *Shemos* 32:7.
4. *Iyun Yaakov, Berachos* 32a.
5. See *Rashi* to *Shemos* 32:7; *Shemos Rabbah* 42:3,7; *Matnos Kehunah; Etz Yosef; Pirkei D'Rav Eliezer* 45; *Pesikta Rabbah* 10:37; *Tanchuma Ki Sisa* 22.

be conducting a tour for her benefit, and you have no further need for the keys to the palace."

Similarly, Moshe had been given the keys, so to speak, to the highest spheres of Heaven because of his role as the leader of the Jewish people. But now that they had sinned and fallen from grace, Hashem took back the keys from Moshe and told him to "descend from your exalted status."[6]

Hashem Expresses His Wrath

Although Hashem had banished Moshe from Heaven, He still had an important mission for him. "Go down at once," Hashem said, "because your nation has become corrupt. They have strayed quickly from the path along which I commanded them to walk. They have turned to idol worship and rejected the Torah entirely.[7] All that was accomplished by the Giving of the Torah has now been destroyed.[8] They have chosen to forget all the great things I have done for them. Instead of showing Me gratitude by adhering to the covenant we have made, they have worshiped idols. In fact, they have violated all three cardinal sins — murder, idolatry and adultery. They deserve to be thrashed for their terrible sins.[9]

"Look at the depth of their depravity. Not only did they construct the Golden Calf, not only did they quickly collect 125 talents of gold for the construction, not only did they show a passionate devotion to the undertaking, not only did they acknowledge it as having powers, not only did they prostrate themselves before it, not only did they bring offerings to it, they also sang hymns to it and danced in front of it in a wild display of joyful celebration.[10]

"It is true that only a minority of the people brought offerings or participated in these celebrations. It is also true that some of the people who brought offerings did so in My honor and not in honor of the Golden Calf. But virtually all of them donated golden ornaments

---

6. *Eliyahu Rabbah* Ch. 4.
7. See *Horayos* 8a.
8. *Ramban* to *Shemos* 32:7.
9. *Shemos Rabbah* 42:1,5; *Yefei To'ar*; *Pirkei D'Rav Eliezer* 45; *Sanhedrin* 57b; *Rabbeinu Bachya* to *Shemos* 32:8.
10. See *Ohr HaChaim; Akeidah; Abarbanel* to *Shemos* 32:7; *Shemos Rabbah* 51:8, 42:8; *Yefei To'ar; Zohar* 192. See *Rashi* to *Shemos* 32:4.

to the collection or even considered the possibility that the Golden Calf might have real powers.[11] Even if they did neither, they should have protested what their friends, relatives and neighbors were doing. For these failings they must bear guilt.[12]

"Instead of following in the footsteps of their patriarch Yaakov, who was loyal in his adherence to the Torah, they acted like his brother Eisav, who worshiped idols.[13] They violated the first two Commandments, which I spoke to them Myself, totally trampling every facet of the Second Commandment by making a molten image, prostrating themselves before it and worshiping it.[14] They have exchanged My glory for the image of a grass-eating bull.[15]

"Mount Sinai was once fragrant with the aroma of roses, but now it is a place of thorns and carries the stench of defilement.[16] It has become like a wedding canopy under which the bride has committed adultery.[17]

"The people were genuinely loyal for only eleven of the forty days you have been away. For the rest of the time, they were already conspiring about how to abandon the Torah.[18]

"The Erev Rav you chose to bring out of Egypt with the people are liars. They may have given lip service to accepting the Torah as the Jewish people did, but in their hearts they were Egyptian all along. It was only a matter of time before they would find a way to return to idol worship."[19]

Moshe recoiled before the Divine wrath.

---

11. *Ramban; Rabbeinu Bachya; Tur; Bechor Shor* to *Shemos* 32:7.

12. *Ohr HaChaim; Abarbanel; Malbim* to *Shemos* 32:7.

13. *Bamidbar Rabbah* 7:4.
   This is a lesson to be learned: If one rejects the Torah and leaves it, he is destined to eventually worship idols (*Sifri Eikev*).

14. *Shemos Rabbah* 42; *Yefei To'ar; Midrash HaGadol; Chomas Anach; Chizkuni; Ohr HaChaim* to *Shemos* 32:7.

15. See commentaries to *Tehillim* 106:20.

16. *Shemos Rabbah* 42:7; see *Radal; Yefei To'ar*.

17. *Lekach Tov* to *Shemos* 37:8. See *Shir HaShirim* 1:12 with *Targum; Tzeror HaMor*.
   Some suggest that Moshe would defend them by arguing that symbolically the *Luchos* were the marriage contract between G-d and the Jews, and since they never received the *Luchos*, the marriage was never consummated. Therefore, there would be reason to give them the benefit of the doubt and they would not deserve death as would normally be the case with adultery (R' *Efraim Al HaTorah* to *Shemos* 32:10).

18. *Shemos Rabbah* 42:7. Others suggest that the Jews kept the Torah for 29 days and the remaining 11 were part of a conspiracy to worship the Golden Calf.

19. *Bamidbar Rabbah* 7:4; *Maharzav*.

"What have I done to deserve this?" he cried out in anguish. "Have I sinned? You call the Jewish people my nation, but are they not also Your beloved nation, the one You have brought forth from Egypt?"

"The Jewish people are indeed your nation," Hashem replied. "They have divorced themselves from Me. They no longer serve or even acknowledge Me, but they are still yours.[20] They still admire you and would follow you when you return. They are yours, because you have risked your life for them.[21] And they are yours, because you are responsible for their present composition. You chose to accept the Erev Rav into the Jewish fold. You brought the treacherous traitors with their pernicious influences into the Jewish encampment."

"Is it all the fault of the Erev Rav?" asked Moshe.

"Come, I will ask the calf itself," said Hashem. "Let it bear witness about its own genesis."

Moshe remained silent, listening intently.

"Calf, who made you?" said Hashem.

"The donkey made me," replied the calf.

The calf had responded with a euphemism. The donkey was a symbol of the pagan peoples from which the Erev Rav had sprung.

"So you see, Moshe," Hashem continued, "the calf itself attests to its makers. It was made by the Erev Rav whom you allowed into the Jewish encampment, and now they have spread their corruption to the Jewish people as well. That is why they are your nation."[22]

In desperation, Moshe snatched the corner of Hashem's garment, so to speak, that represented the Attribute of Mercy.[23]

"Let me say one thing in defense of the Jewish people," he said. "At least they accepted upon themselves the yoke of Torah, unlike the descendants of Eisav who rejected it completely."

"They are hypocrites," said Hashem. "They said they would 'do' the Torah, but instead they 'did' the Golden Calf."

"It is true," said Moshe, "that they have failed miserably. There is no justification for constructing the Golden Calf. But they have

---

20. See *Midrash Tannaim*; *Pesikta Rabbah* 11:45; *R' Avraham Ben HaRambam*.
21. See *Tanchuma Beshalach* 10; *Ki Sisa* 22; *Midrash HaGadol* 32:7.
22. See *Midrash HaGadol*; *Rashi*; *Hadar Zekeinim*; *Toldos Yitzchok* to *Shemos* 32:7; *Shemos Rabbah* 42:10; *Yeshayah* 1:3; *Yalkut Reuveni Ki Sisa*. See *Ohr HaChaim* to *Shemos* 32:19 who writes that the Golden Calf did not actually speak.
23. See *Berachos* 32a with *Tzlach* as to the meaning of this.

shown You great respect and recognition. They prostrated themselves before You when they went out of Egypt. Which of the other nations has paid You such homage? Shouldn't that work in the favor of the Jewish people?"

"They did gain merit," replied Hashem, "when they bowed down to Me. But then, when they bowed down to the Golden Calf, they forfeited all of that merit."

According to those opinions that the Jewish people brought sacrifices to Hashem on 5 Sivan at Mount Sinai, the same argument counteracted that merit. When they brought sacrifices to the Golden Calf, they forfeited all of that merit as well.[24]

Although Hashem had rejected Moshe's arguments in defense of the Jewish people, the merits Moshe had raised did take the edge off the Divine wrath; it was no longer like a raging fire. Moshe had gained a temporary respite, but the situation was still exceedingly perilous. The Jewish people were in real danger of annihilation unless Moshe could pray successfully on their behalf and arouse the Divine Attribute of Being Slow to Anger.[25]

Moshe now found himself outside the inner sphere of the spiritual firmament in which the *Shechinah* resided. He listened to Hashem speaking to him across the boundary of the spheres and tried to muster new arguments and pleas, but he could think of nothing to say. He stood there as if muzzled.

Hashem continued to speak out again against the Jewish people in order to stimulate Moshe to respond and speak in their defense.[26]

"These Jewish people," Hashem said in a decidedly softer tone, "have a long history of being a stiff-necked, stubborn nation.[27] They are stubborn and headstrong and insist on following the path of their choice.[28] Not only do they refuse to listen to authority, they actually turn their backs on the speakers, refusing to turn their stiff necks, refusing to accept rebuke.[29] They are stuck in the rut of idolatry that they learned from the Egyptians. They saw all the miracles

---

24. *Shemos Rabbah* 42:1.
25. *Shemos Rabbah* 42:1; *Radal*.
26. *Abarbanel* to *Shemos* 32:8; *Yefei To'ar*.
27. R' *Saadiah Gaon*; *Ibn Ezra* to *Shemos* 32:9.
28. *Shemos Rabbah* 42:1; *Ohr HaChaim* to *Devarim* 9:13.
29. See *Rashi*; *Ibn Ezra* to *Shemos* 32:9.

I performed for them, but they are too stiff necked to acknowledge what I have done and change their ways.[30] Even when they suffer blows of retribution, they do not turn their stiff necks to discover the source of their suffering. They just continue along the path they have chosen to follow.[31]

"It is true that their stiff-necked tendencies sometimes work to their advantage. It makes them persevere undaunted in their quest for achievement. It could inspire them to accept martyrdom, rather than compromise their principles. But right now, this obstinate attribute has led them astray.[32]

"Leave Me right now! Detach yourself from Me immediately! Do not hold on to the hem of My garment that might open the gates for prayer and leniency on behalf of the Jewish people. Your presence here interferes with My anger. Leave and let My anger flare against the Jewish people so that I will annihilate them and sever their stiff necks.[33] And what will become of My promise to the Patriarchs that I would make their descendants into a great nation, if I destroy the Jewish people? Fear not, My promise will be fulfilled. I will rebuild the Jewish people through you and your descendants, who will become a nation greater than the Jewish people ever were or would be."[34]

Despite the sharp condemnation, Moshe noticed a number of subtle hints and trigger points that bore an important message for him,

---

30. *Ralbag; R' Avraham Ben HaRambam; Akeidas Yitzchak* to *Shemos* 32:9.

31. *Abarbanel* to *Shemos* 32:9.

Eyes are put in the front so that people can see any peripheral danger that comes their way. One can only be protected from a danger coming from behind by turning one's neck. Hashem tells Moshe that since the Jewish people do not turn their necks, it is impossible for them to avoid impending doom, so what use is it if He strikes them as a potential warning for their sins?

32. See *Shemos Rabbah* 42:9; *Matnos Kehunah, Etz Yosef; Beitzah* 25b.

Some add that Hashem was hinting that this nature of theirs made it predictable that they would worship the Golden Calf, due to their obstinate nature. This hint would give Moshe the impetus to defend the Jews by saying that it was as though they had not been given a fair option to choose between right and wrong, due to a predisposed character flaw.

33. *R' Saadiah Gaon; Abarbanel; Ralbag* to *Shemos* 32:10.

Others suggest that Hashem wanted to send the angel of destruction called Af to destroy them. The words *Api* (My anger) and *malach* (angel) have the same numerical value — 91 (*Rokeach*).

34. *Shemos Rabbah* 42:9; *Berachos* 7a with *Maharsha; Etz Yosef; Devarim* 9:14; *Tzeror HaMor*.

Despite the fact that the Jewish people were saved, Hashem's words held true, as Moshe's descendants numbered 600,000 (*I Chronicles* 23:15-17 with *Targum*).

and he felt a surge of hope. Hashem was speaking to him in a softer, gentler tone.[35] He had made reference to the national character of strong-willed obstinacy and acknowledged that it had some positive aspects.[36] Most important, He had told Moshe to "leave and detach himself right now." Didn't this imply that he would have the opportunity to pray a little later?[37] Further, why was He telling him to leave and detach himself when he had already been transported out of the innermost sphere of the spiritual firmament? And why was He telling him not to hold on to the hem of His garment, so to speak, when he was no longer in the innermost sphere?

Clearly, Hashem was hinting to him that if he would pray and plead for the Jewish people, his efforts would not go to waste. Hashem was telling Moshe to remain silent so that He could destroy the Jewish people, which prompted Moshe to raise his voice in prayer and supplication so that they would not be destroyed.[38]

This exchange can be explained by the following parable.

A king once discovered that his son had committed a terrible crime against the crown. He had the prince thrown into the dungeon, then he stood at the door and yelled, "Let no one dare try to appease me! Let no one try to talk me out of giving my son the punishment he deserves."

A courtier standing nearby understood that the king was sending a message to everyone within earshot. It would be improper for the king to show leniency to his son on his own initiative. But if others would come forward and plead for clemency, he would not be averse to granting it.

Others offer a similar parable.

A king once became angry with his son. He began slapping the son in the presence of one of his favorite courtiers.

The courtier remained silent out of respect to the king.

The king persisted with his slaps and declared to his son, "If it were not for my good friend who is with us right now, I would kill you!"

---

35. *Shemos Rabbah* 42:1; *Alshich*.
36. *Alshich* to *Shemos* 32:9.
37. *Ohr HaChaim* to *Shemos* 32:10.
38. *Shemos Rabbah* 42:10; *Etz Yosef*; *Berachos* 32a with *Rashi* and *Maharsha*; *Rashi* and *Bechor Shor* to *Shemos* 32:9-10.
   Some suggest that Moshe actually grabbed onto the spiritual clothing of the *Shechinah*. This means that Moshe grabbed onto the Attributes in which Hashem is clothed, specifically the Attribute of Mercy. See *Maharsha* to *Berachos* 32a; *Ramban* to *Ki Sisa*.

The courtier heard these words and understood that the king had authorized him to come to the defense of the embattled prince. He argued the prince's case passionately, and the king relented.

Similarly, Moshe deduced that Hashem was sending him a subtle message when He told Moshe to stand aside so that He could annihilate the Jewish people. Hashem clearly wanted His beloved courtier, the friend and champion of the Jewish people, to come to their defense. But it would have been improper to make an explicit declaration to that effect. Therefore, Hashem sent the message in this oblique fashion.[39]

The Angels Seek Destruction

Even as Moshe prepared to advocate for the Jewish people and plead for their survival, a group of angels in Heaven were mobilizing against them. Through their sins, the people had aroused the antagonism of five angels of destruction. By going astray, they had aroused the angel named Af, who represented Divine anger. By constructing the Golden Calf, they had aroused the angel named Ketzef, who represented destruction. By bowing to the Golden Calf, they had aroused the angel named Cheimah, who represented Divine wrath. By sacrificing to the Golden Calf, they had aroused the angel named Hashmeid, who represented Divine harm. By acknowledging that the Golden Calf possessed Divine powers, they had aroused the angel named Mash'chis, who represented persecution.

All along, these angels had resented the giving of the Torah to the Jewish people, but Moshe's arguments had silenced them. But now the Jewish people had sinned and shown themselves unworthy of the Torah, and the angels seized the opportunity. Their intent was to destroy the people and take the Torah back into Heaven.

The way was not clear, however, for the angels of destruction to accomplish their goal. The merit of the three Patriarchs of the Jewish people, which came forward to defend them, neutralized three of the angels: Ketzef, Hashmeid and Mash'chis. The two remaining angels, Af and Cheimah, moved forward to destroy the people. Moshe realized that, by himself, he could only hold back one of them. The two of them together would overwhelm him.

---

39. See *Shemos Rabbah* 42:10; *Tanchuma Ki Sisa* 22; *Rashi* to *Shemos* 32:9-10.

"Please, Hashem, I beg You!" he cried out. "Rise up against Af and subdue him, so that I can stop Cheimah from destroying the Jewish people."

Hashem complied, and immediate disaster was averted.[40]

According to some versions, Moshe also contended with the destructive angel Charon. He dug a cave in Heaven, so to speak, and imprisoned Charon inside it. The cave was named Pe'or, a reminder of the idolatrous and adulterous sins that the Jewish people would commit in front of the idol Pe'or. In the future, when they would commit these sins, the angel Charon would be released from his imprisonment in his celestial cave, and would threaten the very survival of the Jewish people. As long as Moshe was alive, he would utter one of the esoteric Names of Hashem and drive the angel back into the cave.

But what would happen after his death? It is said that Moshe requested that he be buried near this cave, in order to protect the Jewish people. Thereafter, whenever Charon would be released from his imprisonment, he would see the vision of Moshe's burial place and flee, terror stricken, back into his cave.[41]

Moshe now realized that the angels of destruction had been thwarted only temporarily. If he descended from the mountain as matters stood now, it would only be a matter of time before the angels regrouped and presented their case for the destruction of the Jewish people. With no one to stand against them, they would surely be successful. Clearly, he had to seize the moment and pray for the salvation of the Jewish people. Otherwise, all would be lost.[42]

---

40. See *Shemos Rabbah* 42:1,7; *Tanchuma Ki Sisa* 20; *Midrash Tehillim* 6, 18:13; *Tosafos* to *Shemos* 32:7; *Rokeach* to *Shemos* 32:11; *Kli Chemdah*. See *Tehillim* 7:7, 106:23. See *Shemos* 32:12; *Midrash HaChefetz*; *Targum Yonasan ben Uziel* to *Devarim* 9:19 as a reference for Hashem blocking Charon and Af from annihilating the Jews.

Others suggest that he contended with Mash'chis and not Cheimah (*Kli Chemdah*).

Others add that it was the angel Charon and not Hashmeid that came to attack the Jews and it was Charon and Mash'chis that remained, as opposed to Af and Cheimah (*Yalkut Reuveni*).

Others further suggest that the five angels of destruction came as a result of five instruments used during the celebration of the Golden Calf (*Meam Loez*).

41. See *Yalkut Reuveni* 32:10; *Pirkei D'Rav Eliezer* 45; *Shemos Rabbah* 41:7; see *Sotah* 14a; *Tosafos* to *Devarim* 34:6.

See *Radal* who writes that Moshe did not do this at this time, but years later after the sin of Peor was committed, prior to his death.

42. *Shemos Rabbah* 42:1; *Maharzav*; *Shemos Rabbah* 41:7; *Yefei To'ar*; *Tanchuma Ki Sisa* 20. See *Ramban* to *Shemos* 32:11.

Moshe Prays for Forgiveness[43]

Ideally, Moshe would have wanted to remove the idol, the cause of the Divine wrath, before he even began to pray. But there was no time to go down from the mountain into the Jewish encampment, smash the idol and then return to stand in prayer.[44] Nonetheless, he did make important preparations before he began to pray. He turned his attention to silencing Satan and the accusing angels so that they would not interfere with his prayers by shouting accusations against the Jewish people.

This can be explained by the following parable.

The king's son was accused of a crime against the crown. The prince was brought to trial, and the prosecutor demanded a harsh sentence. The prince's tutor asked to make a statement to the king, on behalf of the prince.

"Your majesty," he said. "I am not asking to stand before you as the prince's attorney for the defense. If so, the prosecutor would have every right to be present and raise objections to what I have to say. Rather, I want to plead for the prince, as a friend and servant of the royal family. What I have to say, Your Majesty, is personal between you and me, and I respectfully request that the prosecutor be asked to step outside."

Similarly, Moshe asked that Satan and the prosecuting angels be asked to remove themselves, and Hashem acceded to his request.[45]

---

43. There is much discussion on the various supplications that Moshe offered in defense of the Jewish people and when they took place. The *Ibn Ezra* suggests using *Devarim* 9:25 as a basis to say that Moshe did not begin to pray until after the Golden Calf was destroyed. It seemed inappropriate for him to pray for the welfare of the Jewish people while the idol still remained. In addition, Moshe felt it unseemly to address Hashem during His furious anger at the Jewish people, as written in *Avos* (4:23): "Do not appease your friend during his anger." The *Ramban* disagrees and suggests that Moshe prayed two times, once before his descent from the mountain, and once again, after the Golden Calf was destroyed, when he returned to the heavens for an additional forty days, as seen in *Shemos* 32:31. In addition, Moshe ascended a third time and finally returned on Yom Kippur. It was only then that Hashem forgave the Jewish people with the famous words, *Salachti kidvarecha* (I have forgiven because of your word).

I have chosen to go in the order in which the Torah writes the information, according to the view of the *Ramban*. In addition, there are various opinions about the order of prayers which Moshe supplicated on behalf of the Jews, and I have chosen to write them in a manner that is easily understood. For further discussion on this subject see *Ramban, Ibn Ezra; Chizkuni; Abarbanel* to *Shemos* 32:11; *Ralbag* to *Shemos* 32:15; *Shemos Rabbah* 44:1; *Tanchuma Pekudei* 11; *Yalkut* 1:744; *Rashi* to *Devarim* 9:18; *Rashash* and *Maharsha* to *Shabbos* 30a; *Tosafos Bava Kamma* 82a s.v. *Kedei; Shitah Mekubetzes* to *Bava Kamma* 82a.

44. *Ramban* to *Shemos* 32:11.

45. *Shemos Rabbah* 43:1.

"Hashem, why does Your anger burn against the Jewish people," Moshe began, "whom You brought forth from Egypt with the power and might of Your hand?"[46]

At first glance, Moshe's question seems strange and presumptuous. Didn't he know why Hashem was angry? Didn't he know that the people had sinned grievously with the Golden Calf? Rather, his question was: Why was Hashem angered to the extent that He had shut out reasonable arguments in defense of the people?[47] Furthermore, Moshe was questioning why Hashem had moved away from the Attribute of Mercy He had displayed when taking the Jewish people out of Egypt, and was now judging them with the Attribute of Strict Justice. In other words, why was He allowing His anger to burn to this great extent?[48]

"Why are You prepared to destroy the Jewish people with one mighty blow?" he was asking. "You exhibited patience and forbearance when You dealt with the wicked and hateful Egyptians. You did not destroy them with one blow, but gave them a progression of ten plagues. Surely, the Jewish people deserve, at least, as much consideration.[49]

"Why can't You mitigate the bitterness of the decree against the Jewish people, just as You sweetened the bitterness of the water at Marah? You accepted my prayers at Marah and made the bitter water sweet to the taste.[50] Please accept my prayer now and make the decree against the Jewish people easier to endure. After all, they are not the only ones who have sinned. The pagan nations are full of sin. Divert Your anger from the Jewish people and direct it against the sinful pagan nations.[51]

"Please, for the sake of those among the Jewish people who have remained innocent and righteous, do not annihilate the entire nation. Do not group the evil and the righteous together as one.[52]

"Let me say this in defense of the Jewish people. If we look closely at the language of the first two Commandments, they are

---

46. *Shemos* 32:11; see *Ibn Ezra* to *Shemos* 32:11; *Tehillim* 106:23.
47. See *Shemos Rabbah* 43:1; *Devarim Rabbah* 11:2; *Berachos* 32a with *Maharsha*; *Zohar Noach* 67b.
48. *Ramban*; *Rabbeinu Bachya* to *Shemos* 32:11.
49. *Lekach Tov* to *Shemos* 32:12.
50. *Shemos Rabbah* 43:3.
51. *Midrash HaGadol Vayikra* 26:9.
52. *Ohr HaChaim*; *Abarbanel*; *Sforno* to *Shemos* 32:11; *Derashas Even Sho'eiv*.

addressed in the singular rather than the plural, as if You were speaking to me alone and not to the entire people. It is a technicality, I admit, but it is an argument for their defense.[53]

"Why are You so angry at the Jewish people when You know it was the Erev Rav that led them astray? In fact, You just proved to me by questioning the idol that the Erev Rav, symbolized by the donkey, made it. And it was also the Erev Rav who worshiped the idol as a god. It is true that it was my decision to bring them along when we went forth from Egypt, but You could have told me not to do it. You allowed me to make that decision on behalf of the entire people, so why should the people suffer for it now?[54]

"Even if they are guilty for letting the Erev Rav have their way and not protesting and stopping them, should they be annihilated for it?[55] After all, the Jewish people just came out of Egypt where they were steeped in idol worship for so many years. It is a wonderful thing that they have turned away from idol worship themselves, but isn't it asking too much from them to fight against the idolatry of the Erev Rav? For this they should be destroyed?"[56]

Moshe's arguments can be illustrated with the following parable.

A man opened a perfume shop in a degenerate district in the center of a city. Many promiscuous people visit this district, and while they are in the neighborhood, they patronize the perfume store. The storekeeper became prosperous, but his son fell victim to the temptations of his surroundings. The furious father threatens the boy with severe punishment, but his wife comes to their son's defense.

"Why are you so angry at our son?" she says. "Is he to blame, or are you to blame? If you wanted to shelter your son from all these harmful influences, you should not have opened your business in such a district. You have to take responsibility for his behavior."

This is, in essence, what Moshe was saying to Hashem. "How could You expect the Jewish people not to sin, considering the circumstances in which they found themselves? They spent centuries in a land steeped in idol worship that revered Capricorn, the astrological sign of the lamb. When the power of this sign was destroyed,

---

53. *Devarim Rabbah* 3:11; *Midrash HaGadol* to *Shemos* 32:11. See *Rashi* to *Shemos* 20:2.
54. See *Midrash HaGadol*; *Ohr HaChaim*; *Pane'ach Raza* to *Shemos* 32:11; *Shemos Rabbah* 43:7; *Yalkut Reuveni Ki Sisa*.
55. *Ohr HaChaim*; *Malbim* to *Shemos* 32:11.
56. *Ohr HaChaim*; *Akeidas Yitzchak*; *Malbim* to *Shemos* 32:11.

it was only logical that they would have a latent tendency to turn to Taurus, the bull, the next astrological sign.

"Furthermore, You showered them with so much treasure and riches on the shores of the sea. How could You expect their satiated hearts not to turn to sin? The lion does not roar when he consumes a basket of straw, but he does roar when he fills his belly with fat meat. The Jewish bellies and pockets were filled to overflowing. How could You expect their hearts not to roar with desire?[57]

"Another thing. When You first sent me to take the Jewish people out of Egypt, even though they were steeped in idol worship, I asked why they were worthy of deliverance. You told me that it was in the merit of their future acceptance of the Torah and Your sovereignty. You knew their past. You knew they were idol worshipers. You surely foresaw that they would slip in these circumstances. So why are You so angry with them?[58]

"Why don't you look at it this way? What have they done? They made this entity to assist You in the management of world affairs. You made the sun to serve in the daytime, and it provides illumination for the moon at night. You caused the dew to descend, and it causes the wind to blow. You caused the rains to fall, and they cause the foliage to grow. All they wanted was to make another vehicle for Your control of the world."

"This is a foolish argument, Moshe," said Hashem. "It is unworthy of you. How can a Golden Calf do My bidding in the world when it has no power or authority?"

"Then why are You so angry?" Moshe quickly replied. "A wise man does not feel challenged by a fool. A strong man does not feel challenged by a weakling. If this calf is indeed nothing, then why does it bother You so much? It is nothing, a piece of metal slated for destruction. True, the Jewish people erred in attempting to construct an agent to assist You, but in the end they did nothing. All they made was a hunk of metal."[59]

---

57. See *Shemos Rabbah* 43:7; *Bamidbar Rabbah* 13:33; *Maharzav*; *Yefei To'ar*; *Midrash HaGadol*; *Berachos* 32a; *Rashi* to *Shemos* 32:31. See *Berachos* 32; *Sanhedrin* 102a for a variation of this parable.
58. *Shemos Rabbah* 43:8.
59. See *Rashi*; *Pane'ach Raza*; *Akeidas Yitzchak* to *Shemos* 32:11; *Shemos Rabbah* 43:6; *Etz Yosef*; *Tanchuma Ki Sisa* 22.

"I cannot simply forgive the Jewish people," said Hashem, "when I explicitly told them that whoever brings offerings to idols will be destroyed. I made an oath. So how can I forgive them?"

"In the Torah," Moshe replied, "You made provisions for oaths and vows to be annulled if need be, if the one making the oath or vow regrets having made it. If, in the light of developments, he realizes that he should never have made them in the first place, then he can have them annulled by a court or even by a single sage."

"Then I ask you, Moshe, to annul My oath."

"*Muttar Lach, Muttar Lach, Muttar Lach,*" Moshe immediately said. "You are released from Your oath."[60]

The release of the oath averted the danger of annihilation to the entire nation, but those Jews who had sinned personally still faced the consequences of their actions. They were still in peril.[61]

The Defense Continues

"I want to talk about the Erev Rav," Moshe continued. "Let us say for a moment that they deserve to die. But if so many thousands of people in the Jewish encampment will die, what will the world say? They will not appreciate the fine distinction between Jews by birth and the last-minute Egyptian converts. In their eyes, a Jew is a Jew. And they will witness You initiating a wholesale slaughter of Jewish people.

"What will the Egyptians say? They will accuse You of taking the Jewish people out of Egypt to the mountains of Sinai with evil intentions. They will say Your intent all along was to destroy them.[62]

"You told Pharaoh, 'Send forth My people so that they can serve Me.' And now when they witness this terrible slaughter they will say it was all a fabrication. And if You single out the Erev Rav for destruction, they will say that You tricked them into coming along so that You could destroy them with impunity in the desert. They will claim that You had malicious intentions against these idol-worshiping ethnic Egyptians, that You brought them to the desolate wilderness where they would be defenseless, where they would have nowhere to run or hide, and where their corpses would rot without being brought to burial.

---

60. See *Shemos Rabbah* 43:1; *Yefei To'ar*; *Yedei Moshe*; *Berachos* 32a with *Maharsha*.
61. See *Moshav Zekeinim* to *Shemos* 32:14.
62. *Ohr HaChaim*; *Toldos Yitzchak* to *Shemos* 32:12.

"Such a massacre would be an unimaginable desecration of Your Name.[63] People will say that anyone who tries to convert to Judaism will be accepted and then murdered.[64] I am not condoning what the Erev Rav have done, but I think You should carefully reconsider before You visit swift and total destruction on them.[65]

"Pharaoh's astrologers predicted that the star Raah, the blood symbol, awaits us in the desert. Should there be a wholesale slaughter in the Jewish encampment, they will be vindicated. They will say You could not overcome the power of the star and that you slaughtered an entire nation to preserve Your dignity. They will say terrible things about You. They will question Your wisdom, Your power, Your integrity. There will be a worldwide desecration of Your Name, and all peoples will lose faith in You.[66] All the miracles and wonders You performed for the Jewish people in Egypt will be wasted. The sanctification of Your Name and the recognition of Your sovereignty over the entire world will fall by the wayside. They will call You a murderer, Heaven forbid.[67]

"If You want to punish the people for the Golden Calf to preserve Your sovereignty, I want to point out that it will have exactly the opposite effect. It will cause the world to turn away from You."[68]

The Merit of the Patriarchs

Now Moshe addressed Hashem's offer to destroy the Jewish people and fulfill His promise to the Patriarchs by rebuilding the nation through Moshe and his descendants.

Moshe never considered accepting Hashem's offer. He was so devoted to the Jewish people that he did not want to survive if they were destroyed. Furthermore, how could he think about his own personal interest when the entire people was imperiled? People would compare him to Noach who saved himself while the entire

---

63. See *Abarbanel; Alshich; Malbim* to *Shemos* 32:12.
64. *Kli Yakar* to *Shemos* 32:12.
65. *Abarbanel* to *Shemos* 32:12.
66. See *Midrash HaGadol; Ibn Ezra; Ralbag; Akeidas Yitzchak* to *Shemos* 32:12; *Rashi; Targum Yonasan* to *Shemos* 10:10.
   The vision of blood the astrologers of Pharaoh saw would in fact be that of a massive circumcision performed by the Jewish people in the time of Yehoshua.
67. *Berachos* 32a with *Maharsha; Rosh; Chizkuni; Bechor Shor; Akeidas Yitzchak; Sifsei Kohen; Malbim* to *Shemos* 32:11.
68. See *Degel Machaneh Efraim*.

world was inundated by the Flood. Clearly, the prayers Hashem sought were not for his own survival and success but for the salvation of the Jewish people.

On the other hand, wouldn't people suspect his motives in advocating for the Jewish people? Wouldn't they accuse him of doing it to preserve his own role, as the leader of a great nation? Where would he be, if his entire nation were destroyed from under him? These thoughts, however, did not concern him too much. He would pray for the Jewish people but not for himself.[69] He would be satisfied if they would survive, even if he himself would perish.[70] Nonetheless, he was confident that Hashem wanted him to pray for the Jewish people and that he would also be saved.[71]

"Hashem, remember the patriarchs," Moshe prayed, "to whom You swore in Your Name that You would increase their descendants until they would be as numerous as the stars in the heavens, and You also promised to give them the Land of Canaan as an eternal heritage. You did not swear by the heavens and the earth, which will some day come to an end, but by Your own Name, which will endure forever. If You go back on this oath, Your Name will be desecrated.[72]

"When You were about to destroy Sodom, You were willing to spare the city if ten righteous people could be found in it. There were not ten righteous people to be found, so You destroyed the city. Well, let us see if there are ten righteous people to be found now. There are Aharon and his four sons. There are also Yehoshua and Kalev."

"That is only seven," said Hashem. "You are still missing three."

"I call upon the merit of the three Patriarchs," said Moshe. "Let them come forward and complete the number of ten."[73] Moshe could

---

69. See *Etz Yosef*; *Rif* to *Berachos* 32a; *Tanchuma Ki Sisa* 22; *Lekach Tov* to *Shemos* 32:9-10; *Zohar Noach* 67b; *Devarim Rabbah* 11:3.
70. *Bechor Shor* to *Shemos* 32:10; *Zohar Noach* 67b; *Zohar Vayikra* 14b.
71. *Alshich* to *Shemos* 32:10.
72. See *Berachos* 32a; *Rashi*; *R' Saadiah Gaon* to *Shemos* 32:13.
73. *Tanchuma Yashan Ki Sisa*.
   Others suggest that the count included Moshe, Aharon, his younger children Elazar and Isamar, Pinchas, Yehoshua and Calev. Others suggest that the number being considered was 80. This included the 70 elders (accordingly, this view does not agree that they were killed during the worship of the Golden Calf), Aharon, his four children, Moshe and Chur. See *Tzeror HaMor*; *Yedei Moshe* to *Devarim Rabbah* 3:15 as to why these people were chosen to act as merits.

have chosen other righteous Jews who were living at the time, but he chose to call, instead, on the great merit of the Patriarchs.[74]

"First, let me address the transgression of making the idol," Moshe said. "Avraham smashed the idols his father Terach manufactured. May the merit of this courageous deed come to the defense of the Jewish people. For the transgression of bringing offerings to the idol, I call upon the merit of Yitzchak, who offered himself up as a sacrifice to You. For the transgression of bowing down to the idol, I call upon the merit of Yaakov, who destroyed the idols of Shechem.[75]

"What punishments did You have in mind for the transgressors? Did You intend to burn them? Then, let them be protected by the merit of Avraham who risked his life in the furnace of Ur Kasdim. If You intended to put them to the sword, then let them be protected by the merit of Yitzchak, who stretched out his neck to receive the slaughtering knife. If You intended to drive them into exile, then let them be protected by the merit of Yaakov, who was forced to go into exile in Charan.[76]

"It is true that they transgressed the first words of the verse, 'You shall not have other gods,' but let us not forget the final words, that You are 'a L-rd Who shows kindness for thousands of generations.' Thousands of generations have not yet passed. There are only seven generations since Avraham. Show kindness to him.[77]

"Let us turn again to the merit of Avraham. Did You ever reward him for passing the ten tests? Well, perhaps You can grant that reward now. His descendants have violated the Ten Commandments. Let them be protected by the merit of Avraham who passed the ten tests.[78]

"Remember the merits of the Patriarchs. Do not destroy their descendants as You destroyed the generation of the Great Flood.[79]

---

74. See *Tanchuma Ki Sisa* 24; *Shemos Rabbah* 44:4-7; *Devarim Rabbah* 3:15.
  Some suggest that since they would be brought back to life at the time of *techiyas hameisim* (resurrection of the dead), it is as though they are alive and available to be used for their merits (see *Midrash HaGadol*).
75. *Moshav Zekeinim* to *Shemos* 32:13. See R' *Samson Raphael Hirsch* to *Bereishis* 35:2.
76. See *Rashi* to *Shemos* 32:13 and *Gur Aryeh* as to why these were chosen as possible punishments.
77. See *Shemos Rabbah* 44:9; *Tanchuma Ki Sisa* 24.
78. *Tanchuma Ki Sisa* 24; *Shemos Rabbah* 44:4; *Rashi* to *Avos* 5:3; *Rashi* to *Shemos* 32:13. See *Shemos Rabbah* for its parable in making this point.
79. *Aggadas Bereishis* 5:3.

"As for Your offer to recreate a new and great Jewish nation through me and my descendants, will You do this for me at the expense of slaughtering the entire people, disregarding the merit of the Patriarchs? And what good will it do me to have such a nation if, as soon as they sin, they will be destroyed? If a stool with three legs, the Patriarchs, cannot remain standing, how can a stool with only one leg, me, remain standing?"[80]

Moshe continued to pray with utmost intensity, begging Hashem to reconsider His decree of annihilation against the Jewish people.[81] His efforts were so strenuous that he became feverish and gravely ill. He was so weakened that he felt as if he had been ill for thirty days.[82] He knew his very life was at risk, but he was ready to die for the survival of the people.[83]

In the end, Hashem reconsidered because of the merit of the Patriarchs.[84] He retroactively considered His decree of annihilation to be contingent on their persisting in their rebellion. Should they repent, the decree would be considered null and void.[85]

Moshe's arguments prevailed, and Hashem retained him as the leader of the Jewish people. Unlike a mortal king who might feel resentment and demote a minister who rescinds a decree with persuasive arguments, Hashem accepted Moshe's arguments against His decree with joy.[86]

---

80. *Berachos* 32a; *Rashi*; *Abarbanel* to *Shemos* 32:13.

81. *Berachos* 32a with *Maharsha*; *Midrash Aggadah Devarim* 9:15.

See *Shemos Rabbah* 44:1; *Rashash* to *Shabbos* 30a and *Maharsha* which state that Moshe prayed for forty days for the survival of the Jewish people. When he mentioned the *Avos*, Hashem forgave them. This view is in accordance with the *Ibn Ezra's* position that Moshe's prayer took place in the second ascension.

82. *Berachos* 32a; *Midrash Aggadah*; *Ralbag* to *Shemos* 32:11. The word *Vayechal* (and he pleaded) alluded to the word *choli* (sickness).

83. *Berachos* 32a.

84. See *Eliyahu Rabbah* 18; *Midrash Aggadah* to *Devarim* 9:15.

85. See *Hadar Zekeinim* to *Bamidbar* 23:19.

This view is suggestive of the *Ibn Ezra* and *Ralbag's* view that Moshe's prayer was after the destruction of the Golden Calf and when, in fact, the Jewish people showed remorse. Some go so far as to suggest that Hashem's reconsideration was only on Yom Kippur, almost three months later. See *Pirkei D'Rav Kahana* 14:119; *Zohar Vayikra* 14b.

See *Yerushalmi Taanis* 2:1; *Lekach Tov Shemos* 32:14 that the suggestion of Hashem changing His mind is so that we can understand the chain of events. In reality, the whole event goes far deeper than we can comprehend.

See fn. 26 in Ch. 12 as to Hashem's reconsideration of His annihilation of the Jewish people. See *Sanhedrin* 111 with *Rashi* and commentaries; *Bava Kamma* 50a with *Rashi*, *Tosafos* and *Maharsha*; *Pesikta D'Rav Kahana* 26:166; see *Shemos* 32:12; 33:19; 34:6.

86. See *Pesachim* 119a; see *Tehillim* 106:23.

Moshe's impassioned prayers had appeased Hashem. He once again referred to the Jewish people as "My nation." Although He did not indicate that He had completely forgiven the Jewish people or that they would escape punishment, Moshe was satisfied for the time being. He now had a respite to descend from the mountain and deal with the situation in the encampment. He would put the Jewish house in order and then return to the mountain to plead for full forgiveness. For the moment, the danger of destruction had passed.[87]

---

87. *R' Saadiah Gaon; Ramban; Ohr HaChaim; Abarbanel* to *Shemos* 32:14; *Shemos Rabbah* 41:12; *Bamidbar Rabbah* 9:48; *Midrash Tehillim* 18:23. See *Shemos* 32:31.
  See *Rokeach* to *Shemos* 32:14.
  However, those who created and worshiped the idol were still subject to Hashem's wrath (*Toldos Yitzchak; Abarbanel* to *Shemos* 32:14).

15 Moshe Returns

Having stilled Hashem's anger, Moshe felt reinvigorated. He now had the strength to descend from the mountain and confront the sinners in the Jewish encampment. But a major obstacle stood in his way.[1]

As he prepared to descend, Moshe saw angels of destruction coming toward him, intent on killing him and taking back the Torah. Bewildered and confused, Moshe looked around for an avenue of escape, but he could not find any. In desperation, he grabbed hold of the Heavenly Throne, and Hashem wrapped a *tallis* around him for safety.

"Hashem!" Moshe cried out. "What shall I do? I need to go down to the encampment immediately, but if I let go of the Heavenly Throne, the angels of destruction will surely kill me."

---

1. See *Bamidbar Rabbah* 9:48; *Lekach Tov* to *Shemos* 32:15. See *Ralbag* to *Shemos* 32:15.

"Do not worry, Moshe," Hashem replied. "I will create an opening for you underneath the Throne. Pass through that opening, and you will be able to descend in safety."[2]

Hashem then castigated the angels of destruction, and they shrank back. Moshe seized the opportunity to escape.[3] He backed away from the *Shechinah* in respect and deference, slipped through the newly formed opening and descended from the mountain.[4]

As he descended, Moshe carried the two *Luchos* with him. According to some, he carried both *Luchos* in one hand,[5] while according to others, he carried one in each hand.[6] Although he knew that the people did not deserve the *Luchos* and would not receive them, he did not want to leave them in Heaven, where their very presence would bear testimony against the Jewish people.[7] Perhaps he also wanted the *Luchos* to bear witness to the people themselves about the sins they had committed.[8] Others suggest that he was hoping that the sight of the *Luchos* would inspire the people to repent.[9]

Moshe Meets Yehoshua

On the morning of 17 Tammuz, exactly on schedule, Moshe descended from the mountain. Some of the people in the encampment caught sight of a figure in the distance, descending from the mountain. As they strained their eyes, they suddenly recognized Moshe.

---

2. *Shemos Rabbah* 42:4; *Matnos Kehunah*; *Maharzav*; *Shemos Rabbah* 41:7.
3. *Midrash HaChefetz* to *Shemos* 32:15.
4. See *Rabbeinu Bachya*; *Ohr HaChaim*; *Alshich* to *Shemos* 32:15.
    This is similar to how one is supposed to walk away from his rebbi. It is disrespectful to turn one's back when parting from one's rebbi.
    Others suggest the complete opposite. Out of embarrassment, he turned his face away from the *Shechinah*, unable to look into Hashem's eye, after what the Jewish people had done (*Tzeror HaMor*).
    Others suggest that the reference to turning refers to Hashem and not Moshe. His anger having subsided, Hashem turned His face toward the Jewish people (*Tosafos*).
    Some suggest that Moshe did this as a precaution. In case the *Shechinah* reconsiders being merciful and returns to Its Attributes of Judgment, Moshe could immediately repel it with his prayer once again (*Zohar Shemos* 84a).
5. *Alshich* to *Shemos* 32:15.
6. *Rokeach*; *Abarbanel* to *Shemos* 32:15. See *Ibn Ezra* for his view.
7. *Chizkuni* to *Shemos* 32:15.
8. *Abarbanel* to *Shemos* 32:15.
9. *Sforno* to *Shemos* 32:15.

"Look over there!" they shouted. "There is Moshe coming down the mountain. He is alive! Our leader is alive!"

The word spread through the encampment like wildfire. Within minutes, loud arguments and brawls broke out all over. Tensions between the Jewish people and the Erev Rav reached a fever pitch.

"What have you done to our people?" the Jews screamed at the Erev Rav. "You've corrupted us, and it was all for nothing. Moshe is back! Who needs you here? You are nothing but an evil influence. Go back to Egypt. We don't want you here."

While these confrontations were taking place, many others continued with their wild revelry, while the music continued to play. Others sat by the wayside and hung their heads in shame and sorrow over the death of Chur.[10]

From the distance, Moshe could not see any of this. All he saw was activity in the encampment. At the foot of the mountain, he met his disciple Yehoshua,[11] who had set up the tent there when Moshe had ascended the mountain, and had remained there for the entire forty days of his absence. Yehoshua was just about the only person among the Jewish people who had no idea about what was going on in the encampment.[12]

As Moshe and Yehoshua walked toward the encampment, a strange mixture of sounds greeted them.

"Do you hear what I hear?" Moshe asked Yehoshua.

"Indeed, I do," Yehoshua replied. "I hear sounds of celebration — singing, dancing, music — but I also hear angry shouting and fighting. It sounds like there is a civil war going on, to the accompaniment of music and song in the background."[13]

Moshe knew what was going on. Moreover, his purified spiritual nature sharpened his senses to the point where he was able to differentiate and identify sounds barely audible to others.[14]

---

10. *Tosafos R' Efraim Al HaTorah; Malbim* to *Shemos* 32:17.
11. *Chizkuni* to *Shemos* 32:15.
12. See *Lekach Tov; Abarbanel* to *Shemos* 32:17; *Rashi* to *Shemos* 24:13; *Rashi* to *Yoma* 76a.
13. See *Rashi; Targum Yonasan; R' Saadiah Gaon; Ibn Ezra; R' Avraham Ben HaRambam; Malbim; Lekach Tov* to *Shemos* 32:17.
   Yehoshua intimated that these sounds had to be emanating from the Erev Rav. The Torah's use of the word *berei'oh* (in its shouting) spelled backwards is *ha'erev*, referring to the Erev Rav (*Lekach Tov*).
14. See *Korban HaEidah* to *Yerushalmi Taanis* 4:5; *Zohar* 195a.

"A civil war you say?" Moshe said to Yehoshua. "Do you think this sounds like war? Where are the shouts of triumph by the victors or the agonized wailing of the vanquished? This is no war.[15] Yehoshua, you've been through the war with Amalek. You heard the sounds of battle. Does this sound anything like that? Someday, you will lead the people into Canaan and fight a war for years. You should know what war sounds like.[16] These are not the sounds of war. They are the sounds of idol worship and blasphemy.[17] I hear laughter, singing and dancing, and I hear the music of horns, tambourines, drums, cymbals and flutes.[18] I also hear the sounds of torment and remorse, as if the people are lamenting the dead and eulogizing him, as if they are regretting a terrible sin.[19] Let us hurry and investigate. Let us find out what is happening."[20]

Moshe knew full well what was happening. He had already heard all the details in Heaven. However, he did not tell Yehoshua the terrible things he had heard. They would go and see it for themselves.[21]

Moshe Shatters the Luchos

Although Moshe knew what awaited him in the Jewish encampment, he could not mete out their punishment until he had actually witnessed the crime with his own eyes. Furthermore, Moshe assumed that the Jewish people had sinned impulsively out of fear; they thought that their leader had perished and that they had been abandoned in the desert. Perhaps it was essentially only the Erev Rav that had sinned, and even if the rest of the people had also participated, perhaps they would express remorse the instant they caught sight of him. Perhaps, then, they could still be deemed worthy of receiving the *Luchos*.[22]

---

15. See *Rashi; Lekach Tov; R' Avraham Ben HaRambam; Akeidah; Malbim* to *Shemos* 32:17-18.
16. *Yerushalmi Taanis* 4:5; *Tanchuma Va'eschanan* 2; *Shemos Rabbah* 41:1; *Tzeror HaMor*.
17. See *Rashi; Targum Yonasan* to *Shemos* 32:18; *Shemos Rabbah* 41:1.
18. See *Rabbeinu Bachya; Ramban; Tzeror HaMor* to *Shemos* 32:18; *Daniel* 3:5; *Midrash Ohr Afeilah*.
19. *Midrash Ohr Afeilah; Tur* to *Shemos* 32:18. See *Rashi* to *Shemos* 32:18.
20. *Akeidah*.
21. See *Ramban; Abarbanel* to *Shemos* 32:18.
22. See *Moshav Zekeinim* to *Shemos* 32:19. *Yerushalmi Taanis* 4:5; *Korban HaEidah; Shemos Rabbah* 46:1. See also *Devarim Rabbah* 3:12.
   Of course Hashem speaks only truth and there was no doubt in Moshe's eyes of the validity of Hashem's accusation, but Moshe wanted to set an example for future generations as to the proper procedure one must take before deciding on a punishment for a violator (*Maharsha* to *Yevamos* 64a).

Unfortunately, he was bitterly disappointed. The people saw Moshe approach together with Yehoshua well before they actually reached the encampment. Nonetheless, the sounds of celebration did not cease. The people did not come running out to greet and embrace him, nor to express their deep remorse over the corruption that had infected the encampment in his absence. They simply shrugged and continued with their festivities, as if nothing had happened.[23] Only one group showed remorse and disgust at what they had done, and expressed their feelings by kicking the Golden Calf.[24]

Moshe saw the Golden Calf and the instruments, and he was beside himself with rage. It was bad enough that the people had sinned but, at least, they could have shown some remorse. This indifferent reaction to his return, however, was beyond toleration. How could he deliver the *Luchos* to such people? It was unthinkable.[25]

Moshe and Yehoshua entered the outskirts of the encampment, and suddenly, the *Luchos* elicited an unexpected reaction. The essence of the *Luchos* were the letters of the Commandments, pure and holy spiritual entities fashioned from the very sounds that Hashem had uttered on the mountaintop. These letters now recoiled when they neared the contaminated earthly domain of the Jewish encampment.

"Woe to this people," the letters cried out, "that heard the Commandment not to make other gods, and violated it."

The letters, miraculously retaining their shape and their form, wrenched themselves free from the stone into which they were engraved and fled Heavenward, to be reunited with their Creator.[26] After the departure of the letters, Moshe could no longer carry the 200-pound *Luchos* in his right hand with ease, as he had done

---

23. See *Targum Yonasan*; *Malbim* to *Shemos* 32:19; *Midrash Rabbah* 43:1.
24. *Ramban* to *Shemos* 32:1; *Ohr HaChaim* to *Shemos* 32:19.
  They vanished from the area of the Golden Calf, making Moshe see only the Golden Calf and the remaining instruments that were left there.
25. See *Targum Yonasan*; *Malbim*; *Sforno* to *Shemos* 32:19; *Midrash Rabbah* 43:1.
26. *Yerushalmi Taanis* 4:5; *Maharsha* to *Pesachim* 87b; *Targum Yonasan*; *Tosafos* to *Shemos* 32:19.
  Others suggest that the letters flew toward the foot of Mount Sinai and eventually Moshe would throw the *Luchos* to where the letters were (*Kli Yakar*).
  All the Jewish people were able to see them because they flew high and could easily be seen at a distance. This was important so that the Jews could witness the ramifications of their sinful deeds.
  See *Shaarei Aharon* to *Devarim* 9:17 who brings a source that the words *Zachor* and *Shamor* remained on the *Luchos* and did not fly away.

before. He was also weakened and demoralized by the scenes he had encountered. He tried to grasp the *Luchos* with both hands, but they were still too heavy. A human being, rendered buoyant by his soul, can be carried while he is alive but becomes exceedingly heavy when he dies and his soul departs; he becomes dead weight. In the same way, the stone *Luchos* were rendered buoyant by the spiritual letters. Once the letters departed, the *Luchos* became lifeless, dead weight; they were as worthless as a candle without a flame. Moshe could no longer carry them.[27]

Moshe declared, "In the Commandment of the *pesach* sacrifice, the Torah tells us that no pagan or apostate may share in it. Here we have virtually an entire people that have become apostates. Surely, they are not permitted a share in the entire Torah."[28]

Moshe lifted the lifeless, worthless slabs of stone that the *Luchos* had become after the departure of the letters,[29] and hurled them down at the base of the mountain, in full view of all the people.[30] In his heart, he hoped that this drastic action — seeing before their very

---

27. *Rabbeinu Bachya; Chizkuni; Rokeach* to *Shemos* 32:16,19; *Pirkei D'Rav Eliezer* 45; *Radal; Avos D'Rav Nassan* 2:3; *Tanchuma Ki Sisa* 26; *Yerushalmi Taanis* 4:5; *Korban HaEidah; Rashbam* to *Shemos* 32:19; *Ohr HaChaim* to *Devarim* 9:17.

Others add that the *Luchos* were easily breakable because without letters the stone became almost a hollow shell (*Bechor Shor*).

This is similar to a letter from the king, signed with his seal or signature. If the signature or seal is erased from the paper, it makes the paper worthless.

This was also comparable to a candle whose fire was extinguished, leaving the candle useless. The stone of the *Luchos* had no value once the letters were gone (*Avos D'Rav Nassan* 2).

Some suggest that the *Luchos* were actually over 600 pounds (*Meam Loez*).

28. See *Rashi* to *Shemos* 32:19; *Shabbos* 87a. See *Tosafos* there that this *kal vachomer* argument can be refuted.

29. Only because of Moshe's superhuman strength was he capable of holding onto the *Luchos* (see *Rashi; Sifsei Chachamim,* end of *Devarim;* see *Avos D'Rav Nassan* 2:3).

30. See *Rashi; Lekach Tov* to *Shemos* 32:19; *Pirkei D'Rav Eliezer* 45; *Radal; Pane'ach Raza; Tanchuma Eikev* 11; *Shemos Rabbah* 46:1; *Tosafos* to *Nedarim* 38a.

See *Riva* to *Devarim* and *Ibn Ezra HaKatzar* who write that there is a difference of views whether Moshe dropped the *Luchos* due to anger, simply because he was overwhelmed by their heaviness due to the absence of letters, or because Hashem told him to do so.

See *Abarbanel* to *Shemos* 32:19 and *Bamidbar Rabbah* 9:54 who write that Moshe threw them where he had built an altar during the *sheloshes yemei hagbalah,* the three days of separation.

Some add that Moshe intentionally broke the *Luchos* so that he would be as culpable as the Jewish people. Their sins were the cause of the letters parting from the *Luchos,* and now with Moshe breaking the stones, he considered himself as guilty as they were. Moshe hoped to respond to Hashem that he not be made into a great nation at the cost of the Jews being annihilated. He reasoned that if they die, so would he,

own eyes the destruction of the gift he had brought from Heaven — would awaken them from their spiritual torpor and inspire them to feel remorse and repent.³¹

Moshe also chose to smash the *Luchos* rather than return them to Heaven, because he didn't want the *Luchos* to endure as an everlasting accuser against the Jewish people. Without the *Luchos*, all that remained of the compact between Hashem and the people was a verbal agreement.³² Others add that the *Luchos* represented the *kesubah*, the nuptial agreement between Hashem and the people. The smashing of the *Luchos* would nullify the marriage and thereby minimize the severity of the sin.³³

There are other versions of the events that culminated in the shattering of the *Luchos*. According to one opinion, when Moshe saw the Jewish people cavorting around the Golden Calf, he cried out, "How can I give the *Luchos* to such sinners?" He turned around and prepared to return the *Luchos* to Heaven. Aharon and the elders discerned his intentions and came running to stop him. They tried to grab the *Luchos* out of his hands, and a struggle ensued. In the end, Moshe was the stronger. He wrested the *Luchos* from them and smashed them on the ground.³⁴

Others suggest that the *Shechinah* grabbed the *Luchos*, so to speak, to prevent Moshe from delivering them to the Jewish people. Moshe maintained his grasp on two *tefach* measures, Hashem gripped two *tefach* measures of the other side, and no one held the middle two *tefach* measures. Hashem allowed Moshe to wrest control of the *Luchos* and smash them on the ground.³⁵ According to some, Hashem explicitly told Moshe to smash them on the ground.³⁶

---

31. *Moshav Zekcinim; Akeidah; Aharbanel* to *Shemos* 32:19.
32. *Zohar Shemos* 84a; *Moshav Zekeinim; Tzeror HaMor* to *Shemos* 32:19; *Shemos Rabbah* 43:1; *Tanchuma Ki Sisa* 31.
33. *Ibn Ezra* to *Shemos* 32:19.
34. See *Avos D'Rav Nassan* 2:3; *Rokeach* to *Shemos* 32:20.
35. See *Tanchuma Eikev* 11; *Shemos Rabbah* 43:1; *Yerushalmi Taanis* 4:5; *Korban HaEidah*.

Many add that the struggle was not over the *Luchos*, but between mercy and judgment. Moshe prevailed over Hashem by having mercy triumph over judgment. Some add that with the *Luchos* acting as a witness of the Jewish people's violation of the Torah, Hashem wanted them back to cast judgment upon the people. With Moshe winning the struggle and having mercy prevail, destroying the *Luchos* signified that the prosecutor was defeated and mercy had prevailed.

36. *Avos D'Rav Nassan; Yerushalmi Taanis* 4.

After the fact, Hashem told Moshe, "*Yeyasher kochacha* — Thank you for breaking the *Luchos*. You did the right thing." Hashem approved of his action, because the people had sinned.[37] Although the *Luchos* had the status of holy writings, even after the letters were erased, it was permissible for Moshe to break them, under the circumstances. The people needed to be taught a lesson.[38]

The breaking of the *Luchos* had a dramatic and lasting effect on the Jewish people. After the Giving of the Torah, they had been on the verge of reaching an exalted level, enjoying the best of human and angelic existence. Hashem had given each of them a *neshamah yeseirah*, an enhanced dimension to their souls. They were about to gain their freedom from their evil inclinations and the angel of death eternally. They were also blessed to forever retain in their memories the Torah they learned. But with the breaking of the *Luchos*, their evil inclinations did not depart. They remained vulnerable to the angel of death. They would have to struggle to remember the Torah they learned.[39] And the *neshamah yeseirah* left them, returning only on Shabbos and Yom Tov.[40] Ultimately, the broken *Luchos* would cause the destruction of the Second *Beis HaMikdash*.[41]

As for the day on which Moshe smashed the *Luchos*, 17 Tammuz, it would prove to be a fateful day, a day of tragedy in Jewish history.[42]

---

37. *Yerushalmi Taanis* 4:5; *Shabbos* 87a; *Yevamos* 62a.
    See *Bava Basra* 14b and *Maharsha* to *Yevamos* 62a for proof that Hashem approved of Moshe's decision to break them. See also *Avos D'Rav Nassan* 2 for another view and *Binyan Yehoshua* on it.
38. R' *Yehudah HaChassid* to *Shemos* 32:19.
39. See *Shemos Rabbah* 41:7; *Vayikra Rabbah* 18:3; *Maharzav*; *Yefei To'ar*; *Eruvin* 54 with *Rashi*; *Maharsha*; *Ohr HaChaim* to *Shemos* 32:19; *Tikkunei Zohar* 146; *Zohar* 32:7; *Zohar Mishpatim* 113a; *Yalkut* 1:391 p. 232.
    They would also have to learn Torah in pain, poverty, exile and illness. (See *Bamidbar Rabbah* 7:1.)
40. *Yalkut Reuveni Ki Sisa*; *Reishis Chochmah*.
41. *Yalkut Reuveni Ki Sisa*.
    See *Tosafos Al HaTorah* who writes that the sadness and lamenting Yehoshua heard was that of the Jews knowing that the sin of the Golden Calf would have a part in the destruction of the First *Beis HaMikdash*.
42. *Taanis* 26a, 28a.
    Some add that it is for this reason that the Torah refers to the holiday of Shavuos as *Chag HaKatzir* (the Festival of the Harvest) and *Bikkurim* (of the first fruit), and not *Chag Matan Torah* (the Festival of the Giving of the Torah). The breaking of the *Luchos* caused a void in the celebration of the Giving of the Torah. It wasn't until Yom Kippur, when they received the second *Luchos*, that the Giving of the Torah was completed (*Miluim* to *Torah Shleimah* §15).

Moshe Pulverizes the Golden Calf

After smashing the *Luchos*, Moshe now directed his anger at the source of the rebellion. He marched into the encampment, his face grim, and his piercing eyes scanning the faces of the crowds. Despite having worshiped the Golden Calf, most of the people were overcome with remorse and self-loathing as soon as Moshe returned, and shrank back, shame faced, as Moshe passed.

In order to deal with the crisis, Moshe grouped the Jewish people who had become involved with the Golden Calf into three categories. First, there were those who had been given *hasraah*, adequate warning, and had nonetheless worshiped the Golden Calf in front of witnesses. They would be executed by the sword. Second, there were those who had worshiped the Golden Calf in front of witnesses but had received no prior warning. They would die in a plague. According to some opinions, those guilty of sacrificing to the idol were to be executed by the sword, while those who embraced and kissed it were to die by plague.

Finally, there were those who had sinned without warning or witnesses, or who had joy in their hearts that they did not show on their faces. They would be treated as a *sotah*, a woman suspected of infidelity to her husband, who is given a special potion to determine her guilt or innocence. In the same way, Moshe would prepare a potion to determine the guilt or innocence of the people regarding their infidelity to Hashem to Whom they had been symbolically married at Mount Sinai, by worshiping the Golden Calf.[43]

For the potion of the *sotah*, earth was taken from the ground of the Mishkan and dissolved in water, which she was given to drink. Moshe decided to follow a similar regimen. He would pulverize the Golden Calf and its accessories and ornaments. He would dissolve the powder in water and give it to the people to drink immediately before the solution broke down and the powder settled to the bottom.[44]

---

43. *Yoma* 66b with *Rashi*.
   See *Bamidbar Rabbah* 9:45. For various other opinions see *Lekach Tov* 32:29; *Pesikta Rabbah* 10. See also *Shaarei Aharon* for an additional explanation.
44. *Rashi*; *Sifsei Chachamim*; *Tzeror HaMor*; *Ramban* to *Shemos* 32:20.
   Some suggest that this dust would be placed in the Mishkan and actually used for a real *sotah*. See *Bamidbar* 5:17; *Bamidbar Rabbah* 9:54; *Pirkei D'Rav Eliezer* 45.
   In fact, according to the Midrash, the whole section in the Torah dealing with the *sotah* is connected to the Golden Calf. Here, Moshe was the Kohen who cautioned the

In another similarity to a *sotah*, whose head is uncovered, the heads of the Jewish people were also uncovered after they sinned with the Golden Calf. The two gold crowns engraved with the Name of Hashem that they had received at Mount Sinai were now removed.[45]

Moshe built a huge fire, from highly flammable substances.[46] He then tossed the Golden Calf into the flames, where it burned with such ferocity that its former form was completely obliterated; it was charred, scorched, blackened beyond recognition and reduced to ashes.[47] Others suggest that the gold would not have burned. Rather, the canopy over the idol and its combustible accessories and ornaments burned.[48] Moshe then ground the Golden Calf into a fine powder.[49]

According to some opinions, Moshe spoke to the calf before consigning it to the flames. He said, "All this gold, more precious than any other metal! Is this why you were created, to become an idol for the Jewish people?" The gold was miraculously transformed into wood and burst into flame from the heat of Moshe's radiance, and turned to ash.[50]

Moshe took the ash or powder, the residue of the Golden Calf, and scattered it over a stream running through Mount Sinai and gave the water to the people to drink.[51]

According to some opinions, Moshe had difficulty finding water in which to dissolve the powdered idol. There was no water in the

---

Jews about the ramifications of their actions. The powder of the Golden Calf represented the earth that would be placed in the water for a *sotah* to drink. Like a guilty *sotah*, the belly of the Jews would bloat, to signify their guilt.

See *Radal* and *Rokeach* who write that Moshe's dialogue with Aharon and his call for those loyal to Hashem to gather around him, a call answered by the entire tribe of Levi (*Shemos* 32:21-26), took place before the destruction of the Golden Calf.

45. *Targum Yerushalmi; Tosafos* to *Shemos* 32:25.
46. *Ibn Ezra; Chizkuni* to *Shemos* 32:20.
47. *Ramban* to *Shemos* 32:1; *R' Avraham Ben HaRambam; Ohr HaChaim* to *Shemos* 32:20.
48. *Abarbanel* to *Shemos* 32:19.
49. *Ramban* to *Shemos* 32:1.
   See *Alshich* as to why it was necessary to burn it, when he could have ground it without having to burn it.
   See *Tosafos* and *Rabbeinu Bachya* who write that the word "*vayitchan*" (he ground) can be understood as a combination of two words, *vayet chein* (he put forth grace). Moshe saw that eventually, through the destruction of the Golden Calf, Hashem would pardon the Jewish people and put forth mercy and grace toward them.
50. *Sifsei Kohen* to *Shemos* 32:19.
51. See *Lekach Tov; Ibn Ezra; Abarbanel* to *Shemos* 32:20.

desert. As for the Well of Miriam, Moshe had no intention of putting the accursed powder of the idol into the blessed waters of the Well.[52] As he considered his problem, he saw a great tidal wave approaching across the desert to inundate the Jewish encampment.

"What are you doing?" Moshe asked the water.

"I am coming to destroy the world," the water replied. "Now that the *Luchos* and the Torah it represents are broken, there is no longer any reason for the world to continue to exist."

Moshe threw the powder into this towering wall of water and said, "I will give the people to drink of the water in which the powder of the idol is dissolved, and the sinners will be exposed. The world will be rid of these vile people and the Torah will once again be whole."

The water's progress was arrested, but the waters continued to roil and churn; they did not recede until after Moshe had administered the potion to the people.[53]

After drinking the potion, the people passed it from their bodies in the form of urine and solid wastes. The idol that had once been revered and worshiped was humiliated and reduced to waste products, all its glory culminating in an ignominious end.[54]

After drinking the potion, the bellies of many of the guilty swelled, and they were stricken by an affliction called *hydroken*, which caused facial contortions.[55] They suffered all night, and were dead by morning.[56] The lips of those who had kissed the idol turned a pale yellowish color.[57] Many were afflicted with *tzaraas* lesions on their foreheads, a readily visible sign of shame, and suffered abnormal discharges of bodily fluids, relegating them to the ritually contaminated status of *metzora* and *zav*. This spared them from death, because a *metzora* is already considered like the dead. Nonetheless, the shame and humiliation were shocking. A nation that had been cleansed of all blemishes and sickness as they stood at Mount Sinai were now beset by affliction.[58]

---

52. Some suggest that the "Well of Miriam" had its source from the rock Moshe had hit to give the Jewish people water (*Rabbeinu Meyuchas* to *Devarim* 9:21).
53. See *Zohar Mishpatim* 113b.
54. *Rabbeinu Bachya; Ramban; Abarbanel* to *Shemos* 32:20.
55. *Rashi.*
56. *Zohar.*
57. *Pirkei D'Rav Eliezer* 45; *Midrash HaGadol; Rabbeinu Bachya* to *Shemos* 32:20.
58. *Pesikta Rabbah; Vayikra Rabbah* 18:4; *Etz Yosef.*
 This was so because the Jews were *motzi shem ra* (slandering themselves) by claiming

Moshe Confronts Aharon

After he pulverized the Golden Calf, dissolved its powder in water and gave the potion to the people, Moshe turned his angry attention to Aharon, determined to discover the root of the rebellion.[59]

"Aharon, I am shocked," Moshe said furiously. "Why did you cause this catastrophe to happen?[60] What drove you to do this?[61] I know this must have caused you great torment, so they must have done something really horrific to compel you to make the idol for them. What was it?[62] I see that they killed Chur but spared you.[63] Explain this to me, Aharon. What was going on?

"Aharon, don't you realize that you deserve to die because of what happened, even if you were only an indirect cause?[64] In the end, you created an idol that the people worshiped. Did you harbor some deep unexpressed hatred to the people that led you to lead them to the brink of complete destruction? I don't understand what you could have been thinking, Aharon.[65]

"And if that were not enough, you actually made matters worse for them when you struck the Golden Calf and demonstrated to the people that it was a lifeless form. Had you not done so, they might have been able to say in their defense that they acted in error, thinking they were worshiping something of substance. But you proved to them that the Golden Calf was nothing, and yet they worshiped it. This constitutes purposeful and premeditated transgression. So you see, you just added to their guilt.[66]

"And if that were not enough, you went and established a holiday for the idol? How could you do such a thing? Because of you, they not only worshiped the idol, they celebrated in front of it. They

---

"*eileh elohecha*" (this is your god) when they knew it was not the case. See *Targum Yonasan; Ibn Ezra* to *Shemos* 32:20 for their views.
59. *Tzeror HaMor; Ibn Ezra* to *Shemos* 32:21.
60. *R' Saadiah Gaon; Ralbag* to *Shemos* 32:21.
61. *Malbim* to *Shemos* 32:21.
62. See *Rashi* to *Shemos* 32:21.
  In fact, this was the case since Aharon feared for his life and, as discussed earlier, the premise of wanting a leader was not enough for which Aharon should risk his life (*Tosafos Al HaTorah*; see *Tanchuma Tetzaveh* 11).
63. *Tanchuma Tetzaveh* 11; *Etz Yosef*.
64. *Midrash Aggadah* to *Shemos* 32:21.
65. *Ramban* to *Shemos* 32:21.
66. *Vayikra Rabbah* 7:1.

rejoiced in their sin! Can you imagine how much that magnified their guilt?[67] At the very least, why did you not protest the construction of the Golden Calf?"[68]

Aharon looked at his younger brother with dismay. "My master Moshe," he said, "please do not be angry with me. I did the best I could under the circumstances. You know, as well as I do, the character of this nation. After living in Egypt for centuries, they are deeply rooted in evil. They are full of flaws and weakness, and they are miserably deficient in faith. We have both seen them repeatedly fail the tests that Hashem has given them.[69]

"What did you expect from them when you left them for forty days? With their leader absent, their natural evil tendencies that were developed in Egypt rose to the surface. Anyone could have seen that it was only a matter of time before there would be a disastrous eruption.

"On top of everything, they had to contend with the pernicious influence of the Erev Rav.[70] And let us not forget who allowed the Erev Rav to join the Jewish people in the desert. It was you, Moshe. You allowed these incorrigible idol-worshipers to join a nation of fragile, newly emancipated slaves. It was your choice, Moshe, so why are you blaming me for the consequences?[71]

"And even those among the Jewish people who really were righteous deep down, how did you expect them to deal with the images Satan showed them, of you lying dead in your casket?[72]

"Considering the situation, Moshe, I think I did all that could have been expected from me. I tried with all my might to prevent this catastrophe from happening. The people cried out for a leader to lead them, an idol to worship, and I tried to engineer all sorts of delays and postponements. Everything was futile. The people were so intent that I simply could not stop them.

---

67. *Sforno* to *Shemos* 32:21.
  Some suggest that Moshe endorsed Aharon's plan to make a holiday the next day. The intention was that the delay would allow the righteous Jews to protest the Golden Calf and prevent it from being worshiped (*Tosafos*).
68. *Malbim* to *Devarim* 9:20.
69. See *Rashi*; *R' Avraham Ben HaRambam*; *Akeidah*; *Maasei Hashem* to *Shemos* 32:22,25.
70. *Lekach Tov*; *Sforno*; *Malbim* to *Shemos* 32:22,25. See *Netziv*.
  The letters of the word "*v'ra*" (in evil, toward evil) backwards spells Erev, a reference to the present evil being that of the Erev Rav (*Tur* to *Shemos* 32:22).
71. *Tzeror HaMor*; *Abarbanel* to *Shemos* 32:22.
72. *Targum Yonasan* 32:22.

"I told them I would need a lot of gold, hoping they would be reluctant to part with it. I even told them to take the gold from their wives and children. Nothing stopped them. In no time at all, they brought me a veritable mountain of gold. What could I have done with this gold? Am I a goldsmith that can make figures out of gold? So I told the people that all I had to do was throw the gold into the fire. If the image had any value, it would emerge on its own. Of course, I expected that nothing would happen and the people would realize how foolish they were being. How was I to know that Satan and the Erev Rav's sorcerers would conspire to have a seemingly live calflike creature emerge from the flames?[73]

"Anyway, look at it this way, Moshe. You and I are very much alike. You broke the *Luchos* because you wanted to draw Hashem's anger onto yourself and divert it from the Jewish people. I did the same thing. I took the lead in this business in order to take the blame on my shoulders and spare the Jewish people from responsibility for their shortcomings.[74]

"It is true that the travesty took place despite all my best-intentioned efforts. But at least I did my best. I didn't cause this terrible sin. I simply failed in my efforts to prevent it."

Despite Aharon's impassioned plea in his defense, Moshe saw that Aharon bore some responsibility for what had transpired. The cloud pillars that had protected the Jewish encampment in Aharon's merit had departed, leaving the people exposed to the desert and their enemies, a clear indication that, for the time being, Aharon had lost his merit.[75]

"The people have exposed themselves," Moshe said to Aharon, "by showing the world that the *Shechinah* does not reside in their midst.[76] They have shown themselves lacking in mitzvos, faith and gratitude to Hashem for all the great miracles He has performed

---

73. See *Rashi*; *Gur Aryeh*; *Sefer HaZikaron*; *Targum Yonasan*; *Sforno*; *R' Avaraham Ben HaRambam*; *Sifsei Kohen* to *Shemos* 32:22-24.
   See *Ramban* that Aharon gave only a brief and general description of the actual events to Moshe.
74. *Midrash* in *Torah Shleimah* to *Shemos* 32:22.
75. *Targum* to *Shir HaShirim* 2:17; *Nachal Kadmonim*; *Tosafos* to *Shemos* 32:25.
   See *Shemos Rabbah* 32:3.
   It would only be through Moshe's prayer that the clouds would return to guide them and to protect them from the desert elements.
76. *Lekach Tov*; *Ohr HaChaim* to *Shemos* 32:25.

for them.⁷⁷ Even the righteous among them have been tainted by their association with the sinners.⁷⁸

"The Jewish people now stand humiliated in the court of world opinion. The nations of the world have witnessed how the Jewish people have desecrated the Name of Hashem. Always considered a wise, sober and judicious people, the Jewish people have been exposed as a laughingstock, a nation of fools and scoundrels. Our enemies mock and taunt us for our foolishness. They speak and gossip about us with scorn and ridicule. They no longer fear the Jewish people, knowing that our merits have been diminished. They know that they can attack us with impunity and even expect to be victorious.⁷⁹

"This shame will last long into the future. Future generations will revile the Jewish people for their terrible sin. Many centuries from now, King Yeravam will build his own golden calves and claim he is only following the traditions of the Jewish people who came forth from Egypt.⁸⁰

"Drastic steps have to be taken immediately," Moshe concluded. "The damage needs to be repaired, and the dignity and reputation of the Jewish people need to be restored."

Moshe would do so, but at the cost of many lives.⁸¹

---

77. R' Avraham Ben HaRambam; Chizkini; Rashbam; Sifsei Kohen to Shemos 32:25.

See Sforno who writes that Moshe also suggested that no righteous Jews existed among them since, if there were any, they would have and should have protested the worshiping of the calf. It is interesting to note that the tribe of Levi did not participate in the sin of the Golden Calf, and would soon be identified as followers of Hashem when Moshe called out "Mi laHashem eilai — Whoever is for Hashem, join me."

78. Moshav Zekeinim to Shemos 32:25.

79. See Rashi; Raev; Ramban; Targum Yonasan; Sforno; Bechor Shor to Shemos 32:25.

See Tosafos to Pesachim 3b on the word shemetz. The root of the word used in Shemos 32:25 in relation to the Golden Calf is associated with idol worship.

Despite Moshe's remarks, the Jewish people would have a good response to his concern as to how the enemies of the Jews would use the sin of the Golden Calf as a basis to degrade and taunt them when they would be guilty of the same actions. A parable can best explain this scenario. A queen once had some dirt on herself. The maidservants came to the king suggesting that he divorce his queen and replace her with one of them. They explained that the queen was dirty and it was unbecoming for her to remain queen. The king replied to the maidservants that they were fools. The queen, in one small instance, had a speck of dirt on her while they, as maidservants, were constantly unclean and full of dirt. Similarly, it was foolish for the enemy nations of the Jews to mock them when they were far guiltier of idol worship. Some add that this suggestion of the maidservants in the parable is in and of itself foolish, for one cannot compare a maidservant to a queen. Despite the fact that the nations of the world were guilty in their own right, the Jews (the queen) were held to a higher standard (Raev; Bechor Shor to Shemos 32:25).

80. Lekach Tov; Ramban; Rabbeinu Bachya; Targum Yonasan to Shemos 32:25. See I Melachim 12:28.

81. See Abarbanel; Ramban; Rabbeinu Bachya; R' Avraham Ben HaRambam to Shemos 32:25.

Some suggest that, until now, their dedication to idol worship was just in their hearts and minds, leaving them innocent of any practical violation in this matter. However, with the physical act of worship, they were, once and for all, exposed as to who they really were all along and were now eligible for a death sentence (HaKesav VeHaKabbalah).

16 Remorse and Retribution

Moshe realized that he had a small window of opportunity to reestablish the reputation and the stature of the Jewish people, to show the nations of the world that the Jewish people enjoyed genuine strong leadership, and that justice prevailed. The desecration of the Name of Hashem had to be avenged publicly. There had to be a clear demonstration that there would be no tolerance of idol worship.[1]

There was no time to be wasted. Hashem's wrath had subsided, but it could flare up again very quickly if no positive steps were taken right away. By the middle of the day of 17 Tammuz, the day of his descent from Mount Sinai, Moshe had already broken the *Luchos* and destroyed the Golden Calf. He had also given the Jewish people a potion to drink made from the powdered remnants of the idol, thereby assuring retribution for those who had been involved with

---

1. *Ramban; Abarbanel; Moshav Zekeinim; Sifsei Kohen* to *Shemos* 32:26.

the idol albeit not in the presence of witnesses. Without any further delay, he now turned his attention to those idol worshipers who had been forewarned and whose crimes had been committed in the presence of witnesses.[2]

Moshe marched to the court in which the Sanhedrin was in session, and called out,[3] "Whoever is for Hashem, rally around me! Whoever has the fear of Hashem in his heart, come to me! Whoever is inspired to defend Hashem's honor, come to me! Whoever's hands are clean of involvement with the Golden Calf, who did not donate to its construction, who wants to be deemed worthy of serving Hashem in the future, come to me! Let us judge the accused and condemn the guilt."[4]

Thousands of Jews answered Moshe's rallying cry — the elders who served on the Sanhedrin, the princes of the tribes and others who were without guilt, plus the entire tribe of Levi. Not a single member of the tribe of Levi failed to respond to Moshe's call.[5]

It came as no surprise that the tribe of Levi was completely untarnished by the sin of idol worship. Yaakov, who had received the Torah from his father Yitzchak, entrusted the Torah into the care of his son Levi. For hundreds of years, the Levites had been the guardians of the Torah on behalf of the Jewish people.[6] Of all the people, only the tribe of Levi, which was exempt from forced labor, had practiced the mitzvah of *milah*, circumcision, even in the land of Egypt. More important, only the tribe of Levi had been free of idol worship in Egypt. Unlike the other tribes, they had led exemplary lives of holiness and piety and had never sunk to the level of idol worship.[7]

---

2. See *Chizkuni* to *Shemos* 32:30; *Tanchuma Ki Sisa* 26.
   See *Pirkei D'Rav Eliezer* 45 and *Ibn Ezra* to *Shemos* 32:20 who suggest that it was these very people bearing a symbol that showed they had worshiped the Golden Calf who were identified by the tribe of Levi to be killed.
   Although a majority of the Jewish people were guilty for failing to protest, it is conceivable that the *Nesiim* (tribal leaders), the elders and the tribe of Levi had all warned the violators and were witness to their worship.
3. *Targum Yonasan*; *Tzeror HaMor* to *Shemos* 32:26.
4. *Midrash Tehillim* 1,18; *Targum Yonasan*; *Rokeach*; *Abarbanel*; *Malbim* to *Shemos* 32:26; *Yalkut* 393.
5. *Pirkei D'Rav Eliezer* 45; *Bechor Shor*; *Daas Zekeinim* to *Shemos* 32:26,28.
   See *Midrash Ohr Afeilah*; *Malbim* to *Shemos* 32:29 who write that the firstborn did not come, due to the fact that they had idolaters among them.
6. See *Rambam, Hil. Avodah Zarah* 1:3.
7. *Ramban*; *Abarbanel*; *Sifsei Kohen* to *Shemos* 32:26.
   The words "Mi Lashem" — composed of the letters *mem yud lamed hei* — spell out the word *milah* (circumcision), a symbolic reference to Levi's candidacy. The sword

In the end, of all the thousands of volunteers who had answered his call, Moshe chose only the tribe of Levi to stand by his side.[8] He did not feel the innocent members of the other tribes would be completely reliable in fulfilling the difficult task that faced them. They would have to execute the sinners without mercy, and what if the sinners turned out to be their relatives or neighbors? Better to rely on the tribe of Levi that was pure in its entirety. The members of the tribe of Levi were unlikely to encounter relatives or neighbors in the course of their holy mission in defense of Hashem's honor.[9] Furthermore, since Aharon of the tribe of Levi had been indirectly responsible for the construction of the Golden Calf, it was only appropriate that the members of his tribe should atone for his actions.

When the tribe of Levi was fully mobilized and assembled around him, Moshe declared, "This is what Hashem has said, 'Let each man strap on his sword and go to the courts of the tribes. Put those accused of idol worship on trial and, if they are found guilty, put them to death by the sword. Do not show them any mercy. Even if they are your half brothers, the sons of your mothers by fathers from a different tribe, or even if they should be your grandchildren, the sons of your daughters from fathers from a different tribe, or even if they should be close friends or relatives, show them no mercy or compassion. You must carry out the letter of the law and bring them to justice. Remember, you are soldiers defending the honor of Hashem.'"[10]

---

that they were to bring with them would also allude to the knife with which they had performed circumcisions. Only those who had previously used the knife for milah should come with their swords raised to kill the sinners.

See *Let My Nation Go* p. 37 fns. 16 and 17.

8. *Bechor Shor; Hadar Zekeinim* to *Shemos* 32:26.

Some suggest that since the innocent of each tribe had to deal with the sinners among them, only the tribe of Levi had the freedom to judge the entire Jewish population, since there was no one in their own tribe who had sinned (*Sifsei Kohen*).

9. *Yoma* 66b; *Rashi; Bechor Shor; Hadar Zekeinim; Sifsei Kohen* to *Shemos* 32:26.

See *Pane'ach Raza* who suggests that the tribe of Levi did indeed start the process, but were later joined by others who were also clean of sin.

10. *Ramban; Ibn Ezra; Moshav Zekeinim; Abarbanel; Sifsei Kohen* to *Shemos* 32:27,29.

The Torah uses the words son and brother as possible members of the tribe of Levi that were to be killed, were they to have worshiped the calf. Having established that no one in their tribe sinned, the reference to son refers to one's grandson who is the son of his daughter, and a brother refers to one's half brother having the same mother but not the same father. In both cases, these children had mothers from the tribe of Levi, yet their tribal affiliation follows the father.

Only Levi had the fortitude to kill the sinners, regardless of their relationship. This was another reason why they were chosen to judge, as opposed to anyone else (*Tzeror HaMor*).

The Levites followed Moshe's instructions and arrested those who were accused of worshiping the idol in public in front of witnesses.[11] Three thousand men,[12] two-thirds of the worst idol worshipers, were convicted and summarily executed on that very same day. Some say that the 3,000 were all from among the Erev Rav,[13] including the sorcerers and archvillains Ianus and Iambrus, whose deaths were as significant as the deaths of 3,000 others.[14] The corpses of the executed criminals were left to molder like excrement in the sun, in order to strike fear into the hearts of the people and remind them of the consequences of idol worship and the desecration of the Name of Hashem.[15]

Although innumerable Jewish people saw the execution of the condemned, not a single person stepped forward to protest. The people were clearly in agreement with the verdicts; they understood full well that these sentences were just and appropriate.[16] Ironically, the same people who bore guilt for remaining silent in the face of rampant idol worship were now forgiven as a reward for remaining silent in the face of justice.[17]

Their mission accomplished, the tribe of Levi assembled once again in front of Moshe to receive further instructions. Moshe was concerned that they might feel despondent for having just put to death 3,000 people. Even though these people deserved to die, killing 3,000 people was no simple matter to be taken in stride.

---

11. *Tanchuma Ki Sisa* 26; *Sifsei Kohen* to *Shemos* 32:26.

Some suggest that the Levites simply searched for those who were recognized as having worshiped the calf, either because they themselves were eyewitnesses or because the sinners were recognized by the symbols and signs previously mentioned. See *Ramban*; *Targum Yonasan*; *Ibn Ezra HaKatzer*; *R' Avraham Ben HaRambam* to *Shemos* 32:27,28.

See *Imrei Shefer* who writes that because the Levites were free of guilt, they could act as legal witnesses. As witnesses, it would be their duty to be the first to prosecute and punish the violators. See *Devarim* 17:7.

12. Most authorities believe that the 3,000 who were killed were under the umbrella of having received warning and having been witnessed worshiping the idol. Some suggest that the number 3,000 included all the deaths that took place due to the Golden Calf, including those who did not have witnesses or warning (*Tanchuma Ki Sisa* 26).

13. *Zohar* 237.

14. *Zohar Balak* 194.

Others suggest that because of the death of Chur, who was considered as valued as 3,000 people, 3000 people died as revenge (*Yalkut Ohr Afeilah*).

15. *Shemos Rabbah* 42:3; *Etz Yosef*.

16. *Akeidah*; *Sifsei Kohen* to *Shemos* 32:28.

17. *HaKesav VeHaKabbalah* to *Shemos* 32:28.

Therefore, Moshe sought to placate the tribe of Levi and lift their spirits, reassuring them of the righteousness of their mission, and to reward them.[18]

"My dear brothers from the tribe of Levi," Moshe announced. "You have just done a marvelous thing. You have sanctified the Name of Hashem, and for this you will be given eternal reward. You will be separated from the rest of the Jewish people and consecrated for service in the holy domains. You will be the priests and the attendants. The sacred service will be in your hands. Originally, this role was supposed to have gone to the firstborn of all the tribes, but because many of them were guilty of idol worship, Hashem has stripped them of this great privilege and honor. It is now given to you.[19] You will be the priests who perform the sacred service. You will be the ones who pronounce the blessings over the Jewish people. You will be the attendants, the singers and the musicians.[20] You, my brothers of the tribe of Levi, did not receive an individual blessing from our ancestor Yaakov on his deathbed, but now, as an additional reward, I will rectify that omission. You will be specifically included in the blessings that I will give the Jewish people before I pass away.[21]

"Nonetheless, even though the killings were perfectly just," Moshe continued, "you should still do an act of atonement. Bring sacrifices to atone for any remote aspect of guilt in your actions.[22] These sacrifices will also inaugurate you into the sacred service."[23]

A few questions arise regarding this incident. One, we have no record of Hashem telling Moshe to execute the idol worshipers by

---

18. *Sifsei Kohen* to *Shemos* 32:29.
19. See *Rashi; Rabbeinu Bachya; Midrash HaChefetz* to *Shemos* 32:29. See *Bamidbar* 16:9.

It was this very point that angered Korach. Korach, a firstborn in his own right, protested the loss of status taken from the firstborn by the tribe of Levi (*Ibn Ezra; Chizkuni* to *Shemos* 32:29). It is interesting to note that, although the firstborn had lost their status, Korach remained a Levi, and therefore consecrated for service.

20. *Tzeror HaMor; Haamek Davar* to *Shemos* 32:29.

This would be similar to the blessing Pinchas received for his vigilance against Zimri (*Sifsei Kohen*).

It is further interesting to note that Zimri was from the tribe of Shimon. The Erev Rav, now guilty of creating the Golden Calf, married daughters of the tribe of Shimon (*Zohar*).

Some add that *Tehillim* 135:19,20 can be interpreted as saying that in some ways the Leviim were on a higher level than the Kohanim.

21. *Reav Al HaTorah; Chizkuni; Bechor Shor* to *Shemos* 32:29. See *Devarim* 33:8-11 with *Rashi*.
22. *Targum Yonasan* to *Shemos* 32:29.

Some add that Moshe told the Leviim that their killing of the sinners, in and of itself, was as though they had brought a sacrifice, atoning for the creation of the calf (*Tzeror HaMor*).

23. *Lekach Tov* to *Shemos* 32:29.

the sword. Where did Moshe get the authority to do so? Two, the punishment for idol worship in the Torah is stoning. Why then did Moshe command that they be put to death by the sword? Three, the law states that capital punishment may not be administered to more than one person on any given day. If so, how could Moshe order the death of 3,000 in one day?

Some suggest that the penalty of death by the sword appears in the Torah with regard to the instance of "whoever brings sacrifices to a false deity shall be condemned to death," the implication being death by the sword.[24] Others suggest that during Moshe's negotiations with Hashem to gain a reprieve for the Jewish people, the specific fate of the idol worshipers was indeed discussed. They also suggest that the Jewish people on that day were comparable to an *ir hanidachas*, an entire city that was subverted into idol worship. In that case, because of extenuating circumstances, the entire city must be executed on the same day, even though its residents are numerous. In the case of the worshipers of the Golden Calf, there were also extenuating circumstances.[25]

According to others, the rules and guidelines of capital punishment were not yet established at this time. Although the specific punishment for idol worship would eventually be stoning, the Jews were still subject to the Noachide Laws under which idol worship is punishable by the sword.[26]

Others suggest that Moshe gave the instructions of his own accord, following his own thinking, but he told them to the people in the Name of Hashem. Why? Because Moshe was concerned that some people might remind him that a court that executes a person once in seventy years is considered a "deadly court." If so, how could he command that 3,000 people be executed in one day? Therefore, he spoke in the Name of Hashem to preclude argument and recrimination.[27]

---

24. *Rashi; Chizkuni; Nachal Kadmonim* to *Shemos* 32:27. See *Rashbam* to *Shemos* 22:19.

25. See *Moshav Zekeinim; Sifsei Kohen* to *Shemos* 32:27. See *Ramban* to *Shemos* 32:27 for his opinions. See *Sanhedrin* 56a and *Tanna D'Vei Eliyahu*.

Some add that when Hashem told Moshe to descend from the mountain, He was hinting to him that the Jews need to be smitten. The word *"reid"* (descend) is also the root word for *"mardus"* which means smite. Moshe regarded this as meaning that he should judge how the Jews should be punished (see *Shemos Rabbah* 42:5; *Radal; Yefei To'ar*).

26. *Yoma* 66b with *Rashi; Malbim* to *Shemos* 32:27. See *Maharsha* for his opinion. See *Ramban* to *Shemos* 32:27 for his opinion. See *Sanhedrin* 56a.

27. *Eliyahu Rabbah* 4; *Tuvei Chaim; Rimzei Eish*. See *Makkos* 7a. See *Ramban, Tzeidah LaDerech*. See *Devarim* 13:16.

Moshe Removes His Tent[28]

That long and arduous day, 17 Tammuz, finally drew to a close; it would go down in history as a day of infamy for the Jewish people. At the end of the day, although Moshe had destroyed the Golden Calf, given the people to drink of its powdered remains and executed 3,000 of the worst offenders, the Jewish people were still not forgiven for their terrible sin. Despite their show of remorse, all they had was the temporary reprieve that Hashem had granted Moshe before he descended from the mountain.[29]

On the following day, 18 Tammuz, Moshe addressed the Jewish people.

"There is something else I must tell you," he said, "Up until now, Hashem has escorted you through the desert Himself, affording you His Divine protection and guidance. But that was when you were a distinguished people. Now that you have sinned with the Golden Calf, you have fallen in status and are no longer worthy of such a great honor.[30] But Hashem will not abandon you to the perils of the desert. He will send his angel Michael to lead you and protect you from the elements and your enemies.[31]

"In a certain sense, this is a favor to you. If Hashem were your escort Himself, there would be no latitude left to you. Should you ever sin again in such a grievous manner, He would annihilate you immediately. But with only an angel escorting you, you might still have a reprieve."[32]

The people were deeply saddened by this latest news.[33] Their crowns that they had received when they said, "We will do and we

---

28. I have chosen to write a brief synopsis of what took place during Moshe's middle forty-day ascension. Unique to the rest of this book, I have decided to stay on course on the overall subject matter which relates to the breaking of the *Luchos* and their return in Moshe's third ascension. With the subject of the Golden Calf concluded, I am bridging the gap that separated the final events of the Golden Calf and the time period leading to Rosh Chodesh Elul when Moshe ascended for the third and final time.
29. *Tzeror HaMor; Meam Loez* to *Shemos* 32:30.
30. *Shemos Rabbah* 32:3; *Rashi* and *Sifsei Chachamim* to *Shemos* 32:34; *R' Avraham Ben HaRambam* to *Shemos* 32:34; 33:1-3.
   See fn. 81 to Ch. 15 where it states that the Jews lost the clouds of glory due to Aharon's participation in the sin of the Golden Calf.
31. *R' Avraham Ben HaRambam; Tur* to *Shemos* 32:34; *Aggadas Bereishis.*
   Eventually, Moshe would change this decrees and Hashem would once again lead and guide the Jewish people on their travels (*Midrash HaGadol*).
32. *Rashi; Ramban* to *Shemos* 33:1-3.
33. These events can best be explained according to the *Gra*, who suggests that despite

will listen," had already been removed from them. They now expressed their grief and distress by removing the royal garments and jewelry that they had worn at Mount Sinai. They felt banished and abandoned.[34]

Moshe also reacted to this latest development with great distress. He uprooted his tent and placed it just under 2,000 cubits from the encampment. If the Jewish people are banished from their Master, he declared, then they are also banished from His disciple. He would be available to them if they needed him, and would not be too far away for them to come to him on Shabbos. But he would remain in self-imposed exile, as long as the Jewish people were not completely reconciled with Hashem. He also vowed that the people would not travel into the desert as long as Hashem would not lead them Himself. They would remain at their encampment at Mount Sinai.[35]

According to some opinions, the decree of banishment and Moshe's removal of his tent took place after Moshe came back down from the mountain on Yom Kippur.[36]

Asking for Forgiveness[37]

Moshe understood that he could not ask Hashem to forgive the Jewish people as long as the Golden Calf existed and the offenders were on the loose. Their very existence militated against the people and called down retribution on

---

Moshe's forty-day ascension, he descended each evening and ascended the following morning for forty days straight.

34. *Rashi; Rabbeinu Bachya* to *Shemos* 33:4.
35. *Rashi; Targum Yonasan* to *Shemos* 33:7,15.
36. There is a glaring difference of opinion between *Rashi* (to *Shemos* 33:11) and the *Ramban* (to *Shemos* 33:7) as to when this event took place. *Rashi* is of the opinion that Moshe removed his tent upon his final descension after Yom Kippur and remained outside the tent till Rosh Chodesh Nissan when the Mishkan was finally erected. The Mishkan was symbolic of Hashem's presence among the Jewish people and thus, once the Master returned, his student could also return. *Ramban* disagrees because once Yom Kippur had passed, Hashem had forgiven the Jewish people, once and for all, and there was no further need for Moshe to remove his tent. Rather, Moshe removed it on the 18th of Tammuz and, despite the fact that Hashem had forgiven them on Yom Kippur, returned to the Jewish camp only when the Mishkan was erected on Rosh Chodesh Nissan. Being unable to lean toward any one authority, I have chosen to write this in the context in which the Torah relays the information. According to *Rashi*, the Torah's rendition of this event is not in sequence. According to the *Ramban*, it is in sequence.
37. On the 18th of Tammuz Moshe addressed the Jewish nation, telling them he would ascend to the heavens again and beg Hashem to absolve them of their sins. (See *Seder*

their heads. But now that the idol had been pulverized and the offenders executed, he could at last plead for forgiveness.[38]

And so Moshe continued to advocate for the Jewish people and plead for them.

"Hashem, when it came right down to it," said Moshe, "there were only 3,000 people executed for worshiping the idol. Three thousand! How can you annihilate a nation of over 600,000 people, not even counting women and children, converts and servants, because of the guilt of only 3,000 people?[39] Besides, You gave them all that gold when they left Egypt. With so much riches, how could you expect them to avoid sin?[40]

"And now, Hashem, if You forgive and pardon them for their sin, then all is fine and well. But if You do not, them erase me from

---

Olam 6; Chizkuni. See Rashi to Shemos 32:30.)

There are various opinions as to the second of three ascensions Moshe made. All are in agreement that Moshe came down on the 28th or 29th of Av and went up the third time to make the third Luchos on Rosh Chodesh Elul, and descended on Yom Kippur, which signified Hashem's final forgiveness for the Bnei Yisrael. The 10th of Tishrei would be set aside for all times as a day of forgiveness and atonement for the Jewish sins. See Chizkuni to Devarim 9:18 who writes that the choice of words that Rashi uses, "Salachti kidvarecha," suggesting Hashem's final pardon of the Jewish people is, in fact Rashi's own words, since those words were actually said regarding the tragic incident of the meraglim, and not at this time.

It is this middle ascension that is in question. According to Seder Olam Ch. 6 as well as most authorities, Moshe ascended on the 18th day of Tammuz. See Sifsei Chachamim who offers one opinion about the contradiction of Rashi in Shemos 33:11; Rashi in Devarim 9:18; Shemos 18:13.

Some are of the opinion that in this middle ascension Moshe came down and ascended each day until the 28th of Av (Yaavetz; Gra to Seder Olam). See Tanna D'Vei Eliyahu 4 that Moshe set up his tent outside the camp during this time.

See Tosafos to Bava Kamma 82a; Rashi to Taanis 30b; the Rosh at the end of Rosh Hashanah for further sources to this discussion. See Radal 16 to Pirkei D'Rav Eliezer 46 who explains the various opinions on Moshe's middle ascension.

In conclusion, opinions as to when Moshe ascended vary anywhere from the 17th to the 20th of Tammuz. Moshe descended on the 28th or 29th of Av. Some explain that the difference of opinions is due to how many days there were in each of those particular months. In addition, it is also based on when the count begins since, like the first set of days, the count does not begin until a night was joined with the day.

38. See Midrash HaGadol; Tzeror HaMor to Shemos 32:30,31; Tosafos to Devarim 9:18.

One cannot console a mourner while his dead relative lies before him. Once the deceased is buried, only then can one accept consolation for his bereavement. In a similar vein, Moshe knew that only after the calf had been removed and its sinners wiped out could he ask Hashem for atonement.

This dialogue follows all views regardless of whether this was the first time Moshe prayed or the second. See Ramban and Ibn Ezra for their difference of opinion.

39. See Tanna D'Vei Eliyahu 4.

40. See Rashi to Shemos 32:31; Yoma 86a; Berachos 32a; Sanhedrin 102a. See Ch. 14 fn. 57.

Your book. I do not want my name mentioned in the Torah. It would be too great a humiliation for me. People will say that this Moshe, the leader of the Jewish people, was incapable or unworthy of securing clemency for his people."[41]

Furthermore, Moshe realized that his name was always mentioned in the Torah in association with the Jewish people, either regarding things he said to them or they said to him or wonders he performed for them as Hashem's messenger to His people. What would be the point of having his name in the Torah if there were no Jewish people with whom he would be associated?[42] What good is a shepherd if his flock is taken from him?[43]

Some suggest that when Moshe asked to have his name erased from "Your book" he was not referring to the Torah but to the book of life in which Hashem inscribes the fate of people every Rosh Hashanah. In other words, Moshe wanted to die if his people would not be granted clemency. He did not want to live and see the destruction of his people.[44]

According to others, Moshe wanted to die, regardless of Hashem's decision about the Jewish people. First, he wanted his merits to be transferred to the people and his death to atone for them. If all this proved inadequate, and Hashem decided to annihilate the Jewish people, then he certainly did not want to live to witness their destruction.[45]

By his words and actions, Moshe proved himself to be a leader of the highest order. He was ready to put his life on the line for his

---

41. *Rashi; Tzeror HaMor* to *Shemos* 32:32. See *Gur Aryeh; Mizrachi.*
   This is hinted at in the words *"mecheini na misifrecha asher kasavta."* The final letters of the words *misifrecha asher kasavta* are *chaf, reish* and *taf,* spelling the word *keser* (crown). This is a reference to the *Keser Torah,* as well as to the numerical value of 120 which, as we have seen, are the total letters found in the Ten Commandments (*Yalkut Reuveni*).
   See *Zohar Bereishis* 28b that the Erev Rav were descendants of Amalek. It was on the premise of these words that Hashem would "erase" the memory of Amalek.
42. *Shemos Rabbah* 47:9; *Maharzav; Abarbanel* to *Shemos* 32:32.
43. *Sifsei Kohen* to *Shemos* 32:33.
44. See *Rashbam; Ramban* to *Shemos* 32:32; *R' Saadiah Gaon* in *Iyov.*
   See *Targum Yonasan* and *Chizkuni* who write that Moshe wanted his name erased from the book of *tzaddikim,* one of the three books always open before Hashem. The other two list the names of the wicked, and the names of those neither outright wicked nor righteous.
   The differing views are based on the translation of the Torah's use of the word *"sifrecha."*
45. See *Sforno; Abarbanel; Kli Yakar* to *Shemos* 32:32.

beloved people. He recognized that his first responsibility was to protect the people, no matter what measures were required, even laying down his own life.[46]

Moshe prayed to Hashem that He restore the Jewish people to their former eminence and resume the journey to the land of Canaan. He also pleaded with Hashem to show them favor by leading them through the desert Himself, and not relegating them to the care of the angel Michael.[47]

Hashem Responds

Hashem agreed with Moshe that it would be unjust to have the righteous perish along with the wicked. He also rejected Moshe's offer of martyrdom for the sake of the Jewish people. The sinners who deserved to die would do so, but Moshe would remain alive.[48]

But Moshe had uttered the words "erase me from Your book." Since the words of the righteous are taken seriously, he had brought this judgment upon himself, and it had to be fulfilled in some form. Hashem decreed that Moshe's name be eliminated from *Parashas Tetzaveh*. This would be considered an erasure from "Your book."[49]

In the meantime, Hashem set in motion the wheels of retribution for those who had worshiped the idol in the presence of witnesses but had not been given explicit forewarning of the consequences of their actions. These people were not liable to prosecution in the courts but were still subject to *misah beyedei Shamayim*, Divinely administered death.[50] Their retribution took the form of a plague that Hashem let loose in the Jewish encampment on the day Moshe returned to Heaven.[51] The plague persisted for the entire forty days Moshe spent in Heaven, before returning on Yom Kippur.[52]

---

46. *Mechilta Bo*.
47. See *R' Avraham Ben HaRambam* to *Shemos* 32:34; *Lekach Tov* to *Bamidbar* 11:12; *Ramban* to *Shemos* 33:1,12.
48. *Abarbanel*; *Malbim* to *Shemos* 32:33.
49. *Zohar Pinchas*; *Rabbeinu Bachya*.
50. *Rashi*; *Targum Yonasan* to *Shemos* 32:35; *Yoma* 66b. See *Malbim* who writes that these people too were the Erev Rav.
  Others suggest that the people who perished in the plague were people who had no warning or witnesses. Accordingly, it could only be through a heavenly death that they could be punished (*Tanchuma Ki Sisa* 26; *Ralbag*).
51. *Bamidbar Rabbah* 9:49.
52. See *Eliyahu Zuta* 41.
  See *Ibn Ezra* to *Shemos* 32:35 who writes that the plague occurred after they left Sinai,

Only those who had worshiped the idol before witnesses perished during the plague; according to some views this extended to those who embraced and kissed the idol.[53] The witnesses made sure everyone knew this. As a result, it was perfectly clear to the people that this plague was not a natural catastrophe but a Divine retribution specifically directed against those sinners who had escaped prosecution in the courts.[54]

The Torah tells us that the Levites executed 3,000 men, but it does not reveal to us how many people perished during the plague. Perhaps it is because the Torah wanted to underscore that the dedication of the Levites to Hashem was so great that they did not hesitate to execute 3,000 people, an act that would otherwise have been unthinkable. There is no similar lesson to be learned from the number of people that perished by the hand of Heaven during the plague.[55]

As for the guilt of all the other people who had become involved with the Golden Calf in less obtrusive ways, Hashem accepted Moshe's prayers on their behalf, and agreed not to exact full retribution from them right away. Instead, the punishment would be administered over the thousands of years of Jewish history. The account books would be kept open, and every time the Jewish people, collectively or individually, were found deserving of punishment, a small measure would be added as retribution for the sin of the Golden Calf.[56] The Mishkan and

---

and not during their stay at Sinai, which lasted almost a full year.

53. See *Yoma* 66b; *Bamidbar Rabbah* 9:45.

Some suggest that those who did not protest the worshiping of the Golden Calf, although they did not technically violate any laws, were guilty according to the heavenly court (*Rosh*; *Hadar Zekeinim* to *Shemos* 32:35).

Others add that those who did not bow and were not guilty of worship were still slain by the plague because they recognized the Golden Calf as a form of god. Others say that they were killed for bringing the gold to make the calf (*Ramban*). See *Ohr HaChaim* for his view.

54. *Gur Aryeh* and *Mizrachi* to *Rashi* to *Shemos* 32:35. In the case of drinking the powdered water, everyone knew that the deaths were a result of their worship.

55. *Ramban* to *Shemos* 32:35.

56. See *Rashi*; *Rashbam*; *Ramban*; *Bechor Shor* to *Shemos* 32:34; *Sanhedrin* 102a with *Rashi*; *Shemos Rabbah* 43:3; *Bamidbar Rabbah* 12:1; *Midrash Aggadah*; *Rashi* to *Bamidbar* 19:9.

See commentaries to *Sanhedrin* for explanation of the amount of a *litra* and 1/24th that the *Gemara* suggests was the portion of the calf that Hashem included in His punishment.

Maharsha explains that should one's merits and guilt be equal, then the Golden Calf would weigh down the scale on the side of guilt and thus place the person in the category of the wicked. (See explanation to the Attribute of "*V'Rav Chesed*" [Abundant in Mercy], mentioned in the Thirteen Attributes in Ch. 17.)

the *parah adumah*, the red heifer, would also bring a measure of atonement for the sin of the Golden Calf.⁵⁷

Having shown clemency to the Jewish people and reduced the retribution to which they would be liable immediately, Hashem prepared to fulfill His oath to the Patriarchs and bring the people into Canaan.

The question remained: Who would lead them through the desert, Hashem or the angel Michael?

Hashem took note of the repentance of the Jewish people, added that merit to Moshe's prayers on their behalf, and decided to show mercy to them. He reconsidered His earlier decision⁵⁸ and agreed to lead the Jewish people through the desert Himself, until they reached Canaan. He also told Moshe, "Just as I have shown a kind face to the Jewish people and resumed My earlier place in the Jewish encampment, so shall you do the same thing. Your tent has been outside the encampment for long enough. It is time that you return to your proper place among the Jewish people."⁵⁹

Moshe had made inroads in his attempts to have Hashem forgive the Jewish people, but it was not enough. His first ascension prevented their annihilation, this second ascension secured Hashem's presence among the Jewish people to a modified level, but Moshe continued to pray on behalf of the Jewish people until Hashem would forgive them totally.⁶⁰

Others add that the day of accounting for the Sin of the Golden Calf, a day destined for evil, would be the 9th of Av, when in fact great tragedies would take place, beginning with the Spies (*Rashi*). *Maharsha* adds that it has to be the 17th of Tammuz since that is when the sin of the Golden Calf took place. In fact, on the 17th of Tammuz, great tragedies would take place as well.

Others further add that the Torah's telling us that Hashem would account for the sin of the Golden Calf also refers to His accounting of people's sins in general. This would be done during the Days of Awe, Rosh Hashanah and Yom Kippur (*Tanchuma* 28; *Ibn Ezra*).

Some question how Hashem could punish the Jews of future generations when it has been established that Hashem only punishes the children for the sins of the father for four generations. One answer is that Hashem is not actually punishing future generations for the sin of the Golden Calf. What Hashem is doing is remembering the sin in future generations. That means that when Hashem considers potential punishment and may tip the scales to leniency, He will remember the Golden Calf and reconsider His mercy and punish the person instead (see *Abarbanel*).

57. *Shemos Rabbah* 42:8; *Etz Yosef*; *Yerushalmi Taanis* 4:5.

58. *Ibn Ezra* to *Shemos* 32:33; *Ramban* to *Shemos* 33:4; *Shemos Rabbah* 45:1; *Yefei To'ar*; *Rashi*; *Ramban*; *Targum* to *Shemos* 33:14; *Ramban* to *Shemos* 33:17.

This is based on the view that Moshe prayed for the first time now, after the destruction of the calf. This is unlike the opinion of the *Ramban* and other authorities who say that Moshe prayed two times and the Torah separates and sorts Moshe's prayers accordingly.

59. See *Rashi* to *Shemos* 33:11,14; *Berachos* 63b with *Maharsha*; *Shemos Rabbah* 45:1.

Hashem would have had Yehoshua replace him as the leader of the Jewish people, if he would not heed His command.

60. See *Tosafos* to *Devarim* 9:18.

17 Forgiveness

After Moshe prayed and pleaded for the Jewish people for forty days, Hashem relented and forgave them.[1] Moshe prepared to ascend the mountain on the fortieth day, but the night before his ascent he made a special request to Hashem.[2]

"Hashem, please give the Jewish people a second set of *Luchos*. They have repented for the sin of the Golden Calf and You have forgiven them. They are now once again worthy of receiving the Torah, and the *Luchos* are the seal of the gift. The very existence of the world depends on it."[3]

"Do you really believe they are worthy?" asked Hashem. "It is true that I have forgiven them and agreed not to annihilate them. But

---

1. *HaKesav VeHaKabbalah* to *Shemos* 34:1.
   Depending on the days of the month, this occurred on the 28th or 29th of the month of Av. See *Tanchuma Ki Sisa* 31; *Rashi* to *Devarim* 9:18.
2. See *Shabbos* 86a; *Chizkuni* 34:1.
3. *Tanchuma Re'eh* 1.

that does not change what happened. Where was their gratitude and appreciation? Should I give the Torah to a nation of ungrateful people who sank to the level of idol worship?"

Moshe remained silent.

"I will grant your request," Hashem continued, "but only because you asked for it. You have invested so much effort into these people, and I don't want to disappoint you.[4] I grant you new *Luchos*, but I will not make them.

"Make for yourself *Luchos* of stone like the first ones. You broke the first *Luchos* that I had made. How do I know you won't do it again? If you had made those first *Luchos*, Moshe, you would not have broken them.

"So now you will make the second *Luchos*. You will carve, hew and chisel them until they are the same as the first *Luchos* in size, shape and appearance. When your work is done, I will place My hand on the Tablets and inscribe them with the very same letters that were inscribed in the first *Luchos*. Then I want you to build a special wooden Ark into which you will place the new *Luchos*, as well as the broken shards of the old ones.

"Just like the first *Luchos*, the second *Luchos* will have inferences to the entire Torah and all its esoteric secrets.[5] The placement of My hand on the *Luchos* signifies that just as I am eternal so is the Torah, and whoever learns it will be saved from Gehinnom and live forever in the next world."[6]

---

4. *Tanchuma Ki Sisa* 35.

5. *Tanchuma Ki Sisa* 28,29; *Devarim Rabbah* 3:17; *Tosefta Bava Kamma* 7:4; *Yalkut Shimoni* 854; *Midrash HaGadol*; *Rabbeinu Bachya*; *Tzeror HaMor*; *Abarbanel* to *Devarim* 10:1.

In fact, since Moshe did not break the letters but they flew away and remained intact, he was not required to write the letters. This opinion does not reflect the parable that will be given shortly (*Abarbanel*).

See *Shemos Rabbah* 46:1 and *Yefei To'ar* who write that Moshe felt bad for breaking the first *Luchos*. Hashem reassured him that these second *Luchos* would have more of the Torah written on them, since the first *Luchos* only had the Ten Commandments written on them. This Midrash is in opposition to the opinion in *Shekalim* that the first *Luchos* had all the Oral Torah referenced in them.

There are a number of opinions that argue with the accepted view that Hashem wrote the second *Luchos* as well. Some suggest that Moshe wrote the second *Luchos* and not Hashem, based on *Devarim* 10:2. See *Tanchuma Yashan to Ki Sisa*; *Shemos Rabbah* 47:2; *Radal*; *Tur* to *Shemos* 34:29. See *Yefei To'ar* who suggests that Hashem only placed His hand upon the second *Luchos*, as mentioned above, to assist Moshe with the *mem* and *samech* which needed a miracle to stand, but He did not write these *Luchos*.

6. *Yalkut Shimoni* 854.

The Jews were not worthy of having *Luchos* made solely by the hands of Hashem. In

This incident can be explained with the following parable.

A king once went on a long journey, leaving behind his wife and her maidservants. The king appointed one of his trusted courtiers to attend to his wife's interests in his absence.

The handmaidens were of loose moral character and, in the absence of the king, they allowed themselves to behave in an immoral manner. Rumors spread, however, that the king's wife had been unfaithful. When the rumors reached the king in a distant land, he was beside himself with fury, and he made up his mind to have her executed upon his return to his palace.

The king's courtier heard about the king's intentions. Frightened, he tore up her *kesubah*, her nuptial agreement.

When the king returned, the courtier said to him, "Your majesty, please have mercy on your wife. The public knows that I have torn up her marriage contract, and in their minds, she is no longer associated with you. Therefore, it is not necessary for you to kill her to protect your honor. Please spare her life."

Temporarily mollified, the king let his wife live. He also ordered a full investigation of the incident. The investigation revealed that the wife was blameless and that her handmaidens had committed all the immoral acts. The king forgave his wife for the indiscretions of her handmaidens, and the royal couple was reconciled.

The courtier was delighted with the developments. One day, he said to the king, "I want to remind you, your majesty, that your wife does not have a *kesubah* right now. Perhaps you should write her a new one."

"You are the one who tore up her first *kesubah*," said the king. "I left her in your charge, and you let her reputation suffer because of the laxity of her handmaidens. You tore up her *kesubah* to save her life. Now the responsibility for a new one rests with you. Get the paper and the ink, have it written up, and I will sign it."

The Jewish people were like the king's wife, and the Erev Rav were like her maidservants. Moshe, the courtier, had permitted the

---

this instance, Moshe, a human, had to be a part of their creation (*Ohr HaChaim* to *Devarim* 10:2).

While the first *Luchos* were completely created by Hashem, the second *Luchos* were partly created by Moshe. The first *Luchos* represented the Written Torah while the second *Luchos* represented the Oral Torah which, unlike the Written Torah, was written down by humans, as was the case with the second *Luchos* (*Netziv* to *Devarim* 10:1).

Erev Rav to join the people and besmirch their reputation with their sinfulness. He had broken the *Luchos* to divert the wrath of the King, and now it was his responsibility to replace them.[7]

Moshe Becomes Wealthy

Moshe knew that in order for the second *Luchos* to be a duplicate of the first ones, they would have to be made of sapphire. But where would he find such large sapphire stones? Hashem solved the problem by miraculously preparing for him, right by his tent, a rich lode of sapphire hewn from the Heavenly Throne itself.[8]

Moshe hewed two Tablets of stone and prepared to bring them up to Heaven for Hashem to inscribe. He also built the wooden Ark that would serve as the receptacle for the completed *Luchos*. For the time being, they would contain only the shards of the first *Luchos*.

Although Hashem seems to have told Moshe to build the Ark after the second *Luchos* were completed, Moshe build the Ark first. He reasoned that Hashem was not really instructing him on the sequence of the work. He only spoke about the *Luchos* first, because they were the focus of His instructions. In actual practice, however, Moshe felt that it would be more appropriate to construct the Ark first so that there would be a place to put the *Luchos* as soon as they were made. In erecting the Tabernacle the following year, Betzalel followed the same line of reasoning and constructed the Tabernacle before he produced its furnishings and accessories.[9]

The Ark that Moshe built now served only as temporary housing for the new *Luchos* and the shards of the old. The following year, Betzalel would produce the golden Ark of the Torah, and the *Luchos*,

---

7. According to this parable she was only an *arusah* (betrothed).
  See *Devarim Rabbah* 3:17 for a different parable. See *Tanchuma Ki Sisa* 30; *Devarim Rabbah* 3:14; Rashi to *Shemos* 34:1.
8. See *Targum Yerushalmi* to *Shemos* 34:1; *Pirkei D'Rav Eliezer* 46; *Yalkut Shimoni* 854; *Rabbeinu Bachya*.
  Some suggest that Moshe attained his wealth from other precious gems and stones found in his tent (*Taklin Chaditin*).
9. See *Tanchuma Eikev* 10; *Ramban*; *Abarbanel*; *Malbim*; *Sifsei Kohen* to *Devarim* 10:1-3. See *Chasam Sofer* as well.
  There are various reasons why the first *Luchos* did not need an Ark, as opposed to the second. One reason was because the first *Luchos* never had a chance to be placed anywhere since they were to be broken immediately upon Moshe's descent (see *Ramban*). In addition, Hashem wanted Moshe to put the second *Luchos* into safekeeping so that he would not have them readily available to break (*Bechor Shor*). See *Ohr HaChaim*; *Abarbanel*; *Alshich*.

new and old, would be transferred into it. Afterwards, the temporary Ark would be used to lead the Jewish people into battle or, according to others, placed into concealment and never used again.[10]

The labor of making the *Luchos* would make Moshe a very rich man. Hashem had said to him, "Make for yourself *Luchos* of stone like the first ones." What did He mean by "for yourself"? It was a subtle hint that the small stones and chips that would fall away during the process of making the *Luchos* would belong to him, hence "for yourself." These residual gems made Moshe wealthy.[11]

Moshe had earned this special gift by his selflessness in Egypt. Right before the exodus, the Jews had accumulated vast wealth, which they took along with them. They had fairly emptied Egypt of valuables. But Moshe had not taken any. While the rest of the people had been busy amassing fortunes, Moshe had been occupied with retrieving Yosef's coffin from the river. Hashem did not want Moshe to suffer a permanent loss because of the mitzvah, so He gave him the chips left over from the *Luchos*.[12] It also taught the Jewish people the lesson that one does not lose by dedicating oneself to Torah and mitzvos.[13]

In any case, it was important that Moshe should be a man of independent means. His wealth added to his stature in the eyes of the people. Moreover, it reassured them that his integrity was unimpeachable, and that he could not be influenced by offers of monetary reward or other special favors. If there was anything he could have wanted, he had the means to get it for himself.[14]

With his new wealth, Moshe now assumed the full status of the uncrowned king of the Jewish people.[15]

---

10. *Rashi; Tosafos, Rosh* to *Devarim* 10:1; *Rashi* to *Berachos* 8b; *Bamidbar* 10:33.

See *Ramban Devarim* 10:1; *Shekalim* 6:1 for a full discussion on how many Arks were in use at any one time. See *Malbim* for his view.

Upon completion of the wooden Ark, Moshe placed the *Luchos* inside his tent and put the broken pieces of the first *Luchos* inside the Ark (*Maharsha* to *Berachos* 63b; *Ramban* to *Devarim* 10:2).

I have not found a source that discusses where the broken pieces of the *Luchos* were kept during the days that Moshe ascended to the heavens. It is quite possible, with Moshe's tent acting as an *Ohel Moed* until the Tabernacle would be built, that they were left there until the Ark was built.

11. See *Nedarim* 38a; *Yerushalmi Shekalim* 5:2; *Vayikra Rabbah* 32:2; *Shemos Rabbah* 46:2; *Rashi* to *Shemos* 34:1.

Others add that when Hashem used the words "for yourself" he was in essence telling Moshe that it was due to his merits and not those of the Jewish people that they would once again be worthy of receiving the *Luchos* (*Abarbanel* to *Devarim* 10:1).

12. *Ein Yaakov* to *Nedarim* 38a.

13. *Tanchuma Ki Sisa* 29.

14. *Nedarim* 38a; *Koheles Rabbah* 9:11; *Yefei To'ar*.

15. *Tanchuma Ki Sisa* 29.

The Final Ascent

Hashem instructed Moshe to finish his work that night.[16] Early the following morning he was to take the uninscribed Tablets to the mountaintop and wait there for his final living ascent into Heaven, where he would remain for the next forty days.[17]

Hashem also reminded him that all the old restrictions regarding the perimeter of the mountain were still in effect, and He also added new restrictions.[18] This time, no one at all — not Yehoshua, the elders, Aharon nor any of his children — was to escort Moshe in the early stages of his ascent, neither on the mountain itself nor even at its base.[19]

Some of these people had fallen somewhat in stature as a result of the sin of the Golden Calf. This could possibly explain why they were no longer considered worthy of approaching the mountain.[20] Yehoshua, however, had not even been there, yet he too was barred from ascending any part of the mountain. Why was this so?

The first *Luchos* had been given with great fanfare, accompanied by lightning, fire and thunderous sounds, and they had fallen victim to *ayin hara*, which ultimately led to their being broken. The second *Luchos* would be given in quiet seclusion with no one but Moshe in attendance, and would thereby be protected from *ayin hara*.[21]

Furthermore, the first *Luchos* had been given in honor of the entire people and, therefore, the event had taken place in full view of the public. The people, however, were unworthy of receiving the second *Luchos*. They were being given to them only in honor of Moshe. Therefore, the event was to take place in private.[22]

---

16. See *Shir Rabbah* 2:9; *Abarbanel*; *Rokeach* to *Shemos* 34:2.

Unlike the first revelation, where Hashem waited for Moshe to ascend, this time Moshe would wait for the *Shechinah* to approach him (*Alshich*).

17. See *Shabbos* 86a; *Chizkuni*; *Alshich* to *Shemos* 34:4; *Tanchuma Yashan Vayeira*.

This was either Thursday the 29th of Av or Rosh Chodesh Elul. Moshe would eventually descend on Yom Kippur on a Monday morning.

Some say that the custom of fasting on *Behav* (Monday, Thursday, Monday) is related to the fact that Moshe ascended on a Thursday and eventually descended on a Monday. See *Tosafos* to *Bava Kamma* 82a.

It is interesting to note that the calendar in use throughout the events taking place in this work mirrors that of the Hebrew year 5763.

Moshe's early-morning ascensions every time were indications of his eagerness to fulfill Hashem's wishes (*Lekach Tov*).

18. *Lekach Tov* to *Shemos* 34:3.

19. *Ramban*; *Ibn Ezra*; *Rosh*; *Chizkuni*; *R' Avraham Ben HaRambam*; *Malbim* to *Shemos* 34:3.

Not even animals were allowed to pasture in the immediate area of the mountain.

20. *Abarbanel*.

21. *Tanchuma* 31; *Rashi*; *Rabbeinu Bachya* to *Shemos* 34:3.

22. *Ramban* to *Shemos* 34:3.

The following morning — it was a Thursday — Moshe rose early, took the freshly hewn *Luchos* in his hands and ascended the mountain as Hashem had commanded him to do.[23] As Moshe stood on the mountaintop, Hashem descended and revealed Himself in a Cloud of Glory, which He wrapped around Moshe as a protective shield from the angels who might become jealous of Moshe's privileged status.[24] Immediately, Moshe prostrated himself as the *Shechinah* passed before him.[25]

Hashem had already granted forgiveness to the Jewish people before Moshe's final living ascent into Heaven. Moshe, therefore, focused on the future.

"Hashem, please let me know how You direct the world," he called out. "When the Jewish people will need to pray to You in the aftermath of having sinned, how should they pray?[26] What should they do to divert Your anger from them and avoid destruction, if the merit of the Patriarchs is inadequate to protect them?"[27]

The Thirteen Attributes

Hashem wrapped Himself in His *tallis*, so to speak, and taught Moshe the Thirteen Attributes of Mercy and the order in which they are to be invoked in order to effect forgiveness. Hashem gave Moshe a demonstration by having an angel put on a *tallis* and play the role of a *chazzan*, leading the congregation in prayer.[28]

If a person recites the Thirteen Attributes properly, Hashem

---

23. See *Shabbos* 86a; *Chizkuni*; *Alshich* to *Shemos* 34:4; *Tanchuma Yashan Vayeira*.
24. *Targum* to *Shemos* 34:5; *Pirkei D'Rav Eliezer* 46.
25. *R' Avraham Ben HaRambam* to *Shemos* 34:8. See *Rashbam*.
26. See *Gur Aryeh*; *Sifsei Chachamim* to *Rashi* to *Shemos* 34:5.
27. *Tanchuma Ki Sisa* 32.
28. *Tanchuma Yashan Shemos*; *Pirkei D'Rav Eliezer* 46; *Rosh Hashanah* 17a-b; *Rabbeinu Chananel*; *Lekach Tov*; *Midrash Aggadah*; *Rabbeinu Bachya* to *Shemos* 34:5-6.

Many Midrashim suggest a correlation between *Shemos* 33:13 and the discussion that Moshe now had with Hashem. Some views suggest that this dialogue actually took place during Moshe's second ascension.

There are different views as to who uttered the Thirteen Attributes, and who called out the Name of Hashem. Some suggest that upon Moshe's request, Hashem taught Moshe the Thirteen Attributes and Hashem Himself called out the Name *Hashem*, the Attribute of His Name that represents mercy (*R' Saadiah Gaon*; *Lekach Tov*; *Ibn Ezra*; *Rashbam*; *Sforno*). Others are of the opinion that Hashem responded to Moshe's request by telling him that the Thirteen Attributes will arouse His mercy, at which time Moshe himself responded by proclaiming the Thirteen Attributes of Hashem. See *Gur Aryeh*; *Pirkei D'Rav Eliezer*; *Targum*; *Torah Shleimah* 34:52.

assured Moshe, with the proper understanding of their deep meaning, and if he accompanies his prayers with fasting, his prayers will never go unanswered. Eventually, this promise would be formalized into a covenant.[29] Furthermore, anyone who acts toward another person in a merciful manner, in emulation of the Attributes of Mercy, will also have his prayers answered.[30]

The Thirteen Attributes of Mercy are as follows:

- **Hashem.** This Attribute reflects Hashem's mercy toward a person who has not yet sinned, even though He knows that he will eventually sin.[31]

- **Hashem.** This Attribute reflects Hashem's mercy toward a person who has sinned and repented. Hashem forgives and pardons him completely. Unlike a human being who might still bear a grudge against someone who has wronged him even after forgiving him, Hashem forgives and forgets as if the person has never sinned.[32] Others suggest that this is the Attribute of compassion toward a person who has sinned but not repented. Hashem has mercy on him, as a father has mercy on a needy child who refuses to ask for help.[33]

---

29. *Rabbeinu Bachya; Rosh Hashanah* 17b with *Rashi.*
30. *Tzeror HaMor; Reishis Chochmah, Anavah* 1:3; *Alshich*. This is based on *Yoel* 3:5 and *Etz Yosef* to *Rosh Hashanah* 17b.
31. *Rashi; Rosh; Sifsei Chachamim; Shlah.*
  The numeration of the Thirteen Attributes written here follows most commentaries who start the Thirteen Attributes with *Hashem* and end with *Nakeh (Lo Yenakeh)*, as listed below. This follows the opinion of *Rabbeinu Tam* in *Rosh Hushanah* 17b. The Ran lists *Hashem Hashem* as one Attribute and divides *Notzeir Chesed LaAlafim* into two Attributes. The *Sefer Chassidim* writes that the Thirteen Attributes begin with *Rachum*, and he excludes *Hashem Hashem* and *Keil* from the Thirteen Attributes. The missing three Attributes are found in *Shemos* 34:9: *LaAvoneinu U'LeChatoseinu U'Nechaltanu*. The *Korban Nesanel* quotes the *Arizal* who omits *Hashem Hashem* as well, and makes up for the missing two Attributes by also splitting *Notzeir Chesed LaAlafim* into two Attributes, as well as *Erech Apayim*. The *Rambam* also excludes *Hashem* as the first Attribute.
  See end of *Sefer Erech Apayim*, which defines the Thirteen Attributes using the prayer *Mi Keil Kamocha* said in *Tashlich*. For further in-depth discussion of the matter, see *Korban Nesanel* to the *Rosh* in *Rosh Hashanah* 17b and *Miluim* 3 in *Torah Shleimah* end of *Ki Sisa*.
32. *Rashi; Gur Aryeh; Shlah.*
33. *Rabbeinu Bachya.*

- *Keil.* This Attribute is a variation of Divine compassion.[34] It represents Hashem's unlimited power to feed and sustain all the creatures of the world.[35] Others add that this attribute is only manifest when it is evoked through prayer and repentance inspired by suffering.[36] According to others, this Attribute identifies Hashem as the honest and righteous Judge.[37]

- *Rachum.* This Attribute represents compassion that is like parental love. It is protective and always seeks to anticipate and guard against pitfalls.[38] Others add that it reflects Hashem's special compassion for the poor and destitute.[39] It also reflects Hashem's compassion toward an unrepentant person, in that it prevents his immediate destruction.[40]

- *Chanun.* This Attribute reflects Hashem's gracious kindness in helping those who have fallen on hard times.[41] Others add that it reflects special attention to the rich and wealthy.[42] According to others, this Attribute reflects gracious kindness that bestows gifts and blessings in this world, without any diminution of the rewards in store in the next world.[43]

- *Erech Apayim.* This Attribute reflects tolerance toward, and patience with, a person who has sinned. Hashem withholds His anger in order to give the person an opportunity to repent.[44]

---

34. *Rashi; Mizrachi.*
35. *Tosafos* to *Rosh Hashanah* 17b; *Gur Aryeh.*
36. *Rabbeinu Bachya.*
37. *Tosafos; Chizkuni.*
38. *Ibn Ezra; Tosafos* to *Rosh Hashanah* 17b; *Abarbanel.*
  See *Rabbeinu Bachya* who suggests that this conduct refers to the Attribute of *Hashem* and not to that of *Rachum.*
39. *Tosafos; Chizkuni.*
  See *Rabbeinu Meyuschas* who suggests that this applies to the Attribute of *Chanun.*
40. *Meam Loez.*
  Hashem does not show His Attributes of Mercy and Compassion with sins involving idolatry (see *Midrash HaGadol* to *Devarim* 5:9).
41. *Ibn Ezra; Tosafos* to *Rosh Hashanah* 17b.
42. *Tosafos; Chizkuni.*
43. *Meam Loez.* See *Rashi* to *Bereishis* 32:11.
  See *Taz* that the kindness in which Hashem offers free reward refers to the Attribute of *Notzeir Chesed.*
  See *Abarbanel* who suggests that this refers to intelligence, as in the phrase *Chonen HaDaas* (He Who grants intelligence).
44. *Rashi; Shlah.*

The duality of the language — *apayim* meaning two faces — also suggests that Hashem shows patience to both the righteous and the wicked. He shows a bright and delighted face to the righteous person as He amasses the reward in store for him in the next world. He shows a wrathful face to the unrepentant wicked person as He patiently waits to punish him, by sending him to Gehinnom, reducing his share in the next world and giving him his reward in this world.[45] Others add that Hashem delays His anger by relegating the administration of punishment to angels of destruction, thereby giving the sinner more time to repent and gain forgiveness.[46]

- **Rav Chesed.** This Attribute reflects Hashem's abundant kindness, which He extends even to those who are undeserving and lacking in merit.[47] Furthermore, when a person's merits and faults are equally balanced, Hashem will tilt the scale toward the side of merit and consider the person righteous, even though his faults equal his merits.[48] Others see it as an overflowing abundance of Divine mercy toward all people, both righteous and wicked, which far surpasses Hashem's attribute of administering retribution to the wicked. The first twenty-six generations of humankind, which did not yet have the Torah, enjoyed Divine mercy, even though they did not have the merits to deserve it.[49]

- **Emes.** This Attribute represents truth. Hashem is truthful. He keeps His word and pays His debts, rewarding those who obey Him and earn His kindness.[50] Others see it as pure and genuine compassion without the expectation of anything in return, as in *chesed shel emes*, "true" kindness, i.e., kindness done with the dead, where there will be no opportunity for compensation.[51]

- **Notzeir Chesed LaAlafim.** This Attribute reflects Hashem as the preserver of kindness. He remembers all the good a per-

---

45. *Eruvin* 22a with *Rashi*; *Tosafos* to *Bava Kamma* 50b.
46. *Rabbeinu Bachya*.
47. *Rashi*.
48. *Rosh Hashanah* 17a with *Rashi* and *Gra*.
49. *Rabbeinu Bachya*; *Tosafos*; *Chizkuni*.
50. *Rashi*; *Ibn Ezra*; *Gra*.
51. *Rabbeinu Bachya*.

son does out of love for Hashem, and He rewards that person's descendants for 2,000 generations. He also remembers all that the person does out of fear of Hashem, and He rewards that person's descendants for 1,000 years.[52] Others add that this Attribute also reflects the benefits the Jewish people enjoy from the merits of the Patriarchs, for thousands of years into the future.[53]

- *Nosei Avon.* This Attribute reflects Hashem's mercy in withholding punishment for sins committed intentionally, at the urging of one's evil inclination.[54] Others add that this extends to inappropriate thoughts and emotions.[55]

- *Nosei Fesha.* This Attribute reflects Hashem's mercy in withholding punishment for sins committed intentionally and rebelliously, for no other reason than to antagonize and provoke Hashem. Despite the severity of this transgression, Hashem still responds with compassion.[56]

- *Nosei Chataah.* This Attribute reflects Hashem's mercy in withholding punishment for sins committed in error. Hashem forgives completely, as if the sin had never been committed.[57] Others suggest that this Attribute shows mercy to those who sin because they are overcome by desire and temptation.[58]

- *Venakeh Lo Yenakeh.* This Attribute reflects Hashem's mercy toward unrepentant sinners. The seemingly contradictory language, "and He cleanses but does not cleanse," indicates that Hashem punishes but does not punish all at once. Instead, he administers the punishment in small, tolerable doses. Others interpret the phrase as saying that Hashem forgives those who repent, but does not forgive those who do not repent.[59] According to some opinions, the differentiation is in the form of

---

52. *Rashi; Sforno.* See *Rashi* to *Devarim* 7:9.
53. *Rabbeinu Bachya.*
54. See *Yoma* 36b with *Tosafos; Malbim.*
55. *Rabbeinu Bachya.*
56. See *Yoma* 36b; *Malbim.*
57. See *Yoma* 36b; *Malbim.*
58. *Malbim.* See *Nosei Avon.*
59. *Targum; Rashi; Yoma* 86a.
    See *Meam Loez* who suggests that this conduct is reflected in the attribute of *Rachum.*

the repentance. Those who repent out of love are completely forgiven; their slates are wiped clean. Those who repent out of fear are only partially forgiven, to the extent that intentional sins are considered as if they had been committed in error. Although the punishment is mitigated, the absolution is not complete.[60]

At the close of the Thirteen Attributes, Hashem repeated the statement, made previously in the Ten Commandments, that He would avenge the sins of great-grandfathers on their great-grandchildren. The descendants of sinners who followed in the sinful footsteps of their forebears, would have to pay for the sins of their forebears as well. But Hashem would delay the punishments to allow them to repent and be forgiven.[61]

Moshe was overjoyed at Hashem's explanation of the Thirteen Attributes and their deeper meanings.[62] He was particularly appreciative that Hashem holds back His anger even against the wicked, so that they would have the opportunity to repent,[63] and that His mercy far surpasses His anger.[64] Above all, Moshe was ecstatic that Hashem had agreed to grant the Jewish people absolute forgiveness for their sin.[65] With a happy heart, he bowed to the *Shechinah* and offered expressions of gratitude, appreciation and praise.[66]

---

60. *Sforno.*

61. *Mechilta; Rashi; Targum; Ibn Ezra* to *Yisro* 20:6; *Sanhedrin* 27b; *Ki Sisa* 34:7 with *Rashi*.

A son is the flesh and blood of his father and thus a part of him. By continuing in the path of his father, he reasserts his connection to his predecessors and so, even though he may not have actually committed a specific transgression that makes him guilty, he is, however, guilty by association. Rejecting the father's path makes it clears that he is separating from his father's ways and he is therefore judged as an individual (*Nesivos Olam*).

The *Mizrachi* asks: How it is possible for the Jews to suffer for the sin of the Golden Calf for thousands of years, when Hashem only avenges the sinner up to four generations? He answers that the Golden Calf was an exception and what was done was for the benefit of the Jews. In truth, Hashem wanted to annihilate them immediately but, "out of the goodness of His heart," He spread it over thousands of years, thus making this situation different from what is stated here. In addition, and as mentioned earlier, Hashem is not punishing the Jews thousands of years later for the sin of the Golden Calf. He is only mindful of it to the extent that he will not easily forgive the person who sins even at a later time.

62. *Rabbeinu Bachya; Malbim* to *Shemos* 34:8.

63. See *Sanhedrin* 111b with *Yad Ramah; Rabbeinu Bachya* 34:8; *Midrash Tehillim* 93:8.

Others add that Moshe was particularly thankful for the Attributes of *Emes* and *Rachum*, which he knew would act as merciful protection for sinners.

64. *Pane'ach Raza.* As shown in the *middah* of *Rav Chesed.*

65. *Pirkei D'Rav Eliezer* 46.

66. See *Sanhedrin* 111b; *Targum Yerushalmi; Rabbeinu Bachya; Tosafos* to *Shemos* 34:8. See *Rashi; Rashbam.* See *Ibn Ezra* for a different view.

Moshe understood that this was an exceedingly auspicious moment, a time of deep and extraordinary mercy, and he took advantage of the moment to pray on behalf of the Jewish people.[67] Hashem had promised to travel with the Jewish people, but now Moshe asked Him to dwell in their midst once again, as He had done earlier.[68] He also pleaded with Hashem to return quickly to reside among the people,[69] and beseeched Him to make a covenant with the people that He would never withdraw from them, even if they should sin again.[70]

"Hashem, please have mercy," pleaded Moshe. "The Jewish people are a stubborn and stiff-necked nation, and this makes it conceivable that they might sin again and leave themselves vulnerable to destruction. However, the Thirteen Attributes show Your virtuous nature of forbearance and forgiveness.[71] In fact, the people would have been in greater danger if You had entrusted them to the care and guidance of an angel who does not have the capacity to forgive. Because of Your compassionate nature, the Jewish people are more secure than endangered by Your residence in their midst, because You will forgive the sins of Your subjects, Your chosen people.[72]

"Hashem, I am not only asking You to reside among the Jewish people. I am also asking You to distinguish the Jewish people by not residing among any of the pagan nations of the world.[73] The Jewish people are Your subjects forever, even if they should slip into sin from time to time. Please stay among them and lead them into the Promised Land. Let Eretz Yisrael be given to them and to no other nation."[74]

"I will make a new covenant as you requested, Moshe," Hashem replied, "but only on the same conditions as in the previous

---

67. *Netziv.*
68. *Lekach Tov* to *Shemos* 34:9.
69. *Gra; Malbim* to *Shemos* 34:9.
   Hashem had agreed to do so earlier (*Shemos* 33:14) only to the extent that He would travel along with them, but the *Shechinah* would not actually reside with them.
70. *Tzeror HaMor.*
71. See *Rashi; Sefer HaShorashim; Ramban; Tosafos; Chizkuni* to *Shemos* 34:9; see 33:3,5; *Zohar*.
   Others add that the degree of their stubborn and stiff-necked nature would be greatly minimized with Hashem's presence among them, and greatly intensified should Hashem not dwell among them (*R' Chaim Paltiel*).
72. See *Ramban; Rashbam; Chizkuni; Abarbanel; Malbim* to *Shemos* 34:9.
73. See *Rashi; Lekach Tov* to *Shemos* 34:9.
74. *Targum Yonasan; Ramban.*

covenant. They may not make common cause with the pagans nor worship their idols. If they do so, they will breach the covenant and render it invalid, just as their embrace of the Golden Calf breached the first covenant; the breaking of the *Luchos* abrogated it completely. These are the conditions.[75]

"I agree to distinguish the Jewish people from the other nations, and I will seal this covenant by writing the Ten Commandments on the second *Luchos*. The *Shechinah* will reside only among the Jewish people when the Tabernacle will be built,[76] and it will never reside among the pagan nations of the world. I will further distinguish them by performing miracles for them in full view of the entire world, wonders such as have never been seen before. Yes, the world will know that I dwell among the Jewish people."[77]

These wonders that Hashem mentioned include, among others, the earth opening up to swallow Korach and his cohorts, Bilam's donkey talking and Yehoshua arresting the progress of the sun across the sky.[78]

Hashem taught Moshe the entire Torah during his final forty days in Heaven, just as He had done during his first forty days in Heaven. Once again, Moshe took advantage of every moment. During the days, Hashem taught him the Torah, and during the nights, Moshe reviewed it and studied it in depth.[79] Just as before, Moshe did not eat or drink or experience any physical pleasure or sustenance whatsoever. Just as the spirit is sustained in the body by physical sustenance, Moshe's physical body was sustained during these forty days by spiritual sustenance of the Torah he was learning.[80]

---

75. See *Ibn Ezra; Ramban; Tosafos* to *Shemos* 34:10.

See *Shemos* 34:11-26 (*Parashas Ki Sisa*) and 23:14-33 (*Parashas Mishpatim*). Based on the similarities of these verses, this view suggests that the words in *Mishpatim* were establishing the first covenant, as mentioned in *Shemos* 24:4-7. With the creation of the new *Luchos*, a second and new covenant was now in order.

76. *Rashi; Ramban; Gra* to *Shemos* 34:10.

77. *Ibn Ezra; Ramban; Malbim* to *Shemos* 34:10.

78. See *Midrash Aggadah; Rabbeinu Bachya; Chizkuni; Malbim*.

79. *Sefer HaYashar.*

80. *Lekach Tov; Shemos Rabbah* 47:5-8.

See Ch. 12 for the full details of these events.

Many commentaries mention that Moshe's 120 days in the heavens correspond to the 120 years that he lived.

Knowing that he had only forty days to learn, Moshe did not want to waste them by sleeping during that period. By day he was taught by Hashem the Written Law of the Torah and by night he reviewed what he had learned, and toiled in the depths of the Oral Torah (*Shemos Rabbah* 47:7).

As Hashem prepared to write the Ten Commandments on the second *Luchos*, the prosecuting angels came forward and protested that the Jewish people were unworthy of receiving the Torah. As they had argued before, they insisted that the Torah remain in the domain of the angels.

"How can you claim," Hashem said to them, "that you are more worthy of receiving the Torah? Every child knows that the Torah forbids eating dairy and meat together. The Jewish people do not violate this law. Nevertheless, when you angels were guests in Avraham's house you ate dairy and meat dishes together. And now you ask to be given the Torah?"

The angels were at a loss for an adequate response.[81]

"Quick, Moshe," said Hashem. "Take advantage of their momentary silence and start writing the Torah for yourself."

Even though the Torah would reestablish the covenant between Hashem and the Jewish people as a whole, Hashem told Moshe to write the Torah "for yourself." This was because the Torah was being given to the Jewish people in Moshe's honor and merit. He had risked his life for the people, and he had interceded with Hashem on their behalf and gained forgiveness for them.[82] The Torah was, therefore, considered his. Moreover, while the general body of the Torah was given to the Jewish people, Hashem gave Moshe the keys to the secret depths of the Torah as his personal gift. But Moshe, with his gracious nature and his love for the Jewish people, decided to share this treasure with all the people.[83]

On the morning of 10 Tishrei, the day that would be observed for all future generations as Yom Kippur, Hashem placed His hand upon the *Luchos* and inscribed the Ten Commandments on them exactly as he had on the first Luchos.[84] Moshe picked up the *Luchos*

---

81. See *Pesikta Rabbah* 25; *Tanchuma Re'eh* 17; *Tosafos*; *Malbim* to *Shemos* 34:27.

This is based on the connection to the previous *pasuk*, *Lo sevashel gedi b'chalev imo* (do not cook a kid in its mother's milk).

There are differing views as to the meaning of this *pasuk* (*Shemos* 34:27). Some note that the above-mentioned Midrash supports the view that Moshe himself wrote the second *Luchos*. Most views suggest that Moshe rewrote or renewed the original covenant of the Torah made in *Mishpatim* (24:4-7) but Hashem in fact wrote the second *Luchos* as He did the first. See *Shemos Rabbah* 47:3,9. See *Malbim* who writes specifically that this *pasuk* refers to the Torah and not the *Luchos*.

82. *Tanchuma Ki Sisa* 35; *Nedarim* 38a; *Shemos Rabbah* 47:3; *Ramban* to *Shemos* 34:27.

83. See *Nedarim* 38a with *Shitah Mekubetzes*.

84. See *Targum Yonasan*; *Rashi*; *Rabbeinu Bachya*; *Ramban*; *Ibn Ezra*; *Abarbanel* to *Shemos* 34:28-29; *Shemos Rabbah* 47:6. See *Ibn Ezra HaKatzar* and *Malbim* for their differing views.

with ease, as he had the first *Luchos*, because the spiritual letters rendered them virtually weightless.⁸⁵ The second *Luchos* had the advantage over the first *Luchos* in that they were given on Yom Kippur, whereas the first were given on an ordinary weekday.⁸⁶

Moshe's New Radiance

Before daybreak, Moshe came down from the mountain holding the *Luchos*.⁸⁷ The Jewish people watched him from the distance, but as he approached, they shrank back in fear. Moshe was so engrossed in the Torah that he did not immediately notice their reaction. He did not realize that his face had acquired an otherworldly radiance that made him resemble an angel.⁸⁸ The people simply did not recognize him. They could not bear to look at the brilliance of his radiant countenance, which seemed brighter than the sun.⁸⁹ Thinking an angel had descended into their midst, they recoiled in fear.⁹⁰

It is interesting that the Jewish people were able to tolerate the thunder and lightning and the radiance that accompanied the revelation at Sinai, but they were not able to tolerate the radiance of Moshe's face. Why was this so? Because before they sinned with the Golden Calf they were on an exalted spiritual level, but now, having fallen, even the radiance of Moshe's face was too much for them to bear.⁹¹ Before they sinned, the Jewish people were like a person who has been outside in the bright daylight for a long time. He can even

---

85. *Shemos Rabbah* 47:6.
86. *Ibn Ezra* to *Shemos* 34:1.
   Homiletically speaking, the Ten Commandments represent the ten days between Rosh Hashanah and Yom Kippur. And the first two *Dibros* uttered at one time by Hashem represent the two days of Rosh Hashanah (*Yaaros Devash*).
87. *Chizkuni* to *Shemos* 34:29.
   It is interesting to note that the *Chizkuni* suggests that Moshe came down on a Tuesday, which does not conform to our calendar. This would mean Rosh Hashanah fell on Sunday, which contradicts the rule that Rosh Hashanah cannot commence on a Sunday, Wednesday, or Friday. It would stand to reason, based on the earlier views and the one used for the purposes of this book, that Moshe descended on Monday, thus mirroring the Jewish calendar years of 5763-64.
   See *Yalkut Reuveni* who writes that the *Luchos* were given to the Jewish people sometime in the afternoon. He suggests that the *Luchos* were given during the time of *Minchah*.
88. *Abarbanel; Ramban* to *Shemos* 34:31.
89. *Reishis Chochmah, Yirah; Malbim* 34:30.
90. *Ramban; Chizkuni* to *Shemos* 34:30.
91. *Rashi* to *Shemos* 34:30.

look directly at the sun. After they sinned, they were comparable to someone sitting in a dark room. As soon as he steps outside, he cannot tolerate even a small amount of light.⁹²

What was the source of Moshe's new radiance?

Some suggest that it resulted from Hashem passing His spiritual radiance over him⁹³ or from his extended close proximity to Hashem.⁹⁴ Some say it was sparked by the rays that emanated when Moshe was learning Torah with Hashem.⁹⁵ According to others, Moshe had the glow from the day he was born. The light originated from the hidden light of creation. When Moshe was taken to Pharaoh's house, this supernal light was withdrawn, but when he came down with the second *Luchos*, it returned.⁹⁶

When Moshe returned to the Jewish encampment, he placed a cloth veil over his face to mask its radiance, and to allow the people to approach him.⁹⁷ Then he called for Aharon and taught him everything in the Torah up until this point, including the rules of the construction of the Tabernacle and the manufacture of the priestly garments.⁹⁸ He also gave Aharon the details of the new

---

92. *Reishis Chochmah, Yirah* 7:17.
93. See *Rashi* to *Shemos* 34:29; *Shemos* 33:22.
94. *Tanchuma Ki Sisa* 3; *Yalkut* 406. The *Luchos* were 6 handbreadths. Hashem held onto two, Moshe held onto two, leaving just two handbreadths in between himself and Hashem when they were being given to him.
   Some question why this did not take place after Moshe's first ascension, when he brought down the first *Luchos*. One reason for this was that while the first *Luchos* were given in full public display, the second *Luchos* were given in private. For the Jewish people to be convinced that the *Luchos* Moshe was holding came from Hashem, Moshe needed a radiant glow to attest to the fact that he had come directly from Hashem. Another obvious answer is that by the time Moshe descended with the first *Luchos*, the Jews had already worshiped the Golden Calf, thus making the first *Luchos* obsolete (*Rabbeinu Bachya; Tzeidah LaDerech*).
95. *Tanchuma Ki Sisa* 37.
   One lesson to be learned from this is that although Moshe had not eaten for forty days (or over 120 days when his three ascensions are combined), Moshe did not look ill or sickly. On the contrary, the Jewish people learned from this that through Torah one can remain vibrant and strong, as illustrated by Moshe's saintly appearance.
96. *Yalkut Reuveni*.
97. When not speaking with Hashem or to the Jewish people, Moshe would cover his radiant face. When speaking to Hashem, Moshe would remove the covering so that more glow from the spiritual radiance emanating from Hashem would be added. When speaking to the Jewish people, Moshe would also remove the covering out of respect for them. See *Targum Yonasan; Rabbeinu Bachya; Tzeror HaMor* to *Shemos* 34:33-35. For explanation of the meaning of *masveh* see *Targum; Targum Yonasan; Rashi; Lekach Tov* to *Shemos* 34:33; *Rashi* to *Kesubos* 60a. The various opinions include either a scarf, veil, kerchief or clothlike screen.
98. *Sforno; Malbim; Rashbam* to *Shemos* 34:32.
   Moshe started with the princes of the Jewish people that included the Kohanim and

covenant he had forged with Hashem.[99] After he finished with Aharon, Moshe taught Aharon's sons. After them, he taught the elders, and after them, all the rest of the people.[100] Moshe would follow this pattern of teaching for the remaining stay of the Jewish people in the encampment at Sinai, until they set out into the desert on 20 Iyar of the following year.[101]

The Day of Atonement

Moshe had ascended Mount Sinai for the final time on Rosh Chodesh Elul. It had been a day of profound emotion. The Jewish people had wept tears of deep contrition as they watched him leave the encampment. They had fasted and prayed to Hashem that He pardon them for their sins. For his part, Moshe had wept tears of sympathy, lamenting the sorrow of his beloved people. The prayers and the tears had penetrated the highest spheres of Heaven and aroused Hashem's mercy. Forty days later, the last vestiges of Hashem's angry countenance to the Jewish people were finally removed. At long last, He was appeased, and the stain of the terrible sin was wiped away.[102] That day, 10 Tishrei, became known as Yom Kippur, the day on which the sins of the Jewish people are cleansed every year.[103]

---

zekeinim in order to honor them appropriately. See *R' Avraham Ben HaRambam* to *Shemos* 34:32; *Rashi* to *Bamidbar* 30:2.

Moshe repeated all the laws from *Parashas Mishpatim* through *Ki Sisa*. This includes *Terumah* and *Tetzaveh* which detail everything regarding the building of the Tabernacle and the clothing worn by the Kohanim.

99. *Ramban*; *Ibn Ezra* to *Shemos* 34:32.

100. *Rashi*; *Ramban* to *Shemos* 34:31; *Eruvin* 54b. See *Eruvin* 54b for the details on how Moshe taught the Torah to the Jewish people and how each and every one would have it repeated to them four times.

This would be one of the sources to which the first Mishnah of *Avos* would refer: Moshe received the Torah at Sinai and transmitted it to Yehoshua who transmitted it to the Elders ... (*Lekach Tov*).

101. *Mizrachi*; *Chizkuni* to *Shemos* 34:31-32.

With the completion of Moshe's repetition of the Torah, the Jewish people once again showed their willingness to accept the Torah unconditionally, by saying *Naaseh venishma* (*Sefer HaYashar*).

102. *Tanna D'Vei Eliyahu Zuta* 4; *Tanna D'Vei Eliyahu Rabbah* 1; *Pirkei D'Rav Eliezer* 46; *Radal*; *Bamidbar Rabbah* 12:1.

See *Tur Orach Chaim* 581 regarding blowing the *shofar* during the month of Elul.

103. *Tanchuma Ki Sisa* 31; *Moshav Zekeinim* to *Shemos* 34:1; *Tanna D'Vei Eliyahu Zuta* 4.

See *Midrash Aggadah* which says that since the process of creating the *Luchos* began on Rosh Chodesh Elul, it is customary to begin blowing the *shofar* on that day. Some add that since this process ended on Yom Kippur, it would also explain why it is a custom to blow the *shofar* on Yom Kippur night as well. See *Pirkei D'Rav Eliezer* 46.

Moshe's descent from the mountain triggered a day of joy and celebration. On this day, Hashem had forgiven the Jewish people for the sin of the Golden Calf. On this day, the covenant between Hashem and the Jewish people was renewed. On this day, the Jewish people learned that the *Shechinah* would reside in their midst permanently. For all future generations, this day would be observed as a day of atonement, a day of reassurance that Hashem will accept repentance and forgive.[104]

It was then that the Jewish people began the work of constructing the Tabernacle, the dwelling place for the *Shechinah*. It would be completed on Rosh Chodesh Nissan, three weeks short of one year after their departure from Egypt. On 20 Iyar, ten days short of one year after their arrival at Mount Sinai, they would set out on their journey to Eretz Yisrael, fortified by the possession of the Torah and the assurance that Hashem would always guide them with His merciful hand.[105]

---

104. See *Seder Olam* 6; *Tanchuma Pekudei* 11.
105. See *Beitzah* 5b; *Taanis* 21a; *Seder Olam* Ch. 8.

Appendix: Dating Matan Torah

Shabbos was the day of the week on which the Torah was given to the Jewish people at Mount Sinai. There appears to be no question in the Gemara on this account.[1] There is considerable question, however, regarding the day of the month. We know that the Torah was given in the month of Sivan, but on which day? Rabbi Yosi says it was 7 Sivan, while the Rabbanan say it was 6 Sivan.

The roots of this dispute lie in the day of the week on which the Exodus took place and the number of days in the month of Iyar that year.

The Gemara (*Shabbos* 86b) first assumes that the Exodus from Egypt, which occurred on the first day of Pesach, 15 Nissan, fell on a Thursday. Since Nissan usually has the full complement of 30 days, the final day of Nissan would have fallen on a Friday, with Rosh Chodesh Iyar on Shabbos.

---

1. See *Pirkei D'Rav Eliezer* 41,46 for the view that they received the Torah on Friday.

Rabbi Yosi assumes that the month of Iyar that year had only 29 days, following the standard pattern of alternating 30-day and 29-day months. If the first day of Iyar fell on Shabbos, then the 29th would have fallen on Shabbos as well. The first day of Sivan was therefore on Sunday. Since the Torah was given on the first Shabbos of Sivan, the date was 7 Sivan.

The Rabbanan, however, contend that Iyar of that year also had 30 days. Since the first of Iyar was on Shabbos, the 30th was on Sunday. The first of Sivan was therefore on Monday. Since the Torah was given on the first Shabbos of Sivan, the date would have been 6 Sivan.

The Gemara (ibid. 88a) raises a discrepancy between Rabbi Yosi's opinion and a passage in *Seder Olam* that states that the Jewish people left Egypt on a Friday. If Pesach was on a Friday, then the 30th of

According to *Seder Olam* (*Shabbos* 88a Rabbanan)

			NISSAN			
Sunday	Monday	Tuesday	Wednesday	Thursday	Friday	Shabbos
					1	2
3	4	5	6	7	8	9
10	11	12	13	14	**15**	16
17	18	19	20	21	22	23
24	25	26	27	28	29	30

			IYAR			
Sunday	Monday	Tuesday	Wednesday	Thursday	Friday	Shabbos
1	2	3	4	5	6	7
8	9	10	11	12	13	14
15	**16**	17	18	19	20	21
22	**23**	24	25	26	27	28
29						

			SIVAN			
Sunday	Monday	Tuesday	Wednesday	Thursday	Friday	Shabbos
	1	2	3	4	5	6
		Yom HaMeyuchas	hagbalah	perishah	perishah	

Nissan fell on Shabbos, and Rosh Chodesh Iyar fell on a Sunday. Since there are 29 days in Iyar, the last day of Iyar also fell on a Sunday, and Rosh Chodesh Sivan fell on a Monday. This means that Shabbos was 6 Sivan, not 7 Sivan.

The Gemara answers that this passage follows the opinion of the Rabbanan. This entails a revision of the reasoning behind the opinion of the Rabbanan. Now, we assume that all agree that Iyar had only 29

R' Yosi

NISSAN						
Sunday	Monday	Tuesday	Wednesday	Thursday	Friday	Shabbos
				1	2	3
4	5	6	7	8	9	10
11	12	13	14	**15**	16	17
18	19	20	21	22	23	24
25	26	27	28	29	30	

IYAR						
Sunday	Monday	Tuesday	Wednesday	Thursday	Friday	Shabbos
						1
2	3	4	5	6	7	8
9	10	11	12	13	14	15
16	17	18	19	20	21	22
23	24	25	26	27	28	29

SIVAN						
Sunday	Monday	Tuesday	Wednesday	Thursday	Friday	Shabbos
1	2	3	4	5	6	7
	Yom HaMeyuchas	hagbalah	perishah	perishah	perishah	

Rabbanan

SIVAN						
Sunday	Monday	Tuesday	Wednesday	Thursday	Friday	Shabbos
	1	2	3	4	5	6
		Yom HaMeyuchas	hagbalah	perishah	perishah	

days. The argument between Rabbi Yosi and the Rabbanan is with regard to the day of the week on which the Exodus took place.

Rabbi Yosi says that it took place on a Thursday. Therefore, the final day of Nissan, which has 30 days, was on a Friday. Rosh Chodesh Iyar was on Shabbos, and since it had only 29 days, its last day was also on a Shabbos. Rosh Chodesh Sivan was on Sunday, and the following Shabbos, the day on which the Torah was given, occurred on 7 Sivan.

The Rabbanan say that the Exodus took place on Friday. Therefore, the final day of Nissan, which has 30 days, was on a Shabbos. Rosh Chodesh Iyar was on a Sunday, and since it had only 29 days, its last day was also on a Sunday. Rosh Chodesh Sivan was on Monday, and the following Shabbos, the day on which the Torah was given, occurred on 6 Sivan.[2]

The order of events during the days leading up to the giving of the Torah is also a point of contention between Rabbi Yosi and the Rabbanan. Were there two days of separation of the men from their wives, as would appear from a simple reading of the Torah, or were there three, as the Gemara infers from the language of the Torah?

Rabbi Yosi says that the Jewish people arrived at Mount Sinai on Sunday, and they rested for the remainder of the day to recover from the fatigue of the journey. Nothing happened on that day. Early Monday morning, Moshe ascended the mountain, when Hashem told him that the people would be considered "a kingdom of priests." Moshe returned in the evening and repeated this to the people. On Tuesday, Moshe went back up the mountain. Hashem told him to set boundaries to prevent the people from ascending or even touching the mountain. Moshe came down and reported to the people. On Wednesday, he went back up the mountain. Hashem told him to instruct the people to sanctify themselves for two days, "today and tomorrow," meaning Wednesday and Thursday. Moshe came down and reported to the people. On Thursday, the people observed the second day of sanctification. On Friday, Moshe decided to add one more day of sanctification of his own accord. On Shabbos, 7 Sivan, Hashem gave the Torah to the Jewish people.

---

2. See *Rashash* as to how the previous excerpt from *Seder Olam* could be attributed to the Rabbanan, when it is R' Yose himself who wrote *Seder Olam*?

According to the Rabbanan, the order of events was different. On Monday, the Jewish people arrived at Mount Sinai. On Tuesday, Moshe ascended the mountain, where Hashem deemed the people "a kingdom of priests." On Wednesday, Hashem told Moshe to set the boundaries. On Thursday, Hashem told Moshe to instruct the people to sanctify themselves for two days, which they proceeded to do that day and Friday. On Shabbos, 6 Sivan, Hashem gave the Torah to the Jewish people.

So we see that, according to Rabbi Yosi, there were three days of sanctification, and according to the Rabbanan, there were only two.

Today, we celebrate Shavuos on 6 Sivan, and we also observe special customs during the three days of separation. The *Magen Avraham* points out that according to Rabbi Yosi, who counts three days of separation, the Torah was given on 7 Sivan.

Furthermore, if the Jewish people left Egypt on a Thursday, as Rabbi Yosi contends, and the Torah was given on Shabbos, that means there were 51 days between the Exodus and the Giving of the Torah, rather than 50 days.

The commentators and halachic authorities deal with these issues at great length and offer a variety of insights and solutions. This, however, is not the place to expound on these opinions, only to point out the basic questions and issues.[3]

---

3. See *Shabbos* 86-87-88. See *Tosafos* to *Shabbos* 87b s.v. *Oso lerabbanan*; *Ritva*; *Maharsha*; *Rashash* to *Shabbos* 88a.

See *Magen Avraham* to *Orach Chaim* 494; *Machtzis HaShekel* on this in great length. See *Chok Yaakov* 430; *Maharsha*; *Tosafos* to *Avodah Zarah* 3a; *Kometz HaMinchah, Shavuos*.

See *Torah Shleimah* to *Yisro* Ch. 20 in *Miluim* 31 for his discussion as to why the Torah does not refer to Shavuos as "*Zeman Matan Toraseinu* — the Time of the Giving of Our Torah.

This volume is part of
THE ARTSCROLL® SERIES
an ongoing project of
translations, commentaries and expositions on
Scripture, Mishnah, Talmud, Midrash, Halachah,
liturgy, history, the classic Rabbinic writings,
biographies and thought.

For a brochure of current publications
visit your local Hebrew bookseller
or contact the publisher:

Mesorah Publications, ltd

4401 Second Avenue
Brooklyn, New York 11232
(718) 921-9000
www.artscroll.com